PSYCHOANALYTIC INTERPRETATIONS

PSYCHOANALYTIC INTERPRETATIONS

The Selected Papers
of
THOMAS M. FRENCH, M.D.

Foreword by George H. Pollock

CHICAGO
Quadrangle Books
1970

CONTENTS

FOREWORD

A volume of collected papers spanning four decades nearly constitutes a scientific autobiography. Reading such a collection, one witnesses a scientist's ideas emerge and grow, in the process often being transformed into deeper ideas of a subtlety and complexity scarcely imagined at their inception. Yet a scientist's papers are highly distilled products, refined presentations that leave out the intellectual anguish that frequently accompanies their composition. In the finished performance of a scientific paper the language is carefully chosen, the false leads go unmentioned, the drudgery of gathering and processing facts is omitted. Such a collection of papers falls short of being a full scientific autobiography, then, because to the extent that the papers succeed in being scientific, to that extent will they obliterate the personality and travail of the scientist. Perhaps no further reason is needed for using this introduction to Thomas M. French's *Psychoanalytic Interpretations* to discuss the personal aspects of its author's intellectual development.

Dr. Thomas M. French, author and editor of several important works in the literature of psychoanalysis and Emeritus Director of Research and Associate Director of the Chicago Institute for Psychoanalysis, was born in Philadelphia on September 4, 1892. Although both his parents were raised in rural communities, his father, James B. French, became an engineer of national reputation and a consultant to many of the leading railroads of his day. French's younger brother, doubtless under the influence of the father, became an architect, with a strong interest in the aesthetics of architecture. The Frenches lived in Jamaica, New York, while their children were growing up.

Early on, Thomas French evinced an interest in mathematics, which he has sustained throughout his life. Given this interest and ability in mathematics, his father urged an engineering career on his son. French, however, was only mildly interested in engineering, and at that only in its mathematical aspects, caring little about its practical applications. Still, he did not exclude the possibility of becoming an engineer. When he matriculated at Cornell in 1911 he enrolled in an arts program at the end of which, if he so chose, he could study two additional years and take an engineering degree as well.

At the end of his four years at Cornell, French, then twenty-three years old, decided to leave school to take a job as part of a surveying crew for the Jersey Central Railroad. The job did not hold his interest and before long he went to work in his father's office where he concentrated on the theoretical problems of engineering design. During the six months or so he spent in his father's office, he determined to drop the idea of a career in engineering once and for all and to study medicine instead. He returned to Cornell and took an M.D. in 1920.

Immediately after graduation from medical school, French opened a small practice in a section of Long Island mostly inhabited by poor families. This choice of locale for his practice was at least in part dictated by French's politics of the time, which were, loosely speaking, socialistic. His socialism derived from his college days, when he was much taken with the writing of Sidney and Beatrice Webb. (George Bernard Shaw's more literary brand of socialism interested him less.) His medical practice gave him an opportunity to confront the problems of the poor firsthand. It is doubtful that today, even loosely speaking, French could be described as a socialist, though quite possibly his work over the years with the United Charities and other social agencies in the Chicago area represents an extension of his early political proclivities.

As with engineering, so with physical medicine; French soon found himself bored with his practice and really only fully engaged with the theoretical side of his work—more interested, that is, in biology than in bandages. The time had come once again for him to switch professions. He decided on psychiatry. While still working at his medical practice, he acquired an enormous interest in dreams. He read Freud's *Interpretation of Dreams* and found himself fascinated with the questions Freud raised: What do dreams really mean? How do they function in people's lives? What is their historical derivation? Eventually, French hoped to become a psychoanalyst, but he felt he ought first to have a background in psychiatry, and so he became a house officer at the semi-private Bloomingdale Hospital in New York—now known as the Westchester Division—where he spent better than four years acquiring training in psychiatry.

Even in his pre-psychiatric days, two significant features of French's approach to psychoanalytic research began to emerge: the building of (metaphorical) bridges spanning different sides of a problem, and a keen interest in mathematical solutions to intricate human questions. This bridge-building propensity would later be evident—and can now be seen in many of the papers in *Psychoanalytic Interpretations*—in his studies of the integrative process, in his investigations of the mutual relations between integrative fields, and in his work on the structural, functional, and clinical approaches to the analysis of behavior. French's mathematical pursuits can be found in derivative form in his approaches to dream analysis; these researches, covered in great detail in several of his books and monographs, treat the dream as the solution to a problem that is focal at the time of the dream. The analysis of the dream thus involves discovering and understanding this focal conflict, its antecedent components, and its relationship to the historically older nuclear conflict from childhood.

In the midst of his training in psychiatry at Bloomingdale Hospital, French recognized that the time had come to begin his serious study of psychoanalysis. So in 1926 he applied for and was awarded a year's fellowship to the famous Psychoanalytic Institute in Berlin. He chose Berlin over Vienna because he felt the Berlin school a better place at that particular time. He had also hoped to be analyzed by Karl Abraham, a man he greatly admired who was then at the Berlin Institute. Abraham, however, died, and in his place French chose Franz Alexander as his analyst, a fortuitous decision which was to be the beginning of a lifelong scientific collaboration.

In 1927, French returned to the staff of Bloomingdale Hospital for an additional two years, utilizing the new insights and knowledge gained during his year in Berlin. At the end of two years at Bloomingdale, he returned for further study to Berlin. During this period he became a candidate at the Berlin Institute, again working closely with Franz Alexander and also with such famous names in the pantheon of psychoanalysis as Hanns Sachs, Karen Horney, and Max Eitingon.

When Franz Alexander was invited to come to Chicago in 1930, French came over from Berlin with him. He established a private practice and worked as a psychiatrist at the Institute for Juvenile Research. Alexander, meanwhile, left Chicago after a year, then returned in 1932 to found the Institute for Psychoanalysis. French was asked to be one of the members of the Institute's original staff. The Chicago Institute has ever since remained his home base.

While working at the Institute for Juvenile Research, French developed the technique—again reflecting his integrative or bridge-building approach—of evaluating the entire family and the familial situation when assessing a disturbed child. After leaving the Institute for Juvenile Research, French continued to consult with social and family agencies in Chicago, never relinquishing his "field approach" to understanding behavior in the broadest possible context through treating the individual and understanding the family as well.

As the reader of *Psychoanalytic Interpretations* will soon discover, French's is an essentially synthesizing mind. Nothing quite so elates him intellectually as reconciling opposing views—Freud's and Pavlov's, for example—or bringing knowledge from two discrete fields to bear on a single problem. Thus while French has concentrated on the intra-psychic in his individual work with patients and in his research on ego psychology and therapeutic and dream processes, he has also been deeply engaged in studying such interpersonal social-psychological aspects of behavior as the family, social conflict, problems of democracy, and sources of ethical and political orientation. A number of the papers devoted to his studies in these various fields are included in this volume.

French's collaboration with Franz Alexander is still another instance of his ability to combine differing points of view and put them to work for good purposes. Although the two men had distinctly different personalities, unique personal styles, and quite dissimilar methods of approaching a scientific problem, French and Alexander worked well together, each man bringing his particular perspective to the investigation of any given problem. Their book *Psychoanalytic Therapy,* written in conjunction with some of their colleagues at the Chicago Institute, evoked much controversy both in this country and abroad, and sent both men off on valuable independent studies of the therapeutic process. Their collaboration is perhaps shown to best effect, however, in their work on psychosomatic medicine. In 1948, French and Alexander jointly compiled papers from the Chicago Institute in *Studies in Psychosomatic Medicine,* a work focusing on the physiological and psychological reactions of an organism, which they viewed as two aspects of an essentially unified process. French's dream analysis approach was especially valuable in studying this process in patients with such diseases as bronchial asthma and ulcerative colitis. These were in fact pioneering researches, and they have recently culminated in the publication of the first volume of *Psychosomatic Specificity*, a work on which French has served as one of the editors.

Thomas French's fundamental research in the integration of psychological theories into psychoanalysis, in psychotherapy, in psychosomatic medicine, and in dream theory and interpretation are now properly considered landmarks in the history of psychiatry and psychoanalysis. *Psychoanalytic Interpretations*, a volume which has the special virtue of displaying Dr. French's scientific concerns in all their abundant variety, cannot but enhance the reputation of a meticulous and wide-ranging contributor to the science of human behavior.

GEORGE H. POLLOCK

Institute for Psychoanalysis
Chicago, Illinois
February 1970

PSYCHOANALYTIC
INTERPRETATIONS

Part One

THE THERAPEUTIC PROCESS

Chapter One

INTERRELATIONS BETWEEN PSYCHOANALYSIS AND THE EXPERIMENTAL WORK OF PAVLOV

My interest in the therapeutic process in psychoanalysis began with a comparative study of psychoanalysis and the experimental work of Pavlov. Pavlov pointed out that the learning process on which adaptation to external reality depends is a process first of conditioning, then of differentiation of generalized conditioned reflexes. By the acquisition of conditioned reflexes, the hungry animal learns to seek for food in response to "signal stimuli" which have previously been associated with satisfied hunger; but not all stimuli that are at first treated as "signal stimuli" actually fulfill their implied promise to satisfy the animal's hunger. The second step in the learning process must therefore consist in the (internal) inhibition of the responses to stimuli that are not habitually followed by satisfaction—in other words, by a process of differentiation. Thus the process which in psychoanalysis we call adjustment to external reality is based essentially upon the conditioning and differentiation processes of Pavlov.

However, adaptation to external reality does not always succeed. One of the basic discoveries of psychoanalysis was that neuroses result when conflict becomes too great. Pavlov made a similar discovery. When one of Pavlov's dogs was required to discriminate between one stimulus and another that was too closely similar to it, the dog not only became unable to differentiate these two stimuli, but then even differentiations that had already been acquired were lost and the animal's behavior became very disturbed. Pavlov, too, called this disturbed be-

Reprinted from *American Journal of Psychiatry*, 12, No. 6 (May 1933).

havior a neurosis, an "experimental neurosis." Thus both psychoanalysis and Pavlov's experiments discovered the basic relation between emotional conflict and the onset of neuroses.

In the past 40 years there have grown up in neighboring countries two rather large bodies of scientific literature—both devoted to the task of clarifying the mechanisms of behavior and both characterized by a courageous determination to observe facts quite without reference to former preconceptions. Because of the relative inaccessibility of Russian literature, the finer details of the work of the Pavlov school did indeed remain considerably isolated from the scientific thought of other countries; and the psychoanalytic literature, because of the general unpalatability of its findings, has unfortunately been compelled to develop as a sort of foreign body in scientific thought. Nevertheless it seems somewhat surprising that these two bodies of scientific thought have so little apparent relation to each other.

This fact becomes more understandable, however, once we begin to study the work of the two schools more closely; for both in method and in the character of the material chosen for study, the two disciplines stand at almost opposite poles of scientific approach.

The psychoanalytic method, as its name implies, is an analytic one. It starts with a recognition of the complexity of human behavior and contents itself at first with the discovery of the central trends of a patient's behavior, only step by step pushing the analysis from the surface downward. When correctly done it never loses sight of the patient's total situation in the attempt to analyze details—the analysis of details always retaining its place as a part of a more comprehensive insight into the patient's whole psychic situation.

The studies of Pavlov's school, on the other hand, are synthetic in method. The approach is frankly physiological, with emphasis upon a single detail of the organism's reaction, such as the animal's salivary reflexes. It starts with the conditioned reflex as an elementary form of reaction, and in studying this elementary reaction under more and more complex conditions the obvious goal is to reconstruct the complexity of behavior from its elements—much as an organic chemist seeks to produce a complex organic compound synthetically from simpler and better known substances. One feels convinced from occasional comments in Pavlov's accounts of his experiments that he never does really lose sight of the total behavior of the animal upon which he is experimenting, but the emphasis is placed in every case upon the particular conditioned reflex that is under discussion.

There is also a fundamental difference between the two disciplines with regard to the type of material that they select for study. Psychoanalysis has concerned itself primarily with wishes, impulses, and drives—that is, with tendencies arising within the organism. Thus sex, hunger, anger, fear, and their interrelations and derivatives constitute the principal subject matter of psychoanalytic studies, and the effect of external experience upon the life of the individual is studied for the most part with reference to its influence in transforming and giving new direction to tendencies arising from within.

This fundamental biological point of view is, of course, never really lost sight of in Pavlov's experiments; but here also the emphasis is different in Pavlov's work. The unconditioned reflexes with which Pavlov works for the most part are the alimentary and the defense salivary reflexes, but in studying the alimentary salivary reflex, for example, the fact that the animal is hungry is usually taken for granted as a necessary condition of the experiment. Relatively few experiments are directed to problems concerning the interactions of unconditioned reflexes with each other and there is only an occasional comment as to the effects of variations in the intensity of the animal's hunger upon the experimental results.

In view of such wide divergences both in method and in phenomena studied, it is therefore not surprising that the results of the two types of investigation at first seem to have so little to do with each other. If one is convinced nevertheless that the results of these two very extensive investigations must be fundamentally very closely related to each other in spite of differences in emphasis, one must be prepared to make allowances for the differences of approach that have been discussed. One would expect in the first place to find the closest relations to psychoanalytic findings in the more complex of the phenomena studied by Pavlov, and in the second place one should be prepared to make the most of such hints as Pavlov gives us as to the effects of variations in the intensity of the drives and of interactions between two or more unconditioned reflexes. One might expect also to gain some light from psychoanalytic data as to just how far conclusions reached from the study of salivary reflexes can be generalized to apply also to other aspects of behavior.

One other preliminary comment is perhaps necessary in view of the criticisms by Lashley [1] and others of the anatomical and physiological assumptions involved in the conditioned reflex concept. I think we need not concern ourselves very much with these criticisms here. Pavlov has himself rather carefully refrained from too precise formulations as to the anatomical basis of the conditioned reflex and related phenomena that he describes, and his experimental data and the conclusions drawn from them seem to me to be in no way dependent upon any particular anatomical concept. It is with these experimental data rather than with any implied anatomical concepts that I propose to deal in this discussion.

Let us turn now to possible correlations between the two sets of findings.

The classical experiment upon which all of Pavlov's work in this field is based is, as is well known, the following: Pavlov has already demonstrated that if food be placed in a (hungry) dog's mouth, the stimulus of the food in the mouth excites a reflex secretion of saliva of a certain typical quality. This Pavlov calls an unconditioned reflex. If now, just prior to having food put in the dog's mouth, the dog is exposed to some previously indifferent stimulus such as the sound of a metronome, this previously indifferent stimulus thereafter also acquires the power of exciting a secretion of saliva. This Pavlov calls a conditioned reflex.[2]

That the calling up of one reaction or mental process by another with which it has been previously associated is essentially the same phenomenon as Pavlov's conditioned reflex is of course generally recognized and needs no further comment.

The relation between the inhibition of Pavlov and repression in the psychoanalytic sense is, however, not quite so clear. Pavlov distinguishes between two kinds of inhibition. If a dog, for instance, has been conditioned to respond with a secretion of saliva to the sound of an electric buzzer, but at the time of the sounding of the electric buzzer is exposed also to some other stimulus such as the entrance of a stranger into the room, then the sound of the electric buzzer will for the time being no longer possess the power of exciting a salivary secretion. This Pavlov calls *external inhibition*. If, on the other hand, a dog that has been conditioned to the sound of an electric buzzer is repeatedly exposed to this stimulus without subsequently being given food, then the sound of the electric buzzer gradually loses its power of exciting salivary secretion. This is called by Pavlov the experimental extinction of a conditioned reflex. This is one of the forms of *internal inhibition,* the other forms of internal inhibition being in fact only modifications of this fundamental form.

To which of these forms of inhibition does repression the more closely correspond? The motive force in a great many cases of repression is fear (e.g., castration complex). This would of course correspond to an external rather than to an internal inhibition, inasmuch as the inhibitory effect is called forth by a reflex other than the one that is being inhibited. In other cases, however, such as for example in the repression of the Oedipus complex in women,[3] Freud conjectures that the repression results from the repeated failure of desires to be gratified. This would correspond more closely to the phenomena of internal inhibition.

But before proceeding to speak of repression in the psychoanalytic sense and inhibition in Pavlov's sense as equivalent terms, it will be well first to compare the two phenomena somewhat more closely. The essential feature of repression consists in the fact that although the repressed tendency is barred from obtaining direct motor expression, it nevertheless in indirect ways gives evidence that it still exists—as we say—in the unconscious. Are there similar evidences in the case of a conditioned reflex that has been inhibited in Pavlov's sense?

In the case of internal inhibition, at least, there are many such evidences. A conditioned reflex that has been experimentally extinguished is not permanently destroyed. On the contrary, a well-established conditioned reflex will after a time spontaneously recover its full strength, and will do so more quickly if the animal is in the interim given food even without the conditioned stimulus. Moreover, there is the interesting phenomenon that Pavlov calls disinhibition. We have noted, for example, that the coming of a stranger into the room will tend to inhibit the conditioned salivary response, let us say, to the sound of an electric buzzer; if, however, the stranger comes into the room after the conditioned reaction to the buzzer has been experimentally extinguished, then the effect is likely to be to *disinhibit* the salivary reflex, or in other words to release it from inhibition. Apparently the stranger's presence exerts an external inhibitory effect upon both the original reflex and the internal inhibitory process, and the more sensitive inhibitory process yields. It is clear, therefore, that internal inhibition, just like repression, involves a struggle between inhibiting and inhibited tendencies. Further evidence that this is the case is furnished by the following phenomena: First, it is possible to extinguish a reflex beyond zero; if one continues to sound the electric buzzer without following it by food even after the salivary reflex has been abolished, the later recovery of the reflex can be very much delayed. The struggle between inhibiting and inhibited tendencies is thus a quantitative phenomenon —just as in our psychoanalytic experience we find that there are varying depths of repression. In the second place, when one reflex is inhibited there is a definite tendency for the inhibition to radiate so that other conditioned reflexes are also temporarily inhibited—a phenomenon that corresponds to the repression of indifferent material so often noted immediately after allusions to deeply repressed trains of thought.

The psychoanalytic evidence for the fact that repressed tendencies have not been destroyed lies, of course, in the fact that such tendencies are continually finding outlets in symptoms and substitutive gratifications. It is therefore of interest to note the analogy pointed out in detail by Ischlondsky [4] between symptom formation and the phenomena of generalization and of induction in Pavlov's experiments. Let us postpone for a moment the discussion of the generalization phenomena and explain briefly what is meant by induction. If a conditioned reflex, let us say to stimulation at one point on the skin, is inhibited, there is often observed immediately afterward an increase in the conditioned reflex effect obtained from other skin areas. It is easy to see that this phenomenon, which Pavlov calls *positive induction,* might well play an important part in such mechanisms, for example, as "displacement upward" of repressed genital excitations.

So far we have been discussing internal inhibition. We have already noted, however, that the mechanism of many repressive processes would seem to resemble external rather than internal inhibition. Are there also facts relative to external inhibition that correspond to the phenomena of repression? Upon this point Pavlov's evidence is not so complete —but he does report one series of experiments that indicates definitely that such is probably the case. It is a well-established fact in conditioned reflex experiments that painful stimuli as well as indifferent ones can be conditioned to excite the alimentary salivary response. In such cases the animal turns eagerly in the direction of the expected food and there is no evidence of defense reactions in spite of the painful nature of the exciting stimulus. In one series of experiments, an attempt was made to see how far this suppression of defense reactions could be carried, and not one but many conditioned reflexes were established to painful stimuli of increasing intensity applied to various points upon the skin. For a considerable time defense reactions continued to be inhibited and lively alimentary reactions continued to be obtained. Finally, however, a limit was reached and then the situation was completely reversed. The animal went into a prolonged state of restless excitement in which all types of stimuli were reacted to with violent defensive reactions and all alimentary reactions were inhibited. One could hardly seek a more effective demonstration of the fact that the defensive reactions had been "repressed" rather than destroyed.

The evidence seems fairly complete, therefore, that repression in the psychoanalytic sense contains, at least as one of its essential elements, mechanisms such as Pavlov describes as external and internal inhibition. But does not repression also involve something more than this? Pavlov's implied conception of external and internal inhibition as simple automatic reactions seems perhaps comparable to the avoidance of painfully charged topics in the talk of certain disintegrated schizophrenics, but one gains the impression in the study of the neuroses that repression is a more highly organized process than this.[5] We think of repression as an action of the ego [6] (in response, it is true, to a signal from the more automatic superego) and, what is most important, we regard it as founded upon unconscious insight into the nature of the unconscious tendencies that are being rejected. Is there anything in the inhibition of conditioned reflexes comparable to this?

On the other hand, may we not perhaps ask ourselves (as Schilder [7] for example has done, and as some of the modern trends in psychology [8] suggest our doing) whether the conditioned responses of Pavlov are really so simple as they seem, and whether they also may not contain elements that correspond in at least a rudimentary way to the unconscious insight of our neurotic patients' superegos? I suggest, however, that we postpone the attempt to answer this question until we have discussed the phenomena that Pavlov calls differentiation and the light that they throw upon possible rudimentary parallels for unconscious and conscious insight.

Differentiation is a somewhat complex process of refinement of conditioned reflex responses whose most important component is a form of internal inhibition—differential inhibition. If an animal becomes positively conditioned to respond to a certain stimulus, say a tuning fork of a certain pitch, this conditioned response is at first (to use Pavlov's term) "generalized," that is, it can be obtained not only as a response to a tuning fork of that particular pitch but also as a response to a wide range of other stimuli as well. If now the animal is always fed after the tuning fork of the original pitch, but food is consistently withheld when the pitch is different, then the stimuli that are not followed by food are progressively *"differentially inhibited,"* whereas the tuning fork of the original pitch is stabilized in its initial positively conditioned effect.

It is now of interest to note that differentiation in Pavlov's sense is an essential element in all sublimation—for sublimation, as Sachs [9] has pointed out, consists essentially in retaining the socially acceptable form of an originally undifferentiated tendency while rejecting unsocial forms of the same tendency.

The replacement of the Oedipus wishes by the normal object choice at the time of puberty involves an essentially similar process. The boy's reactions toward women have been learned with reference to his mother. If his development has been approximately normal his sexual wishes toward her have been repressed, his tender impulses retained unrepressed. Thus at the beginning of the latency period, a differentiation in Pavlov's sense has already taken place. In addition to this differentiation, however, a generalization has also taken place, and the repression of direct sexual aims that has been learned with reference to the mother has been extended as the pattern for the boy's attitude to other women as well. Throughout the latency period then—as we psychoanalysts put it—every woman is for the child a mother.

At the onset of puberty, however, the increased intensity of the sexual drive begins to disturb this generalized repression of direct sexual aims. We are fortunate to be able to cite at this point one of the few experimental observations that Pavlov has reported with reference to the effect upon the conditioned reflex phenomena of variations in the intensity of the animal's hunger. This observation is to the effect that when a differentiation has been established, an increase in the intensity of the animal's hunger tends to weaken the differential inhibition upon which the differentiation is based, and so to make of no effect the previously established differentiation. This is, of course, exactly parallel to the changes at the time of puberty that we are discussing. At this time the increased strength of the sexual drive threatens to break down the differentiation that during the latency period had repressed direct sexual aims and had allowed outlet only to the tender components of the sexual drive.

As a result of this weakening of the repressive barriers, the individual is now faced with the necessity of establishing a new differentiation— a differentiation that will discriminate this time as to the object of the sexual drive. If development now continues approximately normal, the sexual wishes toward the mother and toward other similarly inaccessible objects will indeed remain repressed, but sexual wishes toward other women will henceforth be granted outlet.

Thus it is evident that *the establishment of the normal object choice at the time of puberty is equivalent to a process of differentiation in Pavlov's sense.* It is of further interest to note the psychoanalytic observation that in situations in which the normal object love is thwarted (death of love object, disappointment in love, etc.) there is a tendency to regress again to the generalized infantile object choice and again to react toward all women after the pattern learned toward the mother. This is, of course, only another instance of the disappearance of differentiation as a result of an increase in the strength of the underlying drive.

Let us now return to the problem of insight. The more recent psychoanalytic literature has concerned itself a great deal with the functional division of the personality into ego, superego, and id. In these discussions we are accustomed to define the ego as the organ of adjustment to reality. What is there in Pavlov's experiments that corresponds to this adjustment to reality?

If we limit ourselves at first to external reality, the answer is easy. Pavlov has himself pointed out that the learning process is a process first of conditioning, then of differentiation of the generalized conditioned reflexes. By the acquisition of conditioned reflexes the hungry animal learns to seek for food in response to "signal stimuli" which have previously been associated with satisfied hunger; but not all stimuli that are at first treated as "signal stimuli" actually fulfill their implied promise to satisfy the animal's hunger. The second step in the learning process must therefore consist in the (internal) inhibition of the responses to stimuli that are not habitually followed by satisfaction— in other words, in a process of differentiation. It is thus evident that the process which in psychoanalysis we call *adjustment to external reality is based essentially upon the conditioning and differentiation processes of Pavlov.*

Furthermore we note that an animal that has acquired delicately differentiated conditioned responses actually acts as though it had a practical knowledge of external reality. In other words, conditioning and differentiation do constitute a sort of rudimentary equivalent to the acquisition of insight into external reality—and we are again confronted with the question suggested by certain trends in psychology [10] as to whether insight in the true psychological sense may not be an essential feature of the conditioning and differentiation processes.

The external reality function of the ego is therefore based in its rudiments upon the processes of conditioning and of the formation of new differentiations that Pavlov describes. Does this fact help us to throw any light upon the nature of the ego or upon the conditions under which the ego can best function?

If we consider first the process of differentiation as Pavlov describes it, we are struck at once by the fact that differentiation takes place under conditions that psychoanalysts would call a conflict. Suppose we are attempting to differentiate a tone of pitch A as a positive stimulus over against a tone of pitch G as an inhibitory stimulus. Because of the initial generalization of both excitatory and inhibitory responses both A and G at first call forth both excitatory and inhibitory reactions —and there will thus exist at the outset a conflict between the excitatory and the inhibitory reactions. The process of differentiation will then consist in the gradual narrowing of the initial generalizations and in the concentration of the positive responses to the stimuli about A and of the negative responses to the stimuli about G. We see, therefore, that differentiation is a process of solution of a conflict.

There is a similar fact with reference to conditioning. An animal tends to form alimentary conditioned reflexes only when it is hungry. In other words, an important condition for the conditioning process is an unsatisfied drive—a condition that we may characterize as a conflict with external reality.

We may postulate, therefore, that one of the necessary conditions for the external reality function of the ego is the existence of either an external or an internal conflict.

Certain other observations made by Pavlov allow us to postulate another condition for the external reality function of the ego. Pavlov states that one of the necessary conditions for the formation of a conditioned reflex is that the animal must be alert. If the animal is not in good health, therefore, or if there are powerful extraneous stimuli, the formation of a conditioned reflex is interfered with or prevented. A conditioned reflex is typically a reaction acquired to a *previously indifferent* stimulus. In order for conditioning to take place, therefore, it is important that there shall not be prepotent reflexes strong enough to prevent the animal's reacting to essentially neutral stimuli. In psychoanalytic terminology we might say, therefore, that a necessary condition for this most elementary of the adjustments of the ego to external reality is the existence of free psychic energy [11] that can be turned to *previously indifferent* stimuli.

That a similar condition exists for the formation of differentiations is strikingly illustrated by Pavlov's experiments upon the production of functional pathological states. These pathological states are of two sorts. One consists in an excessive predominance of excitation, so that the animal reacts to all stimuli (even previously inhibitory stimuli) with excitation. In the other type of pathological state, on the other hand, the animal reacts to all stimuli with inhibition. Either of these two types of pathological disturbance not only makes impossible the formation of new differentiations or conditioned reflexes, but also destroys for a prolonged period existing differentiations. Interesting for our present argument is the fact that the procedure for producing these pathological states consists regularly in throwing the animal into what psychoanalysts would call an acute conflict. The procedures commonly used as either (1) to attempt to force the animal to form differentiations that in number or fineness of discrimination exceed its capacity; or (2) to exceed the animal's capacity to react to painful stimuli as conditioned alimentary stimuli. It requires no further comment to make it evident that in both of these situations opposing reactions are called forth in such intensity that further conditioning and differentiation become impossible. What apparently happens is that each of the opposing reactions becomes generalized widely, and the stronger of the two or some resultant reaction becomes a stereotyped generalized reaction to all stimuli. Paraphrasing now into psychoanalytic terminology in accordance with our argument, we may say that the conflict has become too intense and generalized to leave any energy free for ego functioning.

The external reality function of the ego would thus appear to be *dependent upon two conditions:*

(1) *There must be conflict, either external or internal;* in other words, the animal must be in a state of deprivation; and

(2) *The conflict must not be too intense; there must be sufficient energy left free to allow the animal to retain its alertness to previously indifferent stimuli.*

This analysis of the external reality function of the ego enables us, moreover, to carry one step further our comparison of repression with external and internal inhibition. In psychoanalysis we are accustomed to distinguish between the repression and the conscious rejection of a wish or impulse. The conscious rejection of an impulse is from beginning to end an act of the ego in accordance with its function of adaptation to external reality. This adaptation to external reality, we have seen, is based upon the formation of differentiations in which *previously indifferent* stimuli (i.e., the real external situation) become the arbiters as to whether or not the particular tendency shall be inhibited. Repression, on the other hand, is characterized as a "flight" of the ego resulting in a withdrawal of the repressed tendency away from the reality-testing functioning of the ego. Repression therefore corresponds to those functional pathological states in Pavlov's experiments in which the "conflict" is too intense to allow essentially neutral stimuli (i.e., real external situation) to become arbiters in the process of differentiation. We have pointed out above that the phenomena of internal inhibition give evidence of a struggle between inhibition and excitation (i.e., between inhibiting and inhibited tendencies). This is particularly true during the phases of initial generalization of both excitatory and inhibitory reflexes. If I understand Pavlov rightly, a completed differentiation involves a concentration of both excitatory and inhibitory reflexes each about its specific differential stimuli; in other words, in a "solution" of the initial "conflict." It is the inhibitions incident to such differentiations ("conflict solutions") that correspond to the phenomena of conscious rejection; whereas the phenomena of repression correspond closely to the inhibitions resulting from the chronically "unsolved conflicts."

Before we proceed further with analogies between psychoanalytic findings and those of Pavlov, however, there are important objections to be considered. Are the phenomena that we are comparing really comparable?

Pavlov is discussing rather elementary automatic reactions, usually to external stimuli. Psychoanalysis deals with wishes and impulses arising from the great diffuse drives, such as hunger and sex, within the organism. Such wishes often manifest themselves in dreams or fantasies rather than in any overt action. The activity to which a wish gives rise is, moreover, goal-directed, tending to persist until the wish is fulfilled, and reducible if at all to reflex terms involving not one but many reflexes. Any serious attempt to correlate Pavlov's work with psychoanalytic findings must therefore undertake at least to sketch a sort of "structural formula" of a wish and of its fulfillment mechanisms in the terms of Pavlov's data.

Before attempting this, however, we do well to realize that the phenomena with which Pavlov is dealing are not so simple as they might seem. The alimentary salivary reflexes investigated by Pavlov are, of course, only one small element in the food-seeking reactions of the animal studied. Pavlov notes the accompanying alimentary motor re-action, but if the animal were released from the stand we know that it would be likely to run to its food, and even if no adequate condi-tioned stimuli were at hand, we know that a really hungry dog would proceed to seek for food until it either was satisfied or was diverted by fatigue or otherwise from the attempt. It becomes evident immedi-ately, therefore, that the alimentary salivary reflexes that Pavlov studies are only isolated elements in a more complex goal-directed activity.

It seems probable, moreover, that we are also underestimating the complexity of the conditioned responses that Pavlov describes. We have already pointed out that Pavlov's formulation of the conditioning process seems to take inadequate account of the animal's hunger. Pavlov apparently takes it for granted as a necessary condition of his experi-ments that his dogs are sufficiently hungry and speaks as though he thought of the alimentary salivary secretion as conditioned to the formerly indifferent external stimulus alone. We know, however, that a hungry man will dream of food and it is thus evident that the state of hunger itself must play an important part at least in sensitizing the receptors for the conditioned stimulus. We must therefore probably think of the conditioning process in Pavlov's experiments as a double one, composed of two more elementary conditioning processes: (1) the state of hunger becomes conditioned to sensitize the receptors for the conditioned stimulus to respond more readily; and (2) the conditioned stimulus becomes conditioned to excite in its turn the salivary secretory reaction.

Let us examine this suggestion in the light of the theory of dreams. Freud [12] has formulated the hypothesis that the wish-fulfilling hallucina-tion or dream arises in the simplest cases in reaction to an unsatisfied drive by hallucinatory reproduction of a previous experience in which this drive was satisfied. What Freud here postulates is obviously an-alogous to a conditioned reflex reaction. A hungry man dreams of food. The man has been hungry before and his hunger has been followed by the sight of food and then by satisfaction of his hunger. Pavlov has in fact demonstrated that internal physiological states may acquire con-ditioned reflex properties, and it therefore seems not unreasonable to suppose that the state of hunger itself might become conditioned to elicit some sort of a reproduction of a previous satisfying experience.

Dreams and hallucinations, however, are subjective phenomena. Conditioned reflexes are objective motor or secretory reactions. Are there any objective evidences that dreams and hallucinations elicit reactions similar to those that would have been elicited by the corresponding real stimuli?

This question must necessarily recall to our minds one of the most fundamental peculiarities of unconscious mental processes—the fact that, in the system Ucs, wish and fact, psychic and external reality, are treated as equivalent. A dream does satisfy the dream wish for a time at least, just as though it corresponded to reality; only in this way, in fact, can we explain the dream's success in prolonging sleep. Moreover, we know that unconscious fantasies call forth reactions of fear, guilt, * etc., such as would correspond, at least qualitatively, to their actual realization. Thirst may, for example, call up a dream of a cooling drink that may for a time give considerable relief; and a passive sexual wish, as in Freud's well-known case,[13] may give rise to a vivid dream calling forth fear such as the real "wolf" might have caused. It appears therefore that we must take quite seriously the idea that hunger may become conditioned to elicit the reactions corresponding to stimuli associated with its satisfaction.

The equivalence of psychic and external reality, however, holds

* The unconscious insight of the superego into the nature of repressed tendencies is of course only another name for the tendency of the superego to react to unconscious fantasies with guilt, fear, self-punishment, etc., as though the fantasies corresponded to external reality.

There is one point, however, in which our psychoanalytic knowledge of the process of repression goes beyond any analogies that physiological studies are as yet able to give us. Repression is sometimes characterized (Freud—Interpretation of Dreams, Chapter 7, section e, Primary and Secondary Processes—Repression) as a flight of the ego from painful mental contents. As such we have seen it offers little to distinguish it from the external and internal inhibition in Pavlov's experiments; and in the case of simple phobias, for example, the repressive process seems hardly more complicated than this.

In many instances, however, in addition to the flight of the ego from the (originally external) danger associated with the repressed impulse, there is also an active rejection of the impulse by the superego (this is, of course, seen most plainly in aggressive impulses to self-punishment—such as suicide). This active rejecting role, as Freud has pointed out in his account of the origin of the superego (The Ego and the Id), is based upon an identification with the forbidding parent. The activity involved in this identification with the role of the forbidding parent is moreover beautifully illustrated in what might be called a sort of intermediate stage in the development of the superego —in which children tend to impose first upon other children the prohibitions and punishments that they have received from their parents.

This process of identification with the behavior of others which is so important for the understanding of our psychoanalytic findings has as yet, however, so far as I am aware, received no thoroughgoing experimental physiological analysis—easy as it might be to speculate upon possible mechanisms involved.

good only for unconscious mental processes or, more technically speaking, only for the system Ucs. Conscious mental processes, or the system Cs, are in fact specifically characterized by the ability to test reality, to distinguish between reality and wish-fulfilling fantasy.

This corresponds, however, to another point that must necessarily follow according to our hypothesis. Dreams and unconscious fantasies do not as a rule lead to real satisfaction. If hunger has been conditioned to elicit a hallucination and the reactions appropriate to the corresponding external stimulus, we must therefore assume that this conditioned reflex will soon be differentially inhibited in contrast to motor reactions that are more successful in bringing real satisfaction. The wide-awake child no longer dreams of sweets but looks for them in the pantry. The above, however, is merely a physiological description of what in psychoanalysis we call the function of testing reality.

There can now be only one possible explanation for the inability of the system Ucs to distinguish between wish and reality. We have found that *the reality-testing function is based upon the establishment of a differentiation to inhibit conditioned reactions that treat wish-fulfilling fantasies as equivalent to reality. The loss of the reality-testing function in the system Ucs must therefore be due to conditions that destroy this differentiation.* (See below, note on p. 20.)

What is here suggested is, of course, a physiological explanation for the distinction between system Cs and Ucs. Our physiological hypothesis confirms Freud's conclusion that the distinction is a dynamic rather than a topographical one. The system Ucs, however, has other peculiarities than the fact that it cannot distinguish between wish and external reality. It functions according to the primary psychic process which differs in many ways from the secondary psychic process characteristic of the system Cs. The primary process [14] is characterized by the ready displacement of psychic energy from one mental element to another, by the ready condensation of mutually contradictory elements, by timelessness, and by the lack of distinction between psychic and external reality. Are any of Pavlov's data comparable to the peculiarities of the primary process?

We have already referred to the functional pathological states or "experimental neuroses" in Pavlov's dogs, and to the fact that these may be either excitatory or inhibitory in character. Similar to the inhibitory types there are also what Pavlov calls "partial sleep states" —induced by limiting the generalization of internal inhibition upon which normal sleep is based. The chief difference between these partial sleep states and the inhibitory type of experimental neuroses lies in the shorter duration of the former.

In either of these types of inhibitory state it occurs frequently that a dog will react with a considerable salivary secretion to a weak stimulus that ordinarily would have elicited only a very slight secretion, whereas a strong stimulus that ordinarily would have elicited a considerable secretion is now reacted to with little or none. This Pavlov calls "the paradoxical phenomenon." Sometimes this peculiarity is even more pronounced in that a stimulus that ordinarily would have inhibited secretion now excites secretion, whereas a previously excitatory stimulus becomes inhibitory—"the ultra-paradoxical phenomenon" of Pavlov. In other cases the effect is less pronounced in that all stimuli, weak and strong alike, elicit approximately equal reactions—"the equalization phenomenon" of Pavlov.

It is, of course, very difficult to compare phenomena of this sort, based wholly upon objective and external observation, with the much more complex phenomena that characterize the primary process of mental functioning of the system Ucs. Nevertheless these paradoxical and equalization phenomena of Pavlov's dogs are at least suggestive of two of the specific peculiarities of unconscious mental processes: (1) the representation of an unconscious psychic element by its opposite, and (2) the displacement of emphasis from psychic elements heavily laden with affect upon relatively indifferent elements. The probability that these two groups of phenomena are essentially equivalent is enhanced further by the similarity of the conditions under which they occur: in psychoanalytic experience, in neuroses (including psychoses), and dreams; in Pavlov's experiments, in "experimental neuroses" and "partial sleep states." *

* This discussion must obviously also raise the question as to just what are the conditions that cause the differentiation between reality and fantasy to break down in neuroses and in dreams.

In the case of neuroses, the breakdown of this differentiation corresponds to the above-discussed general tendency of conflict to break down existing differentiations. Clinical and physiological evidence agree, moreover, also in the fact that neuroses may be either predominantly excitatory (manic or catatonic excitements) or predominantly inhibitory (depressions, catatonic stupors, etc.), depending upon the excitatory or inhibitory character of the undifferentiated reactions called forth by the (conscious or unconscious) fantasy presentations.

In the case of dreams, it is not immediately clear just why the generalization of internal inhibition upon which sleep is based should favor the undifferentiated tendency to react to fantasy presentations as though they were real. The clue to the explanation lies probably in the fact that these undifferentiated reactions to the fantasy presentations are themselves inhibitory in character. The wish-fulfilling dream is by virtue of this very fact sleep-conserving. In other words, satisfying a wish exerts a quieting or inhibi-

If these two groups of phenomena are equivalent, an interesting light is thrown upon the phenomena of repression. We have called attention to the fact that the internal inhibition of a conditioned reflex involves a struggle between inhibiting and inhibited tendencies. This is, of course, especially the case before a particular stimulus has become established as an inhibitory stimulus. It is now of interest to cite the report of Ischlondsky [15] that the above-described paradoxical and equalization phenomena occur not only in experimental neuroses and partial sleep states but also as transient phenomena during the process of establishment of new differentiations. The analogy with psychoanalytic findings is again suggestive—for we have already pointed out that the phenomena of repression (in contradistinction to those of conscious renunciation of a rejected tendency) correspond to those of an incomplete differentiation or "unsolved conflict" and repression also relegates a mental process to the system Ucs.

We have as yet, however, only half sketched the "structural formula" of a wish. We have traced the origin of the wish-fulfillment fantasy as a conditioned reaction to the hunger state, and we have observed how the tendency to react to this fantasy as though it were real has been differentially inhibited. When this fantasy or hallucination ceases to be reacted to as though it were real, what becomes of it? Psychoanalytic experience tells us that it may now become a conscious daydream, a wish, or a purpose. But as a wish or a purpose it acquires new properties. It becomes now a goal for action. The child's dream of sweets, for example, upon being inhibited as a wish-fulfilling hallucination, becomes now a goal and incentive directing the child to the pantry. Can we understand this in terms of Pavlov's data?

Certain of Pavlov's experiments help us to make a first step toward the answer to this question. If an animal is fed regularly—say three minutes after the sounding of a gong—there results what Pavlov calls a delayed conditioned reflex. During the first two and a half minutes or more there will be no salivary secretion, but during the last few seconds an abundant secretion appears. It is possible to demonstrate,

---

tory effect and this "inhibition of satisfaction" (as we may call it) apparently fuses readily with the generalized internal inhibitions upon which sleep is based.

This explanation, however, raises the further question (which will be discussed briefly below—footnote, page 25) as to the exact nature of the relations between this "inhibition of satisfaction" and the inhibitory reflexes in Pavlov's experiments. As indicated below, this point requires further experimental investigation. It seems probable, moreover, that a clinical study, especially of dream material, might throw considerable light upon it.

however, that during the period during which there is no secretion, the secretory reaction is nevertheless latent but internally inhibited. This type of internal inhibition is called the *inhibition of delay*.

It is possible, moreover, so to condition an animal that a stimulus such as, for example, an electric gong will be inhibitory when exhibited alone, but will have a marked positive secretory effect in combination with, let us say, the sound of bubbling water. In other words, the compound stimulus—gong plus bubbling water—acquires a positive secretory effect that may be quite independent of any positive effect of either gong or bubbling water when exhibited alone.

These experimental findings of Pavlov furnish close analogies to the mode of action of a wish, purpose, or other goal presentation. As an urge inciting to appropriate activity, the goal presentation acts essentially as a constantly present element in a series of compound stimulus combinations. To choose a simple example,[16] a student wishing to study will react otherwise to an electric light switch in a dark room than will a student wishing to sleep. The wish to study plus the electric light switch thus form a compound stimulus inducing the student to turn on the light; whereas neither the electric light switch nor the wish to study, alone, would have given rise to this action.

A second function of the goal presentation is an anticipatory or preparatory one. The student looking for the electric light switch will be more likely to find it and react to it than if he were not looking for it. The wish to find the switch implies already an anticipatory sensitization to it. Sometimes also one becomes impatient or overconfident and reacts as though a desired goal were already achieved—as in the case of the well-known tendency to overconfident exultation and relaxation of effort upon the eve of victory; facts which show clearly that the tendency to react to the goal as already realized is, though inhibited, nevertheless latent just as in the case of Pavlov's delayed conditioned reflexes.

The mechanisms so far discussed, however, explain the guiding function of the goal presentation only as a static function after fixed reaction patterns have been formed. In the example given above, for instance, the student presumably already knows that the pressing of the electric light button will turn on the light. Pressing the button, therefore, is already a relatively fixed pattern reaction to the combination, wish for light plus electric light button.

A more difficult and fundamental problem concerns the influence of the goal upon the learning process. Let us suppose, for example, that the electric light switch is of a kind different from any with which the student is already familiar and that the student is uncertain which of several buttons or levers he should manipulate. He tries several and finally finds the particular switch that will turn on the electric light. By this process, however, he has presumably learned something. The next time he wishes light in this room, he will probably proceed immediately to the correct switch and avoid all manipulations that failed to bring the desired light.

I choose this very simple and trite example in order to bring into relief both how it resembles and how it differs from the processes of conditioning and of differentiation described by Pavlov. The similarities will impress us first. The light corresponds to the unconditioned stimulus (e.g., food in the mouth) in Pavlov's experiments; the desire for light, to the animal's hunger. In Pavlov's experiments, to be sure, the response (salivary secretion) is a relatively fixed one and the effect of the conditioning process is to give certain *stimuli* a positive effect and others an inhibitory effect upon salivary secretion; whereas, in our example, the differentiation takes place between different *motor responses*. Nevertheless, just as the unconditioned stimulus (food in the mouth) in Pavlov's experiments converts the stimulus just preceding it into a positively conditioned stimulus, so does the light, in our example, "condition" the student to turn next time to the correct switch; and just as in Pavlov's experiments other *stimuli* acquire inhibitory properties because they are not followed by the unconditioned stimulus, so in our example does the student learn to dispense with *manipulations* that failed to bring the light. Upon the basis of these analogies, therefore, Ischlondsky [17] quite unhesitatingly speaks of motor reactions as well as stimuli as capable of becoming positively conditioned.

There is one important difference, however, between such "conditioned" motor responses and the conditioned reflex phenomena of Pavlov as worked out in experiments upon the salivary reflexes. According to Pavlov's original formulation, a conditioned stimulus acquires the reflex properties of the unconditioned stimulus upon which it is based. This seems quite correct so long as one speaks only of the salivary secretory reflexes, inasmuch as the reflex response acquired by the conditioned stimulus in this instance is indeed "the secretion of saliva of the same quality and character" as that elicited by the unconditioned stimulus. The same could be said of reflexes conditioned upon avoidance and defense reflexes as unconditioned stimuli—the animal in these cases, e.g., withdrawing its paw in response to conditioned stimuli just as it does in response to the unconditioned stimulus (electric shock, etc.).

In our example, however, something quite different occurs. The "conditioned" motor response in this instance is to push the button to *turn on* the light. * The reaction *to the light* will be quite different— perhaps sitting down and starting to study. The effect of the light as a reinforcing stimulus is to "condition" positively reactions that *result in* or *are followed* by the light [18] rather than to condition other stimuli to elicit the same response as the light itself.

I suspect, in fact, that if Pavlov had turned his attention more to the alimentary motor reflexes, he would himself have been compelled to modify or supplement his original formulation. If the conditioned stimulus in this case is the taking of food into the mouth, then the animal's "turning his head toward the expected food and smacking his lips" cannot be a conditioned reproduction of the reflex elicited by the unconditioned stimulus—for the unconditioned reaction to taking food into the mouth is mastication and swallowing. The answer of the physiologist to this criticism might possibly be that in the case of the alimentary motor reflex the unconditioned stimulus is not the taste but the sight or smell of the food and that the turning of the head toward the food is indeed an unconditioned reaction to this stimulus. I suspect, however, that the effect of the sight or smell of the food in this case merely obscures the relations we are here discussing—for, in the case of the maze experiments of American experimental psychologists—in which the actual reaching of the food is plainly the effective reinforcing unconditioned stimulus—the choice of the correct path through the maze is obviously a very different reaction from that of the animal after it has found the food. It would seem therefore that in these cases we must substitute, for Pavlov's original formulation, the more popular formula of common-sense psychology that it is those motor reactions that lead to the satisfaction of a drive or a wish that tend to become positively conditioned, whereas

* For the sake of simplicity I have purposely relegated to this footnote discussion of another difference between our example and the conditioned salivary reflexes of Pavlov. The light in our example is not an *unconditioned* stimulus. The motor response to the electric light switch must therefore be compared with the *secondary* conditioned reflexes of Pavlov, i.e., conditioned reflexes secondarily conditioned upon the basis of a conditioned rather than of an unconditioned stimulus. A further problem is created by the fact that such secondary conditioned reflexes are established with much difficulty in Pavlov's experiments—in marked contrast to the stability of much goal-directed behavior in human beings. Further investigation would seem to be needed to determine whether this is due to differences between dogs and human beings or to differences between salivary and motor reflexes or to other unknown factors.

those reactions that are not followed by the desired satisfaction tend to become inhibited.[19]

But satisfaction is a subjective psychological concept. To what objective physiological phenomena does it correspond?

Let us consider somewhat more closely the function of the unconditioned stimulus in Pavlov's experiments. The function of the stimuli presented by food in the mouth would appear to be twofold. On the one hand are the phenomena upon which Pavlov's experiments lay chief emphasis: introduction of food into the mouth *initiates* the processes of mastication and salivary digestion for which, of course, salivary secretion is a necessary preliminary. But the introduction of food into the mouth exerts another influence that is equally important; it puts an end * for the time to the food-seeking motor activities of the animal. It is obviously this inhibitory effect of the unconditioned stimulus upon the food-seeking activities of the animal that is the physiological correlate to the satisfying psychological character of this stimulus; and the well-known soporific effects of satiety (gastronomical or sexual) point to still more widely generalized inhibitory effects of the internal stimuli corresponding to satiety.

It will be of interest to consider these relations in some detail with reference to the alimentary motor reactions. The *initiatory* unconditioned stimulus for these motor reactions is probably the combination of hunger plus the sight or smell of food. This initiatory combination obviously has an *excitatory* effect. In contradistinction to this excitatory initiatory combination, the introduction of food into the mouth, as already pointed out, serves as a *terminal* stimulus whose function is an *inhibitory* one, *to put an end to* the alimentary motor reactions in question.

We now note that it is the *inhibitory terminal* stimulus that is capable of exercising a positive conditioning or reinforcing effect upon successful

* Pavlov has apparently only just begun [in 1932] to investigate this inhibitory effect of the unconditioned stimulus, and in fact appears to be investigating it only indirectly—still by means of experiments upon the more easily measured salivary reflexes. One series of experiments is, however, suggestive, in that it indicates that a previously positively conditioned stimulus tends to lose its positively conditioned properties and even to become inhibitory for both salivary and motor alimentary reflexes, if exhibited regularly *immediately after* the unconditioned stimulus. The inhibitory effect of the unconditioned stimulus upon stimuli immediately following, Pavlov is inclined to regard as an external inhibition—a suggestion that might imply that the inhibitory effect of food in the mouth upon the food-seeking motor activities of the animal is an external inhibitory effect caused by the prepotent masticatory and secretory reflexes initiated by this unconditioned stimulus.

Certain other well-known facts, however, would seem to indicate that the inhibitory effect of the satisfaction of the fundamental drives has a much more fundamental biological basis.

motor reactions; but it is again the *initiatory* combination whose power to elicit the successful motor reaction is reinforced. The "satisfying" terminal stimulus, however, stands in a relation of direct contrast to one essential element in the initiatory combination. Hunger implies the lack of food; the desire for light, in the example of the student, is, one might say, the negative or opposite of the reinforcing stimulus, the light. The reinforcing influence of the "satisfying" stimulus, light or food, is thus exerted in favor of the power of its *polar opposite* to elicit a motor reaction *upon which the light or food itself exerts an inhibitory effect.*

Such detailed exposition of facts that are matters of everyday knowledge * probably seems exceedingly pedantic. Such an exposition is necessary, however, in order to bring out clearly an analogy that seems to me to be of considerable significance. We are all familiar with the phenomena of mutual spinal induction demonstrated by Sherrington,[20] by virtue of which the activity of one muscle group is accompanied by the simultaneous reflex inhibition of antagonistic groups. In the light of the above exposition, I am inclined to believe that the fundamental biological tendency of living organisms to strive toward the satisfaction of drives is based upon mechanisms of the same general sort as the spinal induction mechanisms of Sherrington. Just as the activity of one muscle group and the inhibition of its antagonist form together an organic functional unit reaction, so also, even more fundamentally, do the inhibitory influence of a "satisfying" stimulus group and the excitatory influence of the need or hunger for that group of stimuli constitute a functional unity—such that the inhibitory influence of the "satisfying" stimulus necessarily involves a reinforcement of the excitatory influence of the "need" for it—with reference to any particular motor reaction.

In the analysis of dreams one finds frequently that the dream wish is a direct denial of the unpleasant experience that was the immediate exciting cause of the dream [21]—an observation that suggests definitely that the wish-fulfilling function of the dream is based upon a mechanism of induction, the wish-fulfilling hallucination being in direct contrast to the "need" that calls it forth.

We have already seen that the wish-fulfilling fantasy presentation is capable of functioning in either of two different ways. When the

---

* The writer of course realizes that such "everyday knowledge" is only rough and approximate. More precise working out of the points here discussed must await further experimentation. See footnote on p. 25 above.

satisfying dream of food fails to be followed by real food, its function as a satisfying substitute for food is inhibited and it becomes then a goal spurring the individual to seek for food. We now notice that these two functions are not only alternate functions; they also stand in polar contrast to each other. The wish for food sets in action just those motor reactions that the dream of food inhibits. The activation of these motor reactions would therefore quite plainly seem to be an effect by induction of the inhibition of the "satisfying" function of the dream.

We have already cited the fact that, for example, inhibition of a conditioned reflex to stimulation at one point on the skin often gives rise by induction to an increase in the conditioned reflex effect obtained from another skin area—and especially a very distant or a very near skin area. We have also noted that the wish for light, in the case of our student, functions (1) analogously to a delayed reflex *to the light* during the inhibitory period of latency, and (2) as one element in a series of compound stimuli, sensitizing the student to react to the otherwise indifferent electric switch. It will be noted that the analogy to the above-mentioned induction phenomena in Pavlov's experiments is very close; and that the sensitization of the student to the electric switch would seem quite plainly to be an effect by induction of the inhibition of the conditioned reaction to the light.

Upon the basis of the above discussion, therefore, we feel justified in advancing the hypothesis that *the activating influence of the wish upon motor activities directed toward its realization is a direct effect by induction of the inhibition of its reality value.*[22]

There is direct evidence also in Pavlov's experimental findings that hunger, like its derivative the wish, is a source of radiation of excitation. Pavlov reports that increase in the animal's hunger tends to break down internal inhibitions of all kinds. It is evident, therefore, that the hunger itself must give rise to a rather widely distributed radiation of excitation. Is it possible, perhaps, that the diffuse alertness that Pavlov postulates as a necessary precondition if new conditioned reflexes are to be formed is also a manifestation of just such a widely distributed radiation of excitation from hunger and other drives?

One of the most fundamental physiological objections[23] to the psychoanalytic formulations has been directed against the psychoanalytic assumption of a free psychosexual energy that can be transferred from one wish or activity to another. The phenomena of substitute gratification, regression, and sublimation seem to make such an assumption inevitable, but it has nevertheless been very difficult to reconcile this assumption with any known physiological data. The evidence just adduced for a widely distributed radiation of excitation corresponding to the hunger state points the way to a fruitful investigation of this problem. Pavlov has already worked out very comprehensive experiments upon the progress of irradiation of excitation and inhibition. If experiments could be devised to work out the relations between the *extent and intensity of such irradiations* on the one hand, and factors such as *hunger* and *fatigue* on the other, we suspect that such investigations might throw considerable light upon the physiological nature of the "psychosexual" energy that psychoanalysis must postulate. From our psychoanalytic evidence, we should be inclined to suspect, for instance, that the effect of external stimulation and of previous conditioning would consist in large part in the *concentration* [24] *in the neighborhood of particular stimuli* of some of the diffuse radiation arising from the hunger state. If this expectation should prove to be correct, then the "functional mosaics" of Pavlov would represent *patterns of distribution* of excitation and inhibition, the total amount of which would depend upon the state of satisfaction of the various drives, the extent and degree of fatigue, and perhaps other similar factors.

For the sake of clarity it will be well at this point to bring together and summarize the several suggestions here made with a view to a theoretical reconstruction of the mode of functioning of a drive and especially of those drives, such as hunger or sex, whose activity involves the seeking of an object.

A drive may be called into activity in one of two ways: either (1) (provided the animal is not completely sated) by an external stimulus such as the sight of food; or (2) by the development of a need as a result of the more or less prolonged absence of gratification. Once called into activity, the drive now tends to give rise to a diffuse radiation* of excitation which makes the animal alert or sensitive to a wide range of external stimuli. The diffuse distribution of this excitation is, however, combated by tendencies toward concentration which are in general of two sorts. (1) There is the tendency toward the concentration of the energy of the drive upon dreams or wishes derived from previous experiences of satisfaction, or, in more physiological terms, upon the receptors corresponding to stimuli that have

---

* Such diffuse "radiation" might conceivably take place either by way of nervous pathways or by means of internal secretions through the bloodstream.

been previously positively conditioned. (2) On the other hand, we must postulate an equally important tendency to concentration of excitation about the external stimuli actually presented at the moment, a tendency to concentration which is of course increased if the external stimulus presented is a positively conditioned one.

We have pointed out that a wish and an appropriate direct stimulus (e.g., the student's wish for light plus the electric switch) function as two elements in a compound stimulus. I should like to supplement this analogy with another one which I suspect is not inconsistent with it and has also the advantage of accounting for a greater number of facts. There is much to suggest that a wish and the external stimuli presented at the moment act by virtue of some sort of difference of potential that tends to activate pathways between them. Thus my hunger may activate wishes for a particular food, for a restaurant where the food is particularly well served, and for ways of getting to that restaurant. But this forms only one component in the determination of my behavior; for my choice of route will in any case be determined in an equal degree by my location at the moment, and even my choice of restaurant and of food wished for must be influenced by their availability.

The reader will recall that Freud [25] has shown that a dream must fulfill two conditions. (1) It must represent the fulfillment of a wish dating from childhood, and (2) it must contain references to material of the day preceding. Thus in dreams, also, we seem to see a suggestion that there is at work a sort of potential difference between a wish and recent direct stimulation; and the tendency to hallucinatory reproduction of previous satisfying experiences, as though they corresponded to external reality, must probably be regarded as another manifestation of the same sort of dynamic polarity between wish and direct stimulation. (That the wish must be an infantile one we would explain by the fact that infantile wishes form the undifferentiated basis for all later ones.)

This suggestion that wish and external reality function as poles activating pathways between them can readily be brought into relation with a recent suggestion of Lashley's. Upon the basis of very extensive experimental investigations, Child [26] has demonstrated that "physiological gradients from points of higher to points of lower excitation" establish themselves as the first step in embryological development, determine the axes of growth, control the details of development, and, in the nervous system, predetermine the pathways of conduction before the anatomical connections have been established. Lashley [27] has tentatively suggested that such physiological gradients play an important part in the function of the cerebral cortex. I am tempted to follow up this suggestion with the further one that the psychological tension between wish and external reality corresponds to the dominant physiological gradient determining behavior.

Returning now to the influence of the wish end of this gradient upon behavior, we have found reason to believe that the radiation of excitation from a wish or goal presentation is analogous to the induction phenomena of Pavlov. Is it possible that the radiation of excitation resulting from the state of hunger is also an induction phenomenon? This suggests questions as to the fundamental relations between "hunger" and "satisfaction," on the one hand, and excitation and inhibition, on the other hand—questions which the present evidence does not permit us to answer with any certainty but which it will nevertheless be well to indicate.

We have already cited the soporific effects of satiety. In most of Pavlov's experiments, however, internal inhibition arises under exactly the opposite conditions. Pavlov reports that every excitatory reflex tends sooner or later to become inhibitory. This replacement of an excitatory by an inhibitory process occurs, however, much more quickly if the excitatory reflex is not promptly followed (reinforced) by the unconditioned stimulus, and Pavlov also suggests that the explanation of this probably lies in the fact that the unconditioned stimulus puts an end to the excitement in the nervous elements corresponding to the conditioned reflex and that the excitatory process is probably much more prolonged in case the conditioned reflex fails to be reinforced.

The replacement of excitation by internal inhibition thus appears to be, as Pavlov indicates, a manifestation of fatigue—in direct contrast to the other type of inhibition corresponding to the soporific effects of satiety.

It would thus appear that inhibitory processes arise under two contrasting sets of conditions: (1) *as a reaction to satiety,* * and (2) as a manifestation of fatigue following upon prolonged or intense excitement *resulting from an unsatisfied drive. The excitatory process* would

* Pavlov compares this inhibitory effect of the unconditioned stimulus to the relief from his duties of "an efficient and watchful signalman who after having performed his responsible duties has to be provided with an immediate rest during which he is refreshed so that he may afterwards perform his task again with the same efficiency as before."

then appear to be *an intermediate episode* * *between the inhibitory states of satiety and of fatigue.* We know from Pavlov's experiments that excitatory states tend to radiate. Is it possible that the phenomena of positive induction represent the next succeeding intermediate stage, in which excitation still continues to radiate from a center in which the (internal) inhibition of fatigue has already set in?

We may note in conclusion that the conditions that we here suggest as necessary for excitatory processes in general are strikingly analogous to the conditions necessary for that optimum degree of excitation that makes possible the learning process: (1) *an unsatisfied drive or conflict,* and (2) an intensity of that drive or conflict *that does not exceed a certain limit.*

But it is time now to wait for further experimental investigation of these fundamental relations and to turn to a more concrete problem, and I should like to conclude this discussion with a few remarks about the mechanism of the therapeutic effect of psychoanalysis.

Psychoanalysis started with the conception that psychoneuroses were the result of psychic traumata. Subsequent experience has indeed taught psychoanalysts not to picture the onset of a neurosis quite so dramatically as some of the early cases of hysteria might tempt us to do, but this modifies Freud's former views only to the extent that it leads us to expect in most cases not one great traumatic event but a series of lesser traumata.

Our discussion of the external reality function of the ego now puts us in a position to understand in physiological terms the nature of a psychic trauma. *A trauma is an experience calling forth a conflict of such intensity that there is no energy left free to be turned to neutral differential stimuli.* As a result of this, *the traumatic experience has been withdrawn from the learning process.*

The therapeutic functions of the analyst correspond to the twofold conditions upon which depend the external reality function of the ego: (1) By various devices, but notably by interpretation of the symptoms, the analyst must reawaken the old conflicts and permit a reliving of the traumatic experiences; and (2) by judicious handling of the transference, he must when possible reduce the intensity of the conflict in its new edition so that energy may now be left free to be turned to

---

* More specifically, the stimuli that give rise to excitatory processes appear in general to be of two sorts: (1) "hunger" from an unsatisfied drive; and (2) "signal stimuli" that (we might say) "offer hope" of possible satisfaction (i.e., if a person is not completely satiated, the sight of food alone arouses hunger).

neutral differential stimuli. Only in this way can the traumatic experience be made accessible to the learning process.

I shall conclude by calling attention to the confirmation which this gives to the views of Freud,[28] Ferenczi, Rank,[29] Alexander,[30] and others upon the importance of "recapitulation with insight" * as the essential therapeutic moment in psychoanalysis.

We may note also the light that the above considerations throw upon the well-known aftereffect of a psychoanalytic treatment, an "aftereffect" which is obviously a result of the learning process that has been made possible by the treatment.

NOTES

1. Lashley, K. S.: Brain Mechanisms and Intelligence, Hafner, 1929.

2. Except as otherwise noted, the following accounts of Pavlov's experimental results are abstracted from Pavlov: Conditioned Reflexes, Dover, 1927.

3. Freud, S.: The Passing of the Oedipus Complex, Hogarth Press, 1924. Collected Papers, Vol. 2.

4. Ischlondsky, N. E.: Physiologische Grundlagen der Tiefenpsychologie, 1930. See especially Chapter 2.

5. I owe the clear recognition of this distinction to a personal conversation with Alexander. See Alexander, F.: Psychoanalysis of the Total Personality, Nervous and Mental Disease Publishing Company, 1927. See especially Chapters 3 and 4.

6. Freud, S.: Inhibition, Symptom and Anxiety, 1926.

7. Schilder, P.: Conditioned Reflexes, Archives of Neurology and Psychiatry, 1929.

8. Koehler, W.: The Mentality of Apes, Harcourt, Brace, 1921.

9. Sachs, H.: Gemeinsame Tagträume, 1924. See also Alexander, F.: Psychoanalysis of the Total Personality, p. 126.

10. See references given in notes 5–8 above.

11. The concept "psychic energy" has been found difficult to reconcile with the physiological data at ·present available. See Lashley: Physiological Analysis of the Libido, Psychological Review, 1924. See also page 28 for further brief discussion of this point.

12. Freud, S.: Interpretation of Dreams. 1900, Chapter 7, section c, The Wish Fulfillment.

13. Freud, S.: From the History of an Infantile Neurosis, 1918.

14. See Freud: Interpretation of Dreams, Chapter 7, section e, also The Unconscious, 1915.

15. Ischlondsky, N. E.: Der Bedingte Reflex, 1930. See page 279.

16. This point has also been stressed by Woodward (Woodward, R. S.: Dynamic Psychology, 1924). Woodward, however, wrote before the publication in English of Pavlov's Conditioned Reflexes and did not bring his discussion so closely into relation with Pavlov's experimental data.

The tendency of the "drive stimulus" to call forth premature anticipatory reactions as through the goal were already present has been stressed by Hull (Hull, C. L.: Goal Attraction and Directing Ideas Conceived as Habit Phenomena, Psychological Review, 1931) and has been made by him the basis of a theoretical reconstruction of the

* The phrase is quoted from Alexander.

mechanisms of goal-directed behavior, which is in some respects similar to the one here presented. Hull, however, looks upon the goal presentation as a part of the anticipatory reaction that has *escaped inhibition* and does not recognize, therefore, the *contrast between the goal presentation as wished for and the achievement of the goal.*

17. Ischlondsky, N. E.: Der Bedingte Reflex, pp. 62–63. Physiologische Grundlagen der Tiefenpsychologie, p. 64.

18. In the American literature, this has been called by Thorndike the "law of effect." (Thorndike, E. L.: Educational Psychology, 1921, Vol. I, Chapter 12.) The contrast between this "law of effect" and the conditioning principle of Pavlov is particularly clearly brought out by K. A. Williams: The Conditioned Reflex and the Sign Function in Learning, Psychological Review, 1929. The "sign function" corresponds roughly to the role of induction in the present discussion.

19. This formula corresponds roughly to the pleasure principle of Freud or to modified forms of the pleasure principle such as the reality principle. Pavlov's original formulation correlates roughly with the repetition compulsion of Freud. See Freud: Beyond the Pleasure Principle, Hogarth Press, 1920.

20. Sherrington, C. S.: The Integrative Action of the Nervous System, 1923.

21. To cite only one example, see Freud's analysis of his own dream that he is riding horseback—dreamed in reaction to a boil upon the buttock. Freud, S.: Interpretation of Dreams, Chapter 5, section c, Somatic Sources of Dreams.

22. This inference is suggested by a number of examples cited by Ischlondsky (Physiologische Grundlagen der Tiefenpsychologie, pp. 51–57), but is not definitely stated by him.

23. Lashley, K. S.: Physiological Analysis of the Libido, Psychological Review, 1924.

24. See Thurstone, L. L.: The Nature of Intelligence, 1926. Thurstone, in agreement (at least to this extent) with the assumptions underlying psychoanalysis, points out that behavior arises from *diffuse* inner tendencies (such as hunger) which then become more and more *concentrated* in reaction to external stimuli.

25. Freud, S.: Interpretation of Dreams.

26. Child, C. M.: Physiological Foundations of Behavior, Hafner, 1924.

27. Lashley, K. S.: Brain Mechanisms and Intelligence, 1929.

28. Freud, S.: (1) Further Recommendations in the Technique of Psychoanalysis. Recollection Repetition and Working Through, 1914. (2) A General Introduction to Psychoanalysis, 1920, Chapter 28.

29. Ferenczi, S., and Rank, O.: Entwicklungsziele der Psychoanalyse, 1924.

30. Alexander, F.: A Metapsychological Description of the Process of Cure. International Journal of Psychoanalysis. 1923.

Chapter Two

REALITY AND THE UNCONSCIOUS

An experiment by Wolfgang Koehler illustrates another aspect of a similar principle. In the first part of the experiment a "mature bitch is brought into a blind alley . . . one end of which is cut off by a railing where she is kept occupied with food, her face toward the railing. When the food is nearly gone, more is put down" at some distance on the other side of the rail; "the bitch sees it, seems to hesitate a moment, then quickly turns" and runs "around the fence to the new food. . . . On repeating this experiment the food was not thrown far out but was dropped just outside the fence so that it lay directly in front of her separated only by the wire." In this case "she stood seemingly helpless as if the very nearness of the object and her concentration upon it (brought about by her sense of smell) 'blocked the idea' of the wide circle around the fence. She pushed again and again with her nose at the wire fence and did not budge from the spot." It is evident that here we see the inhibiting effect of a strong emotion (in this case, the fascination of the dog for the food that is so nearly within its reach) upon the capacity of the animal to take account of just the aspect of the situation that contains the clue to the solution of the problem. The possible detour has not an emotional charge high enough to compete with the food under the dog's nose. Hence the dog remains glued to the spot and ignores the only possibility of really gratifying its hunger.

Starting with this experiment of Koehler's, I tried to study, more in detail, the process of differentiation and its role in the solution of conflicts. As Alexander has pointed out, one of the outstanding features of neuroses and psychoses is their stereotyped character. The neurotic re-

Reprinted from *Psychoanalytic Quarterly*, 6 (1937).

peats over and over again the same unsuccessful solutions of his con-
flicts and learns nothing from his mistakes. Here we see the repetition
compulsion in its pure form. Reality adjustment, on the other hand, is
the product of a learning process. In making adjustments according to
the reality principle, one learns from one's mistakes. Learning too is
based upon the repetition compulsion but involves a modification of it.
Past mistakes must be remembered or tentatively repeated but under the
guidance of the urge to find a way of avoiding unpleasant consequences
in the future.

Thus it is important to realize that it is not the painful elements of
reality that are most conspicuously ignored in neurotic behavior, but
rather those emotionally indifferent aspects of reality whose sole value
consists in the fact that they might serve as differential criteria to enable
one to find new possibilities for gratification while at the same time
avoiding past mistakes.

We have tried to illustrate this principle clinically by comparison of
two dreams that were struggling with similar conflicts which, however,
differed quantitatively. We compared these two dreams with reference
to three quantities: the intensities of the two conflicting impulses and
the span of the synthetic capacity of the ego.

From this comparison we concluded that the fundamental differences
that distinguish rational waking behavior from neuroses and dreams are
based upon the quantitative relationship between the synthetic capacity
of the ego and the intensity of conflict. Because of the ego's inadequate
synthetic capacity, neuroses and dreams are usually able to deal with the
conflict only in a fragmentary way and tend to repeat in a stereotyped
manner reactions to previous traumatic experiences. Rational behavior
requires an ego span sufficient for one not only to view one's situation
as a whole but also to enable one to pay attention to differential criteria
so as to be able to learn from past mistakes instead of repeating them.

1. THE DYNAMIC PROBLEM IN REALITY ADJUSTMENT

The mechanisms of dreams, of wit, and of the common mistakes
of everyday life show plainly that even in normally adjusted adult
individuals there are ever-present tendencies to revert not only to the
wishes and emotional patterns of childhood but to irrational modes of
thinking as well. This fact confronts us with a dynamic problem. If

regression is so easy and attractive, what are the incentives that can induce one to follow the path of normal development? In other words, what are the dynamic or economic conditions that are necessary in order that development may proceed normally in spite of these ever-present regressive tendencies? What are the dynamic and economic conditions that determine whether irrational or rational modes of mental functioning shall prevail?

In the first approach to this problem Freud (1911) distinguished between pleasure principle and reality principle. According to the pleasure principle, one is dominated by the impulse to gain immediate pleasure and to avoid immediate pain. The reality principle demands, however, that a person renounce immediate pleasure and even endure pain for the sake of an assured future pleasure.

This distinction already enables us to state the problem of reality adaptation in dynamic terms. The hope of future pleasure is a notoriously weak force when pitted against immediate satisfaction. We should like to know therefore how one learns to renounce immediate pleasure and endure pain for the sake of future pleasure. What forces are strong enough to induce the psyche to renounce pleasure now and to accept pain for the sake of the future?

2. ARE NEUROSES AND DREAMS ABLE TO IGNORE PAIN?

Certain familiar psychoanalytic findings seem to present us with this problem in an even more perplexing form. Psychoanalysis has demonstrated that neuroses and psychoses (when they are not due to organic causes) are reactions to a conflict situation that is too difficult for the ego to face in reality. Psychoanalysis has also shown that neurotic and psychotic symptoms and dreams represent the fulfillment of wishes. We are tempted to infer from these two facts that dreams and neuroses are somehow able to banish the painful elements of reality, that they are somehow able to ignore the difficulties in the way of fulfilling one's wishes and the unhappy consequences that might result from them. According to Freud's earlier formulations, the unconscious can only wish and is dominated solely by the impulse to gain immediate pleasure and avoid immediate pain. If dreams and neuroses are really able to abolish pain, we might ask, what can induce anyone to wake up and come to terms with unpleasant realities?

When the question is put in this paradoxical form, it becomes evident that we must be making some false inferences. Dreams and neuroses are not unmodified products of the unconscious but rather the products of a compromise between repressed wishes and the censoring activity of the ego. The statement that the unconscious can only wish does not necessarily imply therefore that dreams and neuroses can ignore the painful elements of reality. As a matter of fact, we know that most neuroses and many psychoses are painful and that dreams are often unpleasant. According to Freud's earlier formulations, dreams become unpleasant when they express wishes that are disturbing to the ego. In any case, it is certain that even dreams and neuroses do not possess an unlimited capacity to ignore the painful elements of reality.

Nevertheless an unformulated impression persists that neuroses and dreams are less painful than the real conflicts that they are striving to replace. The chief phenomena upon which this impression is based are (1) wish-fulfilling dreams, and (2) the phenomena of secondary gain in the neuroses. We shall return later to the discussion of wish-fulfilling dreams. In the secondary gain in the neuroses, however, we have not a product of the original irrational process of symptom formation but a new reality adjustment taking advantage of the already formed symptoms in order to improve the patient's situation in reality. The acute onset of a neurosis or psychosis is apt to be painful enough. The symptoms strive to achieve wish fulfillment but must accept symbolic gratification that is usually mixed with much pain. Later, however, the patient is able to capitalize upon his pain to win real advantages, such as, for example, the privileged position of a sick person in the circle of his family or friends. In so doing, however, he renounces the possibility of real gratification of the wishes that originally involved him in conflict and accepts in their place other secondary advantages that are more readily obtainable in real life. The secondary gain phenomena, therefore, must be regarded as a more or less successful adjustment to reality rather than as evidence of the ability of neuroses to ignore pain.

In a later study (1922), as we know, Freud abandoned the idea that the unconscious is dominated solely by the pleasure-pain principle and demonstrated the existence of a still more primitive repetition compulsion, of a tendency to revive and relive even the most traumatic experiences. Freud has in fact laid particular emphasis upon just those extreme examples in which the repetition compulsion is in complete defiance of both pleasure and reality principles.

Such examples have, of course, the advantage that they illustrate the repetition compulsion, as it were, in pure culture, uncomplicated by other tendencies. It would be a mistake, however, to think of the repetition compulsion only in terms of its most extreme and dramatic manifestations. Psychoanalysis has so far not attempted to formulate under just what conditions the repetition compulsion is called into activity. Its most familiar manifestations, however, are best understood in terms of the conditioned reflex principle (French, 1933), which is also the indispensable basis of learning by experience. A good clinical example is the castration fear. Once the fear of castration has been attached to the practice of masturbation it is impossible for the psyche even to wish for the forbidden gratification without being compelled to deal with fear. In other words, in accordance with the conditioned reflex principle, we must expect that the search of a drive for satisfaction will regularly be accompanied by a tendency to call up memories of previously unsuccessful attempts at satisfaction.

In the light of Freud's later studies, therefore, we are able to characterize the activity of the unconscious more completely—as an interaction between repetition compulsion and wish-fulfilling tendencies, as a struggle between painful mental contents that are pressing for recognition and the striving of the unconscious to escape from them and substitute more pleasurable contents. Indeed, if the conditioned reflex principle be universally valid for emotionally significant events,[1] we must expect that even in neuroses and psychoses it will be impossible to withdraw from difficult conflict situations except by some sort of renunciation of the urges that have involved the patient in conflict. We must anticipate that, insofar as neurotic symptoms represent the fulfillment of wishes, they must also represent the unhappy consequences of wish fulfillment. In other words, we must expect that neuroses and psychoses are quite as unable permanently to ignore painful elements of reality as is the reality-adjusted conscious ego.

This thesis was first suggested to me not by the conditioned reflex experiments of Pavlov but by the work especially of Alexander upon the role of the superego in dreams and neuroses. The psychoanalytic literature has in fact been approaching similar conclusions by the route of direct clinical observation. After describing the repetition compulsion, Freud began to direct a greater amount of attention to unconscious self-punishing tendencies and other evidences of an "unconscious sense of guilt." Following out these suggestions of Freud, Reik (1925) postulated a universal unconscious urge to confess forbidden impulses which he closely associated with the desire for punishment. Alexander (1930) focused particular attention upon the contributions of the superego to the dream work and to symptom formation. In the case of dreams with unpleasant content, he showed that the superego functions not only as a psychic censor insisting upon the distortion of the content of repressed wishes but may also play a creative role, giving rise to dreams that express predominantly a wish for punishment. Further, with regard to neurotic symptoms, he arrived at the general formulation (Alexander, 1927) "that neurotic illness has two purposes: to wit, the gratification of forbidden tendencies, and at the same time the relief of the conscience anxiety developing as a reaction to this forbidden gratification."

We know, however, that the self-punishing and inhibiting activities of the superego arise by identification with the punishments inflicted and the prohibitions imposed by the parents in childhood. As Alexander (1929) points out in detail, the ego submits to the superego after the pattern it has learned in submitting to the parents in childhood. The ego's acceptance of self-punishment is thus derived from a previous adjustment to an external situation, and implies the recognition of the painful realities to be deduced from past experience. That unpleasant dreams and neuroses are compelled to incorporate self-punishing tendencies into their content is, therefore, clear evidence of the principle we are here proposing, that neuroses and some dreams are quite as unable to ignore the painful elements of reality as is the reality-adjusted conscious ego.

In the meantime Freud (1926) had already reached the same conclusion directly, with reference to the origin of the anxiety in the phobia of little Hans. In a reexamination of the anxiety problem, he found that Hans's fear of his father was justified in reality as an unavoidable consequence of his hostility toward the father. Finally Ferenczi (1934) came to a similar conclusion about dreams, inasmuch as he suggests that the mastery of traumatic memories is the central function of the dream.

The field of the psychoses has, of course, not yet been adequately surveyed with reference to this point. Freud (1923) has interpreted the alternation between the manic and depressive episodes in circular psychoses as a successive gratification of id impulses and self-punishing tendencies, but this is, of course, not applicable to cases showing only periodic manic attacks. In the psychoses in general there is apt to be a regression to stages of ego development prior to the formation of the superego, and consequently we should not expect to find organized conscience reactions such as would correspond to Alexander's formula for the neuroses; but many examples would suggest that the psychotic also is unable permanently to ignore the painful elements of reality and is under the necessity to portray not only the fulfillment of wishes but also the unhappy consequences of their fulfillment. We must suspect, for instance, that the manic patient is betraying by his flight of ideas his fear of the inevitable consequences if he should carry to a conclusion the aggressive impulses to which he gives abortive expression. Paranoid fears, moreover, as is well known, have not only a significance as wish fulfillments but also a real justification based upon the retaliatory reactions which the patient's own aggressive impulses would inevitably elicit. To cite only one more example, one is able frequently to observe, in patients with grandiose delusions, that these delusions alternate with most intense feelings of inferiority. There seem to be good grounds, therefore, for suspecting that even in psychoses there is a very definite limit to the power of wish-fulfilling tendencies to distort the patient's real situation by ignoring the painful elements of reality.

There is, however, one clear exception to our hypothesis that it is impossible to ignore painful reality. If our hypothesis is correct, the purely wish-fulfilling dream is a conspicuous exception that requires explanation. In the literature there is just one hint from Freud that may furnish us with the needed explanation. In the theoretical chapter of *The Interpretation of Dreams* (1900), Freud calls attention to one difference between hysterical symptoms and dreams. A symptom is always the result of a condensation of a wish from the unconscious with a preconscious "thought stream of reaction against it," such as, "for example, self-punishment." In the dream the reaction against the unconscious wish may be absent, "but the contribution from the preconscious which is missing here may be found in another place. The dream can provide expression for a wish from the unconscious by means of all sorts of distortions, once the dominant system has withdrawn itself in the wish to sleep." Following out this hint of Freud's, we may perhaps expect to find that the wish to sleep may in some way serve as a substitute for the recognition of painful elements of reality that the dream would otherwise be unable to ignore. We shall return to this suggestion in our discussion of illustrative clinical material.

To return now to our original problem: we wished to know what forces are strong enough to induce the psyche to accept pain for the sake of the future. If our hypothesis is correct, that the unconscious is compelled to yield not only to wish-fulfilling tendencies but also to the compulsion to relive painful consequences, then the process of modification of the pleasure principle into reality principle becomes more intelligible. We have concluded that the unconscious is not only subject to urges toward wish fulfillment but is also under compulsion to relive experiences of the most unpleasant sorts. It therefore becomes much less of a riddle to explain how the psyche can be induced to endure pain for the sake of the future. We now see that the establishment of the reality principle really introduces no new dynamic element into the situation. The urge to seek pleasure and the compulsion to recall unhappy consequences are both already present. It is only one-half of the truth when we speak of the reality principle as a modified form of the pleasure principle; it is much better described as a fortunate synthesis of pleasure principle and repetition compulsion, a sort of subordination and utilization of the repetition compulsion in the interests of a moderated pleasure principle. Since the psyche is compelled in any case to come to terms with the memory of its mistakes and of their unhappy consequences, it is therefore only making a virtue of necessity when it frankly accepts a minimum of renunciation for the sake of future pleasure in lieu of a merciless and futile compulsion to repeat its previous sufferings.

3. SIGNIFICANCE OF QUANTITATIVE FACTORS IN LEARNING TO ADJUST TO REALITY

Nevertheless we know that neuroses and psychoses occur as flights from conflicts that are too severe in real life. We may now wish to correct this statement by insisting that these attempts to flee from unpleasant reality do not succeed; but the fact remains that intense conflicts interfere with the normal processes of adjustment to reality and it is still necessary to inquire into the nature of this disorganizing effect of severe conflict upon rational mental functioning.

As I have pointed out in a previous paper (French, 1933), some of the results of Pavlov's experiments upon conditioned reflexes suggest a rather specific answer to this question. Pavlov (1927) has been able to produce what he calls experimental neuroses. The methods by which he accomplishes this consist in every case in putting the dog into what is analogous to an acute conflict situation. The dog, for example, may be conditioned to respond to many different painful stimuli with salivary secretion in expectation of being fed, or one may make the dog face the problem of making a very fine differentiation or discrimination—for example, between a circle and an ellipse with nearly equal axes—by giving the dog food every time immediately after it sees the circle but withholding the food in every case after it sees the ellipse. In either case it is evident that very conflicting reactions tend to be called forth, and the situation is analogous to the acute emotional con-flict situations of our patients. The most conspicuous feature of the experimental neuroses so elicited is the stereotyped character of the dog's subsequent behavior. In some cases the dog will react to all stimuli with excitement and salivary secretion; in others always with excite-ment and defense reactions; and in still others with inhibitory reactions indiscriminately in response to every kind of stimulus. In every case these experimental neuroses not only have the effect of destroying the dog's capacity for forming new discriminatory reactions but also tend to destroy differentiations or discriminations that have already been formed.

In other words, in these experiments the effect of a too severe con-flict is to destroy the animal's capacity for discriminatory learning. Pavlov's experiments have illustrated most beautifully the importance of the previously indifferent stimulus for the learning process. When one is under the influence of very strong emotion, there is a tendency for one's attention to be completely absorbed by those aspects of a situation that are already of prepotent emotional significance. Every new step in learning, however, requires precisely that one should pay attention to some new aspect of the situation whose significance has as yet not been appreciated. Strong emotion or acute conflict make this impossible. The experiments of Pavlov that we have just cited show indeed that too severe conflicts tend not only to prevent new steps in learning but also to destroy discriminations that have previously been learned.

A similar principle is illustrated by a very pretty experiment of Koehler (1917). In the first part of the experiment a "mature bitch is brought into a blind alley, . . . one end of which is cut off by a railing [Figure 1] where she is kept occupied with food, her face toward the railing. When the food is nearly gone, more is put down" at some distance on the other side of the rail; "the bitch sees it, seems to hesitate a moment, then quickly turns" and runs "around the fence to the new food. . . . On repeating this experiment the food was not thrown far out but was dropped just outside the fence so that it lay directly in front of her separated only by the wire." In this case "she stood seemingly helpless as if the very nearness of the object and her concentration upon it (brought about by her sense of smell) 'blocked the idea' of the wide circle around the fence. She pushed again and again with her nose at the wire fence and did not budge from the spot." It is evident that here again we see the inhibiting effect of a strong emotion (in this case the fascination of the dog for the food that is so nearly within its reach) upon the capacity of the animal to take account of just the aspect of the situation that contains the clue to the solution of the problem. The possible detour has not an emotional charge high enough to compete with the food under the dog's nose. Hence the dog remains glued to the spot and ignores the only possibility of really gratifying its hunger.

FIGURE I

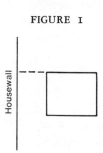

It is not difficult to bring this principle into direct connection with our clinical experience. Alexander (1927) in particular has pointed out that one of the outstanding features of neuroses and psychoses is their stereotyped character. The neurotic repeats over and over again the same unsuccessful solutions of his conflicts and learns nothing from his mistakes. Here we see the repetition compulsion in its pure form. Reality adjustment, on the other hand, is the product of a learning process. In making adjustments according to the reality principle, one learns from one's mistakes. Learning, too, is based upon the repetition compulsion but involves a modification of it. Past mistakes must be remembered or tentatively repeated but under the guidance of the urge to find a way of avoiding unpleasant consequences in the future.

Learning is a process of correcting previously established behavior patterns by taking account of the differences between present and past situations. Conflicts of too great intensity absorb too much energy to permit the individual to pay attention to such differential criteria. They constitute psychic traumata; they interrupt learning and thus lead to the stereotyped attempts at solution that we call neuroses and psychoses.

Thus severe conflicts disorganize rational mental functioning simply because too intense emotion disturbs the discrimination that forms the basis of the learning process. The neurotic is so absorbed in the pain of his conflict and in his vain attempts to wish it away that he fails to heed the new possibilities in his real situation that might offer him a way out of his difficulties. As a result of this disregard of just those features of reality that could serve as a basis for discrimination, he lives in the present as though he were reliving the past and finds himself condemned either to futile attempts at renunciation or to a disastrous repetition of previous traumatic experiences.

Thus the reality principle involves, on the one hand, a modification of the pleasure principle to take account of future pleasure and pain, but also, on the other hand, a modification of the repetition compulsion into learning by taking account of the differential aspects of reality. Conflicts of too great intensity leave no energy free to pay attention to such differential criteria and result, therefore, in a futile struggle between pleasure principle and repetition compulsion. Learning becomes possible only when free energy is left available to pay attention to those less obtrusive aspects of reality that make it possible to distinguish between the painful experiences of the past and more favorable possibilities in the present.

It is important to realize that it is not the painful elements of reality that are most conspicuously ignored in neurotic behavior but rather just those emotionally indifferent aspects of reality whose sole value consists in the fact that they might serve as differential criteria to enable one to find new possibilities for gratification while at the same time avoiding past mistakes.

4. ILLUSTRATIVE MATERIAL (A NIGHTMARE)

In order to test these conclusions, it occurred to me that it would be interesting to compare the tendencies revealed by a patient during some short period of analysis with a hypothetical rational solution of the same conflict.

We have mentioned Freud's suggestion that the wish to sleep may act in some part as a substitute for the need for punishment that is so regularly to be found in neurotic symptoms. In order to throw light also on this suggestion, I have therefore selected for study a nightmare from which the dreamer awoke in acute anxiety. We shall first make a careful analysis of this nightmare and then proceed to compare its manifest content with the psychic adjustments that we surmise might have been necessary in order to enable the patient to achieve a rational solution for his conflict.

The material is from a male patient who had been in analysis about two months, and followed a prolonged period of sexual abstinence. During the two months of the analysis, the patient had discussed rather freely his sexual life in the past but had on only one occasion mentioned any current sexual impulses. In the hour preceding the one to be discussed, occurred a second "confession" of current heterosexual fantasies. That night he went to bed early. He was awakened at midnight by a nightmare and remained awake until early in the morning. He went to sleep again at the hour at which, during his childhood, his father had been accustomed to awaken him. The nightmare was as follows:

> The patient was in a sort of a room. In the background was a girl, the wife of one of the patient's best friends. There was something in the room. The patient wanted to get rid of it. At first it was a small bird. The patient opened the door and it flew out of its own accord. Then something grabbed the patient in the back of the neck. It was a large bird and the patient felt its claws in his neck. The patient thought how he might get rid of "him," but the bird answered as though it had heard his thoughts, "You just think you will. You better ask advice from John if you think you can get rid of me." The patient awoke in acute anxiety.

Of the associations I need mention only the following: the girl in the dream reminded the patient also of a girl to whom he had previously been sexually attracted. His sexual interest in her had begun shortly after she had had an abortion done by a physician to whom the patient had recommended her. In the analytic hour previous to the dream he had confessed to fantasies of getting in touch with her again. The position of the girl in the background seems to the patient to symbolize his recent desire to make confessions to the analyst. Letting the small bird out of the room suggests to him telling his secret thoughts "at the beginning of the analysis." As a boy the patient used to shoot small birds and sometimes would cut off their heads. The large bird reminds the patient of an owl. Its position behind him makes him think of the analyst's position behind the patient's head. He also has the impression that his father once took hold of him by the back of the neck as the big bird did in the dream, but he cannot remember anything about it. Months later in the analysis, however, he recalled that his father used to grab him in the back of the neck in this way when he waked him up in the morning. John in the dream is a friend of the patient's who has been analyzed and has described some of his difficulties to the patient.

The dream is plainly the fulfillment of a feminine and masochistic wish to be attacked by the analyst (father). The associations and the material from the preceding day further make it plain that the masochistic character of this wish has been dictated by the need for punishment. In the hour preceding the dream, the patient had succeeded in confessing heterosexual fantasies whose content pointed to the sadistic wish to attack sexually the pregnant mother and get rid of the unborn child. These wishes bring him into conflict with his still stronger desire to retain the love of the father. In the hour previous to the dream, the patient had attempted to solve this conflict and seek reconciliation with the father (analyst) by confession. For reasons to be mentioned shortly, this attempt failed. The solution in the dream is more drastic. The two sets of conflicting desires are gratified in succession. The little bird [2] in the room symbolizes the mother's pregnancy. The patient first makes a sadistic attack on the mother and gets rid of the unborn child. In the second part of the dream it is undoubtedly not only a threat but also a reassurance and masochistic gratification when the analyst (father) wakes him roughly and reminds him that an analyst is not to be gotten rid of so easily.

After the interpretation the patient recalls that his mother had a miscarriage when he was ten years old. His associations run to various childhood speculations as to the relations between his father and mother and as to his own birth. . . . Once, when the patient was asleep, his father disappeared from the next room. The patient suspected that he had climbed out of the window and had gone out and had a sexual relationship with a neighbor's wife! Then the patient tells how he used to go to his grandmother for love when his parents seemed to favor the younger children.

The allusions to sleeping probably point to the precipitating cause of the dream. At the last analytic session the analyst had been compelled to struggle against a considerable drowsiness. The patient, though not consciously aware of this, has taken unmistakable notice of it in his dream. The analyst is an owl, a bird that sleeps in the daytime and stays awake at night. The patient goes to sleep early and returns to sleep again at the very hour that his father used to wake him up. It is plain that his sleeping [3] is an act of defiance and retaliation. In the second (threatening) part of the dream, appropriately, the feel of the owl's claws on his neck is based upon the memory of his father's awakening him. We may suspect that during the preceding hour the patient had wished to "wake up" the analyst roughly. In the dream the father and analyst retaliate for this impious wish.

The patient's unconscious rage becomes more readily understandable when we recall that the patient had been trying during that hour to win back the analyst's favor by confession of his forbidden impulses. The analyst's drowsiness signaled an abrupt failure of this attempt.

a. An arrested learning process: fixation upon a childhood situation

Let us inquire now as to what the dream has done with present reality. What is conspicuous here is the phenomenon of transference. The patient reacts to a present situation with reactions appropriate rather to a childhood situation. The analysis makes it necessary for the patient to tell of certain sexual impulses. The patient unconsciously reacts to this fact as though he were in the presence of his father in the early Oedipus situation. The patient's rage has indeed been precipitated by an event in the present, but the intensity of the patient's reaction is understandable only when we realize that his struggle to confess was fraught with all the energy of the little child's longing for the love of the father whom he at the same time hates and fears.

In a previous paper (French, 1933) I characterized a psychic trauma as a point at which the learning process had been arrested. The original reaction to the traumatic memory becomes a generalized pattern reaction which may thenceforth be called forth by situations only remotely similar and which is more or less impervious to the modifying influence of later experience. This sort of an arrest of the learning process is well illustrated by the material under discussion. The patient's unconscious reacts as though it had not learned to take account of the differences between his situation in the analysis and his childhood relation to his father.

b. Fate of the painful real elements of the traumatic situation

In order to illuminate what has caused this remarkable arrest of the learning process, it will be of interest to study how the dream handles the traumatic memory of the patient's early Oedipus situation.

We have already pointed out that the dream is a fulfillment of two sets of conflicting wishes. In the first part of the dream the patient is with his mother. The dreaded father is replaced by the helpless unborn brother and the patient succeeds easily in ridding himself of the disturber. The first part of the dream represents, therefore, a successful expression of the patient's defiance. In the second part of the dream, his passive masochistic wishes toward the father are gratified. The dream ends with the reassurance that his hostile wishes cannot really get rid of the father he loves. Better to have a threatening, punishing father than to lose him entirely!

This last "wish fulfillment" reminds us, on the other hand, that the dream has been quite unable to ignore the unpleasant realities of the traumatic situation. If the dream could carry wish fulfillment to its logical conclusion, we should expect it to wipe away all traces of the patient's conflict. Instead of that, the terrifying conclusion of the dream is only an emergency substitute for the tragic realization that if the patient gets rid of his father, he will not have him any more. The patient wants love from the father but he is utterly unable to get rid of the destructive energy that estranges them. When he brings back the father, the best he can do is now to let his own rage be reflected [4] back upon himself. He discharges it in the form of fear.

If we turn now first to the dream's handling of the patient's aggressive wishes, we note a similar inability to ignore the element of frustration in the patient's situation. When the little bird flies away in response to the patient's merely opening the door, it sounds like a bit of infantile omnipotence. Very probably the mother's miscarriage helped to confirm such a claim for omnipotence in the patient's unconscious. But this time the patient's moment of omnipotence is followed immediately by a situation of helpless frustration—with the big bird's claws on his neck.

The patient's frustration in his infantile sexual wishes toward the mother is handled in a somewhat different way. The girl in the dream is in the background; this is a mild way of indicating that the patient's sexual desires are not gratified. Over against this is the fact that the patient is himself in the room from which he has expelled his brother. One may perhaps suspect that the patient's highly symbolic manner of fulfilling his wish for the mother is in itself a compromise between wish fulfillment and a recognition of frustration.[5]

The frustration of the patient's sexual wishes toward the mother is recognized still more plainly in quite another manner. Not only in the manifest dream but also in the emphasis of the dream thoughts is the mother in the background. The dream action centers upon a hostile impulse, upon the removal of an obstacle, the father. This shifting of emphasis from a sexual to a hostile aim is in itself an acknowledgment of frustration. The impulse to get rid of the two birds constitutes a giving up of the patient's primary sexual aim and a concentration of psychic energy upon the fact of frustration and the desire to remove its cause.

Objection will probably be raised at this point that there is nothing in this dream that is not a wish fulfillment. We have, in fact, already recognized that the patient wishes to be wakened and attacked by the father. His love for the father demands also that his aggressive wishes should be frustrated. In accordance with the classical wish fulfillment theory it would be easy to conclude therefore that the frustration and the terrifying awakening in this dream do not necessarily imply a recognition of the real consequences of the patient's aggressive wishes but are merely a fulfillment of the patient's masochistic desire to be attacked sexually by the father and of a desire for his aggressive wishes to be frustrated on account of his love for the father.

I must admit that it is difficult to find absolutely unimpeachable evidence to decide between this classical theory of dream interpretation and my own thesis. The difficulty lies in the fact that all anxiety dreams and most other dreams are the product of a conflict. It follows therefore that recognition in the dream of real difficulties in the way of the fulfillment of one wish is apt to coincide with the fulfillment of the other opposing wish. In all such cases, as in the dream under discussion, it is possible to interpret either in accord with the classical dream theory that the dream is a wish fulfillment and all else is incidental or in terms of my thesis that the dream is also under pressure to recognize disturbing realities.

Nevertheless, there are several considerations that seem to me to speak for my own thesis and against the classical wish fulfillment theory.

1) The fact that this patient awakes in acute anxiety is a sign that the wish to be attacked by the father is an extremely masochistic one. How are we to account for the extremely masochistic character of this feminine sexual wish? Theoretically there are two possibilities. (*a*) The possibility plainly suggested by the material is that the masochism is a secondary masochism, based upon a secondary erotization of the patient's need for punishment (Freud, 1919). This explanation, however, is equivalent to my thesis—that the patient must accept punishment in order to retain the love of the father, that he is quite unable to bring back the father he loves without also bringing back the angry father

whose retaliation he fears, that the feminine desire for sexual gratification from the father has become masochistic only by being condensed
with the patient's need for punishment in order to retain the father's
love. (*b*) A second theoretical possibility would be that the masochism
in the patient's desire to be attacked is primary. We have just seen
in fact that this thesis is a necessary one if we wish to maintain that
this dream is under no necessity to recognize real consequences. The
assumption of a primary masochism in this material, however, is a
purely gratuitous one, supported by no evidence, and particularly unwarranted in view of the fact that the attack the patient fears actually
corresponds to the retaliation the patient should expect as a real consequence of his aggressive wishes.

2) A second point against the classical wish fulfillment theory has
already been mentioned. If the dream is omnipotent in its wish-fulfilling capacities, why does it not wipe out all traces of the patient's
conflict? Why does it not find a wish-fulfilling hallucination that
symbolizes the gratification of both wishes and completely masks their
incompatibility?

3) Finally, although the recognition of a real difficulty in the way
of the fulfillment of one wish is apt to coincide with the fulfillment of
an opposing wish, the converse does not hold true. The classical wish
fulfillment theory furnishes us with no reason why a dream should
gratify one wish in a way that implies recognition of the real unpleasant consequences of the opposing wish. As just pointed out, we
should expect rather the contrary, that the wish-fulfilling tendency in
the dream should attempt to obliterate the incompatibility of the two
wishes. In the present instance, therefore, when the dream chooses to
gratify the patient's sexual wish toward the father by masochistically
accepting his well-grounded fear of retaliation from him, we must
regard this as presumptive evidence that the dream is under compulsion
to recognize painful realities. We must suspect that the dream is merely
utilizing, in the service of its wish-fulfilling function, a fear of real
consequences that it could not have escaped in any case.

c. Absorption of pain by sleep

We conclude, therefore, that the dream as a whole has been quite
unable to avoid recognition of the essential real elements of the childhood situation. If we follow carefully the chronological order of appearance of the manifest dream elements, however, we notice that the
recognition of painful elements increases progressively. Sleep has been

likened to a regression to the intrauterine state in which presumably all or nearly all of the individual's needs are gratified without his having to become aware of them. Such we may assume was the patient's state before he began to dream. The first impression in the dream is significantly symbolic of the intrauterine state—the patient is in a room. The wish for the mother is recognized next but is kept in the background. Then comes the first recognition of a difficulty, but it is only a little one, a small bird. The patient is then compelled to do something, or at least to dream that he is doing something, but his wish to get rid of the disturber is immediately fulfilled without further effort. Immediately afterward, however, it is a big bird instead of a small one that is threatening. The full intensity of the patient's anxiety is apparently reached only after the patient has waked up.

During this dream the patient is awakening out of sleep. We may assume, therefore, with a very high degree of probability, that the depth of sleep is progressively diminishing as the dream proceeds. Thus the progressive increase in the recognition of disturbing elements in the dream apparently runs parallel to a progressive diminution in the depth of sleep. The obvious inference from this fact is that sleep itself to some degree serves as a substitute for painful affects or, stated in quantitative terms, that there is an absorption of painful affects during sleep that is roughly proportional to the depth of sleep.

It is obvious that this capacity of sleep itself to absorb pain must be one of the ego's main resources in its sleep-preserving function. By mobilizing fatigue as a substitute for pain, the ego is able to deprive pain for a time of its sleep-disturbing qualities. Here is obviously the explanation for Freud's observation that we have already quoted, to the effect that the wish to sleep may apparently play the same role in dreams as does the need for self-punishment in hysterical symptoms. Moreover our hypothesis that the absorption of pain by sleep is quantitative and proportional to the depth of sleep would also explain the fact that pain is banished from some dreams much less successfully than it is from others.

In the dream under discussion, the progressively diminishing absorption of painful affects by sleep has had an important influence upon the order in which the most important dream wishes are dealt with in the manifest content. The most disturbing conflict is the ambivalence conflict toward the father which has been intensified and precipitated by the analyst's lack of response to the patient's confessions. In accordance with its sleep-preserving function, however, the dream has turned away from this disturbing conflict to the desire for the shelter and protection of the intrauterine relationship to the mother. It is only later that the obstacles in the way of union with the mother begin to be sensed and usher in the impulse to remove the disturber and lead by this route to the awakening of the whole ambivalence conflict of which the father is the object.

d. Justification in reality for wish-fulfilling hallucinations by allusion to reassuring facts and memories

Freud has postulated that every dream and every neurotic symptom must represent the fulfillment of a wish dating from early childhood. The hypothesis proposed in the present study, if carried to its logical conclusion, would suggest a supplementary and limiting principle— that the wish-fulfilling tendency in symptoms and dreams must find a real basis and justification for its wish-fulfilling hallucinations by reference to actual experiences of the patient or dreamer.

There is much in the psychoanalytic literature that would support such a hypothesis. We often quote Freud's statement that, when properly understood, the neurotic patient is always speaking the truth. What is usually meant, of course, is the subjective truth about his own motives, but instances are numerous in which the patient is shown to be telling the truth not only about his own motives but about objective external reality as well. A well-known example is Freud's suggestion that Goethe's characteristically optimistic attitude toward life may have been due to the fact that most of Goethe's rivals for his mother's love died in early childhood. "I have . . . already declared elsewhere that he who has been the undisputed darling of his mother retains throughout life that victorious feeling, that confidence in ultimate success, which not seldom brings actual success with it" (Freud, 1917). As another example I may cite some neat observations of Pfister (1931). In an analysis of the thoughts that stream through the minds of individuals in moments of great danger he finds that these thoughts regularly lead back to other dangerous situations which have had a happy outcome. Numerous examples of this sort would seem to suggest that the wish-fulfilling tendency in dreams and symptoms cannot manufacture reassurances out of nothing but must draw them in some way from the individual's experience in real life.

In the dream that we have been discussing this hypothesis is beautifully illustrated. In this dream every single wish-fulfillment is represented by a real occurrence in the patient's memory. The patient has undoubtedly been many times in a room with his friend's wife; the little bird's flying out of its own accord refers to a canary of the patient's that once flew away and still more significantly to the fact of his mother's miscarriage, probably also to one occasion when the analyst walked out of the room while the patient was still there. Moreover, we have already mentioned that the sensation of the large bird's claws on the patient's neck is derived from his memory of his father's waking him in the morning. Finally, the reassuring speech at the end of the dream is a reminder that the patient is in analysis and that merely a hostile wish will not take the analyst away from him. The wish-fulfilling function in this dream appears therefore to be achieved by a very clever manipulation of actual memories.

e. Subsequent correction of distortions—similarity to trial-and-error method of adjusting to reality

That every wish-fulfilling hallucination is based upon one or more real memories, which it condenses and reproduces, would probably be a too venturesome assumption; but we may perhaps anticipate that every distortion of reality in the direction of wish fulfillment will be followed by a compensatory tendency to correct the distortion in subsequent material.

A principle of this sort has in fact already been suggested by Alexander in a study of dream pairs (1925). He points out that the two dreams of a pair often tend to supplement each other. "The first dream may, for instance, express the incest wish, the sexual act being disguised symbolically. For example, 'I am driving in a carriage with my sister.' In the second dream the act is disguised less, or not at all, but the incestuous object is replaced by a harmless one."

A very pretty example of such a tendency to correct distortions is contained in Freud's *Fragment of an Analysis of a Case of Hysteria* (1905). Dora, like every other hysterical patient, is unconsciously malingering. She does not admit this to herself or to Freud, but she corrects the omission, as it were, by being very much concerned over the fact that Frau K is malingering in an almost identical manner. This too, of course, is a distortion, a projection; but she betrays this distortion also by the fact that she unconsciously does not expect Freud to believe her, as is shown by the fact that she must reiterate her suspicions of Frau K over and over again.

The most elementary mechanism in dream distortion is displacement, the substitution of one mental content for another, the replacement of a

wish or other affect-laden idea by a content of somewhat similar meaning or by some sort of an allusion to it. Indeed even the acceptance of a
hallucination or a fantasy in place of the real fulfillment of a wish
must itself be regarded as such a substitute gratification. In terms of
our hypothesis, substitutions of this sort must be looked upon as only
incomplete forms of gratification. In terms of the principles just suggested, we must expect to find that the acceptance of less satisfying
substitutes will in every case be followed by evidences of unsatisfied
tension.

It is, of course, this principle that forces one to adjust to reality in
normal waking life. In rational waking behavior one is guided by
wishes and purposes, in other words by goal concepts, but one does
not content oneself with hallucinatory fulfillment of one's wishes. On
the contrary, the realization that one's wishes are not fulfilled spurs one
on to appropriate action.

In dreams one accepts the dream hallucination in place of a real
wish fulfillment. Our discussion so far would lead us to conclude that
the dream is able to content itself with hallucinated satisfactions only
because sleep absorbs the unpleasant realization that one's wishes are
not fulfilled just as it absorbs any other kind of pain. Therefore, as
the depth of sleep diminishes, we must expect a tendency, as in waking
life, for wish-fulfilling hallucination to be followed by some sort of
discontent with a gratification that is merely hallucinated, by some sort
of urge to appropriate action in order to achieve something better than
a hallucinated satisfaction.

We may illustrate this by tracing the dream's handling of the more
important dream wishes and by comparing this with the elaboration
that each would require if it were to seek fulfillment in real life.

1) In real life, if one's way is blocked by an obstacle, one allows
oneself to be diverted for the time from one's original goal and concentrates one's attention upon removal of the obstacle; if a wish is
thwarted, one seeks a substitute gratification, or the energy of a
thwarted wish may be diverted into an impulse to seek revenge. In the
dream the patient has turned from the analyst who has thwarted his
desire for love; he seeks consolation by dreaming that he is in a room
with a mother substitute. He does not become conscious of his desire [6]
for the mother but diverts the energy of that desire into hostile wishes
to get rid of rivals, to get rid of obstacles that separate him from his
mother. His craving for love has been thwarted first by the mother's
pregnancy and second by the analyst's failure to respond to the patient's

confessions; his desire for revenge finds expression in the sadistic character of his desire to attack the pregnant mother.

In real life when one turns from an original goal in order to remove an obstacle it is important that the original goal be retained in some latent form in order that, when the obstacle is once removed, one may then proceed toward one's first destination. In the dream the original desire to be loved is preserved in just such a latent form in the dream setting. The mother substitute in the background probably represents both mother and analyst (as the analyst sits behind the patient) and being in a room with her is symbolic of the patient's desire to be in the mother's womb.

2) Freud (1925) has pointed out that normal thinking is a sort of experimental living through of a possible line of action in one's mind before committing oneself to it in action. Such an experimental living through of necessity implies anticipation of the probable real consequences in case the patient should act upon his hostile wish to get rid of the father. The announcement that the patient cannot get rid of the big bird is a rational conclusion with reference to the childhood situation which the patient is reliving, and his frightened awakening should be compared to the end of a normal train of thought such as, "If you attempt to vent your rage upon the powerful father, you will suffer all that you wish to inflict upon him." It will be noticed that the patient's dream thoughts differ from normal thinking in that the whole energy of the patient's anger against the father becomes concentrated upon this experiment of thought, whereas normal thinking, as Freud (1925) has shown, is best performed with a minimum of psychic energy. The fact that the patient has been concentrating too much energy upon his anticipation of consequences is proved by the fact that he awakens in acute anxiety instead of merely concluding intellectually that it is best not to attack the father.

3) In real life, acting on one impulse may result in consequences that are in accordance with some other desire. In the dream the threat of being attacked by the father, which the patient's fear implies, now constitutes a gratification of the desire for love from the father which the patient attempted to renounce [7] by going to sleep early and dreaming of the mother. We have already called attention to the fact that the statement that he cannot get rid of the big bird is to the patient even more of a reassurance than a threat. This hallucinatory fulfillment of the patient's desire for a sexual attack by the father has, however, now gained a certain justification in reality, for it is also the anticipated

consequence of the patient's desire to attack the father. It is as though the patient had set out to provoke [8] the attack that he so much desires.

4) Thus seen as a whole, the dream resembles [9] the reactions of a person in waking life who is attempting, by a clumsy method of trial and error, to adjust to a reality situation in which he is not very well oriented. Disappointed by the analyst he turns for consolation to dreams of mother; then, beginning to realize that he cannot have undisturbed possession of the mother, he turns his energies to trying to get rid of his rivals, only to discover that in this way he runs the danger of losing the father whom he still continues to love. Faced with this danger, he promptly recalls that his father will not let him get away with his aggressive impulses and awakens to reassure himself that it is all a bad dream. We are reminded of comic heroes on the screen who, oblivious of their total situation, are continually extricating themselves from one difficulty after another, only to find that escape from one difficult situa-ation has precipitated them into another.

f. Contrast with rational elaboration—absence of essential synthetic insights

In some respects, indeed, the dream solution resembles a real solution of the patient's conflict. Freud has called attention to the fact that children are often aggressive and "naughty" in order to provoke their parents to punish them (1918). That such a motive has played an important part in the synthesis of this dream is made certain by a fragment from a dream of two days previous:

> There were two very black horses. One horse bumped into the other.
> . . . (Later) one horse took the harness of the other in his teeth and pulled him over to where he belonged. The patient thought this horse had almost human intelligence.

In association the patient reproached his father for not having shown much intelligence in the way he brought up his children. So also in the analysis (said the dream), if the analyst had anything like ordinary human intelligence, he would "pull the patient over to where he belonged."

In the "owl dream" of two days later, therefore, we are quite justified in assuming that the aggressive impulses in the first part of the dream have also a provocative motive whose aim is achieved when the big bird wakes the patient up.

On the other hand, it is plain that in this dream the wish to provoke punishment has gotten out of hand, for the patient awakens out of his dream in acute anxiety. It is not hard to picture in a rough way what has happened. The wish to provoke punishment implies a subordination of the patient's aggressive impulses to a masochistic aim; but at the moment of the dream the motives of defiance and retaliation prove too strong to be so subordinated and, escaping from the domination of the masochistic motive, seek gratification on their own account.[10] Proof of this is the fact that the patient's ego cannot tolerate the punishment he originally tried to provoke.

We have already compared the dynamic adjustments implied by the chronological order of the manifest dream elements to the struggles of a comic hero who is able to appreciate only one small part of his total situation at a time. When compared with normal reality-adjusted behavior, what seems to be lacking in this dream is the capacity to view the situation as a whole.

We must surmise that the really traumatic moment in the Oedipus complex is the first dawning realization that the little boy's desire to replace the father in the mother's love involves the danger of retaliation from the father and of loss of the father's love. We see in this material that this realization is in a sense still present—punishment follows inexorably upon aggression; but this "knowledge" persists rather as an associative bond than as an insight. In the dream there is almost no recognition of the fact that the patient's getting rid of the "little bird" is the cause of the threatening attitude of the father, that these two events belong together in the relation of cause and effect. We might think of the traumatic memory as having been fragmented.[11] All the essential parts are preserved but they are not perceived in relation to each other. It is as though the traumatic memory had been cut to pieces with a jigsaw to make a picture puzzle.

Let us return now to our original problem. We wanted to know what had arrested the learning process at the time of the patient's early Oedipus conflict. Our recognition of the fragmentation of the memory of this conflict now furnishes us with an adequate reason for this disturbance in the learning process. In order for the patient to profit by his childhood experience, he must recognize that forbidden impulse and punishment are cause and effect. The fragmentation of the traumatic memory makes this impossible. During the first part of the dream the possibility of punishment is suppressed. The threatening figure of the father comes as something unexpected. The causal connection between forbidden impulse and punishment is almost completely ignored. It is, therefore, not surprising that the learning process has been disturbed.

Even more fundamental for the learning process is the maintenance of an adequate incentive. Such an incentive can arise only when the realization of an unsatisfied need and the prospect of satisfaction set up a tension between them and operate together like the two poles of an electric motor. In this dream, the patient is alternately omnipotent and helpless; the two poles of the motor, instead of working together, appear to discharge independently.

Thus the first incentive for the learning process involves a synthesis of elements that in the dream are separated. It is impossible for the patient to find a solution for his conflict so long as he alternates between wish-fulfilling hallucination and helpless fear. In order to find a solution for his conflict, the patient's wish-fulfilling hallucination must become a wish that serves as a guide and a goal directing his activity.

A second requirement, in order that the patient may learn, is insight into the relation between cause and effect. The recognition of causal connections, as Nunberg (1931) in particular has emphasized, is also an act of synthesis. In terms of our dream material, the patient's aggression against the mother's pregnancy and the threatening attitude of the father must be recognized as belonging together in the relation of cause and effect. One might compare this act of synthesis with the union of two states in a federation. The federated state is the ego, whose function begins with the recognition of the causal connection. Armed with this understanding, the ego could now begin to assume the role of arbiter and mediator between the patient's aggression and his fear.[12] The fear must be toned down so as to allow an experimental search for substitutive satisfactions; but then the aggressive impulses must be modified to give place to less dangerous substitutes.

The recognition of this arbitrating role of the ego, moreover, throws into relief the dynamic source of the tendency to fragment the traumatic memory. The two conflicting tendencies—both the patient's desire for the mother and his fear—resist modification. As every analysis shows, the realization that the unconscious desire for the mother is impossible to fulfill is a shattering one. The infantile sexual wishes resist being modified in deference to fear and want no arbitrator; they prefer to take their own course and forget the fear, as the first part of the dream succeeds in doing.

g. *Economic analysis of disappearance of insight*

We are thus brought back to our central problem. We undertook first of all to compare the dream's attempt to solve the patient's conflict with the requirements for a rational solution of the same problem. Upon making this comparison, we were struck first by the fact that the dream was dealing primarily with the realities of a childhood situation, rather than with the realities of the present situation. Our further analysis then disclosed that the wish-fulfilling tendencies in the dream had not been successful in eliminating the unpleasant real elements in this childhood situation, but that the dream material portrayed side by side the hallucinatory fulfillment of the patient's wishes and the frustrations deriving from the fact that these wishes could not be gratified. We then found that the essential differences between the dream solution and a hypothetical rational solution of the patient's childhood conflict were due to the fact that essential synthetic insights were missing—to the fact that the patient was unable to look at this childhood problem as a whole and therefore could not begin to learn the lesson that was contained in it. Because of the absence of this total view of the childhood memories to which the patient is reacting, the patient's dream consists of successive reactions to different fragments of his childhood conflict.

Our next problem is to inquire into the dynamic reasons for this absence of synthetic insights, for this inability of the dreamer to view his problem as a whole. To ask the same question in another way—what dynamic conditions would be necessary in order to enable the patient to gain a view of this unsolved childhood problem as a whole, and so find himself in a position to begin to learn the lesson from it?

(1) THE WISH TO SLEEP

A first answer to this question is so obvious that it may seem a bit ridiculous to have put the question. It is not the function of a dream to achieve a solution for the patient's conflict that would be valid in real life. During sleep one does not wish primarily to find rational solutions for one's conflicts. One wishes first of all to sleep. Wishes derived from one's waking life are first of all disturbers of sleep which the dream is attempting to put to rest as expeditiously as possible.

We have already taken note of the fact that it is only in the process of waking up that this dreamer has been compelled to react to the painful elements in the traumatic situation that he is reliving. The ignoring of painful elements in the first part of the dream has plainly been dictated by the wish to sleep. When the wish to get rid of the analyst becomes so importunate that it threatens the patient with the danger of really losing his father substitute, he saves himself by waking up with what is equivalent to a reassurance that he has only been dreaming. The claws of the bird upon the back of the patient's neck awaken him just as his father used to do and the voice of the bird reminds him that it is quite impossible to get rid of his analyst.

We seem to be dealing therefore with another sort of synthesis of the elements of the patient's conflict, rather than with an evidence of the failure of the ego's synthetic function. The dream has acted as a sort of safety valve to conserve sleep and at the same time to allow a harmless outlet for wishes that might prove disturbing in real life. Then when he has been somewhat refreshed by sleep, the patient wakes up and reminds himself that he has only been dreaming.

This, as we know, is Freud's classical formulation of the function of dreams. It is useful to recapitulate it in order to remind ourselves that the ego's synthetic function is not obliterated during sleep and in dreams but rather focused in large part upon the task of preserving sleep.

(2) INCREASED INTENSITY OF CONFLICT

In the present instance, however, the ego has failed also in this other synthetic function, that of preserving sleep. The patient wakes up, not refreshed and revived by his sleep, but in acute anxiety. If the original purpose of the ego was merely to allow a harmless outlet for forbidden wishes, it is plain that these wishes have proved too strong to remain subordinated to the ego's wish to continue to sleep. On the contrary, they have stirred up infantile fears that compel a precipitate awakening to prevent the ego's being overpowered by destructive forces that have escaped from its control.

We may convince ourselves further that the breakdown of synthesis in this dream is not solely due to the fact that the patient is sleeping, by comparing this dream with the dream fragment already quoted from the hour of two days previous.

There were two very black horses. One horse bumped into the other. . . . (Later) one horse took the harness of the other in his teeth and pulled him over to where he belonged. The patient thought this horse had almost human intelligence.

It will be noticed that this dream implies recognition of the conflict between the patient's hostile wish to attack the analyst (the other horse) and his desire for the analyst's love. The dream is an expression of the wish that the analyst would "pull him over to where he belonged." His wish to be put right is based, of course, upon his wish to be reconciled with his father, to be again accepted as one of the family group. His reproach to the analyst that the analyst does not put him in his place is at bottom a plea for reconciliation. The dream ends with this plea for reconciliation. The hope that he will be corrected and so retain the love of the father remains dominant and the aggressive wish remains subordinated.

The dream of two days later is, in fact, very similar in structure to the earlier dream. In this anxiety dream also an aggressive wish toward the analyst threatens to deprive the patient of his father substitute. In this dream, moreover, the patient's hope that his father would put him in his place is actually realized. The father wakes the patient rudely and assures him that there is no possibility of his getting rid of his analyst.

The difference between the two dreams is plainly a quantitative one. In the dream of the two black horses, the desire for reconciliation is able to retain dominance. In the anxiety dream, the intensity of the hostile wish is so much stronger that it threatens completely to escape from the domination of this wish to be reconciled with the father. In order to regain control in behalf of its synthetic function, the ego must allow the patient to awake in acute anxiety.

If we wish to find an explanation for this quantitative difference between the two dreams, we need only to recall that in the interval has occurred the patient's confession and the frustration caused by the fact that the analyst did not respond. This frustration both intensifies the patient's conflict and weakens the synthetic capacity of the patient's ego. It intensifies the patient's conflict by adding the resentment of frustration to the aggressive impulses that are already threatening to estrange him from the analyst. It weakens his ego by robbing it of the hope of success in its attempt to solve his conflict by seeking reconciliation with a father substitute.

The patient's confessions in the analytic hour preceding the dream constituted in fact a very promising attempt to solve his conflict. Among other things, he confessed his sexual fantasies involving the girl for whom he had once arranged an abortion. It is plain, therefore, that he was already dealing with the aggressive and sexual impulses toward the pregnant mother that play such an important part in the subsequent dream. Moreover, just as in the dream, his admitted fear of telling these fantasies to the analyst is obviously based upon the tendency to react to the analytic situation according to the pattern of his childhood relation to his father. The patient's confessions differ from his dream, however, in one very important respect. The dream deals separately with conflicting tendencies and is unable to view the patient's problem as a whole. Closely associated with this is the fact that in the dream, except at the moment of waking, there is no recognition of the differences between the analytic situation and patient's childhood relation to the father. The patient's confessions, on the other hand, are an attempt at synthesis, an attempt to reconcile the patient's hostility with his desire for the father's love. Moreover, they constitute specifically an attempt to correct the childhood pattern, to determine whether it might not be safe to confess to the analyst impulses that the patient would not have dared to tell the father.

We have already noted that the frustration at the end of this hour both increased the intensity of the patient's conflict and weakened the capacity of the patient's ego by depriving it of the hope of success in its synthetic function. In the subsequent dream the energy of the conflicting impulses is too great to be mastered by the ego in its role of arbitrator.

Borrowing a concept of Pierre Janet (1889), we may picture the ego as having at any given moment a certain "span" [13] or "synthetic capacity."

In the dream of the two black horses we may picture the dynamic situation as in Figure 2. The synthetic capacity of the ego is able to span both the patient's aggressive impulses and his desire to retain the love of the father. The result is an attempt to synthesize the conflicting impulses by provoking punishment and so obtain reconciliation with the father; but the attempt at synthesis follows an old pattern and takes no account of the specific differential features of the present situation.

The situation during the hour preceding the anxiety dream is represented in Figure 3. In this case, the synthetic capacity of the ego is sufficient not only to span the combined energy of the conflicting impulses but also to take some account of the differences between the present situation and past experience. This makes possible an attempt at discriminatory learning, an attempt to determine whether

FIGURE 2

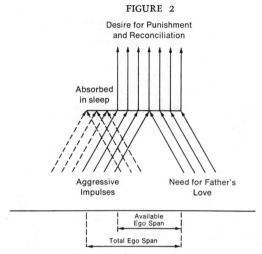

Available ego span is that part of total ego span that is not absorbed in the wish to sleep

FIGURE 3

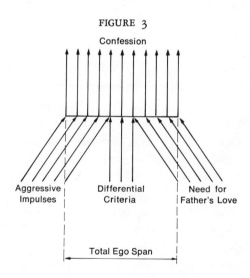

it might not be safe to confess to the analyst impulses that the patient would not have dared to tell his father.

The situation in the anxiety dream is represented in Figure 4. In this case the ego is able to span the conflicting impulses only one at a time. As a result, the patient must discharge in a fragmentary fashion first his aggressive impulses and then his need for punishment in order to retain the love of his father.

FIGURE 4

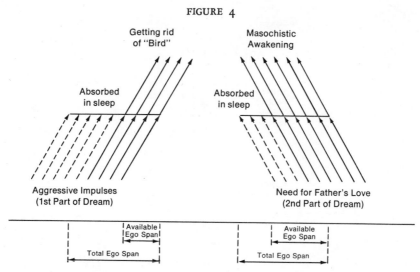

Available ego span is that part of total ego span that is not absorbed in the wish to sleep

5. CONCLUSIONS

We may tentatively summarize our conclusions in the following two main points:

1) In order to understand dreams and neurotic symptoms it is not sufficient merely to find the wish or wishes that the dream or symptom is attempting to fulfill. We must also seek justification in the real memories of the patient for the particular kind of wish fulfillment that the dream or symptom is able to achieve. Neuroses and psychoses are not able to ignore pain. Dreams are able to ignore unpleasant reality only insofar as the state of sleep itself in proportion to its depth is able to absorb the pain. Reassurances cannot be manufactured out of nothing. If a dream or symptom is unable to provide reassurance by reference to the actual experiences of the patient, distortions of reality in the direction of wish fulfillment will be followed by a compensatory tendency to correct the distortions in subsequent material.

2) The fundamental differences that distinguish rational waking behavior from neuroses and dreams are based upon the quantitative relationship between the synthetic capacity of the ego and the intensity of conflict. Because of the ego's inadequate synthetic capacity, neuroses and dreams are usually able to deal with the conflict only in a fragmentary way and tend to repeat in a stereotyped manner reactions to previous traumatic experiences. Rational behavior requires an ego span

sufficient not only to view one's situation as a whole but also to enable one to pay attention to differential criteria so as to be able to learn from past mistakes instead of repeating them.

NOTES

1. In the terminology of the conditioned reflex experiments, the unconditioned reflex (corresponding in the present discussion to the castration fear or other unpleasant consequences of an act) must be a prepotent one if conditioning is to be sure to take place. Hence my qualification that the conditioned reflex principle is universally valid only for emotionally significant events.

2. Reference will be made later to a second overdetermined meaning of this symbolism, bird as phallus, getting rid of the bird as self-castration.

3. The analysis of subsequent nightmares of the same patient tends to confirm the impression suggested by the dream symbolism and associations that the emphasis upon sleeping in this dream is also based upon the reactivation of a primal scene that waked the patient out of sleep. For such a memory sleep is, of course, an appropriate defense and waking up out of sleep is the logical result of the failure of this defense mechanism. It will be noted that the associations to the dream concern themselves a great deal with speculation about the sexual relations between the parents.

4. It will be noticed that the suggestion here offered that the unconscious is quite unable to get rid of the disturbing realities in the patient's situation makes unnecessary the hypothesis of a primary masochism in this material. Theoretically it is helpful to keep separate the two components in the patient's masochistic gratification: (1) the original desire for sexual gratification from the father, and (2) the reflection back upon himself of his own rage. It is the patient's own reflected rage that gives the original passive erotic desires their masochistic coloring.

The mechanisms here cited have of course been abundantly discussed in the psychoanalytic literature (see especially Freud: *A Child Is Being Beaten,* and Alexander: *The Psychoanalysis of the Total Personality*). I recapitulate them here for their bearing upon the dynamics of reality adjustment.

5. It will be noted that the symbolism is of being within the mother's body (a room) rather than directly of coitus. Lewin (1933) has especially called attention to the fact that intrauterine fantasies represent a sort of compromise between the desire for coitus with the mother and the desire to flee to a safe place away from the father. He quotes Freud to the effect that "fantasies of 'returning to the mother' are 'coitus fantasies of the sexually inhibited.' " It will be noted that Lewin's analysis of the intrauterine fantasy makes still more specific our suggestion that the patient's "symbolic manner of fulfilling his wish for the mother is in itself a compromise between wish fulfillment and recognition of frustration."

6. The birds in the dream probably symbolize not only the patient's rivals but also the penis. The realization that there is a little bird in the room therefore is a substitute for beginning awareness of genital desire toward the mother. The further elaboration of this genital desire for the mother is immediately interfered with by a self-castration impulse in deference to the love for the father (see note 7 below). Hence the patient proceeds to get rid of the "little bird."

7. Slight indications of the influence of the desire for the father are already present earlier in the dream. It is undoubtedly partly in deference to the patient's love for his father that the mother is relegated to the background. Moreover, since the little bird also represents the penis, getting rid of the little bird symbolizes self-castration. Dynamically, getting rid of the penis means getting rid of the desires toward the mother that are so disturbing to the patient's bond to the father.

8. This suggestion is elaborated further in Section f.

9. In the following paragraph, I use the chronological order of appearance of the manifest dream elements in order to trace shifts of emphasis that bring into focus one after another during the act of dreaming different parts of the latent dream thoughts. These shifts of emphasis I regard as quantitative indicators of the balance between conflicting tendencies just as conscious thoughts and actions during waking life are indicators of the quantitative balance between the motives that activate them. What we are tracing, of course, is a part of the dream work that takes place during the time the patient is actually dreaming.

10. At this point we have most conclusive evidence that the unconscious cannot ignore disturbing realities. Although the ego's attempt to subordinate its aggressive impulses has broken down, nevertheless the unconscious cannot rid itself of the fear of retaliation, a fear that is so excessive that the patient must awaken in acute anxiety.

11. A single important exception to this fragmentation of the patient's conflict is the overdetermined self-castrative meaning of getting rid of the small bird to which reference has already been made (note 6). This double meaning of getting rid of the small bird gives this symbolic act the significance of an elementary synthesis. By the choice of an ambiguous symbol, the dream is attempting to reconcile the wish to get rid of the father with the wish to make peace with him by getting rid of the offending organ.

12. By fear I mean, of course, not only fear of punishment but also fear of loss of love.

13. Janet uses the term "psychic tension." In a later work (Janet, 1924), I find a paragraph which states the same principle that I am here discussing, though of course without reference to the psychoanalytic concepts of the unconscious and repression. "Psychic force, that is, the power, the number, and the duration of movements, ought not to be confused with psychic tension, characterized by the degree of activation and the hierarchical degree of acts. It is probable that in normal behavior in well-balanced individuals a certain relationship must be maintained between available force and tension, and that it is not good to maintain a great force when tension has lowered; the result is excitement and disorder. A comparison allows the illustration of this little known law: individuals who are not accustomed to order and economy do not know how to behave and run risks if they have at once in their hands a large sum of money. 'If I am disgracefully drunk,' one poor woman told me, 'it is the fault of my employer who gave me seventy francs all at once. I cannot stand more than twenty-five francs at a time. What do you expect? I did not know what to do with seventy francs so I drank them.'"

BIBLIOGRAPHY

Franz Alexander, "Dreams in Pairs and Series," *International Journal of Psychoanalysis,* VI (1925), 446.

Psychoanalysis of the Total Personality (New York and Washington, Nervous and Mental Disease Pub. Co., 1927).

"The Need for Punishment and the Death Instinct," *International Journal of Psychoanalysis,* X (April-July 1929), 256.

"About Dreams with Unpleasant Content," *Psychiatric Quarterly* (July 1930).

Sandor Ferenczi, "Gedanken über das Trauma," *Internationale Zeitschrift fur Psychoanalyse,* XX (1934), 5.

Thomas M. French, "Interrelations between Psycho-analysis and the Experimental Work of Pavlov," Chapter 1 above.

Sigmund Freud, *The Interpretation of Dreams* (New York, 1900).

"Fragment of an Analysis of a Case of Hysteria." *Collected Papers III* (London, Hogarth Press, 1905).

"Formulation Regarding the Two Principles in Mental Functioning." *Collected Papers IV* (London, Hogarth Press, 1911).

"A Childhood Recollection from 'Dichtung und Wahrheit.'" *Collected Papers IV* (London, Hogarth Press, 1917).

"The History of an Infantile Neurosis." *Collected Papers III* (London, Hogarth Press, 1918).

"A Child Is Being Beaten," *Collected Papers II* (London, Hogarth Press, 1919).

Beyond the Pleasure Principle (London, Hogarth Press, 1922).

The Ego and the Id (London, Hogarth Press, 1927).

"Negation," *International Journal of Psycho-analysis,* VI (1925), 367.

The Problem of Anxiety (New York, Norton, 1926).

Pierre Janet, *Les Nèvroses* (Paris, 1889).

Principles of Psychotherapy (New York, 1924).

Wolfgang Koehler, *The Mentality of Apes* (New York, Harcourt, Brace, 1927).

Bertram D. Lewin, "The Body as Phallus," *Psychoanalytic Quarterly* (1933).

Herman Nunberg, "Synthetic Function of the Ego," *International Journal of Psycho-analysis,* XII (April 1931), 123.

Ivan P. Pavlov, *Condition Reflexes* (Oxford, Dover, 1927).

Oskar Pfister, *Schockdenken und Schockphantasien bei höchster Triebgefahr* (Vienna, 1931).

Theodor Reik, *Geständniszwang und Strafbedürfnis* (Vienna, 1925).

Chapter Three

A CLINICAL STUDY OF LEARNING
IN THE COURSE OF
A PSYCHOANALYTIC TREATMENT

After our comparison of psychoanalysis with the experimental work of Pavlov, we attempted next to make "A Clinical Study of Learning in the Course of a Psychoanalytic Treatment." Our method was to compare the dream before and the dream after a three-and-a-half-week period of analysis and to study how the differences between these two dreams could be accounted for in terms of what happened in the interval between them.

By this method we can make it plain that the patient is dealing throughout this three-week period with a single problem in external adjustment, that of overcoming his fear of the analytic task and of adapting himself to the analytic situation. His overcoming of his fear was made possible by his learning to take advantage of the difference between the understanding, tolerant atmosphere of the analysis and the repressive, threatening aura with which the patient had surrounded the memory of his father. Thus, as in most learning processes, the solution of the patient's problem depended upon his acquiring the ability to act upon a discriminatory insight. This discriminatory insight made possible a second, more fundamental adjustment, the diminution of the patient's fear as a result of the diminution of the intense ambivalence that was the cause of the fear.

Neuroses probably in every case represent a permanent fixation upon frustration reactions resulting from traumatic situations in emotional development in which the patient was unable to take the step

Reprinted from *Psychoanalytic Quarterly*, 5 (1936).

in learning that was required of him. Such a concept of a neurosis as the product of a disturbed learning process suggests also the principle upon which therapy must be based. Since the step that life demands of the patient is too great, the treatment must somehow manage to divide this one long step into a number of smaller ones. Psychoanalysis attempts to do this first of all by providing a situation in which impulses that are forbidden in real life are met with understanding and a certain amount of encouragement. Thus the analysis itself facilitates the learning process by substituting a more attainable goal, that of adjusting to the analytic situation itself, in place of the goal which the patient has been unable to reach, that of adjusting to the problems of real life.

We return again to the importance of the influence of quantitative factors upon the learning process. Each step in learning involves the substitution of a new method of obtaining gratification for an old one. The incentive to search for a new method of gratification must be derived from insight into the fact that the old method is no longer adequate. Realization that an old method of gratification is unsatisfactory does not lead to immediate acquisition of a new one but merely initiates a period of experimentation. The first experiments are apt not to be successful. Consequently, the experimentation tends to be punctuated by periods of frustration and despair, because the experimenter has lost his old method of gratification and has as yet found no new one to take its place. It is during this period of frustration and despair that the facilitating influence of the tolerant analytic atmosphere is of crucial importance. In the material studied, it has been possible to follow the way that the patient's conflict is reduced in intensity, at this crucial point, by his latent confidence that the analyst will welcome rather than frown upon his aggressive impulses. It is this reduction in the intensity of the conflict that makes it possible for the patient to learn instead of continuing fixed upon his frustration.

1. Introduction and Preliminary Survey of Case Material

A. Psychoanalytic Treatment as a Process of Reeducation

Freud once compared a psychoanalytic treatment to a process of reeducation.[1] The present paper is an attempt to work out some of the implications of this suggestion.

Psychoanalysis started with the modest objective of attempting to discover the content of unconscious wishes and memories. The repressing forces during this period were looked upon for the most part merely as obstacles in the search for deeper treasures which they were hiding. It was, of course, necessary to understand the obstacles sufficiently to enable the analyst to get past them to the buried wishes and memories, but Freud postponed his attempt at fundamental analysis of the repressing forces until an abundant material had been collected throwing light upon the details of the psychosexual development of the infant and upon the fate during the course of ego development of wishes deriving from earlier periods. Then in a series of studies Freud sketched out his scheme of the structure of the personality and summarized the knowledge of ego development that had grown up, one may say, more or less incidentally during the study of the repressed forces. Alexander [2] early attempted to turn these new concepts of personality structure to practical use and suggested that it was of practical advantage in analytic therapy to attempt to analyze the "total personality" instead of focusing too exclusive interest upon the repressed forces.

The writer's present study is an attempt to carry this suggestion to its logical theoretical conclusion. After attempting to analyze a patient's material in the usual way—as a series of defense reactions to unconscious wishes that are struggling to emerge into consciousness—I shall try to utilize the insight so obtained to understand the patient's whole analysis as a process of progressive adaptation. In other words, in this study I wish to place chief emphasis upon the process of acquiring sublimated and reality-adjusted outlets for the patient's instinctive energy. This process is admittedly the most fundamental therapeutic goal in every analysis, but we often do not consider too closely the intimate mechanisms by which this improvement in external adjustment takes place, tending rather to take it for granted as a consequence of the achievement of our more immediate therapeutic goal, the bringing into consciousness of unconscious impulses and memories.

In the study of organic illness, it is often helpful to focus the center of attention upon the normal tendencies toward recovery in the organism and to regard disease as a disturbance of normal function. Similarly, in this paper I wish to explore the advantages to be gained by looking upon neurotic illness as essentially a disturbance in the normal process of learning to adjust to external reality. Of course, in so doing I shall be merely attempting to see well-known analytic mechanisms from a somewhat new point of view. My justification for this attempt is the hope that, by always keeping in view the learning process underlying analytic therapy, we may improve somewhat our perspective and sense of proportion as to the significance and relative importance of the great multitude of unconscious impulses and memories that press toward the surface in a psychoanalytic treatment.

It will be noticed that the aim of the present paper touches closely upon Alexander's discussion of problems of the psychoanalytic technique.[3] Alexander discusses the fact that there is still disagreement among analysts as to just what factors are most important for the therapeutic effect of a psychoanalysis. There is fairly general agreement that emotional abreaction, the recovery of repressed infantile memories, and intellectual insight all play a role in the "mechanism of the cure," but analysts differ as to the relative importance to be allotted to one or another of these several elements. Following a point of view that has been developed in some detail by Nunberg,[4] Alexander himself is inclined to regard the psychoanalytic treatment as most fundamentally an integrative process that achieves its therapeutic effects by bringing under the conscious control of the ego impulses that had previously been left to unconscious elaboration and synthesis, more or less independent of the central core of the personality. Emotional abreaction, the acquisition of intellectual insight, and the recovery of repressed infantile memories are regarded by Alexander as only partial phases or aspects of this more comprehensive reintegrating process. It is the purpose of the present paper to study this reintegrating process by a rather detailed analysis of the "process of cure" in a single case.

B. Method

The method I propose for this study is to compare dreams and fantasies produced at different periods of the treatment. For the purpose of this comparison, our interest will be directed, as I have already suggested, to the organization of the dream material with reference to the problem in external adjustment with which the patient is at the moment faced. After comparing the organization of dreams produced at different periods, I shall then attempt to account for the differences in terms of the emotional events that have occurred in the interval between them.

After a brief orienting survey of the previous history of the patient, we shall subject to a detailed study of this sort a three-week period occurring early in the analysis during which the patient was struggling with the problem of initial adjustment to the analytic situation. In a later section of the paper, we shall attempt a less exhaustive survey of the whole analysis with special emphasis upon the difficult resistance period which was the turning point in the patient's therapeutic reaction.

The case that I select for study was one of my first supervised analyses during my period of training. I am therefore indebted to Dr. Hanns Sachs for much help in understanding the structure of the case. My theoretical conclusions are based upon a subsequent study of the case record. I have selected this case, in spite of the fact that it is one of my earliest cases, because of the unusually difficult "working through" period that occurred in this analysis. The case appealed to me, therefore, as an especially favorable one for the study of difficult resistance periods.

C. Résumé of Case History

The patient was an impulse-ridden young man of twenty-six, the oldest of six brothers. He had been under analysis for years by a number of analysts in succession. He had originally sought analysis on account of the fixation of his sexual interest upon the compulsive urge to show himself in some uniform, such as a boy scout uniform, with open neck and knees exposed.

His father was a severe silent man with a stern religious background, but subject at times to attacks of rage against the mother. Toward his children he was subtly sadistic. The patient also suspected that he was shy, especially about discussing sexual matters with his children. The patient was intensely afraid of him but compensated for this by tyrannizing over his brothers. The father died about three years before the patient began his analysis with me.

The patient's mother was described as a woman of much charm. She was very religious and subject to many nervous fears, but at the same time she played a rather seductive role toward the patient and his brothers. The patient felt that she subtly encouraged their jealousies of each other and of their father. On a few occasions she encouraged the patient secretly to defy his father.

The patient's eldest brother (one and a half years younger than the patient) was a cripple with an envious, complaining, somewhat cunning disposition. He was, however, deeply attached to the patient, though the latter tyrannized over him and sometimes treated him roughly. This brother died at the age of twenty.

Throughout the patient's childhood he felt himself to be the mother's favorite, but the second brother became successful in business upon coming to manhood and won the mother's favor away from the patient. This was naturally a severe blow for the patient; but the patient's intense hatred of his brother dated from early childhood. The patient recalls kicking and stamping upon his nurse when the mother took his brother as a baby to see a physician in a distant city. Later in his childhood the patient once feared he had killed his brother by hitting him on the head with an iron ball.

The other brothers apparently played less important roles in the patient's life. Toward the youngest, ten years the patient's junior, the patient had at times a somewhat fatherly attitude, but this brother was the father's favorite and the patient was also intensely jealous of him.

The brothers all slept together in one room and used to masturbate together, sharing their fear and defiance of the parents in the next room. During his analysis the patient recalled intense fears dating from early childhood and associated with his sexual impulses. He was terrified by his mother's shears, by his nurse's long fingernails, and by stories that he heard of children being cut up and eaten. Once when the father was about to whip the second younger brother for wetting the bed, the mother cried out, "Not with the ring." The patient thought she was referring to some terrible torture device. Only years later did he realize that his mother meant that the father should take off his wedding ring before striking.

The patient's analytic material showed that he feared castration from the mother as well as from the father, but in his conscious memories the mother played a protecting role. From a very early age, the patient had some inflammation under the foreskin, probably caused originally by accumulated secretions. A physician proposed circumcision but the mother refused to allow this. Instead she irrigated under the foreskin daily for years. The patient naturally derived considerable gratification from this and used to insist on the nurse's doing it on the occasions when the mother was away.

In spite of his fears, however, the patient continued to masturbate. He used to burn the evidences of his masturbation. Nevertheless, he thinks his father knew he masturbated but was embarrassed to speak to the patient about it.

His compulsive interest in exhibiting himself with open neck and bare knees began, he says, in his twelfth year when he saw a boy in a sailor suit with an open neck. This was his favorite masturbation fantasy.

In these fantasies there was an indefinite crowd looking on. The patient used to wish his father and mother would go away so that he could act out his fantasy in real life; and later, when he was sent away to school, he eagerly welcomed the chance to get away from his father and mother so that he could live out his cherished fantasy. As soon as he arrived at his destination, he bought a boy scout uniform, wore it on the street, masturbated in it, and then burned it up.

In addition to his own urge to exhibit himself in this way, the patient was also intensely excited sexually by the sight of younger boys in similar costumes. In this sexual excitement there was a strong sense of identification with the boys whose knees and necks were thus exposed.

One day when the patient was seventeen years old, his father took him for a ride and called his attention to an "idiot" in town whose demented condition, the father said, was the result of his masturbation. The patient at first did not recall that this talk made any particular impression upon him, but for about a year after that he did not masturbate and not long afterward he developed an obscure illness with fever and finally had to have an operation for an infected toenail.

The patient dates from this time his great difficulty in concentrating upon his work at school. Nevertheless he achieved a doctor's degree in theology, after writing a thesis upon the psychology of atheism. Some time later another student hired him to write a thesis, and the patient took delight in hoaxing the professors by getting a thesis accepted that disproved all that his own thesis proved.

He got various positions as a schoolteacher, but he worked erratically, often neglected his work, and did not hold positions for long. He was often out of money and begged or borrowed from his friends. At the time that he began his analytic work with me he was going about in dirty patched clothes, carelessly buttoned, and was spending most of his time either in his room or in bed, or wandering about the streets, or exercising in an athletic suit in various inexpensive boys' clubs.

His sexual energy was at this time completely fixed upon masturbation and upon his exhibitionistic fantasies. In his student days he had been attractive to occasional older married women, but on the one occasion when he had gone so far as to take a woman to a hotel he had been so afraid of impotence that he had been unwilling to attempt coitus.

Owing to external causes, his analysis with me was interrupted temporarily in the seventh month for a period of about seven weeks, then permanently after about two more months of analysis. I cannot say that the compulsion to exhibit his bare knees was entirely cured by the treatment, but the intensity of the patient's absorption in it had tremendously diminished, and in its place there appeared a normal interest in dressing neatly and attractively and a rather playful and defiant but persistent interest in courting the wife of a former school principal of his.

Therefore, although the analysis was not completed, there was at least sufficient therapeutic effect to serve as a basis for this study. Also of particular interest for this study is the prolonged and intense period of "working through" which preceded the patient's most marked improvement. It was this feature that led me to choose this particular case for study rather than others in which the therapeutic success was more complete.

II. Initial Adjustment to the Analytic Task

A. A Comparison of Two Dreams

The patient's analysis opened with attempts to depreciate the analysis by continued reproaches that the analyst was quite unable to help him and by repeated attempts to intimidate the analyst with more or less playful aggressive outbursts. It soon became evident that this behavior was really a mask, hiding intense passive-receptive and masochistic sexual wishes which the patient hoped and feared that the analysis would gratify. The patient's disillusionment with the analyst was further accentuated by his disappointment at having had to give up his former analyst, Dr. Y, toward whom the patient had had what was apparently a very strong mother-transference.

The material that I shall first cite followed a period in which the patient had been attempting to mitigate rapidly emerging fears by playful behavior designed to reassure himself that his fears need not be taken seriously. After repeated interpretations of this mechanism, the analyst decided in the twenty-eighth interview to withhold the reassurance that the patient was craving and to remain entirely silent during the hour. In reaction to this, the patient's questions became more and more importunate. Finally he asked whether the analyst had written Dr. Y and if he had received an answer from him. He repeated this question over and over again more and more demandingly; then finally inquired whether the analyst's motive for not answering the question was "analytic or private."

The next day he reported that he had been violently angry at the analyst, that he had never met anyone that he hated and despised so much, that he wanted to choke the analyst and make the analyst's eyes bulge and then throw him in a corner.

He recalled then how he had kicked and stepped on his nursemaid in childhood and then for the first time told of his rivalry with his second brother, over whom he had tyrannized as a child, until his tyranny had to give way to envious hatred when the brother became successful and won the favor of the mother.

I shall report the next (thirtieth) interview in detail: The patient is ten minutes late and explains that he has overslept. He says that he is doing poorly in school (he had again secured a teaching position some weeks before), that he has no confidence, is only bluffing. He can do nothing, he complains that the analyst retreats from reality by refusing to answer his questions. Yesterday he went to see his mother and she gave him fifty marks. He had a dream. He does not want to tell it. He went to sleep in the hope that he would forget it. . . . Why does not the analyst ask what the dream is? The analyst inquires. The patient asks why he wants the analyst to ask that. Dr. X and Dr. Y always asked.

The dream is as follows:

> He sees his mother. She is very majestic, but is going to die. She has a purse by her side and says that this contains the money for her burial. There is an oven on the side of the room and a shelf with a number of cakes on it. The left wall is very hot. The mother tells the patient to put thick paper against this wall to protect the cakes. The patient protests that the paper will burn, but she says it will burn only very slowly if the paper is thick and then the paper can be replaced.

When the patient saw his mother yesterday, she told him that in moving she had lost a chest with her valuables in it. A man had found it and had written her about it but the man said he was in need and asked her to let him have some money. She was afraid that the man would persecute her, but the patient reassured her, advising her to let the man have the chest so that he would not bother her.

The hot wall reminds the patient of the wall between his bed and the bed his father occupied in the next room when the patient was a child. To the cakes, he associates himself and his brothers. The paper reminds him that the letter this man wrote was on a dirty piece of paper. He also had a dirty newspaper in his pocket.

Three weeks later he revealed some facts that he had been withholding, which make this dream much more intelligible. Some two years previous, before running away from his analysis with Dr. X, the patient had persuaded one of his brothers to endorse an application for a loan of five hundred marks from the university. The brother filled out the endorsement and left the patient to fill in the amount. The patient filled in fifteen hundred marks instead of five hundred. The money obtained on these endorsements was now about used up and the patient was faced with the necessity of securing further loans. In order to do so, however, his only resource was to apply to a friend, a Mr. Z, a very domineering fellow who would be likely to inquire into the details of the patient's previous loans. The fifty marks obtained from the mother were therefore a means of putting off this difficulty a little longer.

Another fact to which the burning of the paper is also an allusion was learned still later—the fact that he used to burn the evidences of his masturbation.

In the dream, therefore, the hot left wall of the oven represents the patient's fear of (wish for) detection and punishment from Mr. Z, the analyst, the father. The paper is the money the patient receives from the mother which protects him for the time being from the necessity of exposing himself to Mr. Z's questions and anger.

As usual, however, it is not really an external but an internal danger from which the patient feels the need for protection. The danger of having to expose himself to his friend's discovery and anger is only an external symbol of the patient's desire for detection and punishment by his father. The fact that the money from his mother staves off the external necessity of having to appeal to his friend is only symbolic of a more fundamental internal economic relationship. Just as the mother's money protects him from the necessity of borrowing from a father substitute, so also is the intensity of his need for the father's love diminished by the gratification and reassurance that he receives from the mother's gift.

It is at this point that we can see most plainly how the analysis is beginning to play a role in the patient's life. His father is no longer living. The hostile impulses, of which his cheating his brother was an expression, make it exceedingly dangerous for him to turn to any father substitute to gratify his intense need for love. The analytic situation tends, however, to encourage these wishes with new hope by its implied promise of immunity from punishment for the expression of hostile wishes. Nevertheless, the fear of retaliation for aggressive impulses is deep seated. This is a dangerous temptation, this encouragement to hope to gratify in the analysis his need for a father's love. It is from this danger most of all that the patient is seeking to escape by turning to his mother for affection and help.

It is interesting to note how much is condensed into the one symbol of the hot wall. We have seen that it represents the patient's intense need for love from the father, also his fear of retaliation for his own hostility to the father and a projection of this hostility toward the father. The heat is also a threat to both mother and brothers—the mother in fact is about to die—and therefore symbolizes also the patient's jealous hatred of all his rivals for the father's love. The reference in the associations to the father's bed on the other side of the wall makes it an allusion also to the patient's feeling of estrangement from the father and to the mystery that attached to what the father might be doing on the other side of the wall. Some months later the patient recalled, in fact, having worked through with Dr. Y some memories of hearing the father's bed creak and suspecting something sexual between father and mother. So also in the manifest content of the dream, the effect of heat upon the cakes in the oven is a pictorial representation of another great mystery of childhood—the role played by the father in the conception of children. Thus we find condensed into this one symbol the sexual riddles of the patient's childhood, and all the ambivalence toward the father and jealous hatred of mother and brothers in which the patient's early sexual investigations must have involved him. The hot wall may be called a symbol of the patient's unconscious. The patient's fear of the analyst is his fear of the unconscious forces which the analysis is encouraging into bolder activity. In the manifest content of the dream, the analyst and the patient's unconscious are condensed together into one common symbol of mystery and danger.

The other elements of the dream all have to do with the patient's attempt to protect himself from these unconscious forces by transferring some of their energy to outlets in his present real life situation. He is seeking to diminish the intensity of his need for love and punishment and for explanations of the mysteries of life, by getting affection and money from the mother; and in the manifest dream some of his hostility to the father is finding outlet in the chivalrous role of helping the mother protect the children from the hot oven.

Thus the problem with which the patient at the moment is dealing is his conflict as to whether or not to accept the analytic task of investigating his unconscious impulses. At the moment his ego is impelled to flight disguised as a sort of heroic resistance. (The figure of the mother, for example, is majestic.) Even his desire for therapeutic help and enlightenment is condensed into the threatening symbol of the hot wall. His protest that the paper is sure to burn through is, of course, an expression of his unconscious hope that the analysis will succeed in spite of him; but it is plain that he is expecting therapeutic help and enlightenment to be forced upon him by the analyst against his own resistance.

I should now like to compare this dream with a dream reported three and a half weeks later, just before the patient confessed to cheating his brother.

> This dream followed immediately upon an admission in the previous interview that the patient wished to compel the analyst to say that the analysis was a failure. This was the first time that he had admitted how much in earnest he had been in his determination to defeat the analysis.
>
> The following dream was reported at the very end of the next (forty-ninth) interview:
>
>> The patient is in a court with many children who are shooting. Either the patient or perhaps the others are afraid and want to open the door but the patient tells them not to do so, that it is better to act as though one is not afraid. Then he receives a wound on his shoulder but he will not admit that he has been wounded.
>
> The court reminds the patient of the room in which he lives—which opens out on a court. It also reminds him of the schoolroom in which he teaches. The children the patient identifies as his pupils. Shooting means "something sexual."
>
> In the next hour after the dream came the patient's confession, long withheld, of having falsified the amount of the note his brother had endorsed.

It will be noticed that this dream is dealing with the same problem as the "hot wall" dream just discussed. This time the patient's unconscious is symbolized by the shooting in the court. The question as to whether or not to open the door is again the question as to whether or not to let the analyst penetrate into the patient's unconscious conflicts. In the previous hour, the patient had admitted that the analyst had been right in saying that the patient wished to defeat the analysis. The wound in the shoulder is a tacit admission that the analyst's interpretations of his passive erotic wishes about the analyst have also been correct. Being hit on the shoulder is probably symbolic of an admission that the patient's "cold shoulder" resistance has been "hit." The revelations of the next hour are, of course, confirmatory of this and we shall note that in the next succeeding dreams, the patient's relation to the analyst is represented as one of cooperation rather than of antagonism.

It is interesting to note the similarities in the organization of the two dreams. (1) In each there is a danger of mysterious origin. Like the hot wall of the oven, the shooting in the court is symbolic of the mysterious sexual activities of the parents, of the riddle of the father's role in the production of children, of the patient's feminine desire for his father's love, of his fear of retaliation for being hostile to the father, and of his jealousy chiefly of the children in the mother's body (court, oven). (2) In the manifest content of each dream the patient is playing a protective role toward the children. (3) In the earlier dream the patient protests that the paper will be burned through. In the later dream the symbolic sense of this prophecy is partially realized by his being wounded in the shoulder.

This enumeration of the similarities of the two dreams now brings into more prominent view the differences between them. (1) In the second dream the patient's fear is not so great, probably because his hostility and consequently his masochism have considerably diminished. Accordingly, his resistance to the analysis has correspondingly diminished. In the earlier dream he was trying to postpone the burning through of the paper as long as possible. In the later dream he acknowledges to himself that he is wounded and merely resists admitting it to others. (2) The figure of the mother as a person is absent in the second dream. The mother is represented only in the impersonal symbol of the court which corresponds to the oven in the earlier dream. This is also due to the diminution in the patient's masochism and resistance. In the earlier dream the mother was (a) a substitute to whom the patient was fleeing for protection from his masochistic attitude to the father; (b) a projection of his own feminine wishes and reactive pride (majesty); and (c) an object of (projected) jealousy (i.e., the hot wall is threatening her). In the later dream he has achieved a passive feminine relationship to the analyst by his readiness to accept the analyst's interpretation of it. Hence he no longer needs to split off and project his feminine wishes, nor to flee for protection to a substitute; and jealousy of the mother is for the moment unnecessary.

Thus it is evident that the patient has made considerable progress in this three-week interval period toward the solution of the problem with which he was struggling in the earlier dream. In the earlier dream he was projecting his wish for help and passive gratification from the analyst and trying to postpone it as long as possible. At the end of this three-week period he is almost ready to cooperate, at least passively, in the analytic task. This, as the next succeeding dreams show, is only preliminary to the urge that the patient will feel shortly to take an active part together with the analyst in the investigation of his unconscious impulses.

B. Survey of Interval Period

Before we discuss this subsequent material, however, it will be of interest to study the process by which the patient has arrived at his present readiness to get passive satisfaction from an interpretation by the analyst that hits the mark. As a preparation for this study of the interval period, let us first inquire how the patient is attempting to solve his problem at the time of the earlier "hot wall" dream.

We have seen that the patient's difficulty in accepting the analytic situation arises from his difficulty in reconciling his intense desire for love from the father with his—also intense—hostility to him. As a consequence, his desire for love must and does assume an extremely masochistic character. The analysis by its implied promise of immunity from punishment is encouraging the transference of this conflict into the patient's relation toward the analyst.

In the dream and the events that immediately preceded it, we can see that the patient is experimenting with a number of possible methods of solving or relieving this conflict. (1) For a long time he had been getting the analyst to play with him. This served the purpose of mitigating the patient's fear by repeated reassurance that the analyst would not take the patient's aggressive impulses seriously and would therefore not retaliate. In this way the patient was managing to get a very precarious and incomplete gratification of his desire for a friendly relationship with a father substitute. This gratification was not only precarious but also incomplete because the patient's playful depreciation of the analyst made him a much less satisfactory father substitute. As already related, the analyst, by remaining silent in the twenty-eighth interview, put a stop to this attempt to make a game of the analysis. The patient's rage and subsequent identification of the analyst with his second brother were symbolic of a transition from a younger brother to a father-transference toward the analyst, inasmuch as this brother was one whom the patient had once been able to depreciate

as a younger brother but who later had become, like the father, a successful rival. In the "hot wall" dream it is already a father-transference to
which the patient is reacting. (2) This dream represents fundamentally
an attempt to relieve the tension of the patient's father conflict by
accepting, as a substitute, a passive-dependent relation to the mother.
If the patient disguises the dependent character of this relationship by
some chivalrous gestures, as he does in the dream, it is probable that
his mother would have a strong inclination to welcome such a relationship to the patient. The obstacles in the way of such a solution would
be the patient's own narcissism, which, as the dream shows, would not
be able to tolerate a frank recognition of his dependence upon the
mother. Moreover the patient's narcissistic protest would quite certainly
be reinforced by his mother's tendency to stimulate the rivalry between
the patient and his father and brothers. (3) In the dream, this narcissistic urge to compete for the mother with the father is already hinted
at in the patient's chivalrous pose of attempting to defend the mother
against the "hot wall" that represents the father. Rivalry with the
father, however, drives the patient back again into the father conflict
for which his only outlet at the moment is (4) the masochistic submission suggested in the symbol of the "hot wall." Inasmuch as the
father is not living, this could be realized only in a passive masochistic
transference to the analyst or to some other father substitute such as
Mr. Z. The obstacle in the way of this solution is obviously the patient's
fear and narcissistic protest against so intense a masochism. (5) We
might also anticipate the possibility of a fifth solution based upon some
synthesis, as yet not definitely indicated, of elements contained in the
other three. We have already indicated that this is precisely what does
occur shortly after the revelations following the "wound in the shoulder"
dream, when the patient's urge to join with the analyst in the task of
investigating his unconscious makes itself evident in his dreams. It
would be difficult, however, to predict this upon the basis of the "hot
wall" dream, and it will now be more profitable to attempt to follow
the course of the analysis in the interval following this dream, in the
light of the problem of adjustment that we have just been outlining.

> The patient opens the hour immediately following the "hot wall" dream
> by noticing the "odor and warmth" of the woman who preceded him. He
> says he has continually been beset with fantasies of men giving birth to
> children. He has had a fantasy of the analyst or his father in a birdcage.
> Everybody was in cages. The cages were taken off for "communication"
> only but then were put back on again.

In another fantasy the analyst had talked over the patient's problem with Dr. Sachs and had been instructed by Dr. Sachs that his questions were not to be answered. There were also fantasies of the patient's going out into the mountains and lying in the snow and freezing to death. . . . At the end of the hour the patient remarks that, if he is wise, he will go to a seminar at the university tomorrow (he was studying at this time for a degree that would enable him to get a license as a regular teacher), but he thinks that the analysis will interfere with this. The analyst thereupon offers him an hour which will not interfere, but the patient says that he wishes the analyst would give him an appointment that would interfere with his going to the seminar.

It will be noticed that the patient seems to be dealing here with reactions of frustration arising out of the analyst's refusal to answer questions in the hour three days previous. This frustration is already condensed in the symbol of the "hot wall." It will be recalled that the patient's father was a very silent man. As became much plainer later, his failure to take notice of the patient's masturbation was felt by the patient also as a frustration of his intense desire for love and notice from the father, the wall between their bedrooms being obviously a symbol of the emotional distance between them. The fantasies of this hour first play with the idea of a child from the father, then try to explain away the analyst's cruel indifference. He fantasies that it is at Dr. Sachs's suggestion that the analyst has refused to talk with the patient. The analyst is really a caged bird (a baby) who can communicate with the patient only when allowed to do so. Finally the patient's exasperation comes out in undisguised form. If the analyst refuses to show any warmth, the patient will go out and freeze himself to death. In summary, we may characterize this interview as a revival of the patient's attempt to make play of the analysis (solution number 1). This leads to attempts to explain away the analyst's silence of a few days previous and ends with a recognition of the frustration of his desire for love.

The next (the thirty-second) interview anticipates the synthetic solution (number 5) with which the patient deals more earnestly only a month or so later, after the change in his unconscious attitude indicated by the "wound in the shoulder" dream. I shall postpone the attempt at economic analysis of this synthesis until we come to the discussion of the more extensive material of this later period. I need only point out at the present time that the patient's active curiosity directed primarily toward the mother is really a displaced attempt at cooperation in the analytic task of attempting to get insight into his own feminine impulses.

The patient opens this hour by telling of an infantile memory of seeing his mother wash her breasts. He recalls going with his mother to the beach where women bathed and seeing women dress and undress. Later he went with his father who simply left him to shift for himself in the water while his father went out to swim. When he was "quite a big child" (at the age of six or seven), he was sent to take something to his aunt on the women's beach. The patient was frightened. His aunt was dressing and the patient was repelled by the sight of her hairy legs.

Tomorrow the patient is to take charge of the play hour at school in place of an older man whom the children ridicule. He is much frightened, especially as he does not know the children's names. He concludes the hour by remarking that he has brought up quite a few memories today but does not see the connection with the present situation. He has heard that analyses are done only for research purposes. He does not want an analysis which is not therapeutic.

It will be noticed that this hour concludes with the abandonment of the patient's active cooperation in the analytic investigation on account of fear of recognizing the masochistic character of his feminine impulses. He fears that the analyst is analyzing him only as a (sadistic) experiment.

The next two interviews are filled with despair.

The patient inquires when the director of the Institute will be back, and says he cannot get along with the analyst. He is getting more and more depressed and the analyst gives him no help to understand and get rid of this depression. The analyst is weak and is always talking about resistance It was a mistake for the patient to have started with the analyst inasmuch as now it is impossible for him either to draw back or to go on. It was also a mistake for the analyst to have started with the patient. The patient is angry at Dr. X who referred him to the analyst. This is the third time that Dr. X has sent the patient to analysts who could do nothing with him.

The patient continues in the same vein also through the next hour. It is no use. He has no confidence. The analyst has accomplished nothing. The patient must have an indifferent third party to judge of the objectivity of his feelings about the analyst.

The next two hours constitute an attempt to solve the patient's problem by acceptance of a dependent mother-transference (solution number 2).

At the beginning of the thirty-fifth interview he is slow to assume the reclining position. His first association is a playful fantasy which he attempts to compel the analyst to take seriously. He is to be operated upon, he takes ether, is nauseated . . . something is wrong with his penis. He has syphilis. He got it by rubbing his penis on the toilet. When the patient went to the doctor to receive injections, the doctor did not believe the patient when the patient said that he had not been with a woman. What will the analyst do about it? He repeats this question many times very playfully. He insists upon the truth of his statements and demands an answer. The analyst finally remarks that it is difficult to believe that the patient means what he says when he is so playful about it. The patient then admits that he does not have syphilis and says that his associations were deflected to this fantasy when two memories occurred to him. From about the age of four until twelve he had an inflammation of the foreskin, and his mother used to give him injections for this. The patient enjoyed these injections. His mother has also told him that the doctor wanted to circumcise him when he was about two years of age, but the mother had refused to allow this. The analyst points out that the patient wishes the analyst to alleviate his castration fears by playing with him sexually under the guise of medical treatment as his mother did.

In the next hour the patient attempts to appeal to the analyst's sympathy by being ill. He complains at length that he has hurt his foot, that his foot is swollen, etc. What should he do about it? . . . He still has inflammation under his foreskin. . . . He thinks he has purposely neglected his foot so as to make it get worse. . . .

We have already anticipated that the patient's attempt to reconcile himself to a passive-dependent relationship to his mother would be shipwrecked upon the obstacle constituted by the patient's inability to reconcile such a passive solution with his own narcissism and with the mother's tendency to stimulate the patient's rivalry with his father and brothers. The next two interviews (thirty-seven and thirty-eight) confirm this anticipation.

The patient is ten minutes late and says he had no interest in coming. He delays assuming the reclining position and then complains at length that he has no interest in working. He remarks that he produced good material the day before, but that he always does poorly the next day after producing good material. Why is this? . . . Then he remembers seeing his father's penis and comparing it in size with his own. He also remembers seeing his father's biceps and comparing it in size with his own. He agrees to the analyst's suggestion that his unwillingness to continue "producing" good material is due to his rivalry with the analyst and promises that he will be on time the next day, but he insists on the analyst's going ahead of him on leaving the room. He denies that this is also an expression of rivalry but afterward agrees to the correctness of this interpretation.

In the following interview (thirty-eight) he relates for the first time the story of his boyhood rivalry with his second brother for their mother's love. In childhood the patient was the favorite. Then the brother became successful and won the mother's preference. Only recently did the patient regain first place with the mother, because the brother shocked her by marrying a Jewess who had been divorced. When the patient was a student in the university, this brother, then seventeen years old, came to live there. At that time the patient was intimate with a Jewess, through whom he had some access to good society. The patient introduced his brother to this Jewess and the brother became very fond of her. Now the brother has married a woman of the same type. Once the patient had gone on an excursion with this Jewess and she had invited him into her room and bed but the patient was impotent. Two days ago a child was born to the brother. The patient's mother was shocked because it was too soon after his marriage. The patient thinks that the present outbreak of rivalry impulses is a reaction to the birth of the brother's child. . . . In childhood the patient looked upon the mother's injections under his foreskin as a sort of sexual relation with her and as a kind of triumph over the brother, but now the brother has triumphed over the patient.

In the next two interviews the patient's rivalry with his brother gives way to self-castrative impulses and then again to reactions of despair.

He insists again that the analyst go ahead of him through the door. Is this a prestige reaction? The patient must overcome this prestige impulse. He insists that he must leave the hour ten minutes ahead of time. Yesterday he was too inhibited to prepare for a review which he had to present in a seminar at the university. He did very poorly and could not even remember the contents of his own doctoral dissertation. He went to a ball at the school and was afraid to go up to the principal of the school who was his host. He interprets cutting off time at the end of the hour as "castrating the hour." . . .

In the next hour he protests that he can do nothing, fantasies that he will get ten physicians to prescribe veronal to kill him off or go off in the mountains to die of the cold. He wishes to know if the director of the Institute is back. . . . He has been sleeping most of the weekend. Either the analysis is no good or his reaction against his brother has completely upset it. He takes a key out of his pocket and throws it violently into the corner.

The next six or seven hours bring the patient's conflict between his rivalry with the analyst and his desire for the analyst's love to a despairing climax.

In the forty-first hour he insists over and over again that he must see the director of the Institute. He cannot get along with the analyst. The patient's personality and the analyst's do not agree. He wishes that the analyst were older. Analysis is impossible without transference. The analyst points out to the patient that there is no lack of transference on the patient's part but that the transference is based on his relationship to his second brother. The patient replies that he does not like a brother-transference. He touched on this several times with Dr. Y but never could solve it.

In the next hour (forty-two) the patient complains that his foot hurts. That morning he did not want to go to school but finally went after a great struggle. He did not want to admit that he felt much better after overcoming his resistance to going to school. In answer to the patient's questions, the analyst discusses at some length the patient's rivalry with the analyst as the motive for his resistance to success in school. The patient remarks that he also gets satisfaction from getting the analyst to talk and feels this as a victory.

In the forty-third hour the patient's conflict achieves concentrated expression in a memory and a fantasy.

He recalls that he used to be pleased when his brother stole things from him secretly as this was a sign of the brother's envy, hatred, and fear of him. Once the patient insisted that his brother leave the room while the patient was talking with his mother. Then follows a fantasy that the patient is a woman and Dr. X (who regularly played a father role in the patient's fantasies) is having sexual relations with the patient and with great expenditure of energy.

To understand the significance of the juxtaposition of this memory and fantasy, we have only to realize that the brother and Dr. X are both represented in the present situation by the analyst. The patient is approaching the acute realization that his envious hatred of and his

desire for love from the analyst are irreconcilable. Actual insight, however, is as yet lacking. The envy and the desire to be loved as a woman
are split apart and displaced upon two different persons, thus making
it impossible for the patient to recognize that envy and feminine desire
for love from the analyst are incompatible.

In the forty-fourth hour the acute frustration arising from this
dawning insight takes form in a sadistic dream.

Dream:

The patient is cutting off the heads of dead fish. He throws the
heads to roosters to devour, and then throws stones at the roosters.

In association he recalls again a childhood incident in which the father
applauded while the patient struck a cat with a shovel. He also recalls
cutting angleworms in pieces and poking at a goose with a stick. He often
used to dream that his father was torturing his mother and that he
attacked his father in order to rescue her.

The specific content of this dream can be understood better by
reference to events and fantasies that occurred at other periods, for the
most part some months later, in the analysis. Very early in his analysis
(before the period that I am reporting in detail) the patient had played
with the fantasy that his mother wanted to castrate him in order to protect him from his father. In the fifth month of his analysis he complained vehemently over and over again that the analyst and his father
had driven him crazy. This was of course a fulfillment of the father's
implied threat when he showed the patient the "idiot" whose demented
condition was supposed to have been due to masturbation. During this
same period the patient recalled stories he had heard in childhood of
children being cut up and eaten. A fantasy toward the end of the fifth
month of his analysis pictures his father as tearing a baby from his
mother's arms and throwing it to the ground so that it nearly died,
and then having sexual relations with the mother. Later the patient
recalled actually fearing as a child that his father would eat him up.

In the dream now under discussion it will be noticed that all of
these fantasies are condensed into a few symbols. Cutting off fishes'
heads is a castration displaced from the penis to the head, a close
analogue to being driven crazy. The roosters eating the fishes' heads
correspond to the stories of children being cut up and eaten and to the
patient's fear that his father would eat him up. In the dream the
patient is playing a role similar to the one his earlier fantasy attributed

to the mother, placating the father by sacrificing the children. The patient's throwing stones at the rooster is probably an allusion to the reproach contained in the later fantasy of the father's throwing the baby to the ground.

Thus, like the cakes in the oven in the former dream, the dead fishes and the stones in this dream represent children. The children are first of all the patient's brothers, probably also the patient's own fantasied children.[5] In the dream and fantasies he is sacrificing the children to the father, thus giving vent to his own sadistic impulses and at the same time seeking to placate the father and to justify his hostility toward the father.

The dream is plainly a reaction to a sort of desperate realization of the conflict between the patient's envy and his need for the analyst's (father's) love. We have noted that every time the patient "produces good material," he is envious and resentful of the analyst's success in eliciting it from him; but at the same time he wishes that the analysis should be productive.

In the dream this conflict is expressed in terms of its infantile prototype. He is envious of his father's genitals and wishes to destroy the children whom the father has "produced"; but he also desires love from the father and is fascinated by the idea of "producing" a child. The dream attempts to reconcile or in any case to condense these conflicting wishes. There is an urge to atone for his phallic envy and placate the father by castrating himself but instead of himself he castrates the dead fishes that symbolize his brothers. He wishes to win the father's love by giving him a child but instead of a child he gives him dead fishes' heads and stones.

It is easy to sense from the material that these attempts at sacrifice are not enough, for the latent dream thoughts contain a whole series of reproaches and attempts at self-justification that we may translate somewhat as follows. To the father: "You demand that I sacrifice to you my genitals. Therefore I have a right to throw stones (reproaches) at you." Throwing the stone, it will be noticed, is a direct allusion to the reproach contained in the later fantasy of the father's throwing the baby to the ground. The fact that there is more than one rooster probably implies that the patient has also a similar reproach against the mother, which he expresses in introjected form by his own behavior in the dream: "You are willing to sacrifice your children to father. You and father are interested in your own pleasure rather than in giving life and love to us children." Other "roosters" are probably the patient's analysts toward whom he directs reproaches of similar content based upon the encouragement that the analysis gives to the patient's unconscious impulses. "You analysts aid and abet my sadism," the dream complains, "in order to get scientific material to devour and to discuss with each other."

Whatever truth there may have been in these reproaches toward his father and mother and his numerous analysts, it is plain that they are a direct reaction to the insight with which the patient is threatened, into the incompatibility of his phallic envy of the father (analyst) and his desire for his father's love.

The next three interviews (forty-five, forty-six, forty-seven) contain the patient's affective expression of this despair.

> He must see the director of the Institute. He is not oriented as to his case, has no one to help him, has no confidence in the analyst. He does not listen to an interpretation that the analyst gives, protests that he does not hate the analyst, simply has no contact with him. . . .

In the next (forty-eighth) hour came the patient's confession that he wished to get the analyst to admit the analysis was a failure.

> He opens the hour by remarking that the same resistance continues. He feels that he will never make anything out of analysis, that the analyst made a mistake in undertaking his analysis. . . . What does the analyst think? The analyst replies that there are often difficult periods in analysis and that it is quite possible that the patient can overcome his present resistances. Thereupon the patient replies that he is angry. He wishes the analyst to say the analysis is a failure. He adds that he had a big setback just before starting work with the analyst upon learning that an analyst recommended by Dr. Y would be unable to undertake the case. Dr. Y was a little unreliable but had no other faults. The analyst then remarks that it was not strange that the patient found it difficult to break off his analysis with Dr. Y of whom he was so fond.

> In the next hour (forty-ninth), the patient complains that his foot hurts. . . . He would like to have an analyst who would encourage him and pat him on the head. . . . Dr. Y made a mistake, he gave in to this desire of the patient's. The patient told him he was making a mistake, that he was making things more comfortable for the patient only to make them worse later. . . . The analyst's comments upon these remarks were then followed by the dream of the children shooting in the court in which the patient was wounded in the shoulder.

C. Emotional Aspects of Learning

We have undertaken a survey of this three-week interval period in order to study the process by which the patient's initial fear of the analysis gave way to an unconscious satisfaction in cooperating, first passively, then actively, in the analytic task. Our attempt to understand this process will be facilitated by a few reflections upon the emotional aspects of learning.

Each step in learning involves the substitution of a new for an old method of obtaining gratification. The incentive to search for a new method of gratification must be derived from insight into the fact that the old method is no longer adequate. However, the realization that an old method of gratification is unsatisfactory does not lead to the immediate acquisition of a new one. It merely initiates a period of experimentation. The first experiments are apt not to be successful; consequently, the experimentation tends to be punctuated by periods of frustration and despair, for the experimenter has now lost his old method of gratification and has as yet found no new one to take its place.

We have just seen how the patient's search for a solution of his conflict is also punctuated by periods of despair. His first playful fantasy—that he can get a baby from the analyst—is followed by rage because he is left out in the cold. His attempt to mobilize his infantile curiosity in the service of the analysis breaks down through inability to face insight into his masochism. The despair occasioned by the failure of this experiment is followed by an attempt to purchase a passive relation to the mother by capitalizing upon his physical symptoms; but this leads directly to rivalry with father and brother and to the realization that the brother has triumphed over him. Finally, insight comes to the patient that he is attempting the impossible; for if he is attempting to down the analyst as a rival, he cannot also expect to receive love from him. It is of great interest to notice that this insight takes definite form before the patient is conscious of it or at all willing to accept it. It is already implicitly formulated when the patient confesses side by side his secret delight in his brother's envy and his fantasy of having intercourse as a woman with Dr. X. In the dream of cutting off fishes' heads, the patient violently repudiates this insight, while at the same time giving concentrated (though inverted) expression to it. "If I wish to be loved by father, I must give up my rivalry with him," is the basic content of this insight. To this the dream replies with retaliatory impulses and angry retorts. "Father demands my penis as a condition of his love. Such a cruel father should have stones instead of children."

Immediately after the abreaction of this rage, however, the patient is able for the first time to admit freely his desire to defeat the analysis. Then his dream of being wounded in the shoulder gives slightly grudging expression to what we may characterize as a sort of cooperative satisfaction in the correctness of the analyst's interpretation of the passive homosexual transference. Immediately thereafter comes his confession of his falsification of his brother's endorsement.

D. Economic Analysis of the Interval Period

It will be of interest to analyze in more detail the nature of these changes in the patient and of the process by which he arrived at them.

We may begin by considering certain economic problems presented by the dream of the hot wall when seen in relation to subsequent material. In the dream of the fishes' heads, sadistic impulses attain undisguised expression. A subsequent dream reported two months after the dream of the hot wall culminates in the patient's being pursued by Mr. Z (the friend to whom he now fears he will have to appeal for financial help) with a revolver. In the dream of the hot wall, these same sadistic impulses and this same fear are projected and condensed into the symbol of the "hot wall." This presents us with an economic problem. At the time of the dream of the hot wall, what is it that prevents an acute outbreak of the patient's sadistic impulses or of his masochism and fear of the father?

Turning to the material, we notice that the dream itself gives a direct answer to these questions. The paper that the patient interposes between the cakes and the hot wall is an allusion to the money that the patient has just received from the mother, which enables him to stave off the necessity of appealing to his sadistic friend, Z.

We have already seen that this is symbolic of a more fundamental internal economic relationship. The mother's money protects the patient from the necessity of borrowing from a father substitute, and similarly the intensity of his need for the father's love is diminished by the gratification and reassurance that he receives from the mother's gift.

It is this diminution in the patient's need for his father that has made possible a series of defense reactions against his sadistic impulses. (1) These impulses have been projected. It is not the patient but the father who is threatening the patient, his mother, and his brothers. (2) In addition to being projected, the specific character of these impulses has to some extent been obliterated by the substitution of impersonal symbols for specific persons and acts. Instead of the father it is a hot wall that is threatening. Instead of the patient and his brothers inside the mother's body, the cakes in an oven are being threatened. The specific content of the sadistic impulses is also considerably obscured though still hinted at by the condensed character of the symbolism. Fire is a rather unspecific destructive agent, but cakes are things to be eaten and dirty paper is something to be thrown away or destroyed. (3) The patient has turned away in fear from this whole complex of unconscious wishes and is seeking help and protection from the mother. It will be noticed that in this dream the figure of the mother is, as it were, reduplicated. As a part of the complex of unconscious wishes from which the patient is trying to escape, she is represented by the impersonal (dead) symbol of the oven. As a person in real life to whom the patient is fleeing for love, help and protection, she is herself, a real person. (4) Finally, the destruction is something threatened, not actual.

We have just seen that the economic basis for these defenses is the diversion of a considerable amount of the energy of the father conflict into an attempt to get real reassurance and relief from the mother. We are obviously dealing here with the actual process of the transference of the energy deriving from infantile conflicts over into reactions toward the real present life situation of the patient. We must assume that physiological needs in their process of elaboration and search for satisfaction tend to call up the not yet solved problems arising out of frustrations of these needs in childhood. Possibilities of gratification or relief in the real situation provide the ego with one means of diverting energy away from these frustrations of childhood. If sufficient energy can be withdrawn into real life,[6] then the residue of energy that still remains attached to the childhood conflict can be projected, treated as a foreign body neither belonging to nor in vital relationship with the ego. (The best examples of this are dreams in which the dreamer is merely an observer of what others are doing.) If still more energy can be withdrawn into real life, the childhood conflict can be, as it were, deprived of life. Living persons can be replaced by inanimate, dead objects. It is already a first step in this process when human beings are replaced by smaller animals. When the process of withdrawal of cathexis from the childhood conflicts has gone further, human beings can even be replaced by inanimate objects without much dynamic quality, such as the oven and the cakes in the patient's dream.

In the situation that gave rise to this dream, a new element has

entered into this picture. The analysis has given new hope of gratification to the never satisfied wishes of childhood. The tolerant analytic
attitude toward unconscious impulses that is personified in the analyst
tends to give new life to these wishes, new hope that this time frustration will not ensue. The effect of this is seen in the dream, in a beginning reversal of the process of calcification described in the last
paragraph. The symbols representing the unconscious have now taken
on the powerful dynamic quality of a threatening fire.[7] The patient is
beginning to transfer his father conflict to the analyst, to hope that
the analyst will gratify his need for a father's love. The sign of this
in the dream is the fact that the analyst and the unconscious wishes
that the patient is beginning to transfer upon him are condensed into
a single symbol, the "hot wall." As a result of this possibility of transference upon a living person, the once-dead symbols have now acquired
a new dynamic power.

In turning to the mother for love and protection, the patient is obviously repeating his attempt to deprive his childhood conflict of life
by diverting energy into the search for a substitute satisfaction in real
life. Even in the dream, however, this is recognized as only a temporary defense. The paper that the patient places against the wall will
eventually burn through. If he is to escape the newly awakened fascination of the analysis, the patient must get ever repeated evidences
of love from the mother. Moreover, in the dream the mother is going
to die. The threatening character of the hot wall is symbolic of the
fact that the patient's fascination for the analysis is growing. The
cathexis now diverted to the mother will shortly revert to the analysis.
The mother will undergo again the process that once before transformed
her into an inanimate oven.[8]

The events of the succeeding three weeks confirm the prophecy contained in this dream. For a time the patient attempts to supplement his
relation to his real mother by giving the analyst a mother role. As we
have already seen, however, the fundamentally competitive character
of the patient's love for his mother soon drives him back again to his
father conflict.

In the dream of the fishes' heads, accordingly, the cathexis that
had been diverted to the mother has reverted again for the most
part to the father conflict. The fishes and their heads represent in
extremely condensed symbolism the mother and brothers, the patient's
own fantasied children, and the patient's genitals. In the dream they

are dead—which signifies the temporary withdrawal of the patient's interest from them as living objects. Besides that, the patient is sacrific- ing them to the father. In the next episode he has stones instead of babies; these he also throws at the father.

Thus the dream shows a temporary almost complete withdrawal of psychic energy from mother and brothers, and from the patient's own genitals. All this energy is concentrated upon a symbolic play centering about ambivalent impulses toward the father. The two episodes of the dream give expression successively to the two sides of this ambivalence. In the first, the patient is making a sacrifice to the father, obviously with the hope of placating him and of winning love from him even in spite of the patient's hostility. The second episode pictures the patient's rage and frustration. The baby that the patient hoped for has become a stone. The patient throws it at the father as a missile and a thing of no value.

Really it is the patient's envious desire to defeat the analysis that is making the analysis unproductive, that is turning the baby into a stone. In the dream the patient has sacrificed to the father his genitals and his babies and thus acquired the right to accuse the father of giving him stones instead of babies.

Thus the dream is first of all a dream of frustration. In the former dream the patient's hostile impulses were projected, replaced in part by reactive fear, and condensed into the symbol of the hot wall. In this dream, the patient's hostile impulses are only in small part projected. To be sure, the roosters eat the dead fishes' heads, but it is the patient who throws the fish to them and afterward pelts the roosters with stones.

In the former dream, the patient was attempting to divert energy away from his father conflict to a real relationship to the mother. As a result of the failure of this attempt, some of the energy so diverted has apparently taken a destructive form and flooded over into the ego. The diversion of energy to the mother enabled the patient to project [9] his father conflict and condense it into the symbol of the hot wall. The reversion of this energy to the father conflict now forces this conflict back into the ego and compels the ego to acknowledge it.

The dream has found means, however, to mitigate the intensity of this frustration. Most notable is the absence of fear in a reaction to the patient's aggressive impulses. It is evident that the patient has found some way to diminish his fear and to reduce the deadly earnestness of his conflict; for he has been able to substitute for the father small barnyard animals of whom he is not afraid. Moreover, the penis that he surrenders is not a penis but a dead fish's head.

The means by which this has been accomplished are twofold: (1) In the first place, the patient's symbolic play with inanimate and dead objects is itself a very important source of satisfaction, similar to the frequently intense absorption of children in play with impersonal objects. Thus, in the dream, to throw stones at the father, for example, not only discharges the patient's frustrated rage against the father but also provides a substitute gratification to replace the patient's unsatisfied desire to give the father a child. This sort of play is, of course, much less dangerous and conflictful than the impulses toward persons that it aims to replace. The satisfaction derived from this symbolic play therefore tends to relieve the intensity of the patient's frustration and so to relieve the acuteness of his conflict.[10] Because the patient has his dead fish and his stones, the real father need not loom so large in his desires. It is this reduction in the intensity of the father conflict that is symbolized by the substitution of roosters for the father. If the patient can be satisfied [11] by throwing fishes' heads and stones at roosters who cannot retaliate, then he need no longer be afraid of the more powerful and dangerous father.

(2) The patient has also found a second means to reduce the intensity of his conflict, by utilizing the analytic situation. His first association to the dream significantly implies a hope that the analyst, like his father, will encourage him in his cruelty to animals. This is indeed a recognition, though a distorted one, of the analyst's real aim. The analyst does wish to encourage him to take conscious responsibility for his unconscious impulses. The patient's hope for encouragement from the analyst, therefore, has a real basis in his intuitive sense of the tolerant and encouraging attitude toward unconscious impulses that forms the essential basis of the psychoanalytic procedure.

The latent recognition of the tolerant and encouraging atmosphere of the analysis is probably responsible, not only for the greater boldness of the patient's sadistic impulses in this dream, but also for the unconscious crystallization of insight into his essential conflict, which we have already noted as the most significant feature of this dream. In the earlier dream, the symbol of the hot wall represented not only a projection but an extreme condensation of the patient's unconscious impulses. The dream of the fishes' heads separates out many of the elements that were condensed in this symbol, and, by elaborating them more fully, brings into clear view the dynamic relations between them. The dream symbolism is based upon a sexual theory of oral impregnation and anal birth and thus makes manifest the sexual curiosity at which the former dream only hinted. More important still, the dream is also at the point of formulating insight into the conflict between the patient's envy of and his desire for love from the father. The desire to attack the father and the desire to placate him and win his love are represented separately, and the dream and associations contain one futile attempt after another to reconcile these two conflicting urges. "If I give father my penis, perhaps then he will love me." "If I let father castrate me, then I shall have a right to attack him." "Perhaps father will really like it if I am cruel to animals instead of attacking him." "I wish father would give me a baby but it must be a dead one." These are the more important formulae with which the patient is attempting to solve a problem which for the moment remains insoluble because of the too great intensity of both of the conflicting impulses.

Nevertheless, this dream already contains the two clues that make possible the temporary solution of his conflict, the solution he soon afterward achieves in his acceptance of interpretations, in the dream of being wounded in the shoulder, and in his subsequent confession. These two clues are the patient's intuitive realization (1) that the analyst will be tolerant of the patient's hostile impulses, and (2) that it will be necessary to sacrifice some of his envious desire to defeat the analyst in order to be helped by him.

We have already noted the fact that the failure of the patient's attempt to turn to the mother has compelled him to allow his father conflict to flood over into his ego. This frustrating experience alone might of course have led to nothing more than a flight from the analysis.[12] In fact, we see in every neurosis an ever repeated cycle of frustrations that lead to nothing. In the present instance, however, the patient's fear has been mitigated somewhat by his sense that the analyst is encouraging him to give voice to his hostile impulses. This gives the patient confidence to put to a practical test his hope that even overt hostility toward the analyst will not lose him the friendly interest and encouragement of a father.

In the next few hours the patient actually puts this hope to the practical test. He faces the despair that is inevitable if his hope of defeating the analysis could be realized. It is significant that the patient's admission of insight into his desire to defeat the analysis follows immediately upon the analyst's assurance that he need not lose hope of being helped, in spite of his despairing resistance.

The value to the patient of this reassuring experience is, of course, the fact that it strengthens the patient's already latent hope that he could differentiate (in Pavlov's sense) or discriminate between the analytic situation and other situations in which he might be impelled to express or act out rage toward a father substitute. Unlike other relationships of the father-son type, the analysis is a therapeutic relationship in which verbal expression of hostile impulses is tolerated, even encouraged. No doubt the patient's previous analyses had contributed to his readiness to expect tolerance from an analyst; but this lesson is one that has to be learned over and over again with each new analyst, and often enough with each new form that the forbidden impulses take. This particular analyst might not be tolerant of this particular impulse—and the test must be made over and over again; but each time it represents a step in a learning process, the acquisition of a new capacity to differentiate between the analytic situation and other situations with which the analytic situation had been identified.

If we examine again the hot wall dream, we now notice that this dream is already attempting to make use of a very old discriminatory insight of a similar sort. The patient had felt afraid of and estranged from his father, but his mother is more indulgent, and even now the patient is able to obtain from her a gift of money. This discriminatory insight is evidently very well established in the patient, but it leads only to another cycle into which he does not have insight. Turning to his mother leads sooner or later to rivalry with his father and brothers, and so to the old dilemma of fear of and estrangement from the father, whose love he so intensely desires. If the patient is to progress in the analytic task, he must be able to recognize in the analyst a father of whom even the patient's rivalrous impulses need not make him afraid.

The patient's father-transference to the analyst involves him in a vicious circle. His hostility to the father aggravates his sense of estrangement from him; this sense of estrangement only renders more desperate the patient's need for the father's love and increases the rage resulting from the frustration of this intensified need. In the dream of the hot wall, the patient is trying to get out of this vicious circle by turning to someone who will give him love and thus make unnecessary such intense frustrated rage; but the desire for the mother's love is too closely entwined with the father conflict and therefore leads only into another vicious circle.

However, if the patient can now reassure himself that the analyst will still be friendly even in spite of the patient's competitive impulse to threaten him, then there can be a chance to divert some of the energy away from the vicious circle of the father conflict. If the patient can be assured in any case of the analyst's friendliness, then he need not feel so frustrated in his desire for love; and this will tend to diminish both the intensity of the patient's hostility and the desperation of his need for love. The energy thus freed from the vicious cycle of his ambivalence toward the father can now be turned to friendly cooperation with the analyst.

In the dream of being wounded in the shoulder, we see the realization of these anticipations. We have already noted the marked similarity between this dream and the earlier dream of the hot wall. We now see that this similarity is based upon the fundamental similarity in the tasks the two dreams are striving to accomplish. Both are attempting to solve the infantile father conflict by finding a substitute for the father that will be more indulgent or more tolerant. Accordingly, in both dreams we find pictorial representation of mysterious forces symbolic of the unconscious and of its repressed infantile father conflict centering about the primal scene. In both dreams we also see an attempt to relieve the intensity of this unconscious need for the father by turning to a more tolerant or indulgent substitute in real life.

The fundamental difference between the two dreams is a mark of the patient's progress in the analysis during the interval between them. In the earlier dream he is trying to evade investigation of his unconscious conflict by turning to the mother as a substitute and getting money from her. In the later dream he has made a first step toward the solution of his unconscious conflict, by turning to the analyst and accepting a bit of unwelcome insight in place of the castration he fears from his father.

In this dream the patient's acceptance of this insight is represented as a wound in the shoulder. This corresponds to the sacrifice of the dead fishes' heads in the dream of a week previous and signifies the giving up by the patient of his desire to compete with the analyst by denying the validity of the analyst's interpretation. The patient is able to make this latter concession, whereas the possibility of real castration only filled the patient with frustrated rage. The reason for this is obvious: merely admitting the truth of an interpretation is an incomparably less masochistic way of winning a father's love than is real castration.

We have already discussed the basis of this diminution of the patient's masochism. In the meantime, the patient has attacked the analyst and has received encouragement instead of reproof. As we anticipated, this reassuring experience has enabled the patient to divert some of the energy away from the vicious circle of his father conflict and so to diminish both the intensity of his hostility and the desperation of his need for love. In the dream the patient not only admits to himself that he has been wounded but he is also playing again a protective role toward the children in the court. In other words, as we anticipated, the energy freed from the vicious circle of the father conflict is now about to be turned to friendly cooperation in the analytic task.

E. Summary and Conclusions

The material we have been discussing suggests many interesting problems concerning types of dream organization and their relation to the economic distribution of psychic energy. I shall postpone discussion of these topics, however, until a later paper in which it will be possible to compare a considerably greater number of dreams.

We started this study by inquiring how far a psychoanalytic treatment could be regarded as a learning process, as a process of progressive adaptation in external adjustment. I shall not attempt to discuss this question exhaustively until we have completed our résumé of the whole case material. However, our analysis makes it plain that the patient is dealing, throughout this three-week period, with a single problem in external adjustment, that of overcoming his fear of the analytic task and adapting himself to the analytic situation. We have also seen that his overcoming of his fear was made possible by his learning to take advantage of the difference between the understanding, tolerant atmosphere of the analysis and the repressive, threatening aura with which the patient had surrounded the memory of his father. Thus, as in most learning processes, the solution of the patient's problem depended upon his acquiring the ability to act upon a discriminatory insight. This discriminatory insight made possible a second, more fundamental adjustment, the diminution of the patient's fear as a result of the diminution of the intense ambivalence that was the cause of the fear.

It will be interesting now to summarize the factors that seem to have contributed toward the solution of this problem.

First of all, the analysis provided him with an attainable goal. Pavlov's [13] and Koehler's [14] experiments have shown most beautifully what we already knew in a general way, that when an individual or animal is pushed to take a step in learning that is beyond its capacity, its attempts at learning tend to be replaced by reactions of frustration or (in Pavlov's studies) by stereotyped reactions that Pavlov himself compares to human neuroses. Neuroses, probably in every case, represent a permanent fixation upon frustration reactions of this sort, resulting from traumatic situations in emotional development in which the patient was unable to take the step in learning that was required of him.

Such a concept of a neurosis as the product of a disturbed learning process suggests also the principle upon which therapy must be based. Since the step that life demands of the patient is too great, the treatment must somehow manage to divide this one long step into a number of smaller ones. Psychoanalysis attempts to do this first of all by providing a situation in which impulses that are forbidden in real life are met with understanding and a certain amount of encouragement. Thus the analysis itself facilitates the learning process by substituting a more attainable goal, that of adjusting to the analytic situation itself, in place of the goal which the patient has been unable to reach, that of adjusting to the problems of real life.

In this particular three-week period of analysis, we notice that the analyst's interpretations of the dynamic character of the patient's conflict serve a similar purpose. They provide the patient with a still more specific and easily attainable goal. The three-week period ends specifically by the patient's admitting his unconscious satisfaction at having been "hit" by the analyst. It will be noticed that the correctness of the interpretations plays an essential part in the patient's satisfaction and relief. The fact that the patient is beginning to sense that the analyst knows his business goes far to relieve the patient's fear of the realization of his envious wish to defeat the analysis. Thus the correctness of the interpretations increases the patient's sense of security and passive satisfaction and gives effective encouragement to the patient's own investigatory impulses, which are so conspicuous as an undercurrent throughout this material. Incorrect interpretations could not have provided the patient with either of these types of satisfaction which were evidently so important in giving him the security and satisfaction that he needed.

It is important to emphasize the fact that the unconscious forces tend of their own accord to concentrate upon such intermediate goals and so to aid the analysis in its attempt to relieve the pressure upon the learning process. The best example of this is the dream of the fishes' heads, in which anal erotic play is substituted as a temporary goal to relieve the intensity of the patient's ambivalence toward the analyst sufficiently to allow the learning process to proceed.

As a result of this spontaneous tendency to adjust its task to its capacity to learn, the patient's material itself usually indicates rather plainly the step the patient is ready to take and can thus serve as a very valuable guide to the analyst in timing his interpretations. If we look back at the dream of the hot wall, we note that it is a sort of prophecy of the step in adjustment that the patient will be working on in the next three weeks. In the dream he is trying to solve his father conflict by distinguishing between a stern father and an indulgent mother. In the next ten days, he tries to test out in the analytic situation whether the analyst may not be a mother rather than a father. After that he experiments with the distinction between the father he remembers and an analyst in the father role.

The patient's progress toward this specific goal of adjusting to the analyst's interpretations is now facilitated by two factors.

1) The first of these is the frustration of the patient's attempt to evade the problem of adjusting to the analysis by fleeing to the mother. So far as I can see in this particular instance, the analyst's interpretations contributed almost nothing to this.[15] The fact that the patient's flight to the mother only drove him back again into the father conflict seems to have been based upon a fundamental cycle inherent in his neurosis and would have occurred with or without analysis.

2) The analysis, however, contributed again most fundamentally by the implicit encouragement given by the analytic situation itself to unconscious forbidden impulses. We have already discussed at length how this encouragement given by the analysis emboldened the patient's aggressive impulses and diminished his fear, so that it was possible for him to acquire the discriminatory insight that the analytic situation was indeed different from his childhood relationship to the father. This reassuring experience, as we have seen, was apparently the effective factor that led to the diminution in the patient's ambivalence and thus made it possible for him to take a cooperative interest in the analytic task.

All of this tends to emphasize the importance of reality-testing in the transference. Striking as are the manifestations of the repetition compulsion, the transference is nevertheless not only a compulsive repetition of earlier events. It is also an experimental attempt to correct the infantile patterns.

In the case we have been studying, this experimental character of the transference was particularly clear. This patient was, as it were, continually trying out the analyst in various roles. He started out by testing how well the analyst would work out in a brother role. This gave the patient the advantage in his desire for prestige but left unsatisfied his desire for a strong father's love. In the ten days preceding the hot wall dream, the fear consequent upon the patient's masochistic need for a father was so strong that it was necessary for the patient to reassure himself continually that the analyst was only playing with him. When the analyst finally decided to stop playing, the patient's unconscious promptly put the analyst in the father role. The identification of the analyst with the patient's second brother marked the transition. This brother was also one who started out as a brother and then became a successful rival like the father. The succeeding three weeks, as we have seen, may be looked upon as a search for someone less dangerous who still could satisfy his need for a father. At the end of this three-week period, the analysis seems for a time to be meeting these requirements.

It would be theoretically interesting to inquire whether the relative proportions of compulsive repetition and of experimental reality-testing in the transference manifestations may not vary in relation to the acuteness and intensity of the patient's conflict. Inasmuch as reality-testing tends to be interfered with by conflicts of too great intensity,[16] we should expect to find that the element of compulsive repetition would be proportionately greater at moments when the conflicting affects were most intense, whereas moments when the patient's conflict was less acute might be expected to show a greater proportion of experimentation in the transference reactions. Comparison of the dream of the fishes' heads with the other two dreams seems to give us some slight corroboration of this suggestion. The dream of the fishes' heads is a dream of acute frustration. The other two dreams were dreamed at times of less acute conflict. In accordance with our hypothesis, the dream of the hot wall and the dream of the wound in the shoulder are, in each case, taking advantage of rather specific facts in the patient's actual situation of the moment. In the dream of the hot wall it is the mother's gift of 50 marks, in the wound in the shoulder dream it is the analyst's correct interpretation, that the patient is using to satisfy his emotional needs. Thus in both the dreams at moments of less acute conflict, the element of experimentation with reality is relatively large. In the dream of the fishes' heads, on the other hand, the patient's hope that the analyst will applaud instead of condemn his sadistic impulses is really patterned much more accurately on the father's applause of the patient's cruelty to the cat, and is only a very distorted allusion to the encouragement given by the analysis to the patient's unconscious impulses. Moreover, the manifest content of this dream is a very transparent symbolization of the patient's conflict in its infantile form (castration wish, anal attack, anal child). Thus, in correspondence with the patient's state of acute frustration, the element of compulsive repetition of his infantile conflict seems relatively great, whereas, as we have seen, at moments of less acute conflict the reality-testing element seems to play a greater role. We hope to return to this question in later studies.

Thus again we return to the importance of the influence of quantitative factors upon the learning process. Each step in learning involves the substitution of a new method of obtaining gratification for an old one. The incentive to search for a new method of gratification must be derived from insight into the fact that the old method is no longer adequate. Realization that an old method of gratification is unsatisfactory does not lead to immediate acquisition of a new one but merely initiates a period of experimentation. The first experiments are apt not to be successful. Consequently the experimentation tends to be punctuated by periods of frustration and despair, because the experimenter has lost his old method of gratification and has as yet found no new one to take its place. It is during this period of frustration and despair that the facilitating influence of the tolerant analytic atmosphere is of crucial importance. In the material studied it has been possible to follow how the patient's conflict is reduced in intensity, at this crucial point, by his latent confidence that the analyst will welcome rather than frown upon his aggressive impulses. It is this reduction in the intensity of the conflict that makes it possible for the patient to learn instead of continuing fixed upon his frustration.

Thus, as Alexander has expressed it, one of the most important of the analyst's tasks is to keep the intensity of the transference at a certain "optimum level."

NOTES

1. Freud, *Introductory Lectures on Psychoanalysis* (London: George Allen & Unwin, Ltd., 1929).

2. Franz Alexander, *Psychoanalysis of the Total Personality* (New York and Washington: Nervous & Mental Disease Publishing Company, 1930).

3. Alexander, "The Problems of the Psychoanalytic Technique," *Psychoanalytic Quarterly,* 4 (1935).

4. Herman Nunberg, "The Synthetic Function of the Ego," *International Journal of Psychoanalysis,* 12 (1931).

5. It will be recalled that a week before this dream the patient was stirred to intense envy of his brother by the birth of the brother's child and still earlier he was beset with fantasies of men giving birth to children.

6. This suggestion may seem to be in contradiction to the fact that projection regularly occurs as a defense mechanism to protect the dreamer from too strong affects. The same is true of the use of impersonal symbols to replace persons. In the dream under discussion, for example, the purpose of the projection and of the impersonal symbolization is precisely to protect the patient from his fear. The act of projection involves the acceptance by the ego of an observing rather than an otherwise active role. We must assume that the act of observing the (hallucinated or real) activities of others is itself a source of considerable satisfaction and thus relieves the intensity of the patient's conflict by absorbing a considerable amount of energy. In a similar way, the gratification derived from symbolic play with impersonal objects may absorb a considerable quantity of energy and so relieve very much a conflict involving persons. (See discussion of dream of fishes' heads, page 94.) Observation of children shows, in fact, that such symbolic play is capable of absorbing very large amounts of psychic energy.

The suggestion made in the text of this paper is not in contradiction with the mechanisms just discussed but constitutes rather a limiting condition to them. Even though a very considerable amount of energy can be absorbed by impersonal symbols or by the act of observing in projection mechanisms, nevertheless the amount of energy that can be absorbed in this way is limited. In this dream, for example, the threatening character of the hot wall shows in fact that the limit of absorption has been slightly exceeded. If the patient were not able at the moment to divert energy to the gratification and reassurance he is receiving from his mother, it is quite certain that the fear, which is now only hinted at, would in that case break through into consciousness and the patient would be reporting an acute anxiety dream similar to the one that he actually did have two months later.

In order still further to safeguard against confusion, I should add that I am here using the term "projection" in a somewhat restricted sense. As is already implied in my argument, I am referring to instances in which a person, instead of acting out his impulses, is content to discharge them by observing or hallucinating others acting them out, without becoming more intimately involved in the activity. I might distinguish this as "total projection." This I would contrast, for example, with a patient who substitutes, for his own desire to attack, a fear that he will be similarly attacked, or with a woman who fantasies a sexual attack that she herself unconsciously desires. These two types of projection I would distinguish as "retaliatory (or inverting) projection" and as "wish-fulfilling projection." In this dream, for example, insofar as the hot wall threatens the patient, it is in part a retaliatory and in part a wish-fulfilling projection. The threat to the cakes in the oven constitutes a total projection. The above discussion applies only to total projection. As pointed out in the next paragraph, the threat to the patient in the hot wall dream constitutes a beginning failure of the pure (total) projection mechanism.

Similarly, we must distinguish between impersonal symbols without dynamic quality (like the cakes and oven) in contrast to dynamic symbols like a threatening fire. In the present dream we note that the dynamic character of the symbol is a sign of a beginning reversal of the process of calcification above discussed.

7. That this is really a case of the coming to life of dead symbols is proved by an earlier dream fragment (the patient's first dream, from the seventeenth interview):

> The patient is in the room where he used to sleep with his brothers. In the next room (where his parents used to sleep) two white figures are sitting up in bed, dead.

In association, he recalled how the brothers all used to masturbate together in this room, each in a different way. He then thinks of the analyst as his brother.

In other words, at the time of this dream, the patient is seeking to deprive of life the infantile problems growing out of the primal scene, by seeking in the analysis a repetition of the mutual tolerance the brothers showed, each in regard to the others' masturbation.

8. It should be noticed, however, that the "hot wall" seems also to be the wall of the oven. (The dream text is not entirely clear in this point. Unfortunately I am not sure whether this indefiniteness is the patient's or due to an imperfection in my notes, which were made from memory after the hour.) This perhaps has a meaning similar to that of the reproaches implied in the dream of the fishes' heads—that the mother at least yields to the sadism of the father toward his children, that it is the intimate relationship (the patient wishes it were a wall or barrier) between the parents that stirs up the patient's violent jealousy and so becomes destructive to the patient and his brothers.

9. See note 7.

10. See note 7.

11. The degree to which the patient can be really satisfied by such a substitute determines, of course, the extent to which the patient's frustration will be relieved.

12. Such flights were in fact not unusual in the patient's analysis. During his analysis with Dr. X he once fled for several months to a distant country, using for that purpose some of the money obtained with his brother's endorsement. Also during his analysis with me, the patient not infrequently missed hours when his fear became too great.

13. I. P. Pavlov, *Lectures on Conditioned Reflexes* (New York: International Publishers, 1927).

14. Wolfgang Koehler, *The Mentality of Apes* (New York: Harcourt, Brace, 1925).

15. In other cases, of course, it is necessary for the analyst to direct his interpretive activity specifically to the task of driving a patient out of his defenses. An example of this was the patient's attempt to make play of the analysis, a defense which he abandoned only after the analyst had reinforced his interpretations by a period of silence.

16. I have discussed this at some length in my paper on "Interrelations Between Psychoanalysis and the Experimental Work of Pavlov," Chapter 1 above.

Chapter Four

INSIGHT AND DISTORTION IN DREAMS

In this paper, again starting with an insight based on Gestalt psychology, we introduce the concept of "practical grasp" of a situation. In his Mentality of Apes (1925), *Koehler describes repeatedly how an experimental animal may for a time stand helpless before a problem, then suddenly gain "insight" into a hitherto unnoticed aspect of the situation. For example, an ape may be quite baffled in its desire to get fruit just out of its reach outside the bars of its cage, until it suddenly discovers the trick of making a longer stick by fitting together two shorter sticks. With its practical grasp of the situation thus enriched by a new insight, the animal then proceeds immediately and directly to the solution of its problem.*

Kurt Lewin and his co-workers have elaborated the concept of the "psychological field" which corresponds very closely to the "practical grasp" of the situation which we are here discussing. (See Lewin, Dynamic Theory of Personality, *1935.)*

The same notion of practical grasp can also be applied to the conflict situations that we encounter in neuroses and dreams. In this paper we compare two successive dreams to illustrate how this concept can be used.

INSIGHT IN DREAMS; ITS FATE IN SUCCESSIVE DREAMS

In the course of a psychoanalytic treatment, an important interpretation is usually followed over a period of days or weeks by a series

Reprinted from *International Journal of Psycho-Analysis,* 20 (1939).

of dreams that have been obviously provoked by the interpretation and are reactions to the dawning insight that has been mobilized by the interpretation. In them one is usually able to detect an urge to confess, side by side with a vehement urge to deny the correctness of the interpretation. Frequently as the analysis proceeds one can observe a gradual decrease in the effectiveness of the denials and an increase in the patient's willingness to accept the proffered interpretation.

The resistance against an interpretation is in some cases expressed by direct denial of its content or by substitution of a content with exactly the opposite meaning, as, for example, when an interpretation of feminine sexual wishes will be answered by a dream of vigorous masculine protest. Direct denial, however, has the disadvantage that, like the negative of a photograph, it leaves practically unchanged the essential relations contained in the proffered insight. The picture remains the same except for the reversal of black and white shades. For this reason, denial is dynamically very close to affirmation; often only a very slight quantitative shift in the dynamic balance is necessary in order to turn a denial into an affirmation. The girl who is too vehement in her rejection of a suitor often betrays by that fact that she is on the point of accepting him. This is, of course, the basis for Freud's well-known rule that in the unconscious a denial is equivalent to an affirmation—that the unconscious knows no negative.

There are, however, other and more effective methods of resistance to an interpretation. In the present paper I wish to call attention to one of these that is often encountered in the first dream after an interpretation. The dreams to which I refer are characterized by the fact that they attempt to deprive the interpretation of all intellectual content by reacting to it, not as an interpretation, but as a disturbing noise or some other kind of disagreeable stimulus.

I shall cite as an example a pair of successive dreams, one occurring before and the other immediately after an interpretation. The first of the two dreams is cited in order to contrast it with the insight-obliterating dream that followed the interpretation. The material is taken from a patient whose most consistent reaction in the analysis had been to attempt to overcompensate for his fears by intimidating the analyst. Three days before the first dream to be reported, the analyst had had occasion to suggest that the patient's very persistent fears were probably a reaction to threats that he had received in childhood concerning masturbation. In reaction to this interpretation, the patient recalled some threats that he had actually received but insisted that they did not mean much to him at the time. On the following day, the patient brought a dream which the analyst was at the time unable to interpret. Two days later he brought the first dream of the pair that I am presenting:

Dream: Patient is fixing a velocipede with his brother. The brother asks patient to get something out of a hall where a meeting is being held. Patient refuses with playful politeness on the ground that his brother is younger. Finally the brother straightens himself up to go but indicates he is afraid. Patient is distressed on learning this and says he would have gone if he had known that this was the brother's reason for not wanting to go. As patient gets up to go he meets people who are coming out of the meeting. There is a black cloud in the rear of the hall of which patient feels very much in awe. One man as he comes out of the hall puts his hand on his pocket and another says: "They have taken in five hundred marks."

In association, the hall reminds the patient of the church where his father preached. The patient used to be very much afraid of his father in church. The velocipede reminds the patient of a velocipede that he and his brothers owned together. Afterward they bought a new one with some money given them by an uncle. The patient was very angry when his father once took this new velocipede to learn to ride on it. Five hundred marks refers to a confession that the patient had made a couple of weeks earlier in the analysis. Some years before he had cheated the brother to whom this dream refers by getting him to endorse a loan and then filling in a larger amount. The analyst interprets the patient's wish to hide his fear of the analysis by representing that the analyst is afraid. Then the patient identifies the black cloud in the rear of the church as his father in a black robe.

It will be noticed that this dream gives evidence of a very considerable latent insight into the patient's emotional situation. Let us begin with the dream's portrayal of the analytic situation. The brother is the analyst. The analyst failed to understand the patient's dream of two days before. The patient concludes that the analyst is afraid. This gives him an opportunity to portray in a projected form his own conflict. The church is his unconscious; the mysterious black cloud in the background is his father conflict. The patient is afraid but it hurts his pride to admit it. The allusion to the five hundred marks and to the people coming out of church probably has the value of a consolation. The patient has already made his confession and is reassuring himself that there is nothing further to analyze.

Thus in the figure of the brother the patient portrays quite clearly the conflict between his fear and his pride. His insight has only one defect. It is projected. He recognizes this conflict in his brother, the analyst, but only partially in himself. His insight needs to be supplemented at just one point. He must recognize that it is his own fear that he is portraying. It was at this point that the analyst had to supplement the patient's insight by pointing out that the conflict between fear and pride attributed to the brother was really the patient's own.

The next dream (reported four days later after two intervening analytic hours) seems at first to ignore the interpretation entirely. The dream is as follows:

> *Dream:* Patient is in the toilet and a small boy who is yellow urinates upon patient's yellow coat.

Associations to this dream are meager. The dream is very distasteful to him, as toilets are associated in his mind with homosexuality . . . he shows considerable reluctance to associate to it but mentions his recent refusal to pay his landlady. When the analyst calls attention to the anal-retentive attitude toward money and associations, the patient remarks that he always likes to use the chamber but does not like to have it emptied. His father was the same way. The patient also has an impulse to eat his own nasal secretions.

This dream seems first of all to be a simple wish-fulfillment dream, fulfilling a passive homosexual wish, probably toward the analyst. As in the previous dream, he compensates for his own passivity by depreciatingly characterizing the analyst as a small boy.

However, the dream is probably also a reaction to the analyst's interpretation of several days previous which the dream is interpreting as soiling. Yellow is the color of urine, but is probably also symbolic of fear. The dream is giving expression to a retort to the analyst's interpretation. "You are afraid yourself; that is why you are reproaching me with being afraid." Thus the dream contains a latent insight similar to that of the previous dream. He is afraid (yellow) and ashamed of it (the dream is very distasteful to him); and still wishes to project his fear upon the analyst. In the manifest dream, however, this insight is indicated only by a symbolic allusion, the yellow color of the little boy and of the patient's coat.

Except for this symbolic allusion, the content of the analyst's interpretation is ignored. "The analyst just urinated upon me," the dream is retorting. The patient chooses to react to the interpretation as a masochistic homosexual gratification rather than to understand the content of it. In reaction to the increased intensity of his conflict, the dream (in its manifest content) has oversimplified the patient's grasp of his conflict by obliterating the insights contained in the former dream. This obliteration of insight has been achieved by a condensed form of presentation that wipes out the essential relations and substitutes a more primitive form of gratification instead of understanding.

QUANTITATIVE LIMITS TO INSIGHT AND TO THE INTEGRATIVE ACTIVITY OF THE EGO

It is clear that emerging insights such as the insight of which the velocipede dream gave evidence have an exceedingly important role to play in the integrative function of the ego. It is for this reason indeed that in therapy we attempt to reinforce such bits of emerging insight by our interpretations. In psychoanalytic therapy we attempt to make unconscious conflicts conscious. In so doing our purpose is to stimulate the ego into renewed synthetic activity. The patient's neurosis has indeed arisen as a compromise between repressed and repressing forces and as such it is itself a product of the synthetic activity of the ego, but an unsatisfactory one. Insight reopens the conflict and confronts the ego again with the task of finding a solution for it. As therapists we hope that the new solution will be a more satisfactory one just because it will be based, we hope, upon a better understanding of the patient's conflict.

At this point, however, our hopes prove to be somewhat premature. What we first encounter is not more intelligent behavior, but resistance. The ego resists being made aware of the intensity of the conflict with which it has to deal. In other words, in accordance with the pleasure principle, the ego shrinks back from its synthetic role and avoids being exposed to the full intensity of the patient's conflict.

This is particularly clearly illustrated in the example that we have just been studying. The analyst's interpretation of the patient's projection of his conflict in the velocipede dream must inevitably increase the intensity of the conflict. If it is the analyst's fear that is responsible for delay in the analysis, the patient's own pride need not be involved. If he accepts the interpretation, the ego is put under pressure to choose between his pride and his fear. If he yields to his fear, his pride will be hurt; if he saves his pride, he must defy his fear.

The succeeding toilet dream, however, does not proceed to find a solution based upon this insight, but rather seeks to reject the proffered insight altogether. In this dream, the ego is evidently striving to diminish the increasing tension by a condensation and partial discharge of the conflicting tendencies. This is achieved by treating the analyst's interpretation as merely an insult which can then be utilized as a source of masochistic gratification.

In other words, these two dreams give us a particularly plastic demonstration of the fact that the synthetic function of the ego is subject to quantitative limitations.

In previous papers [1] I have brought evidence to support the hypothesis that both in the dream work and symptom formation, as well as in the rational behavior, the character and adequacy of the synthetic activity of the ego is fundamentally determined by the quantitative relation between the intensity of the patient's conflict and the span of the ego's available synthetic capacity. Rational behavior requires an ego span sufficient not only to view one's situation as a whole, but also to enable one to pay attention to the differences between present and past situations so as to be able to learn from past mistakes instead of repeating them. If the intensity of the conflict exceeds the ego span, as in dreams and neuroses, the dream ego will be unable to view the patient's problem as a whole and must contrive somehow to understand the conflict in simpler and less conflictful terms. In some cases this is achieved by gratifying each of the conflicting tendencies in succession [2] or by dealing separately and successively with different aspects of the conflict situation.[3] In these cases the ego may be said to have simplified its task by devices of *fragmentation* [4] and *isolation*. In the toilet dream the ego has employed another technique for the same purpose—a technique which we may characterize as *simplification by condensation*.[5]

PROPOSED STUDY OF THE DREAM WORK IN TERMS OF THE EGO'S "PRACTICAL GRASP" OF THE CONFLICT SITUATION

Freud originally studied the dream work by tracing the chains of associations that lead from the latent dream thoughts to the manifest dream content. Comparison of the manifest dream content with the latent dream thoughts made it plain that the latent dream thoughts had been subjected to a series of transformations that contrasted most conspicuously with rational thought processes. These processes of condensation, displacement, translation into simple sensory imagery, etc., Freud termed the primary process. This he contrasted sharply with the secondary process, or rational thinking.

The distinction between primary and secondary processes was derived originally from the comparison of dream work, symptom formation, etc., with rational *thinking*. Primary and secondary processes were compared as thought processes.

In the discussion that has just preceded, we have followed a somewhat different procedure. Starting from Freud's insight that the motive power and incentive for the dream work are derived from unconscious wishes, we have interested ourselves not so much in the transformations undergone by the latent dream thoughts, but rather with the ego's dynamic problem [6] of reconciling conflicting wishes. We have been interested in the dream work not as a distorted intellectual process, as a peculiar mode of thinking, but rather as an attempt by the ego to solve a practical problem. The latent dream thoughts are numerous and heterogeneous and related in many different ways to the conflict which the dream is attempting to solve. Instead of concerning ourselves with these heterogeneous latent dream thoughts as such, we have turned our attention to the ego's practical understanding of the conflict situation as a whole.

If now we wish to compare the dream work with the mental processes of waking life from this more dynamic point of view, it will be appropriate to compare the dream work not with rational thinking but rather with rational *behavior*.

Rational behavior is also motivated by wishes. The significant point for comparison is the way that dream and rational behavior respectively deal with wishes. We must compare the fate and elaboration of unconscious wishes in the dream work with the fate and elaboration of the wishes that motivate rational behavior.

In rational behavior we are guided from moment to moment not so much by logical thoughts as by a sort of practical grasp of what we want and of the real situation that confronts us in trying to get it.

Certain experimental psychologists have interested themselves particularly in this sort of practical grasp of a situation. In his *Mentality of Apes* (1925), Koehler describes repeatedly how an experimental animal may for a time stand helpless before a problem, then suddenly gain "insight" into a hitherto unnoticed aspect of the situation. For example, an ape may be quite baffled in its desire to get fruit just out of its reach outside the bars of its cage until it suddenly discovers the trick of making a longer stick by fitting together two shorter sticks. With its practical grasp of the situation thus enriched by a new insight, the animal then proceeds immediately and directly to the solution of its problem.

At first thought, the "insight" which we attempt to give to our patients in a psychoanalytic treatment seems to be something totally different from the "insight" of which Koehler is speaking in his experiments with apes. In psychoanalysis we are dealing with wishes of which the patient is unaware, wishes that have been repressed, excluded from consciousness. We attempt to help him get "insight" into the content of these repressed wishes. Koehler's apes, on the other hand, know what they want. They are only at a loss as to how to get it. The "insight" of which Koehler is speaking is the sort of practical grasp of a situation that is necessary in order that one may overcome the practical difficulties that stand in the way of wish fulfillment.

On further consideration, however, the contrast between Koehler's and our own use of the word "insight" is not so great as it seems. The insight that we give to our patients does not work by magic. The repressed wish has been repressed because it was in conflict with other motives within the personality. If a patient succeeds in gaining "insight" into a repressed wish, he has only substituted a conscious conflict for an unconscious one. The ego, like Koehler's apes, still has a problem to solve. The ego is still faced with the task of finding a way to reconcile the conflicting tendencies. "Insight" into the repressed wish serves merely to improve the ego's "practical grasp" of the conflict situation.

The problem is indeed more complex than in the case of Koehler's apes. Our patients must reconcile two conflicting wishes, whereas the apes are striving toward a single goal and struggling only with external difficulties in the way of achieving it. With this exception, however, the two cases may be understood in identical terms. In order to perform satisfactorily its task of reconciling conflicting tendencies, the ego must have an adequate "practical grasp" of the conflict situation. Insight into the content of a repressed wish is of course one essential part of this "practical insight."

In analytical geometry one sometimes finds it helpful to change the coordinates of reference and rewrite the equation of a curve in terms of a new coordinate system. The new equation thus derived has, of course, exactly the same meaning as the old one; but in some cases it is possible in this way to bring out certain relations more simply and clearly.

In the following discussion I should like to propose an experiment of thought of this sort. I propose that we attempt to understand the dream work in terms of the ego's practical grasp of the conflict situation, in terms of the ego's attempts to simplify its understanding of the conflict situation in order to bring it within the span of its available synthetic capacity.

The Role of the Ego in the Velocipede Dream

In order to understand the role of the ego in shaping the velocipede dream, we must discuss this dream briefly in its setting in the course of the analysis as a whole.

The patient had originally sought treatment on account of a fixation of his sexual interest upon exhibitionistic and homosexual impulses, accompanied by a total inhibition of heterosexual interest. He had run away from an analysis with a more experienced analyst, Dr. X, but had then come back and been referred by Dr. X to a number of younger analysts in succession.

Early in his analysis, the patient had sought consolation for this fact by comparing the analysis to a scene from his childhood. The patient and his many younger brothers had occupied a room next to the parents' bedroom. Curious about what was going on in the next room, the brothers attempted to relieve their sexual tension by masturbating "each in his own way" in fear and defiance of the parents next door.

It will be noticed that the velocipede dream pictures a similar situation. The patient and his younger brother are represented as two children playing outside of the church where the father is really working. The dream symbolism establishes the connection with the more frank sexual memory and helps us to fill in its subjective content. The hall is the mother, the brother's "straightening himself up" to go into the hall suggests coitus; probably the people coming out of church symbolize the birth of children. Fixing the velocipede parallels the masturbation in the sexual memory. The little boys have a vague impulse to do as the parents are doing. For this their play is a very inadequate outlet. Something is lacking. There remains an indefinite urge to go into the next room to "get something." It is probably the violence of this desire that gives rise to so much fear.

We have mentioned the patient's conflict between pride and fear.

Back of this is a conflict between pride and the dependent attitudes of childhood. He would like to be a man like father, but senses half-consciously that he is emotionally a child.

The subsequent course of the analysis made plain the severity of this conflict. In order for him to become emotionally a mature man, he must undergo a profound emotional transformation. His aggressive energies are now absorbed almost exclusively in the task of attempting to hide from himself and others his deep-seated emotional dependence. When his defense against recognition of his dependence later breaks down, he will pour out the whole of his aggressive energy in destructive and self-destructive resentment on account of the frustration of desires now impossible of fulfillment—resentment because he can no longer be loved like a helpless infant. Only after a period of utter despair and frustration will he gradually become able to reconcile himself to the fact that he is no longer a child. Only then will he be able, step by step, to turn his aggressive energy to the service of real masculinity instead of wasting it in frustrated rage.

It is plain that at the time of this dream the patient's ego is completely unable to grasp the extent of his emotional immaturity. The conflict between his dependence and his pride is too intense. The profound emotional readjustment that is necessary cannot now be grasped in its entirety.

The dream work may be analyzed into three main steps. (1) The first step carries him back to the time when he was really a child, to the time when he was a boy struggling with the riddle of what it means to become a man. (2) The second step simplifies this riddle enormously. In order to fix his velocipede it is necessary to "get something." The latent concept may be reconstructed roughly. "If I wish to be a man like father I need only to take his penis." (3) But the little boy does not dare to castrate the father or to approach the mother sexually. The third step in the dream work is to substitute for these really serious impulses a symbolic play—instead of castration of the father and of coitus with the mother, "raising himself up" to go into a hall to "get something."

It is easy to see that each one of these steps in the dream work has the function of helping the ego to grasp the patient's problem in simpler, less conflictful terms.

1) As a grown man, to sense his emotional immaturity would involve an overwhelming blow to the patient's pride; but it is normal and

taken for granted that a child should be dependent. Moreover, it soothes his pride to be the oldest of many brothers.

2) To grasp the problem of becoming a man as one of "getting something" is a solution that arises out of the needs to receive and to take that are the central core of the patient's infantile fixation. It is impossible for the patient's ego to span the quantities of affect that must be mastered should he sense completely the nature of the transformation that he must undergo in order to become a mature man. He spares himself this overwhelming of his ego by substituting this simplified solution that involves so little modification of his underlying receptive needs.

3) Finally, it is only by the free use of symbolic play that it is possible for the child to learn by emulation of its parents. The disparity between child and parent is too great and real imitation of the parents would too often involve the child in a conflict it could not face. Faced with a step in development that is too great for its capacity, the child divides the one long step into many smaller steps by substituting play for reality. It imitates what it can and fills in the rest with symbolic play.

ALTERNATION BETWEEN INSIGHT AND ACTION IN DREAM AND IN WAKING LIFE

In conclusion I should like to call attention to one more parallel between these two dreams and the ego's mode of functioning in waking life.

The velocipede dream is a dream of insight but does not show any great pressure toward motor discharge. The patient raises himself up to go into the church, but the dream ends before he has to do anything about it.

The toilet dream, on the other hand, is characterized not only by obliteration of insight but also by a partial discharge of tension. Being urinated upon is a masochistic gratification intense enough to stir up a reaction of shame.

Thus in these two dreams, the first is characterized by insight, the second by partial discharge of tension; and the reason for the transition from insight to emotional discharge appears to be the increased conflict caused by the increasing vividness of the patient's insight into his conflict. To this the patient is reacting by rejecting the threatening insight and discharging some of the tension.

It is now interesting to take note of the fact that just such an alternation between insight and discharge of tension also plays an important role in waking life. Planning alternates with activity. In favorable cases one first plans and then executes one's plan. In other cases one becomes impatient of planning and discharges tension in motor activity before one has decided upon a rational course of action.

It is also important to note that, in the course of solving a practical problem, the character of one's practical grasp of the problem situation usually undergoes significant transformations. After the ape has hit upon the idea that the fruit can be brought within reach by fitting together two sticks, then it must focus its attention upon the task of putting the two sticks together. The intellectual faculties of the animal must now be focused rather upon the immediate motor task than upon the situation as a whole.

We must conclude, therefore, that the fact that the toilet dream no longer gives evidence of the more comprehensive insight contained in the velocipede dream is in itself no sign of a deficiency in the adequacy of the ego's integrative function. The criterion for adequacy of the integrative influence of the ego must rather be the relation between the insight achieved and the subsequent motor discharge. In rational behavior, one's activity is intelligent because it is based upon the insight achieved during the period of thought and planning. In the toilet dream, on the other hand, the discharge of tension was associated with a rejection of the emerging insight; the transition from insight to discharge of tension occurred too soon; the ego's synthetic capacity was not great enough to allow insight to proceed to the point where it could serve as the basis for subsequent action, to the point where it could serve as the basis for a real solution of the patient's conflict.

NOTES

1. See especially Chapters 1 and 2 above.

2. For example, see Chapter 2 above.

3. See Alexander, "Dreams in Pairs and Series," *International Journal of Psycho-Analysis,* 6 (1925).

4. See Chapter 2 above.

5. We must leave it to subsequent studies to inquire into the principles that determine just what devices the ego must employ in order to bring a particular task within the span of its synthetic capacity.

6. This direct dynamic approach to dream interpretation is, of course, nothing novel but is the practical intuitive method that we all employ in the actual practice of dream interpretation.

Chapter Five

REALITY-TESTING IN DREAMS

In "Reality and the Unconscious" (Chapter 2), one of the dreams we studied was a nightmare, from which the patient awoke with acute anxiety. In this dream, when we followed carefully the chronological order of appearance of the manifest dream elements, we noticed that the recognition of painful elements increased progressively.

During this dream the patient is awakening out of sleep. We may assume, therefore, that in all probability the depth of sleep is progressively diminishing as the dream proceeds. Thus the progressive increase in the recognition of disturbing elements in the dream apparently runs parallel to a progressive diminution in the depth of sleep. Our inference from this fact is that sleep itself to some degree serves as a substitute for painful affects or, to state it in quantitative terms, that there is an absorption of painful affects during sleep that is roughly proportional to the depth of sleep.

In this paper we make use of this principle to account for the fact that immediately after awakening from sleep a person may be able to solve a difficult intellectual problem with which he had been struggling in vain before going to sleep. An important example of this fact is sometimes encountered in the course of a psychoanalytic treatment.

Since earliest times, dreams have been credited with a prophetic significance. Freud has pointed out that this belief in the prophetic value of dreams is, in part, both justified and explained by the fact that the

Reprinted from *Psychoanalytic Quarterly*, 6 (1937).

function of dreams is to represent wishes as fulfilled. Wishes often succeed in attaining fulfillment also in real life. Hence it is not strange that dreams should often prove to be prophetic.

Freud (1923) has also called attention to the fact that a person, immediately after awakening from sleep, may be able to solve a difficult intellectual problem with which he had been struggling in vain before going to sleep. It has been abundantly demonstrated that both the id and the superego continue to function in dreams. Observations of the sort just cited indicate that the ego's function to find solutions for problems in real life may also be continued in sleep.

A less dramatic, but more frequent, observation points to the same conclusion. I suspect that most analysts can recall dreams that are already, as it were, premonitory of a real conflict solution that the patient will achieve perhaps very soon, perhaps only after a period of weeks or months. Such dreams have been frequently reported in the literature. The following dream, from the first case report in Alexander and Healy's book, *Roots of Crime,* is a dream of this sort.

The patient had been complaining that he would never achieve anything. He could be an elevator boy and slowly advance to a small job in a hotel or a department store, but such a man has no pleasure in life, nothing but duties and children, no hope of advancement. The patient prefers to be a crook.

In the following interview however, he brings a dream that indicates a more hopeful attitude.

> He was going into an office building, as he often did—one of his old tricks. There were raincoats and hats. He took a hat and some stamps from a briefcase. An old white-haired fellow who was working in the elevator shaft saw him through the glass door of the office. He thought he had better "beat it." He went out through another door, came to a lobby, and from there to the street.

He recognized in the old man looking from the elevator shaft the discouraging picture of his future if he goes straight. This is the kind of prematurely aged family man, an old man still an elevator boy, that he had in mind. Associating to the dream he says, "When this fellow looked at me in the dream, I suddenly saw that there were many doors in the room and I took another door, not the one through which the man saw me when I came in." He discovers in the dream that it is not true that there are only two possibilities for him —to become an elevator boy or a crook. In the dream he says, "Maybe there is another way out." In other words, in this dream, rather early in the patient's analysis, there is a reorientation with reference to the patient's future that is anticipatory of the future course of his analysis.

This is, indeed, not an unequivocal instance of conflict solution in a dream. The sudden discovery of the many doors symbolizes a sudden realization that there are new possibilities in life for the patient. In the dream he goes out by another door, thus symbolically accepting the hope that he may find another way out of his conflict, but the rest of the dream indicates plainly that he is not yet able to take the emotional step that is here suggested.[1] The whole façade of the dream is a rejection of it. He is still a thief. As in his conscious associations, the possibility of becoming an honest man is depreciated in the figure of an old man who is still an elevator boy. Moreover, in the first version of the dream, he does not mention catching sight of a new possibility —it is rather the old man who sees him. Finally he decides to "beat it," to run away from the urge to follow further the new possibility that has opened itself up before him.

The second example that I shall cite is a dream that achieves a much more complete conflict solution. The following dream is reported by Ruth Mack Brunswick in her supplement (1928) to Freud's *History of an Infantile Neurosis*.

> The patient stands looking out of his window at a meadow beyond which is a woods. The sun shines through the trees dappling the grass. The stones in the meadow are of a curious mauve shade. The patient regards particularly the branches of a certain tree, admiring the way in which they are intertwined. He cannot understand why he has not yet painted this landscape.

Brunswick points out that this dream is a sort of "clarified" version of the earlier traumatic dream of the wolves in the tree reported in Freud's case history. The landscape is again the landscape of the childhood dream. In childhood "it was night, always a frightening time." "Now the sun is shining. . . . The branches of the tree where the terrifying wolves sat are now empty and are intertwined in a beautiful pattern," symbolizing the parents in sexual embrace. "What was fearful and ominous has become beautiful and reassuring. The patient wonders at his never having painted this scene before, that is, at his failure until now to admire it."

Brunswick points out further that the reconciliation with what formerly terrified him can only mean that he has now, for the first time, overcome his castration fear and "become capable of admiring what others find beautiful, a love scene between a man and woman. So long as he identified himself with the woman he was incapable of such admiration"; his entire narcissism had reacted against the castration threat implied in the female role. If, however, he gives up his identification with the woman, he need no longer fear castration.

However, as Brunswick immediately takes pains to point out, the patient had not in real life progressed so far as the dream seems to indicate. It was really a considerable time before the patient finally experienced the relief which this dream had prophesied.

It will be noticed that Brunswick regarded the dream of the entwined branches as prophetic of an adjustment that the patient would later make in real life. I think that this accords with general analytic experience. When such dreams are properly understood, and if they represent real dream solutions of the patient's most active conflict, we are usually justified in the hope that the dream solution is a sort of prophecy of an adjustment that the patient will be able to make in real life, or at least that it indicates the potentiality of such an adjustment. In other words, the dream has been able to achieve a solution for a conflict that waking thought is still quite unable to solve. The dream work is, by several weeks or even months, cleverer than waking thought. When viewed in the light of our habitual overvaluation of waking thought, this would seem to be a paradox that urgently deserves further investigation.

Before attempting to explain this paradox, let us raise again the question as to whether it exists. Does the dreamer really find the solution [2] for a conflict while he is asleep, or does the dream only bring to manifest expression a solution that had already been found during the preceding day, perhaps without having actually become conscious? It is difficult to decide. As we have already noted, Freud has called attention to the fact that one may solve a difficult intellectual problem during sleep, but in the case of dreams that seem to find solutions for real conflicts, he is inclined to regard the solution as a product of preconscious waking thought which has been incorporated into the dream thoughts as a day residue.[3] Freud recognizes the fact that "many dreams contain attempts to find solutions of conflicts" and that these solutions that are found in the dream are often actually carried out later in real life; but he regards "the function of thinking ahead in the dream" rather as "a function of preconscious waking thought, the result of which may be disclosed to us by the analysis of dreams or by other phenomena."

It is, of course, often difficult to determine when the idea of how to solve a conflict first arises, especially when it is the product of unconscious and preconscious thinking and only later becomes conscious, as in the cases under discussion. For the purposes of the present discussion, however, it is not so important to inquire when the solution of a conflict first arose as an idea. Much more important is the moment when it is first accepted by the ego as a satisfactory compromise product. In this respect, it is interesting to contrast the two dreams we have cited from the literature. The dream reported by Alexander does not in fact register a real acceptance by the ego of the new solution for the dreamer's conflict. In this dream merely the idea of a possible new solution is suggested symbolically and symbolically accepted, but in contrast to this symbolic acceptance, the dream ego is frightened by the new idea and decides to "beat it." The manifest content of the dream reported by Brunswick, on the other hand, registers a real emotional readjustment which anticipates the more permanent adjustment achieved later in the patient's waking life.

Since Freud published *The Interpretation of Dreams,* we have learned to recognize in dreams the products of a compromise between repressed wishes and the repressing forces. In normal, healthy persons, the dream may serve merely as a sort of safety valve allowing the periodic and harmless release during sleep of wishes that might otherwise prove disturbing in waking life. The dreams of neurotic persons, on the other hand, quite typically reflect the failure of the patient to find a solution for his conflict that can be acceptable to him in real life. Let us think of the typical situation in which the neurotic patient has attempted to repress too severely and indiscriminately the impulses deriving from his sexual life. The dreams of such patients only reflect in different language the continuous and bitter struggle between defiant, repressed impulses and the desperately repressive superego. In a psychoanalytic treatment we attempt to help the patient to achieve a redistribution of energy in his psychic economy that will result in a less severe superego, a less defiant id, and a better working compromise between these two parts of the personality. The patient's too rigid superego has been built up in reaction to traumatic experiences in his early life. In order to modify his superego we must help him to reopen and relive the conflicts of which that too rigid superego was a product, and then under more auspicious circumstances to find a new and better solution for a conflict which the patient has never really solved. Prophetic dreams of the sort we have been discussing represent crucial steps in this process of redistribution of energy. In order to understand them, therefore, we must think not in terms of superego and id as fixed structures, but rather in terms of the dynamic interplay of forces that led to the original formation of the superego and that must be now modified in order to permit a correction of the original pattern.

As I have already discussed at length, this dynamic interplay of forces may be most simply pictured in terms that are analogous to Pavlov's experiments upon the differentiation of conditioned reflexes. At some time in his childhood, the patient has had impulses that led or threatened to lead to unpleasant consequences. In order to avoid the repetition of these unpleasant consequences, the patient learns to inhibit the forbidden impulses. Up to this point, the patient's reaction was a simple adjustment to reality, but in the case of the neurotic superego the reaction went further than this. The patient not only inhibited, but vigorously repressed, the forbidden impulses. By excluding the impulses from consciousness, he made impossible the later correction of his reaction pattern. Let us suppose, for instance, that these forbidden impulses were sexual ones directed toward the mother and sister. When puberty comes the patient's too indiscriminate conscience forbids not only sexual impulses directed toward mother and sister, but similar impulses directed toward any woman. The patient's code of prohibitions is in urgent need of revision, but his desperate exclusion from consciousness of all heterosexual impulses makes it impossible for him to recognize that there is a difference between incestuous and other heterosexual longings. In analysis we must help him to bring to consciousness the incestuous wishes in order to compare them with other heterosexual wishes whose social consequences are less disturbing. This is the process that we call reality-testing. The significant feature of the "prophetic," conflict-solving dreams that we have been discussing is the fact that the dream work has achieved a reality-testing during sleep. It will be of interest to study in more detail this process of reality-testing.

In *The Interpretation of Dreams,* Freud demonstrated that a dream in every case fulfills two conditions. (1) It represents the fulfillment of a wish dating from childhood. (2) It contains references to material of the previous day. It is the second of these conditions that is of interest for our present problem. Freud finds that the references to the material of the day preceding need not be allusions to events of emotional importance. He attributes their appearance in the dream to a process of transference over to recent experiences of energy deriving from the infantile conflict.

This transference process is the same sort of transference that one encounters regularly in the neuroses and that we are compelled to study so intensively in the course of a psychoanalytic treatment. Freud only later discovered its fundamental biological significance. It is one of the important manifestations of the repetition compulsion. There is a strong tendency to interpret present situations as though they were merely repetitions of previous experiences and to live in the present as though one were only reliving the past. The most extreme manifestations of this repetition compulsion are bizarre enough, but it is important to recognize that it is only by means of the repetition compulsion in a modified form that we are able to learn by experience. When confronted with a new experience, we tend to recall previous experiences that are similar and to react to the present according to patterns learned from the earlier experiences. If we are to learn to adjust to reality, we must first reactivate the old patterns and then attempt to correct them by comparing the new situation with the old one. This again is the process of reality-testing. In the dream work, this tendency to bring present situations into relation with past experiences persists in the tendency to transfer some of the energy of the infantile conflict over to more recent experiences. The dream work continues to struggle with the task of trying to find a solution for the never solved problems of childhood in terms of the situations of the day before.

That the dream work is still struggling with a problem in adjustment to present reality is seen most clearly in the prophetic conflict-solving dreams that we are now discussing. I can best illustrate this by an example.

The patient is being analyzed in a hospital after a psychotic episode. He had entered upon the analysis rather reluctantly and in a number of dreams had indicated that a very important motive for his accepting the analysis originated in the fact that being analyzed gave him an excuse for remaining in the hospital, where he had no responsibilities and was well cared for. On the day previous to the hour from which material is to be cited, the patient had requested to be allowed to go to a nearby city unattended. The policy of the hospital, however, had made it necessary to insist that his wife meet him at the hospital and accompany him to the city.

He opens the next hour with the following dream:

The patient meets the analyst and the analyst tells him that in the future he shall have more freedom.

He immediately states that more freedom means parole and reminds the analyst of the denial of his request of the day before. He remarks that he had a good time in the city where he met some old acquaintances who had previously worked for him.

After the analyst comments that this was a consolation dream, the patient then brings a second dream:

> He is in a large house made of red brick with light, very neat brown tiles pointing downward. The house resembles his own house in a South African city (where he had had an administrative position), but is larger and finer. The patient and his wife are entertaining there his former employer and the employer's wife. The patient feels he is entertaining well, which is unlike his usual feeling that he is a poor host.
>
> Then the patient is upstairs. He and his wife are in a room near the bathroom. He hears his wife apologizing gracefully to his employer's wife because the employer's room is some distance from the bathroom.
>
> Next the patient is in a large open shower which consists of one very large upright iron column with several bent tubes branching out from it, each tube giving forth a stream which is about half an inch in diameter. The shower has a broken brick floor with a large drain hole. The patient is taking a shower bath. Other people, mostly Negroes, are standing around but not bathing. The patient defecates, then catches the stool in his hand, and it becomes a piece of soap with which he washes himself.

It is this second dream that I am interested in discussing for the purposes of this paper. In association, the patient recalls that he actually did entertain his employer and his wife in this house shortly after his guest had lost a child. He recalls that he felt very uncomfortable in entertaining them, as he is a very poor host. The patient also recalls that his wife hurt her knee while the patient was living in this house. He had to take care of her. He had his own worries at the time (this was at the onset of his depression, which was the beginning of his psychosis) and had the impulse to kill her and commit suicide, provoked by his chagrin at the memory of a previous period of excitement. He also recalls that he and his wife were entertained by his employer one summer. At this time his employer had intestinal cramps and his wife made apologies for him. Ordinarily his employer is an athletic, happy, active sort of man. In association to his apologizing because his guest room was so far from the bathroom, the patient remarks that it is always a matter of considerable concern to him to be near the bathroom whenever he goes anywhere. He gives much attention to avoiding constipation, and for this reason he feels uncomfortable when he goes to strange houses and always informs himself immediately where the bathroom is. Once in his childhood he recalls having defecated in his trousers and the difficulty he had cleaning up. He hates to have to wait to go to the toilet.

We may interpret this dream as a reaction to the patient's chagrin at being reminded that his friends were living active lives and meeting life's responsibilities outside of the hospital, whereas he was continuing in the hospital and allowing his wife to earn her own living as best she could. The dream at first attempts to wish away these feelings of inferiority. The patient is at home with his wife and no longer the recipient of treatment in the hospital. On the contrary, it is he that is entertaining one of the men whose success he most envies, his active, athletic employer. This denial of his chagrin, however, shortly proves unsuccessful. The comparison between the patient and his successful employer stimulates a more infantile competitive impulse. The large upright iron column giving forth a stream of water into a large drain hole is symbolic of the primal scene. But the patient has revised this primal scene so as to draw all attention and glory upon himself. Instead of being merely a frustrated observer, he is between the symbols for father and mother; he is the center of attention. Inferior beings are standing about watching him. As an infantile substitute for ejaculation, he defecates.

There is in fact a real basis for this grandiose fantasy. As an analytic patient, he is indeed the center of attention as compared with the other patients in the hospital (the "Negroes" in the dream).

It is the last incident in the dream, however, that is of special interest for our present discussion. What can be the meaning of the stool's becoming a piece of soap with which the patient washes himself? Washing, of course, is a reaction formation to the soiling impulse. On the other hand, washing is also a sublimated outlet for anal erotic impulses, a sublimated form of smearing. The reaction formation derives its energy in large part from the soiling impulse against which it is a reaction. That the stool becomes soap is a very plastic representation of this fact.

Nevertheless, we are struck by the ease with which the soiling impulse is succeeded by reaction formation without other evidence of shame or guilt in the transition. Instead of feeling ashamed, the patient seems to be boasting: "See, I can turn a stool into soap." It is as though he were performing a feat of magic before an audience. How can we account for the ease with which the patient replaces his shame by such a boast?

We have already mentioned that the patient is one of the few patients in the hospital who is being analyzed. Recalling this, we now discover that his boast is based upon a real fact. The stool that becomes soap is a most significant symbol of the analysis. To tell his dirty thoughts has been most painful for the patient's fastidious ego. This dream represents the patient's first acceptance of the tolerance of the analysis for his anal erotic impulses. In this situation, telling one's dirty thoughts is no longer an offense against good taste, but a means of purifying oneself—which is the patient's conception of being cured of his neurosis.

Thus in this dream the patient has hit upon an element in his real situation that offers a possibility for a better solution of his conflict. In his infantile situation, defecating in his bath could bring only shame and humiliation. In the analysis, telling his dirty thoughts is a kind of soap with which he can wash himself. The dream has taken account of the difference between the shame attaching to his soiling impulses in childhood and the encouragement given to these same impulses in the analysis, and has turned to the analysis as a solution for his conflict.[4] In other words, the dream work has succeeded in a bit of reality-testing of which the patient has not yet been capable in his waking life.

Since we are prone to the prejudice that dreaming is much less capable of finding a solution to a problem in real life than is wide-awake thinking, this sort of paradoxical dream should stimulate us to inquire into the dynamic mechanisms that have made possible the dream's solution. The first step in this solution was the frank appearance of the patient's infantile impulse to compete with his father's potency by an act of defecation. Until this infantile impulse could be brought into consciousness it was, of course, impossible to make a comparison with the analytic situation and so discover that the analysis encouraged rather than discouraged such infantile fantasies.[5] We must next inquire, therefore, why it is that the patient is better able in a dream to bring such a disturbing impulse into consciousness. In waking life we may surmise that his shame is too intense to permit the re-animation of such a fantasy. Even during his psychotic excitement fantasies of this sort had not appeared, and at this period the patient's psychotic excitement had been replaced by the extreme reserve which was normally characteristic of him. In waking life the patient tended rather to react more in accordance with the first part of his dream by priding himself upon his fastidiousness and taste for elegance and striving in this way to overbalance the feelings of inferiority that constantly distressed him.

It will be helpful to weigh carefully the advantages and disadvantages of such a reaction formation as a solution for the patient's conflict. Its obvious advantage is that it protects the patient from the intense shame that a reliving of his infantile impulses must reawaken. Over and against this we must weigh the disadvantage that such a reaction formation leaves the patient a prey to strong inner tensions caused by the constant necessity of holding his infantile impulses in check.

It is plain that in the course of the dream the dynamic balance shifts.[6] In the first part of the dream the reaction formation is in the ascendancy. The wife's apology to the employer's wife is the first sign that the patient's anxiety on account of his repressed impulses is increasing. It is well to be as near as possible to the bathroom. Immediately afterward, the repressed impulses have attained the ascendancy.

How are we to account for this shift of balance? In an attempt to do so, I should like to utilize a hypothesis concerning the dynamic influence of sleep upon psychic equilibrium that was first suggested to me by a study of nightmares that wake patients out of sleep. In such nightmares one can observe that the recognition of painful elements in the dreamer's psychic situation is at a minimum at the beginning of the dream and increases progressively as the dream proceeds, reaching its maximum as the patient wakes up. It is only a short step to infer from this observation that the state of sleep itself absorbs and neutralizes pain. As one becomes refreshed by sleep, we may surmise, the intensity of one's fatigue lessens, the depth of sleep diminishes, and painful affects are released in increasing amounts from the neutralizing effects of deep sleep.

Pain, however, is of two sorts. There is the pain of unsatisfied desire, and then again there is the pain of unpleasant consequences on account of having gratified one's desires. A delicate dynamic balance must determine which of these two sorts of pain one shall choose.

Applying these principles to the dream under discussion, we note that the patient is able at first to abolish or neutralize both of the types of pain to which we have referred. His sense of inferiority is gone.

There are no disturbing infantile impulses. He is successfully entertaining his employer. In the sequel the intensity of the unsatisfied infantile impulses increases rapidly but the fear of consequences appears to be deadened sufficiently to allow the infantile impulses to break through. We might expect the patient immediately afterward to wake up out of his sleep acutely disturbed by the shame attaching to his soiling impulses. Instead of this, the patient's dream ego borrows a trick from the ego of waking life. He promptly recalls that he is in analysis; so it does not matter anyhow. By a sort of pseudo-awakening, the patient reduces the intensity of his sleep-disturbing anxiety and so makes it possible to continue sleeping a while longer.

Since I have been interested in the evidences of the persistence of the reality-testing function in dreams, I have been struck by the frequency with which patients' dreams end by consolations of this sort drawn from the actual facts of real life.

If the above reconstruction of the alternations of dynamic balance in this dream is correct, we are now able to give an answer to the question that we raised a short time ago. We asked why it was that this dream was able to achieve a solution which the patient had been unable to find in real life. The answer is that the state of sleep has absorbed a considerable part of the shame attaching to the patient's soiling impulse and in this way has diminished the intensity of the patient's inhibitions and permitted an experimental reliving of the forbidden impulses under the encouragement of the analysis.

In previous papers (1933 and 1936) I have frequently pointed out that the discriminatory function of the ego is dependent upon maintaining the intensity of conflict at a certain optimum level. In waking life, the patient's conflict was too intense to permit of a discriminating solution. The state of sleep, by diminishing the intensity of the patient's conflict, provided better conditions for ego function. Hence the dream work was able to achieve a solution for a conflict which the dreamer's wide-awake ego could only seek to evade.

NOTES

1. Alexander reports this dream merely as one of a series illustrating the course of an analysis. He does not take time, therefore, to discuss at this point the deeper instinctual basis for the patient's awakening interest in becoming an honest man. Judging from the dream symbolism and from the subsequent course of the analysis, we may suspect that the new possibility that opens itself up before the patient is that of

identification with the analyst, who is perhaps the first successful honest man to whom the patient has become strongly attached. If one is to learn by identification, however, it is necessary that one become quite conscious of the differences between one's own performance and the model one is attempting to copy. As the later analysis shows, the great difficulty in the way of successful identification with the analyst is the patient's emotional resistance to recognizing the great disparity between his own passive desires and his masculine ideal. The subsequent analysis consists of a struggle months long on the patient's part to accept recognition of his passive dependent desires and to overcome his envy of his brother and of the analyst.

2. Maeder (1912, 1913-a, 1913-b) clearly formulated the suggestion that many dreams have a secondary "teleological" function, the function of attempting to find a solution for a conflict in real life. This he compares to the preparatory function of play as practice for real living. Alfred Adler (1912) also ascribed to the dream the function of "thinking ahead." Similar suggestions were also made in a much more vague form by Silberer (1910 and 1911). After Maeder wrote, Freud elucidated the role of the transference in psychoanalytic therapy, described the repetition compulsion, and sketched out a scheme of the structure of the total personality. My own paper is an attempt to reconsider the problems that were raised so long ago by Maeder and others, in the light of these later developments in psychoanalytic theory.

3. *The Interpretation of Dreams,* footnote, page 533, in reply to Maeder and Adler.

4. It is easy to underestimate the importance of unobtrusive and familiar facts. In every analysis it is first of all the tolerant and objective atmosphere of the analysis that makes it possible for the patient to bring repressed impulses to consciousness and give overt expression to them. This is obviously the result of an elementary bit of reality-testing on the patient's part. The patient is taking account of the fact that the analytic situation is different from the childhood situation that first made repression necessary. In the analytic situation it is safe to say many things that one was afraid to say in childhood.

A second familiar fact that is illustrated by every analysis is that the first open avowal of a repressed impulse often takes place in a dream. In other words, a dream is the first sign registering the fact that the patient has taken this elementary step in adjustment to reality. The dream under discussion is only a rather pretty illustration of this very common phenomenon.

5. It is, of course, a matter of everyday experience in psychoanalysis that a patient cannot once and for all accept as a fact the analyst's tolerance for the patient's forbidden impulses. On the contrary, every important new disclosure costs the patient another struggle before he can believe again, with reference to this particular forbidden impulse, that the analyst will be objective and tolerant.

6. It will be noticed that I am here using the manifest content of the dream as an index of the quantitative balance between repressed and repressing forces. This is a procedure that is employed intuitively by all analysts. That repressed wishes are expressed more and more openly in the manifest content of the dream, as the repressing forces weaken, is a fact that can be corroborated during the course of nearly every analysis. I should regard it as superfluous to remark upon it were it not for the fact that Fenichel (1936) has questioned the validity of conclusions drawn from the manifest content of dreams, even though the manifest content may have been studied, as in the present instance, after very careful attention has been paid to the latent dream content.

In the present discussion I am also using the manifest content to trace shifts in this dynamic balance during the course of the dream. This is also a procedure that is not without precedent in the psychoanalytic literature. What I am tracing, of course, is a last phase of the dream work, the part of the dream work that occurs during the act of dreaming.

BIBLIOGRAPHY

Alfred Adler, *Über den Nervösen Charakter* (Vienna. 1912).

Franz Alexander and William Healy, *Roots of Crime* (New York, A. Knopf, 1935).

Ruth Mack Brunswick, "A Supplement to Freud's 'History of an Infantile Neurosis,'" *International Journal of Psycho-analysis*, IX (October 1928), 439-476.

Otto Fenichel, "Review of Alexander and Wilson: 'Quantitative Dream Studies,'" *Psychoanalytic Quarterly*, VI (1936).

Thomas M. French, "Interrelations Between Psychoanalysis and the Experimental Work of Pavlov," Chapter 1 above.

"A Clinical Study of Learning in the Course of a Psychoanalytic Treatment," Chapter 3 above.

Sigmund Freud, *Interpretation of Dreams* (New York, 1900).

"From the History of an Infantile Neurosis," *Collected Papers III* (London, Hogarth Press, 1918).

The Ego and the Id (London, Hogarth Press, 1923).

Alphonse Maeder, "Über die Funktion des Traumes," *Jahrbuch für Psychanalischer Forschungen*, IV (1912).

"Zur Frage der teleologischen Traumfunktion," *Jahrbuch für Psychanalischer Forschungen*, V (1913a).

"Über das Traumproblem," *Jahrbuch für Psychoanalischer Forschungen*, V (1913b).

Herbert Silberer, "Phantasie und Mythos," *Jahrbuch für Psychanalischer Forschungen*, II (1910).

"Über die Symbolbildung," *Jahrbuch für Psychanalischer Forschungen*, III (1911).

Chapter Six

DEFENSE AND SYNTHESIS
IN THE FUNCTION OF THE EGO:
SOME OBSERVATIONS
STIMULATED BY ANNA FREUD'S
THE EGO AND THE MECHANISMS OF DEFENSE

Psychoanalysis began with the discovery of the existence of unconscious memories and wishes and devoted itself first to the study of their content. Later Freud began to inquire into the nature of the repressing forces. Guilt feelings, the unconscious need for punishment, the manifestations of the conscience became the central theme of psychoanalytic interest. More recently the ego and its integrating function have become increasingly central in psychoanalytic thought. Anna Freud's *The Ego and the Mechanisms of Defense* [1] is an important contribution to this increasing interest in the study of the ego.

I

How can one investigate the function of the ego? Anna Freud devotes a considerable part of the first section of her book to the discussion of this question. She points out that it is the ego upon which we have to rely in order to gain information concerning the other two parts of the personality. The ego "is, so to speak, the medium through which we try to get a picture of the other two institutions." It is possible to observe the id only when unsatisfied instinctual impulses attempt to invade the ego. Similarly, the superego is discernible as a separate

Reprinted from *Psychoanalytic Quarterly*, 7, No. 4 (October 1938).

institution only when its claims become disturbing to the ego in the form of feelings of guilt or need for punishment.

On the other hand, the function of the ego itself is a silent and unobtrusive one except at times when the demands of id and superego become a threat to it. The ego knows nothing of successful repression or reaction formation. As observers, we become aware of these successful ego reactions only when we notice "that certain impulses are absent which we should expect to make their appearance in the ego in pursuit of gratification."

In psychoanalytic treatment we become aware of the ego's activity in the ego defenses that are mobilized when impulses from the id threaten to become conscious. The author points out that "from the beginning analysis as a therapeutic method was concerned with the ego and its aberrations; the investigation of the id and of its mode of operation was always only a means to an end." The unconscious impulses were important therapeutically only because they were the cause of symptoms, abnormal character traits, etc., which were disturbing to the conscious personality. The therapeutic goal "was invariably the same—the correction of these abnormalities and the restoration of the ego to its integrity."

In a very interesting review of the various technical procedures employed by the analyst, the author portrays vividly the process of mobilization of ego defenses. I shall cite only a part of her comments upon hypnosis and upon free association. In hypnosis "the goal aimed at was the revelation of the unconscious; the ego was a disturbing factor and hypnosis was a means of getting rid of it temporarily. When a piece of unconscious material came to light in hypnosis, the physician introduced it to the ego, and the effect of thus forcibly bringing it into consciousness was to clear up the symptom. But the ego took no part in the therapeutic process. It tolerated the intruder only so long as it was itself under the influence of the physician who had induced hypnosis. Then it revolted and began a new struggle to defend itself against that element of the id which had been forced upon it, and so the laboriously achieved therapeutic success was vitiated." In free association, on the other hand, "the fundamental rule can never be followed beyond a certain point. The ego keeps silence for a time and the id-derivatives make use of this pause to force their way into consciousness. The analyst hastens to catch their utterances. Then the ego bestirs itself again, repudiates the attitude of passive tolerance which it has been compelled to assume and by means of one or other

of its customary defense mechanisms intervenes in the flow of associations. The inroad of the id into the ego has given place to a counter-
attack by the ego upon the id. The observer's attention is now diverted
from the associations to the resistance, i.e., from the content of the id
to the activity of the ego. The analyst has an opportunity of witnessing,
then and there, the putting into operation by the latter of one of those
defensive measures against the id which I have already described
and which are so obscure, and it now behooves him to make it the
object of his investigation."

II

Thus the functioning of the ego is most readily observed when it
becomes manifest in the form of defense mechanisms against the
eruption of unconscious tendencies. In analysis these defense mechanisms appear as resistance; in life, either as permanent character traits
or as symptoms.

A number of elementary defense mechanisms have been described.
The author offers us a list of ten: repression, regression, reaction
formation, "isolation" and "undoing," projection, introjection, reversal
(of content), turning (an impulse) against oneself (i.e., reversal of
direction), sublimation. This list is incomplete. The most conspicuous
omission is rationalization.

More significant than any mere enumeration, of course, is the problem
as to what determines the ego's choice of defense. What determines
which of its many possible defense mechanisms will be employed by
the ego? This might depend, as Freud has suggested, upon the chronological stage of development of the ego, or, more precisely, upon the
relative stage of development of ego and instinct. The author considers
this possibility, but abandons for the present the attempt to work out
its implications.

As a simpler approach to this problem, she undertakes to classify
the motives that drive the ego to resort to defense mechanisms. These
motives she divides into three groups: (a) "superego anxiety" or fear
of the conscience, which is particularly characteristic of the neuroses
of adults; (b) "objective anxiety" or fear of real consequences, which
is most frequently the motive for defense in infantile neuroses; and
(c) "instinctual anxiety" or fear of being overwhelmed by the strength
of the instincts. This last motive is particularly characteristic of periods

like puberty when there is a sudden accession of instinctual energy threatening to upset a previously established psychic balance.

III

The ego's defenses against "superego anxiety" have already been exhaustively discussed in the psychoanalytic literature. In the present work they are, therefore, not made the subject of separate discussion. The author turns immediately to the study of the defenses against "objective anxiety."

We know that the superego arises by identification with the parents as a means of mastering the objective anxieties of the childhood period. These are fear of punishment and, most important of all, the fear of loss of the parents' love. In adult analyses we encounter these reactions to "objective anxiety" after they have already been modified by the development of the superego. The child's handling of its "objective anxieties," on the other hand, is much more naïve and direct.

In the section that follows, the author presents us with a series of very simple and clear illustrations of defense mechanisms that are characteristic of different periods of ego development—a set of illustrative examples which might well be the beginning of a clinical descriptive study of the development of the characteristic ego defenses from the infantile period up to the time of puberty.

In early childhood, the author points out, it is often impossible for the child to escape painful external impressions and the child is therefore compelled to resort to the somewhat desperate defense of denying the painful fact by means of fantasy. Thus one little boy whom she describes attempts to get rid of his fear of the father by fantasying that he owns a tame lion which terrifies everyone else and loves no one but the little boy himself.

In other cases fantasy alone seems to be an inadequate means of getting rid of painful reality and the child finds it necessary to act out its protective fantasy in play or in talk. This the author calls "denial in word and act." To quote one instance, a little boy must be allowed actually to wear his father's hat or he becomes restless and discontented.

As the child grows older "the ego loses the power of surmounting considerable quantities of objective pain by means of fantasy." To be sure, "even in adult life day-dreams may still play a part . . . but in adult years a day-dream is almost in the nature of a game, a kind of by-product with but a slight libidinal cathexis . . . it seems that the original importance of the day-dream as a means of defense against objective anxiety is lost when the earliest period of childhood comes to an end."

The author raises the interesting question as to why it is that fantasy thus tends to lose its value as a means of defense as the child grows older. She surmises that this change is the result of the strengthening of the faculty of reality-testing and also of the fact that the ego's need for synthesis makes it increasingly impossible for opposites to exist side by side as they do in the fantasy life of the younger child.

However this may be, "when a child is somewhat older his greater freedom of physical movement and his increased powers of psychic activity enable his ego to evade such [painful] stimuli and there is no need for him to perform so complicated"—one might say drastic— "a psychic operation as that of denial. Instead of perceiving the painful impression and subsequently canceling it by withdrawing its cathexis, it is open to the ego to refuse to encounter the dangerous external situation at all. It can take to flight and so, in the truest sense of the word, 'avoid' the occasions of 'pain.' " As one of her examples the author cites the case of a little girl who, much chagrined by a rebuff from an admired boy at her first dance, thereupon loses all interest in dancing and pretty clothes and concentrates her interest upon the ambition to excel intellectually. This sort of withdrawal from activities that have led to painful experiences the author calls "restriction of the ego." Except in its more extreme instances, such "restriction of the ego" may not necessarily be a neurotic manifestation at all, but may be regarded as "a normal stage in the development of the ego." It corresponds to an element in reality adjustment that everyone must make, the recognition and acceptance of one's limitations. It differs from neurotic inhibition, the author points out, in that the neurotically inhibited activity is a substitute for a forbidden instinctual wish which the inhibited person is unable to give up, whereas "restriction of the ego" corresponds to a real renunciation and loss of interest in the abandoned activity.

IV

Up to this point the author has been describing isolated and rather elementary defense mechanisms. In order to understand the activity of the ego it is, of course, profitable to attempt to resolve that activity into its elements. The question might be raised, however, as to whether an enumeration and description of isolated defense mechanisms could ever give us a really adequate picture of the normal functioning of the ego. The defensive activity of the ego is in most cases a much more highly organized reaction, involving not one but several elementary defense mechanisms in conjunction with one another. The essence of the ego function is synthesis and integration, and it must be important therefore not only to resolve the defensive activity of the ego into its elements but also to study how these elementary mechanisms complement each other and become organized into more integrated behavior.

In her next two chapters, the author describes somewhat more complex forms of defensive activity. The mechanism of "identification with the aggressor" may be regarded as a complex mechanism involving a combination of identification and projection. To cite one of the author's prettiest illustrations, the child reacts to its fear of an angry teacher by involuntarily mimicking the teacher's facial expressions. The child defends itself against its fear of the teacher's aggression by identifying with the teacher's aggressive gesture. In another instance a boy vehemently accuses his mother of the curiosity for which he fears that she will reproach him. In this latter case the combination of identification and projection is even more clear, in that the boy identifies with the aggressive role of the mother from whom he fears reproaches, but on the other hand projects upon her the curiosity for which he expects to be reproached.

It is perhaps making the mechanism more complex than it really is, however, to describe it as a combination of identification and projection. What occurs may be more simply described as a reversal of roles. It is only for our convenience that we analyze it into two separate mechanisms of identification and projection.

The next chapter describes a defense reaction which is more highly integrated. The mechanism of "altruistic surrender" may also be called a mechanism of vicarious gratification. It consists in the renunciation of direct gratification of one's own wishes and the substitution of the urge to obtain for someone else the very same gratification that one has renounced for oneself. The author cites the case of a governess who had been a very demanding child but as a grown woman impressed one with her unassuming character and the modesty of the demands which she made upon life. Her own demands upon life had not been completely inhibited, however, but were gratified vicariously in her identification with the love affairs and pretty dresses of her women friends, in her devotion to other people's children, and in her intense ambition for the men she loved. Even the aggressive reactions to frustration which were so conspicuously absent on her own behalf were given free expression in behalf of those with whom she identified, as was illustrated by her indignant anger when a mother refused a child some sweets that it desired. Then she experienced the frustration of the child's wish as if it were her own and became furiously indignant.

In this instance we have not a single defense reaction but rather the organization of a whole personality upon the principle of substitution of vicarious for direct gratification. We should expect this sort of personality organization to put the ego under some tension. To complete the picture we should wish to know whether in these cases there is any evidence of the frustration that would seem to be an inevitable concomitant of such complete renunciation of direct gratifications. The patient's uninhibited anger on behalf of those with whom she identified offers indeed a considerable outlet for such frustration reactions. Under favorable circumstances this sort of outlet may be fairly adequate. A case reported by Helene Deutsch,[2] however, suggests the possibility of a more tragic sequel. After Helene Deutsch's patient had devoted her life to her sister according to the mechanism of "altruistic surrender," the sister finally married and left her. The patient developed a melancholia in which she feared and expected to be abandoned on the street naked and alone—a fear which was in retribution for her own desire for revenge upon the sister by leaving her naked and alone just as the sister had abandoned the patient.

Cases of this sort make it plain that the description of a single defense mechanism gives us a picture of only a fragment of the ego's synthetic activity. If one defense mechanism relieves tension at one point, it must usually be combined with another to counteract the tension which has been increased at another point. Repression must be supplemented by substitutive gratification—by sublimation if the repression is successful, in other cases by symptom formation. Reaction formation may need to be compensated by projection and rationalization. Each individual case is different, but all illustrate the fact that the defense mechanisms must be thought of as elementary parts of the ego's attempts at organization of the total personality. The essential function of the ego is one of synthesis and integration and can be adequately understood only when we attempt to understand it in relation to the total problem of personality organization with which the ego is faced.

V

We have seen that the study of the ego's defense mechanisms seems to offer us the most direct approach to the investigation of the ego activities. It is time now, however, to raise a question. Is a study of the defense mechanisms likely to give us an adequate picture of the normal functioning of the ego?

As the author points out, it is difficult to study the ego when it is functioning smoothly. Even the formation of successful reaction formations takes place unobtrusively. When the ego functions are well performed, they are performed silently and invisibly.

On the other hand, a picture of the ego obtained by a study of its defense mechanisms might be compared to a description of the functioning of a government at a moment when its energies are absorbed in putting down an insurrection. Obviously we see here, not the normal activity of the government, but its emergency activity when its existence is being threatened. Similarly, in studying the defense mechanisms, we are able to observe the activity of the ego only at a moment when its synthetic activity is struggling against the threat of imminent disintegration.

In other words, in studying the ego we are faced with difficulties similar to those that face the biochemist in attempting to study the chemistry of the living cell. It is difficult to determine how far the procedures or disease processes which make possible our observation may themselves have damaged the living activity that we wish to study.

Nevertheless, the various defense mechanisms may perhaps be expected to show us, in isolated and possibly exaggerated form, different aspects of the normal functioning of the ego, and one may perhaps hope to reconstruct a picture of the ego's synthetic activities by piecing together the hints that we get from the nature of its different defense mechanisms.

VI

There can be little doubt that the central function of the ego during childhood is learning—learning to adapt the child's instinctual needs to external reality. It would seem to the reviewer that any adequate understanding of the development of the ego must orient itself about this learning process. What role then is played by the ego's defense mechanisms in relation to this central task in ego development—the progressive mastery of and adaptation to external reality?

Let us attempt to answer this question first with reference to the mechanisms that utilize fantasy in order to deny objective pain and objective danger. As the author points out, denial of objective pain and of objective danger by means of fantasy is a mechanism that belongs to a normal phase in the development of the infantile ego. The dramatization of these protective fantasies in word and act is also a universal feature of children's play.

We have seen that when the anxiety becomes too great, this protective use of fantasy may be exaggerated and fixated into forms that are disturbing to the later development of the ego. This should not lead us to forget, however, that fantasy has a normal function to perform in the process of the child's learning to master its environment. Because of the prolonged period of childhood in human development, much of a child's learning must take place in two stages. The child sees and is told many things which it can for the time master only in its imagination. In the process of education, the child is introduced in advance to an adult world which has little reality for it in direct experience and which can be grasped only by free use of the child's imagination. It is hoped that later the child will make use of this secondhand knowledge in dealing with its own more immediate problems.

The discrepancy between child and adult is so great that, were it not possible to fill in the gaps by means of fantasy, the incentive to become like the parents would be confronted with insuperable obstacles. Identification with the parents can be achieved only by small steps. If it were necessary for the child to make this identification all in one step, the task would be so utterly hopeless that the only possible solutions would be either complete resignation or intense frustrated envy. By means of fantasy, however, the child is permitted to grow up by shorter steps that are within the range of its capacity. Urged on by the pressing need to be like the parents, the child copies what it can and fills in the rest with fantasy. The urge to emulate the parents becomes thus an incentive for a continuous learning process rather than the source of hopeless frustration.

In the pathological cases in which fantasy must be used as a defense against acute anxiety, we see an exaggeration of this normal function which is also a symptom of the beginning of its failure. We have reason to believe that the Oedipus complex and the castration fears that spring out of it are themselves consequences of the fact that in human beings the period of childhood is so prolonged. At the time of the first sexual awakening in the third or fourth year of life, the discrepancy between father and son is so great that real identification with the father is hopeless. Unless this urge to identify with the father can find outlet in fantasy and in play which has the value of fantasy, the energy of the child's phallic sexuality must be concentrated upon envious competition with the father and upon a fear which is the inevitable consequence of such hopeless competition. Under these circumstances, as in the instances cited by Anna Freud, fantasy may now be called in to protect the child from the anxiety that has resulted from the failure of its more normal function. Instead of a means of making possible a gradual and progressive identification with the father, fantasy now becomes an emergency defense against the dangers arising out of the competitive struggle with him.

Thus it would seem that a defense mechanism appears at the point where the normal integrative function of the ego begins to break down. In accordance with a principle to which I have frequently called attention,[3] it would seem that the normal synthetic function of the ego is thrown out of gear when the instinctual tension becomes too great or, more precisely, when there is too great a gap between instinctual need and fulfillment. When the synthetic activity of the ego begins to fail, the elementary mechanisms out of which the ego's normal activity is built up appear now in exaggerated forms. These same elementary mechanisms must now be mobilized as defense mechanisms in order to prevent more complete disintegration of the ego's activity.

VII

The same principle may be illustrated in connection with other defense mechanisms described by the author.

In the mechanism of "denial in fantasy," the infant attempts to get rid of unwelcome facts by the simple device of a fantasy that reverses the painful situation. In other cases, as we have seen, fantasy alone seems to be an inadequate means of getting rid of painful reality. The child finds it necessary to act out its protective fantasy in play or in talk. This the author calls "denial in word and act." From the examples cited, it would seem that in these cases fantasy alone is inadequate to satisfy the child or quiet its anxiety—as in the instance of the little boy who must be allowed actually to wear his father's hat or he became restless and discontented. Even later it was necessary for him to know that he actually had his "stilo" in his pocket. In this case a fantasy of being the father was clearly not enough. The fantasy must be reinforced by some real token.

In this need to supplement fantasy with reality, to give fantasies actuality by living them out upon some real object, it would seem that we have a cruder example of a synthesis that must play an important role in the establishment of the reality principle. We are so accustomed to contrast reality and fantasy as opposites that there is danger of overlooking the fact that the capacity to be satisfied by fantasy is probably one of the dynamic factors essential for the establishment of the reality principle. The reality principle requires that one renounce immediate pleasure and endure pain for the sake of future pleasure. In other words, the incentive of future pleasure must be strong enough to counterbalance the demands of the pleasure principle. But at the moment when it is needed as a force to modify the demands of the pleasure principle, future pleasure can be present only in fantasy. The capacity to be at least temporarily satisfied by fantasy would thus seem to play an important role in learning to wait, in learning to withstand the pressure of immediate needs.

Thus fantasy tends to make one independent of the need for gratification from the external world. Here lies a danger. If fantasy wins too complete a victory over the pressure for immediate gratification, it may tempt one to withdraw completely from external reality.

Fortunately there seems to be a limit to the efficacy of the mechanism of "denial by fantasy." As in the cases described by Anna Freud, denial in fantasy must usually be supplemented by "denial in word and act." In the establishment of the reality principle [4] we seem to see the same principle at work. In both we see a tendency toward synthesis of fantasy with the original pressure for immediate gratification in the external world. The pressure for immediate satisfaction becomes a drive for realization of one's fantasy. By virtue of such a synthesis, fantasy is modified into purpose. In actual clinical experience we can observe all possible stages in this transformation, all possible gradations, for example, between ambitious daydreams and driving ambitions. The proverbial good intentions with which the road to hell is paved are really little more than fantasies without sufficient drive toward realization to be activated into purposes.

But if this is so, why do not Anna Freud's little patients react according to the reality principle? Why must they resort to "denial in word and act"? To attempt to give a complete answer to this question would, of course, take us beyond the scope of the present discussion, but the key to the solution will probably be again the intensity of instinctual need with which the ego is confronted. We must return to the principle that the ego is able to function smoothly only when the instinctual tensions do not exceed a certain limit. The ego is like a delicate electrical instrument that is completely thrown out of adjustment by too intense a current. If the tension is too great, then the more refined adjustment, adaptation according to the reality principle, must be replaced by a cruder adjustment of a similar sort. The normal synthetic activity of the ego must degenerate into a defense mechanism.

VIII

We have already mentioned that the author regards the mechanism of "restriction of the ego" as belonging to a normal stage in the development of the ego. It corresponds to a normal step in reality adjustment, learning to accept one's limitations. It should probably be thought of as a defense mechanism only when the resignation goes too far, when the child gives up rather than make the effort necessary to overcome a difficulty. Here again the defense mechanism arises as an exaggeration of a normal adaptation that is beginning to fail. In general there are two ways of dealing with obstacles in the way of wish fulfillment. Either one struggles to overcome the obstacle or one accepts one's limitations and adapts oneself to them. In normal ego functioning, one chooses between these two principles or combines them according to the nature of the difficulty. When the ego fails in this discriminatory function, either excessive resignation or futile aggressive protest may appear as defense reactions. The mechanism of "identification with the aggressor" is one example of the latter.

Similarly, the principle of substituting vicarious for direct gratification is probably one element in a great many of the normal adjustments of the ego in relation to objects. Sigmund Freud [5] early called attention to the fact that vicarious gratification of their own abandoned narcissism plays an important role in the devotion of parents to their children. As the author points out in a footnote, the mechanism of altruistic surrender is also very similar to one of the mechanisms responsible for fixation upon male homosexuality. The homosexual renounces his claim to the mother's love in favor of a younger man and gratifies his own desires vicariously by playing a maternal role toward the younger man.

Eduardo Weiss [6] has even suggested very plausibly that the transition from homosexual to heterosexual object choice in both sexes probably proceeds by a similar mechanism in that the male, for example, gratifies vicariously his own feminine desires by bestowing upon a heterosexual object the love that he himself desires. It would seem also that the tender components in the sexual urge may quite possibly be based in part upon a similar mechanism.

In these more normal object relations, the principle of vicarious gratification is supplemented by other sources of satisfaction. The mechanism of "altruistic surrender," as described by the author, illustrates this principle of vicarious gratification as a defense mechanism—in an isolated and exaggerated form.

IX

In the concluding chapters the author seeks the clue to some of the perplexing phenomena of puberty in the anxiety of the ego lest it be overwhelmed by the increasing strength of the instincts. The capricious and rather indiscriminate asceticism of the adolescent child and the adolescent's fascination with abstract and idealistic intellectual activity seem to find in this hypothesis a rather satisfying explanation. The asceticism is a desperate attempt to renounce instinctual gratification altogether. The fascination for abstract problems is an attempt at intellectual mastery, an attempt to project the youth's very concrete emotional conflicts into the realm of abstract thought. These attempts at mastery of instinct tend to alternate with impulsive uncontrolled behavior when the rather desperate defenses of the ego fail. The passionate attachments to objects, fleeting as they are intense, are regarded by the author as attempts at recovery, attempts to regain the object relations that threaten to be lost because of the adolescent's attempts to isolate himself from temptation and to renounce instinctual gratification.

In this account the author is evidently treating the reactions of puberty as a series of defense reactions invoked by an ego that is desperately threatened by the increasing strength of instinct, One might speak paradoxically of a normal psychopathology of puberty, a point of view that is quite justified inasmuch as puberty is undoubtedly a period of disturbed equilibrium.

For a more complete understanding of puberty, however, we feel that such an account of its psychopathology should be supplemented by a more detailed study of the processes by which this disturbed equilibrium is regained. After all, in the years of maturity, if development is normal, the ego will find a way of coming to terms with the increased intensity of instinct which is, during puberty, the source of so much disturbance. Puberty is a period of transition. Its difficulties are probably due not so much to the absolute intensity of the instincts as to the fact that the new instinctual demands make necessary a complete reorganization of the ego's relation not only to the instincts but to external reality as well. If the ego does not shrink from its new task, it must henceforth renounce its dependence upon the parents, assume complete responsibility for its own instincts, and accept sexual urges that had been renounced during the latency period, together with the increased responsibilities that are the inevitable consequence of these sexual urges.

If we adhere to the point of view that the essential function of the ego is integration and synthesis, then we must study the reactions of puberty not only as a period of disturbed equilibrium, but also more fundamentally as a process of transition from the relative equilibrium of the latency period to the more permanent equilibrium of the years of maturity. We shall be interested, during this transition period, not only in the ego's attempts to defend itself against a new wave of instinct, but still more in the constructive processes of learning and adaptation that are going on silently underneath these more conspicuous manifestations of distress.

NOTES

1. Anna Freud, *The Ego and the Mechanisms of Defense* (London: Hogarth Press, 1937).

2. Helene Deutsch, *Psychoanalysis of the Neuroses* (London: Hogarth Press, 1932), Chapter 11.

3. See Chapters 1, 2, and 3 above.

4. This is not intended to be a complete discussion of the elementary principles entering into the establishment of the reality principle. In Chapter 2 above I have called attention also to the repetition compulsion as one important factor in this adjustment.

5. Freud, *On Narcissism: An Introduction.* Coll. Papers, Vol. 4, 30.

6. Eduardo Weiss, "Über eine noch nicht beschriebene Phase der Entwicklung zur heterosexuellen Liebe," *Int. Ztschr. f. Psa.,* 11 (1915), 429.

Our next papers have to do with generalizations about the organization of goal-directed behavior and the modifications this organization undergoes in neurotic behavior. The first of these papers is based upon study of reactions to frustration; the second is a more comprehensive attempt to work out the mechanisms on which goal-seeking behavior depends, and the disintegration that these mechanisms undergo when conflict becomes too intense.

Chapter Seven

AN ANALYSIS OF THE GOAL CONCEPT
BASED UPON STUDY OF
REACTIONS TO FRUSTRATION

The concept of goal-directed striving is essential to an adequate orientation for most psychological problems. Nevertheless, there has been a great deal of resistance to the frank recognition of this fact, probably because it was too intimately associated in many minds with teleological concepts derived from theology. Psychoanalysis has recognized it for the most part tacitly in its primary interest in motives, wishes, instinctual drives, all of which are concepts implying a goal-directed striving.

Our fear of teleological concepts often persists, however, even after we seem to have accepted the concept of a goal-directed striving. In order to get away from teleological thinking as quickly as possible, we attempt to understand wishes and purposes upon the analogy of a mechanical force, as though the goal were like the pole of a magnet exerting a direct attraction upon the individual.

Only a little reflection, however, is necessary to convince us that this is not a trustworthy analogy.[1] In the first place, the success of a goal-

Slightly modified from a paper read before the American Psychoanalytic Society in Washington, D. C., December 1937: "Modifications of Instinctual Pattern in Reaction to Opportunity and Frustration." Reprinted from *Psychoanalytic Review,* 28, No. 1 (January 1941).

1. Considerations in many respects similar to those here presented have already been discussed by Tolman in a criticism of Lewin's vector concept (E. C. Tolman, "Lewin's Concept of Vectors," *J. Gen'l Psychology,* 7, 1932). Lewin (Kurt Lewin, "Vectors, Cognitive Processes and E. Tolman's Criticism," *J. Gen'l Psychology,* 8, 1933) replied by emphasizing the fact that the forces that he postulates must be understood as acting in a psychological (cognitive) field rather than in physical space and that Tolman's objections could all be met by paying careful attention to the way that the experimental situation must appear in the eyes of the experimental subject. On the other hand,

directed striving depends upon one's *knowing how* to achieve one's goal. In order to overcome an obstacle in the way of a physical force, it is merely necessary to increase the intensity of the force. In order to find satisfaction for a wish, on the other hand, it is necessary to know how the goal is to be reached. No increase in the intensity of the need or of the energy that can be released in the pursuit of a psychological goal will be of any avail unless there is this knowledge of how the energy must be applied.

In the second place, in order to achieve a purpose it is necessary to subordinate one's motor energies to just the kind of activity that is needed. It is difficult to teach a small and active child how to tie a bowknot. The child has too great a motor urge that can be satisfied only by grosser movements. The finer movements necessary in order to tie the knot require restraint, a capacity to inhibit this urge toward gross motor discharge. It is precisely this restraint of which the child is not yet capable.

It is evident, therefore, that it is misleading to think of a wish as a simple force, tending toward fulfillment, that requires no further analysis. The efforts of an organism to fulfill a wish involve a complex process of integration. The subordination of behavior to purpose requires a very considerable degree of organization.

When a machine is running smoothly there is usually little incentive to study its mechanisms. When it gets out of order, our attention is called to those mechanisms responsible for its failing to function. In order to gain insight into the mechanism underlying goal-directed behavior, we turn, therefore, to an attempt to analyze and classify reactions to frustration.

For a number of years Kurt Lewin and others have been studying reactions to frustration experimentally. The experimental procedure has consisted essentially in interrupting or putting obstacles in the way of an activity in order to observe the subsequent fate of the urge behind the interrupted activity. One of the most thorough of these studies is an article by Dembo [2] which deals directly with the problem

---

Lewin feels that it is better not to attempt to speculate concerning the "mechanisms behind the psychological field." I am very much in sympathy with Lewin's efforts to base dynamic analyses of behavior upon an accurate reconstruction of the individual's cognitive field. I feel, however, that the severe frustration reactions encountered in psychopathology cannot be adequately understood without attempting to analyze "the mechanisms behind the psychological field."

2. T. Dembo, "Der Arger als dynamisches Problem," *Psychol. Forsch.*, 15 (1931), 1–144.

we are discussing. Dembo's procedure was to present her experimental subjects with a task that was impossible to solve while at the same time assuring them that a solution was possible. She then allowed them to struggle for hours or even days with this task in order to observe the symptoms of increasing irritation that inevitably developed.

After classifying her subjects' reactions in detail, Dembo arrives at the fundamental thesis that these reactions are best understood as results of a conflict between the attraction exercised by the goal and the ever-increasing repulsion exerted by the obstacle. Dembo makes this point especially clear in her analysis of the motives impelling a subject to a substitute solution [3] such as, for example, throwing a ring over another bottle which is easier to reach than the one which forms the goal of the experiment. Dembo stresses the point that such a substitute solution does not really ease the tension of the subject. For this reason she rejects the idea of a substitute satisfaction. She regards the substitute solution as first of all a flight from the goal or rather from the frustration that results when the subject attempts to reach it. This impulse to flight, however, is modified by the persistence of the original attraction exercised by the goal, but this attraction is now displaced so that it is felt toward the substitute.

Despite Dembo's rejection of the familiar psychoanalytic concept of substitute satisfaction, I think that we may recognize her analysis of substitution reactions as essentially equivalent to the psychoanalytic concept of displacement. When, for example, a forbidden sexual wish finds expression in a dream of walking into a house, we recognize in the symbolic expression a compromise between the original wish and a flight. Freud long ago demonstrated that dreams and symptoms are compromise products. Hysterical vomiting may, for example, give symbolic expression to a pregnancy fantasy. As such, however, it is a compromise product representing not only a fulfillment of the wish to be pregnant but also a rejection of that wish and probably a punishment for it.

The example that we have cited is, of course, more complicated than a simple reaction to frustration. The pregnancy wish is not frustrated by an external obstacle but it is rejected by another part of the personality, by the conscience. On second thought, however, this distinction is not important. It is merely the distinction between an external and an internal frustration. Moreover, we know that the internal frustration once had its origin in an external frustration. The

3. Dembo states that the substitute has acquired a "goal character."

conscience arises by identification with the parent. Fear of the conscience is derived from fear of punishment from the parent or, still more fundamentally, from fear of loss of the parent's love. The obstacle in this instance is not, as in Dembo's experiments, the impossibility of the task. It is fear of the conscience which is at bottom the fear of the loss of the parent's love. However, the resultant behavior, as in Dembo's experiments, is the result of a struggle between two tendencies—between the urge of the original pregnancy wish and the tendency to avoid or flee from the obstacle.

This tendency to flee from the obstacle deserves perhaps some further analysis. In Dembo's experiment the frustration arises merely because the task set by the experiment was impossible of attainment. This represents the simplest type of frustration situation. As intensity of frustration increases, one has an increasing urge to abandon the original goal because striving for it only leads to more and more frustration. In psychoanalysis also we encounter frustrations of this type. When a child's longing for the mother's love has been frustrated by the mother's turning to a younger child, the child may react by an urge to turn away from the mother and to go and seek solace in another love subject.

When frustration is internal, however, the situation is slightly more complicated. The motive for repression or inhibition must also be considered. If the repressing motive is fear—fear of the father, for example—the avoidance reaction—running away from home, for example—may also in this case be characterized as a flight. If the motive for repression is the need to retain the father's love, then the "avoidance of the obstacle" will be more specifically determined by the character of this specific motive for repression. In order to retain the father's love, one will perhaps submit to the father's demands.

We find, therefore, that Dembo's fundamental conclusion corresponds to one of the most fundamental findings of psychoanalysis, that all of the many possible reactions to frustration are dictated by a conflict between the urge toward the original goal and the urge to avoid the frustrating obstacle. This corresponds closely to the psychoanalytic finding that neurotic symptoms, dreams, mistakes in everyday life, and other reactions of the most varied sorts arise as compromise reactions between repressing and repressed forces.

Successful Reactions

Turning our attention first to the successful reactions, we may divide these roughly into two classes according to the relative strength of these two tendencies: the urge toward the original goal, and the tendency to avoid the frustrating obstacle. These two classes of reactions I should like to characterize as:

1) Concentration of the energy of the original wish upon overcoming the obstacle.

2) Deflection of the energy of the original wish in order to avoid the obstacle.

1) CONCENTRATION UPON OVERCOMING THE OBSTACLE

This is the type of reaction to frustration that involves the least modification of the original wish. One attacks the obstacle aggressively. In many cases there is a mobilization of new energy to attain the goal in spite of the obstacle. In other words, the obstacle stimulates one to increased effort. The urge toward the original goal remains in the ascendancy and suffers little deflection. Instead of avoiding the obstacle, one attacks it aggressively. Any tendency to flee from the obstacle is overcompensated by an aggressive attack upon it.

Nevertheless, this concentration of energy upon the obstacle may represent a most intensive modification of the original urge. At least temporarily the original goal is forgotten. The energy of the original wish is concentrated upon the task of overcoming the obstacle. Not the original goal but the obstacle becomes the center of interest.

2) DEFLECTION TO AVOID THE OBSTACLE

When the degree of frustration is somewhat greater, the urge to avoid the obstacle becomes more important, and it becomes necessary to deflect the energy of the original wish away from a direct approach to the goal. This deflection of energy away from the goal may occur in varying degree.

a) In some cases it is merely a question of getting around the obstacle. If one cannot achieve one's end by one means, one finds another means to accomplish the same purpose. A salesman who has failed to bully a customer into buying his goods may try next to win him by flattery.

b) If it is impossible to get around the obstacle, the next step may be to modify the goal, to accept in place of the fulfillment of the original wish some substitute that is just as good or nearly so. If one cannot get meat, one contents oneself with fish. This is the mechanism in successful sublimation. In place of the gratification of a sexual wish, one is able to content oneself with some socially acceptable substitute.

Unsuccessful Reactions

We may now turn to the consideration of the unsuccessful reactions to frustration which are our main interest. These usually involve an exaggeration of either one, or more usually both, of the mechanisms available for successfully dealing with an obstacle.

Concentration upon the obstacle may be either temporary or permanent. A temporary concentration upon the overcoming of obstacles is part of the normal mechanism of purposeful behavior. In order to achieve one's purpose, one must concentrate attention upon one step at a time. One retains only a general orientation as to the importance of this step with reference to the ultimate goal. When one step has been completed, attention is then concentrated upon the next step.

In our psychoanalytic experience, however, we often encounter instances of a permanent fixation upon this mechanism. One turns from the original goal to overcome the obstacle, but the obstacle is never overcome. Instead of giving up the attempt as hopeless, one continues the futile struggle and the original goal is relegated permanently to the background.

Examples of this sort of fixation are very numerous. I shall content myself with mentioning one, fixation upon phallic competition with the father. In this case the original urge is desire for the mother, an urge whose content is partly genital but in most cases contains important pregenital components. The father's relation to the mother, however, looms up as an obstacle. It is impossible to overcome the father, but nevertheless the futile struggle is never abandoned. The energy of the original urge toward the mother becomes concentrated and fixated upon the never-ending struggle to outdo the father. Nearly the whole energy of the original urge toward the mother may become concentrated upon the competitive urge toward the father. This may go so far that women are valued only as means of competition with men. The original urge toward the mother becomes only a sort of setting and background for the competitive striving toward men.

Turning now to the other mechanism for successfully dealing with an obstacle, either getting around the obstacle or acceptance of a satisfactory substitute may be looked upon as a normal method of dealing with a threatened frustration. In either case, one finds a satisfactory outlet for the energy of the original wish and there is no residual conflict. If a satisfactory substitute is not available the avoidance of the obstacle must go further. One is driven to the mechanism of neurotic substitution. Excellent examples of this mechanism are Dembo's experimental subjects who threw a ring over another bottle instead of over the one which had been designated as the goal.

In our psychoanalytic experience this is, of course, first of all the mechanism of symptom formation. The symptom is a substitute gratification for a repressed wish but it cannot be said to be a really satisfactory substitute. Like Dembo's subjects, people who accept neuroses in place of real gratifications give unmistakable evidence that they also feel frustrated. Neurotics for the most part are not happy people. Many of them are continuously under tension. The symptoms are usually painful or distressing. Guilt, either conscious or unconscious, will not permit them real enjoyment even of the substitute gratifications. In the mechanisms of symptom formation, therefore, we see most plainly the conflict between the urge toward the original goal and the urge to avoid the frustrating obstacle which we have postulated as characteristic of all reactions to frustration. The neurotic symptom serves as a substitute gratification and thus gives evidence of the urge toward fulfillment of the wish for which it is a substitute. On the other hand, the symptom is a displaced and unsatisfactory substitute for the real gratification of the original wish and as such is dictated by the necessity of yielding to the repressing forces, by the urge to avoid the obstacle.

To sum up, there are in general two possible ways of dealing successfully with an obstacle. One may either attack and overcome the obstacle or one may adapt oneself to the difficulties in the way of wish fulfillment. In the first case there occurs what we have called the temporary concentration of energy upon the task of overcoming the obstacle. In the second case one adapts oneself to the difficulties by modifying either the wish or the means chosen to find gratification for it. Thus the two fundamental techniques for successfully dealing with an obstacle are (1) attacking and overcoming it or (2) yielding and modifying one's demands to correspond with what is really attainable.

Corresponding to these two fundamental techniques for dealing with an obstacle, there are also two types of unsuccessful reaction. One may continue to struggle with the obstacle, refusing to recognize that the struggle is futile. This is what we have called permanent fixation upon the struggle with the obstacle. This futile struggle gives one the impression of a stubborn rejection of the other possibility, that of adapting one's demands to the real circumstances. Neurotic substitution, on the other hand, is an unsuccessful attempt at the method of adapting one's demands to reality. In accepting a neurotic substitute one renounces the possibility of an adequate satisfaction. The yielding process has gone too far.

In actual experience, however, one usually finds these two types of unsuccessful solution in close association with each other. Fixation upon phallic competition with the father is apt to alternate with submissive reactions toward him. In other cases the competitive striving itself is displaced from the sexual field, according to the mechanism of neurotic substitution. Instead of competition with the father for the mother, there may be competition in the professional field with an employer or other business associate. This constitutes a sort of integration of fixation upon the obstacle with the mechanism of neurotic substitution. One remains fixated upon the competition with the father, but the competitive struggle is displaced to the professional field according to the mechanism of neurotic substitution. In such a case, even if one should win in this secondary struggle with the employer, one has still not overcome the father and is no nearer to winning the mother. It would not be difficult to demonstrate that all of the unsuccessful reactions to frustration combine elements of struggle and of yielding, that they combine, in other words, the mechanism of fixation upon overcoming the obstacle with that of neurotic substitution.

Disintegration of the Goal-seeking Mechanism

The example just given illustrates very clearly the feature that interests us chiefly in the present discussion, a feature that is to some degree characteristic of all unsuccessful reactions. We see here a beginning disintegration of the goal-seeking mechanism. When one struggles futilely to overcome an obstacle, the struggle with the obstacle has already ceased to be a means toward the achievement of the original goal. The same may be said of neurotic substitution. In accepting an inadequate substitute, one has really given up the struggle to attain adequate gratification of the original urge.

We have already pointed out that the organization of behavior for wish fulfillment involves two steps. The first is a cognitive one. One must understand one's situation so as to know how to reach the goal. The second step is executive. It is necessary to subordinate one's motor energies to just the kind of activity that is needed.

The disintegration of the goal-seeking mechanism may affect one or both of these processes. Even in her experimental studies, Dembo noticed "blurring of the boundaries" of the psychological (cognitive) field. In psychoanalysis, we are dealing for the most part with the results of frustrations more disabling than it is permissible to inflict upon an experimental subject and the distortions are correspondingly greater. In the work of symptom formation in neuroses, the latent content of the symptom has always undergone in the unconscious an elaboration according to what Freud calls the primary process. The primary process is one of the most striking manifestations of this disintegration of the organization for purposive behavior. In the work of symptom and dream formation, one gains the impression of a very free displacement of psychic energy from one mental content to another, guided by the principle of avoiding painful and turning to pleasurable mental contents in apparently complete disregard of external reality and of logical or chronological relations. For our present purpose, it is most important to point out that, whereas in rational thought the stream of thought is successfully subordinated to a goal concept, in the primary process the goal concept loses its dominance. This is exactly what we mean when we speak of the disintegration of the goal-seeking mechanism. The disintegration in this case involves the thought processes, thus having to do with the cognitive step in the organization of purposive behavior.

In other cases, the disintegration involves predominantly the executive aspect of this process. Strong emotions, as we know, tend to undermine this capacity to subordinate one's motor energies to purposive activity. When one is very angry it is difficult to think clearly or to perform tasks that require great muscular precision.

Paradoxically enough, the very intensity of a wish or of a need may make impossible effective efforts to satisfy it. In its desperate attempts at flight a chicken will often run in front of an automobile instead of away from it. In an experiment of Koehler's [4] a dog was unable to pull itself away from meat on the other side of the fence, although it would have been quite possible for it to run around through a door in the rear to get it. Everyone has experienced how impatience or the need for hurry tends to paralyze one's capacity for application to painstaking effort.

All of these cases may be well described as instances of a breaking down of the organization necessary for purposive behavior. The more severe reactions to frustration always show such a disintegration of the goal-seeking mechanism.

4. See note 1.

Factors Influencing Character of Disintegration

The manifold variety of neurotic reactions makes it clear that the products of disintegration may vary enormously. The character and degree of disintegration will depend not only upon both the intensity and the suddenness of frustration but also upon the momentary state of organization of the frustrated activity at the time just before it is frustrated. An attack upon a mobilizing army, for example, is liable to have a very different effect according to whether the attack comes early or late in the process of mobilization. Similarly, if a child is caught in the act of stealing we must expect a different reaction than if he is warned at a time when he is only tempted.

The products of disintegration of a frustrated activity should, therefore, offer us valuable evidence for the study of the distribution of energy involved in the organization of the frustrated activity at the moment just prior to frustration.

In the present paper, however, we may take time only for a few examples to illustrate different degrees and varieties of this disintegration process.

Freud has described acute anxiety as a reaction to a situation of extreme helplessness resulting from an overwhelming mass of excitation which the ego is powerless to master. This primary mechanism of release of anxiety is obviously one of the most extreme examples of the disintegration of the goal-seeking mechanism.

In the mechanism that we have described as permanent fixation upon an obstacle, the degree of disintegration of the goal-seeking mechanism is much less severe. It consists merely in the escape from dominance of the primary goal and concentration on a secondary goal, that of overcoming the obstacle. The original wish is permanently relegated to the background to give place to a struggle with the obstacle which has become pretty much an end in itself. The secondary goal, that of overcoming the obstacle, may, however, retain a very effective dominance.

In other cases, the original urge is replaced by what may be characterized as an organized reaction to the scar left by the frustration. Examples of this are extremely frequent in psychoanalytic experience. Examples very frequently encountered are fixations on revenge reactions. A revenge reaction is of little use in achieving the original goal. It implies rather that the urge toward the original goal has been thwarted. Nevertheless, the example of Hannibal's hatred of Rome will remind us that a revenge impulse may furnish a very effective organizing motive for subsequent behavior. A girl who has been jilted becomes fixated upon the impulse to inflict similar humiliation upon men and deprives herself thereby of the possibility of gratifying her original desire for love, but her revenge upon men is achieved most adroitly.

Other examples of frequent occurrences are narcissistic claims based upon the need to compensate for a humiliating memory. Demosthenes' famous reaction to his speech defect is an instance of this sort. As another example I may cite the case of a compulsively conscientious stockbroker. At one time clients of his lost heavily in a financial panic as a result of buying stocks that he had recommended. In reaction to this exceedingly painful experience he became obsessed with a determination to beat the stock market and for years kept most elaborate charts. In this case, however, the compensatory goal proved to be less stably organized, for the patient developed a psychosis just at the point where he felt he was about to realize his obsessive ambition.

CONCLUSION

In conclusion we need only point out that analysis and comparison of frustration reactions give abundant confirmation of our original thesis that it is misleading to speak of goal-directed strivings as simple forces or tendencies. Seeking fulfillment of wishes is a highly organized process, and severe frustration of these organized strivings does not leave them intact but tends to disintegrate them into more elementary strivings which had previously been subordinated to the original goal. Wish-fulfilling fantasies and symbolic symptomatic acts are to be looked upon as the products of such disintegrations of goal-directed strivings.

Chapter Eight

GOAL, MECHANISM, AND INTEGRATIVE FIELD

I. A BIOLOGICAL PROBLEM

Goal-directed Character of Wishes and Drives

The aim of psychoanalysis is the study of human motives. A motive is a concept that implies striving toward a goal. Everyone knows that rational behavior has a purposive goal-seeking character. Psychoanalysis has demonstrated that irrational behavior also is striving, though less successfully, toward the fulfillment of wishes.

We attempt to understand a person's motives by relating them to other motives. The goals of behavior stand to each other in the relation of means to an end. We trace the chain of motivation back from the subsidiary goal, from the means, to the end goal. In this way we arrive at motives or goals that are more or less universal, not only for human beings but for other animals as well. These we call biological needs or drives.

Thus study of human motives leads us inevitably to problems concerning the adaptive character of biological phenomena. The goals that we seek in our conscious, rationally motivated behavior seem to be derived ultimately from biological needs, from goals that antedate our intelligence, from goals that we inherited, that were somehow inherent in the germ plasm from which we developed.

This method of explaining behavior has been subject to abuses. At all stages in the development of psychoanalytic theory we have too often fallen into the loose habit of explaining behavior by referring it back to some biological goal which we assume to be primary. We content ourselves with explaining a patient's neurosis as a manifestation

Reprinted from *Psychosomatic Medicine*, 3, No. 3 (July 1941).

of oral eroticism, or of eros or the death instinct, or of a need for dependence, a biologically founded receptive tendency. Too often we do not even bother to inquire why or under just what circumstances this particular individual needs to be dependent or craves stimulation of his oral mucous membrane or wishes to destroy. We speak as though we thought that these so-called biological tendencies were operating continuously as primary causes, as though all that we needed to do in order to explain behavior were to refer back to one of these primary causes.

Unfortunately, this loose mode of thinking explains everything so easily that the explanation is worthless. If every kind of neurotic behavior is a manifestation of the death instinct, then we really do not know much more than we did before about the motivation of a particular patient's neurosis. No theory of the drives can be of much value unless it can give us some idea of the specific conditions upon which the activity of each drive depends.

It is evident, therefore, that even the concept of the biological drive is inadequate if we think of the drive itself as a primary cause and do not attempt to define accurately the conditions that call it into activity. If we consider the problem carefully we must realize that an adequate definition of a motive or drive must contain at least three parts: (1) a definition of the conditions that call it into activity; (2) a statement of its goal, i.e., of the conditions that will satisfy it, that will temporarily or permanently put an end to its activity; and (3) an analysis of the adaptive mechanisms by means of which the organism strives to achieve this goal and of the limitations which these mechanisms impose upon its ability to reach its goal.

If we attempt to answer these three questions, it soon becomes evident that the drives cannot be regarded as primary causes at all, that analysis of the drives leads us back still further to more general adaptive principles that guided, and themselves were determined by, the process of evolution of the species. In the present study, I shall attempt to contribute to our understanding of these relations by reviewing and analyzing what we know about the mechanisms of goal-directed activity in general.

A Few Definitions

The terms "biological need," "drive," "instinct" have been defined in many different ways and there is as yet no generally accepted convention as to their meaning. In order to avoid useless controversy over what is after all merely a matter of definition of terms, I wish at the outset to define them in the sense in which I propose to use them in this discussion and also to state briefly my motives for so doing.

I start from the empirically observed fact that human beings and other animals under widely varying conditions and by widely varying means behave in such a way as to achieve certain ends. This is true not only of animals whose hereditary pattern of behavior is relatively fixed, but also of those like the human being whose behavior is in large part a matter of acquired habit. Although we know relatively little concerning the exact mechanisms involved, it is therefore evident that even in the case of the most flexible behavior the universal goals toward which it tends must in some way have antedated and guided the learning of the particular habits by means of which a goal is achieved and must therefore in ultimate analysis be part of a hereditary pattern. I therefore define a "drive" as a hereditary tendency to learn habits [1] that tend to achieve a certain end. I also make use of an old distinction between "instinct" and "drive," using "instinct" to designate relatively fixed inherited reaction patterns and "drives" to refer to those more flexible hereditary patterns whose influence is exerted by serving as a guide to the learning process.

My motives for defining "drive" in this way are three:

1) A first prerequisite of a good scientific terminology is that it should properly reflect our ignorance. We know relatively little about the mechanisms of goal-directed behavior and the object of this discussion is to inquire into them. Therefore, in order to avoid prejudicing the discussion I wish to define wishes and drives in terms that imply nothing as to their mechanism.

2) We also do not know just what role consciousness plays in goal-directed behavior, and indeed it is often difficult to determine in a given instance whether or not an animal is conscious of its goal. I therefore wish to define wishes and drives in terms that also imply nothing as to the state of the animal's consciousness [2] concerning them.

3) We know that goal-directed behavior is merely one manifestation, and probably phylogenetically the latest manifestation, of the regulatory or adaptive principle in biology. In this sense an animal's search for food is just another manifestation of the same regulatory principle that is evidenced in the tendency of the acorn to grow into an oak tree. I wish to discuss motivation in terms that do not destroy our realization of this continuity. I therefore group all goal-directed tendencies together and distinguish only the parts of the integrating mechanism

that are learned in the lifetime of the individual from those that are inherited.

Of course I intend no implication as to what is the inherited nucleus of any particular goal-directed striving. In other words, we are not yet able to enumerate the drives or to describe them accurately. This is still a task for experimental investigation.

Resistance Against Finalistic Concepts

I am aware, of course, that there is a widespread resistance among biologists and psychologists against attempting in this way to trace back behavior to inherited "goals that are somehow inherent in the germ plasm." Indeed, I believe that much of the current confusion in our thinking about the influence of heredity upon behavior springs from the fact that we are disturbed by the finalistic implications of the drive concept. We resist thinking clearly about the drives because we have conflicting emotions about their goal-directed character. As scientists we shy away from such concepts. They remind us too much of animistic and theological explanations of the universe and seem to distract us from the real task of science. Our aim as scientists is to understand the world in terms of cause and effect, in terms of uniform sequences. To speak in terms of wishes, purposes, biological drives—this seems to be a lapse from the discipline of strictly mechanistic thinking.

The far-reaching adaptive character of biological phenomena has impressed men throughout the ages and has led to concepts of a directing intelligence that shapes living beings according to a preconceived scheme or plan. As we know, views of this sort have been a serious obstacle in the way of scientific investigation, because of the implication that usually went with them that one must not question the divine intelligence by inquiring further into the mechanism of these adaptive reactions.

In view of the century-long and bitter struggle between science and theology over this point, it is, of course, not strange that there should be a strong urge among psychologists as well as biologists to get rid of finalistic concepts altogether. From this source springs the widespread resistance against the notion of biological drives in the sense that we have just been using it, as inherited goals of behavior.

Natural as is this wish to get rid of finalistic concepts, I doubt very much if any biologist or psychologist has ever yet succeeded in carrying out such a program. The difficulty of thinking in strictly non-finalistic terms becomes apparent when we consider how many essential biological concepts have finalistic implications. The notion of biological function is, of course, a purely finalistic one. It is possible to discuss the mechanisms of a machine in quite mechanistic terms; but even our discussion of the mechanisms of a machine would lose all point and meaning if we should forget the purpose for which the machine is designed. In inquiring into the mechanisms of an automobile we are interested not in just any physicochemical relations between its parts, but rather in the mechanisms that make it run, that enable it to serve as a means of locomotion. In a similar sense we speak of the functions of the different parts of an animal organism. We could speak in exactly the same sense of the functions of different parts of a machine. We wish in each case to understand the mechanism upon which depends the ability of the part or organ to perform its function, to fulfill its purpose in the total economy of the organism.

Equally important are the often unrecognized but unavoidable finalistic implications in our descriptions of behavior. When we say that a child reaches out and grasps an object, we do not describe geometrically what path his hand takes or physiologically just what is the pattern of muscular contractions involved in this act. On the contrary, we describe the act in terms of its goal, which is to hold the object in the hand. Reaching and grasping are goal-directed activities. For the most part the units of behavior are goal-directed acts. For an understanding of the child's behavior, the exact path which his hand takes or the detailed pattern of muscular contractions involved is usually quite irrelevant. To ignore the goal of the child's act would be only to make his behavior quite unintelligible.

The Mechanism of Goal-directed Strivings

Much of our conflict concerning the use of finalistic concepts in our scientific thinking springs from the false assumption that finalistic and mechanistic thinking are necessarily antagonistic to each other. That this is not the case is proved by the analogy to which we have already referred and which has been so very useful in physiology—the analogy between the animal organism and a machine. A machine also has a function, but that does not prevent us from inquiring in detail into the mechanisms by means of which that function is performed. To make just such an inquiry into the mechanisms of goal-directed behavior is indeed the aim of the present study.

To this one might object that, in the case of the machine, the goal is imposed from without. It is the driver, not the automobile, that wishes to move from one place to another, and it was not the automobile itself but human hands that built it for that purpose. In the case of the animal organism, however, the goal-directed striving seems to arise from within the organism itself. In the animal organism, therefore, we have a somewhat more complex problem. In the case of the organism we must try to understand not only how the machine works but also how it got its design. What are the source and genesis of the goals toward which the organism seems to be striving?

In the present state of our knowledge, of course, we are not able to answer questions of this sort. It is interesting that all of our attempts so far to account for the genesis of goal-directed strivings lead us back to preexistent goal-directed strivings whose mechanisms are not yet clear. Learning, as we shall see,[3] usually implies a preexistent wish or drive as its incentive. On the other hand, the principles of natural and sexual selection [4] take for granted the fact of heredity. Heredity itself is obviously a phenomenon comparable to the most highly adaptive goal-seeking behavior. That the developing germ cell finally arrives at a form and dynamic character so closely resembling that of the parent organism is a fact that can obviously not be just taken for granted. It is evident also that the chain of events that is set in motion by the genes and cytoplasm of the germ cell is not a fixed and unalterable sequence of cause and effect. It would seem rather that development must take place under the influence of flexible directing mechanisms similar to the drives—mechanisms that tend toward final states of equilibrium that are relatively fixed, even though under varying circumstances the route by which the final equilibrium is reached may vary widely. A general, in giving orders for a military operation, cannot prescribe in detail what his subordinate generals shall do, but must give them objectives or goals which they are expected to achieve by whatever means unpredictable circumstances may dictate. The development of the organism must be thought of in similar terms. Experimental embryological studies have demonstrated that in the very earliest stages of embryological development even such drastic interference as the removal of half of the egg will not prevent the development of a normal organism. Later there develop more circumscribed embryological fields each with its own particular goal of development; but even the removal of large parts of a limb field, for example, will not prevent the development of a normal limb unless the mutilation occurs after the limb field has itself become differentiated into a number of still more circumscribed fields.[5]

The obvious analogy for regulatory phenomena of this sort would be a physicochemical system that tends toward an equilibrium that remains the same regardless of the starting point or of the route by which the equilibrium is finally reached. Such a tendency to equilibrium may depend upon the universality of certain forces, as in the case of the tendency of water almost inevitably to find its way to the ocean. In other cases the final state of equilibrium is dependent on a high degree of organization which is peculiar to the particular physicochemical system. It is evident that the equilibria toward which the goal-directed tendencies of living beings tend are of the latter sort, comparable to the mechanisms of a complex machine.

For many years Koehler (16, 19) has been attempting by means of psychological experiments to form some idea of the nature of the physicochemical systems that determine the nature of psychological fields. He has also (18) pointed out analogies between psychological and embryological fields from this point of view. Experimental embryologists are also attempting to work out the physicochemical mechanisms responsible for the formation and influence of the embryological fields; and the new science of physiological genetics is attempting to trace in detail the mechanisms by which the inherited potentialities of the germ plasm influence the actual course of development. It is undoubtedly along these lines that we must hope for the final solution of problems concerning the nature and genesis of goal-directed strivings.

In the present study, however, we wish to attack only one small part of this problem. Our present aim is to attempt a dynamic analysis of the organization of goal-directed behavior in general.

II. ORGANIZATION OF GOAL-DIRECTED BEHAVIOR [6]

Pseudo-Mechanical Concepts

At the present time it is customary to simplify these problems for ourselves by thinking of goal-directed strivings in pseudo-mechanical terms. We attempt to understand wishes and purposes upon the analogy of a mechanical force, as though the goal were like the pole of a magnet exerting a direct attraction upon the individual.

Only a little reflection, however, is necessary to convince us that this is not a trustworthy analogy.[7] In the first place, the success of a goal-directed striving depends upon one's *knowing how* to achieve one's goal. In order to overcome an obstacle in the way of a physical force it is merely necessary to increase the intensity of the force. In order to find satisfaction for a wish, on the other hand, it is necessary to know how the goal is to be reached. No increase in the intensity of the need or of the energy that can be released in the pursuit of a psychological goal will be of any avail unless there is this knowledge of how the energy must be applied.

In the second place, in order to achieve a purpose, it is necessary to subordinate one's motor energies to just the kind of activity that is needed. It is difficult to teach a small and active child how to tie a bowknot. The child has too great a motor urge which can be satisfied only by grosser movements. The finer movements necessary in order to tie the knot require restraint, a capacity to inhibit this urge toward gross motor discharge. It is precisely this restraint of which the child is not yet capable.

It is evident, therefore, that it is misleading to think of a wish as a simple force, tending toward fulfillment, that requires no further analysis. The efforts of an organism to fulfill a wish involve a complex process of integration. The subordination of behavior to purpose requires a complex machinery and a highly organized mechanism of dynamic control.

Hierarchy of Goals—Cognitive Field and Executive Task

The nature of the dynamic organization necessary for goal-directed striving seems most transparent in the case of conscious rational behavior. Upon even the most superficial analysis, our deliberate purposive behavior resolves itself into a whole system or hierarchy of goal-directed acts that stand to each other in the relation of end and means. Knowing how to achieve a goal is first of all a matter of resolving the task of reaching the goal into a number of simpler goal-directed acts which serve as means toward the attainment of the original goal. The desire for the end goal successively activates efforts directed toward subsidiary goals. A mother wishes, for example, to feed her child. In her desire to satisfy the child's hunger she goes to the store, buys food, brings it home, cooks it, calls the child, and finally feeds it. Each of these successive activities is itself a goal-directed act which in process of its execution must itself be resolved into a series of still simpler goal-directed acts.

It is evident further that the end goal, the desire to feed the child, must not only activate the several subsidiary goals, but must also time them in relation to each other and to the total situation. All this takes place under the directing influence of a cognitive field. This cognitive field must itself first be created before it can exert its directing influence. This takes place usually under the impelling force of the original goal-directed striving. One begins to consider by what means one's wish can be satisfied. If we are successful in finding adequate means to reach our goal, we say that we *know how* to achieve it.

Thus the problem as to how behavior is subordinated to a goal-directed striving resolves itself into two parts, one cognitive, the other executive. We must inquire first how the goal-directed striving builds up its cognitive field and, second, by what means one is able, under the guidance of the cognitive field, to direct one's motor energies to just the kind of activity that is needed.

Genesis of Cognitive Field

Just how does a goal-directed striving build up its cognitive field? How does one find out how one's goal is to be achieved?

As we know, there are two possible answers to this question. One's practical knowledge of how a goal can be reached may be based upon what one has learned from previous experience or it may be based upon some inherited capacity that did not need to be learned.

The process of learning has been the subject of the most extensive investigation. Pavlov (25) and others have attempted to reduce it to its simplest terms in their investigations of conditioned reflexes. According to Pavlov, a conditioned stimulus—the sound of a metronome, for example—acquires the reflex properties of the unconditioned stimulus that immediately follows it (for example, the taste of food in the dog's mouth). This formula, however, does not fit the usual case in which the animal is learning how to reach a goal. The acts that enable an animal to reach food are not the same as those provoked by the taste of food in its mouth. It is obvious that Pavlov's original formulation does not fit this sort of learning.[8] The facts would seem rather to correspond to the more popular formula of common-sense psychology, that it is those motor reactions that lead to the satisfaction of a drive or wish that tend to become positively conditioned. This principle has been called by Thorndike (26) the law of effect.

We note now, however, that this common-sense formulation already implies a preexistent goal-directed striving, a wish or a drive. In view of this fact, it would seem to simplify matters to follow the suggestion of the Gestalt school of psychology in regarding the process of conditioning as merely the most elementary example of the process of building up a cognitive field.[9] The cry of an infant, for example, is followed by the satisfaction of its hunger. After this has happened once or several times, the infant integrates crying and the satisfaction of its hunger into a single cognitive field. The infant has gained a new insight. It has learned how to get food by crying for it. At a later time this knowledge can be utilized when the infant again desires food. This interpretation of conditioning as a process of gaining a new insight receives confirmation from the fact that knowledge acquired during the pursuit of one goal may also be utilized in learning how to reach quite another goal.[10] In the process of trying to find out how a new goal is to be reached, one must begin by orienting oneself as to one's present situation in relation to the goal and then proceed to piece together bits of knowledge that one may have acquired at various times and under various circumstances in order to build up a plan of how the new goal is to be reached.

Human experiments indicate that simple conditioning often takes place without the conscious knowledge of the subject. In other words, a cognitive field may be built up and later utilized in the guidance of behavior without the subject's ever having been conscious of it. This, of course, will not surprise psychoanalysts, who are already familiar with phenomena that we are obliged to interpret as evidence of unconscious insight.

In our subsequent discussion, therefore, it will be of advantage to disregard the distinction between conscious and unconscious insight. By "cognitive field" or "practical insight" we mean a mechanism capable of registering and integrating stimuli in such a way as to make possible a more or less flexible adaptation to varying situations in order to achieve an end goal. A purely mechanical example would be a thermostat or a telephone dialing system; or we may turn to physiology and find examples in the mechanisms in the central nervous system for maintaining a constant body temperature, or for maintaining equilibrium in the upright position.

In general, we attempt to understand goal-directed behavior in terms of two factors. We try first to learn what a person wants, what is his goal, and then to determine what he knows about how to get it. Once we have some insight into what he wants, then by comparing what he does under varying circumstances, we can infer what he knows and what he does not know about how to get it. Conversely, if we know both the goal of his behavior and the content and limitations of his cognitive fields, then we should be able to predict precisely the range and flexibility of his adaptive responses to varying conditions.

As we have seen, however, the motives that guide our rational conscious behavior seem to be derived ultimately from biological needs, from goal-directed urges that we inherited. How did these biological drives acquire their apparent "knowledge" of how their goal is to be reached? The accepted biological theory concerning this point accounts most easily for those cases in which the adaptive response is a relatively fixed one. The theory of natural selection, which originated with Darwin, points out that the needs which these adaptive responses serve are vital for the survival of the organism or of the species. The adaptive responses themselves, it is now believed, were hit upon by accident in the course of millions of successive chance mutations of the germ plasm; but only those responses which could best insure the survival of individual organism and race could be passed on to future generations.

In human behavior, however, fixed adaptive responses of this sort play a much less important role than in many other animals. For this reason, we are accustomed to distinguish between these hereditarily fixed responses which we call instincts and other much more flexible goal-directed strivings which we call drives. In the case of these less fixed reactions, the biological need, at least in many cases, must exert its influence upon behavior through the learning process. We have already seen that learning usually implies, as incentive to learn, a pre-existent goal-directed striving, a wish or a drive. From this point of view a drive may be defined as a tendency to learn habits that are effective in relieving the tension of an underlying biological need; or, in still other words, we may define the drive as a tendency to build up cognitive fields[11] that facilitate the relief of such a tension.

From this it follows that the organization of a drive in relation to its goal consists of at least two parts: (1) a physiological tension more or less specific for the particular drive; and (2) mechanisms that have been inherited or learned by means of which this tension can be relieved. We must assume, for example, that a newborn infant may be hungry without having any idea how its hunger is to be satisfied. The tension arising from its hunger is discharged in diffuse motor activity. Only the sucking movements of the lips give us a hint that the infant's tension is to be satisfied by taking something into the mouth. At first the infant knows only that it is uncomfortable. Before it can do anything purposive about it, it must first learn how to satisfy its hunger; it must learn more definitely what it wants and what to do in order to get it. Thus knowledge based upon experience tends to concentrate the diffuse motor restlessness of the child upon more sharply differentiated efforts to achieve a more circumscribed goal. The diffusely radiating excitation of the child's hunger (see Fig. 1-A) is supplemented perhaps by appetite for a particular food which concentrates the child's energies (Fig. 1-B) upon a particular plan for getting it and may

FIGURE 1-A   FIGURE 1-B

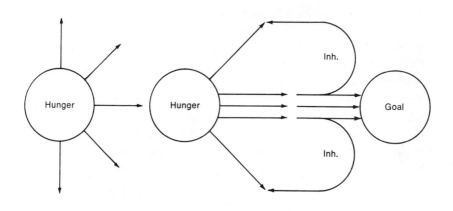

→ indicates tension and its direction

perhaps also inhibit (Fig. 1-B inh.) other and disturbing manifestations of the child's restlessness.

The Executive Task—Subordination of Behavior to Purpose

In order to get a more adequate picture of this process of concentration of energy upon more specific goals, we must now turn to the study of the executive aspect of goal-directed behavior. We may gain some insight into the directive influence of the cognitive field by studying reactions to frustration.

When difficulties or obstacles are put in the way of a goal-directed striving, the task of overcoming these difficulties becomes at once a subsidiary goal. In order to reach the original goal, it is necessary first to overcome the obstacle. In general there are two methods of getting past an obstacle: (1) one may remove or destroy it; or (2) one may avoid the obstacle and attempt to get around it. In either case the energy of the original goal-directed striving must be concentrated upon this subsidiary task.

Concentration upon overcoming the obstacle is the type of reaction to an obstacle that involves the least modification of the original wish. One attacks the obstacle aggressively. In many cases there is a mobilization of new energy to attain the goal, in spite of the obstacle. The obstacle stimulates one to increased effort.

When the degree of obstruction is somewhat greater, the urge to avoid the obstacle becomes more important and it becomes necessary to deflect the energy of the original wish away from a direct approach to the goal. This *deflection* of energy to avoid the obstacle may occur in varying degrees. (*a*) In some cases, it is merely a question of getting around the obstacle. If one cannot achieve one's end by one means, one finds another means to accomplish the same purpose. A salesman who has failed to bully a customer into buying his goods may try next to win him by flattery. (*b*) If it is impossible to get around the obstacle, the next step may be to modify the goal, to accept in place of the fulfillment of the original wish some substitute that is just as good or nearly so. If one cannot get meat, one contents oneself with fish.

Disintegration of Goal-seeking Mechanisms

If the difficulties in the way of a goal-directed striving become insurmountable the original end goal may lose its dominance and the subsidiary goals of overcoming or avoiding the obstacle may become ends in themselves. Examples of this sort of fixation upon a traumatic frustration are very numerous and indeed cover the whole field of psychopathology. In such reactions, flights from the frustrating memory and attempts at aggressive mastery of it are apt to alternate or to be condensed together in all sorts of combinations. A boy who has been frustrated by the mother's preference for an older brother may at one time turn away from women altogether. At other times he may turn his whole energy upon a competitive struggle with other men. This may go so far that women are valued only as a means of competition with men. Or a girl who has been jilted may become fixated upon the impulse to inflict similar humiliation upon men and may deprive herself thereby of the possibility of gratifying her original desire for love. Or instead of attempting to master her frustration by defiant or revengeful behavior, a neurotic girl may accept choking sensations or some other hysterical symptom as an unsatisfactory and unpleasant symbolic substitute for forbidden sexual wishes.

Thus in every psychopathological manifestation there is a disintegration of the goal-seeking mechanism. The goal-directed striving, instead of successfully directing behavior toward a single purpose, now loses its dominance. Goals that have previously played a subsidiary role as means to an end now escape from the dominance of the end goal and become ends in themselves. As a result, behavior becomes some sort of a confused resultant of the struggle for dominance between competing goals.

Neuroses and psychoses, as we know, are the products of psychic conflict. The disruptive influence of competing goals undermines still further the effective dominance of any one goal, and may lead to the most irrational and paradoxical behavior.

The distintegration of the goal-seeking mechanism may affect either its cognitive or its executive aspect, or both. In the cognitive sphere, we find evidence of this disintegration of the goal-seeking mechanism in the peculiar mode of elaboration of mental contents that is characteristic of the dream work and of the process of symptom formation in the neuroses. Freud (6) calls this the primary process. The primary process is one of the most striking manifestations of this disintegration of the organization for purposive behavior. In the work of symptom and dream formation, one gains the impression of a very free displacement of psychic energy from one mental content to another, guided by the principle of avoiding painful and turning to pleasurable mental contents in apparently complete disregard of external reality and of logical or chronological relations. For our present purpose it is important to point out that, whereas in rational thought the stream of thought is successfully subordinated to a goal concept, in the primary process the goal concept loses its dominance. This is what we mean when we speak of the disintegration of the goal-seeking mechanism. The disintegration in this case involves the thought processes, thus having to do with the cognitive step in the organization of purposive behavior.

In other cases, the disintegration involves predominantly the executive aspect of this process. Strong emotions, as we know, tend to undermine the capacity to subordinate one's motor energies to purposive activity. When one is very angry it is difficult to think clearly or to perform tasks that require great muscular precision.

Struggle for Dominance Between Different Goals

Thus analysis of reactions to frustration gives us a picture of subsidiary goal-directed strivings escaping from the dominance of the end goal. This would seem to be conclusive evidence for the fact that even in rational, effective, purposeful behavior, the integrative capacity of the dominant goal-directed striving is quantitatively limited. Each goal exerts its integrative influence through the medium of a cognitive field. Under the guiding direction of its cognitive field, each goal strives toward its own end by activating or releasing subsidiary goal-directed strivings and inhibiting antagonistic goals. If a single goal maintains effective dominance, the subsidiary goals are activated and released according to schedule. If no single integrating goal can maintain its dominance, the conflict between competing goals gives rise to the cognitive confusion of the primary process and to the irrational and paradoxical behavior characteristic of neuroses and psychoses. Except in the most acute phases of a neurosis, however, a curative tendency, a tendency toward integration, can also be noted. Freud (13) has called attention to the fact that the central function of the ego is to reconcile conflicting strivings. Out of this need for reconciliation arise new goals whose aim is to bring the two conflicting strivings into harmony with each other. A child whose forbidden impulses threaten it with loss of the parent's love will seek to win back the parent by confession; or the need to find a solution for an insoluble emotional conflict may find a displaced expression in a compulsive interest in solving philosophical problems.

III. DYNAMIC ANALYSIS OF GOAL-DIRECTED BEHAVIOR

Psychic Tension and Integrative Capacity

We might perhaps expect that the most intense wish would be the one most likely to attain dominance over other goals. Paradoxically enough, however, the very intensity of a wish or of a need may make impossible effective efforts to satisfy it. In its desperate attempts at flight a chicken will often run in front of an automobile instead of away from it. In an experiment of Koehler's (17) a dog was unable to pull itself away from meat on the other side of the fence although it would have been quite possible to run around through a door in the rear to get it. Moreover, everyone has experienced how impatience or the need for hurry tends to paralyze one's capacity for application to painstaking effort.

We gain some insight into this apparent paradox if we recall that a biological need or drive implies a state of disturbed equilibrium or physiological unrest that tends first of all to be discharged in diffuse motor activity, and that this diffuse excitation is only later concentrated upon more circumscribed goals [12] as a result of knowledge gained from subsequent experience. Thus the original urge to escape an unpleasant tension is supplemented by an attraction to a more circumscribed goal that is desired also for its own sake. Hunger is supplemented by appetite. Under the polarizing influence of this compound craving, a cognitive field is built up which must then inhibit any disturbing remnant of the original tendency to diffuse motor discharge and must subordinate activity to the task in hand.

It is evident, therefore, that the capacity of a goal-directed striving to maintain its dominance depends first of all upon the ability of its cognitive field to inhibit and regulate the tendency of its own underlying tension to seek discharge in diffuse motor activity. This ability to withstand tension we may designate quantitatively as the *integrative capacity* of a goal-directed striving.

Fantasy, Confidence, and Integrative Capacity

Our next problem will be to inquire into the dynamic sources of this integrative capacity of a cognitive field.

We gain some light upon this question by recalling the effectiveness of dreams or fantasies in temporarily quieting disturbing tensions. If we are in danger, we recall memories of how we once escaped from other dangers. If we are hungry, we dream of food.

Dreams and fantasies, however, are not permanently satisfying. There is a tendency for the disturbing tension to reassert itself. If one is to achieve more permanent relief, fantasy must be activated into purpose. This occurs apparently by a sort of fusion or synthesis of the satisfaction derived from fantasy with the tension of the original need. As a result of this synthesis,[13] one becomes dissatisfied with mere fantasy. The fantasy takes on the partly unpleasant quality of an unsatisfied wish, and one feels the need to strive for the realization of one's fantasies. On the other hand, just as a satisfying or reassuring fantasy has been able temporarily to quiet a disturbing tension, so now the hope of success in achieving one's purpose is able to diminish the tension of the underlying need [14] and its tendency to diffuse motor discharge.

It is this hope of success, which has all the satisfying value of a fantasy, that now is able to give the cognitive field [15] its integrative capacity. The knowledge of how to achieve one's goal now acquires the quality of hope and expectation of future satisfaction. The hope of achieving one's goal tends to concentrate the tendency to diffuse motor discharge upon more sharply defined efforts directed toward the goal. This hope also gives to one's plans the capacity to withstand antagonistic tensions. For the sake of realizing one's hope of success, one becomes willing to forgo other satisfactions and to withstand the painful pressure of disturbing tensions.

Thus the intensity of a wish is not the only factor that affects its integrative capacity. Equally important is the factor of confidence in one's ability to achieve the goal. It is upon this principle that the war propaganda of which we hear so much today is striving continuously to undermine the enemy's confidence. One is much more ready to make sacrifices in order to attain a goal if one feels sure that one's efforts will meet with success, but by undermining confidence, one weakens the energy of the enemy's purpose. It is evident, therefore, that the effective integrative capacity of a goal-directed striving depends not only upon the intensity of one's desire but also upon one's confidence in the ability to achieve it.

Obviously, the most objective basis for such confidence is the memory of previous success in achieving the same or similar goals. One makes a sort of intuitive estimate of the probability of success based upon one's previous experiences of success or failure. We all know, however, that one's expectations of success or failure are not so objective as this. Sometimes quite generalized moods [16] of optimism or pessimism result from success or failure in quite unrelated spheres or from endogenous physiological factors whose cause may not be easy to discover.

Integrative Capacity and Integrative Task

It is obvious that the success of a goal-directed striving will depend not only upon its own integrative capacity, but also upon the state of readiness of the subsidiary goals that it must employ as means. Much depends, therefore, upon the question of whether these subsidiary mechanisms are enjoyed for their own sake or whether they must be forced into activity by the central integrating field. In other words, we must consider not only the integrative capacity of a goal-directed striving, but also its integrative task.

We may illustrate these relations most clearly by reference to the phenomena of sublimation. Some boys love to build things. Such a boy later may find his work as a carpenter or an engineer quite fascinating, whereas another man might find the same work quite irksome. In the first case the work will require relatively little effort. In psychoanalytic terminology, we should say that the work was highly eroticized for him or that it had a high cathexis of psychic energy. In the second case, the work will require much more effort and may be done only because it is necessary in order to earn a living. Under these circumstances the work will require much more effort. The man whose purpose is to earn a living will be faced with a much greater integrative task than in the case of the man who enjoys his work for its own sake.

We encounter a similar problem in relation to possible competing goals. If it is necessary to interrupt a child's play in order to get the child to do some task, much will depend on just how this is done. Sometimes it is possible to make the task interesting to the child. The child's active interest turns away from its play to the work it is being required to do. The little girl who has been playing house may be induced to feel that washing the dishes is merely a more interesting continuation of her play. In such a case the integrative task in this activity will be relatively light because the work is enjoyed for its own sake. If the mother's devices fail, however, and the work is felt as an interruption to the child's more interesting play, then the play remains as a competing goal and the child's integrative task in compelling herself to work will be much greater.

We have defined the integrative capacity of a goal-directed striving as the amount of tension it is able to withstand without showing signs of disintegration. Similarly, we may define the integrative task of a goal-directed striving in quantitative terms as the amount of tension that its integrative field must withstand in order to subordinate behavior to its end goal. As we have seen, the goal-directed striving, acting through the medium of its cognitive or integrative [17] field, must not only inhibit antagonistic strivings but must also activate one subsidiary goal after another, all in accordance with the time schedule of the cognitive field. The sum of the tensions arising out of antagonistic strivings plus the resistance of subsidiary goals to activation constitutes at any given moment the integrative task. If signs of disintegration of the goal-directed striving appear, we take this as a measure of its integrative capacity, as evidence that its integrative task is now in excess of its integrative capacity.

Functional Readiness and Functional Reluctance of Physiological Mechanisms

Not only subsidiary goals but also elementary physiological mechanisms differ widely as to their functional readiness for activation by a dominant goal-directed striving. In a state of health and rest, most functional activity is pleasurable. A healthy child loves to be active for the very joy of activity and has an eager interest in sensory impressions of all kinds, and its mind is continuously and spontaneously active with all sorts of questions. Activity is interesting for its own sake, quite independent of or in addition to one's interest in the particular goal toward which one is striving. If there is no task at hand, the child is eager to find something to do. In states of ill health or fatigue, on the other hand, one may find that it requires effort to be active and there may be a desire to withdraw from sensory stimuli which at other times would be experienced as pleasurable but which now imply an unwelcome spur to activity. In sleep, this withdrawal from both activity and sensory stimulation is more or less complete.

It would seem reasonable, therefore, to regard these varying attitudes toward stimulation and activity as part of a system of mechanisms for the regulation of the level of functional activity in the various organs. An indispensable prerequisite for the possibility of adaptive or goal-directed behavior is the fact that the organism contains organs and physiological mechanisms that are equally available for many different purposes. It is the function of a muscle to contract, but the contraction of any one muscle may form a part of the most varied patterns of contracting muscle groups and may be subordinated to goals of the most diverse kinds. The same muscle may help one moment to build something, another moment to destroy it. All depends upon the total pattern of innervation to which its functional activity is subordinated.

In order to make this possible, it is necessary that the different organs and functional systems be capable of being activated whenever they are needed by the adaptive mechanisms of the organism, but it is also important that their readiness to respond to such activation be regulated in accordance with the physiological state of the activated organ itself. If an organ is diseased or excessively fatigued, stimulation to functional activity may be harmful. On the other hand, if the organ is healthy and in a good state of rest, functional activity may even be beneficial. In the state of excessive fatigue, therefore, the organ needs protection from activation, whereas in the state of healthy vigor, as in the play of children, one craves stimulation and activity and there may even be an urge to go in search of tasks to occupy one's senses and muscles and mind.

It is not difficult to bring these mechanisms into relation with certain facts from general physiology. One of the fundamental properties of protoplasm is irritability, the capacity to react to stimulation. This property is obviously dependent upon the fact that in each tissue there is stored latent energy that is released or discharged by appropriate stimulation. Just how a tissue will respond to stimulation in a particular instance will depend not only upon the character of the tissue and of the stimulus, but also upon the intensity and duration of the stimulation. A tissue or organ will react with its appropriate functional activity only if the intensity and duration of the stimulus exceed the minimal threshold for functional response of that tissue. In addition to this minimal threshold there is also a maximal threshold. In general, if this maximal threshold is exceeded, the excessive stimulation will result increasingly in destructive changes in the tissue rather than in functional activity.

These thresholds obviously will vary according to the functional state of the organ stimulated. In general, we may expect that fatigue will tend both to raise the minimal threshold for functional activity and to lower the maximal threshold at which functional activity begins to be impaired. On the other hand, we may expect that in states of high functional readiness the minimal threshold will perhaps be lower and the upper dangerous threshold higher.

These variations of threshold according to the functional state of the stimulated organ are also supplemented by regulatory mechanisms on a higher integrative level. In order to protect the fatigued or unhealthy tissue against excessive stimulation, we experience what we may characterize as a sort of reluctance to activity which may or may not be conscious but which exerts an inhibitory influence [18] upon the tendency of any integrative field to activate this particular tissue. Similarly, the increased readiness of the healthy tissue for activation is supplemented by some sort of eagerness for activity which again may or may not be conscious but will exert a facilitating influence upon the tendency of any integrating field to activate that particular organ. Indeed, the frequent need of healthy, happy children to find "something to do" would even seem to imply that in such cases the need for functional activity may play the dominant role, and wishes and tensions derived from other biological needs might play a relatively negligible role, in activating a particular integrative field. A child may ride a bicycle, for example, not so much because it wants to get to any particular place but just for the pure joy of riding.

It is in this way, probably, that we can best understand the craving for stimulation of the various "erotic zones" which plays such an important role in the behavior of even the youngest infants. Freud has pointed out that these cravings for stimulation tend first of all to be attached to other organic functions, to the need for nourishment or for excretion. Finally, many of them are subordinated at puberty as forepleasure mechanisms to the "primacy of the genital zone" [19] and to the biological goal of reproduction of the species. On the other hand, as Freud has pointed out, stimulation of the erotic zones is desired also for its own sake, quite independent of any activation by hunger or by tensions arising out of the reproductive function. It is this independent kernel of desire for stimulation for its own sake that I should like to identify with the need for functional activity of healthy physiological mechanisms. In this connection its significance would be twofold. It is a direct manifestation of the need for functional activity of the sense organs themselves, but it is also an indirect manifestation of a need for activation of muscles and effector systems seeking for stimuli to activate them.

Psychic Tension and Psychic Energy

In psychoanalysis we are accustomed to use somewhat loosely the phrases "free psychic energy," "excess" or "superabundance of psychic energy," "lack of free psychic energy." In the light of the above discussion it is now possible to give these phrases a more precise meaning. Let us assume a hypothetic threshold at which the craving for functional activity of an organ disappears, at which "functional reluctance" appears in place of "functional readiness." At this threshold point we might picture a physiological system as supplied with its normal quota of psychic energy; above or below this threshold we might speak of "excess of psychic energy" or "lack of psychic energy" respectively. Thus, somewhat schematically, if an organ or functional system is in a state of functional readiness, craving activity, we may picture it as filled with more than its normal quota of energy and ready to over-flow.[20] On the other hand, if an organ is in a state of fatigue or functional reluctance, we may picture it as lacking its normal quota of energy and therefore resistant to activation and to discharge of its already deficient stock of energy.

We picture the relation between psychic tension and psychic energy as an extremely flexible and adaptive one. Psychic energy is activated by psychic tensions and psychic tension tends to be neutralized by the activation of psychic energy. Especially the activation of energy that is ready for discharge is experienced as pleasurable and tends to neutralize the activating tension. As an example of this, we may cite the common observation that one can diminish the intensity of hunger or fear by doing something about it, even though food or safety may not be immediately available. We have also called attention [21] to the ability of satisfying fantasies to quiet disturbing tensions. Similarly, children use masturbation or thumb-sucking as a consolation for feelings of frustration or as a means of binding or "erotizing" anxiety. In an obstetrical hospital, for example, I once saw a minor but painful operation performed on a very young infant with no anaesthetic other than a bit of gauze soaked in sugar water which the infant was allowed to suck. It sucked very vigorously but did not once whimper or cry during the whole operation.

Most important are the quantitative relations between psychic energy and the activating tension. If the energy of a functional system is below its "normal" quota, we may picture its "functional reluctance" as opposing any activating tension. If the activating tension is great, however, it may overpower the opposing tension of the functional reluctance until such time as increasing resistance is able to equal and counterbalance the activating tension. We shall designate as "available psychic energy" the amount of energy that may be activated before this point of equilibrium between activating tension and functional reluctance is reached.

If there is no strong activating or inhibiting tension, the need for discharge of energy will manifest itself in spontaneous playful [22] activity that is ready for anything, that seems to run in search of goals to occupy it.

The tendency of excessive energy to discharge may, however, be opposed by an inhibitory tension, thus giving rise to an ever-increasing pressure demanding release of the dammed-up energy. As examples, we may cite the traumatic consequences that ensue when a child's hands are tied to prevent it from sucking its thumb or when toilet training is too early, too sudden, or too severe.

Tension of a Drive and Its Resources

Just as we contrasted integrative capacity and integrative task, so also it is useful to distinguish carefully between (1) the tension of a drive or wish, and (2) the resources or means available to satisfy it. As we have seen, a psychic tension is a state of need that does not imply any knowledge of means or indeed the existence of any means to satisfy it. Sometimes the possibility of satisfying one's desire is dependent upon external circumstances. One cannot satisfy one's hunger unless there is food within reach. But one's ability to satisfy one's needs is not dependent upon external circumstances alone. One must also have resources within oneself. The most important of these necessary internal resources are knowledge of how to attain one's goal, sufficient confidence in the success of one's strivings to encourage one to pursue one's goal effectively, and a state of relative functional readiness in the organs whose functional activity may be required. Thus briefly we may divide the internal resources of a drive into (1) those based upon previous experience, and (2) those dependent directly upon the momentary physiological state of the organism.

1) In much of the current discussion of the drives we seem to ignore the fact that, at least in human behavior, practically every one of the important drives must *learn how* to attain its goal. The drive itself consists only of a rather helpless excitement or tension and a few rudimentary instinctive motor mechanisms plus the capacity to learn and retain other motor mechanisms that may later succeed in reaching the goal of the drive. In a very important sense the drive originally does not even "know" its own goal. The goal exists only as a potential incentive for the learning process, as a tendency to reinforce and cause the retention of motor mechanisms that have once been successful in reaching it. Probably the first step in this learning process is to learn to know what one wants. The latent or potential goal of a drive must become an actual incentive. One must learn that food quiets hunger. This is the most elementary cognitive field by means of which the drive can exert its influence upon subsequent learning. Under the guiding influence of this knowledge, one can then begin to learn how to get food.

It is important, therefore, to keep constantly in mind the modifying influence of the learning process as contrasted with the rather helpless excitement arising out of the tension of the original biological need. The goal of such a tension is a negative one, merely to escape the unpleasant tension, and its tendency is toward diffuse motor discharge. It is knowledge and hope based upon the memory of previous success, on the other hand, that give one a positive and more sharply circumscribed goal. We must distinguish carefully between this positive attraction toward a more circumscribed goal and the negative and diffuse need merely to escape from an unpleasant tension. In general, the goal of one's strivings is also desired for its own sake and not only as a means of escape from an unpleasant tension.

In building up the integrative capacity of a goal-directed tendency, this positive attraction of the goal plays a most important role. Hopes and purposes, as we have seen, are derived from fantasies and retain some of the satisfying character of fantasies. Confident of attaining one's goal, one already enjoys one's success in anticipation. The pleasure derived from the anticipation now tends to neutralize the tension of the underlying need and in this way to diminish its tendency to diffuse motor discharge. Finally, the positive attraction of the goal tends to direct the diffuse motor discharge of tension into more circumscribed channels by facilitating those motor pathways that lead to this particular goal and inhibiting those that would interfere.

It is evident, therefore, that the fate of the tension of a drive at any given time is largely dependent upon the extent of its resources in terms of past learning and of the memory of previous success. If these resources are not available the tension must continue to rise, seeking constantly for discharge in diffuse motor activity which never leads to real satisfaction of the underlying need. On the other hand, if the drive tension is supplemented by knowledge and by confidence that one knows how to reach the goal, then the motor discharge is channeled and integrated and is likely to result in achievement of the goal and quieting of the underlying need.

From all of this it follows how erroneous it is to attempt to jump in one step from the analysis of actual behavior to conclusions concerning "fundamental biological tendencies" in the hereditary constitution of an individual. As we have just seen, the hereditary pattern in the human being consists almost exclusively of drives that are helpless to attain their ends. Only learning and the experience of success can make an individual less helpless. If an individual's behavior is predominantly characterized by attitudes of helplessness and dependence, it is quite unjustifiable to conclude, therefore, that he was born with a very strong dependent or "oral erotic" tendency in his hereditary constitution. It is only after very careful genetic analysis of the resources derived from an individual's life history that we can safely attempt to deduce any conclusions concerning the nature of his inherited drives. Without such genetic analysis, the character of his observed behavior can obviously tell us nothing trustworthy about his hereditary patterns.

2) In estimating the internal resources of a drive it is also important to consider the physiological state of the organism itself. We have already discussed the importance of the state of functional readiness of subsidiary mechanisms. It is also of importance to take into account the functional readiness of the integrative field. We have already called

attention to the fact that confidence in one's ability to achieve one's goals is not always based upon memory of previous successes, but may be part of a quite generalized mood of optimism resulting in some cases from endogenous physiological factors. We may now take account of these endogenous factors in our scheme by thinking of them as affecting directly the state of functional readiness of the integrative field itself. Moreover, it is not only the hope of success that one enjoys. One also enjoys for their own sake the skill and self-mastery of successful purposive behavior. What we have called the integrative capacity of a goal-directed striving is built up out of these two factors—anticipation of success and joy in planful activity for its own sake. We may probably look upon both as manifestations of the functional readiness of the integrative field.

There seems good reason to assume also that the influence of previous success or failure in determining the level of confidence may be effected through the medium of the influence of success or failure upon the state of functional readiness or fatigue of the integrating mechanism. One is frequently able to observe clinically that a short period of the tension of unsuccessful effort or of an unresolved conflict is more fatiguing than a whole day of strenuous but successful work. It seems probable, therefore, that memories of previous failures will tend to induce more rapid fatigue of the integrative field and in this way rapidly to diminish its integrative capacity. Certain observations of Pavlov seem to be in harmony with this conclusion. Pavlov reports that many repetitions of a conditioned reflex will inevitably result in a slow transition to inhibition of the conditioned reflex. The development of inhibition, however, takes place much more slowly if there is prompt reinforcement of the conditioned reflex by its being followed with its proper unconditioned stimulus. Pavlov (25) himself explains this fact by suggesting that the cortical excitation resulting from a conditioned stimulus is probably much more prolonged and results in much greater fatigue if the reflex is not promptly reinforced. He illustrates his concept of the significance of reinforcement by citing the analogy of "an efficient and watchful signalman who after having performed his responsible duties has to be provided with an immediate rest during which he is refreshed, so that he may afterwards perform his task again with the same efficiency as before."

In this way we approach some understanding of the physiological basis for our hypothesis that confidence of success is closely related to the functional readiness of the integrative field, whereas loss of confidence would be correlated with fatigue of the integrative field.

Summary: Dynamic Source and Mode of Operation of an Integrative Field

Let us now make use of these somewhat schematic concepts to summarize in as simple terms as possible our picture of the dynamic relationships (1) between a biological need and the integrative field of a goal-directed striving derived from it, and (2) between this integrative field and subsidiary mechanisms.

1) We have seen that the integrative capacity of a wish or drive tends to be undermined when its intensity becomes too great. On the other hand, confidence based either upon the memory of previous success or upon endogenous factors tends to enhance the integrative capacity. These facts may be readily understood upon the hypothesis that the integrative capacity of a cognitive field results from activation of its "available psychic energy" by the tension of the underlying need. In accordance with the facts to be explained, we assume that memories of previous successes constitute a sort of reservoir of energy in the integrating mechanism which may also be enhanced or diminished by other factors that affect its physiological state of readiness (i.e., the endogenous factors influencing confidence). The paradoxical relations between tension and integrative capacity can then be understood as follows. So long as the tension does not exceed the available energy of the integrative mechanism, so long will the integrative capacity of the goal-directed striving increase with increasing tension (see Figs 2A, B, and C). But as soon as the tension of the need begins to exceed the available energy of the integrating mechanism, the effect of increasing tension will be the opposite. Up to this point, the increasing tension will have merely activated increasing amounts of the available psychic energy of the integrating mechanism. But from the moment that the available psychic energy of the integrating mechanism is exhausted, any excess of tension will now tend no longer to augment the integrative capacity of the goal-seeking mechanism but will rather augment the tension which this integrative capacity must master. Instead of augmenting the integrative capacity it will now augment the integrative task (see Figs. 2D and E).

2) These relations between psychic tension, psychic energy, and integrative capacity may also be used to clarify the varying relations be-

tween the integrative field and subsidiary goals. As we have seen, the goal-directed striving, acting through the medium of a cognitive field, must successively activate one subsidiary goal after another and inhibit other goal-directed strivings, all in accordance with the time schedule contained in the cognitive field. It is obvious that the difficulty of this integrative task will vary greatly according to the amounts of psychic tension and psychic energy that are bound in the various subsidiary goals and motor mechanisms. A subsidiary goal that is not in a state of functional readiness will be difficult to activate. The attempt to activate it may be subjectively felt as effort. It will involve tension between integrative mechanism and subsidiary goal in order to overcome the resistance of the subsidiary goal to activation. This in turn will involve an increased strain upon the integrative capacity of the dominant goal-directed striving.

On the other hand, a subsidiary goal that is endowed with a large amount of free psychic energy will be easy to activate but difficult to inhibit at times when the schedule requires that it be inhibited. This task of inhibition will also increase the strain upon the integrative capacity of the end goal. As a result, there will arise difficulties which we may group together under the general head of impatience and inability to wait.

Finally, if the sum of the tensions between the end goal and its subsidiary goals at any time exceeds its integrative capacity, the result will be a disintegration of the dominant goal-directed striving.

IV. Applications

This analysis of the internal dynamic organization necessary for the success of goal-directed strivings is, of course, still very approximate and will require to be refined and perhaps corrected in many details. We shall learn its deficiencies and inadequacies in the course of attempting to apply it to specific problems that present themselves in our psychoanalytic experience. In conclusion I wish to proceed, therefore, to consider a few of the problems upon which I believe this analysis throws light, even in its present rough and sketchy form.

Frustration and Rage

The significance of frustration and rage is a problem that has necessarily played a very important role in the development of the psychoanalytic theory of the drives. In his theory of the death "instinct,"

Freud (12) postulated that the tendency to self-destruction and, second, to destruction of other objects is one of the two fundamental drives dominating the behavior of all living beings. He believed this destructive urge to be a component in varying degree of all living activity. I have already indicated what I feel to be the chief objection to this sort of formulation. If all kinds of behavior are to be understood as fusions in varying proportions of eros and death instinct, then we have only a single quantitative scale to account for all the manifold and complex variations in human and animal behavior. Moreover, the theory of the death instinct pays no attention to specific conditions that may provoke destructive behavior but seems tacitly to assume that the destructive urge is operating continuously as a primary cause except insofar as it is neutralized or modified by the life instinct. As I have already stated, the difficulty with this formulation is that it explains everything so easily. No theory of the drives can be of much value unless it can give us some idea of the specific conditions upon which the activity of each drive depends.

If we examine the specific factors in the manifestations of rage, three characteristics stand out: (1) the fact that it is released by frustration; (2) its destructive goals; and (3) its tendency to sudden and massive discharge of energy. Let us attempt to bring these three peculiarities of rage reactions into relation with our reconstruction of the dynamic organization of goal-directed behavior.

First, what do we understand by frustration? Frustration occurs when one must recognize that a goal that one has been pursuing with some confidence of success is unattainable. It would throw considerable light upon the other two peculiarities of the rage reaction, therefore, if it should turn out that they are deducible as natural consequences from the profound reorganization made necessary by the more or less sudden realization that a goal toward which one has been striving is unattainable.

We have already seen that confidence in one's ability to attain a goal is one of the important dynamic factors upon which the integrative capacity of the goal-seeking mechanism is dependent. If now this confidence is first threatened, then destroyed, we may expect in succession two sets of reactions. First, while the possibility of achieving the goal is only threatened and not yet destroyed, the integrating mechanism will be stimulated desperately to mobilize all available energy upon the subsidiary goal of overcoming or destroying the obstacle. While the integrative capacity of the original goal is still mobilized upon this

INFLUENCE OF INCREASING TENSION UPON AN INTEGRATIVE FIELD

Fig. 2A. Low tension provides inadequate incentive; task requires too much effort; project not attempted.

Fig. 2B. With rise of tension, integrative capacity becomes adequate to undertake task.

Fig. 2C. Superabundant integrative capacity is now adequate for even more difficult task.

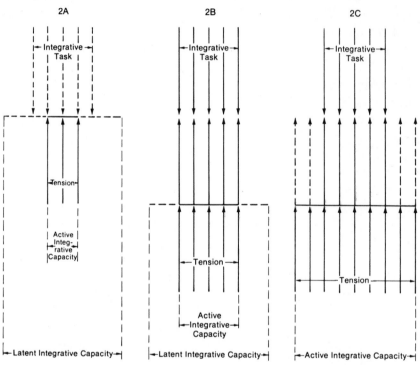

Explanation of Figures 2A, 2B, 2C, 2D, and 2E:
    Horizontal line, including dotted portion, represents available psychic energy of integrative field which we call its latent capacity; to become effective this latent integrative capacity must be activated by tension of underlying need. That part of the latent integrative capacity that has been so activated we call the active integrative capacity, which is represented by the solid portion of the horizontal line. Number of vertical arrows extending upward to horizontal line indicates amount of tension of underlying need. Number of vertical arrows extending upward from horizontal line corresponds to active integrative capacity of integrative field and indicates amount of tension that integrative field is able to exert to overcome resistance of integrative task. Number of arrows extending downward in Figures 2A, 2B, 2C is quantitative measure of integrative task, T. In Figures 2D and 2E, the integrative task, T, is augmented by excess tension, E, of underlying need (the arrows E' and E" extending out beyond limits of integrative capacity). Total integrative task therefore $=$ T $+$ E.
    Figures 2A to 2E represent the effect of progressively increasing tension upon the efforts of an individual to perform a task, T.

Fig. 2D. Excessive tension increases integrative task.

Fig. 2E. Further increase of tension leads to beginning disintegration of goal-seeking mechanism.

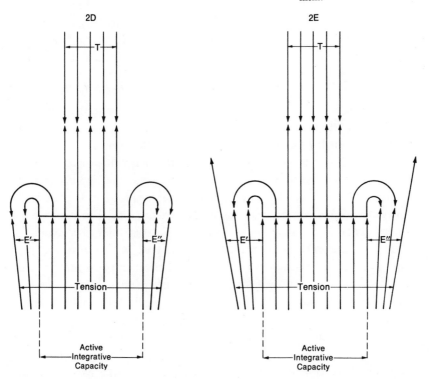

Fig. 2A. Low tension provides inadequate incentive; task requires too much effort;

Fig. 2B. With rise of tension integrative capacity becomes adequate to undertake project not attempted. (Hence no arrows extending upward from horizontal line.) task.

Fig. 2C. Superabundant integrative capacity (see dotted arrows) is now adequate for even more difficult task.

Fig. 2D. Excessive tension (see arrows E′ and E″) increases integrative task.

Fig. 2E. Further increase of tension leads to beginning disintegration of goal-seeking mechanism. (Note arrows extending out beyond restraining influence of integrative field.)

destructive subsidiary goal, there comes now the final realization that the original goal is unattainable. The integrative influence of the original goal is now destroyed completely. Up to this point the integrative capacity of the central integrative field has been utilized not only to activate the subsidiary goal of destroying the obstacle, but also to inhibit discharge of the newly mobilized energy in ways that might interfere with the ultimate realization of the original goal. With the destruction of the original integrative field, this inhibitory influence disappears. The energy that has been activated and that has already been given a destructive goal may now escape from the domination even of subsidiary goals and become a more or less diffuse discharge of motor energy. Moreover, insofar as this energy comes under the influence of any goals at all, its aims will tend to remain predominantly destructive.

Progressive Differentiation and Fixation of Goal-directed Strivings

In considering this sort of disintegration of goal-directed behavior into more or less uncoordinated destructive rage, one gains also another impression which I believe to be of considerable value for the theory of the drives. Even in play, when psychic energy has once become bound in the service of a particular goal, one gains the impression that this process sooner or later becomes irreversible. Play becomes earnest. Sometimes when our patients most fear frustration, they attempt to protect themselves from the possibility of frustration by avoiding committing themselves too completely to any goal. A girl who has once suffered a severe frustration in love will often attempt to protect herself from that time on by taking all love affairs lightly. She attempts from then on to play with love. If she ever really falls in love again, she senses that there will be no drawing back. It is very difficult to relinquish a desire to which one has thoroughly committed oneself.

The same principle holds also not infrequently for the choice of means. Not infrequently one becomes committed to the need not only to satisfy one's desire but to satisfy it in a particular way. One is not only committed to the original goal but becomes fixated also upon a subsidiary goal. The choice of subsidiary goal has also become irreversible. It may be necessary, for example, for some purposes, to solve a mathematical problem. The problem offers difficulties. One becomes involved in it. Sometimes one cannot rid oneself of the need to solve it although it would be much easier to look up the answer.

There would seem to be some analogy between the process of progressive differentiation of goal-directed impulses and the course of differentiation of cellular tissues. The cells of the body are all derived from a single totipotent egg cell. Gradually the cells created by division of this egg cell become differentiated into many different types of somatic cells. At certain points in this development the differentiation becomes irreversible. The nerve cell must continue to be a nerve cell or die. It cannot retrace its development and then become a muscle cell. Similarly, we get the impression that psychic energy, in the course of elaboration of goal-directed tendencies, becomes bound first to a goal, then perhaps more narrowly to particular subsidiary goals. Once one has committed himself to a particular way of obtaining gratification, the particular quantum of psychic energy that has been activated by that goal becomes irreversibly bound to it. It is not easy to stop suddenly in one's course and shift to another method of attaining one's ends, even though one is confronted with plain evidence that another way of attacking one's problem would be much better. There is a strong tendency to remain fixated upon the original plan of procedure. It is for this reason probably that revenge reactions and the talion principle play so important a role in psychopathology. A girl who has been jilted, for example, may perhaps rather easily find another man who originally might have attracted her just as much, but that would require real renunciation, release [23] of the energy bound in her first love affair, and the turning of that energy to another goal. Otherwise she remains fixated upon the original frustration and can only vent the bound energy in an urge repeatedly to seek revenge for her frustration. Thus, if the goal-seeking tendency to which the energy is bound is frustrated, its only possible fate is to undergo destructive degeneration, to discharge itself in some destructive form.

Release of Energy by Easy Success

Another situation that will lead to a sudden release of energy is the unexpectedly easy achievement of a goal toward which one had been striving with intense effort. Freud has twice alluded to this problem. This is, of course, the mechanism of wit (Freud, 8; Kris, 20). The suddenly released energy is discharged diffusely in laughter. Freud (11) has also pointed out that manic excitements of greater or lesser duration may be precipitated as a result of unexpected success. It would be of interest to study such reactions further from the points of view that we have been outlining.

Expansion and Contraction of the Integrative Field

I shall allude very sketchily to only one more possible application of these studies—an application which I think may offer important possibilities for future research.

We have already pointed out that psychic energy that is not bound by any preexisting psychic tension tends to manifest itself in playful activity and, as it were, to go in search of tasks to occupy it. We speak of such a person as "bubbling over," "full of life and energy."

It is not difficult to recognize similar tendencies to expansion of the integrative field. Self-confident individuals tend to reach out for new responsibilities. It is as though one were under necessity to employ the whole of one's latent integrative capacity. It is in this way, probably, that we are to understand the tendency to increased generosity in individuals who are well satisfied and really sure of themselves to which Alexander has frequently called attention. In our psychoanalytic practice we have frequent occasion to observe this in the gradual mellowing of the personality that is one of the surest signs that a patient is achieving mastery of his conflicts.

On the other hand, any strain on the integrative mechanisms such as results from increased tension caused by obstacles, frustration, psychic conflicts, etc., makes necessary a contraction of the integrative field in order to bring it within the limits of the ego's integrative capacity.

Dependent or eliminatory or expansive tendencies may occur as secondary reactions to such expansions or shrinkages of the integrative field. We have already noted that superabundant integrative capacity tends to manifest itself by reaching out for new responsibilities. On the other hand, by seeking help one may attempt to transfer to another person the greater part of an integrative task that is in excess of one's capacity; or the need to diminish the integrative load under stress of an acute conflict may lead, for example, to an impulse to get rid of wife and children in order to concentrate the whole of one's integrative capacity upon the task of solving the immediate conflict.

I suspect that factors of this sort, involving changes in the integrative capacity of the ego or in the character of the task with which the ego is confronted, would throw light upon many of the reactions that have previously been explained as manifestations of presumably continuously active drives acting as primary causes.

NOTES

1. See page 170.
2. See page 170.
3. See page 168.

4. See page 170.

5. For an excellent summary of this work see Paul Weiss (30).

6. The following description of the organization of purposive behavior parallels very closely analyses by E. C. Tolman (28) and by Henry Murray (24). I shall not take time to discuss the rather slight differences between my views and theirs, but shall merely state that Tolman's book is a beautiful analysis of the experimental evidence concerning the mechanisms of purposive behavior, whereas Murray's and his co-workers' analysis is based upon exhaustive clinical attempts to find a method of describing personality adequately. It should also be obvious to any reader who is familiar with the work of Kurt Lewin and his co-workers (for example Lewin, 22, 23) how extensively I have made use of his method of analyzing goal-directed behavior by reference to the psychological field. My views differ from his chiefly in one point, which will be discussed immediately.

7. Considerations in many respects similar to those here presented have already been discussed by Tolman in a criticism of Lewin's vector concept (Tolman, 29). Lewin (21) replied by emphasizing the fact that the forces that he postulates must be understood as acting in a psychological (cognitive) field rather than in physical space and that Tolman's objections could all be met by paying careful attention to the way that the experimental situation must appear in the eyes of the experimental subject. On the other hand, Lewin feels that it is better not to attempt to speculate concerning the "mechanisms behind the psychological field." The writer of the present article is very much in sympathy with Lewin's efforts to base dynamic analyses of behavior upon an accurate reconstruction of the individual's cognitive field. He feels, however, that the severe frustration reactions encountered in psychopathology cannot be adequately understood without attempting to analyze the "mechanisms behind the psychological field."

8. Hull and his co-workers (14, 15) are actively engaged in the task of attempting to understand goal-directed behavior in terms of a complex system of interacting conditioned reflexes. I also once attempted to construct such a system (French, 2). In the present discussion, however, I have tried to avoid these intricate problems.

9. E. C. Tolman (28) carefully analyzes the experimental evidence that proves that the concept of formation of new cognitive fields is more adequate than Thorndike's law of effect to explain the relevant facts.

10. See E. C. Tolman and C. H. Honzik (27).

11. See page 169.

12. See Figures 1-A and 1-B on page 171 above.

13. Sometimes this synthesis fails to take place. The threatening tension may be too intense. One clings to the satisfying fantasy, struggling desperately to banish one's fear or pain; but then finally the disturbing tension becomes too strong and breaks through in some sort of emotional or motor discharge.

At other times a false synthesis takes place. One attempts to give a sort of reality to one's fantasies in symbolic acts. As Anna Freud (5) puts it, "denial by phantasy" is supplemented by "denial in word and act." Similarly, neurotic characters must give reality value to their fantasies by "acting them out."

It is an interesting problem to inquire just what conditions are necessary in order that this synthesis between fantasy satisfaction and underlying tension may lead to the formation of a really effective purpose capable of inhibiting disturbing tensions and concentrating one's motor energies upon the task of achieving one's goal. Probably these conditions are of a quantitative nature. The cognitive field required for the formation of an effective purpose is more complex than the cognitive field required for "denial in word and act" or for the "acting out" of neurotic fantasies. The formation of an effective purpose should therefore require a greater potential integrative capacity.

14. See French (3, 4), Benedek (1).

15. In discussing the cognitive field in its integrative executive function, we shall refer to it as the "integrative field."

16. Indeed, the level of confidence once established may lead to a cyclical chain of causation. Confidence in the success of one's efforts within certain limits will enhance the effectiveness of one's efforts by increasing the capacity of the integrative field; but this in turn will tend to enhance the objective reasons for hope of success. On the other hand, expectation of failure may give rise to a vicious circle tending in the opposite direction. Which of the two cycles gain ascendancy may be determined by a general mood level resulting from quite extraneous factors.

17. See note 15 above.

18. The paradoxical overactivity and resistance to sleep of the tired child, however, should warn us against an attempt to formulate these relations too simply. The exact relations should be worked out by experiment supplementing clinical observation.

19. In *Three Contributions to the Theory of Sex,* Freud (7) demonstrated that the manifold variety of sexual behavior could not be understood in terms of a simple drive whose goal is union of the genitals of the opposite sexes and reproduction of the species. On the contrary, he was able to prove that the sexual urge is a composite one originally directed toward many different goals and only with difficulty subordinated, in the course of individual development, to the biological goal of reproduction of the species.

We may now note that our analysis of goal-directed strivings in general corresponds closely to this early analysis by Freud of the relation between the reproductive urge and the subsidiary partial sexual aims which at puberty must be subordinated to the "primacy of the genitals."

On the other hand, as we have seen, the phenomena of sublimation indicate plainly that these cravings for stimulation and functional activity may be also subordinated to strivings toward all sorts of other goals as well as sexual ones. The question arises, therefore, whether the craving for stimulation and for functional activity of the various "erotic zones" may not have a more general significance. Indeed, this suggestion has already been twice offered by Freud himself (9, 10), only to be immediately somewhat arbitrarily rejected.

20. We must be careful, however, not to think of such a tendency to overflow in too automatic and passive a manner, like water spilling out of an open container. In accordance with the analysis already made, we must picture the process of overflow as a much better regulated process, perhaps analogous to a mechanism whereby an increased strain upon the elastic walls of a container would give rise to a signal for a release mechanism.

21. See page 175.

22. In the play of children, play tends to become earnest, often very earnest indeed. In the above description I am speaking of play that is still playful, that has not become involved in a too earnest striving for any particular goal.

23. This can be accomplished only by a process of living through the reactivated emotional conflict in such a way as to come to the realization that another love affair need not necessarily turn out so disastrously. In a previous paper I have called this "emotional learning" (for more detailed discussion see French, 3). The necessary conditions for such emotional learning are an integrative capacity sufficient to span both (1) the conflicting tensions arising out of the original traumatic memory, and (2) the task of comparing and distinguishing between the original trauma and a present opportunity for satisfaction. The principle is illustrated in the following diagrams:

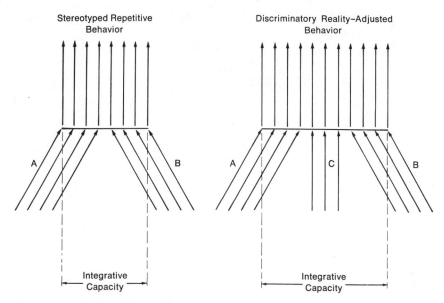

Explanation of above diagrams:

As in Figure 2, horizontal line represents integrative capacity. The slanting arrows (A and B) represent the tensions of two conflicting needs—for example, a forbidden sexual urge and fear of punishment. In the first diagram we picture the integrative capacity as wholly preoccupied with the task of reconciling the two conflicting needs and without any reserve capacity to take account of new features in the present situation that may differ from the original traumatic situation out of which the patient's fear of punishment arose. A patient's fear of punishment, for example, may be based upon memories of his father's very punitive attitude. Because of his preoccupation with the conflicting tensions of his sexual urges and his fear, he will be entirely unable, for example, to take account of the fact that he is now dealing with the analyst whose attitude toward forbidden impulses is much more tolerant. The result will therefore be a stereotyped repetition of behavior which may have been appropriate for the original childhood situation but which is quite inappropriate to the realities of the present situation.

In the second diagram we picture the integrative capacity as somewhat greater and therefore able to take account not only of the two conflicting tensions, but also of the new features of the present situation (represented by arrows C) that differ from the earlier traumatic memories and will thus enable him to correct the pattern of his earlier reaction to the traumatic memories and to behave in a discriminatory fashion that is adequate to the present real situation. Instead of reacting to the analyst as a punitive father, for example, he will take account of the analyst's actual attitude of encouraging the patient to confess forbidden impulses.

BIBLIOGRAPHY

1. Benedek, Therese: Defense Mechanisms and Structure of the Total Personality. Psychoanalyt. Quart., 6: 96, 1937.
2. French, Thomas M.: Interrelations Between Psychoanalysis and the Ex-

perimental Work of Pavlov. Amer. J. Psychiat., *12:* 1165, 1933; Chap. 1 this volume.

3. French, Thomas M.: Reality and the Unconscious. Psychoanalyt. Quart., *6:* 23, 1937; Chap. 2 in this volume.

4. French, Thomas M.: Defense and Synthesis in the Function of the Ego. Psychoanalyt. Quart., *7:* 537, 1938; Chap. 6 in this volume.

5. Freud, Anna: The Ego and the Mechanisms of Defense. First Ed., Hogarth Press, London, 1936.

6. Freud, Sigmund: The Interpretation of Dreams. Allen & Unwin, London, 1932.

7. Freud, Sigmund: Three Contributions to the Theory of Sex. Fourth Ed., Nerv. & Ment. Dist. Pub. Co., N.Y., 1930.

8. Freud, Sigmund: Wit and Its Relation to the Unconscious. Fisher & Unwin, New York, 1917.

9. Freud, Sigmund: On Narcissism, an Introduction, Collected Papers. Vol. IV, Chap. II. Hogarth Press, London, 1925.

10. Freud, Sigmund: Introductory Lectures. Chap. XXI. Allen & Unwin, London, 1929.

11. Freud, Sigmund: Mourning and Melancholia, Collected Papers. Vol. IV. Hogarth Press, London, 1925.

12. Freud, Sigmund: Beyond the Pleasure Principle. Hogarth Press, London, 1922.

13. Freud, Sigmund: The Ego and the Id. Hogarth Press, London, 1927.

14. Hull, C. L.: Mind, Mechanism and Adaptive Behavior. Psychol. Rev., *44:* 1, 1937.

15. Hull, C. L., and co-workers: Mathematico-Deductive Theory of Rote Learning, A Study in Scientific Methodology. Yale University Press, New Haven, 1940.

16. Koehler, Wolfgang: Die Physischen Gestalten in Ruhe und im stationaeren Zustand, Eine Naturphilosophische Untersuchung. F. Vieweg & Sohn, Braunschweig, 1920.

17. Koehler, Wolfgang: The Mentality of Apes. Harcourt, Brace & Co., New York, 1921.

18. Koehler, Wolfgang: Zum Problem der Regulation. Wilhelm Roux. Arch. EntwMech. Org. Festschrft. f. H. Diersch, *112:* 315, 1927.

19. Koehler, Wolfgang: Dynamics in Psychology. Liveright, New York, 1940.

20. Kris, Ernst: Das Lachen als mimischer Vorgang. Int. Z. (ärztl.) Psychoanal., *24:* 146, 1939.

21. Lewin, Kurt: Vectors, Cognitive Processes and E. Tolman's Criticism. J. Gen. Psychol., *8:* 315, 1933.

22. Lewin, Kurt: Dynamic Theory of Personality. McGraw-Hill, New York, 1935.

23. Lewin, Kurt: The Conceptual Representation and the Measurement of Psychological Forces. Duke University Press, 1938.
24. Murray, Henry: Explorations in Personality. Oxford University Press, New York, 1938.
25. Pavlov, I. P.: Conditioned Reflexes, An Investigation of the Physiological Activity of the Cerebral Cortex. Oxford University Press, New York, 1927.
26. Thorndike, E. L.: Educational Psychology, Vol. II. New York Teachers College, Columbia University Press, New York, 1913.
27. Tolman, E. C., and Honzik, C. H.: Introduction and Removal of Reward and Maze Performance in Rats. Univ. Calif. Publ. Psychol., 4: 257, 1930.
28. Tolman, E. C.: Purposive Behavior in Animals and Men. Century Co., New York, 1932.
29. Tolman, E. C.: Lewin's Concept of Vectors. J. Gen. Psychol., 7: 3, 1932.
30. Weiss, Paul: Principles of Development. Henry Holt & Co., New York, 1939.

Chapter Nine

THE INTEGRATION OF SOCIAL BEHAVIOR

In this paper we return to a clinical study of a series of interviews in a psychoanalytic treatment. This time our focus of interest is on the integration and disintegration of goal-directed behavior involving the patient's relations to other people.

The first of the patient's dreams in this series, which we shall call the bridge dream (10-a), offers a particularly good starting point for an inquiry into the dynamics of purposive behavior, for it gives evidence of a subordination of means to an end goal clearly comparable to the integrated mechanisms of rational purposive behavior in waking life. The dream is dominated by the wish to please the mother. To this end, the patient renounces his erotic impulses toward a young girl, and, assuming a protective role toward her, he takes her home to her mother. In this way he wins the mother's thanks and receives from her a glass of milk. Thus in this dream we see an example of successful subordination of means to an end goal.

In the succeeding dreams this subordination of means to an end is less successful. We see increasing threats of the disintegration of the goal-seeking mechanism.

The bridge dream seems to have been inspired by the analyst's expression of interest in dreams during the previous hour, which apparently awakened the patient's hope of winning the analyst's approval by bringing her a dream. The manifest content of the dream records similar hopes of winning a mother's love and approval in his adolescent years, and betrays as well the fact that behind this hope lies hidden a fear of losing her love because of his sexual impulses toward a sister

Reprinted from *Psychoanalytic Quarterly*, 14, No. 2 (April 1945).

figure. The manifest content of the dream is evidently inspired by the hope that he may win back the mother's love by returning her daughter safely to her.

. The patient did not see the analyst on the following day and consequently could not immediately realize his hope of pleasing her by bringing her a dream. It seems clear, moreover, that the reassuring influence of this hope could not be sustained a day longer, for, in the dreams of the next few nights, the threat that he is in danger of losing the mother because of his disturbing wishes emerges much more plainly. Thus, the increasingly desperate tension of the patient's need for the mother does not increase his ability to make sacrifices in order to win her. It is rather the hope of success, in the bridge dream, that enhances his capacity to hold disturbing tensions in restraint and successfully to subordinate his means to the end of winning the mother. When the tension of his need for love is not any longer reinforced by his hope of winning love, the mounting tension increases the integrative task, but not the integrative capacity, of his dominant urge to please the mother.

In other words, when hope of success diminishes, tension rises and is with much greater difficulty subordinated to the task in hand. Obviously one is less ready to make sacrifices to attain a goal once one has begun to doubt whether the goal is really attainable.

One of the central interests of pre-Freudian psychology was the problem of the nature and mechanism of intellectual processes. (Under the term "pre-Freudian" I include not only studies made prior to Freud but also later studies not significantly influenced by Freud.) Psychoanalysis, on the other hand, has interested itself primarily in problems of motivation. Psychoanalysis started with a study of pathological symptoms and was therefore compelled to take normal behavior more or less for granted as a standard for comparison. Disturbances of the cognitive processes were studied as distortions of an adequate perception of reality. As a consequence, psychoanalysis has usually quite consistently disregarded the fact that normal cognitive processes probably require a more delicately balanced equilibrium and are therefore more difficult to explain than are the mechanisms of most pathological distortions.

In the present paper I wish to return to the earlier interest of psychology in the mechanisms of the intellectual functions. In doing so, however, I shall avail myself of the very rich material bearing upon problems of this sort that has resulted from the intervening development of psychoanalytic psychology. We shall attempt to analyze some of the dynamic factors involved in the process of integration of social behavior, or, in other words, in the process of integration of our behavior in relation to other people.

A report of some clinical material from the analysis of one of Dr. Helen McLean's patients, who was analyzed in our research upon bronchial asthma, will illustrate the discussion.

The patient, a forty-six-year-old laborer, had just started an analysis for bronchial asthma. He was the oldest of six children. His father was a big, powerful man, a blacksmith, who allowed no one in the home to question his authority and who insisted that the children keep quiet when he was at home. The mother was an attractive woman who protected the children from the harsh words and blows of the father and in this way drew them upon herself.

The patient himself was a sickly child who needed constant care. He slept with his mother until he was three, when his brother was born. After that he slept with her whenever he was ill. With this brother he quarreled constantly. The next sibling, a sister, is the one to whom reference will be made in the material that follows. She was born when the patient was eight and died during the patient's adolescence.

Of the subsequent history, we need mention only that the patient ran away from home at the age of twenty after a quarrel with his father. He emigrated to America, where he married a woman to whom he was not particularly attracted but of whose mother he was very fond. The marriage was satisfactory until the birth of his first child (a boy) a year later, after which the patient and his wife began to quarrel, and the patient developed asthma. For many years prior to analysis, he had held a job cleaning out cattle and freight cars in a railroad yard where the exposure to cattle hair aggravated his asthma. His comrades were often indulgent enough to allow him to sit or sleep in a warm room while they did his work.

Beginning of Analysis—The First Dream: During the first few hours of his analysis, this rather inarticulate man found talking freely about personal matters very difficult. He was very uncomfortable during these hours because of his severe asthmatic wheezing. In the sixth hour he experienced much relief when he was finally able to voice freely his resentments against his wife, who, he complained, was fat, sloppy, and quarrelsome and neglected the two children and himself.

In the ninth hour, the analyst had expressed an interest in dreams. At the beginning of the next hour the patient reported the following dreams, the first in the analysis. He introduced the first dream with the remark that he had had a dream—"That's what you want," he added. The dream was dreamed New Year's Eve and reported January 2. It ran as follows:

> *Dream 10-a.* Dream of school-days—in weekend I was going home—we always walked unless someone picked us up. I walked alone until I got to bridge—a girl was there leaning on bridge, watching boats. I stopped and pinched her on back, and then we walked on home. Getting dusk. Her mother met her and thanked me and asked me in and gave me a glass of milk.

After telling his dream, he proceeded immediately to tell two dreams which he dreamed the following night:

> *Dream 10-b.* Last night kind of embarrassing. I was in railroad station, with a lot of people—wife and me—we were separated, she in one end and I in other—old friends around—they came and asked me why I married her. I dodged her too.

> *Dream 10-c.* Something toward morning about doctors and ladies—I was taking some kind of treatment—doctors taking culture—lady comes along and says now we've hit spot.

Associations: The patient insisted that the woman in the last dream was not like the analyst, but like a servant girl. The bridge was one where he used to play. It shook when the wagons went over it. "Lots of fun there. Road leading home. It was level. There were trees around and on both sides fields and gardens; nice scenery." The girl lived along the road. No, the patient was not interested in her. He was seldom in her company, only met her going and coming from school. He used to meet girls on the bridge. The mother in the dream was elderly, pleasant. Her son came along with her to meet the girl. The old lady took him to the basement for a cold glass of milk. It was good milk with cream in it, refreshing in summer. The mother . . . had gray hair and was stooped like a farmer's wife. Yes, exactly like the patient's mother. The boy hung around behind his mother and said nothing. A boy of about twelve. The patient was fourteen or sixteen when he went on this road, the boy was younger. Yes, his next younger brother was two years younger. The patient had a sister who died at about ten of scarlet fever. . . . "We all liked her." The girl in the dream was older and taller than the sister.

In association to the railroad station the patient remembered that the railroad was close to the lakefront. He could see the lake (an obvious reference to the analyst's home where she saw the patient). . . . The patient and his wife were there. The wife was not well dressed: she was sloppy. The patient was sidestepping her. One lady asked why the patient married her. She said she was sorry the patient had married her. The dream was embarrassing.

At this point the analyst interpreted the dream as the fulfillment of a wish that she sympathize with the patient in his desire to leave his wife. The patient replied that he had not liked his wife at first but was talked into marrying her. He boarded with her sister and in this way became associated with the family. Her mother said she would not mind if the patient married her daughter. He was tired of eating around. The sister was a good housekeeper and cook and he figured she was like a home girl. The analyst remarked that the patient married her for a home, that he wanted someone to take care of him like a mother.

Dream Interpretation—The Immediate Situation: The last two dreams seem to relate most directly to the patient's immediate situation in the analysis. As the analyst says, the patient wishes her to sympathize with his desire to leave his wife (dream 10-b). His embarrassment also implies that he wishes to turn to the analyst for the affection he cannot get from his wife. In the last dream (10-c), he tries to give this wish a professional setting, consistent with his professional relation to the analyst as his physician. The dream suggests that he is in a clinic, or at any rate receiving treatment. The "lady" in the dream gives him the sympathy that he craves from the analyst in the form of a reassurance that the treatment has "hit the spot."

It is probable that in the last dream (10-c) medical treatment has been substituted for analysis as an expression of the patient's fear of the analysis. He would prefer even a painful treatment because its dangers are much less mysterious. The substitution of a railroad station in place of the analyst's home also suggests a fear of the analytic situation, a desire to go away. His wishes for affection from the analyst are too personal and he is vaguely afraid of the consequences. Therefore he also seeks safety in numbers. Instead of his being alone with the analyst there are "old friends around" or "doctors and ladies."

The First Dream in Relation to the Life History: The first dream seems to transport us back into the patient's adolescence rather than to deal directly with the present situation. The connecting link with the two subsequent dreams is the patient's desire for affection from the analyst. Evidently in his boyhood he used to know how to win affection and appreciation from mothers by being protective and chivalrous toward their daughters. He seems also to have a similar motive in bringing the dream, for he presents it to the analyst as though it were a present, commenting "That's what you want."

But why does the dream not express his desire for affection from the analyst more directly, in terms of the present situation, as in the two dreams of the next night? What takes him back to the adolescent period?

To answer this we must turn to the patient's life history. We may mention the fact that, in contrast to the dream, his own mother did not always approve of his interest in women. Once she rebuked him sharply for making sexual advances to a young married woman who was visiting in the home, and he was very much afraid that she would learn of his sexual affair with a maid. In the light of this history, the dream now seems like a reassurance. The patient starts by making a playful erotic gesture, pinching the girl in the back; but then he seems to think better of it and keeps on good terms with the mother by escorting the young lady safely home.

What brings this old conflict to the surface now? In the light of the two succeeding dreams, we must suspect that the patient is experiencing some erotic stimulation from being alone with a woman analyst. If so, he is attempting to protect himself against his erotic desire, first by substituting a younger woman in place of the analyst (mother), and then by promptly escorting the girl home to win the thanks of the mother. This suggestion is indeed confirmed by the patient's denial of interest in the girl. He repudiates any connection between the "lady" in the last dream and the analyst, and depreciates the "lady" as "like a servant girl." As already indicated, we learn later in the analysis that he once had a sexual affair with a "servant girl," which he very much feared his mother would discover.

The next hour brought a displaced confirmation of this suggestion, for he confessed, in answer to the analyst's question, that he never put any value on dreams, and then complained that he could not stand loud talking nor sleep with any kind of noise. He spent the rest of the hour protesting against his wife's loud talking and against the idea of "wives and mothers" talking about sex.

Two More Dreams: However, even though the patient resented what he felt were sexual implications in the analyst's interpretation, the next dream indicated that he was much impressed by it. In the twelfth hour, three days later, he brought the following dream:

Dream 12. Can't remember it—about father and mother—seems mother doing blacksmith work—she had hot iron and was hammering.

When the analyst reminded him that his father was a blacksmith, he added a few details:

Father was also in the dream but not so clear as mother; he was standing on side of shop—kind of dark. Plainly see my mother—she had hot iron and working at it, flattening it out and bending it, doing clean work, good job too.

In association he stated that his mother had never done any blacksmith work although she might have come to the door of the shop.

Corresponding to the patient's inarticulate character, he had quickly finished with his associations; so the analyst tried to help him out. She suggested that perhaps she seemed like a woman doing a man's job.

The patient did not reply to the analyst's comment but continued to dwell admiringly upon the details of the mother's work in his memory of the dream:

Father standing on side. Mother took iron out of fire—performing the work on it—long piece of heavy iron.

The iron resembled iron used on a locomotive to pull out clinkers. His mother was shaping it. There was a hook on the end of it.

The analyst remarked that if she was bending the patient like iron, he must be afraid. He agreed that he really was afraid of the analysis. He did not know what it was all about and felt helpless because he was in the dark.

It will perhaps facilitate the discussion of this dream if we immediately report the material of the next two hours. In the next hour, three days later, the patient reported that he vomited and had a stomachache the day before, after drinking three glasses of beer and winning twenty dollars at poker. He also had lumbago on his left side. The rest of the hour was spent discussing his bad conscience when he won at poker and his need to give at least some of the money back.

In the fourteenth hour, four days later, he complained of a stiff neck. . . . He continued: the last time he was here he had a pain in his back; the next day he had a stiff knee and could hardly walk. . . . Then he reported a dream:

> *Dream 14.* My younger boy had awful large snake—tame. He played with it. I was scared . . . snake would sneak into pillowcase. Snake had V-face and flat and pointed—run around eyes—on face a smile or laugh—snake awful fat.

The patient's associations were repeatedly interrupted by complaints about the pain in his neck which filled up most of the hour. His younger son, Vincent, was playing with the snake. He looked contented, and was not scared, but liked it. The patient noticed the snake sneak into the pillowcase. The child walked over and pulled it out. The patient laughed when asked to associate to the snake's going into the pillowcase. He doesn't like snakes, gets sick. There are a lot of snakes where he works. They are harmless but he doesn't like them. The other men caught them and put them in his coat pocket. Had he been aware of their doing this he would never have worn the coat.

He commented that the snake was very big and was reminded of his fat wife. The analyst suggested that the reference was to his wife's pregnancy with the patient's younger child and that his stiff neck was a reaction to his jealousy of his wife's caring for the baby.

More Interpretation: As already noted, the associations to these dreams are meager. Nevertheless, they enable us to fill in some of the gaps in our picture of the patient's psychological situation as revealed by the preceding dreams.

The "anvil dream" in the twelfth hour expresses the patient's admiration for a woman's ability to do a man's job well. As the analyst's comment indicates, we may now surmise that the patient had been somewhat disappointed at being assigned to a woman analyst, but he was evidently quite fascinated by the analyst's interpretation of his dreams of a few days before and was beginning to feel that she could do a good job just as if she were a man. Looking back at the clinic dream (10-c), we find confirmation of this suggestion. In our discussion of this dream it was not clear why the patient introduced "doctors and ladies" in place of his analyst, and then depreciated the lady. Now we realize that the patient was already wishing that a man instead of a woman was his "doctor." This is also consistent with, or rather complementary to, the motive that we have already discussed for his depreciation of his female analyst. If this analyst were a man, he would not be exposed to heterosexual temptation that so frightened him.

The theme of sexual temptation and his reaction to it is also depicted in the anvil dream (12). As the analyst's comment indicated, if the mother's beating an iron bar on the anvil represents the patient's treatment, he must be thinking of himself as the bar that is beaten and bent. Indeed, in the material of the next two hours, the dream of being beaten on the anvil seems to be a prophecy of the severe muscular and arthritic pains that follow! But why is he in such need of punishment? Apparently he is intensely chagrined by the sexual interest which the analyst unconsciously awakens in him. Hence the analyst's job, he feels, is to hammer him into shape, just as his father used to bend iron bars on the anvil. Actually in his young manhood, as we learn later in the analysis, his choleric father had twice beaten him for his sexual episodes.

Further indications as to why the patient feels he should be beaten are found in the dream of the snake (14). Plainly in this dream he has some desire to hurt his younger son, or perhaps at this moment it is the analyst's child, whom the patient encounters occasionally in the house and resents because it comes between him and his need for a mother's love. In the dream he projects this wish. It is not he but the snake that might hurt the child. Thus the dream seems successful in reassuring the patient that the child has nothing to fear.

The evidence of this hostile wish against a child now enables us to understand a detail of the dream of the girl on the bridge (10-a) to which we have paid little attention. In the dream, the girl's mother was accompanied by her son, a boy about the age of the patient's next younger brother. This was the brother whose birth displaced the patient from his mother's bed. As we learn later in the analysis, it was this brother whose baby carriage the patient once pushed down the hill and whom he lost in the hayfield. Thus even in this first dream (10-a) we have evidence that his fear of losing his mother's love arose not only because of his sexual interest in girls, but also because of his resentment of his brothers and sisters. Indeed, his pinching the girl in the dream may have been an erotized expression of a hostile impulse as well as a playful erotic gesture. That the sister to whom the dream alludes was the one who died in the patient's late adolescence tends to confirm this formulation.

In childhood the patient was sickly and in this way found his way back to the mother's care and attention. Otherwise the brother might have displaced him to a still greater extent. Indeed it was only when he was sick that he was again taken into the mother's bed. In the clinic dream (10-c) he again employs the same device for finding his way back to the parent's care and attention.

In the dream of the railroad station, on the other hand, he is fleeing from the temptation situation as he did when his landladies became pregnant. This time, however, he takes care to assure himself beforehand that there will be another mother to whom he can flee.

Summary of the Psychological Situation: To sum up our impressions from these five dreams, we find a consistent though still somewhat sketchy picture of the patient's psychological situation in the early hours of the analysis. He is frightened at being alone with a woman analyst and reacts to the situation as a sexual temptation. On the other hand, he wishes to be loved by the analyst as by a mother and resents her child as a rival. He is intensely chagrined by these wishes (which are probably for the most part unconscious) and tries to protect himself from them by stressing the fact that he is in a professional situation, that the analyst is a "good clean" workman, not a woman who wants to tempt him sexually. Even so, a man analyst, who would not be a sexual temptation, and who would give him the beating that he feels he deserves, might be better.

Integration and Disintegration of Goal-directed Behavior: The first of the dreams cited above, which we shall call the bridge dream (10-a), offers a particularly good starting point for an inquiry into the dynamics of purposive behavior, for it gives evidence of a subordination of means to an end goal clearly comparable to the integrated mechanisms of rational purposive behavior in waking life. The dream is dominated by the wish to please the mother. To this end, the patient renounces his erotic impulses toward the young girl, and assuming a protective role toward her, he takes her home to her mother. In this way he wins the mother's thanks and receives from her a glass of milk. Thus in this dream we see an example of successful subordination of means to an end goal.

In the succeeding dreams this subordination of means to an end is less successful. We see increasing threats of the *disintegration of the goal-seeking mechanism.* In the railroad-station dream (10-b), as we have seen, the patient is running away from sexual temptation as from a danger. Instead of renouncing his sexual wishes with the confidence that he will thereby win the mother's approval, he is now running away from them and anxiously seeking consolation and re-assurance from an older woman. In the anvil dream (12) he is so disturbed by the threatening sexual tensions that he must conceive of the analysis as a good beating. He still maintains what has now become an admiring and very submissive relationship to the mother, but only on condition of being beaten into shape by her—of having the bad impulses, as it were, hammered out of him.

Our next problem is to find the reason for this progressive tendency to disintegration of the goal-seeking mechanism.

Neutralization of Tension by Hope: The bridge dream (10-a) seems to have been inspired by the analyst's expression of interest in dreams during the previous hour, which apparently awakened the patient's hope of winning the analyst's approval by bringing her a dream. The mani-fest content of the dream records similar hopes of winning a mother's love and approval in his adolescent years, and betrays as well the fact that back of this hope lies hidden a fear of losing her love because of his sexual impulses toward a sister figure. The manifest content of the dream is evidently inspired by the hope that he may win back the mother's love by returning her daughter safely to her.

This dream occurred on New Year's Eve. The patient did not see the analyst on the following day and consequently could not immedi-ately realize his hope of pleasing her by bringing her a dream. It seems clear, moreover, that the reassuring influence of this hope could not be sustained a day longer, for in the dreams of the next night the threat, that he is in danger of losing the mother because of his dis-turbing wishes, emerges much more plainly. In the dream of the rail-road station (10-b) he is running away from his wife, who has be-come a symbol of sexual temptation, and he is seeking consolation and reassurance from an older woman who represents the analyst.

Thus it appears that the second dream (10-b) differs from the first (10-a) primarily because of an increase of the tension of unsatisfied desire. There may be two reasons for this. First, as a result of the patient's attempt to renounce sexual wishes, it is quite possible that there may have been an increase in sexual tension during the inter-vening day. Second, the power of the hope of future satisfaction to quiet disturbing tensions is evidently quantitatively limited, for the patient is unable to sustain his hope for another day. In the bridge dream (10-a), the dream or hope of winning the mother's approval has partially satisfied the patient's wishes for the moment and thus diminished their tension; but when once the satisfying hope of winning the mother must be abandoned, the result is a still further increase in the tension of the patient's unsatisfied desires.

Let us now repeat and summarize these conclusions: The hope of winning the mother's approval at the time of the bridge dream (10-a) partly satisfied the patient's wishes for the moment and thus in part neutralized their tension; but he was unable to sustain his hope for another day, and the result was an increase of tension. The differences between the bridge dream (10-a) and the railroad-station dream (10-b) were primarily a result of this increase of the tension of unsatisfied wishes.

Following this method of analysis, we note that in this series of dreams the tension of the patient's need for the mother seems to be steadily rising. Nevertheless, his efforts to win her are at once becoming less successful and more desperate. We have already cited the reason for this. In the bridge dream (10-a) his desire to please the analyst had been reinforced by his hope of success. At the time of the railroad-station dream (10-b) it appeared that this hope could not be maintained. A sign of his continually diminishing hope of pleasing the mother was that his means of seeking a reconciliation with her became increasingly desperate in the succeeding dreams. In the clinic dream (10-c), he must accept illness, and in the anvil dream (12) he is symbolically portraying himself as accepting punishment, in order to maintain his relationship to her.

Thus it is evident from these examples that the increasingly desperate tention of the patient's need for the mother does not increase his ability to make sacrifices in order to win her. It is rather the hope of success, in the bridge dream (10-a), that enhances his capacity to hold disturbing tensions in restraint and successfully to subordinate his means to the end of winning the mother. When the tension of his need for love is no longer reinforced by his hope of winning love, the mounting tension increases the integrative task, but not the integrative capacity, of his dominant urge to please the mother.

This observation is, of course, quite in accord with everyday observations concerning the factors that determine the effectiveness of conscious purposes in waking life. We might perhaps expect that the most intense wish would be the one most likely to attain dominance over other goals. Paradoxically, however, the very intensity of a wish or of a need may make effective efforts to satisfy it impossible. Everyone has experienced how impatience or the need to hurry tends to paralyze one's capacity for application to painstaking effort.

We gain some insight into this apparent paradox when we take into account the fact that a biological need or drive implies a state of disturbed equilibrium or physiological unrest which tends first of all to be discharged in diffuse motor activity and that only later, as a result of knowledge gained from subsequent experience, is this diffuse excitation concentrated upon more circumscribed goals. Thus the original urge to escape an unpleasant tension must be supplemented by an attraction to a more circumscribed goal that is also desired for its own sake. The hope of winning the mother must supplement and give direction to the motor discharge stimulated by the fear of losing her. The original tendency to diffuse motor discharge must be concentrated upon and subordinated to the task in hand, and any disturbing remnant of the urge to discharge motor energy diffusely must be inhibited. As we have seen in the bridge dream (10-a), the hope of winning the mother has first temporarily diminished the tension of the underlying needs and concentrated the remaining tension as far as possible upon the goal of pleasing her. However, the remnants of sexual tension that cannot be so concentrated must be inhibited. We may designate quantitatively this ability of a goal-directed striving to withstand antagonistic tensions as its *integrative capacity.*

Yet, as our examples plainly show, the integrative capacity of a wish is not dependent upon its intensity alone. Indeed, as we have seen, if the intensity of a wish becomes too great, its integrative capacity will diminish. The integrative capacity appears to be much more directly dependent upon a second factor—the factor of hope and confidence in the ability to achieve one's goal. When hope of success diminishes, tension rises and is with much greater difficulty subordinated to the task in hand. Obviously one is less ready to make sacrifices to attain a goal once one has begun to doubt whether the goal is really attainable.

Destructive and Erotic Impulses in Relation to the Integration of Goal-directed Strivings: The importance of this distinction between the tension of a wish and the integrative capacity based upon hope of fulfilling it becomes still more evident in our patient's material if we now take into account our deeper analysis of the motives underlying these dreams. In the bridge dream (10-a), we recognized that behind the patient's sexual interest in the sister there lurks a still deeper hostility toward both her and his next younger brother. The erotic impulse toward the sister has apparently been substituted for a hostile one toward both brother and sister.

We have, moreover, already pointed out that the patient's jealous hostility toward rivals is itself derived from his need for a mother. He resents brother and sister because they are obstacles in the way of his receiving the mother's exclusive interest and attention.

In the light of this deeper conflict, we now see clearly illustrated that we are dealing with a threatened disintegration of the goal-seeking mechanism, whose aim it is to make the patient secure in the mother's love. The patient wishes to get rid of his brother and sister in order to keep exclusive possession of the mother, but his aggressive impulses toward the brother and sister tend only to estrange him from the mother and to increase the danger of his losing her love entirely. The very motive that threatens to estrange him from the mother has itself arisen directly out of his desperate need to keep her love. In other words, quite transparently, the patient's intense need for the mother is threatened by the very tensions to which this same need has given rise.

The bridge dream (10-a), however, succeeds much more satisfactorily in subordinating the means to the goal of winning the mother. The dream is dominated by the wish to please her. In the dream work we are able to detect two steps in this attempt. The hostile impulses are first mitigated into erotic ones. Unfortunately, however, the mother is also unwilling to tolerate the patient's sexual impulses toward the sister and the attempt at mitigation must therefore be carried further. To this end he tries to renounce his erotic impulses toward the sister and to please the mother by assuming a protective attitude toward her. In this dream he even goes so far as to be willing to share the mother's love with both brother and sister. He is rewarded by receiving the mother's thanks and a glass of milk.

Thus, in the bridge dream, the erotization of the patient's hostile impulses toward the sister and brother seems to be only a part of the more general modification of the patient's impulses, a modification induced by his hope of pleasing the mother. It would seem that the hope of winning the mother has diminished the tension of his desperate need for the exclusive possession of her love. When the tension diminishes, his hostile impulses toward rivals can be mitigated. Instead of wishing to destroy them, he can content himself with giving the sister a playful pinch.

Thus it would appear that, with decreasing tension, destructive impulses tend to be modified into erotic ones, whereas with increasing tension erotic impulses take on an increasingly destructive character.

In our interpretation of the patient's material, we spoke of the erotization of his hostile impulses toward his brother and sister. By this we meant the substitution of erotic for hostile impulses. The term *erotization* was first introduced by Freud in his attempt to account for phenomena of this sort in terms of a theory of fusion and defusion of erotic and destructive drives. This theory, however, gives us no answer to the question as to just what circumstances determine when erotic and destructive "drives" shall fuse and when they shall again be dissociated.

Our analysis of this patient's material has led us to a somewhat different concept of this problem. Freud's hypothesis was that two different kinds of drives, destructive and erotic, tend to fuse or be defused. Our hypothesis is, rather, that the hope of satisfaction of any wish tends temporarily to neutralize part of the tension of that wish. In accordance with this hypothesis it is no longer necessary to regard erotic and destructive impulses as manifestations of two separate and antagonistic "drives." The modification of erotic into destructive impulses or of destructive into erotic impulses of similar content is, rather, to be explained as a consequence of the respective increase or decrease of a single factor—the tension of unsatisfied needs or desires. As tension increases, it tends to take on more destructive forms; as it decreases, originally destructive impulses are eroticized. Thus the hope of satisfaction by neutralizing the tension of unsatisfied desire tends to lead to the erotization of hostile impulses; conversely, as the neutralizing effect of the hope of satisfaction diminishes, erotic impulses tend to be modified into hostile ones.

In accordance with this principle we should expect that increase of tension from any cause would tend to bring about the reemergence, in their original destructive form, of impulses that had previously been erotized. This is what actually occurs in the dreams that follow the bridge dream (10-a). In the railroad-station dream (10-b), the hope of winning the mother has disappeared and the anxious tension of the patient's need for her has accordingly increased. As a result the protective attitude toward the sister has vanished; instead he is trying to flee from sexual temptation and to seek justification in the eyes of a mother figure by condemning his wife. The attempt to renounce his sexual interest in her has resulted in the reemergence of the underlying hostile and rivalrous attitude toward her. Instead of sharing the mother with her as in the bridge dream, he is now seeking to get the mother to take sides with him against her.

In the anvil dream (12) three days later, the patient's impulses have already taken on a violently aggressive character, and he is able to conceive of reconciliation with the mother only in terms of being beaten into submission.

Dependence as a Mechanism of Social Integration: It will now be of interest to attempt to form a concept, in terms of the hypotheses just described, of the integrative pattern involved in certain types of social relationships. Let us consider first what we mean by dependence. In clinical analysis it is often difficult to discover the genetic source of deep underlying dependent cravings that seem to run more or less as an undercurrent through a patient's whole life history. It is usually much easier to discover the dynamic source of a more superficial dependent wish that arises for the first time as a reaction to a particular situation in the analysis. As an example, we may cite a wish that began to appear in the material of the patient we have just been studying, when the analysis first began to make him aware of the inadequacy of his efforts to please his mother. At this point in the analysis, he began to struggle to protect himself against the insight that his impulses were not pleasing to a woman, by turning to the hope that the analyst would teach him how to behave toward her.

Let us ask, what is the significance of this need for instruction in relation to the patient's fundamental integrative problem? We have only to put the question in order to point to the answer. The patient is seeking to make his integrative load lighter by relegating part of it to someone else, in this case to the analyst. He senses the need to please the analyst, but since the analyst is not impressed with his attempt to renounce and deny his sexual and hostile impulses, he does not know how to make his impulses acceptable to her. In the face of this helplessness, the tension of his need to be loved by a mother tends to rise enormously. He protects himself from this increase in integrative load by a simple device. The analyst shall solve this problem for him. Trusting in her therapeutic interest in him, he protects himself with the hope that she will teach him how to make his impulses acceptable to her, that she will instruct him how to bridge the gap between his own actual impulses and what she requires of him.

We notice that what we have just done is to define dependence as as integrative mechanism. Dependence upon another person consists in the attempt to lighten one's own integrative load by transferring the whole or a part of the integrative task to someone else to solve.

Responsibility for Others as a Mechanism of Social Integration: Our definition of dependence now implies, as a corollary, a definition of what is involved in taking responsibility for the needs of another person. Taking responsibility for another person implies an integrative capacity adequate to span not only one's own needs but the needs of another person as well. In the bridge dream (10-a) we already have a rudimentary example of this type of social integration. In this dream the patient was reacting to the hope that he could please the analyst as he had pleased the mother, by renouncing his sexual and hostile impulses. The attempt to please another person implies a cognitive field that includes a sense of the other person's needs as well as one's own, and in relation to one's own. Thus the bridge dream implies a cognitive field that includes the mother's anxiety to have her daughter returned to her as well as the patient's own impulse to treat the daughter as a rival or as an object of his sexual impulses.

Upon careful scrutiny we find in fact that the cognitive field implied in the bridge dream (10-a) is even more complex than this, in that it takes account not only of the patient's needs and the needs of the mother whom he wishes to please, but also of those of the sister figure. He is able to sense that the young girl also needs the protecting love of a mother, and it is upon this realization that he bases his impulse to share the mother's love with his sister and brother and his hope of pleasing the mother by so doing.

Thus the capacity for taking responsibility for others would seem to be based upon an integrative capacity in excess of that required for the integration of efforts to satisfy one's own needs. The original goal that gave rise to the patient's conflict was a dependent one, to be loved and fed by the mother. This goal takes account only of his own needs and requires the help of the mother to satisfy them. In terms of the patient's own dependent needs, brother and sister are only obstacles in the way of their gratification, and the impulse to get rid of them is a logical means of again securing for himself the exclusive love of his mother. The only defect in this logic is its failure to take account of the psychology of the mother, to realize that the mother will resent impulses to get rid of her other children. In the bridge dream (10-a), however, the goal of the patient's strivings has been expanded into one that takes into account the needs of all three persons concerned, that integrates the hope of pleasing the mother with the hope of sharing the mother's protecting love and care with his sister. Thus the bridge dream may be cited as an elementary example of socially integrated behavior, of behavior whose goal includes satisfaction of the needs of other persons as well as of oneself. According to our analysis, the necessary precondition of such an expansion of the goal of one's strivings is an integrative capacity in excess of that required for the integration of efforts to satisfy one's own needs.

According to our hypothesis, in the partial disintegration of the goal-seeking mechanism that follows, loss of hope of pleasing the mother has resulted in a diminution of integrative capacity, so that the goal of the patient's strivings cannot expand to include the needs of others. With emphasis concentrated upon the patient's own needs, brother and sister again become merely obstacles in the way of his need for exclusive possession of the mother. The result, as seen in the dreams that follow, is the reemergence of the conflict between hostile impulses toward brother and sister and the fear of estranging the mother.

Earlier in our discussion, we attempted to explain the erotization of the patient's hostile impulses toward the young girl in the bridge dream (10-a) as a consequence of the temporary neutralization of tension by the hope of pleasing the mother. According to our hypothesis, the resultant decrease in tension found expression in the mitigation of what had originally been a hostile impulse into an erotic one. This mitigation now finds more complete explanation in terms of our hypothesis that an increase or decrease of integrative capacity gives rise to expansion or contraction of the number of persons included in the goal of this patient's strivings. As long as the goal of the patient's strivings includes only the satisfaction of his own dependent needs, his brother and sister will remain only obstacles in the way of his exclusive possession of the mother; but when the goal of the patient's strivings is expanded to include the girl's dependent needs as well as his own, then the girl ceases to be an obstacle. Moreover, the patient's protective interest in the safety and welfare of the young girl, as well as his own, will tend to exert a mitigating influence upon any remnant of the original hostility that may still be present.

Chapter Ten

THE INTEGRATIVE PROCESS

Implicit in our common-sense knowledge of behavior is the assumption that it can be analyzed into two components: motivation and know-how, motivation and insight. When we wish to predict what a person will do, we inquire first what is his motive. What does he want, and how much does he want it? Then, when we know what he wants, we try to find out what he knows or thinks he knows about how to get what he wants.

Some of the Gestalt psychologists have been particularly interested in the insight by which behavior is guided. For example, in one of Koehler's (1931) many experiments of this kind, an ape is at first baffled in its desire to get fruit just beyond its reach outside the bars of its cage and then suddenly discovers how to make a longer stick by fitting two shorter sticks together. Kurt Lewin (1935) and his co-workers try to help us understand an experimental subject's behavior by making diagrams of his psychological field; they try to map out what the experimental situation looks like to the subject. For example, Kurt Lewin may picture a child separated from his goal, a piece of candy, by a negatively charged barrier of parental prohibition.

However, insight is not always conscious. To take account of this fact, we must rid our concept of insight of any implication that it must be conscious. Machines often seem "intelligent." A thermostat "recognizes" the differences between a temperature lower and a temperature higher than a desired temperature; it "responds" to the lower temperature by turning on the heat, to the higher temperature by turning it off. Even though other influences may cause the temperature

Reprinted from *Dialectica*, 5 (1951).

to fluctuate widely, the thermostat continues to "react" so as to restore its "goal temperature." Without any conscious awareness, it is guided by an elementary kind of insight. Its "behavior" has a goal or "motive" and is guided by a cognitive mechanism.

The other component in the determination of behavior is its motivation. Integrative fields are polarized by an urge to get from where one is to a desired goal. Yet cognitive and integrative fields differ in the amount of motivating pressure that activates them. Sometimes we have insight on how to achieve a goal without any desire to make use of it. For example, I may be able to tell someone else how to get to a certain place although I have no desire to go there myself. The intensity of one's desire to achieve a goal is its motivating pressure. The motivating pressure of a plan is the urge to put the plan into execution.

We should distinguish between motivating pressures according to the nature of their goals. Some motivating pressures have only negative goals. They are urges to get away from something, to escape from pain or from the object of one's fear, to put an end to the distressing physiological state of hunger. These states of unrest we call needs or drives; they are characterized by painful subjective pressure which tends to seek discharge in diffuse muscular activity, like the restless thrashing about of a hungry infant.

Other wishes arise out of hopes. Stimulated by opportunities for satisfaction or by memories of previous satisfaction, they are longings to realize these hopes. The goals of such wishes are positive. They are wishes for something, not wishes to get away from something.

In the integration of goal-directed behavior, needs and hopes play complementary roles. They are the poles, negative and positive, about which all behavior is oriented.

We summarize as follows the process of activation of goal-directed behavior: First, the motivating pressure of a need seeks discharge in diffuse motor activity. Next, hope of satisfaction, based on present opportunity and on memories of previous success, stimulates the integrative mechanism to form a plan for realizing this hope. Finally, hope of satisfaction activates this plan so that it exerts a guiding influence, channeling motor discharge into efforts to put the plan into execution.

We should expect, perhaps, that when one's desire for a goal increases, his efforts to achieve it will become more effective. When the motivating pressure is not excessive, this is often true; but excessive pressure has just the opposite effect. When pressure becomes excessive the patterns of goal-directed behavior disintegrate, giving place to poorly

*directed and diffuse motor discharge. In everyday life we call this
"losing one's head."*

*"Losing one's head" can best be accounted for by the hypothesis
that, when motivating pressure is excessive, the necessary guiding
insight cannot control motor discharge: The pressure of a need first
seeks diffuse discharge in motor activity. In order to achieve a goal,
one must bring this motor discharge under the control of an integrative
field. The difficulty of this task of channeling motor discharge into
effective effort increases in proportion to the amount of pressure that
must be controlled or bound. The amount of pressure that has to be
bound by an integrative field is its integrative task. To account for the
fact that an integrative field sometimes cannot exert effective control
over motor discharge, we assume next that the integrative field itself at
any given moment has a quantitatively limited capacity to bind motivational pressure. For effective goal-directed behavior, integrative capacity
must be adequate to the integrative task. Disintegration of the mechanisms of goal-directed behavior occurs whenever the integrative task
exceeds the integrative capacity.*

*Our thesis is that, in irrational behavior, the integrative mechanisms
that must be postulated to account for rational behavior have undergone
fragmentation, followed usually by partial reintegrations of some of
the fragments.*

Implicit in our common-sense knowledge of *behavior* is the assumption
that it *can be analyzed into two components:* motivation and know-how,
motivation and insight. When we wish to predict what a person will
do, we inquire first what is his motive. What does he want, and how
much does he want it? Then, when we know what he wants, we try
to find out what he knows or thinks he knows about how to get what
he wants.

THE GUIDING INFLUENCE OF INSIGHT

Some of the Gestalt psychologists have been particularly interested
in the insight by which behavior is guided. For example, in one of
Koehler's [1] many experiments of this kind, an ape is at first baffled in

1. W. Koehler, *The Mentality of Apes* (2d ed.; New York: Harcourt, Brace & Co.,
1931).

its desire to get fruit just beyond its reach outside the bars of its cage, and then suddenly discovers how to make a longer stick by fitting two shorter sticks together. Kurt Lewin [2] and his co-workers try to help us understand an experimental subject's behavior by making diagrams of his psychological field; they try to map out what the experimental situation looks like to the subject. For example, Lewin may picture a child separated from his goal, a piece of candy, by a negatively charged barrier of parental prohibition.

The situation as the experimental subject understands it is, of course, not necessarily identical with the actual situation as it looks to an outside observer. Sometimes the experimental subject is unaware of aspects of the situation that are important for the solution of his problem. For example, Koehler tells of a dog's being so fascinated by a piece of meat which it could see just on the other side of a fence that it neglected to turn around and discover how it might have run around the end of the fence.

In many of these experiments, insight is assumed to be conscious; the psychological field is assumed to correspond to the situation as the experimental subject consciously sees it. However, insight is not always conscious. Conditioned response experiments show that a person can acquire an adaptive response without conscious awareness of the process. The finer details of most motor skills are automatic; conscious attention often interferes with them instead of improving them. In psychopathological states, one may perform even complex purposive acts without being aware of what he is doing.

To take account of these facts, we must rid our concept of insight of any implication that it must be conscious. Machines often seem "intelligent." A thermostat "recognizes" the difference between a temperature lower and a temperature higher than a desired temperature; it "responds" to the lower temperature by turning on the heat, to the higher temperature by turning it off. Even though other influences may cause the temperature to fluctuate widely, the thermostat continues to "react" so as to restore its "goal temperature." Without any conscious awareness, it is guided by an elementary kind of insight. Its "behavior" has a goal or "motive" and is guided by a cognitive mechanism.

The notions of unconscious insight and of the "cognitive mechanism" of a machine may be confusing at first. Yet, actually, at any particular time, most of what we know is not conscious; it is only capable of becoming conscious.

2. Kurt Lewin, *A Dynamic Theory of Personality* (New York: McGraw-Hill, 1935).

Still, we can form a concept of unconscious insight only by analogy with conscious knowledge. By reflecting on the nature of conscious perception and knowledge, we realize that it involves patterning of the data with which it deals. We see or understand things in relation to each other. By analogy with conscious knowledge, we postulate that the same kind of patterning occurs without our being aware of it or we contrive a machine that can discriminate between different kinds of patterns.

An early step in the evolution of biological regulatory functions is the differentiation of cognitive from executive systems. Primitive nervous networks are found in the simplest metazoan organisms and have increased progressively in complexity as more highly differentiated organisms have evolved. Instead of allowing external forces to activate directly the effector systems, such a nervous network is selectively sensitive to stimuli and elaborates them in patterns before transmitting their activating influence to the effectors. When the result is to pattern response so as to achieve an adaptive goal, a nervous system corresponds to the concept of cognitive mechanism that we have been outlining.

MUTUAL INDUCTION BETWEEN INTEGRATIVE FIELDS

The simplest possible cognitive mechanism is a cognitive field.[3] A cognitive field selects and patterns incoming stimuli and activates effector mechanisms to react not to the separate stimuli but to their pattern.

Another distinction is useful. One may know something without doing much about it. The term "cognitive" focuses our attention on the process of patterning incoming impressions. Yet cognitive fields also exert a guiding influence on behavior. When we are particularly interested in this guiding influence of a cognitive field, we call it an integrative field.

To estimate the influence of an integrative field in actual behavior we must first know the goal toward which the organism (or machine) is striving and the pattern of the insight by which it is guided in this striving. Then we compare the behavior actually observed with the sum of the reactions that we should expect if the organism had reacted independently to the stimuli impinging on it. The effect of the guiding insight or cognitive field is the difference between the behavior actually observed and this hypothetical sum or resultant. For example, in Koehler's experiment, the ape, before discovering the trick of fitting

3. We have borrowed this term from the Gestalt psychologists.

the two sticks together, was reacting successively to various aspects of the situation. The difference between its behavior after and before acquiring this insight is the effect of the integrative field that had taken form in the meantime.

However, the guiding influence of a single integrative field can account for only the simplest goal-directed behavior. To account for more complexly integrated behavior, we must assume that two or more integrative fields act upon each other. For example, in efforts to achieve a purpose, a plan for achieving an end goal must activate a plan for achieving the next subsidiary goal.

Sometimes we put our integrative fields on paper; we make maps or plans. We can illustrate the functional relationships between integrative fields by considering how we use maps in planning a trip. Let us suppose that I am in Chicago and want to drive to Cleveland, Ohio. A map of the Midwestern states tells me that the most direct route to Cleveland is Route 20, leading through South Bend and Toledo; but since I do not happen to be on Route 20, I must next consult a street map of Chicago. Guided by the street map, I drive to the nearest point on Route 20. Then, following the street map, I turn right on Route 20. Later I can check my conclusion that this is the right direction, for I soon find Lake Michigan on my left, as both maps tell me it should be if I am driving away from the center of Chicago and toward Cleveland.

In this example, the two maps function as two integrative fields. The interstate map serves as an integrative field polarized and activated by my desire to drive from Chicago to Cleveland; and my desire to drive to Cleveland is transferred from the interstate map to the street map as an incentive to get from where I am to the nearest point on Route 20. Thus in the integrative process that guides me in driving from Chicago to Cleveland, the essential steps are transfers of incentive from one integrative field to another—first from the interstate map to the street map of Chicago, then from the street map to the actual roads as perceived, and finally, by means of the musculature, to the steering wheel and engine of the automobile.

In the orderly execution of a plan, such a transfer of incentive from one integrative field to another is dependent upon a certain equivalence of pattern between them. In our example, the street map corresponds in pattern to a part of the interstate map; and the actual landscape, as perceived, is equivalent to a part of the street map. If there were no such equivalence between the two maps we would not transfer incentive from one to the other. For example, if we did not find the lake where the maps show it or if one map showed it and the other did not, we should probably be unwilling to proceed until we had decided how to reconcile our conflicting guides. A discrepancy between two of our guiding integrative fields would make us want to bring them into harmony with each other, to correct one of the two maps to make it agree with the other, or to correct both to bring them into harmony with the perceived landscape. In other words, each of the three cognitive patterns tends to impose on the others an equivalent or homologous pattern. Such a need to establish and maintain equivalence of pattern between two cognitive fields we call *resonance* or *mutual induction* between them.

This need to bring two interacting cognitive fields into harmony with each other is not only significant for the integrative process involved in execution of plans; it also furnishes the motivating drive for the process of forming plans. The guiding integrative field itself must first take form by mutual induction between a perceived real situation and wish-fulfilling fantasy. For example, I may fondly imagine myself climbing mountains in Colorado; but actually I find myself sweltering in the hot streets of Chicago. Then I get out my road maps and plan how I can get from Chicago to Colorado. The planning process has two poles: (1) what one fantasies as fulfilling one's desires; and (2) what one perceives as real. Its task is to find a bridge between reality as perceived and wish-fulfilling fantasy. The gap between reality and fantasy must be bridged by a process of mutual induction, by finding a plan that is in resonance at one pole with perceived reality and at the other with wish-fulfilling fantasy.

INTEGRATIVE FIELDS AND MOTIVATING PRESSURES

We turn now to the other component in the determination of behavior, its motivation.

Integrative fields are polarized by an urge to get from where one is to a desired goal. Yet cognitive and integrative fields differ in the amount of motivating pressure that activates them. Sometimes we have insight on how to achieve a goal without any desire to make use of it. For example, I may be able to tell someone else how to get to a certain place although I have no desire to go there myself. *The intensity of one's desire to achieve a goal is its motivating pressure. The motivating pressure of a plan is the urge to put the plan into execution.*

We should distinguish between motivating pressures according to the nature of their goals. Some motivating pressures have only negative goals. They are urges to get away from something, to escape from pain or from the object of one's fear, to put an end to the distressing physiological state of hunger. These states of unrest we call needs or drives; they are characterized by painful subjective pressure [4] which tends to seek discharge in diffuse muscular activity, like the restless thrashing about of a hungry infant.

Other wishes arise out of hopes. Stimulated by opportunities for satisfaction or by memories of previous satisfaction, they are longings to realize these hopes. The goals of such wishes are positive. They are wishes for something, not wishes to get away from something.

In the integration of goal-directed behavior, *needs and hopes* play complementary roles. *They are the poles, negative and positive, about which all behavior is oriented.* Although we try first to escape from painful pressures arising from our needs, our efforts tend to be focused more specifically on positive goals based on our hopes. Whereas the activity stimulated by an unsatisfied need tends to be diffuse, hope of satisfaction tends to concentrate this activity on a more circumscribed goal. Hunger gives rise to diffuse motor restlessness, but the sight of food directs this restless activity into efforts to achieve the specific goal of getting food. In general, the motivating pressure of a need gives rise to motor discharge in many directions, but a hope channels this motor discharge into efforts to achieve a particular goal.

The negative and positive goals of behavior differ also in their relation to learning from experience. Some lower animals inherit highly developed adaptive patterns; but a human being must learn how his needs can be satisfied. Only after an infant has learned that the mother's breast satisfies hunger does his primary need, hunger, give rise to a wish for the mother's breast. Only by insight acquired by experience is the motivating pressure of a primary need (drive) channeled into efforts to achieve a positive goal.

Thus we are reminded again of the essential part played by insight in the integration of goal-directed behavior. The motivating pressure of a need seeks discharge in motor activity; but a well-directed effort

4. It is customary to speak of the "tension" of a need. However, pressure (push) is a more suitable term than tension (pull), since it is directed primarily away from a negative goal rather than toward a positive goal. Accordingly, deviating from customary usage, we use the term "motivating pressure" to designate both the dynamic influence exerted by a need and the unpleasant subjective feelings by which this motivating pressure is manifested in consciousness.

to achieve a goal is something more than mere motor discharge of pressure. To achieve a goal it is not enough just to do something. One must also know what to do. To be of any use at all, efforts to achieve a goal must be guided by practical understanding of the problem to be solved, by some kind of plan for achieving one's purpose. Efforts to achieve a goal result only when motor discharge of the pressure of a need is integrated with the guiding influence of a plan.

It is in this way that hope of satisfaction can focus motor discharge on circumscribed efforts to achieve a goal. These circumscribed efforts to achieve a goal are efforts to execute a plan. Hope tends to activate a plan. By activating the guiding influence of a plan on motor discharge, hope concentrates this motor discharge on efforts to achieve a positive goal.

We summarize as follows the process of activation of goal-directed behavior: First, the motivating pressure of a need seeks discharge in diffuse motor activity. Next, hope of satisfaction, based on present opportunity and on memories of previous success, stimulates the integrative mechanism to form a plan for realizing this hope. Finally, hope of satisfaction activates this plan so that it exerts a guiding influence, channeling motor discharge into efforts to put the plan into execution.

EFFECTS OF EXCESSIVE MOTIVATIONAL PRESSURE

We should expect, perhaps, that when one's desire for a goal increases, his efforts to achieve it would become more effective. When the motivating pressure is not excessive, this is often true; but excessive pressure has just the opposite effect. When pressure becomes excessive, the patterns of goal-directed behavior disintegrate, giving place to poorly directed and diffuse motor discharge. In everyday life we call this "losing one's head."

As a dramatic example of such disintegration of the patterns of rational behavior, I like to use a story once told by a mountain guide: One day, while lost in a forest, he suddenly found himself out of breath. He had been running. He knew that running was the worst thing he could do when lost in the woods, so he made a strenuous effort to "collect himself"; but in a moment he was again out of breath. He had again been running. This second time, fortunately, he did succeed in restraining his overpowering impulse to run. Climbing a tree instead, he was able to spy at some distance a familiar house. Then his importunate fear disappeared.

"Losing one's head" can best be accounted for by the hypothesis that, when motivating pressure is excessive, the necessary guiding insight cannot control motor discharge: The pressure of a need first seeks diffuse discharge in motor activity. In order to achieve a goal, one must bring this motor discharge under the control of an integrative field. The difficulty of this task of channeling motor discharge into effective effort increases in proportion to the amount of pressure that must be controlled or bound. The amount of pressure that has to be bound by an integrative field is its *integrative task*. To account for the fact that an integrative field sometimes cannot exert effective control over motor discharge, we assume next that the integrative field itself at any given moment has a quantitatively limited capacity to bind motivational pressure. For effective goal-directed behavior, *integrative capacity* must be adequate to the integrative task. Disintegration of the mechanisms of goal-directed behavior occurs whenever the integrative task exceeds the integrative capacity.

An integrative capacity that is inadequate to its integrative task may also be reflected in an earlier step of the integrative process, by limitation of the *span of the guiding integrative field*. In a comic moving picture, for example, the screen hero is sometimes pictured as unaware of important aspects of his situation. He steals an apple and then discovers that the owner of the fruit stand has been standing behind him all the time; then he runs off only to bump into a policeman a few yards away. To designate the delimitations of what is included in an integrative field, we use the term *integrative span,* or the span of the integrative field. In the example just mentioned, the screen hero's integrative span included at first only the apple as object of his desire, then only the fruit-stand owner and the desire to escape from him, then only the policeman.

In our patients we often observe behavior that is not so different from these caricatures on the screen. At one moment a patient will be acting on an overpowering forbidden impulse, apparently quite oblivious of any fear of consequences; but a few moments or hours or days later he will be overwhelmed by fear of punishment for what he has done. Such behavior we interpret as evidence that the patient is able to span only one-half of his conflict at a time. If his integrative span had been adequate, he would not have acted on his forbidden impulse until he had first considered how to deal with the consequences that were to be expected.

From the preceding discussion, it is evident that the integrative task increases roughly in proportion to the motivating pressure of the underlying need or to the sum of the pressures of conflicting needs.

Since it is hope of success that activates the guiding influence of a plan, we must expect that integrative capacity should increase with increasing confidence of attaining one's goal. Everyday observation confirms this expectation. When one is confident of success, he becomes willing to forgo other satisfactions and to withstand the painful pressure of disturbing needs in order to realize his hope of success. Conversely, when one expects to fail, his capacity to make sacrifices and to withstand pressures for the sake of a goal disappears.

We started this paper with a discussion of the part played by insight in the integration of rational behavior; but our study of the effects of excessive motivational pressure is now leading us back to the problems with which psychoanalysis is becoming increasingly preoccupied: to inquire into the integrative processes in neuroses, psychoses, and other kinds of irrational behavior. Our thesis is that *in irrational behavior, the integrative mechanisms that must be postulated to account for rational behavior have undergone fragmentation,* followed usually by partial reintegrations of some of the fragments.

In the early years of psychoanalytic investigation, Freud concentrated his interest on the repressed and unconscious parts of the personality. He resolutely postponed study of the "higher" mental functions until he had thoroughly explored the unconscious. Later he began to correct this one-sided orientation.

Especially his analysis of the structure of the personality has won wide acceptance in the psychoanalytic literature. Yet our use of Freud's structural concepts has not really corrected the original one-sided orientation. We tend to think too schematically about the ego and the id and the superego, trying to fit our patients' material into a uniform mold, instead of observing and analyzing clinically both sides of our patients' conflicts and the attempts of the integrative mechanism to find a solution for them. In our next three papers, we shall carry Freud's analysis further, trying to find a still more flexible dynamic approach to the study of the total personality.

We shall start with the superego. The concept of the superego implies that the motive for repression and inhibition of disturbing motives is guilt; but the motives for inhibition are not always the same. In each case, as we point out in "Structural and Functional Approaches to the Analysis of Behavior," there is a specific inhibiting motive, an appropriate reaction to the particular wish that is being censored. Probably it is based in every case on the disturbing consequences of past attempts to fulfill a similar wish. For example, an intense dependent wish may arouse protest from the dreamer's pride; a hostile impulse may give rise to a guilt reaction; a sexual impulse in a man may stir up fear of the *father; or the same sexual impulse may lead to fear of rebuff from the mother figure toward whom it is directed.*

When we now study a dreamer's reaction, we find that it is more than an attempt to give disguised expression to the disturbing wish. The dream work must struggle somehow to reconcile the two conflicting motives. The conflict between them is a problem *which the integrative mechanism must try to solve. For example, the dreamer's pride, threatened by a dependent wish, may react with compensatory fantasies of independence or achievement, or may try to conjure up a situation in which the dependent craving would not be too incompatible with self-respect. The dreamer whose guilt has been aroused by his hostile wishes may imagine himself unjustly treated in order to justify his hostility; or his guilt may demand appeasement by a fantasy of being punished.*

In the paper on "Analysis of the Dream Censorship," we outline a method for analysis of dream censorship.

First we try to discover the dream wish that is most intensely cathected. This is the "disturbing motive" of the dream.

Then we compare this disturbing wish with the manifest dream. From the nature of the manifest dream's reactions we try to deduce just why this wish was disturbing. The motive that is responsible for the dream censor's reactions to the disturbing wish is the dreamer's "reactive motive."

The conflict between the disturbing motive and the reactive motive is the dreamer's "focal conflict." By comparing this focal conflict with the manifest dream we try next to determine how the problem-solving function of the dreamer's ego has dealt with the focal conflict. The focal conflict presents the patient with a problem. The problem is to find a way in real life to reconcile the dreamer's disturbing motive and his reactive motive. Often the dreamer's ego continues in the dream work to search for a solution of this problem.

On the other hand, the dreamer's conflict is usually too great for the ego to face. Then the ego's task becomes one of trying to reformulate the problem. By substituting a similar problem in which the dreamer is much less intensely involved, the ego tries to achieve some degree of detachment from the problem and to get a better perspective on the question at issue. In this way the ego tries to diminish the dreamer's "integrative task" and to bring it within the span of the dreamer's "integrative capacity."

In the course of a patient's treatment, his capacity for understanding his conflicts keeps fluctuating. The kind of precise analysis of the dream censorship that we have just outlined helps us to improve our understanding of these fluctuations and of the reasons for them. In this way we can improve very much our ability to follow intelligently the vicissitudes of the therapeutic process.

In the third paper, "Guilt, Shame, and Other Reactive Motives," we attempt a more extended survey of the kinds of reactive motives that we encounter in the analysis of many different kinds of patients.

Chapter Eleven

STRUCTURAL AND FUNCTIONAL
APPROACHES TO
THE ANALYSIS OF BEHAVIOR

I

In the early years of psychoanalytic investigation, Freud concentrated his interest on the repressed and unconscious parts of the personality. He resolutely postponed study of the "higher" mental functions until he had thoroughly explored the unconscious. Later he began to correct this one-sided orientation.

Especially his analysis of the structure of the personality has won wide acceptance in the psychoanalytic literature. Yet our use of Freud's structural concepts has not really corrected the original one-sided orientation. We tend to think too schematically about the ego and the id and the superego, trying to fit our patients' material into a uniform mold, instead of observing and analyzing clinically both sides of our patients' conflicts and the attempts of the integrative mechanism to find a solution for them. In this paper I am raising the question of whether we cannot find a more flexible dynamic approach to the study of the total personality.

When Freud (5) first studied the dream work, he attributed the act of repression to a dream censor. This was one of his first structural concepts. The dream censor, he postulated, distorts and disguises unacceptable wishes so as to make them unrecognizable. At a time when he was not yet ready to study the repressing forces, this suggestive

Reprinted from *Mid-Century Psychiatry: An Overview* (Springfield, Ill., 1953).

analogy with a political censorship personified and dramatized a hypothetical repressing agent and permitted him to postpone further analysis of the motives that activate the dream censorship.

Now that we are interested in the functioning of the personality as a whole, *the motives that inspire the dream censorship are just as important* to discover *as the motives that are repressed.* Yet the great suggestive value of Freud's analogy with a political censor has made it easy to take the dream censorship for granted. In the psychoanalytic literature, it is astonishing how often we neglect to inquire critically in each particular case what motives are responsible for repression.

When we do inquire, we find that the motives for repression are by no means always the same. The dream censorship is neither a person nor an impersonal system of the mind. In each case it is a specific inhibiting motive, an appropriate reaction to the particular dream wish that is being censored. Probably it is based in every case on the disturbing consequences of past attempts to fulfill a similar wish. For example, an intense dependent wish may arouse protest from the dreamer's pride; a hostile impulse may give rise to a guilt reaction; a sexual impulse in a man may stir up fear of the father; or the same sexual impulse may lead to fear of rebuff from the mother figure toward whom it is directed.

When we now study a dreamer's reaction we find that it is more than an attempt to give disguised expression to the disturbing wish. The dream work must struggle somehow to reconcile the two conflicting motives. The conflict between them is a *problem* which the integrative mechanism must try to solve. For example, the dreamer's pride, threatened by a dependent wish, may react with compensatory fantasies of independence or achievement, or may try to conjure up a situation in which the dependent craving would not be too incompatible with self-respect. The dreamer whose guilt has been aroused by his hostile wishes may imagine himself unjustly treated in order to justify his hostility; or his guilt may demand appeasement by a fantasy of being punished.

On the other hand, when we content ourselves with the notion of a dream censor which we do not further analyze, we can easily fail to recognize the problem-solving activity that is hidden behind tangled chains of associations in the latent dream thoughts.

II

Freud's two successive reconstructions of the origins of the conscience are two classical examples of an analysis that tries to take account of all the interacting motives.

The first of these reconstructions was part of his elaboration of the concept of narcissism (6). One form of infantile narcissism is a kind of megalomania: the infant likes to imagine himself omnipotent and perfect. Yet his actual helplessness and the criticisms of his parents make it impossible for him to maintain this illusion. He protects himself from disillusionment by attributing the wished-for perfection to an ego-ideal. The conscience arises as a need to achieve this ideal in reality.

Later, supplementing this account, Freud derived the conscience from the child's attempts to resolve the Oedipus complex (7). In the Oedipus complex, the little boy's ambition to be powerful like the father fuses with his desire to possess the mother sexually. Thwarted in this desire by his fear of castration by the father, he is driven to seek another way of identifying with the father's power. He achieves this goal by imposing on himself the father's prohibitions, threats, and punishments. The part of the personality that splits off thus to identify with the father's prohibitive role is the conscience or superego.

The inverted Oedipus complex also contributes to the formation of the superego, since the little boy is thwarted also in his desire to be loved sexually by the father. When the superego takes over the father's role, submitting to the restraints and punishments imposed by the super-ego can serve as a substitute for gratification of the boy's feminine desire to submit to the father.

III

However, since the publication of *The Ego and the Id*, we often use the superego concept as we once did the concept of the dream censor. Instead of emulating Freud's method of analyzing an interplay of motives, we personify the ego and the superego and use them as explanatory concepts that seem to make further analysis unnecessary. For example, we may say that the ego accepts an id impulse, is punished by the superego, and submits to this punishment. By thinking of ego and superego as persons, we seem to "understand" their "behavior" by a kind of empathy.

Yet personifying the ego or the superego, instead of helping, tends to divert us from the task of analyzing the integrative functions. The ego and the superego are both complex mechanisms. When we personify them, we ignore their complexity. In order not to be diverted from the task of trying to analyze complex functions into their component parts, it is better, instead of thinking of the ego, to think of the integrative mechanism; and, instead of attributing an inhibitory reaction to the superego, we should try to find out whether a patient is reacting with guilt, or pride, or fear of punishment, or fear of loss of love, or some other specific conflicting motive.

IV

Fortunately, we do not always make such schematic use of Freud's analysis of the structure of the personality. I shall not attempt an extensive review of the literature but shall merely mention a few studies that call attention to particular kinds of conflict that we frequently encounter clinically.

In an early paper discussing the differences between child analysis and the analysis of adult patients, Anna Freud (4) called attention to the fact that the child's superego can usually not be counted upon to inhibit disturbing impulses unless it is supported by prohibitions from the parents or from the analyst. Evidently in these children the process of introjecting parental prohibitions has not been completed, and the prohibitions imposed by the superego must therefore be reinforced either by fear of punishment or by fear of loss of the parents' love.

In many adult patients, the process of introjection of parental inhibitions is similarly incomplete, and fear of punishment or fear of loss of love is often the dominant inhibitory motive, supplementing or even replacing guilt. For example, in our studies of bronchial asthma at the Chicago Psychoanalytic Institute (3) we found that asthma attacks are precipitated only by situations in which fear of estrangement (or separation) from a mother figure is the inhibiting motive. During periods when introjection of parental prohibitions was more successful, the patients developed other symptoms, such as neurotic compulsions, but were free of asthma.

Alexander has devoted considerable attention to another motive that is often responsible for repressions and reaction formations. He has pointed out, for example, that feelings of inferiority on account of strong dependent needs are often reacted to with aggressive criminal

behavior: the criminal is trying to prove that he is not soft but tough
(1). Later Alexander called attention to the fact that such feelings of
inferiority often come into direct conflict with guilt feelings (2). Guilt
inhibits aggressive impulses and subdues a man into submissive attitudes;
but such submissive impulses give rise to feelings of inferiority that
drive him again into aggressive behavior.

In a recent paper, Piers (8) has elaborated this contrast further, insisting on the distinction between guilt and shame. The word "shame,"
which he uses in a somewhat broader sense than usual, corresponds to
Alexander's "feelings of inferiority." Piers finds the essential difference
between guilt and shame in the fact that guilt inhibits and condemns
transgression whereas shame demands achievement of a positive goal.
He adds a structural distinction between guilt and shame: guilt, he
believes, proceeds from the superego, shame from the ego-ideal.

V

In trying to understand the reactions of the personality as a whole,
our basic task is to reconstruct the problem that the integrative mechanism is struggling to solve. To illustrate this approach I shall next
discuss a dream analysis:

The dreamer was a forty-six-year-old married man under analysis by
Dr. Helen McLean (3) for bronchial asthma. He worked in a railroad
freight yard where, on account of his asthma, he was treated very in-
dulgently. In the twenty-fifth hour of his analysis he reported the
following dream:

Boxcar, in a room or building, like in office where we work. Door open
in boxcar. Switchman called my attention to it. We both walked over and
opened door further. Full of all kinds of merchandise, all unpacked. I
pulled out pad of paper, kind of cheap so I threw it back. Then picked
up a lot of pencils, all No. 1. Then took any pad, said I might need it
later. Policeman or watchman came in and asked if door was closed. I
said no and closed it—felt guilty about taking this pad and pencils. All I
remember.

As the patient woke up from this dream he was wheezing hard. He
had to use adrenalin.

His associations were as follows: In his work, the patient often had
to inspect boxcars. When the door of a boxcar was open the switchman
wanted a man to go with him as a witness that nothing was taken.

When asked to inspect a car, they often teased by saying "Bring it into the office." The analyst inquired if the paper and pencils resembled the paper and pencils that the analyst used to take notes. . . . The patient said "No," that the pencils were like those that the railroad furnished. "Maybe I wanted to write a letter," he added. "Maybe I do, to father or brothers. . . . I only think about writing home but don't do it. Didn't see father or brother in dream, only the two men I work with, one a switchman, the other a watchman. Here I was stealing, felt guilty, felt he would think I took those articles."

I shall not take time to report the hours just preceding this dream, from which it is evident that the patient is reacting to his treatment by a woman as a temptation. In the dream text he tells us that he felt guilty. Apparently stealing pencils and a pad from a boxcar has been substituted for some sexual impulse that disturbs him.

If some analyst were so disposed, I do not doubt that he could force this dream into the pattern of a superego based on the Oedipus complex. The watchman is an authoritative figure who is calling the dreamer to account. The dream text also calls him a policeman. He might well be a projected image of the patient's superego. If the analyst to whom the patient feels attracted is a mother figure he should feel guilty toward the father, and it is therefore fitting that his superego should be represented by a man.

However, this interpretation has not attempted to bring the details of the dream text and associations into relation with the dreamer's actual conflict situation. Whom does the switchman represent? And what is the meaning of his showing the dreamer the open door of the boxcar? When the watchman appears he asks whether the door was closed. What is the meaning of this question?

To understand these details, we must reconstruct the patient's conflict more carefully. He is probably reacting not only to the seductive implications of being alone with a woman but also to the permissiveness of the therapeutic situation. In the therapeutic situation he is encouraged to talk freely even about forbidden topics. The open door of the boxcar symbolizes this seductive permissiveness of the analytic situation; and the switchman who is calling attention to the open door is the analyst. When the watchman asks whether the door was closed he is asking about this permissiveness of the analytic situation. "Were you not forbidden to take those pencils?" is the meaning of his question; and the patient answers "No," putting the blame on the analyst.

However, in the actual therapeutic situation the patient is not sure of the analyst's permissiveness. We suggested a moment ago that the watchman might be a projected image of the patient's conscience; but the dreamer's actual situation suggests a simpler explanation, that both the switchman and the watchman represent the analyst who, in spite of her seeming permissiveness, is also a forbidding mother figure to him. Although she seems to be encouraging his forbidden wishes, she might be offended as his mother would have been.

This conflict situation is the immediately effective stimulus for this dream. By comparing it with the dream text we can deduce what features of this stimulus situation are most disturbing to the dreamer and how he would wish to correct them.

1) The dream text pictures temptation as occurring not in the analyst's office but in the freight yards where he works. Actually the patient is consulting the analyst as a physician; his relationship to her is a professional one. To protect himself from temptation he needs to reassure himself that the situation is really a professional one, not a personal relationship with sexual implications. The dream work has tried to carry this reassurance further, substituting his relationship to the men on the job for his too personal relationship to the analyst. A number of references in dream text and associations emphasize this substitution of the less conflictful job situation.

2) To protect him from temptation from a woman, the dream work has substituted two men. For his sexual impulse toward her, the dream has substituted the rather trivial symbolic act of stealing pencils from a boxcar.

3) In reality the woman who is tempting him is the same one whom he is afraid of offending. To relieve him of this embarrassment, the dream work has assigned the analyst's two conflicting roles to two different substitutes. By this device, the dreamer is able first to respond to the temptation and then to deal with his fear of offending a parental figure. In this way the dream permits him to avoid confronting the two sides of his conflict.

VI

Following Freud, we usually think that the dream censorship is exercised by the superego. Yet it is evident from our analysis that this dream's distortion of its picture of the conflict situation has not been motivated by guilt. The distortion in this dream is not a reaction of the dreamer's conscience to a forbidden wish. On the contrary, his guilt and his fear of offending the analyst are part of the conflict situation that has served as the dream stimulus. It is not only the forbidden impulse but the conflict situation as a whole that has been given distorted representation in the dream text.

To understand the motive and mechanism of the distortion in this dream, we must reconstruct the problem which the dreamer's integrative mechanism faces. The patient's conflict in real life, which we have just reconstructed, is too great to be spanned by his integrative mechanism. It presents an integrative task that is in excess of his integrative capacity. In order to bring the dreamer's problem within the span of his integrative capacity, the dream work has substituted an analogous but less disturbing problem. Similarly in waking life, when a problem is too complex to be grasped all at once, we may try first to solve an analogous but simpler problem. (This is, e.g., a technique frequently used in solving difficult mathematical problems.) Or, if one is too much involved in a controversy in actual life, it is often wise to withdraw to a distance for a time in order to view the points at issue with better perspective.

For our understanding of this device it is important to recognize that one cannot get rid of a disturbing conflict. For example, this dream could not wish its problem away; all that the dream work could achieve was to substitute a less disturbing but analogous hypothetical problem. And even this device gave only temporary relief; for the dreamer soon awoke with an acute attack of asthmatic wheezing.

VII

One of Freud's earliest insights was his discovery that hysterical symptoms are reminiscences; a hysterical symptom is the precipitate of a traumatic memory. His reconstruction of the origin of the conscience follows the same pattern: The conscience is a precipitate of the Oedipus complex. The normal conscience results from resolution of the Oedipus complex. An unresolved Oedipus complex leaves a neurosis or a neurotic character as its residue.

The Oedipus complex is, of course, not the only traumatic memory that can leave its traces in a patient's character. Even the dream that we have just been discussing involves a conflict that differs considerably from Freud's classical picture of a little boy's competition with the father for the mother.

From our analysis, it appears that it is not his conscience but the analyst that this patient is afraid of offending. He reminds us of Anna Freud's child analysands. He has not yet acquired a superego that is independent of support from a parental figure. He has not yet introjected parental prohibitions and imposed them on himself. He is much more afraid of a mother's disapproval than of his own conscience.

On the other hand, the inhibiting motive in this dream is not simply fear of loss of love. The watchman, when he appears, is not immediately offended but asks the patient to justify himself. The need to justify oneself implies a rule of conduct acknowledged by both accuser and accused. The rule of conduct to which appeal is here made is one that is familiar in the nursery: "Don't take things without permission." The patient's reply to the watchman's question is a kind of shamefaced admission that he has taken the analyst's permissiveness too seriously. However, in the end the dream's attempt to justify him fails; for he awakens wheezing with asthma.

When we transpose this scene back into the patient's childhood, it is evident that this little boy was too afraid of offending his mother to come into active competition with his father. If our reconstruction of this dream is correct, he has fled from a too ambivalently personal relationship with a woman to a less threatening camaraderie with the men on the job; and when the watchman appears it is not as a dreaded rival but as one who comes to enforce the mother's authority.

The fantasied episode with the two men on the job is also patterned on a familiar scene in the nursery—one in which a little boy and his brother are caught by a parent in some trivial forbidden act. And the substitution of two men on the job for the analyst suggests a pattern that may well have become established in childhood—a pattern of turning for companionship to brother or father figures when his relationship to his mother became too conflictful.

VIII

And now, from this example, we can see the essential error in our structural approach to the analysis of behavior. When we read the superego and the ego into our analysis of a patient's behavior, we are trying to force the reactions of a particular individual into the pattern of a life history described by Freud as typical. But no individual is entirely typical. Instead of using Freud's account of the Oedipus complex as a Procrustean bed into which everything must fit, we should try rather to find the actual memories which have shaped the patterns of this particular patient's behavior.

Thus we return to the method that was always basic in Freud's attempts to interpret the neuroses. We search in our patient's thoughts and behavior for the *persistent dynamic effect of particular traumatic memories*. Now that we are interested in the personality as a whole, we modify this basic method of Freud's only by one slight shift of emphasis for which he has already shown us the way. We must now pay attention to both sides of our patient's conflict and try to reconstruct the problem with which the integrative mechanism is struggling. Once we have succeeded in reconstructing the patient's integrative problem and the integrative mechanism's method of handling it, we can often recognize easily the situations in the past that have patterned his behavior.

BIBLIOGRAPHY

1. Alexander, Franz, M.D.: *Roots of Crime*. A. Knopf, New York, 1935.
2. Alexander, Franz, M.D.: The Relation of Inferiority Feelings to Guilt. *Int. J. Psychoanal.*, 19:41, 1938.
3. French, Thomas M., Alexander, Franz, *et al.: Psychogenic Factors in Bronchial Asthma*. Parts I and II. *Psychosom. Med. Monographs*, 1: no. 4, 1941, and 2: nos. 1 and 2, 1941. National Research Council, Washington, D. C.
4. Freud, A.: *Introduction to the Technic of Child Analysis*. New York, Nervous and Mental Disease Publ. Co., 1928.
5. Freud, S.: *The Interpretation of Dreams*. New York, Macmillan, 1913. Also in: *Basic Writings*, Book II, The Modern Library, New York, 1938.
6. Freud, S.: *On Narcissism—An Introduction*. In: *Collected Papers*, Vol. IV. Third Edition. London, Hogarth Press, 1946, p. 30.
7. Freud, S.: *The Ego and the Id*. Fourth Edition. Hogarth Press, London, 1947.
8. Piers, G., and Singer, M.: *Guilt and Shame*. Charles C. Thomas, Springfield, Ill., 1953.

Chapter Twelve

ANALYSIS OF THE DREAM CENSORSHIP

A central trend in the work of Sandor Rado is his development of an adaptational approach both to the science of psychodynamics and to the art of psychoanalytic therapy. One of the most important underlying concepts in this adaptational approach is the concept that psychoanalytic therapy should concern itself first of all with the patient's current problems in the here and now. This principle is most important not only for psychoanalytic therapy but also for psychodynamic science, since observations made during the course of psychoanalytic therapy are our most important source of data on which to base a science of psychodynamics, and these data are usually most adequate when they pertain to the patient's current behavior and current problems.

Such interest in a patient's current problem is the starting point of both of these lectures given in Dr. Rado's honor. In this one, we shall describe and illustrate a method of using a patient's dreams to reconstruct with precision his focal conflict at the moment of dreaming and his successive ways of dealing with this focal conflict. The first dream that we use as an example may be of some personal interest to Dr. Rado, since it is from the record of a case from the Berlin Psychoanalytic Institute which was first discussed by me at a case seminar in Dr. Rado's home.

The second lecture (Chapter 14 below) will report a case history to elaborate a thesis which Rado (1953)[1] has already proposed, that

Reprinted from George Daniels, ed., *New Perspectives in Psychoanalysis* (New York, 1957).

1. S. Rado, "Recent Advances in Psychoanalytic Therapy," in *Psychiatric Treatment, Proceedings of the Association for Research in Nervous and Mental Disease* (Baltimore: Williams & Wilkins, 1953), 21: 42–58.

in psychotherapy it is our aim to help the patient advance "from un-
warranted despair to warranted hope."

I

The problem that I shall be discussing is based directly on
Freud's *Interpretation of Dreams.* Freud postulated (1) that every
dream represents the fulfillment of a wish, and (2) that in the manifest dream the latent dream thoughts have undergone distortion. He
combined these two propositions in the statement that a dream represents
a disguised fulfillment of a repressed wish.

Freud attributed the distortion of the underlying dream thoughts
to a dream "censor." In the early years, he was interested chiefly in
discovering the repressed thoughts that the censor had tried to hide.
He paid only fleeting attention to the motives that had inspired the
dream censorship. Just why were these particular thoughts unacceptable
to the dreamer's conscious ego? Just why did they have to be given this
particular kind of distorted representation? Often the answers to these
questions seemed self-evident. Freud did not concern himself further
with them.

Years later, however, he identified the dream censor with the superego—which seems to imply that the dream censorship is motivated
by guilt.

I should like to examine more carefully the question of what moti-
vates the dream censorship.

II

I start with the proposition that guilt is only one of the motives
that may activate the dream censorship. To illustrate this fact, I shall
report a dream in which the motive responsible for distortion is pride
(shame) rather than guilt.

The dream is one that I reported many years ago. It is taken from
the record of a patient whose most consistent reaction in the analysis
had been to attempt to overcompensate for his fears by intimidating
the analyst. Actually, this was my own first supervised analysis, and
I was a little afraid of this patient. Three days before this dream, I had
had occasion to suggest that the patient's very persistent fears were
probably a reaction to threats that he had received in childhood concerning masturbation. In reaction to this interpretation, the patient

had recalled some threats that he had actually received but he insisted that they did not mean much to him at the time. On the following day, he brought a dream which the analyst was at the time unable to interpret. Two days later, he reported the following dream:

Dream: The patient is fixing a velocipede with his brother. The brother asks the patient to get something out of a hall where a meeting is being held. The patient refuses with playful politeness on the ground that his brother is younger. Finally, the brother straightens himself up to go but indicates that he is afraid. The patient is distressed on learning this and says he would have gone if he had known that this was the brother's reason for not wanting to go. As the patient gets up to go, he meets people who are coming out of the meeting. There is a black cloud in the rear of the hall, of which the patient feels very much in awe. One man, as he comes out of the hall, puts his hand on his pocket, and another says: "They have taken in five hundred marks."

In association, the hall reminds the patient of the church where his father preached. The patient's father was a Lutheran minister and the patient used to be very much afraid of him in church. The velocipede reminds the patient of a velocipede that the patient and his six younger brothers all owned together. Afterward, they bought a new one with some money given them by an uncle. The patient was very angry when his father once took this new velocipede to learn to ride on it. Five hundred marks refers to a confession that the patient had made a couple of weeks earlier in his analysis. Some years before he had cheated the brother to whom this dream refers by getting him to endorse a loan and then filling in a larger amount. The analyst now interprets the patient's wish to hide his fear of the analysis by representing that the analyst is afraid. Then the patient identifies the black cloud in the rear of the church as his father in a black robe.

In this dream it is easy to recognize that the dreamer is reacting to his analysis. The brother is the analyst. Fixing the velocipede is the patient's treatment. In order to "fix" him up, it is necessary to "get something out of" the patient's unconscious, which is represented in the dream by his father's church. The mysterious black cloud in the background is his father conflict. The patient is afraid, but it hurts his pride to admit it. Instead of recognizing his own fear, he has recognized that his brother (the analyst) is afraid. The analyst had failed to understand the patient's dream of two days before, and the patient has interpreted this failure as evidence of fear on the analyst's part. In his childhood the patient used to compensate for his own fear of his father by gloating over the fear that he himself inspired in his six younger brothers. He has used a similar defense in this velocipede dream.

Finally, the dream ends with a reassurance against his fear. The people coming out of the church are a sign that the meeting (analysis) is over. The allusion to the five hundred marks makes this reassurance more specific. The patient has already made his confession and is telling himself that there is nothing further to analyze.

This interpretation illustrates the first step in what we shall call "analysis of the dream censorship." We have recognized the dream as a reaction to a conflict between two motives. We shall call these two motives his "disturbing motive" and his "reactive motive," respectively. His "disturbing motive" is fear, fear of trying to cooperate with the analyst in the investigation of his unconscious. His "reactive motive" is shame. He is ashamed of his fear. The conflict between a dreamer's disturbing motive and his reactive motive is his "focal conflict."

Before we discuss further just how we can analyze the dream censorship, we should first discuss a possible objection. Every dream has many meanings. How, then, can we speak as if the dream had only one disturbing motive? Which of the dreamer's many "overdetermined" wishes is *the* disturbing motive of the dream? Still, we may reassure ourselves that Freud, too, sometimes spoke of *the* dream wish. He, too, seemed to imply that one of the many dream wishes is more important than the others.

The distinction implied is one between varying intensities of cathexis. *The* disturbing dream wish is the one that is most intensely cathected. We think of cathexis as both converging on and radiating out from the disturbing dream wish as a center. Many wishes from deeper in the dreamer's unconscious may converge on the dreamer's disturbing motive. For example, in the velocipede dream, the patient's fear of investigating his unconscious probably has its source in a number of different infantile fears. But then, cathexis from his focal conflict between fear and shame has radiated out again and found expression in many different elements of the manifest dream—in the playfully polite interchange between the brothers, in the brother's betrayal of his fear and the patient's pretended consideration for the brother, in the black cloud in the rear of the hall, in the people leaving the church, and in the remark about the five hundred marks at the end of the dream.

Our analysis of the dream censorship begins only after we have found *the* disturbing wish at the center of the dream thoughts. Then we are ready to search for the dreamer's reactive motive. This we do by comparing our postulated disturbing motive with the manifest dream. We ask: Just how has the manifest dream reacted to the disturbing wish? From the nature of the manifest dream's reactions we try to deduce just why this wish was disturbing. If in the manifest dream the dreamer is trying to punish himself, then we may conclude that his reactive motive is guilt. In the velocipede dream, he is trying to hide from himself his fear, to make play of it, to pretend that his brother is the one who is afraid, and to pose as the magnanimous older brother. All this suggests that he is ashamed to admit his fear, that his reactive motive is shame.

When we have discovered both the disturbing motive and the reactive motive, we have not yet completed our analysis of the dream censorship. In order to be convinced of this fact, we need only to compare the dreamer's focal conflict with the manifest dream. For example, another patient with the same conflict might have been able to admit to himself frankly, "I am afraid but ashamed of being afraid." After thus facing his conflict, he might have chosen any one of several possible rational solutions. Refusing to be intimidated, he might have plunged with determination into the investigation of the next deeper layer of his unconscious conflict. Or he might have yielded to his fear and given up his treatment. Or, following the procedure that we encourage in psychoanalysis, he might have admitted his fear and shame to the analyst as well as to himself, in order to get the analyst's help in finding the reason for his fear and his resistance.

The patient's response in the velocipede dream does not correspond to any one of these three possible rational solutions. At this point the dream censorship entered in to distort his picture of the conflict. We can recognize three successive steps in the process that ended in substitution of the manifest dream for a frank understanding of his focal conflict. First, the dream work has substituted a complicated symbolism for the infantile sexual conflicts out of which his fears have arisen. Then the censor has substituted a playful interchange with his younger brother for the earnest preoccupation with his emotional problems that his analysis requires. Finally, instead of facing his own conflict, he has pictured his brother, the analyst, as the one who is in conflict between fear and shame.

The second of these three steps is our best clue for understanding the motivation of the censorship. Throughout the early part of his analysis, one of this patient's most important resistances was to try to make play of the analysis, to avoid taking his treatment seriously. In this way he was trying to forestall too intense reactivation of the intense fears that had been part of his infantile neurosis. Actually, the patient had employed the same technique even in his childhood. The patient and his six younger brothers had occupied a room next to the parents' bedroom. Curious about what was going on in the next room but too afraid to look in, the brothers attempted to relieve their sexual tension by masturbating "each in his own way" in fear and defiance of the parents next door. It is true that a child's play often becomes very earnest; but "playful" behavior is behavior to which one does not allow himself to be very intensely committed. In the velocipede dream, going into the church would have involved intense reactivation of his fear of his father; but by sparring "with playful politeness" with his younger brother, he protected himself from becoming too intensely involved in his conflict. The dream ended without his having to go into the church after all.

By symbolic portrayal of the patient's conflict, the dream censor has achieved a similar purpose. The patient's treatment involves the danger of reactivating intensely his infantile neurosis, but fixing a velocipede is harmless play. Going into his father's church while the father was preaching would have been dangerous, but not so dangerous as it would have been to intrude on the parents' sexual relationship in their bedroom.

Such symbolic portrayal of disturbing conflicts is common in children's play. Much depends on whether such substitution of playful activity occurs before or after the disturbing conflict has been activated. If the playful activity has been substituted *only after* the disturbing conflict has already been activated, then the intense affects of the disturbing conflict will be transferred over to the otherwise harmless play. The resulting play will be anxiety-laden and will be transformed into neurotic symptoms. On the other hand, sometimes substitution of the harmless play occurs *before* the disturbing conflict has been intensely cathected. According to the mechanism that Freud has described, anxiety resulting from only very slight activation of the disturbing conflict can serve as a warning signal. Under these circumstances, transfer of the child's interest over to harmless symbolic play serves to protect him from further activation of the disturbing conflict. This is what we believe to have occurred in the velocipede dream. By turning his interest to fixing a velocipede, the patient succeeded for a time in forestalling the further activation of his infantile neurosis that was about to result from his treatment.

Until now we have been discussing the influence of the dream censor on the patient's fantasied (dreamed) behavior. Now we ask: What has the censor done to the dreamer's understanding of his conflict?

In search of an answer to this question, we compare the dreamer's focal conflict with the manifest dream. Frank understanding of the focal conflict would have involved his admitting to himself, "I am afraid of my father but ashamed of being afraid." In the manifest dream, instead of admitting his fear and his shame, he has pictured his brother as in conflict between fear and shame. In other words, he has given only projected recognition to his insight into the nature of his conflict.

Traditionally, we think of such projection of an important insight as a distortion of the latent dream thoughts. We picture the dream censor as deliberately trying to deceive the dreamer's ego. A political censor tries to protect a monarch from being exposed to frank criticism by his subjects. Similarly, in this case, the dream censor has tried to flatter this dreamer's ego by assuring him that he is not cowardly but magnanimous. Up to this point the dream censor has been acting in response to the dreamer's reactive motive, to his shame.

But then, from this point on, the dream censor acts not in response to only one motive but in the service of the problem-solving function of the dreamer's ego. The dreamer's ego is not only shrinking back from looking at the truth about himself. He also has a problem to solve. What should he do about this conflict between fear and pride? The dream contains an answer to this question. He should "straighten himself up." He should continue with his investigation of his un-conscious (go into the church). This is a good answer—except for the fact that the manifest dream has treated the problem as though it were the analyst's (brother's) rather than the patient's.

Yet, even though he has not recognized the problem as his own, he has found an answer that is also applicable to himself. He, too, should "straighten himself up." He should continue with his task of looking into his unconscious.

In order better to understand this problem-solving function of the dream censorship, let us compare it to a device that we often use in waking life to clarify our thinking. Let us suppose that I am confronted with a problem in which I am intensely involved: I want to think objectively about it and to come to a sound conclusion, but my feelings are too strong. So I try to think of the problem as though it were someone else's. I try to achieve some degree of detachment from the problem. It is as though I were withdrawing to a distance in order to get a better perspective on the question at issue.

In other words, the projection mechanism in this dream *is not only a distortion* of the latent dream thoughts for the purpose of sparing the dreamer the pain of looking at his conflict. *It is also a technique of intellectual mastery.* The dreamer has a problem—which is to find a way of reconciling or arbitrating between his fear and his pride. In order to do so, he must face the fact that he is both afraid and ashamed. If he should allow his conflict to be fully activated, it would be greater than he is able to face. So he has found a way of detaching himself from his conflict and thus preventing its being further activated. If the analyst is the one who is afraid of the unconscious and also ashamed of being afraid, then the patient need not be so intensely emotionally involved and can be better able to think clearly about it. It is easier for him to decide what the analyst should do than it would be to make the same decision for himself.

We can formulate these relationships more precisely in technical terms. The understanding by which a person's behavior is guided (at a given moment) is his "integrative field." The adequacy of his understanding is measured by how much of the information essential for solving his problem is included in the "span" of his integrative field. In order to deal with a conflict intelligently, a patient must be able to span both of his conflicting motives in a single integrative field. His integrative field must also include an adequate understanding of the real situation in which his conflict is embedded. The difficulty of thus spanning and understanding his conflict is his *"integrative task"* —which is roughly proportional to the intensity of the conflict. On the other hand, the ego's capacity to span its conflict is limited. *If*, at any moment, *the ego's integrative task is in excess of its "integrative capacity,"* then adequate *understanding* of the problem *will no longer be possible.*

If the integrative task suddenly becomes excessive, then confusion and panic may be the result, as in some nightmares. In other cases, by prophylactically detaching itself from the conflict, as in the dream that we are now studying, the ego may forestall too intense mobilization of its conflict. Under such circumstances, a compromise can usually be found between the ego's need to shrink back from its conflict and its need to continue with its normal function of problem-solving. Such a compromise may be achieved by reformulating the problem. For example, in the velocipede dream, the patient's conflict about allowing his infantile neurosis to be reactivated has been reformulated as though it were his brother's (analyst's) conflict about venturing into his father's church. By thus substituting a similar problem in which his ego is less involved, the patient has diminished his integrative task and increased his available integrative span. Behind the mask of his projection, the patient's increased integrative span can now make possible a really good insight into the nature of his focal conflict.

This kind of analysis can be of great value in helping us trace the therapeutic process in a psychoanalytic treatment.

In the course of a patient's treatment, his capacity for understanding his conflicts keeps fluctuating. In order to follow the course of the treatment intelligently, it is important to understand these fluctuations and the reasons for them. One of the chief advantages of the precise analysis of the dream censorship that we have just illustrated is the fact that it makes such fluctuations in the patient's insight much more intelligible than they would otherwise be.

For example, let us first inquire what we expect the effect of the analyst's interpretation of the velocipede dream to be. Then we can compare our theoretical deduction with what actually happened as indicated by the patient's next dream.

As we have already reported, the analyst interpreted to the patient his fear of the treatment and his projection of his fear in the velocipede dream. In the light of our analysis of this velocipede dream, it is now easy to predict that one effect of this interpretation of the analyst's must be to increase the intensity of the conflict. So long as the patient believes that it is the analyst's fear that is responsible for delay in the analysis, the patient's own pride need not be involved. On the other hand, if the patient accepts the analyst's interpretation, his ego will be put under greater pressure to choose between his pride and his fear. If he yields to his fear, his pride will be hurt; if he saves his pride, he must defy his fear. Since such increased mobilization of his conflict will involve increase of the integrative task, we must expect that the ego's integrative span will decrease accordingly. In other words, we must expect his next dream to show less evidence of understanding of his conflict.

This deduction now gives us a clue for better understanding of his next dream.

Dream: The patient is in the toilet and a small boy who is yellow urinates upon the patient's yellow coat.

Associations to this dream are meager. The dream is very distasteful to him, as toilets are associated in his mind with homosexuality . . . he shows considerable reluctance to associate to it, but mentions his recent refusal to pay his landlady. When the analyst calls attention to his anal-retentive attitude toward money and associations, the patient remarks that he always likes to use the chamber but does not like to have it emptied. His father was the same way. The patient also has an impulse to eat his own nasal secretions.

If we were not interested in the precipitating stimulus, we should be tempted to interpret this dream as a simple wish-fulfillment, as fulfillment of a homosexual wish to be urinated upon, probably by the analyst. But, if so, what could have activated such a homosexual wish just at this time?

As soon as we ask this question, we can recognize this dream as a retort to the analyst's interpretation of several days before. The analyst had told the patient that he was afraid. This new dream is ignoring the content of the analyst's interpretation entirely. This dream is reacting to the analyst's interpretation as only an insult. Now we can understand the stimulus for the homosexual wish. The analyst's "insult" has been erotized, converted into a fantasy of being urinated upon, which is then enjoyed erotically.

Let us next contrast these two successive dreams. In the velocipede dream, behind the defense of projection, the patient achieved a good insight into his conflict between fear and shame. In the yellow boy dream, this understanding of his conflict disappeared entirely.[2] It was replaced by an erotic fantasy of being urinated upon. We can now understand this disappearance of the patient's understanding, this shrinkage of his integrative span. It is a consequence of the increased mobilization of his conflict that we should expect to occur in reaction to the analyst's interpretation.

2. Unless possibly yellow is a symbol of fear, as it would be in American English. The dream was reported in German and the patient understood only a few words of English.

III

We shall next discuss two dreams to illustrate another kind of motivation of the dream censorship and another kind of reformulation of the dreamer's problem.

These dreams are taken from the record of the patient whom we shall discuss at much greater length in Chapter 14. For our present purpose, we need recount only a few essential facts from her life history. She was a twenty-eight-year-old married woman whose mother had died soon after childbirth, when the patient was four and a half and probably at the height of her Oedipus complex. Some months later, although she had had reason to believe that she was the father's favorite daughter in a very large family, she had been sent, together with her younger brother, Lewis, to foster-parents hundreds of miles away. To this uprooting from her childhood home she had reacted with a deep dependent and basically compliant attachment, largely unconscious, to a foster-mother who tended to exploit her by making her a sort of maid of all work. Her brother Lewis later married, as did she, but the brother moved away to another town, whereas she continued to live in an apartment in the house which her foster-mother owned and in which the foster-mother lived. The patient continued also to do much of the foster-mother's work, in addition to her own house-work and her job. The dream that we shall now report occurred not long after the brother, his wife Helen, and their children had come for a visit to the foster parents.

Dream 45: There was a box with kittens or puppies in it down at work. They didn't belong there. I called the attention of the boss's secretary to it, but she was more concerned with the question of who had put them there than with getting them out.

Associations: "I couldn't understand how no one had noticed them before. I thought she should call someone to take them away." (A.: "What about the secretary?") The patient and the secretary don't like each other; the secretary is a fixture there and is bossy. The girls resent it that she is an old friend of the boss's wife and that she tells the latter about all the office affairs. The patient then brought up Lewis' visit again and spent the rest of the hour in ventilating, with the analyst's encouragement, her resentful attitudes toward Lewis. She did not smooth things over for him with her mother this time, she says, when the mother criticized him to her and said that he did not care anything about his home, etc. The patient and Lewis have nothing in common. Before he got married he used to stay out every night until 5:00 a.m., presumably with Helen. He said to the patient, "She is the only girl in the world, I love her. *You* don't even know what love is." The patient wondered if he realized how right he was. When the analyst commented on her resentments in regard to Lewis, she continued: "He always is hurting my feelings. This time he didn't come up to see me at all when he arrived, in fact he didn't see the family until late. When he did come up I knew it was because Dad sent him. . . . He still doesn't act the part of an adult. . . . When he married Helen he insisted she become a Catholic, but they never have been in church except for the baby's baptism. . . ."

Two hours later this dream was followed by another one:

Dream 47: A man was walking up and down in an empty room. I thought Lewis was going to be punished, but I don't know what for, or the connection.

She then reports that Lewis and Helen are going to have another baby in six months. They plan to drive up to Chicago once a month for prenatal care so the child can be born in a Chicago hospital. The patient thinks this is crazy, especially if they should move to Arizona. . . . "Helen said Lewis' asthma was caused by his nerves. He has had no trouble with it since leaving Chicago except when they have a fight. Is this possible? They told him at the hospital that he should get away. He solved everything by just moving." She then goes on to tell how she never had thought anything bothered Lewis. He had always been able to do pretty much as he pleased and to get away with it with the family, in contrast to herself. They even accepted his marriage to Helen! "I don't think it would help for me to go away because I couldn't help feeling sorry that my parents were left alone."

The key to the interpretation of these two dreams is the fact reported immediately after the second one. Helen's expected child gives poignant meaning to the contrast between the symbol of kittens or puppies in a box in the first dream, and the empty room in the second dream. Helen already has two children and is expecting another, whereas the patient is childless. In her associations to the first dream, the patient's jealousy of Lewis' affection for his wife is little concealed; and, after the second dream, she gives expression to a similar envy of Lewis' ability to leave home and "do what he pleases"—whereas she is tied to her parental home by her loyalty to (and dependence on) her foster-parents. In this context, we can recognize that the disturbing motive in the first dream is a wish that she could be the one to have children by Lewis. The second dream is motivated by the spiteful wish that Lewis should be "punished" by Helen's being childless (her room empty) as the patient is.

Each dream has also another meaning. The empty room in the second dream is also a reference to the patient's own childlessness which she is accepting as a punishment for her wish that Helen should be child-less. In the first dream, masked behind the thought that she would have to get rid of her own incestuous child (get the puppies out), is the still more disturbing wish to get rid of Helen's children.

Jealousy is a double-pronged motive. Wishing to have Lewis' love and Lewis' children instead of Helen's having them implies both wishing to have the children and wishing for Helen not to have them. In both dreams these two wishes are closely integrated but in different ways. In the first dream the wish to be the mother of Lewis' children is *the* disturbing dream wish, whereas in the second dream the spiteful wish that Helen should be childless has moved over into the central position.

The need for punishment in the second dream is a sign that the patient's reactive motive is guilt. In the first dream, the patient's guilt has found expression in her feeling that the kittens "didn't belong there" and that the secretary should get them out.

When we carefully analyze the censorship in many dreams, we learn that there are many kinds of guilt. In these two dreams the patient's guilt has a very personal character, closely integrated with love for the mother figure (sister-in-law) who is being attacked and with a longing for harmony with this mother figure. This longing for harmony with the mother is the reason for the close identification with Helen in both dreams. In the second dream she must accept her own child-lessness as a punishment for her wish that Helen be childless. In the first dream her feeling that her own fantasied babies (kittens) do not "belong there" corresponds to her own (repressed) jealous feeling that Lewis' children should not have been given to Helen, but to the patient herself. Identification implies an illusion of union with the mother. The mechanism is similar to what Freud calls hysterical identification—in which a patient's deep love of her rival finds expression in identification with the suffering that she wishes to inflict on the rival. In the patient's case, her traumatic loss of her mother after childbirth, at the height of the patient's Oedipus complex in early childhood, is almost certainly the reason for her need to get her mother back by identifying with her.

An important principle in analysis of the dream censorship is to try very carefully to account for the exact details of the manifest dream. Often such details are references to significant features of the dreamer's present real situation. Traditionally, we often overlook such details. We have the habit of interpreting the patient's present behavior as if it were only a repetition of the past. In so doing, we are in danger of missing those very features of the patient's actual situation to which the patient is turning in her hope of finding a real solution for her conflict.

In the kitten dream, such a detail is the patient's attempt to call the boss's secretary's attention to the kittens and her feelings that the secretary is more concerned with the question of who had put them there than with getting them out. Our clue for understanding this statement is to recognize the boss's secretary as a substitute for the analyst. If the patient should tell the analyst that she is pregnant, she thinks that he would be more interested in finding out who the father was (who put them there) than in helping her get out of her jam by getting rid of them. In other words, this dream indicates that the patient is questioning whether she should act on the analyst's encouragement to talk freely about her preconscious fantasies, and in particular about her pregnancy fantasy. Her dream is an argument against telling the fantasy (which in the dream thoughts she is thinking of as reality). The analyst will only want to analyze her fantasy. He will tell her that Lewis is the father. In her dream thoughts she also carries her distrust of the analyst further. In her associations she says that the boss's secretary tells the boss's wife about all the office affairs. This is the patient's frequently recurring fear that the analyst will talk about her to her foster-mother.

We now notice that the analyst has become a woman in this dream. This confirms our earlier impression that the reactive motive in this dream is guilt toward a mother, closely associated with fear of loss of a mother's love. This fear has found even more direct expression in her fear that the analyst (secretary) will tell her foster-mother (the boss's wife) about her (fantasied) pregnancy.

Now we are ready to ask: How has the problem-solving function of the ego dealt with the focal conflicts in these two dreams?

We must begin by recognizing that at this time there is no possible rational solution for the focal conflict in either of these dreams. To turn her erotic interest to a non-incestuous object is a solution that the patient could be expected to achieve only after a long period of analysis, at best. The ego's problem must, therefore, resolve itself in each dream into one of so reformulating her conflict that it can be spanned by the patient's ego's integrative capacity.

The essential contribution of the censorship in each dream has been to reformulate the dreamer's problem in such a way as to eliminate the necessity for jealousy between the sisters-in-law. In each dream this has been achieved by a condensation, by the identification of the patient and Helen, to which we have already referred. In each dream a single symbol has been substituted for both women.

The box with kittens in it represents both the patient's wish for children and the children that Helen actually has. Since the two women are represented as one, what is left to stir up jealousy between them? This act of condensation has been supplemented by the replacement of pregnancy, which is the central issue in the patient's jealousy conflict, by the harmless symbol of kittens in a box. There has also been elimination of any allusion to Lewis—except in the question, "Who put them there?"

The empty room in the second dream is also a symbol that makes no distinction between the two women. It is a symbol both of the patient's own childlessness and of the childlessness that she wishes to inflict on Helen. It is also a symbol that is not immediately recognizable as a symbol of childlessness—one, therefore, that need not stir up further the patient's jealousy.

Now, comparing the contributions of the censorship in the two dreams, we can again best account for the differences between them on the assumption that, in the first dream, substitution of the harmless symbol occurred *before* the patient's spiteful jealousy had been activated, whereas, in the second dream, the symbol of the empty room was substituted *only after* the jealous hostility had already been mobilized. This assumption would account for the fact that the patient's disturbing wish was the erotic one to have children by Lewis in the first dream, whereas in the second dream it was the hostile wish toward Helen.

We get further confirmation of this hypothesis when we try to reconstruct quantitatively the displacement of cathexis that made possible the reformulations of the patient's problem that we have just described.

In the first dream, the patient's pregnancy fantasy apparently served as a warning signal before it had been intensely activated. This signal stimulated the patient promptly to turn her interest away from the fantasy itself to questions about whether she should tell the analyst about it.

In the second dream, the censor reacted only after the patient's jealousy had been activated. The reaction was to substitute Lewis as object both of her hostile wish toward Helen and of her own need for punishment. The underlying thought is that Lewis is responsible for both women's attachment to him and is therefore guilty of making them jealous of each other. Consequently, he is the one who deserves punishment.

This difference in the timing of the displacement mechanisms in the two dreams now accounts for the two basic differences between them.

In the first dream, because of the patient's early turning away from her preoccupation with the disturbing pregnancy theme, the manifest content shows little evidence of mobilized affect. In the second, a man's walking up and down in an empty room implies restless agitation, and it is specifically stated that Lewis is going to be punished. This implies clearly that the patient's jealousy of and guilt toward her sister-in-law must already have been mobilized before they were turned against Lewis.

In view of the less intense mobilization of affect, we should expect the integrative task to be less and the integrative span to be greater in the first dream than in the second. In other words, we should expect the intellectual content of the patient's conflict to be spelled out more precisely in the manifest content of the first dream. This anticipation corresponds to the facts. The symbolism of kittens or puppies in a box, of their not belonging there, and of the need to get them out spells out in considerable detail the intellectual content of the patient's pregnancy fantasy and of her conflict about it. This we contrast with the manifest content of the second dream, in which the empty room is the only hint suggesting that her conflict has to do with jealousy of Helen's pregnancy.

We can also reconstruct the reason for the increased mobilization of her conflict in the second dream. In the first dream, her pregnancy fantasy had served as a warning signal before it had really been mobilized. In response to this signal she had turned away to the question of whether she should tell her analyst about it. Then, at the end of the dream, she had found reasons for not telling him. Consequently, cathexis must be expected to revert to the underlying pregnancy fantasy with resulting reactivation of the associated jealousy conflict. In the second dream we see the effects of this reactivation of the jealousy conflict.

IV

We shall now summarize our conclusions:

We believe that, in dream analysis, one should not be content with discovering and enumerating overdetermined dream wishes. It is also possible to analyze the dream censorship.

Our procedure is as follows:

First, we try to discover *the* dream wish that is most intensely cathected. This is the "disturbing motive" of the dream.

Then we compare this disturbing wish with the manifest dream. From the nature of the manifest dream's reactions, we try to deduce just why this wish was disturbing. The motive that is responsible for the dream censor's reactions to the disturbing wish is the dreamer's "reactive motive."

The conflict between the disturbing motive and the reactive motive is the dreamer's "focal conflict." By comparing this focal conflict with the manifest dream, we try next to determine how the problem-solving function of the dreamer's ego has dealt with the focal conflict. The focal conflict presents the patient with a problem. The problem is to find a way in real life to reconcile the dreamer's disturbing motive and his reactive motive. Often the dreamer's ego continues in the dream work to search for a solution of this problem.

On the other hand, the dreamer's conflict is usually too great for the ego to face. Then the ego's task becomes one of trying to reformulate the problem. By substituting a similar problem in which the dreamer is much less intensely involved, the ego tries to achieve some degree of detachment from the problem and to get a better perspective on the question at issue. In this way, the ego tries to diminish the dreamer's "integrative task" and to bring it within the span of the dreamer's "integrative capacity."

In the course of a patient's treatment, his capacity for understanding his conflicts keeps fluctuating. The kind of precise analysis of the dream censorship that we have just outlined helps us to improve our understanding of these fluctuations and of the reasons for them. In this way, we can improve very much our ability to follow intelligently the vicissitudes of the therapeutic process.

Chapter Thirteen

GUILT, SHAME, AND OTHER REACTIVE MOTIVES

It is now generally recognized that neuroses are reactions to unconscious conflicts. In order to understand an unconscious conflict, we should distinguish two kinds of motives—a "disturbing motive," which has usually been repressed, and a "reactive motive," which is responsible for the disturbing motive's having been repressed.

Psychoanalysts were at first interested chiefly in the disturbing motives. The patient's struggle to keep these disturbing motives repressed was usually called "resistance," but the motives for resistance were often not carefully analyzed. Sometimes resistance was attributed to a "psychic censor," but little attempt was made to analyze the reactive motives that had inspired the censorship.

Still, in order to understand a neurosis or a patient's personality structure, we should know both of the motives that are involved in an underlying conflict. When we are interested in the functioning of the personality as a whole, *the motives that inspire the censorship are just as important* to discover *as the motives that are repressed.* We should try to find out not only the patient's disturbing motive but also the reactive motive that has caused him to repress, or to inhibit, or to try to explain away, his disturbing motive.

In this paper, I shall try to distinguish a number of different kinds of reactive motives. Since Freud published *The Ego and the Id,* psychoanalysts have been much interested in reactions to guilt, but the word "guilt" is often used loosely to include many other kinds of reactions. For example, guilt should be distinguished from fear of loss of a parent's love, from fear of punishment, and from shame.

As a basis for understanding the distinction between guilt and fear of loss of love, we recapitulate Freud's two successive attempts to explain how the conscience is formed in the course of a child's development. The first of Freud's reconstructions (1914) was part of his elaboration of the concept of narcissism. One form of infantile narcissism is a kind of megalomania: the infant likes to imagine himself omnipotent and perfect. Yet his actual helplessness and the criticisms of his parents make it impossible for him to maintain this illusion. He protects himself from disillusionment by attributing the wished-for perfection to an ego-ideal. The conscience arises as a need to achieve this ideal in reality.

Later, supplementing this account, Freud (1923) derived the conscience from the child's attempts to resolve the Oedipus complex. In the Oedipus complex, the little boy's ambition to be powerful like the father fuses with his desire to possess the mother sexually. Thwarted in this desire by his fear of castration by the father, he is driven to seek another way of identifying with the father's power. He achieves this goal by imposing on himself the father's prohibition, threats, and punishments. The part of the personality that splits off thus to identify with the father's prohibitive role is the conscience or superego. Sometimes we describe this process by saying that the superego arises by "introjection" of the father's prohibitive role.

The inverted Oedipus complex also contributes to the formation of the superego, since the little boy is thwarted also in his desire to be loved sexually by the father. When the superego takes over the father's role, the boy's submitting to the restraints and punishments imposed by the superego can serve as a substitute for gratification of the boy's feminine desire to submit to the father.

GUILT AND FEAR OF LOSS OF LOVE

By means of this reconstruction we can now distinguish between guilt and fear of loss of a parent's love. In an early paper (1928), Anna Freud insisted on the importance of this distinction as a basis for understanding the differences between child analysis and the analysis of adult patients. She called attention to the fact that the child's superego can usually not be counted on to inhibit disturbing impulses unless it is supported by prohibitions from the parents or from the analyst. In children the process of introjecting parental prohibitions has usually not been completed; and the prohibitions imposed by the superego must therefore be reinforced either by fear of punishment or by fear of loss of the parents' love.

The same distinction between guilt and fear of loss of love as reactive motives is also important sometimes for understanding adult patients. In these patients, too, the process of introjection of parental inhibitions has been incomplete; and fear of loss of love is often the dominant inhibitory motive, supplementing or even replacing guilt. This distinction may be important in determining what symptom a patient will develop at a particular time. For example, in our studies (1941) of bronchial asthma at the Chicago Psychoanalytic Institute, we found that asthma attacks are precipitated only by situations in which fear of estrangement (or separation) from a mother figure is the inhibiting motive. During periods when introjection of parental prohibitions was more successful, the patients developed other symptoms, such as neurotic compulsions, but were free of asthma. In other words, at such time the patient's conscience, which caused him to condemn himself, served as a kind of buffer, protecting him from the danger of offending a mother figure, which might otherwise have precipitated an asthma attack.

GUILT AND INFERIORITY FEELINGS

Another distinction that is important for understanding the behavior of patients is the distinction between guilt and feelings of inferiority or shame. Alexander (1935) pointed out, for example, that feelings of inferiority on account of strong dependent needs are often reacted to with aggressive criminal behavior; the criminal is trying to prove that he is not soft but tough. Later (1938), Alexander called attention to the fact that such feelings of inferiority often come into direct conflict with guilt feelings. In inhibited and compulsive characters, this alternation between guilt and feelings of inferiority may be exceedingly disabling. The patient's guilt inhibits the patient's aggressive impulses and subdues a man into submissive attitudes; but his pride will not permit him to accept his submissive attitudes, and this gives rise to feelings of inferiority, which tend to drive him again into aggressive behavior.

More recently, Piers (1953) has elaborated this contrast further, insisting on the distinction between guilt and shame. The word "shame," which he uses in a somewhat broader sense than usual, corresponds to Alexander's "feelings of inferiority." Piers finds the essential difference between guilt and shame in the fact that guilt inhibits and condemns transgression, whereas shame demands achievement of a positive goal.

He relates this contrast between shame and guilt to Freud's two earlier terms for the conscience. Shame, when its goal is positive achievement, he thinks of as a reaction to the ego-ideal; whereas guilt, he believes, proceeds from the superego.

FURTHER CLASSIFICATION OF REACTIVE MOTIVES

The distinctions between guilt and fear of loss of love and between guilt and inferiority feelings do not nearly exhaust the possible variations in a patient's reactive motives. Indeed, each of the kinds of reactive motive that we have enumerated should be classified further into subgroups.

An important distinction is one between the negative and positive goals of a reactive motive. For example, feelings of inferiority and shame are uncomfortable or disturbing feelings of which a person tries to rid himself by compensatory behavior. Therefore, we call them negative goals (i.e., goals to be avoided); but ambition and pride in achievement are positive goals. Similarly, hopes of winning a parent's love or of reconciliation with a parent are positive goals, which we contrast with fear of estrangement or fear of loss of love. Desires to justify oneself should similarly be contrasted with guilt feelings.

Another distinction that is important has to do with the realistic or unrealistic character of reactive behavior and with its effectiveness in achieving its positive goals. A Demosthenes or a Hannibal compensates for inferiority feelings by a lifelong ambition culminating in supreme achievement, whereas another man's compensation may consist only in idle boasting or in daydreams of being a great man.

THREE KINDS OF PRIDE

We often think of pride as satisfaction in being admired by others, which psychoanalysts usually regard as a form of exhibitionism; but pride as a reactive motive probably takes its origin in more elementary urges toward active mastery, which are independent of any concern about being observed. We shall group such reactions together under the concept of "presocial pride."

Presocial Pride

The stimulus for such reactions may be fear, or the memory or fear of helplessness in the face of strong desire, or the threat of an obstacle interfering with the goal-directed striving. The reaction is increased effort in response to an obstacle, or, if the stimulus is fear, there may be a counter-phobic braving of the danger.

The essential satisfaction of this kind of pride can be translated into the words "I can." It is a pride of self-assertion, power, or achievement.

A child will often react with a kind of triumphant delight when he first learns to stand or walk or climb stairs. One child I knew, when he first succeeded in standing by holding on to the side of his playpen, remained in this position until he fell asleep. Then he fell back on his pillow. He immediately climbed up again as soon as he woke up, and repeated this performance all day and all night until his parents became alarmed at his loss of sleep. His delight in his achievement was quite independent of any encouragement from his parents—since he had received none.

Such reactions to achievement or to the mastery of difficulties can be recognized not only in human beings but in animals as well. They probably are analogous to such physiological reactions as the compensatory hypertrophy of an overloaded heart, or to the development of callous in reaction to irritation of skin or bone. For example, a dog may first run with its tail between its legs when threatened by another dog—but then, detecting some sign of fear in the other dog, it will turn and give chase with its tail high in the air! Or a cat will sit motionless, keeping watch over a captured mouse, only to pounce upon it when the mouse gives the least sign of trying to get away. Does the cat derive any satisfaction from thus teasing the mouse? If it were human, we would suspect that it is gloating in its power over its helpless prey.

In later life pride in achievement is the motive that most facilitates learning and constructive efforts. On the other hand, in our patients we can observe how the inhibition of aggressive impulses will often give rise to intense feelings of inferiority, because inhibition of aggression makes a person feel weak.

"Exhibitionistic" Pride—Pride in Being Admired or Approved

We must suspect that pride in self-assertion, power, and achievement is based on an inherited mechanism; but other kinds of pride are more or less deliberately inculcated in the child by parents and teachers, by the peer group, and by society at large. Very early, the child develops desires to call attention to himself, to be admired, and to be praised; and feelings of inferiority or shame begin to appear whenever he is seen in an unfavorable light. Because society values a number of different kinds of behavior, such socially oriented pride may take any one of a number of different forms.

a) Aggressive efforts to overcome difficulties and to brave danger are important for the survival of the community as a whole. Therefore, the community tends to idealize toughness and boldness and to give honor to the virtues of courage and bravery; and the child's pride in aggressive behavior and achievement tends to be supplemented by pride in exhibiting his prowess or skill to others.

b) On one hand, the parents and society in general demand compliance from all, and especially from children and women. To this demand, the individual may respond by wishes to be approved for being good.

On the other hand, the desire to be good may come into conflict with the ambition to be tough; and, consequently, a man may be despised as a weakling if he is too compliant.

c) The criteria for sexual attractiveness are related in somewhat complex ways, which differ for the two sexes, to the two codes of behavior that we have just mentioned. In men, aggressiveness tends to enhance sexual attraction, and being too good or compliant to detract from it. On the other hand, in women, aggressiveness tends to detract from sexual attractiveness except when it can be used provocatively in order to provoke aggression from the male. Moreover, a woman must draw the line with considerable subtlety between being too good and being too seductive.

d) The word "shame" is used in both a general and a more specific sense. As we have already mentioned, Piers (1953) uses the word in its more general sense as equivalent to feelings of inferiority of any kind. In its narrower, more specific sense, it is a *reaction to being seen* by others in an unfavorable light.

Two kinds of experiences are particularly likely to give rise to such feelings of shame (in the narrower sense). One is an experience which almost every child undergoes at some time. At first, the infant is admired for showing himself without clothes to his elders; but then, one day, the elders suddenly hold him up to shame for showing himself in the very way that had previously provoked so much admiration. Experiences of this kind probably account for the very close association of shame and exhibitionism to which psychoanalysis has called attention.

The other situation which can activate intense shame is one of betraying erotic feelings toward another person and receiving either no response or a negative response from the object of one's affection. Such an experience might be compared to taking off one's armor (as an expression of trust and affection) and then discovering that the person to whom one has thus exposed oneself is really an enemy.

Development of Ego-ideals

We have already quoted Freud's concept of the development of the superego by introjection of parental prohibitions. By a similar process of internalization, the standards according to which a person expects to be judged by the family or by society at large may be incorporated into his own personality and may become an ego-ideal by which he judges himself. If, then, in the course of time, the standards of society change, or if the individual moves into a new society, he may cling loyally to his own introjected ideals and standards, even though they may now conflict with those of the society in which he lives.

DIFFERENT KINDS OF BEHAVIOR INSPIRED BY NEED FOR LOVE

The need for love or fear of loss of love may also result in a number of different kinds of behavior.

Sometimes a person develops patterns based on realistic efforts to win the love of parents and others. The simplest pattern of this kind is one of winning parental approval by being good, by compliance with the consciously expressed moral demands of the parents. Others, during childhood, are not concerned so much with what the parents teach that they should do but learn, rather, how to please the parents as persons. Later, such a person may find it very important always to make himself (or herself) pleasing to other people, but not necessarily by being good or complying with the demands of society as a whole. In still other cases, a child may become very skillful in adapting to the weaknesses and peculiarities of the parents and others, and in exploiting the weaknesses of others to his own ends, in adroit defiance of the standards of society.

In the last thirty years, the psychoanalytic literature has had a great deal to say about the need for punishment, which is usually thought of as a manifestation of a conscious or unconscious sense of guilt. However, such needs for punishment can often be recognized in the child long before there has been introjection of parental prohibitions. The basic mechanism starts with the child's realization or fear that he has offended the parent. To this realization the child then reacts with a hope of reconciliation with the parent by accepting or even provoking punishment. This hope is usually a realistic one, since parents are often willing to accept a child back into their good graces after they have inflicted punishment on him.

Another reaction pattern, which is often confused with a need for punishment and attributed to guilt, is based, I believe, on a much more elementary mechanism. This is the mechanism which I shall call "simple reversal of aggression." By this I mean the mechanism in which an aggressive impulse is turned back against the aggressor in its original form, in which an aggressive impulse is inhibited and then replaced by the fear or wish that someone will do to the aggressor what he originally wished to do to his victim.

A moment ago, we pointed out that a child's hope of reconciliation by means of punishment is a realistic one, based on the actual behavior of parents. But in the mechanism of simple reversal of aggression, the patient's expectation of being attacked or hurt is not based on any remembered real experience of punishment from a parent. On the contrary, the form of the aggression expected from someone else reproduces the form of the patient's own original aggressive impulse. To account for this reversal, we need only assume that *fear of estrangement* from the parent has first caused the original aggressive impulse to be inhibited; and then—because this aggressive impulse must still seek some kind of outlet even after it has been inhibited—it is turned back against the patient himself.

Transition to True Guilt Reactions

The transition from behavior motivated by fear of loss of love to true guilt reactions involves at least two steps.

In the first step, the authority of the parents is replaced in part by acceptance of certain generalized ethical principles that are valid for others as well as for the child himself, and the unconditional desire for the love and approval of parental figures is replaced by a need for self-justification. For example, at a certain stage in ethical development, a child will often use the parents' own words to pass judgment on brothers, sisters, or even on the parents themselves. When an ethical rule has once been accepted by a child, it can be thrown into the balance to help justify the child in a controversy between the child and someone else.

But when a child has learned to use an ethical rule to justify himself, the child has not yet developed a conscience. The child can be said to have a conscience only when he has begun to turn the rule back against himself to condemn himself. Then his conscience may stir up in him a need for punishment that is independent of the more personal desire to win reconciliation with a parental figure.

ANALYSIS OF THE CENSORSHIP IN A DREAM

Having now sketched out how reactive motives can be classified, we ask next how one can determine, by analysis of a patient's behavior, what reactive motives have been responsible for his inhibition, repression, or other reaction to a disturbing motive. One particularly good way to investigate reactive motives is to try to find out what has motivated the censorship in dreams.

In the manifest content of dreams, the latent dream thoughts seem to have undergone distortion. Freud (1900) attributed this distortion to a dream censor. Like a political censor, Freud believed, the dream censor finds certain thoughts unacceptable and excludes them from consciousness. Other thoughts the censor permits to enter consciousness, provided they first submit to distortion; they are permitted to enter consciousness in disguised form.

Now, in order to study the dreamer's reactive motives, we attempt to analyze the dream censorship:

Let us suppose that we have already discovered the disturbing dream wish. We ask next: Why did this wish have to be censored? What was the reactive motive that caused the dream censor to repudiate this particular wish? In order to determine this, we examine the manifest dream and ask how the dreamer has reacted to the disturbing dream wish. For example, if the patient is reacting with feelings of inferiority to an intense dependent wish, in the manifest content we may find him boasting of his independent achievements. If he is reacting with guilt to a hostile impulse, the manifest content may picture him as being condemned and submitting to punishment. If the dreamer is reacting with fear of estrangement, the manifest content may picture him as seeking reconciliation with a parental figure. The following rather unusually simple example will illustrate how we proceed.

In his first analytic hour, a patient had told of telling both his father and his wife about a current extramarital relationship. The analyst asked why he had done so. In response to this stimulus, the patient that night dreamed as follows:

I found myself helpless, unable to use arms and legs, and being tortured by two individuals. I promised them that I wouldn't hurt anybody even if I didn't like them. The two individuals seemed to be my father and my brother. I struggled and tried to bite.

Even from the text of this dream it is evident that it is motivated by the patient's need to justify himself. He has reacted to the analyst's question of the preceding hour as though it were an accusation to the effect that his having told his father and his wife was motivated by a desire to hurt them. In the dream text he has pictured a situation in which he would be justified in trying to hurt someone. Being tortured by his father and brother would be ample justification for struggling and trying to bite. Moreover, his "promise" that he wouldn't hurt anybody even if he didn't like them is a protestation of innocence that should still further justify him.

However, the desire to justify himself does not fully account for the manifest dream. The fact that he is unable to use his arms and legs and that, instead of hurting someone, he is being tortured, points to an intense reaction formation to his hostile impulses, giving rise first to motor paralysis and then to the turning back of aggression against himself. To account for these two successive reaction formations, we must probably postulate guilt as a reactive motive.

Now, putting together these two bits of evidence, we can reconstruct the genesis of this dream as follows: The analyst's question stirred up the patient's guilt on account of his desire to hurt both his father and his wife. The dream text implies that he wanted to hurt them not only indirectly by his confession but also by attacking them physically. In the dream work he first reacted to his guilt by a fantasy of having his arms and legs paralyzed, and then by one of being tortured. Then, as a second step, he utilized this fantasy of being tortured to justify himself and even to give him an excuse for biting.

BIBLIOGRAPHY .

1. Alexander, F. 1935. *Roots of Crime.* New York: A. Knopf.
2. ————. 1938. "The Relation of Inferiority Feelings to Guilt," *Internat. J. Psychoanal.,* XXIX, 41.
3. French, T. M. 1953. "Structural and Functional Approaches to the

Analysis of Behavior." In: *Mid-Century Psychiatry,* ed. Roy R. Grinker. Springfield, Ill.: Charles C. Thomas.

4. French, T. M.; Alexander, F.; *et al.* 1941. *Psychogenic Factors in Bronchial Asthma.* ("Psychosomatic Medicine Monographs," Vol. I, No. 4; Vol. II, Nos. 1 and 2.) Washington, D. C.: National Research Council.

5. Freud, A. 1928. *Introduction to the Technic of Child Analysis.* New York: Nervous and Mental Disease Publ. Co.

6. Freud, S. 1900. *The Interpretation of Dreams.* New York: Macmillan Co., 1933.

7. ———. 1914. "On Narcissism—An Introduction." In: *Collected Papers,* IV, 30, 3rd ed. London: Hogarth Press, 1946.

8. ———. 1923. *The Ego and the Id.* 4th ed. London: Hogarth Press, 1947.

9. Piers, G., and Singer, M. 1953. *Shame and Guilt.* Springfield, Ill.: Charles C. Thomas.

Chapter Fourteen

HOPE AND REPUDIATION OF HOPE
IN PSYCHOANALYTIC THERAPY

A fact that we all know but sometimes forget about psychoanalytic therapy is that the deep unconscious is not directly accessible to therapeutic influence. The direct impact of the therapy is at the level of the system preconscious. We influence the unconscious only indirectly and very slowly through the medium of its preconscious derivatives.

In the course of a psychoanalytic treatment, patterns from the past are repeated over and over again. When our attention is focused on the past, nothing seems to change. What changes from week to week is much closer to the surface. Consequently, if we wish to understand the therapeutic process, we must follow very strictly Freud's advice to "analyze from the surface downwards." We must focus our attention first on what is happening in the system preconscious.

Traditionally, when we analyze the patient's orientation toward present reality, we concentrate our interest chiefly on his resistances. Sometimes we take his therapeutic incentive for granted. We may even lose sight of the motives that keep him coming to the treatment in spite of his resistances.

In this paper by David R. Wheeler and myself, we attempted to correct this omission by reviewing the course of a psychoanalytic treatment at the Chicago Institute for Psychoanalysis and tracing the source of "the therapeutic incentive that makes successful therapy possible." Our patient's therapeutic incentive, we found, had its basis in latent and suc-

Reprinted from *International Journal of Psychoanalysis*, 44 (Part 3, 1963). The co-author of this paper is the late Dr. David R. Wheeler.

cessively emerging hopes, based always in part on the realities of the therapeutic situation, of finding a solution for her conflicts. Such therapeutically significant hopes are rarely if ever conscious. They are preconscious hopes which the patient must struggle energetically to repudiate. In our patient's case, repudiation of her therapeutically significant hopes was her most important resistance.

These hopes are based on present reality. Why, then, do they have to be repudiated? In our review we found that these present reality-based hopes were too closely associated to other hopes, dating back to the patient's childhood, that had been followed by disastrous consequences. As a result, similar hopes, if reactivated during the therapy, would lead inevitably to mobilization of disturbing emotions arising out of the old traumatic memory. The patient's present hopes in the therapy had to be repudiated in order to prevent such reactivation of the associated traumatic memory.

In therapy, however, the analyst must encourage the patient's reality-based hopes to emerge progressively, as incentive for the therapeutic process. The analyst does this by giving explicit recognition to the present realities toward which the patient's new hope is oriented. The effect of encouraging the patient's new hope, however, will not be immediately beneficial. Instead of helping, reactivation of the new hope leads to more or less reactivation of the associated traumatic memory pattern. When this occurs, the patient may then be preoccupied for weeks or months with disturbances resulting from this reactivation.

The therapist's interpretation is designed not for present but for future effect. Ultimately, he expects, the disturbing affects will be dissipated or discharged. Then hopes similar to those that were repudiated will begin again to emerge. When this occurs, he expects that his earlier interpretations will have had a latent effect. His previous explicit recognition of the patient's new hopes will have increased their integrative capacity, even though they have remained latent. Now these hopes will emerge more boldly and persist longer before they are repudiated. Ultimately, they may become dissociated from the memory of earlier traumatic consequences, so that they can be lived through to fulfillment in the therapeutic situation.

I

In one of the technical papers, Freud (1913) tells of a therapeutic experiment. He told a patient (a young woman) about a repressed homosexual experience of which the girl's mother had informed him. The patient went into a convulsion each time Freud mentioned this incident. She finally "simulated imbecility and total loss of memory" to defend herself against what Freud had told her.

This experiment illustrates a fact that we all know but sometimes forget about psychoanalytic therapy. We know that the deep unconscious is not directly accessible to therapeutic influence. The direct impact of the therapy is at the level of the system preconscious. We influence the unconscious only indirectly and very slowly through the medium of its preconscious derivatives.

In the course of a psychoanalytic treatment, patterns from the past are repeated over and over again. When our attention is focused on the past, nothing seems to change. What changes from week to week is much closer to the surface. Consequently, if we wish to understand the therapeutic process, we must follow very strictly Freud's advice to "analyze from the surface downwards." We must focus our attention first on what is happening in the system preconscious.

II

Traditionally, when we analyze the patient's orientation toward present reality, we concentrate our interest chiefly on his resistances. Sometimes we take his therapeutic incentive for granted. We may even lose sight of the motives that keep him coming to the treatment in spite of his resistances.

This leads us to our most important thesis in this paper. This is that the therapeutic incentive which makes successful therapy possible must have its basis in the patient's latent and successively emerging hopes of finding a solution for his conflicts. This thesis is based on a more general one—that hopes play a centrally important part in the motivation and integration of all rational behavior. They are the central core of the ego's integrative function.

Psychoanalytic literature, until recently, has given very little recognition to the significance of hope in human and animal behavior. It is rather to poets and philosophers that we must turn for evaluations of

hope and of its influence on behavior. In general psychological literature, probably the first to pay systematic attention to hope was Alexander
F. Shand. In a book entitled *The Foundations of Character* (1914),
Shand collected and tried to organize into a comprehensive system what
literary men and anecdotal observers of animal behavior had written
about the part played by different emotions in the formation of character. He devoted a number of pages to hope, which he includes among
the emotions subsidiary to desire. "Hope increases the activity of
desire," he writes, "aids it in resisting misfortune and the influence of
its depressing emotions, and in both ways furthers the attainment of
its end." He quotes a number of poets and essayists in praise of hope.
Of these, a quotation from Amiel's *Journal intime* is particularly explicit
and dramatic. "At bottom," says Amiel, "everything depends on the
presence or absence of one single element in the soul—hope. All the
activities of man presuppose a hope in him of attaining an end. Once
kill this hope and his movements become senseless, spasmodic, and
convulsive, like those of someone falling from a height."

In her paper "Adaptation to Reality in Early Infancy," Benedek
(1938) emphasized the importance, for the development of the infant's
ego, of his "confidence" in relation to his mother in earliest infancy.

In *Childhood and Society* (1950), Erikson sketched an outline of the
psychosocial "crises" that furnish the emotional background for the
development of the ego from infancy to maturity. This development,
he postulated, starts with the infant's "basic trust" in his mother.

In a recent essay, Erikson (1962) has included hope as the earliest
of the "virtues" which guide the ego in its development toward integration within itself, with the mother, and then into the life of the
family and the community.

In scientific literature on the motivation of behavior, one reason for
the relative neglect of hope has been failure to distinguish between
hopes and other kinds of wishes. In two earlier papers (1941, 1945)
and then in a series of volumes entitled *The Integration of Behavior*
(1952, 1953, 1958), French has made this distinction a starting point.
He distinguishes between two kinds of wishes, two kinds of goals or
poles of behavior—between what one is trying to get away from or
get rid of and what one is seeking. We try to get away from pain or
from something that we fear, to put an end to hunger, to get rid of
sexual tension. "Need-pressure" is the name we give to such an urge to
escape from or put an end to disturbing stimuli. We contrast such need-
pressures with the positive attraction or pull exerted by *hopes*—which

may be based either on present opportunities for satisfaction or on memories of previous satisfaction, or both.

Starting with this distinction, French elaborated the thesis that hope of success in carrying a plan through to execution is the essential dynamic source of the integrative capacity that makes it possible for the ego to subordinate effort to purpose in rational behavior. Our thesis (above quoted) concerning hope as the essential basis for therapeutic incentive was elaborated and illustrated in detail in the third volume of this series.

More recently, Menninger (1959) has spoken and written in praise of hope. Starting with the pessimistic Greeks who condemned hope as an illusion and a curse, in contrast to St. Paul who eulogized "faith, hope, and love," Menninger traces through history the strangely and intensely ambivalent feelings about hope that have permeated the thoughts of philosophers, of religious teachers, and of poets. He concludes by citing much general and clinical evidence in support of his conviction that hope is a potent and "indispensable factor in psychiatric treatment and psychiatric education."

The ambivalence of philosophers and poets toward hope is of considerable interest in relation to our present thesis. As the title of this paper suggests, our patients, too, give evidence of considerable conflict about entertaining hopes.

III

Let us now repeat our thesis: The patient's therapeutic incentive is based always on specific hopes, which are in part realistic, of what the therapy can do for him.

We wish at the outset to forestall a possible misunderstanding. When we talk about hope we do not have in mind only some vague anticipation on the patient's part that the therapy will help him, or an equally vague confidence in the therapist, based probably on a rather unspecific positive transference. What we are talking about are specific hopes of exactly what the treatment can do for him. These hopes are usually only preconscious. They are always in part based on the realities of the therapeutic situation.

We must also warn against another possible misunderstanding. The hopes that we are speaking of are not the therapist's hopes for the patient. They are the patient's own hopes. They are not even hopes of which the patient is conscious. They are preconscious hopes which the patient must struggle energetically to repress and to repudiate. Indeed, repudiation of his therapeutically significant hopes is usually one of the patient's most important resistances.

To illustrate this thesis, we shall now report parts of the analysis of a patient in whom this resistance against hope was unusually strong and persistent. This patient had been in an analysis for some 300 hours before we had begun our detailed cooperative study of her material. At this time, and for many months before, the patient's hours on the couch had seemed to be characterized by a consistent, deadly monotony. Much of the time she was silent except when prodded by the analyst. Content, when it did emerge, was limited to seemingly natural and unavoidable reactions to the numerous petty irritations of everyday life. Interpretations seemed to elicit no response except on the most mundane and matter-of-fact level, completely devoid of fantasy or affect. The result was a profoundly bored and discouraged reaction on the part of the analyst. He had lost much of his own hope of being able to help the patient.

This was the state of affairs when we became interested in reviewing this patient's case. Somewhat to our surprise, we then discovered that the patient's monotonous resistance had not been at all in evidence at the beginning of the treatment. It had developed at definite points in the analysis in reaction to specific dynamic situations.

In this paper we shall try to give the reader some picture of how our insight into the interplay of hope and disillusionment that constituted this patient's therapeutic process gradually deepened.

IV

We will begin with an abbreviated summary of the patient's anamnesis, as reported in her first three hours.

The patient had come to analysis with a diagnosis of ulcerative colitis and had been accepted as a research patient. She had already had some psychotherapy from Dr. E, a woman internist working in a university clinic. When first seen at the Institute she was 28 years old, rather frail and colorless in appearance, most subdued and shy in manner. She had been married for four years but was childless. She worked full time in a clerical position. Her husband was employed as an engineer in an industrial plant and also attended night school, working for a college degree.

The patient was born in a small town in South Dakota, the third from the youngest in a Catholic family which included nine children. The true father was a rural mail carrier who was in disrepute with the rest of the family because he drank. According to family accounts, the patient was his favorite child. He used to take her with him on his mail delivery rounds.

The mother had died only a day or two after the youngest sibling, a boy, was born. The patient herself was then about four and a half. Thereupon a maternal aunt took the new baby, while the older children continued to live in the home, except for the patient and her next younger brother, Lewis. They were soon afterward brought to Chicago to live with the father's sister and her husband, who became foster-parents. The patient and her brother were never legally adopted because the father would not give his consent. The foster-parents nevertheless changed the children's surnames to conform to their own.

The patient could recall nothing of her real mother or of anything antedating the mother's death. She did remember an older sibling's telling her that Lewis and she were lucky, that they were going to be able to go to Chicago to live. The patient was surprised. "My grandmother later said that I was my father's favorite," she recalled, "and she couldn't understand how he ever let me go."

The patient stated that the major disappointment of her life occurred when she was eighteen, when she had to give up training as a nurse because of the acute and fulminating onset of her ulcerative colitis. After several weeks' hospitalization with high temperature and hemorrhage from the colon, she returned home to the family apartment for convalescence. Two years later her hopes of being allowed to reenter training were finally denied by the nursing school authorities. Then, for once in her life, she allowed herself to weep. Being in training and living at the hospital had enabled her to associate with other girls and to be free of the restrictive demands of her foster-parents and grandparents at home.

Her position at home was in many respects that of a slavey. The foster-mother had no taste for homemaking, and managed to keep busy running the apartment building which the couple owned and in which they lived. As a result, from her early teens on, the cooking, cleaning, and sewing for the most part devolved upon the patient. There was also the invalid grandmother to take care of. The patient had to come home directly from school every day to take care of these duties, and she was not encouraged to participate in activities with other young people or to invite them to her home. The patient returned repeatedly to these complaints about her foster-parents.

Seven years before she came for treatment, the foster-parents had adopted an infant boy who had been found abandoned in a nearby alley a few hours after birth. Taking care of this child, little Bobby, also became chiefly the patient's responsibility, though it was one which she rather enjoyed. But she complained bitterly that the foster-parents had allowed his teeth to become decayed through neglect, just as had happened in her own case. She was also bitter about the fact that her foster-parents had decided that she should not have any children because of her health, and had talked her into setting aside the rules of the Catholic church and practicing birth control. She added that since giving up contraception some time ago, she had been worrying if anything might be wrong with her, because she was still not pregnant.

V

In her fourth hour, her first on the couch, the patient unwittingly gave her first hint of what she hoped for from her treatment.

She told of her husband's having protested because she had stayed out until 11 P.M. one night recently to visit a sick woman acquaintance. She had promised to be home at 8 P.M. She agreed that he had every right to be angry, just as her foster-mother had been on similar occasions earlier. She added that if the analyst should change her in therapy it would be unfair to her husband, because then he would not have the submissive, dutiful wife he had contracted for.

In other words, she was already hoping that the treatment would free her from her compulsively compliant attitude.

In the next hour, she reported a dream about an overflowing sink.

Dream: A sink was leaking onto the floor, but I couldn't see where the water was coming from. It went on and on. I kept trying to mop it up but it was an endless job, it went on and on.

The analyst asked whether the overflow was clean or dirty. The patient "guessed it was clean."

In the next hour, she admitted that she had not reported the dream honestly. With much squirming, embarrassment, and painful affect, she confessed that it was not a sink but a toilet that was overflowing. It was filthy, not clean. "I have a quirk," she added. "I could never talk to anyone about sex, and I hate dirty stories." She explained that it was due to her Catholic education. The nuns in school were always talking about chastity, but she did not know what that meant. She would never have gotten married if she had known what the priest was going to tell her just beforehand—that sex was not a sin after marriage, that her duty as a Catholic wife was to have intercourse as often as her husband wanted it.

It is evident that the patient had come to her analysis with an intense conflict about sexual thoughts, and much conscious guilt and shame.

A dream reported in her tenth hour next gave evidence of how the patient hoped that the analyst would help her deal with this sexual conflict:

> *Dream:* I was at work. Mr. B, the assistant boss, came out of his office— he is rather indifferent and cold—and stood in front of my desk and said matter-of-factly that he thought that I should go out and have a sand- wich. Much later I was with a group from the office having dinner, and hoped that he didn't think that I was eating because he told me I should.
>
> In association she added that Mr. B had recently been calling another girl in the office to ask about mistakes the patient had made. She protested to the analyst that she did not want any special consideration because she was ill. The analyst, taking the dream as a reference to himself, suggested that she felt that he, too, was telling her she could have something for herself. To this permissive remark she immediately gave a sexual mean- ing: "A speaker at a parent-teachers meeting [she was attending a parent- teachers meeting at Bobby's school] the other night said that it was up to the parents to teach their children that sex is a beautiful thing, and that they should warn them against making fools of themselves."

This dream well illustrates the importance of keeping our attention focused on the patient's preconscious responses to her treatment. We might be content to interpret it only as evidence of the patient's sexual transference wishes toward the analyst. Were we to do so, we should miss a more superficial, but much more significant, preconscious hope oriented toward the therapeutic situation. The key to this hope is the exact form of the manifest dream content. The patient is hoping that the analyst will play a role similar to that of the priest who spoke to her just before her marriage. She is hoping that the analyst will now tell her that she should enjoy sex. (It was the patient, and not the analyst, who related his permissive remarks explicitly to sex.) She is reacting to this hope with great embarrassment. She repudiates it most energetically. She is shocked at the idea that the analyst might think she would be receptive to such a suggestion.

This dream also illustrates the fact that our patients must energetically repudiate the therapeutically significant hopes inspired by the treatment. This fact is understandable. If these hopes had not been unacceptable to the patient's ego, they would long ago have exerted their therapeutic effect and the patient would not have had to come for treatment.

It was a sign of the patient's growing response to the analyst's tacit support that only three hours later she was able to tell of some disturbing memories.

In hour 13 she asked for further reassurances that her material was confidential. Then she said that there was something which she could not confess even to the priest. The story came out with agonized affect and many pauses:

One summer night in South Dakota when the patient was twelve or thirteen, her father was driving her home from her uncle's.—He had been drinking. It seemed like a nightmare!—He told her that she was so much like her mother, then asked how long it had been since her last menstrual period and said that he wanted to do something with her but couldn't take the chance.

In the following hour the patient concluded that she might as well tell it all. She went on to confess sexual activities, which she first thought were actual intercourse, with an older brother during several subsequent summers in South Dakota. When she met this brother, Harold, on her first vacation there, she found him so considerate and obliging that she wished he had come to Chicago with her instead of her younger brother, Lewis. "But after the first few summers things changed. There was all that attraction, all that filthy petting and stuff. . . . I think I was probably as guilty as he was. . . . I'm so disgusted with myself for letting things like that happen. It didn't matter to him. . . . He tried to do it, but I wouldn't agree. Then he said I had no right to get him all bothered and then not give in to him. But I didn't, I don't know why. I knew every summer that I should not go up there, but no one knew anything about it and I couldn't give any good reason for not going."

The hours that immediately followed these confessions were for a long time baffling to us. For a long time we were unable to find a continuing dynamic chain of events that could make these next few hours intelligible as part of a therapeutic process. Then, finally, it began to dawn on us that the hopes directed toward the therapy that we had already recognized gave us the key to understanding what happened next.

The reasoning that led us to this insight was as follows:

Why, we asked ourselves, must a patient's therapeutically significant hopes be repudiated as they begin to emerge? Our answer was that they are related to hopes that were once very important in childhood but had to be rejected because they were associated with disastrous consequences. In view of this fact, we must expect that the beginning emergence of similar hopes in the therapy will soon be followed by beginning mobilization of disturbing emotions arising out of the old traumatic memory.

With this thought as our clue, we shall now review and try to understand the next period (hours 16 to 30) in this patient's treatment.

In her sixteenth hour, the patient told of old fears. In her delirium at the time of her acute attack of ulcerative colitis, she might have talked about her sexual play with her brother.

In the seventeenth hour the patient expressed fear that her dentist, the one person aside from her husband whom she had told about her analysis, would tell her family of it.

Her next (eighteenth) hour she opened with a period of silence. Then she asked abruptly, "Do I have to hate my parents?" The analyst asked what she meant. She continued: "Dr. E said I have to learn to hate them; she said I had every reason to. Then I went home and hated her instead. But I really don't think I ever hated anyone. Oh, I'm all mixed up! Maybe I did hate them."

Why, we must ask, does this question of hating her parents come up now?

Instead of answering our question, the patient told of another incident which would tend to justify her hostility toward her foster-mother: "Once my mother gave away a doll that I liked, and she didn't tell me about it. I decided to punish her by never playing with another doll, and I didn't. I wouldn't tell her why I wouldn't play with them. It was the satisfaction of knowing that it bothered her. I must have been stubborn or I would have forgotten about it. At first I thought that she had no right to give away my things, but later when she did it I felt that nothing was really mine, and then it didn't bother me so much. About the doll I knew that she would have said, 'That poor little girl has nothing. You should be glad to give her your toys.' The things came out of her pocket in the first place, so she had the right to take them back and give them away. I never felt anything was really mine, it was just mine to use. I guess it's too bad I didn't throw tantrums when I was a kid."

We are impressed with this patient's attitude of pious resignation toward her foster-mother. We are also impressed with her profound reaction to the loss of the doll. She herself explains her reaction as one of spite against the mother, but this hardly seems adequate to account for her resolve, which she actually carried out in later years, never to play with dolls again. Her explanation was a rationalization, hiding behind an aggressive motive the realization of how grievously she had been hurt. Her real motive was to protect herself from any possible repetition of her disillusionment by never letting herself become so attached to a doll again.

Why did this doll mean so much to her? We begin to get some inklings of the underlying traumatic memory from a dream reported in the next hour.

> *Dream:* A girl at the office was showing me some jewelry in a box. She said it was jeweled initials for a purse. They were *my* initials.

She recalled that the foster-mother once gave her some initials for a purse. They were the wrong kind, but, of course, she couldn't tell her. The girl in the dream is only an acquaintance whom she sees at lunch. She is nice, a happy person, good company. The initials might have been hers, too; she has the same first name as the patient. They were hard to read, like fancy script. She couldn't be sure they were her initials, and she wanted to look again, but avoided it. She thought they were R.B., her initials before she was married.

She has had so many names in her life. She recalls resentment at the foster-parents' changing her name to theirs even though she was not legally adopted. She had thought of running away. She tells of her embarrassment whenever the fact that her name had been changed comes out, usually in connection with legal documents and records. The girl in the dream once said at lunch that she was glad to change her name when she married. The patient also liked it when she heard this girl once mention having to go over and help her mother clean house, while her husband stayed at home and slept.

In the next hour, the patient again said that the girl who figured in her dream had remarked at lunch the other day that she was glad to have got rid of her maiden name when she married. The patient admitted that she liked this girl and again mentioned her speaking of having to go over and help her mother clean house on Saturday. She was struck by the fact that this girl didn't seem to mind.

A little later her thoughts reverted to the time when she was first brought to Chicago. "They said that Lewis wouldn't eat a strange dish when we came to Chicago unless I ate it first. My grandmother remarked, 'You'd think that the food was poisoned.' I suppose it's hard for kids of that age to go into a house full of strangers and accept everything." After a silence she continued: "I think changing my name when I married bothered me, I don't see why it had to be that way. It seems as though you give up your identity or something." The analyst agreed, and brought this feeling into relation with the loss of her own parents, adding that perhaps she always wondered what she did have that was her very own, that could not be taken away. "Yes," she replied, "but isn't it that I'm not able to adjust myself? If that was the way it had to be, I should have accepted it. They had a right to take away what they had given."

Again we are struck by the patient's attitude of fatalistic resignation.

For a long time we were unable to understand this dream. Finally, the patient's twice-repeated reference to the girl who did not mind helping her mother gave us the clue.

The patient, herself, is longing for a good mother-daughter relationship, but the treatment seems to be leading her in a direction that threatens her relation to her foster-mother. "Do I have to hate my parents?" she had asked. Hating her foster-mother would destroy the possibility of a good mother-daughter relationship.

Now we must ask: Why does she expect the analyst to tell her she must hate her foster-mother? And why is she so afraid of losing her mother?

In the light of her history, we can understand why she so longs for a mother. When she was barely four years old she was suddenly deprived of her true mother by death. Then she expected to stay with her father, whose favorite she thought she was. Yet, only a few months later, she was sent away to strange foster-parents and had to change her name. From the associations of the last two hours we can reconstruct the impact that these events must have made on her. Unconsciously she is talking about herself when she remarks how hard it is to go into a house full of strangers. The way that she dwells on the change of her name reflects her feeling at that time that she had completely lost her identity. First losing her mother and then being sent away to strangers by her father must have left this little girl with a feeling of being utterly uprooted.

No wonder that her longing for a mother is so intense! The trauma of being uprooted must not happen again! At all costs, she must see to it that her hostility does not cause her to lose her foster-mother too. Hence her resigned, submissive attitude.

This patient's questions about hostility toward her foster-parents had emerged suddenly not long after her confessions about her sexual play with her brother.

To account for this fact, we recall that her mother's death occurred when she was a little over four years of age, when she must have been at the height of her Oedipus complex. We also know that she was recognized as the father's favorite before she came to Chicago, that he liked to take her with him on his rural mail delivery rounds, etc. Putting this together with the later account of his sexual advance, we may surmise that his relationship to her even before the mother's death had been a seductive one.

Now, in her treatment, the reawakened memories of the father's sexual suggestion and of her incestuous play with her brother have begun to make her aware of where her hopes of sexual release (as a result of the analysis) are leading her. In order to be released from her sexual inhibition, she would have to break away from her desperately submissive tie to her foster-mother. Dr. E (the internist at the hospital where she had been treated for her colitis) had actually advised her to to leave home. She had assured the patient that she had every reason to hate her parents; but the possibility of hating her foster-parents and leaving them only reactivates the memory of how completely uprooted she felt when she really did have to leave home to go to live with strangers.

The intensity of her reaction to the doll incident also begins to make sense. The doll had served as a substitute, consoling her for the loss of her mother. In her fantasy she had probably given to the doll the mother whom she herself had lost.

Relating back to an earlier fantasy, the doll was probably also a baby that she had wished that the father would give her—just like the baby that he was giving her mother. In reality, instead of giving her a baby, he had sent her away to strangers. Indeed, intense resentment of this disillusionment by her father was the one emotional reaction to these events that had persisted in consciousness until the time of her treatment. For example, in her eleventh hour, while discussing her feelings toward her foster-parents, she had suddenly blurted out, "I didn't see how anyone could honor my own father." She added vehemently, "I didn't matter much to him, so why should he matter to me? Obviously he didn't care a hoot about us. I wouldn't let a family of mine be split up. I suppose I'll always hold that against him."

Thus this patient's Oedipus wishes seem to have culminated in the wish for a child by her father. This was followed by the death of her mother, and then by the loss of both her home and her father. In view of these disastrous consequences, it is not surprising that she became a compliant, good girl, in this way clinging desperately to her new home and her new mother. Now she must fight off energetically any hope of being freed by the treatment, any thought of permitting herself to enjoy sexual pleasure.

In these last three hours the patient has given us a glimpse of a traumatic memory of great intensity. However, what happened next in the therapeutic situation was not at this level. At this time, she did not relive this traumatic experience in her relationship to the analyst. This was fortunate, since at this time her ego would have been utterly incapable of mastering such an intense shock of being uprooted.

At this time, the ongoing therapeutic process was focused on preconscious hopes much closer to her real relationship to the analyst in the therapeutic situation. To discover these hopes we turn again to the manifest content of her dream.

> *Dream:* A girl at the office was showing me some jewelry in a box. She said it was jeweled initials for a purse. They were *my* initials.—I wanted to look again but avoided it.

From this dream we now conclude that she is hoping that the analyst, represented in the dream by the girl, will restore to her (show her) the memory of the close relationship she once had with her own mother. Yet in the dream she must avoid even looking to see whether the initials in the box are really hers. The memory of losing her mother (and of the events that followed) is so traumatic that she must shrink back from even looking at it.

Can this insight help us understand the treatment hours that immediately follow?

In the twenty-first hour, after a silence, the patient suddenly asked, "Why do I want to live without emotions? I can't remember ever having been hurt *that* much. I just want everyone to leave me alone." She continued with feelings of guilt toward her husband. "I feel that

Joe was terribly gypped when he got me for a wife. He deserves something better. His relatives are so interested in us, but I don't ever want to be bothered with them or to have to talk to them on the phone. Yet I like them, too."

Continuing this theme in the twenty-third hour, she protested that she had never wanted to ask her foster-parents for anything. "I don't like to accept things from them even now," she continued. "Things they give me seem like a bribe. . . . I don't think they ever gave me anything because they wanted to. They did it for their own reasons."

In this series of hours we detect a new trend. In her introduction to her usual complaints about how badly her foster-parents treated her, we learn that she is really more distressed when people treat her well, as, for example, in the case of her husband's relatives.

At the close of the twenty-third hour, the analyst pointed this out to her. He remarked that she seemed to need to feel herself unloved and exploited and to get gratification out of self-commiseration.

This interpretation made a great impression on her. She could not sleep that night. In the next hour, she wondered if "all this colitis and stuff" was not something that she had because she enjoyed it. A week later, she was still worried. She had been unable to sleep ever since the discussion of the week before.

In the twenty-sixth and twenty-seventh hours, she unexpectedly brought her concern into connection with sex. She told of her unhappiness in her marriage because of her feeling that sexual relations are disgusting and abhorrent and often painful. She wants her husband to "leave her alone." Instead, he insists on intercourse almost every night. She continued, almost moaning, "How can I stop feeling sorry for myself and enjoying it? I think that is what is wrong with me about sex. That discussion last week bothered me. I thought maybe there must be some reason . . . I just about decided that I spoiled . . . [labored and gasping breathing] . . . that I spoiled sex by feeling sorry for myself and feeling abused."

Thus, for the first time, this patient is consciously calling into question her whole masochistic orientation and in particular her repudiation of sexual pleasure. This beginning realization that she has "spoiled sex" may well be an important step toward therapeutic progress. It implies the possibility of her taking seriously an emerging hope. Perhaps her repudiation of sexual pleasure is unnecessary. Perhaps it is something from which her treatment can free her.

We know, however, that such a masochistic pattern cannot be given up easily. We must expect that her new hope of sexual release will be followed promptly by reactivation of the underlying fears that had made it necessary for her to "spoil sex."

In the next (twenty-eighth) hour, she asked suddenly, "After a woman has five kids, is she apt to be nervous in having the next one?" She went on to explain that yesterday was her twenty-eighth birthday and that her grandmother often told her about her mother's becoming nervous before she was born because the doctor was away. She continued, "I was wondering if she was a coward. I don't think I'm afraid of pain. I'm conscious of being close to thirty, and you should have kids when you are young."

We know that the patient's mother later actually died after childbirth. Preconsciously, the patient seems now to be wondering whether she too must die in childbirth, probably in retribution for her own earlier death wishes against the mother, which had been fulfilled by the mother's death.

Her anxiety began to take another form in the twenty-ninth hour. "Have you talked to my family?" she asked. Her foster-parents and her husband had suddenly become much more agreeable to her wishes in small things, so that she thought that the analyst must have been talking to them. The analyst told her that he had not contacted her family, but that perhaps she wished that he would. She vehemently denied any such wish, but the next hour she berated herself for having been so stupid as to distrust him. She added that she would not have come back again if she had not been sure that he had not communicated with her family.

For a long time we were puzzled to explain why this sudden distrust of the analyst had emerged just at this time. Then it dawned on us that this, too, was a logical consequence of the hopes that she had been preconsciously entertaining. She had begun to anticipate the probable consequences of her hopes that the analyst would make her freer sexually. If he did, what would her family say? Then a possible solution had occurred to her (preconsciously). Perhaps the analyst might talk to them and secure their acquiescence in what he was trying to do for her. This preconscious hope actually became conscious in a less disturbing form. She suspected that the analyst really had talked to them. That was why the parents had been nicer to her lately. However, her disturbed reaction to this seemingly pleasant thought betrayed her underlying intense need to repudiate this dangerous hope. If the analyst should tell the parents of her hope that the treatment will give her sexual release, there is no question in her mind what their reaction would be.

VI

At this point, we shall interrupt our detailed report of this patient's therapeutic sessions. We shall skip ahead to a later dream in which the hopes that we have just reconstructed came to overt expression.

This patient's basic character defense was one of masochistic submission to her foster-mother. Even after her marriage, she continued to do many household chores for her foster-mother, in addition to holding down a full-time job and also working hard taking care of her own home. All this did give her sufficient justification so that she could do a great deal of griping about her foster-mother, as well as about others. Although she herself was always accepted as the compliant, good girl, she also spent a good deal of time in her therapeutic sessions complaining about others on the job and elsewhere who got away with things. She had especially mixed feelings toward her brother Lewis. On the one hand, she was protective of him and his wife in their conflicts with the foster-parents; but she also expressed rather openly her envy of him because he had been able to get his own way much more than she. She was especially envious of him because he had finally been able to leave home after his marriage and to establish himself in another town some hundreds of miles away.

In the therapeutic situation, whenever the patient recoiled from her hopes of release by the treatment, this whole masochistic pattern was intensified, together with her griping protest against it. Her rebellious protest became stronger and more determined whenever she began to feel more secure in the analyst's support.

A particularly good opportunity for such a rebellious protest was reported in the seventy-sixth hour—when her brother Lewis was evicted from his home. At this time he asked the foster-parents for a loan so that he could buy a trailer for himself and his family. This, the patient said, would put him just where his parents wanted him—under their domination. She was sure the foster-mother would maneuver him back into their apartment building and make him work there as janitor. To prevent this, the patient herself secretly offered Lewis a loan in case the parents should refuse. When they did refuse, she let Lewis have the money.

Her reaction to this secret defiance was the following dream, which was reported in her eightieth hour, just after Lewis and his family had left the foster-parents to drive back to their own home.

Dream: I was in the apartment downstairs. My parents and I were at the door saying goodnight to some callers who were leaving. I thought they would never go. When they finally did, I went into the dining room and you were there. I had realized that you were in the apartment, that was why I was anxious for them to leave. Then you were talking to my mother. She looked as if she was pretty sore. You sent me out of the room, indicating that you could fix it up. I wondered how I was ever going to explain this. I thought I had put you in a heck of a spot because I knew you were there, they didn't. I was responsible for you being there and the least I could have done was tell them. I was willing to let you try to fix it, but you didn't know what you were up against. As far as I know, no one has ever crossed her yet. At the end of the dream I looked out the front window, and there weren't any sidewalks, rather deep trenches in their place, but it didn't seem unusual or remarkable.

Her only association was to recall how hostile the parents were toward the doctors at the hospital because they had told Lewis that his asthma had an emotional basis and had advised his getting away. In the light of this, she was awfully glad that she had never told them anything of her treatment "here."

This dream illustrates a principle that we believe to be very important for the understanding of psychoanalytic therapy. The principle is: As soon as a patient begins to take her hopes seriously, she must reckon seriously with the consequences and find a plan for dealing with them.

Our patient is nourishing hopes of becoming free of her foster-parents. With the encouragement of the doctors at the hospital, Lewis did leave the parental home. Now, by lending him money, she herself has just been supporting him in his desire to remain independent. In this way she is living out vicariously her own wish to become free. She is already preoccupied (consciously) with fear that they will find out what she has done. This time she dreams openly of her hope that the analyst will intervene for her with her foster-mother. But her dependent need for the mother is too great. She cannot conceive how even the analyst's support could prevail against her foster-mother.

VII

At the beginning of this paper, we called attention to a fact which we all know but which we sometimes forget when we try to understand the therapeutic process in a psychoanalytic treatment. The influence of the therapy on the patient's neurosis is not exerted directly on the patient's deep unconscious but rather at the level of the conflicts that are focal in the system preconscious.

Just below the surface of the patient's consciousness, in every analysis that is progressing satisfactorily, there is a continuing interchange, a kind of dialogue, between the analyst and the patient's preconscious ego. It is at this level and in this way that the effective impact of the therapy on the patient's behavior is achieved.

In this paper we have just been trying to follow and understand such a dialogue. We shall now summarize briefly the main steps in this interchange between the analyst and the patient's preconscious ego.

In the first twenty hours of her treatment, our patient's dawning hopes of release from sexual inhibition had begun to awaken a traumatic memory. Early in her childhood, she had entertained sexual wishes toward her father and fantasies of having a child by him. Then her mother died and she lost both her father and her home. She was left with a sense of having been completely uprooted—abandoned to the care of strangers. Now, in the therapeutic situation, this memory was so disturbing that she was compelled to shrink back from looking at it. An old defense was reactivated, a shrinking back from all emotions. She had to shrink back especially from human contacts that threatened to reawaken her own deeply traumatized longings for affection.

At this point, the analyst entered into the conversation, calling attention to her need to pity herself, to feel herself unloved and exploited. This interpretation caused the patient great distress, which disturbed her sleep for over a week. Behind all this distress, however, a therapeutically significant hope was hidden. The analyst's interpretation of her masochism had reinforced once more her hope of sexual release as a result of her treatment. This time her reawakened hope was based on her beginning realization that she herself was "spoiling sex" quite unnecessarily.

Still the dialogue in the patient's preconscious continued. Again her hopes were answered by fear of inevitable consequences. What would her foster-mother think? Her preconscious ego answered with a new hope. Perhaps the analyst might intervene for her with the foster-mother. However, even as late as her eightieth hour, the patient's hope of support from the analyst was no match for her desperate need to cling to her foster-mother.

VIII

If time permitted, we could trace this kind of a dialogue all through the patient's very long treatment. Within the limits of this paper we shall have to content ourselves with a very brief summary of how some of her hopes, after being repeatedly repudiated, could finally be accepted in consciousness and find fulfillment in real life.

It was imperative for this patient to get some kind of parental support for her wishes for sexual release. When she finally realized that she could not expect such support from her foster-mother, she turned next to her husband.

Just before marriage, the priest had instructed her always to yield to her husband's sexual demands. These instructions furnished the justification for her marital adjustment—on condition, of course, that she must not enjoy it. Later, her glimpse of the possibility of enjoying sex led to an intense reaction formation. She began to find excuses for refusing her husband. He, thus provoked, would not be put off. He became all the more insistent and demanding. On a number of occasions, he had intercourse with her while she was asleep and she succeeded in sleeping through it, only realizing in the morning what must have happened.

Under these circumstances, it is understandable that her husband should wish that the treatment would produce some change in her attitudes toward sex. The following dream reported in the 133rd hour is one of several that seemed to be trying to put her husband's authority behind a hope, which she herself must repudiate, that the treatment might change her sexual attitudes:

> *Dream:* Sunday morning while I was putting my shoes on I remembered that Joe said that some of my shoes needed repairing. I asked him which ones it was, and he said that he had never mentioned anything like that. So I must have dreamed it, but I can't remember the dream. [Silence.]

In association to this dream, she spent the whole hour complaining vehemently about her husband's sexual demands on her.

Another dream, reported months later, revealed that this hope had been allowed to develop much further before being repudiated.

> *Dream:* Sunday morning I recalled that I had been dreaming that I had been cooking cabbage. I was thinking that he [the husband] was going to be very pleasantly surprised to find this in the house.

Her first association repudiated this wish. The patient and Joe don't have cabbage because she cannot eat it and Joe does not like it.

As in other dreams of this patient, food has been substituted for sexual gratification. The dream has chosen a food that neither the patient nor her husband like in order to repudiate her hope of "surprising" her husband by enjoying his sexual demands.

Once before this (in her 165th hour), the patient had reported having enjoyed her sexual relations with her husband. It was only much later that she came to accept and enjoy the marital relationship consistently.

The doll incident, reported as early as the patient's eighteenth hour, has already given us a hint that wishes for a child must have played a very important part in her childhood. They were later energetically renounced as a protection against disillusionment. Later in her treatment, this wish emerged repeatedly and was repeatedly repudiated.

The following dream was reported in her 102nd hour:

Dream: I dreamed that I woke up in the morning and somebody said that I had given birth to a baby. I didn't know about it—everyone knew more about it than I. I was showing the baby to someone, but it was more like showing off a new dress or coat.

The background for this dream was the fact that her foster-mother had been remarking what a shame it was that Joe didn't have any kids —since he got such a bang out of them and liked to fix up Bobby's toys so much.

During this period and for a long time afterward, this patient's wish to have many children (like her mother) was finding expression chiefly in a vicarious form. The patient's foster-mother was very critical of Lewis' wife, Helen, because she was having pregnancies one after another with almost no interval between them. The patient protested defiantly on Helen's behalf that she had a right to have children just as often and as many as she wanted.

It was not until two years later that the patient herself first thought consciously that it would be nice to have a baby of her own. The thought came to her while she was looking at patterns, in order to make some baby coats for Helen's children.

We recall that early in the treatment the patient had very much envied her brother Lewis' having been able to move away from the parental home. Then, by lending him money, she had given vicarious expression to her own desire to do the same. Still, in her dream at that time, she had been unable to conceive how even her analyst could prevail against her foster-mother.

Some months after this, however, she and her husband began to dream and then to plan for building a house of their own in the suburbs. Her unconscious resistance toward these plans took the form at first of exaggerating enormously all the practical difficulties that intervened to delay them. As the plans came closer to realization, she became much alarmed at the thought of how offended her foster-mother would be. These fears, too, proved to be much exaggerated. The foster-parents finally became fairly well reconciled to the move. In the patient's 415th hour, she reported, though with a characteristic lack of enthusiasm, that they had actually made the move. In spite of her disavowal of enthusiasm, her satisfaction in the new house became more and more apparent in the succeeding months. Finally, she resigned from her job in order to be able to spend more time in her new home.

We hope that these few episodes will suffice to illustrate the fact that the therapeutic hopes this patient brought with her at the very beginning were all premonitory of the therapeutic progress that she was actually to achieve in the course of her very long treatment.

IX

We shall conclude by summarizing our concept of the therapeutic process—based on our analysis not only of this one case, but of others as well.

In rational behavior, the subordination of behavior to purpose is made possible by integrative capacity based on hope of success in carrying a plan through to execution. We believe that hope plays a similar role in psychoanalytic therapy. Specific hopes, oriented always in part toward the realities of the therapeutic situation, keep emerging. Such hopes are essential for the maintenance of the gradually increasing integrative capacity on which success in therapy depends.

Unfortunately, these therapeutically significant hopes are closely associated with other hopes from the past which once ended in disastrous consequences. For this reason, the newly emerging hopes must at first be repudiated. Unless they are promptly repudiated they begin to reactivate the associated traumatic memories.

At this point, the analyst can help by giving explicit recognition to the present realities toward which the patient's new hope is oriented. He should also explain that the patient's need to repudiate her new hope is a consequence of disturbing events in the past.

The therapist should not expect such an interpretation to have an immediately beneficial effect. The immediate effect of his interpretation will be weak indeed in comparison to the patient's own need to repudiate her new hope. If the associated traumatic memory pattern has begun to be activated, the patient may be preoccupied for weeks or months with disturbances resulting from this reactivation.

The therapist's interpretation is designed not for present but for future effect. Ultimately, he expects, the disturbing affects will be dissipated or discharged. Then hopes similar to those that were repudiated will begin again to emerge. When this occurs, he expects that his earlier interpretations will have had a latent effect. His previous explicit recognition of the patient's new hopes will have increased their integrative capacity, even though they have remained latent. Now these hopes will emerge more boldly and persist longer before they are repudiated.

The analyst must remember that it is not his own hopes but the patient's repudiated hopes that need recognition and encouragement. In order to achieve the maximum therapeutic effect, he should be alert to recognize therapeutically significant hopes even when they are only hinted at. If he can recognize the patient's own emerging hopes early and repeatedly, he should be able to hasten very much the patient's ultimate recovery.

BIBLIOGRAPHY

Benedek, T. (1938). Adaptation to Reality in Early Infancy. *Psychoanal. Quart.,* 7.

Erikson, E. H. (1950). *Childhood and Society* (New York: Norton).

———. (1962). The Roots of Virtue. In: *The Humanist Frame,* ed. by Julian Huxley (New York: Harper).

French, T. M. (1941). Goal, Mechanism, and Integrative Field. *Psychosom. Med.,* 3; Chapter 8 of this volume.

——— (1945). The Integration of Social Behavior. *Psychoanal. Quart.,* 14; Chapter 9 of this volume.

——— (1952, 1953, 1958). *The Integration of Social Behavior* (Chicago: University of Chicago Press).

Freud, S. (1913). On Beginning the Treatment, *S.E.,* 12.

Menninger, K. (1959). Hope. *Amer. J. Psychiatry,* 116.

Shand, A. F. (1914). *The Foundations of Character* (London: Macmillan, 1920.)

Psychoanalysis is almost unique among sciences in the predominant use that it makes of introspection and empathy as methods of investigation.

The concept of empathy implies that one person imagines himself in the situation of another person and has a sense of experiencing directly what the other person feels. In order to rid the concept of empathy of its mysticism, we must probably assume that the observer is responding to cues in the other person's behavior, many of which have been perceived at a level below the threshold of consciousness. By means of these cues, together with his own associated subjective feelings, the observer is able to create in his imagination a vivid sense of what the observed person is feeling.

Intuitively gifted observers are often very sure of their empathic impressions and do not like to have them questioned. Yet if we are to use empathy as a scientific tool, it is imperative that we find some way of checking our empathic impressions.

An important therapeutical difficulty seems to arise from Freud's earliest and most important discovery. Freud traced back neurotic symptoms, dreams, etc., to emotional responses that have been repressed. We think of empathy as sensing what another person feels. How can we "empathize" with "feelings" that are not conscious?

Fortunately, this riddle suggests its own answer. We can make a distinction between "direct empathy" and "empathic understanding." "Direct empathy" is experienced as though it were a direct perception of what another person is consciously feeling. "Empathic understanding" is understanding why a person behaves as he does.

In order to understand a person's behavior, we must often assume that he is activated by motives and guided by insight of which he is only partly or not at all conscious. We attribute to him motives and insight which, if conscious, would make his behavior intelligible. This is the way in which we arrive at the concepts of unconscious or preconscious motives and of unconscious or preconscious insight.

"Empathic understanding" is the name that we give to understanding that is arrived at by this kind of empathic inference. Empathic understanding can be checked against the observed person's subsequent behavior and against empathic inferences from such subsequent behavior. Empathic understanding, much more than direct empathy, seeks to reconstruct the relations between a whole sequence or constellation of events. Checking our empathic understanding is like fitting together the pieces of a jigsaw puzzle. The parts of our empathic reconstruction should fit together precisely. When more and more details or features of our patient's behavior fit together accurately in our reconstruction, we are justified in becoming more and more sure of our empathic understanding.

In our chapter on "The Integrative Process," we pointed out that two basic assumptions are implicit in our empathic understanding of behavior. One is that behavior is goal-directed, motivated. The other is that, in order to achieve a goal, one must know how. Goal-directed efforts, in order to be successful, must be guided first by an understanding of the problem to be solved, and ultimately by a plan for achieving the goal.

Prior to the development of psychoanalysis, psychology paid relatively little attention to questions about how behavior is motivated. Finally, psychoanalysis focused interest on the motivation of behavior. On the other hand, psychoanalysts have tended to take for granted the part played by knowledge and understanding in the guidance of behavior. In our chapter on "The Cognitive Structure of Behavior," we attempt to integrate our psychoanalytic studies of motivation with systematic studies of the "practical understanding" or "cognitive structure" by which all behavior must be guided.

Three kinds of knowledge are involved in the guidance of behavior. These are practical understanding of things, verbal understanding, and practical understanding of people. Practical understanding of things and verbal understanding have already been studied by many authors. After a brief review of some of what is known about these two kinds of knowledge, this chapter will be devoted to discussion of practical understanding of people, which is the kind of knowledge that is most essential as a background for psychiatrists but has often been taken for granted and usually not adequately distinguished from verbal thinking.

As clinical samples of analysis of different parts of the cognitive structure of case histories, we may cite our reconstructions of the focal conflicts of two dreams in our chapter on "Analysis of the Dream Censorship"; and also the latent and emerging hopes of finding solutions for focal conflicts on which the therapeutic process in the case studied in "Hope and Repudiation of Hope in Psychoanalytic Therapy" was based. In a subsequent chapter, "Cognitive Structure of a Case of Ulcerative Colitis," based on this same case, we attempted to trace these same therapeutically significant hopes in the opposite direction, back into the past. Starting with periods of reactivation of traumatic memories, we tried to carry our analysis back to interpretative reconstruction of the genesis of the patient's neurosis.

In our "Review of Our Studies of the Therapeutic Process," we summarize our preceding papers on this subject.

Chapter Fifteen

THE COGNITIVE STRUCTURE OF BEHAVIOR

Psychoanalysis and Empathic Understanding

Psychoanalysis is almost unique among sciences in the predominant use
that it makes of introspection and empathy as methods of investigation.

Empathy and Its Limitations

Many psychoanalysts are reluctant to admit this fact. The concept
of empathy seems too mystical. It implies that one person imagines
himself in the situation of another person and has a sense of experiencing directly what the other person feels. How can we trust such a
mystical act as a scientific procedure?

In order to rid the concept of empathy of its mysticism, we must
probably assume that the observer is responding to cues in the other
person's behavior, many of which have been perceived at a level below
the threshold of consciousness.[1] By means of these cues, together with
his own associated subjective feelings, the observer is able to create in
his imagination a vivid sense of what the observed person is feeling.

Intuitively gifted observers are often very sure of their empathic
impressions and do not like to have them questioned. Yet we know
that empathic impressions may be very much distorted by emotional
bias on the part of the observer. If we are to use empathy as a scientific
tool, it is imperative that we find some way of checking our empathic
impressions.

Empathy also has limitations resulting from other causes.[2] It is most
trustworthy in situations that are closest to the observer's own subjective experience. This fact limits greatly our ability to understand the
behavior of animals, especially that of nonmammalian vertebrates and

even more that of invertebrates. The same principle limits our capacity to understand people from unfamiliar cultures. Even more important is the fact that many of us find it difficult to empathize with infants or very young children.

Empathic Understanding and How It Can Be Checked

A still greater theoretical difficulty seems to arise from Freud's earliest and most important discovery. Freud traced back neurotic symptoms, dreams, etc., to emotional responses that have been repressed. We think of empathy as sensing what another person feels. How can we "empathize" with "feelings" that are not conscious?

Fortunately, this riddle suggests its own answer. We can make a distinction between "direct empathy" and "empathic understanding." "Direct empathy" is experienced as though it were a direct perception of what another person is consciously feeling. "Empathic understanding" is understanding why a person behaves as he does.

In order to understand a person's behavior, we must often assume that he is activated by motives and guided by insight of which he is at most only partly conscious. We attribute to him motives and insight which, if conscious, would make his behavior intelligible. This is the way in which we arrive at the concepts of unconscious or preconscious motives and of unconscious or preconscious insight. In other words, this is our *operational definition* of unconscious or preconscious motives and of unconscious or preconscious insight. "Empathic understanding" is the name that we give to understanding that is arrived at by this kind of empathic inference.

Direct empathy feels like direct perception. We do not know in any detail how this illusion of direct perception is created. We can check it only by asking the other person what he feels. Even then we cannot always be sure that the observed person will tell the truth.

Empathic understanding, on the other hand, can be checked against the observed person's subsequent behavior and against empathic inferences from such subsequent behavior. In some of Freud's early hysteria cases, this kind of confirmatory evidence [3] was very dramatic. In many cases the repressed memory that Freud had reconstructed emerged later in the patient's consciousness and was lived through again with intense affect. The patient's symptom could then be empathically understood by its being fitted into the context of the memory that was being relived; and the patient's abreaction of the affect belonging to this memory would then be followed by symptomatic relief.

For purposes of scientific reconstruction, empathic understanding is much superior to direct empathy. Empathic understanding, much more than direct empathy, seeks to reconstruct the relations between a whole sequence or constellation of events. Checking our empathic understanding is like fitting together the pieces of a jigsaw puzzle. The parts of our empathic reconstruction should fit together precisely. When more and more details or features of our patient's behavior fit together accurately in our reconstruction, we are justified in becoming more and more sure of our empathic understanding. In many cases, what has been empathically understood can also be repeatedly checked against new evidence. This follows from the fact that patterns that are really significant in a patient's life will be sure to repeat themselves over and over again in one form or another.

Still, capacity for empathic understanding differs widely from one person to another. Our scientific conscience would be better satisfied if we could learn to follow with greater precision the steps by which a psychoanalyst or other observer arrives at his empathic understanding. Kubie (1952, 1953) has offered a promising suggestion. He regards an interpretation of a patient's behavior as only a hypothesis to be tested. Then he invites the patient to join with him in testing this hypothesis and also in extending or revising it. This suggestion has been followed in great detail by Walter Bonime (1962), who has reported, with many examples, how he and his patients collaborate in interpreting a patient's dreams.

French (1944, 1952) and French and Fromm (1964) have elaborated extensively an almost identical suggestion. The basic principle of their method is to try to trace in detail the evidence on which the investigator has based his interpretations. Usually, they find, the interpreter's initial empathic impression has taken into account only part of the available evidence. Step by step, they then try to revise and expand an initial interpretation to take account of evidence that had previously been neglected. This process can also be continued later as still other evidence becomes available, using the new evidence to confirm or reject or to revise or expand conclusions that had previously been drawn.

AN OPERATIONAL APPROACH TO INTERPRETATION AND THEORY

Another principle is involved if we wish to check our interpretations adequately. This principle concerns the relationship between interpretation and theory.

Theoretical concepts "are not the foundations of science," Freud [4] has written. We must be ready to replace or modify our theoretical concepts, he says, whenever such modification is necessary for the understanding of empirical observations. We must take care not to be misled by our theories. Any science that is developing will be continually making new observations. Our science will become stagnant unless we keep rechecking our theories in the light of new observations. Our theories must be built up about the methods of observation that we employ. In our theory-building in the psychoanalytic field we should remain in sensitive and ever renewed contact with our empathic understanding of actual behavior.

From the point of view of interpretive method, our psychoanalytic concepts range between two extremes. Some (like the psychodynamic mechanisms) are based directly on empirical observations; others (like the drives) are much further removed from the actual data of observation. Theories that are not in close contact with observations should not yet be either accepted or unconditionally rejected. Our first concern should be to learn all that we can directly from empathic understanding of actual behavior. Moreover, even our best empathic understanding needs to be *re*checked whenever we can make new and pertinent observations.

Our *theories* should be based on generalizations from the behavior of many patients, interpreted one at a time.

We outline three rules, accordingly, for guidance in our interpretive approach:

1) We should ignore our theories while we are interpreting. Instead of becoming preoccupied with our theories, we should try to resonate sensitively with what is focal in the patient's thoughts.

2) In formulating our interpretations and theories, we should use only concepts that we can define in terms of the interpretive procedures by which they were arrived at.[5] This is our *operational approach* to interpretation and theory.

3) Our operational approach should be further guided by the "prin-

ciple of parsimony" ("Ockham's razor"). We reduce our theoretical thinking to the simplest possible terms. In other words, in our theoretical framework we use only concepts that are *necessary* to account for all pertinent evidence that is available at the time.

Making use of these principles, we shall now try to work out some of the theoretical implications of the interpretive approach that we have just sketched. In everyday life, our concept of human behavior is based on empathic understanding. Psychoanalysis has extended and refined our common-sense method of understanding behavior, by applying it to the empathic understanding of irrational as well as rational behavior. In this paper, our purpose is to spell out the conceptual system that emerges when we recognize explicitly the role played by empathic understanding in our common-sense and psychoanalytic understanding of behavior.

MOTIVATION AND INSIGHT

Two basic assumptions are implicit in our empathic understanding of behavior. One is that behavior is goal-directed, motivated. The other is that, in order to achieve a goal, one must know how. Goal-directed efforts, in order to be successful, must be guided first by an understanding of the problem to be solved and ultimately by a plan for achieving the goal.

Prior to the development of psychoanalysis, psychology paid relatively little attention to questions about how behavior is motivated. Finally, psychoanalysis focused interest on the motivation of behavior. On the other hand, psychoanalysts have tended to go to the opposite extreme. We have tended to take for granted the part played by knowledge and understanding in the guidance of behavior. What is needed now is an integration of our psychoanalytic studies of motivation with systematic studies of the "practical understanding" or "cognitive structure" by which all behavior must be guided.

Need-Pressure and Know-how

In formulating our concept of motivation, psychoanalysts often start with notions like "instincts," "drives," or "needs," which are assumed to constitute the hereditary basis for goal-directed behavior. This is exactly the opposite of an operational approach. What is most directly accessible to empathic understanding is usually the immediate goal or goals of behavior. So much has happened in the twenty or more years since a patient's birth that it is impossible to disentangle how much is inherited pattern and how much was acquired later. It is important, therefore, that we examine critically the concepts of "instinct," "drive," and "need." We sometimes think of a person's longing to be loved, for example, as a need or a drive or even an instinct, born with the infant as he emerges from the mother's body. This kind of loose usage is particularly deeply ingrained in persons who idealize empathy with the infant or the child. The assumption of inborn "urges" is probably based on the adult observer's subjective identification with the infant's behavior. *We read back into the infant our own understanding, as adults,* of the significance of his behavior. This is a very uncritical use of empathy. A need for maternal love, for example, implies a conceptualization of which the infant is not capable at birth. At birth the human infant is not even capable of realizing that the mother exists as a person. How, then, can he wish to be loved by her?

What is left out of account in this loose usage is the fact that any goal-directed striving involves not only some kind of an urge toward a goal but also some equivalent of knowledge of what the goal is and how it is to be achieved. We shall next inquire into the part played by this factor of intelligence or knowledge in the hereditary transmission of behavior patterns.

We start with the concept of need. The word "need" has two different meanings. We should take care not to confuse these two meanings with each other. We should distinguish between "objective needs" and "need-pressures." [6]

Adult observers know that an infant "needs" food. By this we mean that if he does not receive food, he will become sick, starve to death. In this sense, food is an objective need of the infant. Scientists even know that the baby's food must have certain chemical constituents if the baby is to live. "Objectively," the infant "needs" proteins, fats, and carbohydrates, a certain minimum caloric intake, a certain minimum assortment of amino acids, vitamins, minerals in small amounts, if he is to live and grow normally.

Only adults and scientific investigators know about the baby's "objective needs." Presumably, all that the baby knows is his intense discomfort (hunger). His hunger is a "need-pressure." His hunger is a "physiological state of unrest" which exerts a "need-pressure," stimulating him to cry. Fortunately, the baby has parents who can be called to his aid. The baby's mother, hearing the baby cry, understands that he "needs" (objectively) to be fed. She feeds him and "satisfies" his hunger.

It is impossible to discuss need-pressures or "drives" intelligently unless we consider them in relation to the "knowledge" that must be utilized in order that they may find "satisfaction." Need-pressures and understanding are two complementary factors in behavior, neither of which is effective without the other.

The next important question is: *Where,* in each particular case, *does the knowledge reside* that is essential in order that satisfaction may be achieved? It is important not to forget that it is the mother, not the baby, who knows both that the baby "objectively needs" food and that food will "satisfy" his hunger. There is no evidence, in the first few days of his life, that the baby even knows that it is food that he wants. For this reason, except when or until we have definite evidence to the contrary, it is better to assume as a working hypothesis that inherited need-pressures do not have positive goals. A baby at birth is not capable of desiring food.[7] The baby must *learn* to desire food. Only after he has been fed repeatedly does he begin to *learn* that mother and being fed bring "satisfaction," i.e., are followed by cessation of his hunger.

What evidence do we have to tell us when a baby has learned to desire food? We know that he has made this beginning step in learning when his crying begins to take on a new character. He shows signs of beginning to expect his mother to come when he cries and of wishing for her and the food that she brings. His crying has then ceased to be a "blind instinct," a stereotyped response to hunger. It has become a means to an end. From this point on, the baby "knows" one way to seek satisfaction of his hunger—by crying in order to call mother and food.

At this point, however, we should pause to give heed to an enormous body of evidence that seems to throw doubt on the working hypothesis that we have just formulated. Walter Cannon wrote of the "wisdom of the body." In this phrase he expressed a wondering admiration of the adaptive perfections of the organism. In earlier ages these perfections had been attributed to the wisdom of God or of Mother Nature. What was new in Cannon's use of this phrase was that it summed up much of what he had learned in a lifetime spent in investigating the details of physiological responses.

This "wisdom of the body" seems to throw doubt on the working assumption that we have just made. Our working assumption was that the baby at birth knows nothing about how to fulfill his objective needs, that he is not born with any positive goals of behavior, that he must learn from experience, for example, even to wish for mother and food. He must even learn, we postulate, how to utilize his instinctive crying response as a way of calling mother and getting food.

Another phrase that is sometimes used contrasts sharply with Cannon's notion of the body's "wisdom." This other phrase seems to be more in accord with the working assumptions that we have just summarized. We sometimes speak of "blind instinct." Konrad Lorenz (1952) has reported a dramatic example. One day he was holding a black rag in his hand, whereupon a flock of jackdaws which he was raising swooped down upon him just as they would have done if it had been one of their number, a black bird, that he was holding. It seems that the birds did not "know" the difference between a black rag and a black bird. Just as the word "wisdom" implies a marvelous perfection of understanding, so does the phrase "blind instinct" give recognition to the fact that an animal's "understanding" has definite and sharp limits.

How can these two seemingly contradictory concepts be reconciled? In recent years the designers of computers have dramatized the answer to this question. They have designed and built machines whose capacity to solve certain kinds of problems far exceeds that of the human brain. The "wisdom," or, better, the knowledge, "know-how," that enables the machine to solve problems is the knowledge of the designer that he has caused to be built into the machine. The machine's capacity to solve problems, however, is based on the coordination and integration of numerous detailed reactions to particular stimuli. In many machines, each of these detailed reactions is automatic, like the "blind instinct" of an animal which reacts in a stereotyped way to its "innate releasing stimulus." Still the machine has been so designed that automatic coordination of its "blind instincts" will achieve the goal or solve the problem that the designer intended. In other words, the designer's knowledge has been built into the machine as a constellation of "blind" automatic mechanisms.

This answer still leaves unanswered an age-old question: Where did the animal organism get its design? Where did it get its built-in "wisdom" or "know-how"? Probably we do not know the whole answer to this question. Today the accepted answer is: through the action of natural selection in the course of evolution, through the dying out of variant forms and species whose "design" was not good enough to enable them to survive in the competitive struggle for existence.

The human infant is born with a very meager repertory of "blind instincts." This fact keeps him for a very long time dependent on his mother. Other animals have instincts that make it possible for them to forage for their own food much sooner. The human baby, for example, is for a very long time dependent on *the mother's knowledge* of how to provide food for him. This prolonged dependence on the mother for food now gives him time for a much more prolonged and extended process of learning from experience. In this way, a much more flexible adaptation to a wide range of possible environments is made possible. Instead of rigidly fixed patterns for getting food, the "wisdom" that has been built into the baby's body has equipped him with mechanisms for learning from experience. This built-in capacity to learn makes it possible for him to adapt slowly to any one of a wide range of possible environments by discovering new ways of getting food. This mechanism is the mechanism of the inherited "drive."

Thus we arrive at the conclusion that a "drive" is not a single "urge" which can be recognized empathically. According to the concept that we propose,[8] a "drive" consists of three parts. The first and last of these parts are built into the organism as automatic mechanisms in its inherited "design." The middle part is left to be filled in by insight ("know-how") acquired by learning from experience during the lifetime of the individual concerned.

The first of these three parts is a "need-pressure" in response either to appropriate external stimulation, such as pain, or to an internal "physiological state of unrest," like hunger. The last part is the mechanism of "reinforcement" by "satisfaction" of this need-pressure (the "law of effect," according to Thorndike).[9] This is the mechanism by which the middle part of the drive mechanism, which has been left blank by heredity, can be filled in by insight (know-how) based on past experience.

The Cognitive Structure of Goal-directed Behavior

Our next task is to reconstruct the process by which learning from experience fills in the gap between unsatisfied need-pressures and memories of satisfying experience. As a first step we must distinguish between two kinds of goals of behavior. One tries to escape from pain or from the object of one's fear, or to put an end to a distressing physiological state like hunger. "Need-pressure" is the name we give to such an urge to escape from or put an end to disturbing stimuli. We contrast such *need-pressures* with the positive attraction exerted by *hopes,* which may be based on present opportunities for satisfaction, or on memories of previous satisfaction, or on both.

As we have already stated, primary need-pressures do not have positive goals. Only after an infant has learned that the mother's breast satisfies hunger does his primary need-pressure, hunger, give rise to a wish for the mother's breast, which then becomes his positive goal. The primary need-pressure had tended to be discharged diffusely; but from this time on, hopes, based at first on memories of previous satisfaction, tend more and more to channel the primary need-pressure into efforts to achieve positive goals. Later, with increasing experience and practice, one learns progressively to recognize present opportunities for satisfaction and to focus the originally diffuse need-pressure more and more on effective efforts to achieve circumscribed positive goals.

We must next examine this focusing effect of hope more carefully. If efforts to achieve a positive goal are to be successful, not only hope but also insight is necessary. A well-directed effort to achieve a goal is something more than mere motor discharge of need-pressure. If efforts to achieve a goal are to be effective, they must be guided by an adequate practical understanding of the problem to be solved or by some kind of plan. Misunderstanding of the problem to be solved may lead a person to false hopes. Therefore, if efforts to achieve a positive goal are to be successful, the channeling effect of hope must be guided by adequate understanding.

Transformation of Fantasy and Play into Planning and Purpose

This leads us to the problem of how plans are constructed. Our key for the answer to this question is the role of fantasy in our mental life.

Freud contrasted pleasure principle and reality principle. According to the pleasure principle, one seeks immediate pleasure and avoids immediate pain. The reality principle demands that one renounce immediate pleasure and even endure pain for the sake of an assured future pleasure. In accordance with this distinction, it is unfortunately now customary in psychiatric and psychoanalytic thinking to disparage fantasy as a regressive form of thinking.[10] On the other hand, Freud also pointed out that the reality principle is a modified form of the pleasure principle.

By systematically studying practical understanding we can trace the actual process of transformation of pleasure principle into reality principle. This transformation is usually not an abrupt event. Difficulties in the way of simple wish fulfillment are often recognized only one at a time. In its purest form, daydreaming is playful. It is dominated by a wish-fulfilling tendency and does not take seriously difficulties in the way of wish fulfillment. Yet play often becomes earnest. Children may take their play very seriously. When play begins to become earnest, then fantasy must begin to take account of obstacles in the way of wish fulfillment.

In other words, play, fantasy, and even dreams often serve as a preliminary and exploratory phase in the elaboration of the planning that is essential for rational behavior. Planning begins with fantasy. Daydreaming grades into making plans. When we begin to take our daydreams seriously, they become tentative plans. In this way, fantasy and play are transformed step by step into planful thinking and purposive behavior.

Very important for the course of development of purposive behavior is the timing of this transition from playful fantasy to serious purpose. While a person is only exploring his problem, it is desirable that he not let himself become too involved in it. At first, he should only play tentatively at planning. On the other hand, if he lets himself be committed to one plan too soon, his plan may turn out badly. His efforts to carry it out end in failure and in other disturbing consequences. In such a case, his reactions to frustration will seriously interfere with his search for a better plan and will lead to neurotic or psychotic behavior.

THREE KINDS OF KNOWLEDGE

Three kinds of knowledge are involved in the guidance of behavior. These are practical understanding of things, verbal understanding, and practical understanding of people. Practical understanding of things and verbal understanding have already been studied by many authors. Practical understanding of people is the kind of knowledge that is most essential as background for psychiatrists, but it has often been taken for granted and usually not adequately distinguished from verbal thinking.

Practical Thinking About Things

Our discussion of goal-directed behavior in our last two sections is most simply and directly applicable to the practical understanding of things. We shall next review briefly some of what is known about this kind of intelligence.

Practical thinking begins with what Jean Piaget (1936) calls "sensorimotor intelligence." Piaget has traced in great detail how the infant builds up, step by step, an ability to grasp spatial relationships within the range of his immediate perception and to manipulate objects inventively within that range. This "sensorimotor intelligence," which culminates around the eighteenth month of the infant's life, continues later to develop into a grasp of spatial and temporal relationships beyond the range of immediate perception, and to acquisition in varying degree of mechanical sense, of an increasing understanding of and skill in manipulating objects. All this we call practical understanding of things, of inanimate objects.

Practical understanding of the inanimate world has been most systematically studied by Gestalt psychologists. Wolfgang Koehler (1931) emphasized the importance of "insight" for the learning process. For example, in one of his experiments, an ape, baffled at first in its desire to get fruit just beyond its reach, suddenly discovers how to make a longer stick by fitting two shorter sticks together. Kurt Lewin (1935) helps us understand the meaning of an experimental subject's behavior by making diagrams of his "psychological field"; he tries to map out what the experimental situation looks like to the subject. For example, Lewin may picture a child separated from the piece of candy which is his goal by a negatively charged barrier of parental prohibition. Similarly, E. C. Tolman (1948, 1951) speaks of "cognitive maps" by which behavior is guided in maze-running experiments. Karl Duncker (1926, 1945) and Max Wertheimer (1945) have applied similar concepts to the study of problem-solving and productive thinking. In my own *Integration of Behavior* (1952, 1954, 1958), I have used the terms "cognitive field" and "integrative field" to correspond to the "psychological field" of Lewin and to Tolman's "cognitive map."

However, only the simplest behavior can be adequately guided by a single integrative field. In rational purposive behavior, a plan for achieving an end goal must usually be supplemented by plans for achieving one or more subsidiary goals. Such a hierarchy of plans for achieving an end goal constitutes the "cognitive structure" of purposive behavior. Such cognitive structures may be exceedingly complex, as, for example, in the case of the master plans and numerous detailed working drawings which an architect must use in order to show how a building is to be constructed.

The Syntactical Structure of Verbal Understanding

From late in the infant's first year on, the development of practical understanding becomes intertwined with the child's learning to talk and to understand language. With the development of language, understanding and thinking take on an entirely new character.

Language has two functions. For our present purpose, it is important to distinguish between communicating by means of speech and thinking in terms of words and sentences. When speech is used for purposes of communication, the original thinking or perception is practical understanding. Then this practical thinking has been translated into words and sentences. On the other hand, in pure verbal thinking, words and sentences are manipulated logically to lead to new conclusions.

COMMUNICATION BY MEANS OF SPEECH

In other words, words and sentences have meaning. That which is designated by a word or formulated by a sentence is its meaning. Somewhere in the background of all verbal thinking is a nonverbal meaning. At the most elementary level, concrete particular things or events that are perceived or understood without words are described or explained in words. This is descriptive or expository speech.

In order to be communicated, what is perceived or understood without words must be put in a form that can be understood by someone else. For example, let us suppose that we wish to explain to someone else how a mechanical operation is to be performed. In this case what is to be communicated is not verbal but practical (mechanical) understanding. In order to communicate our mechanical understanding to another person, we may translate it into words and sentences. In order to understand, the other person must translate the speaker's words back into mechanical understanding. If the hearer is able to do this, he will be able to perform the operation that has been explained. On the other hand, the hearer may understand only the syntactical structure of the speaker's sentences but not their nonverbal meaning. In such a case, the speaker's explanations will have been useless.

There are radical differences of structure between practical and verbal understanding. In practical thinking, we perceive things directly in relation to one another as parts of a whole, whereas in verbal thinking we think in terms of the syntactical structure of words organized into sentences. In everyday life, we are so accustomed to describing what we perceive in words and to translating our descriptions back into perceptual imagery that we usually do not notice how radically our descriptions have transformed the perceptual imagery. To become aware of this difference, we need only compare an architect's plan of a house with an attempt to describe it in words. The plan gives us a picture of the whole, but our description must use many sentences, analyzing and then focusing our attention successively on details of the picture and on detailed relations between them.

ABSTRACT CONCEPTUAL THINKING

There is another important difference between practical thinking and verbal thinking. Verbal thinking interposes the syntactical structure of sentences between our direct perception and our understanding. When this detachment of our understanding from direct perception becomes greater, thinking becomes relatively independent of nonverbal practical understanding. In abstract, conceptual thinking, the meanings of words are defined, not by reference to the immediate data of perception, but in terms of other verbal concepts. In this way, the concepts of abstract conceptual thinking are two or more steps removed from the immediate data of perception. For example, kinetic energy is defined as equal to one-half the product of the mass of a moving object multiplied by the square of its velocity. In other words, kinetic energy cannot be directly measured but is defined in terms of two verbal concepts, mass and velocity, which can be directly measured. Mass is measured (roughly) by the weight of the object, and velocity by the distance traversed in a unit of time. Thus, the concept of kinetic energy is two steps removed from data of direct observation.

This detachment of abstract conceptual thinking from direct perception has great advantages to compensate for its obvious disadvantages. By building up conceptual systems that are two or more steps removed from the data of immediate perception, abstract conceptual thinking is able to arrive at broad generalizations whose validity could not be recognized by direct observation. This was a momentous step in the development of thinking. It was the step that made possible, first, such practical disciplines as arithmetic; later, many differing philosophies; and finally, the widely ramifying conceptual structure of modern science. Thus, the highly specialized technique of abstract conceptual thinking, with its detachment from direct perception, is uniquely valuable for purposes of scientific and philosophical generalization.

Verbal thinking is less well suited for some other purposes, however. For understanding people and interpersonal relations, another kind of cognitive structure, which does not depend on syntactical logic, is much superior.

Practical Thinking About People
THE STRUCTURE OF EMPATHIC UNDERSTANDING

Practical thinking about people begins with and is organized about what we call empathic understanding. Yet empathic understanding itself is not a simple and elementary act. We have described empathy as a sense of experiencing directly what another person feels. Such imaginative identification with another person may go much further than empathy. In watching an absorbing movie, for example, we may become so completely identified with one of the characters on the screen that for a time we lose all sense of a separate identity. Such complete absorption in what another person is feeling we call "sympathic resonance." In contrast to sympathic resonance, empathic understanding implies a split in the observer's ego. With one part of his ego, he remains in sympathic resonance with the person who is understood. The other part of his ego, remaining detached, "understands" by observing the part of his own ego that is in sympathic resonance with the observed person.

This "split in the ego" is something that we recognize introspectively whenever we reflect consciously on the phenomenon of empathy. In the psychoanalytic literature, Richard Sterba (1934) was the first to call attention to such splitting off and detachment of an observing part of the ego.

At other times there may be a further split in the observer's ego. It is sometimes possible, at least to some degree, to understand two other persons at the same time. While watching a movie in which there are two actors, for example, one may identify predominantly with one of the characters. Usually there is also some degree of empathic understanding of the other character. If so, the observer has succeeded in achieving *"empathic grasp" of an interpersonal situation.* To account for empathic grasp of an interpersonal situation involving two other persons, we must postulate a three-way split of the ego. For example, a child may see two persons struggling with each other or in some kind of sexual embrace. With the detached part of his ego, he sees what they are doing to each other. His "understanding" of the scene, however, may go much further than just looking. He also participates in the scene with his imagination, as though he were one or both actors—i.e., he identifies with one or both actors. In order to account for a double identification, we must postulate that two parts of the observer's ego get into sympathic resonance, one with each of the actors. Then the detached, observing part of the ego projects these feelings of sympathic resonance back into the observed scene, and experiences them as the respective feelings of the two observed persons.

The essential feature of empathic grasp of a situation is that one is able to experience at the same time a number of different sets of feelings and to keep these feelings separate, attributing each to the appropriate person. We call this kind of grasp of an interpersonal situation an understanding of its "role structure." [11]

Practical thinking about people is based on empathic grasp of interpersonal situations. For example, a salesman must use his empathic understanding of other people in order to get them to buy from him. In this interpersonal situation, the salesman must be both an understanding observer and an active participant. His empathic grasp of the task of selling must involve an integration of empathic understanding of the roles of others and introspective understanding of his own role. Strictly speaking, such practical thinking about an interpersonal problem is "introspective-empathic thinking." However, for the sake of brevity, we shall often use the term "empathic thinking."

We distinguish between empathic fantasy and empathic thinking. Empathic fantasy is fantasy in terms of role structure. Empathic thinking is thinking in terms of role structure. In empathic fantasy or empathic thinking, role structures, undergoing change and being substituted one for another, become the units of more complexly organized fantasy or thinking.

ROLE-GIVING PLAY, EMPATHIC FANTASY, AND EMPATHIC THINKING

Earlier in this paper we pointed out that fantasy has an essential part to play in the practical thinking that makes purposive behavior possible. Planning begins with fantasy. Daydreaming grades into making plans. When we begin to take our daydreams seriously, they become tentative plans.

When we first made these statements we had in mind practical thinking about things. Empathic fantasy is related in the same way to empathic thinking. Empathic fantasy is an essential preliminary or first stage in the elaboration of empathic thinking.

The structure of empathic fantasy is often transparent in the role-taking and role-giving play of children. In the symbolic play of very young children, inanimate objects are substituted freely in the roles of persons or animals. In later role-giving play, roles are given to imaginary or real persons whose imagined motives and feelings are lived out empathically with more or less intensity. This kind of play is empathic fantasy. In its purest form, empathic fantasy is dominanted by a wish-fulfilling tendency. It seeks to modify real interpersonal situations in the direction of fulfillment of the wishes of one or more of the participants.

In other play of this kind, recognition is given to the real difficulties in the way of wish fulfillment. With increasing recognition of real difficulties, empathic fantasy is increasingly transformed into efforts to find solutions for real interpersonal problems. When thus transformed, empathic fantasy increasingly approximates empathic thinking.

For example, a shy little girl, ignored by other children, may imagine that she is a beautiful princess, loved and admired by everyone. This is empathic fantasy. As she grows older, however, she may gradually learn how to make herself attractive and win love from others. In other words, in her behavior, pleasure principle will have been modified into reality principle and her introspective-empathic fantasy will have been converted into introspective-empathic thinking.

DIFFICULTIES IN STUDYING EMPATHIC THINKING

We tend to underestimate the importance of empathic thinking in everyday life. According to our definition, any thought processes which involve attempts to understand other people by identifying with them are empathic thinking. Any thinking which tries to understand interpersonal situations in terms of role structure is empathic thinking. Empathic fantasy is fantasy that conceives of interpersonal situations in terms of role structure.

Empathic thinking is practical thinking, interested primarily in influencing interpersonal situations rather than in just being communicated to others. For this reason, it is often taken for granted instead of being made a subject of serious study. Empathic thinking is unobtrusive and evanescent. If we succeed in understanding another person well enough for our practical purposes, we need not retain in memory how we arrived at our correct conclusions. We seem to have "understood" by a kind of mystical "intuition." Because of this, scientists sometimes dismiss empathic thinking as not being thinking at all.

Yet we should abandon the notion that "intuition" and empathic understanding are something mysterious. On the contrary, psychoanalysis has discovered how a person's conscious fantasies and errors and slips in his thinking or in his overt behavior often give us clues for reconstructing the steps in his empathic thinking. Our art of psychoanalytic interpretation is based on the utilization of such clues.

The art of understanding empathic fantasy and empathic thinking is a very different art from that of understanding words and sentences. In order to understand empathic thinking we must penetrate behind a person's spoken words. We listen to his intonations, watch his gestures, and sense the emotional tone of his words. By these means, we reconstruct in our imagination the emotional implications of what he is thinking. It is as though we were listening to a message in another language that is hidden behind the meaning that is directly described or explained by the syntactical structure of the speaker's sentences. Psychoanalysts often call this other language the language of the unconscious. Freud (1912) explicitly described the process of interpretive understanding as one in which the analyst uses his own unconscious to get into resonance with the patient's unconscious. The patient cannot describe or explain to the analyst what he is unconsciously feeling, but his emotionally colored words, his intonations, and his gestures are able, nevertheless, to evoke in the analyst an empathic understanding of the patient's empathic fantasy and empathic thinking.

The psychoanalyst also aims to do something more. As we have already said, empathic thinking is usually unobtrusive and evanescent. The psychoanalyst, however, tries to fix his attention on the emotional implications of what his patient is feeling and thinking so he can reconstruct in his own imagination the cognitive structure of the patient's empathic fantasy and thinking.

EMPATHIC AND VERBAL THINKING IN THE DREAM WORK

Freud called dreams the "royal road to the Unconscious." We shall now say the same thing in another way. The analysis of dreams is our most precise and comprehensive approach to understanding the cognitive structure of empathic fantasy and empathic thinking.

Every dream has many meanings. This fact can be used to buttress our resistance to checking our interpretations. Even if some of the evidence seems to point in another direction, we can still maintain that we have only found one more of the dream's overdetermined meanings. In opposition to this resistance, our working assumption is that the various meanings of a dream fit together intelligibly. Each dream must also fit intelligibly into the dreamer's real-life situation at the moment of dreaming. These two working hypotheses prevent us from being content with a mere list of possible overdetermined meanings of a dream. They are our most rigorous check—indeed, our only adequate check—on our interpretations. We try to make our standards very strict. When we really succeed in interpreting sensitively and correctly, the parts fit like the most beautifully constructed jigsaw puzzle, and each new bit of evidence makes the fit more perfect.

We use the term "cognitive structure" to designate the way in which the meanings of a dream fit together and the way they fit into the context of the dreamer's situation in real life. We think of the cognitive structure of a dream as a constellation of related problems. In this constellation, there is usually one problem on which deeper problems converge and from which more superficial problems radiate. *This was the dreamer's focal problem* [12] at the moment of dreaming. Every focal conflict is a reaction to some event or emotional situation of the preceding day which served as a "precipitating stimulus." As a check on our whole reconstruction, it is most important to find the dreamer's focal conflict and the precipitating stimulus that activated it.

Our reconstructions of the thought processes of the dreamer differ in one important way from the usual psychoanalytic approach to interpretation. The practical, empathic thinking that underlies dreams becomes much more intelligible when we recognize that the functional units in this living process are problems, not wishes or fantasies. Wishes are the dynamic stimuli that activate problems. Every wish will have consequences if it is fulfilled. A wish and its expected disturbing consequences constitute a problem. The problem is: How can the wish be modified so that it can find fulfillment with a minimum of disturbing consequences? Wish-fulfilling fantasies are attempts, often fleeting attempts, to solve problems. Both wishes and wish-fulfilling fantasies are only parts or phases of a more comprehensive problem-solving effort.

In other words, when we reconstruct the empathic fantasy underlying a dream, we find that every dream is struggling, more or less successfully, to solve a problem. Since this conclusion differs somewhat from Freud's classical formulation of the dream work, we shall next review the evidence on which Freud's formulation (1900) was based.

In his interpretation of dreams, Freud's first and basic discovery was that dreams have a wish-fulfilling function. Then, in order to account for the distortion in dreams, he introduced a distinction between the latent dream thoughts and the manifest dream. The process by which the latent dream thoughts are converted into the manifest dream is the dream work.

The latent dream thoughts, Freud insisted, always make good, logical

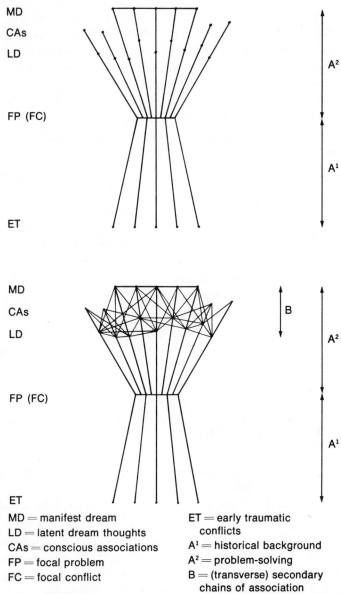

MD = manifest dream
LD = latent dream thoughts
CAs = conscious associations
FP = focal problem
FC = focal conflict

ET = early traumatic conflicts
A¹ = historical background
A² = problem-solving
B = (transverse) secondary chains of association

We conceive of the cognitive structure of a dream as centered about the dreamer's focal conflict (see accompanying diagram). On the one hand, the focal problem itself has arisen by condensation out of a whole constellation of subfocal problems based on the dreamer's past. (In our diagram we have represented this "historical background of the dream" by a number of lines leading upward and converging on the focal conflict.) On the other hand, the focal conflict has given rise, one after another, to a series of attempts to find a solution for this conflict. (This part of the dream work is represented in our diagram by lines leading upward from the focal conflict to various parts of the manifest dream.)

sense. On the other hand, when he reconstructed the chains of association that lead from the latent dream thoughts to the manifest dream,
he found that they do not make sense. Basing his explanation on these
facts, Freud postulated that the dream work involved successively two
kinds of thought processes. The latent dream thoughts, with which the
dream work started, are the products of logical and reality-oriented
thought processes, which Freud called the secondary process. In the next
phase of the dream work, however, these logical and sensible thoughts
had been subjected to another kind of thought process. This was the
primary process, which seemed to involve "free and massive displacement of energy from one psychic element to another, guided only by
the pleasure principle, along any available associative pathway, without
regard for reality or logic." In the course of the dream work, Freud
postulated, the latent dream thoughts, which had at first been elaborated
according to the secondary process, were "drawn down into the Unconscious" and elaborated according to the primary process.

We now have a good opportunity to illustrate our operational approach to interpretation and theory. The facts on which Freud based
his concept of primary and secondary processes are unquestioned. We
are beginning to become aware, however, of new factual relationships
which we have only dimly recognized before. We are learning to distinguish sharply between empathic thinking and verbal thinking and to
recognize that the really significant thinking in the dream work is introspective-empathic fantasy in the process of being transformed into
introspective-empathic thinking. As we have already stated, when we
succeed in reconstructing the empathic fantasy and thinking underlying
a dream, we find that every dream is struggling, more or less successfully, to solve a problem.

Our next task, therefore, is to look back at the facts. Now we shall
try to reformulate Freud's account of the dream work so as to take account of our distinction between empathic thinking and verbal thinking.

In the latent dream thoughts, two kinds of thinking are linked together. These latent thoughts are the product of the dreamer's empathic
fantasy and empathic thinking, concerned with the dreamer's wishes and
emotions. Afterward, this empathic thinking has been translated into
words. In the dream work the resulting verbally expressed thoughts have
undergone disintegration, involving *destruction of their syntactical structure*. The result is what seems to be a free displacement of energy without regard for reality or syntactical logic. On the other hand, the under-

lying empathic fantasy and empathic thinking persist with relatively little modification.

We get confirmation for this way of understanding the dream work by paying close attention to Freud's own approach to the interpretation of dreams. When we carefully study Freud's many samples of dream analysis, we find that he has two ways of listening to the dreamer's free associations. Part of the time, he is listening to catch the meaning that is hidden behind the dreamer's words. At other times, Freud is interested in the words themselves, rather than in their meaning. He is trying to analyze how the dreamer's words and verbally expressed thoughts are linked together. His aim is to trace the chains of associations that lead from the latent dream thoughts to the manifest dream.

What interests us now is that, when he listens for the meaning of the dreamer's words, Freud finds that the dreamer's thoughts make sense. He discovers the latent dream thoughts which make sense, and, underlying these latent dream thoughts, he discovers the wish-fulfilling function of the dream. On the other hand, when he listens primarily to the dreamer's words, he finds that the chains of associations that lead from the latent dream thoughts to the manifest dream do not make sense. This observation confirms the conclusions we have already stated. When the interpreting analyst succeeds in listening empathically, what he hears is the dreamer's empathic fantasy and empathic thinking, which make good sense. On the other hand, when the interpreting analyst concentrates his interest on studying how the dreamer's words are linked together in chains of associations, what he finds is disintegration products of the dreamer's verbal thinking. *The dreamer's chains of associations are not the dreamer's actual thought processes.* They are, rather, disintegration products, which have become a mask behind which the really significant empathic thought processes are hidden.

Thus, we realize more than before that the really significant thought processes in dreams are in terms of empathic thinking. In spite of appearances to the contrary, this empathic thinking always makes good sense. This fact has often been obscured for us in the past by Freud's original description of a seemingly chaotic primary process. When we separate the dreamer's empathic thinking from the disintegration products of his verbal thinking, then it becomes evident that the dream work is struggling with a task of problem-solving, of trying to find a solution for a focal conflict, of trying to reconcile a disturbing motive with the reactive motive to which this disturbing motive has given rise.

NEUROTIC OR PSYCHOTIC BEHAVIOR RESULTING FROM BREAKDOWN OF
THE EMPATHIC PLANNING PROCESS

Study of the way in which a dream struggles with the task of resolving a conflict now gives us a new perspective not only on the dream
work but also on the thought processes that give rise to neurotic or
psychotic behavior. Freud was predominantly interested in tracing back
the genesis of neurotic symptoms to the patient's past. Especially for our
day-to-day guidance in psychoanalytic therapy, however, it is important
also to trace the process in the present by which rational efforts to solve
problems in waking life sometimes lead into the insoluble conflicts that
result in neurotic behavior.

This process that we wish to trace from one moment to the next is
the transition from rational to irrational behavior as a result of the development of excessive conflict. Such excessive conflict interferes with
the orderly progression from empathic fantasy to empathic planning on
which rational behavior depends.

To illustrate such a transition we may cite an incident already reported
in an earlier work (Alexander and French, *et al.,* 1946, p. 76)—the
case of an attractive young woman who spent the greater part of one
analytic interview talking in glowing terms of a minister with whom
she was closely associated in church work. She concluded by remarking
that it sounded as though she were in love with the minister. The therapist quietly agreed that she must indeed be in love with him. Then the
remaining few minutes of the hour were spent in friendly discussion of
the problem created by the fact that the minister was married. Two days
later this patient had a violent temper tantrum; when she was seen by
the analyst (before her anger had subsided), she was quite unaware of
the cause of her outburst.

In order to understand such an incident, we must first take account
of a variable quantitative factor. This factor is the degree of a person's
"involvement in" or "commitment to" his wishes. For example, in the
case of the religious worker just mentioned, the patient had been able
to discuss intelligently her feelings for the minister because she had not
yet fully sensed the conflict into which they must plunge her. She had
thought of her feelings for the minister in terms of her pleasure in
working with him professionally. Even after it occurred to her that she
was talking as if she were in love with him, she did not take the idea
very seriously. She was able to agree with the therapist that she must be
in love with the minister because at the time she had no sense of the

intensity of her feeling for him. In other words, she was not yet very intensely involved in her disturbing wishes. When she awoke in the morning two days later, however, the conflict in which her wishes for the minister involved her must have suddenly been activated in its full intensity. The result was the violent temper tantrum of whose cause she was not aware.

In many cases, careful dream analysis enables us to trace a similar transition in the dream work. At first, the dreamer is playing tentatively with one fantasy after another, trying to find a solution for his focal problem. Such turning from one wish-fulfilling fantasy to another is possible only when the dreamer is not too intensely involved in his successive fantasies. As he becomes more involved, he continues longer with one fantasy before he turns to the next. With more prolonged involvement he must begin to deal more and more seriously with difficulties in the way of wish fulfillment. Finally, he may become involved so intensely that he can no longer turn away to another fantasied solution. Such irreversible involvement we call "commitment." The patient has become committed to this fantasy and to any disturbing consequences that acting upon it would involve.

If the fantasy to which he has been committed now proves to be an adequate solution for a dreamer's focal conflict, then we say that his dream has achieved "resolution" of his conflict. Such a resolution dream is essentially equivalent to the resolution of a conflict in the rational planning underlying purposive behavior in waking life.

On the other hand, in waking life, if the conflict to which a person has committed himself threatens to end in failure or disturbing consequences, or both, then his commitment makes it impossible for him to draw back from his disastrous plan. He is frustrated.[13] His reactions to frustration seriously interfere with the search for a better plan. The result is neurotic or psychotic behavior.

NOTES

1. See L. Kubie (1952, 1953) and the experimental studies of O. Poetzel (1917), C. Fisher (1954, 1956, 1957), C. Fisher and I. H. Paul (1959).
2. See H. Kohut (1959) for an excellent discussion of the limitations of empathy.
3. See Gedo, Sadow, *et al.* (1964).
4. S. Freud (1914), p. 77.
5. This is a rule proposed by P. W. Bridgeman (1927). Bridgeman bases this rule on, and illustrates it by, the reasoning which Albert Einstein used in discussing the

formulation of time relations (at the velocity of light) between events occurring at a distance from each other.

6. Henry A. Murray, *et al.* (1938) have used the word "press" in a sense that has some similarity to our term "need-pressure." Murray's term "press," however, is used in an entirely different context. He speaks of the "press" of a situation rather than of the "pressure" of a need.

7. This hypothesis is in accord with a basic principle of scientific interpretation, with the principle of parsimony (Ockham's razor). According to this principle, we should make only the minimum assumptions that are necessary to account for all the pertinent evidence that is available at the time.

8. This concept is very close to the concept of drive proposed by Lorenz (1957). Lorenz distinguishes between innate instinctive acts and appetitive behavior. Innate instinctive acts are completely stereotyped behavior patterns which do not undergo modification in response to changing environmental conditions. The ethologists maintain that innate instinctive acts cannot be modified by learning. They are activated, in each case, by what the ethologists call an innate releasing mechanism, a very specific set of stimuli to which the organism responds with the characteristic instinctive act.

Wallace Craig (1918) was the first to point out that an animal strives to achieve discharge of its instinctive acts by "appetitive behavior." Appetitive behavior is goal-directed behavior. Ethologists sometimes use the term "drive" to designate such appetitive behavior. The ethological concept of drive is similar to, but more precisely defined than, the drive concept as it is sometimes used by the psychoanalyst. For the ethologist, a drive always has, as its specific goal, achievement of the innate releasing stimulus for a particular instinctive act.

9. E. L. Thorndike's "law of effect," first proposed in 1911, has given rise to very extensive discussion in the psychological literature which has been thoroughly reviewed by L. Postman (1947). For another excellent review see E. R. Hilgard and D. G. Marquis (1940). For reviews of crucial points in this discussion, the reader is referred to C. L. Hull (1932, 1933, 1935), K. W. Spence (1946), H. C. Blodgett (1929), E. C. Tolman (1932, 1933), K. Lewin (1942), R. Leeper (1935). The authors mentioned in this brief note fall into two main groups. Of these two groups, one, including Thorndike, Hull, and Spence, puts chief emphasis on reinforcement by satisfaction; the other group, including Blodgett, Tolman, Lewin, and Leeper, is predominantly interested in cognitive structure. In this paper we are distinguishing the building up of cognitive structures and the mechanism of reinforcement by satisfaction, respectively, as the second and third parts of the drive mechanism.

10. Ernst Kris's concept of "regression in the service of the ego," however, is an exception to this tendency to disparage regression and fantasy.

11. This concept of role structure is one that plays a very important part in sociological and social psychological thinking. In sociological literature, the roles are usually conventional or standardized, corresponding to a community's concept of what should be the role of a father in a family or of the president of a country, for example. Our concept of a psychological role structure is slightly different in that it does not necessarily correspond to the habitually accepted or legally prescribed role structure of an institution. Psychological role structure is much more individual, based on the individual's concept of the meaning of other people's behavior. This individual concept may even be very much distorted as, for example, in the case of a very young child who observes parental intercourse.

12. See T. M. French and E. Fromm (1964).

13. We define frustration as loss of hope of achieving a purpose in which one has become irreversibly involved (committed). See French, 1952, p. 126.

BIBLIOGRAPHY

Alexander, Franz, and French, Thomas M., et al. *Psychoanalytic Therapy.* New York: Ronald Press, 1946.

Blodgett, H. C. "The Effect of the Introduction of Reward upon the Maze Performance of Rats." *Univ. Calif. Publ. Psychol.* 4:113–34, 1929.

Bonime, Walter. *The Clinical Use of Dreams.* New York and London: Basic Books, 1962.

Bridgeman, P. W. *Logic of Modern Physics.* New York: Macmillan, 1927.

Craig, Wallace. "Appetites and Aversions as Constituents of Instincts." *Biol. bull.* 34:91–107, 1918.

Duncker, Karl. "A Qualitative (Experimental and Theoretical) Study of Productive Thinking (Solving of Comprehensible Problems)," *Ped. sem.* 33:642–708, 1926.

———. "On Problem Solving." *Psychol. monogr.* 58, 1945.

Fisher, Charles. "Dreams and Perception; the Role of Preconscious and Primary Modes of Perception in Dream Formation." *J. Am. psychoanal. assn.* 2:389–445, 1954.

———. "Dreams, Images and Perception: A Study of Unconscious Preconscious Relationships." *J. Am. psychonal. assn.* 4:5–48, 1956.

———. "A Study of the Preliminary Stages of the Construction of Dreams and Images." *J. Am. psychonal. assn.* 5:5–60, 1957.

———, and Paul, I. H. "The Effect of Subliminal Visual Stimulation on Images and Dreams: A Validation Study." *J. Am. psychonal. assn.* 7:35–83, 1959.

French, Thomas M. "Clinical Approach to the Dynamics of Behavior." In J. McV. Hunt (ed.), *Personality and the Behavior Disorders.* New York: Ronald Press, 1944.

———. *The Integration of Behavior.* Chicago: University of Chicago Press, 1952, 1954, 1958.

———, and Fromm, Erika. *Dream Interpretation; A New Approach.* New York and London: Basic Books, 1964.

Freud, Sigmund (1900). *The Interpretation of Dreams.* Standard Edition, Vols. 4 and 5; London: Hogarth, 1955.

———. (1912.) "Recommendations to Physicians Practising Psychoanalysis." Standard Edition, Vol. 12; London: Hogarth, 1955. Pp. 109–20.

———. (1914.) *On Narcissism; An Introduction.* Standard Edition, Vol. 14; London: Hogarth, 1955. Pp. 67–104.

Gedo, John E., Sadow, et al. "Studies on Hysteria; A Methodological Evaluation." *J. Am. psychoanal. assn.* 12:735–51, 1964.

Hilgard, E. R., and Marquis, D. C. *Conditioning and Learning.* New York: Appleton-Century, 1940.

Hull, C. L. "The Goal Gradient Hypothesis and Maze Learning." *Psychol. rev.* 39:25–43, 1932.

———. "Differential Habituation to Internal Stimuli in the Albino Rat." *J. comp. psychol.* 16:255–73, 1933.

———. "Special Review of Thorndike: The Fundamentals of Learning." *Psychol. bull.* 32:807–23, 1935.

Koehler, Wolfgang (1931). *The Mentality of Apes.* New York: Harcourt, Brace, 2nd ed., 1931.

Kohut, Heinz. "Introspection, Empathy and Psychoanalysis." *J. Am. psychoanal. assn.* 7: 459–83, 1959.

Kris, Ernst. "Psychology of Caricature." *Int. j. psychoanal.* 17:285–303, 1936.

———. "On Preconscious Mental Processes." *Psychoanal. q.* 19:540–60, 1950.

Kubie, Lawrence S. "Problems and Techniques of Psychoanalytic Validation and Progress." In Eugene Pumpian Mindlin (ed.), *Psychoanalysis as Science.* Stanford, California: Stanford University Press, 1952. Pp. 46–124.

———. "Psychoanalysis as a Basic Science." In Franz Alexander and Helen Ross (eds.), *Twenty Years of Psychoanalysis.* New York: Norton, 1953.

Leeper, R. "The Role of Motivation in Learning: A Study of the Phenomenon of Differential Motivational Control of the Utilization of Habits." *J. genet. psychol.* 46:3–52, 1935.

Lewin, Kurt. *A Dynamic Theory of Personality.* New York and London: McGraw-Hill, 1935.

———. "Field Theory and Learning." In *41st Yearbook, Nat. Soc. Study Educ.* Bloomington: Public School Publishing Co., 1942.

Lorenz, Konrad. *King Solomon's Ring.* New York: Thomas Y. Crowell, 1952.

———. "Comparative Study of Behavior." In C. H. Schiller (ed.), *Instinctive Behavior* (9th ed.). New York: International Universities Press, 1957. Pp. 239–44.

Murray, Henry A. *Explorations in Personality.* New York: Oxford University Press, 1938.

Piaget, Jean (1936). *The Origins of Intelligence in Children.* New York: International Universities Press, 1952.

Poetzel, Otto. "Expermentell erregte Traumbilder in ihren Bezieungen zum indirecten Sehen." *Z. F. neurol. u. psychiat.* 37:278–349, 1917.

Postman, Leo. "The History and Present Status of the Law of Effect." *Psychol. bull.* 44:6, 1947.

Spence, K. W. "Theoretical Interpretations of Learning." In F. A. Moss (ed.), *Comparative Psychology*. New York: Prentice-Hall, 1946.

Sterba, Richard. "The Fate of the Ego in Analytic Therapy." *Int. j. psychoanal.* 15:117–26, 1934.

Thorndike, Edward L. *Animal Intelligence: Experimental Studies*. New York: Macmillan, 1911.

Tolman, E. C. *Purposive Behavior in Animals and Men*. New York: Century, 1932.

———. "Sign-Gestalt or Conditioned Reflex?" *Psychol. rev.* 40:246–55, 1933.

———. "Cognitive Maps in Rats and Men." *Psychol. rev.* 55:189–208, 1948.

———. *Collected Papers in Psychology*. Berkeley and Los Angeles: University of California Press, 1951.

Wertheimer, Max (1945). *Productive Thinking*. Enlarged ed. New York: Harper, 1959.

Chapter Sixteen

COGNITIVE STRUCTURE OF A
CASE OF ULCERATIVE COLITIS

I

This paper is a sequel to the paper, appearing as Chapter 14 in this volume, published by David R. Wheeler and myself, in which we reviewed the course of a psychoanalytic treatment with the purpose of tracing the source of "the therapeutic incentive that makes successful therapy possible." Our patient's therapeutic incentive, we showed, had its basis "in latent and successively emerging hopes," based always in part on the realities of the therapeutic situation, of finding a solution for her conflicts. Such therapeutically significant hopes are rarely if ever conscious. They are preconscious hopes which the patient must struggle energetically to repudiate. In our patient's case, repudiation of her therapeutically significant hopes was her most important resistance.

These hopes are based on present reality. Why then do they have to be repudiated? Because, we found, these present reality-based hopes were too closely associated to other hopes, dating back to the patient's childhood, which had led to disastrous consequences. As a result of this, similar hopes, if reactivated during the therapy, would lead inevitably to mobilization of disturbing emotions arising out of the old traumatic memory. The patient's present hopes in the therapy had to be repudiated in order to prevent such reactivation of the associated traumatic memory.

In therapy, however, the analyst must encourage the patient's reality-based hopes to emerge progressively, as incentive for the therapeutic process. The analyst does this by giving explicit recognition to the present realities toward which the patient's new hope is oriented. The effect of encouraging the patient's new hope, however, will not be immediately beneficial. Instead of helping, reactivation of the new hope leads to more or less reactivation of the associated traumatic memory pattern. When this occurs, the patient may then be preoccupied for weeks or months with disturbances resulting from this reactivation.

The therapist's interpretation is designed not for present but for future effect. Ultimately, he expects, the disturbing affects will be dissipated or discharged. Then hopes similar to those that were repudiated will again begin to emerge. When this occurs, he expects that his earlier interpretations will have had a latent effect. His previous explicit recognition of the patient's new hopes will have increased their integrative capacity, even though they have remained latent. Now these hopes will emerge more boldly and persist longer before they are repudiated. Ultimately, they may become dissociated from the memory of earlier traumatic consequences, so that they can be lived through to fulfillment in the therapeutic situation.

In the earlier paper, we were primarily interested in tracing in detail the influence of the patient's reality-oriented present hopes on the course of the therapeutic process. In this paper, we plan to trace these hopes in the opposite direction, back into the past. Starting with periods of reactivation of traumatic memories, we shall try to carry our analysis back to interpretative reconstruction of the genesis of the patient's neurosis.

Historical reconstruction was always one of Freud's main goals in his development of psychoanalysis. In the early years, most psychoanalysts shared this interest. Later, many psychoanalysts became cautious and skeptical. There were two good reasons for this increased caution. Premature and too exclusive preoccupation with the patient's past tended to distract the analyst from the patient's situation in the immediate present. The other main reason was a tendency for attempts at historical reconstruction to become uncritically speculative.

In my opinion, such repudiation of historical reconstruction has now gone too far. Often exact facts from the patient's past are the only really trustworthy check on interpretations of unusual or puzzling behavior in the present. Instead of searching in the patient's past for the precise source of puzzling details of a patient's behavior, we are now too often content to interpret in terms of vague and stereotyped concepts (like dependence, aggression, oral or anal erotic character traits, etc.) which cannot be adequately checked in any particular case because of their extreme lack of precision. Instead of repudiating reconstructions, we should concentrate our efforts rather on developing systematic methods of checking historical reconstructions.

In our method of historical reconstruction, we follow Freud closely. In the early days of psychoanalysis, Freud's chief check on his reconstructions was to wait for the patient to recover conscious memory of the events that he had reconstructed. Usually, he had to wait a long time. Many times he and other analysts were unsuccessful in getting their patients to bring back their repressed memories to consciousness.

Later (1914), Freud discovered that the patient tends to relive past events that he cannot bring back to consciousness. Such reliving of past events constitutes an elementary kind of remembering. Freud utilized this principle both to reconstruct the patient's past and also to check his reconstructions. The method of reconstruction that we propose in this paper is based on very strict application of this principle (French, 1954). We try first to understand a patient's behavior as a "natural" reaction to his situation in the immediate present. Much of his behavior, however, cannot be accounted for in terms of present reality only. Our interpretive principle is that any feature or detail of the patient's behavior that is not adequately explained as a response to present reality should be traced back to its origin in some situation or event in the past. We also make use of a corollary principle. We do not use the past to explain present events that can already be adequately accounted for as reactions to the present.

In the course of the development of psychoanalysis, Freud's understanding of the emotional factors responsible for a neurosis was, step by step, elaborated further. At first, Freud was predominantly interested in disturbing wishes from the past. Later, he and other analysts began to take more account of guilt, feelings of inferiority, fear of loss of love, and other disturbing consequences of wishes. More recently, we have paid increasing attention to the fact that a wish cannot long be separated in one's mind from anticipation of its disturbing consequences. Together, a wish and its expected consequences give rise to a problem. In order to reconstruct a patient's problem (French, 1958) at a given moment, we must first discover his disturbing motive. Then we compare the patient's manifest behavior with his disturbing motive in order to determine the nature of the consequences he fears. For example, if his disturbing motive is a dependent craving and he reacts with compensatory fantasies of independence and achievement, then we conclude that he is ashamed of his dependent wish. If his disturbing motive is a hostile impulse and his reaction is to inflict injury on himself, then we may conclude that his reactive motive was guilt; in other words, his hostile impulse made him feel guilty. When now we have discovered, first, the patient's disturbing motive, and next, the nature of the consequences he fears, then we can recognize the nature of his problem. His problem is: How can his disturbing wish be modified so that it may find fulfillment with a minimum of disturbing consequences? A further development in our interpretive approach is the one that Wheeler and I elaborated. When once we have recognized the problem with which a patient is preoccupied (at a particular time), then we begin searching for the opportunities in the present and the memories of success in the past about which he has organized his hopes of solution for his focal problem. These are our first steps in reconstructing what we call the "cognitive structure" of a patient's behavior.

The theoretical basis for this newer approach to interpretation can now be formulated in more general terms (French and Fromm, 1964). When we study the practical thinking that guides our behavior, we discover that the functional units in this living process are problems, not wishes or fantasies. Wishes are the dynamic stimuli that activate problems. Wish-fulfilling fantasies are attempts—often fleeting attempts—to solve problems. Both wishes and wish-fulfilling fantasies are only parts or phases of a more comprehensive problem-solving effort. When we inquire further into the practical thinking with which a patient is preoccupied, we soon find ourselves reconstructing not just one problem but a constellation of problems. Such a constellation of intimately interrelated problems is the cognitive structure of the patient's behavior at that particular time. In this cognitive structure we expect to find one problem on which deeper problems converge and from which more superficial problems radiate. This is the patient's focal conflict at that particular time.

This leads to questions about the role of problem-solving in the integration of both rational and irrational behavior. Two basic assumptions are implicit in all attempts to understand behavior empathically. These assumptions are: (1) that behavior is goal-directed, motivated; and (2) that goal-directed efforts, in order to be successful, must be guided by knowledge of how to achieve the goal (French, 1954). Our purpose in this paper, as in a number of earlier papers, is to apply these two working assumptions systematically to the task of improving our art of psychoanalytic interpretation. Our thesis is that psychoanalytic studies of the motivation of behavior need to be rounded out by systematic studies of the "practical understanding" by which all behavior must be guided. In this paper we shall try to apply this principle to the task of interpretively reconstructing the emotional factors responsible for a patient's neurosis.

When now we begin to focus attention on a patient's problems, we also come gradually to another realization. With few, if any, exceptions, the problems that patients take to psychoanalysts are problems of interpersonal adaptation (French and Fromm, 1964). Most exceptions to this statement are only apparent. For example, a patient may be in conflict between a hostile impulse toward a younger brother and guilt. His conflict at this time is an internal one, between his hostile impulse and his conscience. Then we trace back his guilt feelings to their source in the patient's early childhood. We find that his inhibiting motive had originally been not an internal but an external one. His hostility had originally been in conflict with fear of estrangement from his mother. In other words, in early childhood his conflict had been an interpersonal one involving himself, his brother, and his mother. Later, substituting a conscience of his own for his mother, he let his conscience take over the role of being offended by his hostile impulse. He learned to protect himself from the danger of estrangement from his mother by internalizing his conflict, by himself taking over the task of inhibiting his hostile impulse at the behest of his conscience.

A psychoanalyst treats individuals. As an individual therapist, he is interested primarily in the development of one individual and is in danger of losing sight of the fact that the individual's problems cannot be really understood except as an indissoluble part of the problems in mutual adaptation within the family or in some other group to which the patient has belonged.

The personality structure of an individual and the structure of his neurosis are cognitive structures. Both are *precipitates* of his successive *attempts to fit into the groups* to which he has belonged. In general, his personality structure, insofar as it has not been disturbed by neurosis, has been built around the patterns of his successful adaptations to groups. His failures in adaptation to groups constitute the nucleus about which his neuroses have been organized.

The simplest and surest procedure for trying to understand both a patient's neurosis and his personality structure involves two stages. First, we reconstruct, as precisely as possible, the nature of the problem with which he is preoccupied now. Then we trace this problem back, step by step, to the earlier problem of fitting into groups from which his present problem is derived. If our reconstruction of a significant early problem has been correct, then the analysis of later problems that emerge into focus in the course of treatment should lead us back repeatedly to the same earlier problem.

II

To illustrate our approach to reconstruction of a case history, I shall now review the case which David R. Wheeler and I have already reported.

We shall begin with a brief anamnesis:

The patient had come to analysis at the age of twenty-eight, with a diagnosis of ulcerative colitis. She had been accepted as a research patient at the Chicago Institute for Psychoanalysis.

The patient was born in a small town in South Dakota, the third from the youngest in a Roman Catholic family which included nine children. The true father was a rural mail carrier who was in disrepute with the rest of the family because he drank. According to family accounts, the patient was his favorite child. He used to take her with him on his mail delivery rounds.

The mother had died only a day or two after the youngest sibling, a boy, was born. The patient herself was then about four and a half. Thereupon a maternal aunt took the new baby, while the older children continued to live in the home, except for the patient and her next younger brother, Lewis, who were soon afterward taken to Chicago to live with the father's sister and her husband, who became foster-parents. The patient and her brother were never legally adopted because the father would not give his consent. The foster-parents nevertheless changed the children's surname to their own.

The patient could recall nothing of her real mother or of anything antedating the mother's death. She did remember an older sibling's telling her that Lewis and she were lucky, that they were going to be able to go to Chicago to live. The patient was surprised. "My grandmother later said that I was my father's favorite," she recalled, "and she couldn't understand how he ever let me go."

In her foster home the patient became a kind of maid of all work. The foster-mother had not any taste for homemaking and managed to keep busy running the apartment building which the couple owned and in which they lived. As a result, from her early teens on, the cooking, cleaning, and sewing for the most part devolved upon the patient. There was also the invalid grandmother to take care of. The patient had to come home directly from school every day to take care of these duties, and she was not encouraged to participate in activities with other young people or to invite them to her home. In her treatment, the patient returned repeatedly to these complaints about her foster parents.

At the age of eighteen, the patient went on probation as a student nurse in an excellent hospital. In this hospital, she said, for the first time in her life she was really happy. At last she had an opportunity to associate with other girls, and now she was free of the parental domination that had been so intolerable. She wished that training would go on forever. Her father had predicted that she would get sick and break down physically. However, she actually gained weight and felt fine—except for one day, about three months after she started, when she noted that she was extremely weak and exhausted and then observed a considerable quantity of fresh blood in her stool. The next day she was all right again. She made no mention of the incident to anyone.

At the end of six months' training, she started on a month's vacation, which she dreaded. On her way home she noted that she was feeling exceptionally weak and tired. The next day she felt even more exhausted and miserable, and early the following morning she woke up with a fever of 104 degrees, followed by diarrhea and severe back pain. When blood appeared in her stool a few days later, she returned to the hospital, but this time as a patient. Because of the high nocturnal temperatures and marked prostration, typhoid was first suspected, but this and also amoebic dysentery were ruled out by stool examinations and bacteriologic tests. The diagnosis of nonspecific ulcerative colitis was made after proctoscopy. After a month in the hospital she went on outpatient treatment, but after one or two years she was told definitely that she could not resume nurse's training. She was completely desolated by this rejection, and for one of the very few times in her life she wept. Soon afterward she obtained employment in a clerical position.

Ten years later, at the time that she was accepted for psychoanalytic treatment, she had been married four years. She had continued to work full time at her job, however, as well as working hard taking care of her own home. She and her husband were living in her (foster-) mother's apartment house, in the apartment just above her mother's.

Except for one brief period of hospitalization, one year after her marriage, she had lost no time from her work. However, at times of emotional upset, she had continued to have brief exacerbations with abdominal pain, followed by variable amounts of bleeding and, sometimes but not always, by an increase in the number of stools, up to six or seven movements of formed stool a day. These flare-ups occasionally lasted the greater part of a week, but typically the duration was less than a day, usually beginning in the evening before bedtime.

In our earlier paper, Wheeler and I tried to elucidate the therapeutic process in the whole course of this patient's treatment. Our thesis was that the therapeutic incentive that makes successful therapy possible must have its basis in the patient's latent and successively emerging hopes of finding a solution for her conflict. Reviewing briefly the first part of our earlier paper, I shall now report the initial hopes with which her treatment started and then try to reconstruct the cognitive structure of this patient's neurosis, as revealed by the first twenty hours of her treatment.

The patient's initial response to her treatment by a male analyst could be inferred from two dreams, discussed in her fifth and sixth hours, and in her tenth hour, respectively. In her fifth hour, the patient reported a dream of a sink overflowing and then in her sixth hour admitted, with much squirming, embarrassment, and emotional distress, that it had been a toilet that was overflowing, and that she had never been able to talk to anyone about sex. She added that she would never have married if she had known what the priest was going to tell her just beforehand—that sex was not a sin after marriage, that her duty as a Catholic wife was to have intercourse as often as her husband wanted it.

Her next dream, reported in her tenth hour, revealed how the patient hoped that her analyst would deal with this sexual conflict.

> *Dream:* I was at work. Mr. B, the assistant boss, came out of his office—he was rather indifferent and cold—and stood in front of my desk and said matter-of-factly that he thought that I should go out and have a sandwich. Much later I was with a group from the office having dinner, and hoped that he didn't think that I was eating because he told me I should.

In association, she added that Mr. B had recently been calling another girl in the office to ask about mistakes the patient had made. She protested to the analyst that she did not want any special consideration because she was ill. The analyst, taking the dream as a reference to himself, suggested that she felt that he, too, was telling her she could have something for herself. To this permissive remark she immediately gave a sexual meaning: "A speaker at a parent-teachers meeting [she was attending a parent-teachers meeting at her step-brother Bobby's school] the other

night said that it was up to the parents to teach their children that sex is
a beautiful thing, and that they should warn them against making fools
of themselves."

When we are trying to reconstruct the cognitive structure of a dream,
it is usually best to try first to understand the dream as a response to
the dreamer's emotional situation at the moment of dreaming. With this
purpose in view, we depart somewhat from an approach that has become
habitual with many analysts. We postpone until later an attempt to
understand the dream as fulfillment of an infantile wish. In the case of
this dream, for example, we are just now not primarily interested in
finding evidence of this patient's sexual transference wishes toward the
analyst. Instead, we pay attention first to the patient's immediate situation in the therapy. Our method is to try to account in detail for the
exact form of the manifest dream content.

With this hint we can recognize that this dream was giving expression
to a hope that the analyst would play a role similar to that of the priest
who spoke to her just before her marriage. She was hoping that the
analyst would now tell her that she should enjoy sex in her marriage.
She was reacting to this hope with great embarrassment. She repudiated
it most energetically. She was shocked at the idea that the analyst might
think she would be receptive to such a suggestion. Actually, at this time,
she was sexually frigid and claimed that she submitted to her husband's
very frequent demands for intercourse only because the priest had told
her it was her duty.

Pursuing our purpose of understanding cognitive structure, we ask
next why this patient had to repudiate so energetically her hopes of
enjoying sex. We shall keep this question in mind as we review her
next few hours. A few hours later in her treatment, she was able to tell,
with agonized affect, an incident that she could never confess even to the
priest—how, when she was twelve or thirteen, her father, when drunk,
had once made sexual overtures to her. In the next hour she continued
with a confession of sexual activities with her older (by two years)
brother, Harold, during several subsequent summers in South Dakota.
On one occasion, she thought she had had intercourse with her brother
but, after confessing to the priest, she realized that it had not been intercourse, though, of course, it was still a sin.

Continuing her account in her fifteenth hour, the patient recalled that
this brother had visited her while she was in nurse's training in the hospital. Although the patient herself did not bring the two events into

associative connection, her isolated attack of rectal bleeding (already mentioned) seemed to have occurred about the time of this visit. At the time of his visit, she had been planning to go three months later to South Dakota for her vacation (where she would probably have seen her brother again). As we have already mentioned, the acute onset of the patient's ulcerative colitis occurred while she was returning home before she was to go on this vacation. Instead of going to South Dakota, however, she returned to the hospital as a patient. While the patient was sick in the hospital, her brother visited her, together with a sister, but she was too sick to care, she said.

Her preoccupation with memories of the onset of her colitis continued in her next two hours. She told of talking to her roommate and lingering on in the hospital on the night of her departure. On her return home, she was irritated when her foster-mother asked if she were sick, because she did not want to lose the sense of release from dependence on her family that she had had while in the hospital. She also recalled that in her delirium at home (before she returned to the hospital), she had been afraid that she would tell her foster-mother about her brother. A similar fear also emerged at this point in her treatment. She feared that her dentist, the one person aside from her husband whom she had told about her analysis, would tell her family of it.

In her next few hours, as reported in our earlier paper, the patient's associations seemed to be leading back to a traumatic memory. Our reconstruction of this traumatic memory was based on a conscious memory reported in the patient's eighteenth hour and on a dream discussed in her nineteenth and twentieth hours.

She opened her eighteenth hour with silence, which was followed by an abrupt question: "Do I have to hate my parents?" She explained that Dr. E (her psychotherapist at the university hospital) had told her that she would have to learn to hate them, that she had every reason to hate them. In further explanation, she then told of her (foster-) mother's having once given away a doll that the patient liked, without even telling the patient that she had done so. The patient had decided to punish her mother by never playing with another doll. She would not tell her mother why she would not play with dolls, but took spiteful satisfaction from knowing that this bothered her mother.

In our earlier discussion, we were impressed by the patient's intense reaction to the loss of this doll. We concluded that her love of the doll had served as a consolation for loss of her true mother at the age of four and a half. In her (preconscious) fantasy, she had probably given to the doll the mother whom she herself had lost. When her foster-mother had given away the doll, it was as though she had again lost her mother. Spite toward her foster-mother was probably only an aggressive rationalization, hiding the real reason for her determination never to play with dolls again. Her real motive had been to protect herself from any possible repetition of her loss by never letting herself become so attached to a doll again.

This reconstruction of the impact on this patient of her mother's death could be confirmed and expanded by analysis of a dream reported in her nineteenth hour:

> *Dream:* A girl at the office was showing me some jewelry in a box. She said it was jeweled initials for a purse. They were *my* initials.

Our first key for interpreting this dream was the associations, twice repeated, commenting on the good relations between the girl in the dream and the girl's mother. These associations suggested that the patient herself was longing for a good mother-daughter relationship. The initials in the purse in the dream led to associations about the patient's resentment and embarrassment about having her name changed when she was first sent to her foster-parents. She told how her younger brother, Lewis, who was sent with her, was frightened at going into a house full of strangers. She added a moment later that changing her name had made her feel as though she were giving up her identity. From these associations we sensed how first losing her mother and then being sent away to strangers by her father must have left this little girl with a feeling of being utterly uprooted.

We were impressed by the intensity with which the patient had reacted to the loss of her doll. Now we can realize why her longing for a mother had been so intense. The trauma of being uprooted must not happen again! At all costs, she must see to it that her hostility would not cause her to lose her foster-mother, too. Hence her resigned, submissive attitude to her foster-mother and her compliant acceptance of the role of maid of all work.

Now we must ask: Why did this memory begin to be reactivated just at this time in her treatment? This patient's question about hostility toward her foster-parents had emerged suddenly not long after her confessions about her sexual play with her brother. To account for this, we recall that her mother's death occurred when she was a little over four years of age, when she must have been at the height of her Oedipus complex. We also know that she was recognized as the father's favorite before she came to Chicago, that he liked to take her with him on his rural mail delivery rounds. Putting this together with her later account of his sexual advance, we may surmise that his relationship to her, even before the mother's death, had been a seductive one.

Now, in her treatment, the reawakened memories of the father's sexual suggestion and of her incestuous play with her brother had begun to make her aware of where her hopes of sexual release (as a result of the analysis) were leading her. In order to be released from her sexual inhibition, she would have to break away from her desperately submissive tie to her foster-mother. Dr. E had actually advised her to leave home. She had assured the patient that she had every reason to hate her parents; but the possibility of hating her foster-parents and leaving them only reactivated the memory of how completely uprooted she had felt when she really had had to leave home to go to live with strangers.

We can summarize the most important features of the cognitive structure of this patient's neurosis, insofar as we have been able to reconstruct them from the first twenty hours of her treatment, as follows.

Her sexual neurosis, we believe, had its roots in a traumatic series of events dating back to her fourth year. This traumatic chain of events, we suspect, started with sexual wishes arising out of a seductive relationship (details not yet known) to her father. Then there occurred two events which she must have felt to be consequences of her guilty wishes. First, she lost her mother (a few days after the birth of a child). Then, less than a year later, her father, whose favorite child she had been, sent her hundreds of miles away to foster-parents who were strangers to her. Thus, her sexual wishes toward her father seemed to have had as consequences the loss of her mother, then of her father and her home.

The neurotic pattern that developed later can be readily understood as a reaction to intense fears that consequences like these traumatic ones might occur again. First, she developed an intensely compliant reaction to her foster-mother, out of fear of losing her foster-mother as she had lost her own mother. Her sexual inhibitions developed only later— after she had submitted, over a series of summers, to sexual seduction from an older brother. We still do not know why her sexual inhibitions did not develop in time to prevent her from yielding to her brother's seduction. Evidence to answer this question emerged only later. The patient unconsciously responded to this brother, who was older, as a parental figure, replacing her foster-mother, who was in Chicago. For this reason, the brunt of the responsibility for their sexual play could be borne by the brother and, as long as they were together, his love could serve as a substitute for the mother's love. (Such an incestuous relationship to a parental figure is often encountered in the histories of catatonic patients and usually ends, in such cases, with onset of a cata-tonic psychosis when the moral support of the parental figure is with-drawn—by death, separation, etc.)

The immediate effect of the therapy upon this neurotic pattern was to arouse (preconscious) hopes of release from her sexual inhibitions. The immediate effect of these hopes was paradoxical. Instead of dimin-ishing, their effect was to reactivate her conflict. As her sexual wishes began to be released, they began to reawaken her fear of (again) losing her mother.

We shall discuss in a moment how in her treatment the patient re-sponded to this fear. When we do, it will also be necessary to consider whether reactivation of this traumatic conflict had anything to do with the onset and exacerbation of her somatic disease.

III

Ever since Freud discovered that hysterical symptoms have meaning, psychoanalysts and many others have been puzzling about a "mysterious leap" from mind to body. This is an old philosophical problem, but there is really no good reason why psychoanalysts need to get involved with this riddle in its philosophical form. The psychoanalyst can best understand somatic symptoms in the same way that he does any other symptom. He must try to understand psychosomatic disorders and symp-toms by asking how they fit into the context of the emotional problems which the patient is struggling to solve. In other words, his task is to try to understand how physiological disturbances fit into the cognitive structure of the problems with which the patient's mind is preoccupied.

We make too much of a mystery of the psychogenesis of somatic symptoms. Let us suppose, for example, that a man, feeling estranged from his mother on account of something he has done or may wish to do, seeks reconciliation with her by making a confession. In this case, the motivation and content of his confession are psychological. The act of confession requires innervation of the physiological mechanisms in-volved in speech, including some modifications of respiration. Let us now suppose that this man is so afraid of offending his mother that he inhibits and represses his urge to confess and develops an attack of bronchial asthma instead. In this case, the relation between mind and body is not much different than it was in the first case. The essential difference is in the intensity of the patient's conflicting motivations. In the second case the intensity of his conflict is so much greater that it has overwhelmed the integrative mechanism. Excessive intensity of the conflict has made it impossible for the integrative mechanism to subordinate the activated physiological mechanisms to the purpose of making a confession.

Our confusion about psychosomatic relationships springs from two causes—first, that we usually start our thinking by trying to understand *pathological* psychosomatic relationships, and second, that we start our thinking with *psychology,* rather than with physiological function.

A prerequisite for understanding psychosomatic pathology is understanding the physiology of normal behavior. For example, we know that in bronchial asthma there are vagal innervations of the bronchial musculature, and that epinephrine or sympathetic innervations relieve bronchial spasm. Next, we should like to know whether vagal or sympathetic innervations play similar roles in normal speech or in crying. Our best working hypothesis is that we ought to be able to understand psychosomatic disease processes either as pathological *exaggerations* of normal physiological responses or as *disintegration products* from more complexly organized physiological patterns.

According to this working hypothesis, our best point for understanding psychosomatic relationships is not psychoanalytic psychology but the kind of thinking about physiological function that is exemplified by Walter Cannon's *The Wisdom of the Body.* As the designers of computers are now teaching us, the mind itself should be regarded as a very highly specialized physiological organ whose function is problem-solving. In the course of evolution the body has learned to solve many very complex problems automatically. The mechanisms that Cannon investigated most thoroughly were of this kind. Other problems the body is not able to solve automatically. The mind is an organ whose function is to solve *new* problems, problems that the body has never solved before.

After careful experimentation to work out the details of physiological reactions, Cannon turned philosopher. He tried to divine the functional purpose served first by each detailed response and then by the system as a whole. The designers of computers do something similar, though in reverse order. They start with a problem to be solved and then work out the detailed mechanisms that are necessary in order that a machine may solve it. If we are to understand psychosomatic relations we must emulate both Cannon, the philosopher, and the designers of computers. We must try to discover the problem with which both the patient's mind and his body are struggling.

We should be challenged by the fact that our task is more difficult than either Cannon's or that of the machine designer. Cannon had already worked out the detailed physiological reactions. The computer designer starts with knowledge of the problem to be solved. In our attempts to understand a psychosomatic illness, neither we nor the patient know at first either what the problem is or the detailed mechanisms that the patient is using in his unsuccessful attempts to solve it. All this we must learn by appropriate modification of our art of psychoanalytic interpretation.

IV

To illustrate this kind of approach to the study of a psychosomatic symptom, we shall now continue our account of Dr. Wheeler's case. But first, we must mention a fact that we learned only much later in this patient's treatment. The patient had originally been accepted for analysis as part of a research project for the study of emotional factors in ulcerative colitis. This diagnosis had been made twice, each time after a thorough medical survey in a hospital of excellent reputation. The first medical investigation and diagnosis had been made shortly after the acute onset of the patient's symptoms. The diagnosis was confirmed ten years later in a university clinic. Later, during the first twenty-one months of her psychoanalytic treatment, she refused stubbornly to submit to any physical examination. Although she never said so explicitly, her chief resistance was probably against being examined by a male physician. Finally, she agreed with great relief to accept referral to a private woman physician. At this time amoebae were found in her stools. Of course, this finding introduced an element of uncertainty even as to the nature of the patient's physical disease. Still, it does not seem probable that two thorough medical surveys, ten years apart, should both have missed her amoebic infestation. Obviously, we do not know just when she acquired it.

On account of this uncertainty, we were for a long time reluctant to publish the results of our studies. During the period of her analysis, this patient's most frequently reported physical symptom was rectal bleeding, in most cases not accompanied or followed by diarrhea but usually preceded by abdominal pain. For this symptom the amoebae in her intestinal tract furnished an adequate physical cause. How then could we be sure whether emotional causes played any part in precipitating these hemorrhages?

Finally it occurred to us that there was other evidence that should be taken into account. In this particular case, the symptoms in which we were interested occurred during brief episodes at intervals that were sometimes long, sometimes short. This suggested a question: Did this patient's brief episodes of abdominal pains and rectal bleeding fit, in any consistent and convincing way, into the cognitive structure of her ongoing emotional problems as revealed by her free associations, dreams, and behavior?

With this question in mind, we shall return now to our review of Wheeler's case.

In our earlier paper we did not mention the fact that, at the beginning of her twenty-second hour, the patient, for the first time since the beginning of her treatment, reported symptoms of her ulcerative colitis. Abdominal pains which could not be suppressed by phenobarbital and belladonna began on a Monday, two days after she reported dream 19, and lasted a week, culminating in a small amount of rectal bleeding the night before her twenty-second hour on Saturday. During this whole week she had felt extremely tired in spite of getting her usual amount of sleep.

We now ask: Do these symptoms make any sense in the context of the patient's dream and of our interpretation of it?

During the three hours (eighteen, nineteen, twenty) that we have already studied, the patient gave us a glimpse of a traumatic memory of great intensity. What is important for our present purpose is how intensely this memory was *reactivated* at the time of her symptoms and in the days just preceding. We shall start with hour nineteen. In dream 19, there was as yet little evidence that this disturbing memory was intensely reactivated. In her manifest dream, there was no evidence of the reliving of intense affect. The shock of her having "lost her identity" when she was sent away from home was mentioned only in her twentieth hour. In her dream (19), the patient's initials in a box had been only an allusion to this shock. The focal conflict in this dream was centered rather on a present hope—that the analyst (represented in the dream by the girl) would restore to her memory (show her) the close relationship she had once had with her mother. In the dream, she had had to avoid even looking to see whether the initials in the box were really hers. This suggests that the memory of losing her mother and of the events that followed had been so traumatic that she had to shrink back from even looking at it. In other words, the evidence suggests that this was an instance of anxiety which, though only slightly activated at this time, had nevertheless served as a "warning signal" (see Freud, 1926) to forestall further reactivation of her traumatic memory.

In the days immediately following, however, the disturbing memory does seem to have begun to reemerge. In her twentieth hour, her memory of being sent away from home was reported much more vividly; and real emotion related to the present began to emerge in her twenty-first hour. She opened this hour with silence, then suddenly asked, "Why do I want to live without emotions? I can't remember ever having been hurt *that* much. I just want everyone to leave me alone. I'm not even friendly." She continued with feelings of guilt toward her husband. "I feel that Joe was terribly gypped when he got me for a wife. He deserves something better." "His relatives are so interested in us, but I don't ever want to be bothered with them or to have to talk to them on the phone. Yet I like them, too. . . ." Bringing this outburst into relation with her repressed memory of losing her mother and her home, we can now sense that her love for her mother had ended so tragically that she could not tolerate ever becoming warmly attached to anyone again.

These two hours corresponded to the time when the patient was suffering from abdominal pains and just preceded the twenty-second hour, when she reported her rectal bleeding. In view of this, it is attractive to hypothesize that the patient's abdominal cramps were another manifestation of the emotions arising from her traumatic memory. They were probably an attempt to bind the reactivated disturbing emotions. Her rectal bleeding occurred when this attempt failed.

Further analysis of the cognitive structure of dream 19 can now help in our reconstruction of the relation between the patient's colitic symptoms and her traumatic memory.

We have not yet accounted for one important detail of the symbolism of this dream. Why should she have dreamed that her initials were jeweled and in a box? We get a key to the meaning of this symbolism when we bring it into relation with the patient's desperate need to protect herself from becoming warmly attached to anyone. The symbol of the jeweled initials in a box has two meanings, one warm and highly personal, the other impersonal. The warm, personal meaning corresponds to the focal meaning of the dream, her desire to have her mother restored to her. In accordance with this longing, the dreamer's initials in a box symbolize a fantasy of her being inside the mother's body, the most intimate fantasy possible of union with her mother. (Such a fantasy would almost certainly have been suggested by seeing another child inside her mother just before her mother's death.) On the other hand, jewelry in a box is an impersonal symbol with a still more impersonal meaning. Jewels and money are symbols of a stool to which she clings (Freud, 1915).

In the reconstruction of cognitive structure, it is an important principle of interpretation that, if a symbol has two different meanings, both meanings are intimately related parts of a single creative imaginative train of thought. Our hypothesis in this case is that in the course of the dream work these two fantasies were activated successively, the second fantasy replacing the first. Such a substitution, we postulate, is always meaningfully motivated. In this case, we postulate, the dream started with the intimately personal fantasy of being inside the mother's body. Then, to protect her from reactivating the excessively painful memory of losing her mother, the dream work had substituted the impersonal symbol of jeweled initials in a box.

As a check on this reconstruction we ask: Do we have any other evidence for the motive that we have postulated for this substitution? Actually, the motive that we are looking for soon comes to conscious expression. We have already quoted her distressed question in her twenty-first hour, "Why do I want to live without emotions?" This question dramatized the reason why in her dream she had needed to substitute an impersonal fantasy for her intimate personal one. She needed desperately to avoid activating her memory of how she had loved her mother. Only in this way could she protect herself from reliving the pain of losing her.

In analogy with this dream substitution, we can also guess how this patient's abdominal cramps fitted into the cognitive structure of her traumatic memory. Instead of reliving her intense frustrated longing for her mother, she was substituting the impersonal mechanical act of clinging to her bowel content.

We have already suggested that the meanings of psychosomatic symptoms are closely related to the functional significance of physiological mechanisms. Physiologically, we do not know how our patient's abdominal cramps were produced, but we do know that the lower bowel's function is not only to excrete but also to delay excretion until absorption of nutrient materials and water from the bowel can be completed. The bowel differs from other excretory organs in that regulation of the speed and timing of the eliminatory process is of central importance. The function of the lower bowel may be described as one of coordinating eliminatory and retentive reactions. When this coordination fails, we may expect the mutually antagonistic functions to be activated at the same time and thus to come into conflict with each other. In our patient's case, for example, we suspect that her abdominal cramps are evidence of such a conflict between the two mutually antagonistic functions of excretion and retention.

In the dream that we have just analyzed, we find that this conflict between elimination and retention occurred in relation to the wider context of the patient's childhood memory of her mother's death. In the underlying thoughts, the act of defecation has been converted into a symbol of reliving the loss of her mother, and the cramplike clinging to her intestinal contents has become a symbol of desperate clinging to prevent reliving of her traumatic memory of being abandoned by her mother.

At one time, symbolic interpretations of this kind were very popular. More recently, analysts have become skeptical of such interpretations, especially when applied to psychosomatic symptoms. This skepticism was at first justified because symbolic interpretations were often made very loosely and without adequate checking. Now, I believe, our skepticism has gone too far, because it is possible often really to check our interpretation of symbols against other evidence. The check that we have just employed in this case is one of the most convincing—we found that the motive that we had to postulate to account for a symbolic substitution actually appeared in consciousness soon afterward.

In this case, the patient's desperate clinging did not long succeed in binding her intensely frustrated longing for her mother. The result seems to have been an intensification of the destructive processes in the mucosa of her colon that culminated in her bleeding from the anus.

In summary, we reconstruct somewhat as follows the chain of events in this patient's treatment that culminated in the activation of her somatic symptoms. In the early hours of her treatment, our patient's dawning hopes of release from sexual inhibition had begun to awaken a traumatic memory. Early in her childhood, she had entertained tender and sexual wishes toward her father and fantasies of having a child by him. Then her mother died and she lost both her father and her home. When she was sent away to strangers, she was left with a sense of having been completely uprooted—abandoned. Now, in her treatment, the memories of her father's sexual overtures and of her sexual play with her brother have reminded her that release from her sexual inhibitions would bring her into disturbing conflict with her foster-mother. In her eighteenth hour she warned herself about how her foster-mother had once taken from her the doll to which she had clung as a compensation for the loss of her mother. In her eighteenth hour, however, this incident was only remembered, not intensely reactivated in her feelings. In the dream thoughts underlying dream 19, her traumatic memory was again only slightly activated. It served rather as a "warning signal" (Freud, 1926) stimulating her to protect herself from reliving her past by turning instead to present hopes that her analyst would restore her mother to her. In the next few days her abdominal cramps were a sign that her attempts to ward off the painful pressure of her frustrated longings for her mother were beginning to fail. In her twentieth hour, her associations came closer to betraying her feelings of having been completely uprooted when she was sent away to her foster-parents. In her twenty-first hour, she blurted out that she had to fight off all warm, personal feelings. Her abdominal cramps were an attempt to bind her emerging longing for her mother. Her rectal bleeding occurred several nights later, just before her twenty-second hour, discharging the excitation that her cramps had failed to bind.

We now note that the patient's account suggests that the original acute onset of her ulcerative colitis had also occurred as a reaction, much delayed, to fear of estrangement from her foster-mother as a result of her sexual play with her brother. In her treatment hours, the patient's confession of the sexual episodes with her father and brother was followed immediately by her detailed reminiscences about the onset of her colitis, which occurred just as she was leaving the hospital, where she was in nurse's training, to take a vacation at her childhood home in South Dakota. In South Dakota she would have been exposed again to temptation from her brother. An isolated episode of severe rectal bleeding three months before the recognized onset of her colitis seems also to have corresponded roughly in time with a visit from this brother. During his visit (as she reported later in the treatment), she had told her brother that she did not want to see him again. On the other hand, she was late in returning to the hospital, which suggested that the old attraction had been revived. We also have another bit of evidence that her colitis was associated in her mind with her earlier sexual play with her brother. We have already mentioned that, at the time of onset, she feared that in her delirium she would tell her foster-mother about her brother.

On the other hand, there remains one question to be answered if this explanation of the onset of her colitis is correct. Her sexual play with her brother had continued for several summers and had then been discontinued when she stopped going to South Dakota for her summer vacations. Why, then, had she not developed her ulcerative colitis several years sooner?

We have already suggested a probable answer to this question. The patient's submissive attitude to her foster-mother, and her compliant acceptance of the role of maid of all work, had served to protect her from the danger of again losing her mother and her home. However, when she started training as a student nurse she was very happy in the feeling that she was at last free from her mother's domination. Unfortunately, this freedom made her vulnerable again. When she was again exposed to temptation from her brother, she no longer had any adequate defense to protect her from the danger of once more being uprooted.

V

As a further check on the hypothesis outlined in the preceding pages, we shall next review a number of other emotional situations, in the course of this patient's treatment, which were associated with abdominal cramps, or rectal bleeding, or both.

In the patient's thirty-fourth hour (on a Saturday), she was very tense and talked unusually volubly. "My true father came in from South Dakota Thursday night," she said. "Joe [her husband] can't understand why I am upset when he comes, or that he puts me in a heck of a spot. *My ulcers were bleeding yesterday.*" (This was the first time since her twenty-second hour.)

"We had to go down [to her foster-parents' apartment] that evening and also last night. My father was telling me what the rest of the family were doing and I just wasn't interested. Joe thinks my father is a nice guy. That burns me up. He always arrives without warning like this. I wish he would stay in South Dakota." "Once he bought a rifle for Lewis [the patient's younger brother] and a bicycle for me, but I left it there. I didn't want anything from him."

"Thursday night I was getting dinner. Joe was not home yet and the doorbell rang. I feared it was Dad. I didn't answer and finally Joe let himself in and asked what was the matter."

The analyst suggested at this point that perhaps she was afraid to be alone with her father. "Maybe that is it," she admitted, becoming extremely tense. "He is not drinking now.—It happened once but probably never would again.—I don't see why I can't forget about that thing. It bothers me to have to act as though everything were all right.— Couldn't it be that I feel the way I do because he didn't want me as a kid?—I suppose I was hurt, so I want to hurt him now. If you love a child, you don't part with it."

In her next (thirty-fifth) hour, the patient seemed depressed. "Joe asked my father," she said, "what my mother looked like. He got the usual answer, that I was just like her." "Joe said later that he thought my father was lonesome, that he felt sorry for him, and that I hurt his feelings. I replied that I didn't care, I'd have more sympathy for a total stranger.—I wish he'd go home! Last night I thought I heard a doorbell ringing. I guess I was dreading that he might come up if possibly he was going back today, and I didn't want him to come. I absolutely dread having him kiss me, and I can't avoid it when he comes and when he leaves.—I've always tried to be out of the house when old friends or relatives were leaving, so that I wouldn't have to let them kiss me."

In answer to the analyst's question about her (true) father's attitude toward her, she continued, "He seems to be so anxious to be friendly. He included me among his daughters in a remark to Joe. I resented it, for I don't think he has any right to claim me as one of his daughters." After a silence, the analyst asked why. "You can't give something away and then claim it back again," she replied. "He has twenty-two grandchildren. I'm the only daughter by whom he doesn't have any.—Dad said the other night that it would be nice to have a baby in the family again. He said something about my perhaps wanting to take time out for a family some day. I didn't want to talk about it and I didn't see any reason why I should. I'm not interested in him, and I wish he wasn't so interested in everything that I do."

In the first part of her thirty-sixth hour, the patient spoke relatively fluently about feelings of aversion toward her husband which she thought were becoming increasingly manifest. She thought that he was noticing a change in her in this direction. For example, he was increasingly protesting that she wanted to shut him out of her life com-

pletely. Whatever she does for him is strictly out of a sense of obligation and duty, she said. He came home from work sick the other day
and she could muster up no feelings of interest or concern about it
such as he always exhibits toward her. Then, without pause, she mentioned that her father was supposed to return to South Dakota that
morning.

After a silence, the analyst commented that perhaps she wanted to
shut her husband out of her life just the way she would like to shut
out her father. "But that's not the same," the patient protested. "But
I don't think I am capable of loving anyone.—I think Joe probably
knows I'm not." After a silence, the analyst repeated and expanded his
interpretation, ending with the statement that the patient probably had
more positive feelings than she cared to admit. To this, the patient responded, with some surprise, "You are assuming I have natural, warm
impulses?"

A dream reported in her thirty-seventh hour was probably a reaction
to this twice-repeated comment of the analyst's. It was a dream of the
night before:

Dream 37: We were back in school days; Joe and I were in Lincoln Park;
it was awfully crowded. A guy was giving away money—you just walked
across the bridge and he gave you some money. Then Joe said he knew a
shortcut to go back by, it seemed that he was to rent a boat, but that
wouldn't get you back . . . but I thought that was what he meant. It
seemed as though the man gave you money *before* you crossed the bridge.
I could not remember the man or receiving the money. I did not even
wonder why it was being given away.

In her associations the patient said that her jaw had recently started
to swell. She feared that her dentist might make something serious of it.
"So I supposed the guy giving me money was my dentist telling me there
was nothing wrong." The analyst replied that perhaps she felt that *he*
was giving her something, as, for example, in his remark at the end of
the last hour. The patient rejected this interpretation, then said that her
father had left for South Dakota that morning, but she had already left
for work and so was spared having to bid him goodby. Then she added,
"My ulcers were bleeding this morning."

In her next hour (thirty-eight) she referred back to dream 37 as the
dream "where you are always giving me something."—"I feel guilty
about not paying the full price for this treatment," she added. "I feel

I'm taking advantage of something I've no right to, like the people who can afford to pay but go to County Hospital as charity cases."

Commenting on these five hours, we note that the patient's two episodes of rectal bleeding occurred one at the beginning and one at the end of a visit from her true father. In each case, the bleeding was associated by the patient with her intense reluctance to relate herself to him warmly. On the first day of his visit, she was frightened at the prospect of his visiting her when she was home alone. At the end of his visit, she mentioned her bleeding ulcers just after expressing her relief that she did not have to kiss him goodby. In her associations she insisted at first that she was just not interested in him. Later, she expressed bitter resentment because he had sent her away when she was a child. Underneath both of these reactions was not only resentment but also fear of having warm, affectionate feelings toward him (both dependent and sexual) reawakened, and of being abandoned as a consequence, as had occurred after her mother's death.

In dream 37, however, this conflict had been transferred into the therapeutic situation. The analyst's twice-repeated assurances that she was capable of "warm, natural love" must have pleased her, in spite of her inability to admit it to herself, but they also threatened to activate affectionate feelings toward the analyst himself. Her defense, as in dream 19, was to substitute money for love. She pictured the analyst as offering her money for nothing. In the background again was the fear of losing home and mother. The water in the dream, to be crossed by bridge or boat, was the water in Lincoln Park that she would have to cross to get back home to her foster-mother.

VI

The patient's next episode of rectal bleeding occurred over a weekend (Saturday and Sunday) and was reported Tuesday, in hour forty-four. The apparent precipitant was the news that Lewis had come to Chicago to visit their foster-parents. (Lewis was the younger brother who had been sent to the foster-parents at the same time as the patient, when she was four and a half. The patient had always been fond of this brother but also envious of him, because he had been able to get his own way with the foster-parents much more than she.) In her forty-fourth hour the patient said that she wished that he and his wife Helen would stay away. "I was nothing but trouble for her," she said, because she had to act as buffer or conciliator between them and her foster-mother; and she herself did not care much for Helen.

Then she reported a dream which, she said, "made no sense."

Dream 44: I was back in the St. Vincent grade school taking a test or something; I was writing. A nun was there and you were there. That is all I can remember.

Associations: It was the second-grade room. Four months ago, she had to revisit it to see the nun about Bobby's erratic schoolwork, since her mother would not go. The nun in the dream was Bobby's present teacher.

The patient had started school in the second grade and had never seen nuns before. "I think I was afraid of the nuns, I could never talk to them or tell them of my family, of my brothers and sisters, like the other kids could. I would never think of talking to any of them. I suppose they thought I was a well-adjusted little girl because I did such good work and was no bother."

Before discussing this dream we shall mention two other dreams, reported at the beginning of the patient's forty-fifth and forty-seventh hours, respectively (See French, 1957, pp. 11–18):

Dream 45 came at the beginning of the next hour: There was a box with kittens or puppies in it down at work. They didn't belong there. I called the attention of the boss's secretary to it, but she was more concerned with the question of who put them there than with getting them out.

Dream 47: A man was walking up and down in an empty room. I thought Lewis was going to be punished, but I don't know what for, or the connection.

The key for our understanding of all three of these dreams is a fact that the patient reported just after telling dream 47—that Lewis and Helen were expecting to have another baby in six months. They had come to Chicago in order to make arrangements for prenatal care once a month so that the child could be born in Chicago. Helen's pregnancy gave poignant meaning to the contrast between the symbol of kittens or puppies in a box in dream 45 and the empty room in dream 47. Helen already had a child and was expecting another, whereas the patient was childless. In her associations to dream 45, the patient's jealousy of Lewis' affection for his wife had been little concealed. "Before he got married," she complained, he used to stay out every night until 5 A.M., presumably with Helen. He said to the patient, "She is the only girl in the world, I love her. *You* don't even know what love is." The patient wondered if he realized how right he was. Later, she continued: "He always is hurting my feelings. This time he didn't come up to see me at all when he arrived.—When he did come up, I knew it was because Dad sent him." On the other hand, after dream 47, she expressed envy of Lewis' ability to leave home and "do what he pleased," whereas she was tied to her parental home by her loyalty to (and dependence on) her foster-parents. In this context, we can recognize that the disturbing motive in dream 45 was a wish that she could be the one to have children by Lewis. Dream 47 was motivated by the spiteful wish that Lewis should be "punished" by Helen's being childless (her room empty), like the patient.

The pregnancy wishes in these two dreams (45 and 47) now make clear the meaning of dream 44. The "test" she must take had to do with the sexual wishes toward Lewis which must have preceded her wishes to be impregnated by him. The "test" was being expected to tell the analyst about these sexual wishes. This interpretation was confirmed by her associations about her inability to talk to the nuns at school, in which she mentioned specifically that she could not tell them about her family, about her brothers and sisters. The patient's associations to dream 45 confirmed this interpretation even more pointedly. With reference to the puppies in the dream, she said, "I couldn't understand how no one had noticed them before. I thought she [the secretary] should call someone to take them away." The patient and the secretary, she said, don't like each other. The girls resent the secretary's being an old friend of the boss's wife who tells the latter about all the office affairs. In connection with the last sentence in the dream, we can now recognize that this dream was struggling with the question of whether to tell the analyst about her pregnancy fantasy. The analyst (represented in the dream by the secretary) would only want to analyze her fantasy. He would tell her that Lewis is the father. In her dream thoughts she carried her distrust of the analyst further. In her associations she said that the boss's secretary tells the boss's wife about all the office affairs. This is the patient's frequently recurring fear—that the analyst might talk about her to her foster-mother.

An interesting question is: Why was the dream of the test immediately preceded by rectal bleeding, whereas there was no mention of rectal bleeding in connection with the two later dreams (45, 47)? The probable answer is that in the first of these three dreams, fear of losing (the love of) the mother was more intensely activated, as was indicated by the patient's reference to her fear of talking to the nuns in childhood and by the fact that the manifest dream pictured her as taking (being put to) a test. In the dream of the puppies (45), the danger of her foster-mother's being told of her disturbing wishes was more remote; and in the dream of the empty room (47), her guilty wish was to be punished by childlessness rather than by loss of the mother.

In her seventy-second hour the patient reported, with seemingly complete lack of affect, that her (true) father had died in South Dakota. After a long silence, and in reply to the analyst's urging, she discussed how she felt about his death. "I can't feel anything. I am not even sorry he is dead. I couldn't be expected to have any feeling for him, I hardly knew him. But I guess it is the same way with me when anyone dies—I just don't seem to feel anything."

She attended the funeral, together with her foster-parents and her brother Lewis, and was very critical of the perfunctory and disgruntled way in which the priest conducted the ceremony. He expressed reluctance to bury the father from the church because the father was such a backslider and had already gone to hell, and he harangued the rest of the family, telling them they had all better get busy and save their souls. "Country priests are all like that," the patient added.

During the two weeks after her father's death, there were no symptoms of colitis. Then, in her seventy-seventh hour, she reported that some of her sisters and brothers had stopped on their way back from the funeral. The patient took the opportunity to ask one of her sisters "about the time we were riding in a car' at night before we came to Chicago—my father [true father] was driving, I guess he was upset because he said nothing all the way. It was then my older brother, Harold, told me that maybe I was going to Chicago with Lewis. . . . It was an old car, it was raining, we were driving fast and Father wouldn't stop to put up the side curtains. It impressed me as being very unusual." Next (in her associations), the patient reverted to the topic of her distress when other children found out that her foster-parents were not her real parents. They would ask, "If your father lives in South Dakota, why don't you live with him? Why did he send you away?" The patient was afraid they would think he didn't want her brother and herself, and she would make up excuses for him. "But he didn't even come to Chicago to see if we were happy as kids—I suppose he just thought that that was two of them off his hands." On the day following this hour (seventy-seven), the patient had *another episode of rectal bleeding.*

In our earlier paper, we described this patient's basic character defense of masochistic submission to her mother. Even after her marriage, she continued to do many household chores for her foster-mother, in addition to holding down a full-time job and working hard taking care of her own house. In this way she had continued to protect herself from the danger of repeating her traumatic memory of being uprooted, from the danger of losing her foster-mother. Her submission to her foster-mother was also adequate to justify her in doing a great deal of griping. She had especially mixed feelings toward Lewis. On the one hand, she was protective of him and his wife in their conflicts with the foster-parents; but she also expressed rather openly her envy of him because he had been able to get his own way much more than she. She was especially envious because he had finally been able to leave home after his marriage and to establish himself in another town some hundreds of miles away.

In the therapeutic situation, whenever the patient recoiled from her hopes of release by the treatment, this whole masochistic pattern was intensified, together with her griping protest against it. Her rebellious protest became stronger and more determined whenever she began to feel more secure in the analyst's support.

A particularly good opportunity for such a rebellious protest was reported in her seventy-sixth hour. Lewis had been evicted from his home, and he asked the foster-parents for a loan so that he could buy a trailer for himself and his family. This, the patient said, would put him just where his parents wanted him—under their domination. She was sure the foster-mother would maneuver him back into their apartment building and make him work there as janitor. To prevent this, the patient herself secretly offered Lewis a loan in case the parents should refuse. When they did refuse, two weeks later, she let Lewis have the money. In this way she was supporting him in his desire to remain independent and thus giving vicarious expression to her own desire for freedom. Then she promptly became preoccupied (consciously) with fear that they would find out what she had done.

In reaction to this secret defiance, she reported a dream in her eightieth hour, just after Lewis and his family had left the foster-parents to drive back to their own town. In the dream, the analyst was in her foster-mother's home talking to her mother. Her mother was pretty sore, but the analyst said he could fix it up. The analyst didn't know what he was up against, the dream continued. "As far as I knew," the patient thought, "no one has ever crossed her yet." To emphasize the hopelessness of escape, the dream ended with the discovery that there weren't any sidewalks around the house, "but rather deep trenches in their place."

No rectal bleeding was reported at the time of this dream or of the secret defiance which preceded it. Her dream makes clear the reason for this. The patient was secure in her realization that there was no danger of her really losing her foster-mother. Not even the analyst, she felt sure, could prevail on the mother to let her go, and her mother's home in the dream was surrounded by deep trenches to make flight impossible.

VII

The evidence cited so far suggests that both the original onset of this patient's colitis and a number of episodes of rectal bleeding during the course of her treatment were precipitated by reactivation of a traumatic memory from her early childhood. This statement should be formulated more precisely. What we have just called a traumatic memory was really a chain of memories: first, sexual wishes toward her father, involving wishes for a child by him and stimulated by her mother's pregnancy at the time; then the birth of a baby brother, followed, in a few days, by the death of her mother; and finally, less than a year later, her being uprooted from her home and family by her father's sending her away to foster-parents who were strangers to her.

The complexity of this chain of events 'accounts for a fact of considerable significance—that the precipitating stimuli for this patient's episodes of rectal bleeding varied over a wide range, depending on which events were, in each particular case, most intensely reactivated. We have reported two examples of this fact. Of the six precipitating situations so far reported, the disturbing events started in five cases with sexual temptation from her father or one of her brothers. The bleeding episode after the seventy-seventh hour was an exception, however. This episode followed reactivation of her memory of being sent away to Chicago by her father. The abdominal cramps after hour nineteen and the rectal bleeding just before hour twenty-two were also an exception, in that the colitic symptoms in this case did not follow immediately on her confession of sexual play with her brother (in hour fourteen). The immediate precipitant in this case was, rather, reactivation of her feelings of being uprooted, which came to most acute expression in hour twenty.

Still another report of her "ulcers raising hell" occurred in hour ninety-three at a time when she was most distressed because she felt that her husband's family were neglecting his grandmother, who was in a hospital and dying. The patient herself had not known this grandmother well, but she was reminded of the time when her own grandparents were sick for weeks while the family were expecting them to die. She admitted that it was a relief after they were gone, but it was all "mixed up with fear." All the time she had hoped that she wouldn't be home when it happened and that they wouldn't be afraid when the end came. It also seems probable that the immanent death of her husband's grandmother had unconsciously reactivated the traumatic memory of her own mother's death.

We must remember, also, that reactivation of these traumatic memories depended not only on external precipitating events but also on the state of the patient's defenses at each particular time. We have already mentioned several instances of this. The circumstances of original onset of the patient's ulcerative colitis are a particularly instructive example. Several years elapsed between the patient's sexual play with her brother and the acute onset of her colitis. We have already suspected that the reason for this delay was the fact that, as long as this patient remained at home with her foster-mother, her submission to her foster-mother's domination protected her from the danger of repeating the trauma of losing her mother. When she left home to go into nurse's training, however, she was hoping to become free of her mother's domination. This made her much more vulnerable to the danger of being uprooted again, when her planned vacation threatened once more to expose her to temptation from her brother.

The same principle was illustrated by her reaction to lending her brother money when her parents refused to do so. By this act she was vicariously living out her own wish to be free of her mother, but in her dream (80b) she succeeded in reassuring herself that no one had ever crossed her foster-mother yet and that there were deep trenches around the house to make flight impossible. This successful reassurance accounts for the fact that no rectal bleeding was reported in connection either with her lending Lewis money or with the dream that we have just mentioned.

Another defensive urge literally permeated this patient's character. This was a desperate need to protect herself from developing warm and dependent emotions. Over and over again, this patient protested that she was unable to be even friendly with her husband's relatives and other people, even though she liked them. At one time she reproached herself about having paid no attention when her husband hurt himself —in marked contrast to her husband's solicitous concern whenever she was ill. In fact, she often described herself as incapable of love.

A particularly perplexing example of her need to inhibit warm feelings occurred at the time when Dr. M (the elderly dentist who had long treated her with tender solicitude) was slowly dying. To the news of his fatal illness, the patient reacted with the feeling that she could not pay her bill to him now because it would have the unfortunate appearance of trying to pay him off before he died. This strange thought implied, of course, that the patient did have a compulsive need to pay him off before he died. Why? In order to account for it, we must bring it into relationship with this patient's distress at having any really tender feelings toward anyone in her life. Such distress served as a safeguard against becoming involved—as she once had been—in tender feelings toward her true mother, who had died. Consequently, she must try, contrary to fact, to think of her relation to Dr. M as only one of professional service and financial obligation.

This seemingly paradoxical need to repudiate all tender feelings toward him came out even more dramatically in a reaction reported in her 176th hour. "Last Christmas, Joe asked if I hadn't got anything for Dr. M, and said we should. I didn't think so. He ordered a magazine subscription for him, although I didn't think he'd like it. But he [the old dentist] was surprised and pleased, even had tears in his eyes. I was so sorry we had done anything about it, I knew we shouldn't have."

We have already reported this patient's dream "where you are always giving me something," and her feeling of guilt "about not paying the full price" for her psychoanalytic treatment. Thus, in order to protect herself from the danger of loss of a loved object, this patient found it necessary to transform feelings of love and longings to be loved into relatively impersonal feelings of financial obligation.

In the symbolism of this patient's dreams this transformation found expression in the well-known substitution of money for love. Psychosomatically, a similar transformation seems to have been achieved by substituting clinging to her stool for receiving love. We have already illustrated these two mechanisms by the analysis of two dreams which were closely associated with colitis symptoms. The substitution of money for love was most indicated in dream 37, in which the analyst's assurances that the patient was capable of "warm, natural love" were symbolized by a man who "gave you money" without her doing anything to earn it. In dream 19, which was also followed soon afterward by abdominal cramps and rectal bleeding, our analysis of the dream symbolism suggested that the dream work had substituted the impersonal symbol of jeweled initials in a box for the intimately personal fantasy of being inside her mother's body as a baby.

This pattern of substituting money for love probably also accounted for several episodes of rectal bleeding in connection with her relation to her foster-mother. We shall report the two of these in which the connection seems clearest. In hour ninety-nine, the patient *reported bleeding* the night before. The night before the bleeding she had visited her foster-father, who was in the hospital. He had asked her to take care of some business matters for him. Her foster-mother had volunteered but was too unreliable, the patient thought. She thought her foster-mother resented it when her father asked the patient to take care of things. "I always get caught in the middle with them," she continued. "But she kept out money that he gave her to pay bills with. No wonder he never trusted her."

In her 115th hour, on a Tuesday, she reported that since Sunday morning she had had abdominal pains and blood in her stools. Her mother had told her that her father had been extremely upset Saturday night because the patient had refused to go down and work on his books. In spite of her own husband's objection, she had gone down that night to help her father. "It was a great strain," she said. Her father just wanted to guess on such matters as the amount of dividends he had received and the number of shares of stock that he possessed. The patient felt there was not any point in recording mere guesses. So she had refused to continue on Sunday. Later, after an enumeration of difficulties at work, she complained that everyone wanted her to do something and she didn't have time to do it all, ending with the statement that she wanted to get the floors scrubbed. "Keeping my father calmed down worries me the most," she added. "He tells me that the only way he can keep his mental balance is by having everything down in black and white in his books. When he is upset, he keeps the whole family up in the air. But Joe resents it if I help him and then can't do something that he [Joe] wants me to do."

At this time, the patient's father was in a hypomanic mood, preoccupied in a grandiose way with business affairs and the stock market. In her 114th hour, she had told how her father was fussing at her to come downstairs evenings, regardless of the fact that she was tired, to help him with his books and his accounts. When she suggested that he get a neighbor girl, who also had had bookkeeping experience, to do it, he demurred, saying that the mother would object to his working with a young, pretty girl. The patient felt that he was flattering himself in this. "After all, he is a very old man." Thus, in the background of her father's demands that she help him with business affairs we can sense that the patient was reacting to unrecognized sexual temptation, competition with her foster-mother, and fear of losing her mother's love, as in our earlier examples. Again, she was trying to protect herself from sexual temptation, and from loss of her mother's love—by substituting money for love.

BIBLIOGRAPHY

Cannon, W. (1932). *The Wisdom of the Body.* New York: Norton.

French, T. M. *The Integration of Behavior.* Chicago: University of Chicago Press, 1952, 1954, 1958.

———. (1957). "Analysis of the Dream Censorship." In *New Perspectives in Psychoanalysis: Sandor Rado Lectures (1957–1963),* ed. by George E. Daniels. New York: Grune & Stratton, 1963. Pp. 1–19. Chapter 12 of this volume.

——— and Fromm, Erika (1964). *Dream Interpretation: A New Approach.* New York: Basic Books, Inc.

——— and Wheeler, D. R. (1957). "Hope and Repudiation of Hope in Psychoanalytic Therapy." In. *New Perspectives in Psychoanalysis: Sandor Rado Lectures (1957–1963).* Pp. 20–44. Reprinted from *Int. j. psychoanal.* 44: 304–16, 1963. Chapter 14 in this volume.

Freud, S. (1914). "Remembering, Repeating, and Working Through." *Standard Edition,* 12. London: Hogarth, 1958.

———. (1915). "Instincts and Their Vicissitudes." *Standard Edition,* 14. London: Hogarth, 1956.

———. (1926). "Inhibition, Symptom and Anxiety." *Standard Edition,* 20. London: Hogarth, 1956.

Chapter Seventeen

REVIEW OF OUR STUDIES
OF THE THERAPEUTIC PROCESS

PSYCHOANALYTIC THERAPY AS A "CORRECTIVE EMOTIONAL EXPERIENCE"

These studies on the therapeutic process have as their background Freud's description (1914) of the process of working through the transference neurosis. Our studies have as their starting point three statements by different authors of an almost identical insight:

Freud's suggestion (1917) that psychoanalytic therapy is a kind of reeducation.

French's concept (1933, 1936, 1937, 1946, 1952) of psychoanalytic therapy as the resumption of a learning process that had been interrupted by a traumatic experience in the past.

Alexander's concept (1946) of psychoanalytic therapy as a "corrective emotional experience."

Before discussing our own further studies, we shall first summarize the earlier formulations which served as background for them.

1) Freud's description (1914) of the process of working through the patient's infantile neurosis in the transference was the final decisive step in Freud's elucidation of psychoanalytic therapy. We may summarize briefly this classical discussion of the culminating phase of the therapeutic process as follows:

In his resistance, a patient often reacts to the therapist not as he really is but rather as though he were one of the significant figures in the patient's past. He "transfers" to the therapist the role of his father or mother or of some other important person. Instead of bringing a repressed memory back to consciousness, a patient often relives it as though it were occurring in the present, distorting his understanding of present reality so as to make it fit the reality of the past. Such reliving of a repressed memory Freud calls "compulsive repetition."

When such compulsive repetition occurs, the patient's therapeutic task is to "work through" the reactivated memory. The analyst should not expect, Freud warns, that his interpretations will immediately put an end to the patient's reliving of past conflicts. He should rather try to keep the patient at the task of associating freely and of trying to understand his unconscious motives, in spite of his resistance. Only by reliving the repressed instinctive trends that feed his resistance, Freud points out, can the patient be convinced of their existence and of their power over him. Only by this kind of direct demonstration of the power of his unconscious motives can the most important therapeutic changes in the patient's behavior patterns be achieved.

2) Freud's comment about psychoanalysis as a reeducational process was added several years later (1917), almost incidentally, and supplemented by a description of how the process of working through makes it possible for the patient's ego to regain control of the libido that had previously been bound in the patient's symptoms.

3) Alexander's concept of a "corrective emotional experience" spells out more explicitly Freud's suggestion that psychoanalysis is a process of reeducation. Alexander (1946) writes: "In all forms of etiological psychotherapy, the basic therapeutic principle is the same: to reexpose the patient, under more favorable circumstances, to emotional situations which he could not handle in the past. The patient, in order to be helped, must undergo a corrective emotional experience suitable to repair the traumatic influence of previous experiences" (p. 66).

This concept, we believe, is an outstanding contribution to understanding of the therapeutic process in psychoanalytic treatment. Alexander writes further: "In the formulation of the dynamics of treatment, the usual tendency is to stress the repetition of the old conflict in the transference relationship and to emphasize the similarity of the old conflict situation to the transference situation. The therapeutic significance of the *differences* between the original conflict situation and the present therapeutic situation is often overlooked. And in just this difference lies the secret of the therapeutic value of the analytic procedure. Because the therapist's attitude is different from that of the authoritative person of the past, he gives the patient an opportunity to face again and again, under more favorable circumstances, those emotional situations which were formerly unbearable and to deal with them in a manner different from the old" (p. 67).

Traumatic Interruption of a Process of Discriminatory Learning

4) Alexander's concept of corrective emotional experience was based on direct clinical observation. In the meantime (1933, 1936, 1937), I had arrived at an essentially similar formulation on theoretical grounds. My formula is that the therapeutic effect of a psychoanalytic treatment results from the *resumption* of a *previously interrupted* process of *discriminatory learning*. What was new in this formulation is the obvious fact that the learning process in psychoanalytic treatment is one that had been begun but *interrupted,* usually long ago in the patient's childhood.

This formula was first suggested by a comparison of familiar psychoanalytic observations with some of the conditioned reflex experiments of Pavlov (1927). For example, a young boy's sexual interest is usually turned first to his mother, which brings him into conflict with his father. But then, during the latency period, his sexual needs become less intense and his attachment to his mother becomes predominantly a tender one which no longer involves him in conflict with his father. During adolescence his physical sexual urges again become more intensely activated, but now, if development proceeds normally, he begins to turn his sexual interest away from his mother to girls of his own age, who need not involve him in conflict with his father. What now impressed me was the fact that in principle this normal development is very similar to what Pavlov (1927) calls differentiation of a conditioned reflex. In one experiment, for example, a dog was first conditioned to respond to a circle with salivary secretion. This was done by regularly feeding the dog after showing it the circle. Afterward, food was regularly withheld after the dog had been shown an ellipse with semi-axes in the ration of 2:1. The result was that the dog secreted saliva after being shown the circle but inhibited salivary secretion after being shown the ellipse. Both of these examples—both the psychoanalytic observation and the Pavlovian experiment—are instances of discriminatory learning. "Discriminatory learning" is a technical phrase, equivalent to Alexander's more vivid clinical concept of "corrective emotional experience."

In this case, however, the Pavlovian experiment went further. After the first differentiation had become established, Pavlov tried successively to establish finer differentiations, using ellipses with semi-axes of 3:2, 4:3, etc. He was successful until an ellipse with semi-axes of 9:8 was reached. At this point, also, a considerable degree of discrimination did develop for a time, but after three weeks of work discrimination not only failed to improve but became worse and finally disappeared altogether. Then the behavior of the animal underwent an abrupt change. The hitherto quiet dog began to squeal in its stand, kept wriggling about, tore off with its teeth the apparatus for mechanical stimulation of the skin, and bit through the tubes connecting the animal's room with the observer—none of which had ever happened before. On being taken into the experimental room the dog now barked violently, which was also contrary to its usual custom. In short, it presented all the symptoms of a condition of acute neurosis. When the cruder differentiations were tested they also were found to be destroyed, even the one with the ratio of the semi-axes 2:1. Thus in this case discriminatory learning came to an abrupt end. Pavlov himself called the dog's behavior "an acute neurosis."

We now return to our clinical parallel. Our adolescent boy's sexual urges have become more intensely activated at puberty, and he is in the process of learning to turn his sexual interest away from his mother to girls of his own age. But let us now suppose that, before he has fully succeeded in making this discrimination, his sexual interest in the mother is too intensely activated and that this in turn reactivates intensely his early conflict in relation to his father. Under these circumstances, we know that the boy will develop a neurosis. One feature of his neurosis will be that he will be inhibited sexually in relation to other women as well as in relation to his mother. He will *no longer be able to discriminate* between his mother and other women.

Thus the parallel between this human neurosis and the neurosis of Pavlov's dog is very close. In both cases a process of normal discriminatory learning has been interrupted by excessive conflict and in both cases the capacity to make the necessary discriminations has been lost. Pavlov's dog can no longer discriminate between one stimulus and another that is too closely similar to it, and then even discriminations that have already been acquired are lost. In our clinical experience, a patient, years after a traumatic event, will often react to his analyst or to someone else in his present environment as though this person were one of the significant figures in the patient's past. Instead of bringing a repressed memory back to consciousness, the patient will relive it as though it were occurring in the present—distorting his understanding of present reality so as to make present reality fit the reality of the past.

Impressed by this close analogy, we conclude that human neuroses, too, are the result of *interruption* of a process of *discriminatory learning*. This leads us to a concept similar to Freud's original traumatic theory of neuroses. Our theory differs from Freud's only in the fact that we define the concept of a traumatic event more broadly than Freud did. A traumatic event, according to our definition, is *any situation or event that more or less permanently interrupts the process of learning by experience.*

RESISTANCE AGAINST RESUMING AN INTERRUPTED LEARNING EXPERIENCE

If neurosis is the result of a permanent interruption of a process of learning by experience, then recovery can occur only if in some way it is possible for the patient to *resume and carry to completion* the process of discriminatory learning whose long-ago interruption gave rise to his neurosis. This is the formulation I have proposed as the principle on which psychoanalytic therapy must be based.

Our next question is an empirical one. Is such resumption of an interrupted learning process possible? If so, how can it be made possible? These are the crucial questions for the understanding of psychoanalytic therapy.

When we try to answer these questions it is important to distinguish between normal learning and a patient's attempt to resume a learning process that was interrupted long ago. Alexander sometimes does not make this distinction sharply enough. For example, at one point he illustrates a corrective emotional experience as follows (1956): "The simplest examples of the working of this therapeutic factor are seen in self-assertive and aggressive attitudes which may have been repressed in the past due to parental intimidation. If the therapist wants to revive these repressed and self-assertive impulses during the treatment, he must reverse the intimidating influence of the parents. . . . The patient's expression of aggression, self-assertion, or resentment must be met objectively without any emotional response or retaliation on the part of the analyst. In this way the analyst corrects the original intimidating influence of the parents. The parental intimidation is undone and the tolerant attitude of the therapist has now replaced the parent's role in the patient's mind" (pp. 40–41).

Unfortunately, in this example Alexander has failed to take account of the patient's resistance. The traumatic memory patterns of neuroses cannot be corrected so easily. What Alexander is describing at this point is normal emotional learning, such as can be achieved by a person who has no neurosis.

Therapeutic resumption of an old learning process is a much more difficult and disturbing experience than normal learning. Resumption of an interrupted learning process corresponds to what Freud calls "working through" a traumatic memory. This the patient will inevitably resist energetically. When Pavlov's dog reached the limit of its capacity for discriminatory learning, it tore apart the experimental apparatus with its teeth.

Two Phases of Therapy: First Mobilization, then Resolution, of a Traumatic Conflict

If the patient must resist reactivation of his conflict so desperately, how can we make it possible for him to resume the learning process that was interrupted?

In order to answer this question, we must study the patient's defenses.

A traumatic memory pattern tends to be reactivated when an individual is faced with a similar problem in the present. Such a tendency to relive disturbing memories would be very disturbing in real life if it were not possible to find devices to protect oneself against it. Neuroses consist of such devices to protect the patient against having to reactivate his traumatic memory patterns. These devices are the patient's "defenses."

On the other hand, in therapy a patient cannot learn how to solve a problem so long as he is struggling to avoid it. Our first task in therapy is to induce the patient to set aside his defenses and to deal again directly with his conflict. This part of the treatment is the phase of "mobilization" or reactivation of the traumatic conflict. Resumption of the interrupted learning process, in order to make possible "resolution" of the traumatic conflict, can occur only after the conflict has been "mobilized."

The outstanding characteristic of the phase of mobilization of conflict is the fact that it is energetically resisted by the patient. We should remember that a *patient has good* and rational *reason to resist* setting aside his defenses, since his reliving an infantile neurosis is likely to interfere seriously with his rational behavior in everyday life. Our therapeutic task, accordingly, has two sharply contrasting objectives. First, we must induce the patient to *set aside his defenses,* in spite of his resistance. We must also try to *protect him from setting aside his defenses too rapidly*—since too intense reactivation of his conflict will make resumption of learning impossible.

A New Approach to the Study of Defenses

To know how to regulate the process of mobilization of a patient's conflict, we must study the patient's defenses from a new point of view.

Ordinarily we think of defenses as directed against a disturbing wish or drive. This concept is not useful when we are trying to regulate the process of mobilization of a patient's conflict. A disturbing wish is only one side of a conflict. The disturbing wish is opposed by a reactive motive—guilt, for example. If his disturbing wish is a hostile wish against some loved person, then it is customary to think of his guilt as the motive for his defense. But now we are interested in the therapeutic task of regulating the intensity of activation of the patient's whole conflict in order to make therapeutic learning possible.

From this new point of view, the patient's guilt is not part of his defense but part of the conflict against which he is defending himself. Now we are interested in studying not only his defense against his disturbing wish, but rather his defense against excessive reactivation of his conflict as a whole.

This new approach simplifies the study of defenses in relation to the therapeutic learning process. How can a patient protect himself from activating a conflict? Essentially, there is only one way—by diverting his interest elsewhere. If, for example, a hostile impulse is beginning to be activated, then the patient must quickly turn away to some relatively harmless impulse and thus prevent both his hostile impulse and his reactive guilt from being activated.

Is it possible for the ego thus to turn away from a disturbing conflict? Sometimes, but not always. It depends on the degree to which the ego has allowed the patient to become involved in or committed to the disturbing conflict. At a time when the disturbing impulse in question has been only slightly activated, the ego may be able to turn away promptly. Freud (1926) speaks of the use of anxiety as a "warning signal." He points out (p. 162) that anxiety may arise in either one of two ways in later life. In one, it is an involuntary, automatic, and quantitatively appropriate reaction to danger. In the other, the ego "subjects itself to anxiety as a sort of inoculation, submitting to a slight attack of the illness in order to escape its full strength—with the unmistakable purpose of restricting the distressing experience to a mere indication, a signal." To illustrate this mechanism (discussed at greater length in French [1958], pp. 34–35, and French and Fromm [1964], pp. 69–70) we cite a classical hypothetical example.

A forbidden sexual impulse begins to be activated. The ego responds with castration fear. If the disturbing impulse has been only slightly activated, then the castration fear will need only to be hinted at. In such a case the ego may be able to respond to the hint of castration as a warning and to turn quickly away from the dangerous impulse. We call this kind of defense a "prophylactic defense," since it is able to prevent the disturbing conflict from being activated to any significant degree.

In other cases the ego does not respond so promptly. As a result, the disturbing impulse is much more intensely activated. In such a case, the patient's involvement in the disturbing conflict may become irreversible. Such an irreversible involvement we call "commitment." This concept of commitment is a very important one, for it enables us to follow closely the process of reactivation of a traumatic conflict. Until it begins to be reactivated, the conflict has been in a state of latency. In fact, relatively normal behavior is possible only when the patterns of traumatic conflicts from a person's past are in a state of latency. But once a patient's involvement in a reactivated conflict has become irreversible, the conflict can no longer be "wished away." Then the patient's defenses are unsuccessful, his conflict becomes excessive, and his behavior becomes neurotic.

Mobilizing a Patient's Conflict

We are now ready to consider the problem of mobilizing the patient's conflict.

When a patient seeks treatment for a neurosis, this already implies that one or more conflicts have been activated excessively as a result of failure of his defenses. This kind of mobilization we call "neurotic mobilization" or "mobilization by frustration of defenses" (French [1958], pp. 40–41). Since failure or frustration of the patient's defenses inevitably results in excessive activation of the patient's conflict, this kind of mobilization by frustration is not favorable for therapeutic learning.

Another kind of mobilization of a patient's conflict is "mobilization by hope," which we also call "therapeutic mobilization" (French [1958], pp. 39–40). The conflicts at first activated by this kind of mobilization are usually closer to the surface than those activated by neurotic mobilization. To facilitate therapeutic mobilization of a patient's conflict, the psychoanalyst must first try to discover the nature of the patient's own therapeutic incentive. Just what does he hope for from his treatment? Before he came for treatment, his hopes may have been rather vague. In response to the analyst's encouragement to talk freely, more specific therapeutic hopes usually emerge. These specific therapeutic hopes always have their basis in the reality of the immediate therapeutic situation but are usually only preconscious. The therapist's first task is to discover these specific therapeutic hopes and how they can be utilized to make the patient willing to relax his defenses and, step by step, to let his disturbing conflicts be mobilized.

As a first step the therapist usually should give prompt recognition to the patient's emerging hope. Such recognition lends support to the patient's hope and increases his confidence, enabling him to entertain his new hope more boldly. *The immediate effect,* however, *is usually not a corrective emotional experience.* On the contrary, the patient's emerging therapeutic hopes are always closely associated with old hopes that once ended disastrously. As the patient's new therapeutic hope becomes activated more intensely, fear of the traumatic consequences of the associated old hope is soon activated with corresponding intensity. Thus the effect of the patient's new hope is paradoxical. After first seducing the patient to dream, or to fantasy, or to act more boldly, the emerging therapeutic hope ends up by reactivating the patient's underlying conflict. This is what we call a "therapeutic mobilization" of the patient's conflict.

For example, in the case that Wheeler and I describe in Chapter 14 above, the severely inhibited patient quickly developed a hope that her treatment would free her from her sexual inhibitions. This hope she repudiated energetically and did not allow to emerge into consciousness. Nevertheless, she continued to entertain her repudiated hope preconsciously. Then fear of the consequences began to be reactivated. If she responded thus to the analyst's anticipated encouragement, what would her foster-mother think? In her early childhood (at the age of four), while in the midst of an intense Oedipus attachment to her father, she had suddenly lost her mother by death and had then been sent away to strange foster-parents. Consequently, her hopes of sexual release in the treatment soon began to reactivate unconscious fears of being utterly uprooted from her home just as she had been after her own mother's death.

But what right have we to say that this kind of mobilization of a patient's conflict is therapeutic? Mobilization by frustration, we pointed

out, makes therapeutic learning impossible. If the conflict is too intensely activated, the same will be true of mobilization by hope. If the
patient's conflict is less intensely activated, however, hope, by increasing
a patient's integrative capacity, tends to facilitate discriminatory learning. The intensity of a conflict mobilized by hope usually undergoes
certain characteristic changes. Usually tension first rises (slowly or
rapidly) to a height, then gradually recedes. At the point of maximum
activation of his conflict, the patient usually is not capable of discriminatory learning, but learning often becomes possible after the intensity
of the patient's conflict has begun to diminish.

Unfortunately, we shall have time only to cite a hypothetical example
(see Alexander and French [1947], pp. 93–94): A patient has come
to therapy with generalized inhibitions that make it impossible for him
to entertain sexual feelings for any woman. After a period of treatment
he begins to date an unmarried woman of his own age. The analyst
notices that in certain physical features this woman resembles the
patient's mother. He expects, accordingly, that the patient will soon
develop fears or guilt feelings. These feelings will rise to a high point
until finally he stops dating the girl. Then his fears or guilt will begin
to recede. After a time the patient may turn to other interests, and his
fear or guilt will disappear.

We shall consider next two possible ways in which the analyst may
handle this patient and what their effects on the sequence of events
described above will be.

Suppose first that the analyst promptly calls the patient's attention to
the fact that the girl resembles the patient's mother. The effect of such
an interpretation will be to accelerate and intensify the development of
the patient's fear or guilt. In other words, the result will be to accelerate
the neurotic mobilization of the patient's conflict that would have occurred spontaneously in any case. The increased intensity of the patient's
conflict will then make it impossible for the patient to learn to discriminate between the girl and his mother, and nothing therapeutic will
be accomplished.

But let us consider another way in which the analyst may deal with
the patient's emerging heterosexual interest. This time the analyst will
say nothing about the patient's mother but will respond sympathetically
to the patient's positive interest in the girl. The patient at first will
probably interpret the analyst's comment as approval and will approach
the girl more boldly. However, the more boldly he acts, the greater will
be the fear or guilt that follows. The analyst knows that at this point

it will be impossible for the patient to respond to further encouragement. He waits for the patient's fear or guilt to rise to a high point. Only after the patient's fear or guilt has begun to recede does the analyst mention the mother, pointing out then that the patient has been reacting as if the girl were the patient's mother—which, of course, she is not. In choosing this moment for his interpretive comment, the analyst is guided by the principle that discriminatory learning cannot take place so long as the patient's conflict is excessive. For this reason, he has postponed his interpretation until the intensity of the patient's conflict has spontaneously begun to diminish.

Abreaction as an Auxiliary Mechanism

When Breuer and Freud (1895) first described their method of cathartic hypnosis for treating hysteria, they ascribed a very important role to *abreaction* of the patient's conflict. Later, Freud learned that the therapeutic effects of abreaction are not permanent. Since then, there has been a tendency in the analytic literature to deny altogether the therapeutic value of abreaction.

This is throwing the baby out with the bath water. I agree that abreaction is not the sole therapeutic mechanism in psychoanalytic therapy, but it does play an essential auxiliary role in making therapeutic learning possible. Resolution of a traumatic conflict can take place only if the conflict is first mobilized; but even mobilization by hope is at first usually excessive. Partial abreaction must first take place in order to make the initially excessive conflict accessible to learning.

SUMMARY

1) As starting point for our analysis of the therapeutic process, we took Alexander's concept of a "corrective emotional experience." A corrective emotional experience is a process of discriminatory learning, of learning by experience.

2) Learning by experience, however, is not always possible. In every neurosis the patient has built up defenses which prevent his traumatic conflict from being reactivated sufficiently to make discriminatory learning possible. Unless the patient can first be induced to set aside his defenses and allow his conflict to be adequately mobilized, a corrective emotional experience cannot take place.

3) To make therapeutic learning possible, the mobilization of the patient's conflict must be regulated. His conflict must be reactivated

sufficiently but not excessively. In order to regulate the intensity of re-activation of the patient's conflict, the therapist must keep in close touch with the patient's therapeutic incentive (as well as with his resistance). Therapeutic incentive is based on hope, on specific hopes oriented to-ward the realities of the therapeutic situation. Our thesis is that such specific hopes, repeatedly emerging and continually undergoing modi-fication in adaptation to the therapeutic situation, are essential for the maintenance of the gradually increasing integrative capacity on which success in therapy depends.

However, hopes have consequences to the extent that one becomes emotionally committed to the possibility of realizing them. Unfortu-nately, these therapeutically significant hopes are closely associated with other hopes, from the past, which once ended in disastrous consequences. The resulting conflict may be excessive and for a time irreversibly so; but when reversible, this kind of reactivation of a traumatic conflict can end in "therapeutic mobilization by hope."

4) Such therapeutic mobilization may make possible a process of "working through." To this end, the therapist should postpone inter-pretation until enough of the excessive pressure of the underlying trau-matic conflict has been abreacted to make therapeutic learning possible.

BIBLIOGRAPHY

Alexander, F. *Psychoanalysis and Psychotherapy*. New York: Norton, 1956.

Alexander, F. and French, T. M. *Psychoanalytic Therapy*. New York: Ronald, 1946.

Breuer, J. and Freud, S. (1895). *Studies on Hysteria*. New York and Wash-ington, D.C.: Nervous & Mental Disease Press, 1936.

French, T. M. "Interrelations Between Psychoanalysis and the Experimental Work of Pavlov." *Am. j. psychiatry, 12:* 1165–1203, 1933. Chapter 1 of this volume.

―――. "A Clinical Study of Learning in the Course of a Psychoanalytic Treatment." *Psychoanal. q., 5:* 148–94, 136. Chapter 3 of this volume.

―――. "Reality and the Unconscious." *Psychoanal. q., 6:* 23–61, 1937. Chapter 2 of this volume.

―――. *The Integration of Behavior*. Vol. I. *Basic Postulates*. Chicago: University of Chicago Press, 1952.

―――. *The Integration of Behavior*. Vol. III. *The Reintegrative Process in a Psychoanalytic Treatment*. Chicago: University of Chicago Press, 1958.

――― and Wheeler, D. R. "Hope and Repudiation of Hope in Psychoanalytic Therapy." *Int. j. psychoanal. 44:* 304–16, 1963. Chapter 14 of this volume.

———— and Fromm, E. *Dream Interpretation: A New Approach.* New York: Basic Books, 1964.

Freud, S. (1914). "Remembering, Repeating and Working Through." Standard Edition, 12. London: Hogarth, 1956.

————. (1917). "Introductory Lectures: Analytic Therapy." Standard Edition, 14. London: Hogarth, 1963, 451 ("after education"), 454–55.

————. (1926). "Inhibition, Symptom and Anxiety." Standard Edition, 20. London: Hogarth, 1961.

Pavlov, I. P. *Conditioned Reflexes.* London: Oxford University, Humphrey Milford, 1927.

Part Two

THERAPEUTIC METHOD AND RESEARCH METHOD IN PSYCHOANALYSIS

Chapter Eighteen

CLINICAL APPROACH TO THE
DYNAMICS OF BEHAVIOR

Psychoanalysis was first discovered and studied as a method of therapy rather than as a method of scientific investigation. Discussion of psychoanalysis as a scientific contribution, on the other hand, very often starts with psychoanalytic theory. This approach to psychoanalysis has led to some confusion. Plunging into the theoretical conclusions at which psychoanalysts have arrived, one gains the impression that psychoanalysis is a body of scientific doctrines based in very considerable part upon rather unrestrained speculation. Quite the contrary is the case. The most important scientific contribution of psychoanalysis has been not its conclusions but its method. In this paper, accordingly, we shall discuss psychoanalysis as a method of scientific investigation, as a clinical approach to the study of the dynamics of behavior.

Psychoanalysis as a scientific method is based upon a single, very simple principle. If we do not understand a person's behavior, we seek to make it intelligible by finding its emotional context. If a man behaves as though he is angry, for example, we try to learn more about the circumstances until we find something that seems adequate to account for his anger. If we learn that someone has made an insulting remark to him, we shall then find his anger quite "natural."

This method of attempting to understand human behavior was not invented by psychoanalysis. It is the method of the common-sense psychology of everyday life. It is essentially an intuitive method based upon the psychological knowledge, for the most part unformulated, that makes

Reprinted from J. McV. Hunt, ed., *Personality and the Behavior Disorders* (New York, 1944).

one person's behavior seem "natural" to us, whereas another person's behavior seems "strange" and "unaccountable." Psychoanalysis has merely extended the range of application of this method and has succeeded in demonstrating that even the most irrational behavior becomes "natural" and "understandable" to us if we succeed, after a long search, in finding its proper emotional context in the life history of the individual concerned.

It will be seen from this example that the psychoanalytic method, when properly practiced, really involves no theoretical preconceptions whatsoever other than the quite unformulated psychological assumptions that guide us in our everyday relations with other human beings and for the validity of which our everyday contacts with our fellow men offer us constantly repeated empirical tests. When we have succeeded by this method in "understanding" a person's behavior, we have not yet in most cases formulated the reasons for the patient's behavior in scientific terms. What we have done first of all is to enlarge our knowledge of the emotional context of the patient's behavior. After we have done this we may have little more than an intuitive sense that this person's feelings and actions are quite normal. Nevertheless—and with justice—we speak of this kind of insight into a person's behavior as a "psychological understanding" of his reactions.

We must next inquire what must be added to this sort of "psychological understanding" in order to use it in arriving at valid scientific formulations. It is useful to distinguish two successive steps in the scientific utilization of our clinical studies. We begin with the interpretation, with the attempt to find the emotional context that will make the patient's behavior seem "natural" to us. Once we have grasped the true sense and meaning of a patient's behavior, however, we are then ready to subject our imperfectly formulated "psychological understanding" to more careful analysis. The first step in this process is to subject our interpretations to critical examination and analysis. When we have arrived at an interpretation, we must next inquire how completely it "explains" the available facts. In most cases we find that our interpretations when thus critically examined leave a number of questions still unanswered. Usually there are a number of facts that are still not adequately accounted for. This leads to a search for a still wider emotional context in order to answer the questions arising successively from each interpretation. It was in this way that Freud, in seeking a "psychological understanding" of the neuroses, was led farther and farther back into the life histories of his patients.

Thus a critical application of the interpretative method leads us inevitably into the task which has been a central preoccupation in the psychoanalytic literature, that of dynamic reconstruction of the life histories of individuals. Usually we find that a particular bit of "peculiar" behavior has been influenced by a considerable number of events, both present and past. We seek, therefore, to study the dynamic interrelations between these events and to reconstruct the steps by which they contributed to and cooperated in the chain of causation of which the patient's behavior was the result.

The goal of science is not merely to find explanations for particular cases, but rather to formulate generalizations that are valid for many different cases. In this task of formulating valid generalizations, we begin again with "common-sense psychology." We have based our interpretations upon the psychological assumptions that guide us in our everyday relations with other people. These assumptions already imply generalizations about human behavior, but these generalizations are for the most part unformulated. Our first task is to formulate them, to make them explicit.

In this task we are aided by the fact that psychoanalysis has succeeded in extending the application of these assumptions to behavior that at first sight seemed quite peculiar. The elucidation of "peculiar" behavior has the advantage of throwing into relief relationships which we might otherwise take for granted. For this reason, as Freud has often pointed out, the study of psychopathology has been of enormous service in contributing to our knowledge of the "normal" psychology of everyday life. By studying the psychological contexts that throw light upon the symptoms of mental illness, we are able to see in isolated and exaggerated form dynamic relationships that can easily be overlooked and taken quite for granted in our everyday "understanding" of more usual behavior.

A first step in this kind of generalization was the description of psychodynamic mechanisms that are encountered over and over again in our patients' material.

Freud and others have also made considerable progress in describing features that are characteristic of the life history of individuals suffering from particular types of disorders. We know, for example (Freud, 1913), that severe childhood conflicts over toilet training are regularly found in the life history of patients who later suffer from compulsion neuroses. Depressive reactions (Freud, 1917) are particularly likely to occur in reaction to the loss of a loved object toward whom the patient has also entertained strong but repressed feelings of hostility. And so forth.

The extremely rich clinical material that has been accumulated by the psychoanalytic method of observation also offers us an orientation that should be extremely valuable in guiding us to problems that can be profitably investigated by experimental methods. The problems suitable for clinical and experimental investigation are not always the same, however. Those who wish to make use of the insights that have resulted from psychoanalytic investigation should, therefore, not content themselves with summarizing psychoanalytic concepts and theories, but should rather familiarize themselves sufficiently with the fundamental psychoanalytic method of interpreting behavior by searching for its emotional context so that they will be able to evaluate clinical data upon their own merits.

Human behavior is exceedingly complex. If we wish to gain an understanding of it, there are in general two methods open to us. We may create artificial, highly simplified situations. We may investigate experimentally, for example, whether one can train an individual to react with a knee jerk to the sound of an electric bell. In so doing we are attempting to follow a sound experimental principle. We attempt to simplify our problem by isolating the separate dynamic elements and investigating them one at a time. With this purpose in view, for example, we disregard the fact that our experimental subject is a struggling young professional man who is having the greatest difficulty in earning enough money to support his wife and three children. For the purpose of this investigation we regard this fact as irrelevant. For the present we are interested only in whether we can condition his knee jerk to respond to a new stimulus.

But the disadvantages of such a procedure are also evident. In the first place, we cannot be entirely sure that the emotional difficulties of our experimental subject are really irrelevant in relationship to the conditioning of his knee jerks. In the second place, we may not be entirely sure that the problem we have set ourselves is the one that is most likely to throw light upon the dynamics of behavior. We should probably be able to proceed more wisely in the choice of questions to investigate if we first made some attempt to get an orientation as to the problems presented by behavior when studied as a whole.

In the clinical approach to the study of behavior we have the advantage that we are compelled to see a person's behavior in its proper perspective. Thus we avoid the danger of studying some isolated detail of an individual's reaction entirely out of its usual context. On the other hand, we have the disadvantage that a clinical approach compels us to study behavior in all of its complexity. We are in danger, therefore, of being completely bewildered by the intricate patterns of interacting motives with which the everyday activity of any individual confronts us.

Ordinarily the attempt to understand human behavior by direct observation meets with another difficulty. People usually do not wish to tell us about the matters which touch them most deeply. Often the matters that are most important in an individual's life are a cause of some disturbance to him and are closely guarded as a secret from all except his closest friends. There is one situation, however, which may call forth a motive strong enough to overcome this natural reticence. The patient who consults a physician for treatment of a psychoneurotic illness can often be induced to talk freely about disturbing and intimate matters which he would otherwise keep to himself. It is for this reason that attempts to understand human behavior by direct observation have been so closely associated with the development of psychotherapy.

PSYCHOANALYSIS AS A METHOD OF SCIENTIFIC INVESTIGATION

It is usual to discuss the psychoanalytic method as a method of therapy rather than as a method of scientific investigation. Discussion of psychoanalysis as a scientific contribution, on the other hand, very often starts with psychoanalytic theory. This approach to psychoanalysis has led to some confusion. Plunging into the theoretical conclusions at which psychoanalysts have arrived, one gains the impression that psychoanalysis is a body of scientific doctrines based in very considerable part upon rather unrestrained speculation. Quite the contrary is the case. The most important scientific contribution of psychoanalysis has been not its conclusions but its method. It therefore seems appropriate in this chapter to discuss psychoanalysis as a method of scientific investigation, as a clinical approach to the study of dynamics of behavior.

As a scientific method, psychoanalysis is indeed influenced by the fact that it is not only a method of scientific investigation, but also a method of therapy (see Alexander, 1936). In other words, the method is a clinical one and must always consider the therapeutic interests of the patient. For this reason, the first objective of a psychoanalytic investigation must be to understand the individual case in order to know how to handle the therapeutic problem. The most important complication that the therapeutic requirements introduce into the task of scientific investigation is the fact that in some cases it is necessary, in the interests of therapy, to make a quick diagnosis of a situation and to act upon conclusions that are in the nature of guesses and not yet definitely proved. This would indeed be a complication if these guesses were accepted as final scientific formulations instead of for what they are—tentative hypotheses that are to be tested and either proved or disproved by subsequent evidence. If this tentative attitude toward the interpretation of the patient's material is maintained, however, it is surprising to what degree the interests of therapy and the requirements of scientific investigation coincide.

The Fundamental Principle of Psychoanalytic Interpretation

Psychoanalysis as a scientific method is based upon a single, very simple principle. If we do not understand a person's behavior, we seek to make it intelligible by finding its emotional context. To cite a very trivial example, if we see a man strike himself violently in the face, his behavior is likely to seem peculiar to us, but if we discover that he was killing a mosquito, we are no longer perplexed. If a man behaves as though he is angry, we try to learn more about the circumstances until we find something that seems adequate to account for his anger. If we learn that someone has made an insulting remark to him, we shall then find his anger quite "natural."

This method of attempting to understand human behavior was not invented by psychoanalysis. It is the method of the common-sense psychology of everyday life. It is essentially an intuitive method based upon the psychological knowledge, for the most part unformulated, that makes one person's behavior seem "natural" to us, whereas another person's behavior seems "strange" and "unaccountable." Psychoanalysis has merely extended the range of application of this method and has succeeded in demonstrating that even the most irrational behavior becomes "natural" and "understandable" to us if we succeed, after a long search, in finding its proper emotional context in the life history of the individual concerned.

Psychoanalytic literature is full of examples of the application of this method to the more perplexing types of behavior that are clinically known as psychoneuroses and psychoses. In order to make our discussion concrete, let us cite as illustration a brief analysis of a single life history.

A married woman with one child has an extramarital affair while her husband is in prison. She becomes pregnant. The husband is released from prison before the second child is born, but a divorce is secured and the patient wishes now to marry her lover. The lover, however, becomes evasive and is extremely reluctant to marry her, but the patient is insistent that the lover shall marry her, openly calls the children by his name, and wishes to get legal help in compelling him to marry her.

So far, perhaps, her behavior sounds not so very irrational. She has the two children to take care of, and it seems natural that she should wish to get the support of the man who is responsible for her second pregnancy. In the light of other facts, however, this appearance of rationality disappears. She admits confidentially to her therapist that she had deliberately allowed herself to become pregnant while she was still married to her husband in the hope that she might compel her lover to marry her. Moreover, it is not difficult to convince her that the marriage will almost certainly turn out badly, inasmuch as the lover is so utterly reluctant to assume any responsibility for her. Nevertheless, she is determined to force through the marriage, even though she suspects she may want to divorce the man afterward, and she gives as her motive for this determination her wish to legitimatize the child.

The question arises at once as to why the child needs to be legitimatized. Both children were conceived while she was still married, and the most practical way of avoiding unpleasant comment would be to say nothing about the paternity of the second child and to let it be tacitly assumed that the children are the children of her husband. Nevertheless, as we have seen, the patient's behavior is exactly contrary to these rational motives of social discretion. She has openly called the children by the lover's name and now insists upon giving the second child a legitimatization that by any practical standard he would not have needed, by forcing through a marriage that she herself realizes can only result in unhappiness. This behavior is obviously not intelligible in terms of the context of what we know about her present situation.

We get some light upon this patient's motivations, however, when we learn something about her early history. The patient was one of several children, but her parents separated very soon after her birth. All the other children remained with the father, but the patient was put in an orphan asylum. She was later taken into a foster home where she was well cared for until the foster-father died. After a time economic difficulties forced the foster-mother to place her with the foster-mother's own parents, who were unsympathetic and frequently asked why her own father had not kept her. After she was grown, she looked up her parents and learned that her mother had been sexually promiscuous. The father was very cold to her and expressed doubt as to whether he was really her father.

In the light of this story, the patient's behavior with reference to her lover and to her own illegitimate child becomes much more understandable. The patient has evidently brooded a great deal about the circumstances concerning her own birth. Why did the father reject her alone when he took all the other children to live with him? This is a question about which she probably would have been curious anyhow, but her foster-grandparents undoubtedly made the question all the more important to her by constantly reproaching her with it. Finally, she learned that her mother was promiscuous in her sexual relations and that the reason for her father's rejection was that he believed the patient was the child of an extramarital relationship. It will be noticed that the patient in her own behavior has identified very closely with her mother. It looks, indeed, as though she were under some compulsion to live through again the problems created by her mother's behavior. She, too, has a child from her marriage and now gets another one in an extramarital relationship. Now she is concerned with the problem of legitimatizing the child. It seems plain that her utterly impractical plan to legitimatize a child that she need not have had and that in any case could have passed as the child of her marriage is really based upon a need to legitimatize herself. She is under compulsion to do for her own illegitimate child what she feels her mother should have done for her. Her mother should have married her real father and given her a legitimate home instead of abandoning her to an orphan asylum while her supposed father kept the other children with him. Thus, in her relationship to her lover and his child, the patient is not really guided by the rational requirements of her present situation at all, but by a compulsive urge to set right, as it were by proxy, the wrong that was done to her as an illegitimate child.

Interpretation and Analysis

It will be seen from this example that the psychoanalytic method, when properly practiced, really involves no theoretical preconceptions whatsoever other than the quite unformulated psychological assumptions that guide us in our everyday relations with other human beings and for the validity of which our everyday contacts with our fellow men offer us constantly repeated empirical tests. This common-sense psychology, however, is an unformulated psychology. When we have succeeded by this method in "understanding" a person's behavior, we have not in most cases formulated the reasons for the patient's behavior in scientific terms. What we have done is first of all to enlarge our knowledge of the emotional context of the patient's behavior. After we have done this we may have little more than an intuitive sense that this person's feelings and actions are quite "natural." Nevertheless—and with justice—we speak of this kind of insight into a person's behavior as a "psychological understanding" of his reactions.

We must next inquire what must be added to this sort of psychological understanding in order to use it in arriving at valid scientific formulations. Our task will be to analyze our psychological understanding, to attempt to reconstruct in detail the steps by which different events in the life history of the patient have contributed to his present behavior, and to separate out the component causes that have contributed to it. In other words, it is useful to distinguish two successive steps in the scientific utilization of our clinical studies. We start first with the interpretation, with the attempt to find the emotional context that will make the patient's behavior seem "natural" to us. After the interpretation, we proceed to a more precise analysis. It is with this scientific analysis of behavior that has already been "psychologically understood" that the scientific formulation of our psychoanalytic observations properly begins.

It is imperative that the two steps should not be confused or condensed. As every teacher of psychoanalysis knows, there is no surer way to inhibit a student's capacity for true psychological insight than to allow him to proceed immediately to formulate his patient's material in terms of universal clichés which he has learned from his reading of psychoanalytic literature. The same principle holds true for any attempt at analysis and formulation of the extremely rich observational material that has resulted from psychoanalytic study of many different kinds of "peculiar" behavior. In order to remain upon sound scientific ground, therefore, it is important to distinguish carefully between psychoanalytic interpretation and the scientific analysis of interpreted material.

The psychoanalytic interpretation must come first. It must find, in the life history and present circumstances of the patient, the proper emotional context for his apparently irrational behavior so that his behavior becomes quite "natural" and understandable to us. Upon this psychological understanding rests the whole objectivity of our procedure Until we have an adequate psychological understanding, any attempts at more precise formulation can only lead us astray, for they will certainly have nothing to do with psychological reality. The psychological understanding must, therefore, come first and should preferably be formulated in the language of everyday life with as few theoretical implications as possible. One of the chief ways of going astray in our investigation of psychodynamic relationships arises from the loose habit of formulating our psychological observations in terms of one or another theory that happens to be popular at the moment. Just the opposite rule should guide our dynamic interpretations of behavior. Our interpretations should aim to express as simply and accurately as possible the dynamic relations implied by fitting the patient's behavior into its total emotional context and should endeavor to avoid further implications based on prevailing theories.

Once we have grasped the true sense and meaning of a patient's behavior, however, we are then ready to subject our imperfectly formulated psychological understanding to more careful analysis. A first step in this process will be to subject our interpretations to critical examination and analysis. When we have arrived at an interpretation, we must next inquire how completely it "explains" the available facts. In most cases we find that our interpretations when thus critically examined leave a number of questions still unanswered. Usually there are a number of facts that are still not adequately accounted for. This leads to a search for a still wider emotional context in order to answer the questions arising successively out of each interpretation. It was in this way that Freud, in seeking for a psychological understanding of the neuroses, was led farther and farther back into the life histories of his patients.

Reconstruction of Life Histories

Thus a critical application of the interpretative method leads us inevitably into the task which has been such a central preoccupation in the psychoanalytic literature, that of dynamic reconstruction of the life histories of individuals. Usually we find that a particular bit of "peculiar" behavior has been influenced by a considerable number of events, both present and past. We seek, therefore, to study the dynamic interrelations between these events and to reconstruct the steps by which they contributed to and cooperated in the chain of causation of which the patient's behavior was the result.

We have already illustrated the method that should be followed in such an analysis. We first examine the patient's behavior in relation to the patient's real situation at the time. Perhaps when we have gained a sufficient orientation into the patient's real situation, his behavior will seem quite intelligible. In many cases, however, careful examination of our psychological understanding in relation to the present situation will only raise new problems. In the case cited, for example, we attempted to explain the patient's behavior in terms of her desire to legitimatize the child of her extramarital relationship. Upon closer examination, this could not explain why she had deliberately allowed herself to be impregnated or why she could not allow the fact that she was married at the time to be a sufficient legitimatization of the child. We then turned to the patient's previous history and found an explanation in the patient's brooding over the circumstances of her own birth. In this case we found the explanation for her irrational need to legitimatize the child in her own need to legitimatize herself. The fact of her own "illegitimate" birth, and particularly the reproaches about it that she heard from her foster-grandparents, threw a great deal of light upon her subsequent need to legitimatize the child. We might, however, raise still further questions. This patient no longer lives with the foster-grandparents and, so far as we know, no one reproaches her any more because of the circumstances of her birth. Why, then, can she not forget about the whole matter and accept whatever satisfactions life is able to offer her at present? To attempt to answer this question, we should have to learn still more about her life history and her reactions to it and seek for a still wider emotional context.

Thus, as a rule, when we have once succeeded in finding an explanation for "irrational" behavior, closer examination of our interpretation will usually disclose still other problems that can be solved only by searching farther and farther back into the patient's life history for the wider emotional context that is necessary to explain each new discrepancy. In this way we arrive at more and more complete reconstructions of the psychological sense of the patient's life history.

GENERALIZATIONS FROM PSYCHOANALYTIC DATA

Psychodynamic Mechanisms

The goal of science is not merely to find explanations for particular cases, but rather to formulate generalizations that are valid for many different cases. In this task of formulating valid generalizations, we start again with "common-sense psychology." We have based our interpretations upon the psychological assumptions that guide us in our everyday relations with other people. These assumptions already imply generalizations about human behavior, but these generalizations are for the most part unformulated. Our first task is to formulate them, to make them explicit.

In this task we are aided by the fact that psychoanalysis has succeeded in extending the application of these assumptions to behavior that at first sight seemed quite peculiar. The elucidation of "peculiar" behavior has the advantage that it throws into relief relationships which we might otherwise take for granted. When a machine is running smoothly there is often little incentive to study its mechanisms, but when it gets out of order, our attention is called to those mechanisms responsible for its failure to function. For this reason, as Freud has often pointed out, the study of psychopathology has been of enormous service in contributing to our knowledge of the "normal" psychology of everyday life. By studying the psychological contexts that throw light upon the symptoms of mental illness, we are able to see in isolated and exaggerated form dynamic relationships that can easily be overlooked and taken quite for granted in our everyday "understanding" of more usual behavior. Making use of these highlights which psychopathology can throw upon the dynamic mechanisms of normal behavior, psychoanalysis has already made considerable progress in the task of formulating scientific generalizations.

A first step was the description of psychodynamic mechanisms that are encountered over and over again in our patients' material. It will perhaps be of interest to discuss a few of the more important of these psychodynamic mechanisms.

The first mechanism to be described was the mechanism of repression. In their first studies of hysteria by means of hypnosis, Breuer and Freud discovered that many hysterical symptoms could be traced back to the memory of a disturbing experience that had been pushed out of consciousness and forgotten. Under hypnosis patients could be induced to bring such memories back to consciousness and to relive and discharge the disturbing emotions. The pushing of the disturbing memory out of consciousness, Freud called repression; and the discharge of the repressed affects that took place (in these cases under hypnosis), he called abreaction. After such recall of a repressed memory and the abreaction of the accompanying affects, the associated hysterical symptom often disappeared.

Thus repression was first defined in subjective terms as the exclusion from consciousness of psychic impulses or other psychic content which nevertheless continue to exert a dynamic influence upon behavior. Inasmuch as the repressed impulse is still active, it will usually be replaced in consciousness and in the patient's overt behavior by some substitute. This is the mechanism of substitution or displacement. To cite one of Freud's examples (Freud, 1893), "a highly intelligent man assists while his brother's ankylosed hip is straightened under an anaesthetic. At the instant when the joint gives way with a crack he feels a violent pain in his own hip joint which lasts for almost a year." Indeed, hysterical symptoms are quite regularly to be understood as substitute manifestations for some repressed impulse or affect.

By studying such substitute phenomena in relation to the more complete emotional context, it is frequently possible to infer the memory or other content that has undergone repression. Freud's patient Dora, for example (Freud, 1905a), told him once how Mr. K had suddenly embraced and kissed her. She pulled herself loose and ran away with feelings of disgust. Afterward she could not bear to go near any man whom she saw talking tenderly or earnestly to a woman. Besides this, she often experienced as a hallucinatory sensation the pressure of Mr. K's embrace about the upper part of her body. Piecing these facts together, Freud inferred that Dora's disgust and flight had been a reaction to her awareness of sexual excitement upon Mr. K's part, which, however, she had repressed. The hallucinatory sensations about her chest, Freud suspected, owed their persistence to a displacement of this perception and of her own sexual excitement. Frequently such inferences are confirmed after a shorter or longer period by the patient's recovery of the actual memory.

Very many of the psychodynamic mechanisms may be regarded as special cases of substitution. When a repressed impulse is replaced by another impulse of a character opposite or antagonistic to it, we speak of reaction formation. Dora's disgust in the instance just cited is a good example of this mechanism.

The mechanism of projection may be defined as a tendency to react to dynamic tendencies within one's own personality as though the tendency in question belonged to someone else instead of to oneself. A classical example is the mechanism of the paranoid patient who reacts to his own unconscious recognition of homosexual impulses in himself by imagining that others are accusing him of homosexuality. This is the mechanism that plays a predominant role in cases of paranoia and paranoid schizophrenia; it is also encountered in less virulent forms in many other types of neurotic illness and may even play a role in the behavior of relatively normal persons.

A converse mechanism of introjection has also been described, according to which one reacts to someone else's wishes or tendencies as though they were one's own. This is a mechanism encountered with especial frequency in cases of melancholia. A beautiful example is cited by Helene Deutsch (1932). A woman who had been living alone with her little dog developed a severe melancholia when the dog ran away. So trivial a cause can obviously not offer a complete explanation for the development of a severe psychotic reaction. This patient's psychosis becomes much more understandable to us when we learn that this woman had devoted her whole life to a younger sister and that this sister a few years before had married and moved away to a distant country, leaving the patient to live a lonely life with no other companion than this little dog. The central theme of the patient's psychosis was her delusion that she was to be abandoned naked on the street to die a terrible death. Analysis disclosed that the source of this delusion was the patient's unconscious bitter reproach against the sister who had deserted her after accepting her love and care for so many years. It is not difficult to understand that this woman, who has been left all alone by the sister to whom she had devoted most of her life, should now feel in her bitterness that such a sister deserves to be cruelly deprived of all the love and care that she had received, by being put out naked upon the street to die a terrible death. In the psychosis, however, the patient turned this reproach back upon herself. In her delusion it was she and not the sister who was to receive this punishment. The murderously bitter reproach against the sister has been "introjected."

Two other mechanisms of very general importance are fixation and regression. Traumatic experiences or difficulties in adjustment which cannot be faced and worked out regularly result in an arrest of emotional development at this point. Freud calls this fixation. As an example we may cite the fixation upon the conflicts induced by the training of the infant in cleanliness that is regularly found in cases of obsessional neurosis. In such patients impulses to play with dirt and energetic reaction formations, such as washing compulsions and other forms of obsessive cleanliness, may persist throughout life. In milder cases, however, this conflict may recede into the background but, after some frustration such as disappointment in a love affair, may appear again later in life and give rise to an obsessional neurosis. Such return to a conflict belonging to an earlier period of development Freud calls regression.

Other Generalizations from Psychoanalytic Data—Typical Life Histories

By reconstructing and comparing many life histories, psychoanalysis has also been able to reconstruct certain typical conflict situations which occur with a somewhat restricted number of variations in the life history of every individual. Conflicts over weaning, toilet training, rivalry with brothers and sisters, sexual investigation beginning early in childhood and leading to sexual interest in parents, brothers, or sisters, and often to intense jealousy based upon these sexual attachments—these are some of the earliest conflict situations whose importance had been very little realized until psychoanalysis was able to call attention to them. Other conflicts belonging to later periods, and especially the relations of these later conflicts to the earlier ones, have also had much light thrown upon them by psychoanalytic investigation.

Very considerable progress has been made also in describing features that are characteristic of the life history of individuals suffering from particular types of disorders. We know, for example (Freud, 1913), that severe childhood conflicts over toilet training are regularly found in the life history of patients who later suffer from compulsion neuroses. Depressive reactions (Freud, 1917) are particularly likely to occur in reaction to the loss of a loved object toward whom the patient has also entertained strong but repressed feelings of hostility. Paranoia, as Freud (1911) pointed out in his analysis of the Schreber case, seems quite typically to be associated with strong homosexual impulses which the patient is usually unable to avow and which he therefore attempts to handle by the mechanism of projection, either attributing the homosexual impulses themselves to others or thinking of himself as falsely accused by others. These are but a few examples of the generalizations that psychoanalysis has been able to establish concerning the psychogenic history of well-known clinical syndromes.

Studies of this kind are, of course, only first steps toward the solution of what Freud has called the problem of "choice of neurosis." We should like to be able to predict, from the previous history of an individual, under just what circumstances behavior disorders would develop and just what would be the nature of the pathological behavior to be expected. At the present time, indeed, psychoanalysts of experience are often able to make some shrewd guesses of this sort, but the factors involved are still too complex to admit of any high degree of certainty in such predictions. The problems of "choice of neurosis" still require much future investigation for their final solution.

For such future investigations, a much more minute and detailed study of the voluminous data that are available whenever an analysis is carefully recorded will probably be important. Indeed, we encounter the problem of "choice of neurosis" again in miniature if we make the attempt, for example, to compare the different dreams of a single patient and to account in detail for their similarities and differences by studying the previous life history and the events that have occurred in the intervals between them. Such studies aim to account for the recurrent patterns that run through a patient's life and dreams in terms of the frustrating and facilitating events of his life history. Upon this background, the progressive influence of the analysis can be traced as a sort of emotional learning process correcting the earlier patterns. Studies of this kind are being made especially by Rado (1955) and by the writer (French, 1936, 1937a, 1937b, 1939).

CLINICAL DATA AS ORIENTATION FOR EXPERIMENTAL STUDIES

As will be seen in the following chapters, the extremely rich clinical material that has been accumulated by the psychoanalytic method of observation now offers us an orientation that should be extremely valuable in guiding us to problems that can be profitably investigated by experimental methods.

It should be emphasized, however, that the problems suitable for clinical and for experimental investigation are not always the same. Those who wish to make use of the insights that have resulted from psychoanalytic investigations should, therefore, not content themselves with summarizing psychoanalytic concepts and theories, but should rather familiarize themselves sufficiently with the fundamental psychoanalytic method of interpreting behavior by searching for its emotional context, so that they will be able to evaluate clinical data upon their own merits. Too often attempts to "validate" psychoanalytic conclusions by experiment lead to evidence much less conclusive than the original clinical data upon which the conclusions were based. Experimental data must also be interpreted, and the interpretations of such data can often be less carefully controlled than our clinical data which take so much more careful account of the whole psychological context.

It is quite futile, for example, to try to test by experiment whether there is such a thing as repression of disturbing mental content. In this case the clinical evidence is quite incontrovertible and the experimental evidence not very conclusive. Equally incontrovertible is the accompanying evidence of displaced gratification of repressed impulses. Experimental studies of substitution (see Sears, in J. McV. Hunt, ed., *Personality and the Behavior Disorders*, 1944) have indeed yielded results that are interesting and significant in themselves but can hardly be regarded as a test of the validity of the clinical observations. Probably the clinical and the experimental observations are dealing with data that are not altogether comparable. The laws that govern the displacement of repressed impulses and affects probably differ considerably from those that prevail in the less traumatic situations that result from the artificial interruption of activities. A study of these differences, however, might offer a starting point for a very promising investigation.

In general, a much more fruitful kind of cooperation between clinical and experimental approaches is to use the clinical observations as cues to point to problems that are in need of much more detailed investigation. Every psychoanalyst whose eyes are open to the scientific as well as to the therapeutic implications of his work is aware of many such problems which the exigencies of the therapeutic situation or the complexity of the clinical data do not permit him to follow further but which might be quite suitable for experimental analysis. The psychoanalytic mechanisms, for example, are phenomena isolated enough to to be quite suitable topics for experimental investigation. As one example out of very many, I may cite the question as to what conditions determine whether projection or introjection shall be used as a defense. A good example of the kind of attempted synthesis of clinical and experimental studies that I have in mind is Dr. Sears's analysis of the concepts of fixation and regression in the light of a long series of experimental studies. Very interesting and significant also are attempts like those of J. McV. Hunt (1941) and D. M. Levy (1934 and 1938) to subject animals to experimental procedures similar to some of the common traumata of childhood in order to reproduce and subject to experimental analysis the disorders that are encountered clinically in persons who have histories of similar childhood traumata. It is along lines such as these that clinical and experimental methods will best be able to supplement each other.

BIBLIOGRAPHY

The following list is not intended as a complete bibliography. Such a bibliography would cover almost the entire psychoanalytic literature. It is intended rather as a selected reading list for those who wish to make themselves more familiar with psychoanalysis as a method of scientific investigation. I have therefore included in it a number of Freud's own descriptions of the development of his method and also a considerable amount of illustrative case material, and have added a few papers on mechanisms of particular neuroses and on experimental studies of problems suggested by clinical observations.

PSYCHOANALYTIC METHOD

Alexander, F. 1936. Medical value of psychoanalysis. (2nd ed.) New York: Norton.

Freud, A. 1937. The ego and the mechanisms of defense. London: Hogarth.

Freud, S. 1893. On the psychical mechanism of hysterical phenomena. In *Collected papers.* Vol. 1. London: International Psycho-analytical Press, 1924. Pp. 24–42.

———— 1904a. Freud's psychoanalytic method. In *Collected papers.* Vol. 1. London: International Psycho-analytical Press, 1924. Pp. 264–72.

———— 1912. The dynamics of the transference. In *Collected papers.* Vol. 2, London: Hogarth, 1924. Pp. 312–23.

———— 1914. Further recommendations in the technique of psycho-analysis. Recollection, repetition and working through. In *Collected papers.* Vol. 2. London: Hogarth, 1924. Pp. 366–76.

———— 1920. Introductory lectures on psycho-analysis. London: Allen & Unwin, 1936.

ILLUSTRATIVE CASE MATERIAL

Alexander, F., & Healy, W. 1935. Roots of crime. New York: Knopf.

Deutsch, H. 1932. Psycho-analysis of the neuroses. London: Hogarth.

Freud, S. 1900. The interpretation of dreams. In *The basic writings of Sigmund Freud.* New York: Modern Library, 1938.

———— 1904b. Psychopathology of everyday life. London: Fisher & Unwin, 1914.

———— 1905a. Fragment of an analysis of a case of hysteria. In *Collected papers*. Vol. 3. London: Hogarth, 1925. Pp. 13–146.

———— 1905b. Wit and its relation to the unconscious. In *The basic writings of Sigmund Freud*. New York: Modern Library, 1938.

———— 1909. Notes upon a case of obsessional neurosis. In *Collected papers*. Vol. 3. London: Hogarth, 1925. Pp. 296–383.

———— 1911. Psychoanalytic notes upon an autobiographical account of a case of paranoia. In *Collected papers*. Vol. 3. London: Hogarth, 1925. Pp. 390–470.

ADDITIONAL PAPERS ON MECHANISMS OF PARTICULAR NEUROSES

Freud, S. 1913. A predisposition to obsessional neurosis. In *Collected papers*. Vol. 2. London: Hogarth, 1924. Pp. 122–33.

———— 1917. Mourning and melancholia. In *Collected papers*. Vol. 4. London: Hogarth, 1925. Pp. 152–73.

———— 1922. Certain neurotic mechanisms in jealousy, paranoia and homosexuality. In *Collected papers*. Vol. 2. London: Hogarth, 1924. Pp. 232–44.

MICROSCOPIC AND COMPARATIVE DREAM STUDIES

French, T. M. 1936. A clinical study of learning in the course of a psychoanalytic treatment. *Psychoanal. Quart.*, *5*, 148–94. Chapter 3 of this volume.

———— 1937a. Reality-testing in dreams. *Psychoanal. Quart.*, *6*, 62–77. Chapter 5 of this volume.

———— 1937b. Reality and the unconscious. *Psychoanal. Quart.*, *6*, 23–61. Chapter 2 of this volume.

———— 1939. Insight and distortion in dreams. *Int. J. Psycho-Anal.*, *20*, 287–98. Chapter 4 of this volume.

EXPERIMENTAL STUDIES

Hunt, J. McV. 1941. The effects of infant feeding-frustration upon adult hoarding in the albino rat. *J. Abnorm. Soc. Psychol.*, *36*, 338–60.

Hunt, J. McV., & Willoughby, R. R. 1939. The effect of frustration on hoarding in rats. *Psychosom. Med.*, *1*, 309–10.

Levy, D. M. 1934. Experiments on the sucking reflex and social behavior in dogs. *Amer. J. Orthopsychiat.*, *4*, 203–24.

———— 1938. On instinct satiation; an experiment on the pecking behavior of chickens. *J. Genet. Psychol.*, *18*, 327–48.

Chapter Nineteen

EGO ANALYSIS AS A
GUIDE TO THERAPY

In his earliest therapeutic efforts, Freud interpreted to the patient his repressed psychic contents. Later he learned that the repressed mental contents could only be brought to consciousness by analysis of the ego's defenses against them.

The ego's defenses, however, are only one aspect of the ego's central function of synthesis or integration. The aim of therapy is to improve this synthetic integrative function. It follows, therefore, that as therapists we should focus our attention primarily neither upon the repressed impulses nor upon the ego's defenses alone, but rather upon the integrative function of the ego, upon the specific integrative task that confronts the ego at each point in the analysis, upon the problem that at each particular moment the ego is attempting to solve.

In our psychoanalytic thinking we are accustomed much of the time to think of a patient's irrational behavior as a compulsive repetition of traumatic childhood events. It is this concept that underlies Freud's definition of the "transference." We think of the patient as having transferred, to his present situation in the analysis, attitudes and reaction patterns that first arose in and were appropriate reactions to a childhood situation. In therapy, however, it is equally important to recognize a tendency in exactly the opposite direction. Every patient has innumerable memories. One day one of these memories will emerge, another day, quite a different chain of memories. One of the principles that determines the selection of particular memories for reactivation at particular times is the principle that each situation in the present tends to reactivate

Reprinted from *Psychoanalytic Quarterly*, 14 (1945).

memories of similar situations with which the patient has been faced in the past.

It is easy to see that this principle has an adaptive significance. Every reaction to a present situation must be based in large part upon past experience. Past experience, however, is a vast storehouse of memories. The reaction patterns from the past that are likely to be most useful in the present situation are obviously those that dealt with similar situations in the past. One must search in the past for precedents that could be useful in solving a present problem. In therapy, therefore, it is not only important to recognize the influence of patterns from the past upon present behavior; but, for our practical guidance from day to day, it is even more important to recognize that the choice of particular memories for reactivation is determined in largest part by the particular problem in adaptation with which the ego is struggling at the moment.

In this chapter we have utilized this principle as a guide in the discussion of a number of technical problems: (1) in interpreting two different kinds of dreams of seduction; (2) in permitting the analyst to read directly from the material a valid critical judgment upon his own handling of the therapy as well as important indications as to what his own next step in the therapy should be; (3) in indicating to the analyst times when, instead of trying to "overcome" the patient's resistance, he should actually encourage the resistance as a much needed buffer to keep the patient from plunging into disturbing material too rapidly; and (4) in cultivating a flexible approach to the problem of terminating the analysis.

1. THE EGO'S PROBLEM IN ADAPTATION AND ITS IMPORTANCE IN THERAPY

We are all familiar with Freud's account of the historical development of his own attitudes toward psychoanalytic therapy. In his early therapeutic efforts he directly interpreted repressed psychic contents and was even somewhat annoyed, as the dream of Irma's injection shows, if the patient was not able to accept his interpretation. Later, however, he came to realize that repressed mental contents could only be brought to consciousness by analyzing the ego's defenses against them.

It has now become a standard principle of psychoanalytic technique, therefore, not to interpret the repressed content of id impulses directly without first carefully orienting oneself as to the nature and strength of the ego's defenses against them. The fascination of deep unconscious material is so great, however, that even the most experienced analysts are frequently tempted to violate this important technical principle, and beginners in psychoanalysis usually find it much easier to recognize and interpret immediately repressed unconscious wishes than to restrain their delight in discovery until they have gone to the trouble of orienting themselves carefully as to the relation of these repressed impulses to the patient's conscious attitudes and behavior.

In the following discussion I wish both to illustrate this well-recognized and well-established technical principle and to propose an extension of it. The principles that I wish to suggest are, I believe, practiced intuitively, at least at times, by most experienced psychoanalysts, but I wish to propose a systematic elaboration and application of them.

Analysis of the resistances focuses our attention on the ego's defenses and upon the defensive function of the ego. The ego's defenses, however, are only one aspect of its more important and central function, the function of synthesis or integration. The aim of therapy is to improve this synthetic or integrative function. It seems to follow, therefore, that in therapy our attention should be focused primarily neither upon the repressed impulses nor upon the ego's defenses alone, but rather upon the integrative function of the ego, upon the specific integrative task that confronts the ego at each point in the analysis, upon the problem that at each particular moment the ego is attempting to solve.

How can this be done? Obviously, in order to understand the ego's integrative task at a particular moment we must first discover both the nature of the repressed wishes that are struggling to emerge into consciousness and also the nature of the defenses of the ego against these repressed wishes. But we must also attempt to reconstruct something more. We need to know not only the motives that have been repressed but also the motives that have given rise to the defensive reaction. It is important to determine, for example, whether a disturbing sexual impulse has been repressed on account of fear of punishment, of fear of loss of the mother's love, of guilt, or of pride. Then, when we have determined the motive of the defense, we are ready to reconstruct the integrative problem with which the ego is faced at this particular moment.

In each of the four cases above mentioned, for example, the ego's problem will be different. In one case the patient's problem will be either to find some outlet for his sexual impulses without incurring punishment or to find some way of reconciling himself to the punishment. In another the problem will be either to find some way of making the disturbing impulse acceptable to the mother or to find some substitute that will make the patient less dependent upon the mother. In still another case, the problem may be either to find some way of compensating for the patient's injured pride or to modify the disturbing sexual impulse so as to make it consistent with the patient's pride.

In order to reconstruct the ego's problem, however, we must not only determine the nature of the conflicting motives but also take into account the patient's real situation in relation to them. A patient whose central problem is to reconcile sexual impulses with his need for his mother's love, for example, will find his problem much simplified if some mother figure has just indicated to him what he might do to please her.

Formulated from a somewhat different point of view, the ego's integrative problem at any particular moment is the problem in adaptation presented to the ego by the actual situation at that time. For the sake of clarity, however, it is important to emphasize that it is not only the real external situation that constitutes the ego's problem, but more the conflicting needs with which the patient is reacting to this situation. It will be noticed that such an approach to therapy focuses our attention systematically upon the patient's actual conflict at the moment, rather than upon infantile memories.

In our psychoanalytic thinking we are accustomed much of the time to think of a patient's irrational behavior as a compulsive repetition of traumatic childhood events. It is this concept that underlies Freud's definition of the "transference." We think of the patient as having transferred, to his present situation in the analysis, attitudes and reaction patterns that first arose in, and were appropriate reactions to, a childhood situation. Our psychoanalytic experience in fact furnishes us with numerous dramatic examples of almost complete reenactment in the analytic situation of traumatic events from the patient's past.

Such complete and dramatic reenactments of a past event are exceptional, however, even in an analysis. This can be explained only on the assumption that the tendency to react according to the pattern of the past is only one of the tendencies that contribute to ordinary behavior. Equally important for the understanding of our therapeutic situations is a tendency in exactly the opposite direction. Every patient has innumerable memories. Different memories emerge on different days. One of the principles that determines the selection of particular memories for reactivation at particular times is that each situation in the present tends to reactivate memories of similar situations with which the patient has been faced in the past.

It is easy to see that this principle has an adaptive significance. Every reaction to a present situation must be based in large part upon past experience. Past experience, however, is a vast storehouse of memories. If all of these memories could be reactivated at once, the result would be hopeless confusion. If past experience is to serve a useful function in guiding behavior in the present, it is necessary that the present exert a selective influence on the choice of the particular memories that are to be reactivated. The reaction patterns from the past that are likely to be most useful in solving present problems are obviously those that dealt with similar situations. One must search in the past for precedents that could be useful in solving a present problem. It is therefore to be expected that there is a tendency for a present situation to select for reactivation those memories and behavior patterns that dealt with similar problems in the past.

The application of these principles to our therapeutic problem can be formulated thus: in therapy it is not only important to recognize the influence of patterns from the past upon present behavior, but, for our practical guidance from day to day, it is even more important to recognize that the choice of particular memories for reactivation is determined in largest part by the particular problem in adaptation with which the ego is struggling at the moment. It is this problem in adaptation about which our therapy must be oriented.

A thesis such as this could probably best be illustrated by a somewhat extended account of the therapy of particular cases. Because of the limitation of time and other motives, however, it will be necessary in this paper to illustrate it only by a series of anecdotes.

2. Significance of Dreams of Seduction

Frequently a patient brings us dreams or other material in which the analyst is accused of seducing the patient. If we are interested only in the repressed wish, we may interpret such material as evidence of the patient's wish to be seduced. The defense in this case would be projection, one of accusing the analyst of seducing rather than acknowledging the wish to be seduced. Both of these interpretations would be correct as far as they go, but they would miss the point of the material insofar as therapeutic indications are concerned. In a very considerable proportion of cases, dreams of seduction are a reaction to the therapeutic process itself. The patient comes to the analysis with certain forbidden sexual wishes which have been repressed on account of guilt. The analysis then surprises the patient by seeming to give encouragement to these disturbing wishes. The patient's conscience is startled and then reacts to the analysis as a dangerous seduction. It follows that this accusation against the analyst is not only a projection but has also some basis in reality. The therapeutic indication is, therefore, to recognize the truth contained in the patient's accusation and then to proceed further to point out the differences between psychoanalysis and seduction, to point out that the purpose of the analysis is only to encourage a patient to become conscious of her sexual impulses and to enable her to discuss them freely; but that the question of what she should do about them is obviously one that she herself must decide, after taking into account both the disturbing impulses themselves and the reactions of her conscience against them.

In other cases, the accusation implied in the patient's material goes further than this. The patient in a dream will perhaps picture the analyst as indulging quite openly in unabashed sexual activities with her, the implication being that the therapy has become some kind of perverse sexual activity for both therapist and patient. Again if we were interested only in the repressed mental content we would be compelled to interpret such material as evidence of an extremely open avowal of sexual wishes toward the analyst; and again the defense is projection. From the point of view of the therapeutic problem, however, such interpretations would once more miss the point entirely. Most frequently such material is a sign that the patient has forgotten the therapeutic purpose for which she originally consulted the analyst, and without admitting it to herself is utilizing the analysis primarily as a source of erotic gratification; but the accusation against the analyst also usually has its justification in reality, in that the analyst has failed to recognize this transference resistance. Thus, having failed to recall her to her therapeutic task by pointing out the resistance, the analyst has laid himself open to the charge that he also is responsible for the patient's resistance. In such cases the therapeutic indication is to do just what the patient's material is accusing the analyst of failing to do—to interpret the patient's self-indulgent utilization of the analysis as a source of erotic gratification and thus to call her back to her therapeutic task. Here it will be noticed that the dream, when properly interpreted, practically prescribes what the analyst's next therapeutic step should be.

3. THE PATIENT'S MATERIAL AS A THERAPEUTIC GUIDE

It will be noted that in both these cases the patient's material not only gives us definite indications as to the nature of the patient's own conflict, but also permits the analyst to read directly from the material a valid critical judgment upon his own handling of the therapy as well as important indications as to what his own next therapeutic step should be. This I believe to be a principle of quite general validity. In supervising the analysis of students, I have frequently noted rather sharp changes in the character of the transference relationship as soon as the student analyst corrected an important error in his handling of the case. A frequent change of this sort is the following: The patient, throughout his material, may be identifying the analyst with an indulgent mother. The supervising analyst then discovers that the student analyst has been failing to interpret important material or to follow up his interpretations properly with interpretation of confirmatory evidence. The student, returning to the patient, then makes the necessary interpretations and follows them up energetically by pointing out the supporting evidence in the succeeding material. As a result of the student's more energetic interpretations, the patient's material now promptly identifies him no longer with an indulgent mother but rather with a punishing father. In Chapter 3 above, I have already given an illustration of such a sudden transition in the patient's material from a "depreciated younger brother" transference to a "dangerous father" transference immediately after I had taken effective measures not to cooperate further in the patient's attempt to make play of the analysis.

In other cases the patient's material may indicate that the analyst has plunged too quickly into disturbing emotional conflicts. Fortunately, if we can learn to read them, the patient's behavior and associations usually give us very precise day-to-day indications as to how much interpretation the patient can tolerate. If the therapist is alert to such indications, he can usually become quickly aware of the patient's inability to tolerate a disturbing insight. As an example, I may cite a patient to whom a premature interpretation of a homosexual conflict was made. The next day the patient made no reference to this interpretation but in his associations revolving about a dream there repeatedly occurred the theme of people going insane. It was obvious that the patient feared unconsciously that facing this interpretation would drive him "crazy."

The therapist therefore wisely refrained from pressing the interpretation further and simply remarked, "I think my interpretation yesterday must have frightened you." The patient thought a moment, then said, "To tell you the truth, Doctor, I can't remember what your interpretation was." Interpretation for a considerable period thereafter centered upon the patient's fear. After a period of about a month, however, this fear had diminished sufficiently so that the original interpretation could be repeated, and this time the patient was much better able to face and discuss it.

4. RELIEVING ANXIETY BY ENCOURAGING RESISTANCE

Not infrequently the natural reactions of the analyst tend to mislead him as to the significance of particular types of material in relation to the therapeutic process. It is especially easy for most of us to be misled in this way by defenses that have an aggressive character. As an example, I may cite a social worker who began her analysis with an elaborate case history of her parents and a desire to discuss the parents' problems as she might have discussed the problems of some of her clients. After this there was a very evident need to be extremely technical in the discussion of her own mechanisms. It was obvious that the patient was attempting to play the role of analyst instead of accepting the role of patient. An analyst susceptible to such competition from his patients might have interpreted this as an aggressive and competitive masculine identification. He might easily have justified such an interpretation, for competitive motives of masculine identification did actually play a considerable role in this patient's behavior.

Such an interpretation would have missed the real significance of this patient's need at this time to emphasize her profession by discussing herself technically as a case history. As was abundantly confirmed by later material, this patient's need to maintain her role as a case worker in relation to the analyst was an attempt at intellectual mastery of the unconscious but intense anxiety with which the patient was approaching the beginning of her treatment. The problem in adaptation with which the patient was struggling was therefore the problem of overcoming her anxiety sufficiently to make it possible for her really to discuss her own personal problems. If the analyst had interpreted this resistance as motivated by an aggressive impulse toward himself it would only have increased the patient's anxiety. It would have driven the patient into a vicious circle, since an increase in her anxiety might easily have caused her to react more aggressively and thus stimulate further the analyst's own need to "overcome her resistance."

As soon as we realize, however, that the patient's therapeutic problem is not one of overcoming a resistance, but one of mastering anxiety, we see that the indication is not to push the patient at all to overcome her resistance. Our task is first to interpret her anxiety, and then to compare the analytic process to a child's gradually overcoming his fear in learning to swim or ride horseback, and to explain to her that there is no hurry.

In this particular case the analyst even went so far as to encourage her resistance. The patient herself was consciously very determined to "overcome" her "resistance" and kept reproaching herself about her difficulty in bringing associative material. To this the analyst replied that her attempt to drive herself was having the same effect upon her anxiety that an attempt on the part of the analyst to do the same thing might have had. It was only frightening her the more. Making use of the analogy of learning to swim or ride horseback, the analyst explained to her that the best way to overcome her fear was not to drive herself but to try to relax. She must wait patiently until a gradual relaxation of her anxiety permitted her material to emerge spontaneously. In these explanations the analyst even went so far as to point out to her the essentially protective function of the resistance as a much needed buffer which kept her from plunging into disturbing material too rapidly. In other words, the therapeutic indication at this time was to put the patient as much at ease as possible and to wait for the effect of a diminution of anxiety, which would make it possible for her in good time to bring out the content of the disturbing conflicts.

As the analysis progressed, there appeared at first dreams which gave expression to the patient's acute anxiety or which attempted to reassure her against it. In one such dream she was on a narrow, insecure bridge, walking over a stream far below. Later the anxiety gradually began to appear in consciousness. It then became possible to sense that the anxiety was in reaction to extremely masochistic impulses in the transference. These masochistic impulses toward the analyst were themselves, as is so frequently the case, a reaction to a conflict between aggressive competitive impulses toward her mother and the patient's need to remain secure in her mother's love, a need which proved to be very important in this patient's life.

Just as hints of this masochistic transference were beginning to appear in the material, the patient one day confessed that she was withholding something. She asked if it were really necessary for her to tell it. Then for several days she was tortured by acute anxiety which made sleep impossible, while she was struggling in vain to overcome her resistance against telling me the thoughts that she was suppressing. After this futile procedure had continued for several hours in succession, it finally occurred to me to ask myself a very simple question. Since this material seemed to be so painful, why was it that the patient had not succeeded in protecting herself more effectively against it by repressing it? This question gave me the clue to the real meaning of her behavior. It was evidently necessary for the patient to suffer. Her telling me that she had some associations that she was withholding was motivated by the unconscious wish to provoke me to extract the disturbing material from her painfully. The patient must have had a need to convert the analysis into a painful process, in which she was to be compelled to make most disturbing confessions. When this was pointed out to her, she brought immediate confirmation by recalling a time when another psychiatrist, years before, had actually succeeded after a long struggle in dragging disturbing material out of her. In the light of the hints that had preceded, we can now sense that this need to make the analysis such a painful process was motivated by the urge to justify herself in utilizing the analysis for emotional gratification with the analyst as a father figure.

5. The Problem of Terminating the Analysis

The problem of termination of the analysis is one about which much has been written. Sometimes for long periods nothing new seems to be brought out by an analysis. It seems to be dragging out indefinitely. The analyst's conscience then may be disturbed by what seems a futile procedure. It is probably in reaction to such feelings of discomfort that proposals have frequently been made in the psychoanalytic literature for the analyst to set a definite date for the termination of the analysis. As we know, Freud experimented with this device of setting a date for termination; but he discussed it in terms which implied that he considered it an authoritative act, one which would probably injure the prestige of the analyst in the patient's eyes should the analyst be compelled later to change his mind.

The question as to termination or interruption of the analysis looks different, however, if we consider it in terms of the concept of the analysis as a learning process. The therapeutic problem then becomes one of whether the patient will learn more inside or outside the analysis.

From this point of view, an analysis may be divided into three phases. In the beginning the patient is usually dealing with a problem of adjusting to the analysis itself. In the example cited above, the problem was one of overcoming the patient's fear of the analysis. Some such resistance to the analytic process itself must be dealt with at the beginning of every analysis.

Later the problems with which the patient must deal are those in his or her real life situation for which he has in the past been unable to find a solution. Then, as a result of the emotional support which the patient receives from his relationship to the analyst, the intensity of these conflicts is somewhat reduced, so that he becomes able step by step to find a more satisfactory solution for these problems in real life.

If the analysis proceeds satisfactorily, the patient's adjustment in real life situations ultimately becomes relatively satisfactory and his problem then begins to take on another character. It becomes more and more one of dispensing with the emotional support derived from his relationship to the analyst and attempting to test out his newly won adjustments to real life without the aid of the analyst. Quite obviously the therapeutic indication will now be to broach the problem of interrupting or terminating the analysis.

In my experience it is usually neither necessary nor desirable to do this in an authoritative manner. Often at first the mere suggestion that the analysis ought to be terminated at some time will mobilize quite sufficiently the patient's conflict about getting along without analysis. The motives that induce the patient to cling to the therapy can then be analyzed. After these motives have been analyzed, either patient or therapist may then proceed to more definite plans for interruption or termination.

In the discussion of the patient's reactions to the prospect of termination, the analyst may profitably compare the problem to that of a child learning to accept weaning or learning to walk without support.

There need be nothing arbitrary about a decision to terminate analysis on a particular date. Such a suggestion can be made as a quite tentative or experimental one. It may be that both patient and analyst have misjudged the intensity of the weaning conflict, and in such a case, when approached in this way, there can be no harm in postponing the date agreed upon. When this happens, the patient's discovery that his resistance to leaving the analysis is so intense will in itself be an instructive experience. Usually for the same reason it is well not to think in terms of irrevocable termination of an analysis but rather in terms of an experimental interruption to determine whether the patient can permanently dispense with the analyst's aid.

Very fortunately if the analyst keeps alert and considers the patient's reactions as a learning process, the material will usually give definite indications of when the possibility of interruption or termination should be broached. One of the surest signs is material alluding to the length of the analysis—projected material protesting that the analyst is dragging out the analysis unnecessarily, or associative trends finding excuses for continuing in analysis, or unconscious material centering about birth, weaning, or other problems of separation from parental support.

Such associative trends are very often interpreted as resistance against bringing out unconscious material. The analyst, stimulated perhaps by the desire to recover some suspected infantile memories, may allow the analysis to be dragged out for a long time. Instead of thus clinging vainly to the hope of satisfying his curiosity, the analyst should rather concentrate attention on the patient's own unconscious realization that he is clinging to the analysis for emotional support and that he is neglecting the task that lies ahead, which is to learn to get along without the analyst. Very often in such cases the only way to induce the patient to bring out the suspected memories may be to confront him with the problem in adjustment to real life of which the particular memory may have been just one example.

To illustrate, we may cite the case of a patient who during a long analysis had developed keen insight into very many of her problems. At the time we are now considering she was bringing many dreams which were relatively easy to interpret. These she discussed in the analytic hours with a great deal of interest. She seemed to be the ideal cooperative patient, but the numerous dream analyses brought out merely the same insights that had been discussed many times.

After a time, however, she herself began to be impatient and to protest that her analysis was lasting too long. Finally she proposed that the analysis ought soon to be terminated. The analyst did not discourage her in this decision, and after a short discussion a date was set for termination after about one month more of analysis.

The next day, however, the patient reported that in the preceding twenty-four hours she had been obsessed with a sudden and complete skepticism about the validity of her whole analysis. All that she had previously learned about herself and that she had come so enthusiastically to accept, she now felt to be "all hooey."

The meaning of this sudden skepticism was, of course, not difficult to guess. This patient's acceptance of interpretations had been only one side of an unconscious bargain. If the analyst would give her the emotional satisfaction and support of listening to and appreciating her keen intuitive understanding of dream analysis, then the patient would be quite content to believe what he told her and to accept his interpretations; but if the emotional satisfaction that she derived from the analysis must be renounced, then she was no longer willing to pay him the compliment of accepting his interpretations.

This reaction now made doubly clear the approaching problem in adaptation. Her next task must be to struggle through to an independent insight that no longer need be supported by the reward of fascinating intellectual discussions with the analyst. Inasmuch as the patient's reaction indicates so clearly that this is the problem, we may take this reaction as an excellent confirmation of the decision of the previous day, namely, that it is now time for her to experiment with the problem of trying to walk alone.

Chapter Twenty

RESEARCH IN PSYCHOTHERAPY

*Research in psychotherapy is often confused with evaluation of thera-
peutic results. In reviewing his efforts and their results, a therapist
usually has a strong urge to evaluate his performance as a whole as
"good" or "bad." But evaluation of a therapy as good or bad is quite
irrelevant for scientific inquiry, and the underlying motives of pride or
guilt may seriously distract the therapist from his scientific purpose. His
task as a scientific investigator is not to evaluate but to try to understand quite objectively what has happened, as a chain of cause and effect.*

*There is a good reason why it is impossible to learn very much from
our usual statistical methods of evaluating therapeutic procedures. In
evaluating therapeutic results, we usually compare the patient's behavior
before and after treatment and attempt to judge the success of the
treatment as a whole. But a psychotherapeutic treatment may last many
months, and in the course of such a long time the therapist usually says
or does or fails to say or do many things that are of significance to
the patient. Such a treatment is not one but a long series of many clinical experiments. If the patient's reactions to the treatment are to be
understood as a chain of cause and effect, then obviously the results of
each experiment must be studied separately, not jumbled all together
in an attempt to evaluate the therapy as a whole.*

*In the brief paper that follows, we shall illustrate this procedure by
several hypothetical examples.*

Reprinted from *American Journal of Psychiatry,* 105 p. 229 (Sept. 1948).

A therapist's first obligation is to his patient. While treatment is still in progress, it is not easy for him to free himself from the emotional pressure of his therapeutic responsibilities; but even after the therapeutic task has been completed and therapeutic obligations have been discharged, he often continues to focus his interest upon evaluating his efforts as a therapist and may find it difficult to achieve the detachment of a scientific observer toward what has occurred in the course of the treatment.

It is for this reason that research in psychotherapy is so often confused with evaluation of therapeutic results. In reviewing his efforts and their results, a therapist usually has a strong urge to evaluate his performance as a whole as "good" or "bad" from the point of view of the patient's interest and the goals of therapy. In this he is motivated by a continuing sense of therapeutic responsibility, by pride, or by guilt. But evaluation of a therapy as good or bad is quite irrelevant for a scientific inquiry, and the underlying motives of pride or guilt may seriously distract the therapist from his scientific purpose. His task as a scientific investigator is not to evaluate but to try to understand quite objectively what has happened, as a chain of cause and effect.

There is a good reason why it is impossible to learn very much from our usual statistical methods of evaluating therapeutic procedures. In evaluating therapeutic results, we usually compare the patient's behavior before and after treatment and attempt to judge the success of the treatment as a whole. But a psychotherapeutic treatment may last many months and in the course of such a long time the therapist usually says or does or fails to do many things that are of significance to the patient. Such a treatment is not one but a long series of many clinical experiments. If the patient's reactions to the treatment are to be understood as a chain of cause and effect, then obviously the results of each experiment must be studied separately, not jumbled all together in an attempt to evaluate the therapy as a whole.

As an example of a single therapeutic experiment, let us consider a hypothetical but typical case. We observe that a patient regularly reacts to certain topics by boasting or showing off. We infer that these topics are associated with something that is very humiliating to him. By alluding to these topics in various ways, we attempt to establish whether our initial observation is correct or in error. If further observation confirms this initial impression, we plan a procedure to desensitize him so that it will become easier for him to discuss the disturbing topics and ultimately even to tell us the experience that was so humiliating to him.

In all essential respects this procedure is equivalent to an experiment in a laboratory: first, we observe the patient's behavior and make a hypothesis concerning its motivations; then, if observation of further behavior confirms the hypothesis, we plan a simple procedure to modify the behavior in a way that we predict; next, we carry out the plan and observe whether the results are those predicted. This simple therapeutic experiment is designed to test the validity both of our initial diagnosis of the patient's emotional situation and of our predicted results based on a deliberate plan to change the initial behavior pattern.

The method just described is employed with variation as part of the teaching program in a number of training centers in this country. In order to utilize it for scientific investigation of the therapeutic process, we need only repeat the experiment a number of times in similar situations. As an example the situation cited is more or less typical and will undoubtedly occur at some time in the treatment of many patients.

To set up an experiment in therapy, it is suggested that a group of therapists meet at specified intervals to discuss their handling of a series of more or less similar cases. At each meeting the current emotional situation of one or more of the patients is discussed. Each therapist makes a diagnostic interpretation of the situation, proposes a therapeutic procedure, and predicts results. The therapist responsible for the case carries out the procedure that seems best to him. After an interval, he reports to the group the patient's reactions to the therapy; these are studied and checked against the predictions. Ultimately, we should be able to assemble and compare these data, gathered from the treatment of similar conditions of frequent occurrence in different patients, and to derive from them both diagnostic rules for recognizing typical conditions and general principles to guide us in handling them.

Chapter Twenty-One

ART AND SCIENCE IN PSYCHOANALYSIS

Freud recommended that the analyst listen to everything the patient says with the same "evenly-hovering attention," avoiding any selection of anything in particular and allowing his "unconscious memory" full play.

What Freud is describing is, of course, an intuitive art, not a scientific procedure. In the following paper our first question is: Can the analyst's intuitive insights be checked systematically by objective and critical examination of the evidence, as in a genuine scientific procedure? And, if so, how? A serious difficulty is that every bit of the patient's behavior has many meanings. We must, therefore, try to specify in advance just which meaning we are looking for. For our present purpose, it is best to try to find the wish or the conflict that the patient has most intensely cathected at a given moment. This conflict we shall call the patient's "focal conflict." To the question, "What is the patient's focal conflict?" at a particular time, there is presumably only one correct answer.

What objective check can we have on the correctness of our understanding of a patient's behavior?

We have more or less abandoned our practice of making reconstructions that can be checked by the patient's ultimate recovery of childhood memories. However, we do have even better opportunities for checking our understanding of the patient's behavior at short range.

An important part of the analyst's task is to interpret to the patient his resistances. Every such interpretation may profitably be regarded as a therapeutic experiment. If it is to be an intelligent experiment, the analyst must know what he is doing. His decision to make each par-

Reprinted from *Journal of the American Psychoanalytic Association,* 6 (1958).

ticular interpretation should be grounded in his understanding of the patient's psychodynamic situation at the moment. If possible, he should also have some idea of what he hopes to accomplish by his interpretation. If he has, he is now prepared to learn something from the patient's response. If his understanding of the patient's immediately preceding behavior has been correct, then perhaps the patient's response will be the expected one. On the other hand, if the patient reacts differently than expected, then the analyst knows that his previous "understanding" of his patient's behavior was either incorrect or incomplete.

We should cultivate the habit of trying to formulate our intuitive understanding explicitly. After we have formulated explicitly what we have intuitively grasped, we can reexamine our "insight" and the evidence for it to determine whether it is truth or fantasy.

How can this be done? The correct answer to this question is a corollary to our fundamental principle of free association. The analyst should not try to guide the stream of the patient's associations. He should let the patient's own (unconscious) interest determine his train of thought. This is the principle of free association. A similar principle should guide the analyst in deciding when and what to interpret. The analyst should keep his attention always focused on the conflict with which the patient himself is preoccupied.

Thus we are led back again to our concept of the patient's "focal conflict." We try first to discover the disturbing dream wish which was most intensely cathected at the moment of dreaming. Then we do one thing more. We examine the manifest dream to see how the dreamer has reacted to this disturbing dream wish. We ask ourselves: Why did this wish have to be censored? What was the "reactive motive" that caused the dream censor to repudiate this particular wish? For example, was the dream censorship motivated by guilt? or by fear? or by shame?

The patient's focal conflict is the conflict between the disturbing wish with which he is preoccupied and the reactive motive that must be postulated to account for the way the censorship has dealt with this disturbing wish.

When I am interpreting to the patient, my rule is to interpret at the level of the focal conflict. The great advantage of an interpretation at this level is the fact that it adds no new factor to complicate the patient's emotional situation and the analyst's picture of it. When a patient is preoccupied with a single focal conflict, there are three dynamic facors that must be taken into account: (1) his disturbing motive; (2) his reactive motive; and (3) his hopes for a possible solution of or *defense against his conflict. When the analyst now interprets at the level of the focal conflict, he does not add a new dynamic factor, but by his interpretation he may change the quantitative balance between the factors that are already active. He achieves this by allying himself in an understanding relationship with one or more of these already activated factors.*

Thus, when the analyst interprets at the level of the focal conflict, the dynamic situation continues to be relatively simple and therefore not too difficult to understand.

Our recommendation is that, when a psychoanalyst makes an interpretation to a patient, he should first try to predict to himself what the effect of his interpretation will be. Then he should be alert to check whether his expectations are fulfilled in the same hour and in the next few hours. Such a policy of trying to anticipate what will happen next should improve both (1) the analyst's immediate conduct of the treatment, and also (2) his gradually deepening understanding of the patient.

In conclusion, we return to the problem of the analyst's countertransferences. The analyst's first line of defense should be not to allow his curiosity to be lulled to sleep by fragmentary bits of insight. If he sets himself the task always of discovering the conflict with which the patient is preoccupied, then the patient's material itself will often serve as a clue to warn the analyst of his own disturbing emotional reaction.

In a well-known passage in one of his technical papers, Freud makes some recommendations about how a psychoanalyst should listen to his patient's free associations. "The technique . . . is a very simple one," he writes. "It . . . consists in making no effort to concentrate the attention on anything in particular, and in maintaining in regard to all that one hears the same measure of calm, quiet attentiveness—of 'evenly-hovering attention,' as I once before described it. In this way a strain which could not be kept up for several hours daily and a danger inseparable from deliberate attentiveness are avoided. For as soon as attention is deliberately concentrated in a certain degree, one begins to select from the material before one; one point will be fixed in the mind with particular clearness and some other consequently disregarded, and in this selection one's expectations or one's inclinations will be followed. This is just what must not be done, however; if one's expectations are followed in this selection there is the danger of never finding anything but what is already known, and if one follows one's inclinations anything which is to be perceived will most certainly be falsified. It must not be forgotten that the meaning of the things one hears is, at all events for the most part, only recognizable later on." Later he adds, "All conscious exertion is to be withheld from the capacity for attention, and one's 'unconscious memory' is to be given full play. . . . One has simply to listen and not to trouble to keep in mind anything in particular."

Still later in the same paper he suggests that the analyst "must bend his own unconscious like a receptive organ towards the emerging unconscious of the patient, be as the receiver of the telephone to the disc. As the receiver transmutes the electric vibrations induced by the sound-waves back again into sound-waves, so is the physician's unconscious mind able to reconstruct the patient's unconscious."

When we reread these words of Freud, we realize that what he is describing is an intuitive art, not a scientific procedure.

Still, we should not distinguish too sharply between our art and our science. Scientific investigation, too, is an art, requiring imagination and scientific intuition. The distinguishing feature of scientific investigation is not that it should be unimaginative but rather that it tries systematically to check its intuitive insights by objective and critical examination of the available evidence.

In psychoanalysis, one of our most important therapeutic goals is to help the patient understand himself. This goal cannot be achieved didactically. Much of what the analyst hopes that the patient will learn is not yet known to the analyst himself. If the patient is to learn, his own ego must collaborate with the analyst in an investigation of the unknown parts of himself. Our question now is whether this investigation must depend only on the analyst's gradually increasing intuitive understanding of the patient. Or can the analyst's intuitive insights be checked systematically by objective and critical examination of the evidence, as in a genuine scientific procedure?

But first we ask: Should we not be content to let our therapeutic art be a purely intuitive one? The unconscious of an intuitively gifted analyst is an exceedingly subtle and penetrating tool, capable of insight which it would be impossible for any more rational or intellectual procedure to achieve. Why, then, should we try to put checks on it?

Unfortunately, intuition is very dependent on the gifts of the artist. We begin to realize this when we try to teach our therapeutic art. An intuitive art can be learned by example and by practice, but it cannot really be taught by precept or instruction. No one can teach a student to listen to his own unconscious. The best we can do is to help him release the capacities for intuitive understanding that he already has but that may have been buried beneath inhibitions as a result of early training and neurotic conflict. Then we can expose the student to case reports that have been elucidated in the literature and help him understand patients whom he is treating himself. Finally, if he has the requisite intuitive capacity, he will "catch on" and begin to use his own unconscious to understand his patients' behavior.

I recall an early learning experience of my own. I had just started work in a psychiatric hospital under the leadership of Dr. Samuel Hamilton and was assigned the case of a young man whose chief complaints were convulsions and blindness. After the customary routine examinations, I told Dr. Hamilton that my diagnosis was hysteria. "You will have to prove that," he replied. He advised me to try to exclude epilepsy by other physical investigations, and then added that in order to confirm a diagnosis of hysteria I must discover its psychogenic stimulus. Thus challenged, I went back to the patient. I took as exhaustive an anamnesis as I knew how. I also interviewed relatives in droves, and kept pressing for more and more facts. Finally, an uncle spoke up reluctantly, "Well, I'll tell you, Doc. We didn't want to say anything about it." Then he told of the boy's having come home one day to discover his mother in sexual intercourse with a stranger.

This experience occurred long before the beginning of my formal psychoanalytic training; yet I now regard it as one of the most important learning experiences in my psychoanalytic development. It fired my imagination with a hope which I never lost. If I were persistent enough, I might discover the psychogenesis of other cases which I did not yet understand. This, I believe, is an example of the principle involved in each step in the learning of our therapeutic art. From reading Freud's clinical examples, I had already acquired a vague notion of the way one can intuitively grasp the meaning of a patient's behavior. Probably I did not realize yet what was involved, but after the experience just described, I had been awakened to hope that I, too, could understand patients by listening to my own unconscious.

But let us return to our question: Why should we not be content with our therapeutic art?—which each of us must learn as best he can from the example of others and from his own experiences. The most important reason is that a person's own unconscious is not always a reliable guide.

We are becoming increasingly aware of the distorting and disturbing influences of an analyst's "counter-transferences." Our answer is that the analyst himself should first be analyzed before he tries to analyze others. Then he should keep on trying to analyze his counter-transferences, even after his own personal analysis has been interrupted. We know, of course, that this analysis of counter-transferences is never perfect; still, we cling to a kind of mystical faith in the reliability of the "well-analyzed analyst's" unconscious as a guide for his therapeutic judgment.

Obviously we need to do more than just to try to analyze away our counter-transferences. We need some kind of an objective check on our intuition. We ought to try systematically to evaluate our intuitive insights—objectively and critically. Such an attitude toward our intuitions may even do something to counteract our remnants of counter-transference. It is easiest to see ghosts in the dark. If we examine our ghosts in broad daylight it is easier to see whether they are really there.

Now we have the answer to our question. We should not be content to let psychoanalysis be only an intuitive art. We should also try to convert it into a scientifically oriented procedure.

Can this be done? And, if so, how?

In the early years of psychoanalysis, our chief check was a long-range check. Freud's interest centered on getting the patient to bring back to consciousness his repressed memories. After a long period of analysis of resistances, the patient finally recovered a deeply repressed memory. The emergence of such a memory into consciousness served as an objective confirmation of the essential correctness of the analytic work that had preceded.

In the early years of psychoanalysis, analysts made many attempts to reconstruct the disturbing events that were presumably responsible for their patients' neuroses. Then, while they tried to analyze the patients' resistances, they waited patiently for the reconstructed memories to emerge into the patient's consciousness. Sometimes they were successful. At other times, as in Freud's "Analysis of an Infantile Neurosis," the memory itself never became conscious, although the accumulated evidence for it seemed to be overwhelming. In still other cases, Freud discovered that the memories that hysterical patients had obligingly recovered were only fantasies.

In later years, many analysts have begun to distrust historical reconstructions. They prefer now not to try to anticipate what is coming but to wait until the patient first relives his infantile neurosis and then, perhaps, consciously remembers the events that he has been reliving.

This policy is certainly in line with scientific caution. Yet, by being so cautious, the analyst also protects himself from putting his interpretive powers to the test. If he makes no predictions, then he cannot be proved wrong.

Our flight from putting ourselves to the test often goes even further. Some years ago, I took part in a forum on validation of psychoanalytic interpretation. I was amazed to discover that what was being discussed was the interpretations that the analyst makes to the patient. What I had expected to discuss was the interpretations that the analyst makes to himself before he tells the patient anything. What we tell our patients is usually not a scientific hypothesis that needs validation. It is, rather, a stimulus to which the patient will probably react emotionally and which we hope will activate further free associations. What most needs validation is the intuitive understanding on which we based our decision to make an interpretation to the patient. Yet we are often reluctant to formulate this understanding explicitly so that we can put it to the test.

When we do try to formulate our understanding of our patient's behavior, we find that each of a number of analysts will interpret the same material in a different way. Of course, we reassure ourselves immediately that we know the reason for this. Every bit of the patient's behavior has many meanings. So we politely concede to one another that we have each recognized a different one of these many overdetermined meanings.

Yet this is a serious difficulty in the way of our developing an objectively critical attitude toward interpretation. Since there are so many overdetermined meanings, we are tempted to assume that almost any interpretation may be one of these meanings.

In order to overcome this difficulty, we must find ways of distinguishing between different kinds of overdetermined meanings. We should try to specify *in advance* just which meaning we are looking for. For example, we may try to find the wish or the conflict that the patient has most intensely cathected at a given moment. This conflict we shall call the patient's "focal conflict." To the question, "What is the patient's focal conflict?" at a particular time there is presumably only one correct answer.

We return to our problem of how to convert our therapeutic art into a scientifically oriented procedure. What objective check can we have on the correctness of our understanding of a patient's behavior?

We have more or less abandoned our practice of making reconstructions that can be checked by the patient's ultimate recovery of childhood memories. However, we do have even better opportunities for checking our understanding of the patient's behavior at short range.

An important part of the analyst's task is to interpret to the patient his resistances. Every such interpretation may profitably be regarded as a therapeutic experiment. If it is to be an intelligent experiment, the analyst must know what he is doing. His decision to make each particular interpretation should be grounded in his understanding of the patient's psychodynamic situation at the moment. If possible, he should also have some idea of what he hopes to accomplish by his interpretation. If so, he is now prepared to learn something from the patient's response. If his understanding of the patient's immediately preceding behavior has been correct, then perhaps the patient's response will be the expected one. On the other hand, if the patient reacts differently than the analyst expected, then the analyst knows that his previous "understanding" of his patient's behavior was either incorrect or incomplete. Now the analyst is confronted with a question. He should ask himself how his previous "understanding" must be modified to account for the patient's new behavior.

Yet now we seem to be confronted with a conflict between our intuitive art and our science. "Intuition" is an art of making judgments without knowing consciously how we arrive at them. But if we do not know how we arrived at our understanding of the patient, how can we test our conclusion objectively and critically? The answer is that we should cultivate the habit of trying to formulate our intuitive understanding explicitly. After we have explicitly formulated what we have intuitively grasped, we can reexamine our "insight" and the evidence for it, to determine whether it is truth or fantasy.

Freud advises the analyst to listen to his unconscious as to a telephone receiver. We should not misunderstand this advice. He does not tell us to be *guided only* by what the unconscious tells us. The art of psychoanalytic understanding is an art that requires collaboration between the analyst's ego and his unconscious. The analyst should *use* his unconscious to help him understand the patient's unconscious. Then he should *check* what his unconscious tells him against his *objectively critical intelligence*.

Probably many analysts have had experiences like one that has sometimes happened to me. Occasionally, I have found myself in unusual rapport with a patient, able by my comments to touch off highly significant responses from the patient. Yet, thinking back after the hour,

I have not known just what unconscious understanding prompted me to say what I did. Under such circumstances it is very instructive for the analyst to try to analyze retrospectively the evidence and the reasoning on which his intuitive understanding was based.

We must now return again to Freud's warning: "As soon as attention is deliberately focused one begins to select from the material before one." Yet, sooner or later, selection cannot really be avoided. The patient talks about many topics, and much that he says has many meanings. As soon as the analyst decides to make an interpretation to the patient he must make a selection. He must decide which of many possible therapeutic experiments to make. To let his unconscious be his guide is no adequate way. If the analyst does not choose consciously, his unconscious must make the selection.

Freud's advice is to interpret the patient's resistance. However, there are many topics which the patient resists bringing into consciousness. The analyst must decide which resistance to interpret. In a given case, not every analyst would make the same interpretation. Some analysts, for example, are particularly fascinated by the Oedipus complex; others, by one or another kind of pregenital conflict. In view of this fact, how is the analyst to avoid being guided by his own expectations or by his inclinations?

The correct answer to this question is a corollary to our fundamental principle of free association. The analyst should not try to guide the stream of the patient's associations. He should let the patient's own (unconscious) interest determine his train of thought. This is the principle of free association. A similar principle should guide the analyst in deciding when and what to interpret. The analyst should keep his attention always focused on *the conflict with which the patient himself is preoccupied.*

Thus we are led back again to our concept of the patient's "focal conflict." Let us spell out in greater detail how we try to find the patient's focal conflict.

In *The Interpretation of Dreams,* Freud (1900) sometimes speaks of *the* dream wish. This suggests a concept similar to our notion of focal conflict. When we are searching for the dreamer's focal conflict, we, too, try to discover *the* disturbing dream wish which was most intensely cathected at the moment of dreaming. Then we do one thing more. We examine the manifest dream to see how the dreamer has reacted to this disturbing dream wish. We try to analyze the dream censorship. We ask ourselves: Why did this wish have to be censored? What was the "reactive motive" that caused the dream censor to repudiate this particular wish? For example, was the dream censorship motivated by guilt? or by fear? or by shame?

The patient's focal conflict is the conflict between the disturbing wish with which he is preoccupied and the reactive motive that must be postulated to account for the way the censorship has dealt with this disturbing wish.

Traditionally, in psychoanalysis, we tend to relate anything that the patient does back to patterns from the past that he is supposedly repeating in the transference. This habit, however, may distract us from the task of discovering the patient's focal conflict. The focal conflict is always a reaction to a "precipitating situation" in the immediate present. To find the focal conflict, accordingly, we must keep in close touch with the patient's current situation. We explore both what is happening in the patient's real life outside the analysis and also the patient's emotional orientation toward the therapy. Sometimes an interpretation by the analyst will have served as the precipitating stimulus. Even more frequently, the patient's focal conflict will prove to be a reaction to what Alexander calls the "emotional climate" in the immediately preceding therapeutic sessions.

In order to avoid misunderstanding or confusion, we should state further that the focal conflict is seldom, if ever, conscious. It is usually just below the surface of consciousness. On the other hand, it is not the same thing as the nuclear conflict of the patient's neurosis. (However, in the course of therapy, after overlying defenses have been worked through, the nuclear conflict may become focal.) The focal conflict is much more superficial. It is usually preconscious rather than unconscious. It is also continually changing, from dream to dream or from hour to hour.

With this concept of the patient's focal conflict we return now to the task of integrating our art with our science.

As always, when we try to understand our patients, our first step must be an intuitive one. The analyst must first listen to his own unconscious; but, as soon as he has a good hunch, the focal conflict concept gives him an objective criterion with which to check it. Our objective criteria for the correctness of our interpretation are (1) that the focal conflict must be recognizable as a "natural" reaction to some aspect of the patient's actual situation, and (2) that the details of the patient's thoughts and behavior must all be recognizable as "natural" reactions to our postulated focal conflict.

Sometimes psychoanalysts have told me that one cannot expect to discover the patient's focal conflict in every interview, that one may have to wait a long time. They buttress this impression with the statement of Freud's that we have already quoted—that "the meaning of what one hears is, at least for the most part, only recognizable later on."

My own conviction, on the contrary, is that such complacency in the face of inability to discover the problem with which a patient is preoccupied is a serious defect in an analyst's orientation toward his therapeutic task. At the time that Freud made this statement, he and other analysts were interested chiefly in the deep unconscious meaning of the patient's associations, in the infantile wishes underlying the patient's thoughts. It is true that we often have to wait a long time before we can understand the deep unconscious meaning of much that the patient says. Yet, for the analyst's guidance in his day-to-day conduct of the treatment, the deep unconscious meanings of the patient's behavior are not those that are most important for him to grasp; what is most important for the analyst to understand is the patient's focal conflict. An analyst should not be complacent if he cannot decide what conflict is focal for the patient. If, for any period longer than a few days, the analyst cannot find the patient's focal conflict, he should know that something is wrong, that he is missing something of crucial importance. For example, I remember a patient whose associations I was long unable to bring into vital and focal relationship with anything that I knew was happening in his daily life. Fortunately, I was not happy or complacent about this fact. After two months of puzzled discussion with the patient about the obscurity of his material, I was finally given the answer. Not long after he had started treatment, he had begun an unprofessional relationship with a client of his about which he dared not tell me. Of course, his associations were obscure because the conflict about which they were focused was being withheld. If I had allowed myself to be satisfied with bits of insight on the periphery of his thoughts, I might never have learned what was really the matter.

A basic rule, if one's understanding of the patient is to be adequate, is not to be easily satisfied. The complacent analyst is likely to be wrong most of the time. Glib interpretations tend to put the analyst's curiosity to sleep. Even if an analyst feels that he is on the right track, he should keep questioning the adequacy of his understanding. "Is there anything in this patient's material that is inconsistent with my interpretation?" "What parts of the patient's behavior are still unexplained?" Such questions should keep him continually alert and dissatisfied.

Different analysts may understand in different ways Freud's concept of "evenly-hovering attention." There are different kinds of listening. One may listen passively, almost inertly, merely registering what the patient says. In order not to be influenced by his own preconceptions, the analyst may avoid any active attempts to understand what he hears; he may content himself with whatever fragmentary bits of insight may occur to him without effort and hope that the meaning of the rest will become clear to him later on.

Or the analyst's orientation may be exactly the opposite; while he is listening he participates actively with his imagination, intuitively identifying with the patient as far as possible, in order to catch the full significance of what the patient is saying.

To some extent these two ways of listening may be the expression of different temperaments, perhaps even of the degree of fatigue of the analyst. But passive registering of the patient's communications should not be mistaken for the evenly-hovering attention that Freud recommends. The analyst's attention should be alert and inquiring, as well as evenly distributed.

It is particularly important that the analyst should not be content with fragmentary bits of insight. His constant aim should be to understand how the different trends and themes in the patient's associations fit together into a single intelligible context. Trying to understand a patient's associations is like trying to piece together a jigsaw puzzle. This kind of fitting together into a single intelligible cognitive structure is our only reliable immediate check on the correctness of our interpretations. Consequently, we should not be complacent but actively puzzled if the pieces do not fit together intelligibly.

With the best understanding that he can muster at a given moment, the analyst can use the focal conflict concept as a guide in designing his therapeutic experiments.

The question of the best depth for interpretations to the patient is one that is much discussed in the psychoanalytic literature. It is generally agreed that interpretations that are "too deep" may be too disturbing to the patient. Or, if his defenses are more adequate, the patient may not be able to understand what the analyst is trying to tell him. On the other hand, interpretations that are too superficial may not tell the patient anything that he does not know already.

Freud (1913) suggested that important interpretations should not be made (1) until a dependable transference has been established, and (2) until the patient is almost ready, of his own accord, to understand what the analyst is about to interpret to him. Fenichel, paraphrasing this latter principle, suggested that the analyst should keep just ahead of the patient's own insight. Horney, to illustrate the same point, used an obstetrical analogy. She advised that the analyst interpret the "presenting" material—i.e., thoughts and wishes that are not yet conscious but are almost ready to emerge to consciousness.

The rule that I now propose has similar implications. Its only advantage is that it makes use of criteria based on objective analysis of the patient's associations. My rule is to interpret at the level of the focal conflict.

Interpreting at the level of the focal conflict has two advantages:

1) The patient should be much better able to understand and assimilate an interpretation that has to do with the problem with which he is already preoccupied. This is a well-recognized principle of education.

2) The effect of an interpretation at the level of the focal conflict should be easier to predict than the effect of other interpretations.

Just now we are interested in predicting the effect of the analyst's interpretation. The great advantage of an interpretation at the level of the focal conflict is the fact that it adds no new factor to complicate the patient's emotional situation and the analyst's picture of it. When a patient is preoccupied with a single focal conflict, there are three dynamic factors that must be taken into account: (1) his disturbing motive; (2) his reactive motive; and (3) his hopes for a possible solution of or defense against his conflict. When the analyst interprets at the level of the focal conflict, he does not add a new dynamic factor, but by his interpretation he may change the quantitative balance between the factors that are already active. This is achieved by allying himself in an understanding relationship with one or more of these already activated factors.

Thus, when the analyst interprets at the level of the focal conflict, the dynamic situation continues to be relatively simple and therefore not too difficult to understand. On the other hand, if the analyst should interpret some conflict that is at the moment on the periphery of the patient's interest, the effect may be to activate a competing focus and thus to make the patient's behavior much more difficult to understand or to predict.

Our recommendation is that, when a psychoanalyst makes an interpretation to a patient, he should first try to predict to himself what the effect of his interpretation will be. Then he should be alert to check whether his expectations are fulfilled in the same hour and in the next few hours. Such a policy of trying to anticipate what will happen next should improve both the analyst's immediate conduct of the treatment, and also his gradually deepening understanding of the patient.

Let us consider each of these advantages in turn.

1) To the patient, an interpretation is a stimulus. An interpretation of the focal conflict often activates it more intensely and centers the patient's reaction even more sharply on the analyst and on what the analyst has said. If the analyst understands what is happening, he will now point out to the patient how he is reacting to the first interpretation. The patient will probably respond to this second interpretation also; and in this way a chain of interpretations and responses will be started which the analyst should use to make a kind of laboratory demonstration to the patient of the motives that underlie the patient's behavior in a reasonably well-controlled situation.

If now the analyst is trying to anticipate at each point how the patient will react, he will be more alert to recognize the patient's responses when they do occur and then to use them for purposes of demonstration; but if he is merely passively registering what the patient says, he may fail to recognize that the patient is reacting to the interpretation of the preceding hour, and much valuable time will be lost. Failure to follow up in this way on a correct and important initial interpretation is one of the most frequent mistakes that inexperienced analysts make.

2) But now let us suppose that the analyst's prediction proves to be wrong. This should set the analyst again to thinking and asking himself questions. *Discrepancies* between what actually occurs and what he had expected are his *best clues* for discovering relationships that have not yet been suspected. In scientific investigation, it has long been recognized that an unexpected observation is often a most fruitful stimulus for new and valuable hypotheses; but, if the observer has no expectations, he will not even realize that what he observes is different from what he might have expected.

Now it is time to entertain some doubts. Is it really possible for the psychoanalyst to be critically objective toward his own formulations as well as toward the patient's behavior? Is it possible for him to think of his intuitive insights as only hypotheses and to subject them to critical scrutiny?

We have just suggested that the analyst should try to predict the effect of his interpretations to the patient. Trying to predict the patient's reaction, we suggest, serves the purpose of making the analyst alert in the next few hours to check the correctness of his prediction and may enable him to recognize the significance of a reaction that he might otherwise have overlooked. Now we ask: May not the analyst, instead of really checking his prediction, try to force his understanding of the associations of the patient's next hour into the pattern suggested by his prediction? If the analyst is too fascinated by his own interpretation, he will, of course, be tempted to do just this.

In other words, at the beginning of each succeeding interview the analyst must steer his course between two dangers. He should be alert to recognize the patient's reactions to the preceding hour; but he must also be on his guard not to be too much under the influence of preconceptions based on his understanding of that hour.

Let us now try to spell out what the analyst's orientation should be if he is to avoid both of these dangers. There are two possible approaches, and I believe that either one is reliable if properly checked.

As an example of one approach, let us suppose that in the preceding hour the analyst has made an interpretation which he believes is important to the patient. If the interpretation to the patient really was important and properly timed, then the analyst knows that the patient cannot help reacting to it, unconsciously at least (whether or not he reacted consciously). So, at the beginning of the next hour, the analyst listens for the patient's unconscious response. With this clue, the analyst may be able easily to understand the associations of the second hour, and most of the associations of the two hours will fit intelligibly together into a single cognitive structure.

However, the analyst must take care not to force the patient's reactions in the second hour into the preconceived pattern suggested by the associations of the preceding hour. Perhaps the analyst cannot find any significant relation between the associations of the second hour and the interpretation that he made in the preceding hour. Then the analyst must consider three possibilities: (1) The analyst's interpretation may have been incorrect or not so important as he believed it to be; or (2) the patient may have suppressed his reaction and failed to tell the analyst about it; or (3) the patient's reaction to the analyst's interpretation may be so disguised that the analyst is unable to recognize it for what it is.

The analyst, of course, does not know yet which of these three possibilities is the correct one. So he turns to the other possible approach to the associations of the second hour, an approach which he might well have adopted in the first place: He listens to the patient's associations of the second hour without reference to his understanding of the preceding hour. Let us now suppose that most of the associations of the second hour fit well into a single context of their own which cannot be recognized as having any significant relation to the analyst's understanding of the preceding hour.

Once more there are three possibilities: Either (1) the analyst's understanding of the preceding hour was wrong (or partly wrong); or (2) his understanding of the second hour is wrong (or needs some kind of revision); or (3) there is a significant link between the patient's reactions in the two hours which the analyst has not yet discovered.

The important point now is that the analyst should not be complacent or oblivious. He should be puzzled; the question of how these two hours are related to each other should remain as an unsolved riddle in his mind, to make him alert to evidence that may later help him find an answer.

This brings us back to the suggestion that we made a moment ago. The key to an objectively critical attitude toward our own formulations is to be *alert to discrepancies*.

Some analysts are so on their guard against being biased by what they already know that they postpone formulation of a patient's material just as long as possible. Such an analyst might ask: If the analyst's attitude is to be an actively inquiring one, how can he avoid being led astray either by his expectations or by his inclinations? We have tried to answer this question. Our answer is: The analyst should always be alert to discover the problem with which *the patient* is preoccupied. We answer further: Instead of being led astray by his expectations, the analyst should be always alert to discover discrepancies between what he expects and what actually happens. Discrepancies are his best clues for finding out facts that he does not yet know about his patient.

If the analyst has no expectations, how can he recognize discrepancies? The most important objection to a policy of postponing formulations is that it makes the analyst less sensitive to apparent discrepancies in the patient's behavior and associations, less inclined to ask himself pertinent questions, and less alert to evidence that might help him find the answer to important questions.

There is, of course, still another fundamental question to answer: How can the analyst combat the disturbing and distorting influence of his own counter-transferences?

If counter-transference reactions are very severe, there is really no good answer to this question. Further analysis of the analyst may help in his future analytic work, but the corrective results of the analyst's personal analysis are not likely to be prompt enough to help a patient with whom he is already involved.

On the other hand, the analyst's disturbing emotional reaction to his patient may be only a temporary one, not grounded in any deep-seated unresolved neurotic pattern. In such a case, an objectively critical attitude toward his attempts to understand the patient may facilitate greatly the analyst's prompt discovery of his own disturbing reaction. We have pointed out that, when an analyst is unable to discover his patient's focal conflict, he is usually missing something crucial. It may be that the patient is successfully withholding some important fact. On the other hand, it is equally possible that the analyst may be blind to some important link underlying the patient's associations. Or the "precipitating situation" for the patient's focal conflict may have been an emotional reaction of the analyst's which the analyst himself has not yet recognized. The analyst should be particularly alert to this last possibility.

By careful analysis of a patient's associations and dreams, one can often deduce a valid criticism of the analyst's way of conducting the analysis. An example from my own early experience was very instructive to me. The patient's neurosis centered about intense fears of castration at the hands of both father and mother. To these fears he had reacted with attempts to intimidate his many younger brothers. In his analysis he tried immediately to intimidate me. He succeeded. At one point his resistance took the form of trying to make play of the analysis. Interpretation of this behavior as a defense against his fears had no effect. Finally, mustering up my courage, I stopped playing with him and remained silent during a whole hour. The effect was immediate. Both rage and fear emerged, and from this time on he began to identify me with his father instead of with a younger brother.

Since this time, in my supervisory work, I have often noticed that a patient's identification of his analyst with an indulgent mother is a sign that the analyst is not pressing his interpretation of the patient's disturbing motives actively enough. When the analyst begins to follow up his interpretations more energetically, the mother-transference is promptly replaced by fears of a stern father.

I should add, of course, that at other times the patient's material will indicate that the analyst has been pressing too hard to penetrate the patient's resistances.

Sometimes one can make more specific deductions from the patient's responses. A patient's unconscious fantasies will often picture the analyst in a seductive role. If such a fantasy is reacted to with the usual shame or guilt, it can often be recognized as a response to the analyst's normal role of encouraging the patient to become conscious of forbidden wishes. In other cases, however, a fantasy will emerge in which the analyst is joining the patient in orgiastic activity. Such a fantasy is not only one of simple wish fulfillment, it is also a sign that the patient's erotic transference has become a resistance, which the analyst has failed to recognize. The analyst has failed to recognize that both he and the patient have forgotten their task of analyzing the underlying conflict that is focal for the patient. They have allowed discussion of erotic fantasies to become only a source of unrecognized gratification for both of them.

In general, the analyst should pay close attention, not only to the patient's unconscious wishes, but also to the way the patient's ego is trying to relate these wishes to external reality. If the analyst does this systematically, he will often find that there is, hidden in the patient's material, a very accurate prescription of just what kind of therapeutic intervention the patient needs from the analyst at that particular time.

In conclusion, we return to the problem of the analyst's counter-transferences. The analyst's first line of defense should be not to allow his curiosity to be lulled to sleep by fragmentary bits of insight. If he sets himself the task of always discovering the conflict with which the patient is preoccupied, then the patient's material itself will often serve as a clue to warn the analyst of his own disturbing emotional reaction.

Chapter Twenty-Two

HOW DIFFERENT APPROACHES TO
THE STUDY OF BEHAVIOR
CAN BE INTEGRATED

In this paper we started with our discontent with the psychoanalytic concept of the drive. The drive concept, especially as applied to human beings, is unsatisfactory because it is so remote from actual observed behavior. For example, the theory of the "death instinct" does not ask what specific circumstances provoke destructive behavior; and we do not know as well as we should when a craving for stimulation of any particular erotic zone is likely to be activated.

The best approaches to the study of human heredity are (1) direct observation of human infants, and (2) comparison with the investigations of innate behavior patterns in other species being made by ethologists. Examples of direct observation of infants are Spitz's work (1946) on the smiling response and his study of anaclitic depressions. Bowlby's paper on "The Nature of the Child's Tie to His Mother" (1956) illustrates beautifully how the ethological approach may be applied to the study of human infants. Ethologists have predominantly studied animal species that are lower in the vertebrate scale, especially birds and fishes. Bowlby, applying similar methods to the observation of the human infant, reminds us of the fact that sucking is not the infant's only innate response to the mother. There are also crying, smiling, and clinging responses, and a tendency to follow the mother, first with his eyes, and later in other ways after he has become able to move about more freely. In our psychoanalytic thinking, we have tended to lump together

A paper presented to the American Psychoanalytic Association panel on ethology, New York, 1959.

all of these responses, thinking of them all as subordinate to a basic craving to suck at the mother's breast. Bowlby points out, however, that the elementary responses which he enumerates are initially isolated responses. Only later are these isolated responses integrated in various ways, one of which is the subordination of other elementary urges to the oral craving.

The ethologists distinguish between innate instinctive acts and appetitive behavior. The innate instinctive acts, they say, are completely stereotyped behavior patterns which do not undergo modification in response to changing environmental conditions. The ethologists maintain that these innate instinctive acts cannot be modified by learning. They are activated, in each case, by what the ethologists call an innate releasing mechanism—a very specific set of stimuli to which the organism responds with the characteristic instinctive act.

In contrast to the rigidly stereotyped instinctive acts, the ethologists distinguish what they call "appetitive behavior." Appetitive behavior is goal-directed behavior, behavior whose goal is to seek out the specific innate releasing stimulus for a particular instinctive act. Ethologists sometimes use the term "drive" to designate such appetitive behavior. For the ethologist, a drive always has, as its specific goal, achievement of the innate releasing stimulus for a particular instinctive act.

In psychoanalysis, as it deals with adults or older children, what we are observing and studying is practically always appetitive behavior. We deal primarily with the patient's wishes and his attempts to fulfill them, realistically (i.e., in accordance with the reality principle), or symbolically (in symptoms), or by hallucinations (as in dreams). All this, according to the ethologists' concept, is appetitive behavior.

The ethologists themselves have only just begun to study appetitive behavior.

Another link must be inserted between the behavior studied by the ethologists and adult human behavior. This link is the study of learning. Appetitive behavior, since it is capable of a great deal of variability in the means used to achieve a more or less fixed goal, is the kind of behavior which is accessible to modification by learning.

In psychoanalysis, of course, we study these learning processes—and their vicissitudes—in reverse. Starting with a patient's present behavior, we try to reconstruct the most significant periods of transition in his life history. In particular, we hope to be able to trace the neurotic disturbances in his present behavior to traumatic events in his past. For our present purpose, it is helpful to expand somewhat our usual concept of what constitutes a traumatic experience. A "trauma," as I like to define the term, is "any situation or event that more or less permanently interrupts the process of learning by experience."

I do not know how many psychoanalysts share my discontent with the psychoanalytic theory of the drives.

The basis for my difficulty with the drive concept, especially as applied to human beings, is that its connection with actual observed behavior is so remote. For example, if I hear one man berating another verbally for getting in his way on the street, do I have any direct evidence that this behavior is a manifestation of an inherited destructive drive? He is expressing his aggression by talking, but he did not know how to talk when he was born. Moreover, the stimulus for his aggression was the fact that the other man was an obstacle while he was driving on the street; however, he was not born with the ability to drive an automobile.

I suppose we would all agree that all behavior, if traced back far enough, would lead ultimately to some kind of inherited predisposition; but in the case of actually observed behavior, unless it be the behavior of an infant, we can almost never trace back the chain of causation that far. Consequently, in order to guess at the innate or inherited background of any particular behavior, we have to fall back on certain general assumptions based on features that are common to the behavior of both men and animals. We might postulate, for example (as a first approximation), that all animals inherit a tendency to react to an obstacle by trying to overcome or destroy it.

Such a proposition, however, is very different from the psychoanalytic concept of a destructive or self-destructive drive ("death instinct"). The notion of an inherited tendency to struggle against obstacles has a certain precision. It tells us what kind of circumstances tend to activate this particular hereditary pattern. On the other hand, the theory of the death instinct does not ask what specific conditions provoke destructive behavior. It usually assumes tacitly that the destructive urge operates continually as a primary cause, except insofar as it is neutralized or modified by the "life instinct." It postulates also that life and death instincts are components of all behavior. According to this theory, every active striving is in part a manifestation of the destructive drive. This formulation explains everything so easily and indiscriminately that it is almost valueless.

The concept of erotic zones and partial erotic drives in Freud's libido theory is much more closely related to direct observation. Still, we do not know, as well as we should, when a craving for stimulation of any particular erotic zone is likely to be activated. We do know, for example, that cravings for oral erotic stimulation are increased when a person is hungry. Such cravings may also become intense at other times. When does this happen? In order to answer this question, we should probably turn to our psychoanalytic studies of patients with bulimia.

Anyone who is unhappy about drive theories that are becoming too remote from direct observation must respond with relief both to studies based on direct observation of human infants and also to the investigations of innate behavior patterns that are being made by ethologists. Of these two approaches to the study of innate behavior, the observation of human infants and young children is the one that should contribute most directly to our understanding of hereditary patterns. Spitz's work on the smiling response and his study of anaclitic depressions are extremely promising examples of the value of this kind of investigation. Since 1957, we at the Chicago Institute for Psychoanalysis have also been listening with great interest to his more comprehensive attempts, by direct observation of the infant, to reconstruct the earliest steps that are the precursors to the development of the child's ego. In this discussion, I propose only to make a few comments on the relationships between these ethological studies and psychoanalysis.

The ethologists' investigations are primarily concerned with innate behavior. Consequently, we must expect that they will be more closely related to our direct observations of infants than to anything that we can learn by psychoanalysis of adults (or even of older children). In his recent paper on "The Nature of the Child's Tie to His Mother," Bowlby illustrates beautifully how the ethological approach may be applied to the study of human infants. Ethologists have predominantly studied animal species that are lower in the vertebrate scale, especially birds and fishes. Bowlby, applying similar methods to observation of the human infant, reminds us of the fact that sucking is not the infant's only innate response to the mother. The infant also has crying, smiling, and clinging responses, and a tendency to follow his mother, first with his eyes, and later in other ways, after he has become able to move about more freely. In our psychoanalytic thinking, we have tended to lump together all of these responses as subordinate to a basic craving to suck at the mother's breast. Bowlby points out, however, that the elementary responses which he enumerates are initially isolated responses.

Only later are these isolated responses integrated in various ways, one being the subordination of other elementary urges to the oral craving.

We turn next to the relationships between ethology and what we can learn from our clinical psychoanalytic observation of adults.

The ethologists distinguish between innate instinctive acts and appetitive behavior.

The innate instinctive acts, they say, are completely stereotyped behavior patterns which do not undergo modification in response to changing environmental conditions. The ethologists maintain also that these innate instinctive acts cannot be modified by learning. They are activated, in each case, by what the ethologists call an innate releasing mechanism, a very specific set of stimuli to which the organism responds with the characteristic instinctive act. In later refinements of their observations, the ethologists have called attention to the fact that an innate instinctive act may occur spontaneously in the absence of any external stimulus to release it. They explain this by postulating that, in the absence of its specific releasing mechanism, pressure for discharge of the instinctive act accumulates. As this pressure accumulates, the instinctive act may be elicited by an increasingly wide range of stimuli and, in extreme cases, may be discharged "in vacuo."

In contrast to the rigidly stereotyped instinctive acts, the ethologists distinguish what they call "appetitive behavior," a term which was introduced by Wallace Craig. Appetitive behavior is goal-directed behavior whose goal is to seek out the specific innate releasing stimulus for a particular instinctive act. Ethologists sometimes use the term "drive" to designate such appetitive behavior. The ethological concept of drive is similar to, but more precisely defined than, the drive concept as it is sometimes used by the psychoanalyst. For the ethologist, a drive always has as its specific goal achievement of the innate releasing stimulus for a particular instinctive act. It would be of interest to inquire whether this very specific ethological concept of a drive could be of any value to us in our psychoanalytic attempts to understand the hereditary background of behavior.

I should like to point out next that in psychoanalysis, as it deals with adults or older children, what we are observing and studying is practically always appetitive behavior. We deal primarily with the patient's wishes and his attempts to fulfill them, realistically (i.e., in accordance with the reality principle), or symbolically (in symptoms), or by hallucinations (as in dreams). All this, according to the ethologists' concept, is appetitive behavior. As psychoanalysts, we are interested in the ethologists' stereotyped instinctive acts only insofar as they are the goals of appetitive behavior.

The ethologists themselves have only just begun to study appetitive behavior. Practically all of their work in this area has been directed to the elucidation of elementary tropisms. This sets a limit to the use that we can make of ethology for the elucidation of adult human behavior —indeed, for the elucidation of anything except the behavior of human infants.

Another link must be inserted between the behavior studied by the ethologists and adult human behavior. This link is the study of learning. Appetitive behavior, since it is capable of a great deal of variability of the means used to achieve a more or less fixed goal, is, for this reason, the kind of behavior which is accessible to modification by learning.

In psychoanalysis, of course, we study these learning processes—and their vicissitudes—in reverse. Starting with a patient's present behavior, we try to reconstruct the most significant periods of transition in his life history. In particular, we hope to be able to trace back the neurotic disturbances in his present behavior to traumatic events in his past. For our present purpose, it is helpful to expand somewhat our usual concept of what constitutes a traumatic experience. A "trauma," as I like to define the term, is "any situation or event that more or less permanently interrupts the process of learning by experience."

Thus, we arrive at a scheme, somewhat like the following, for the way in which various approaches can be coordinated in our attempts to understand human behavior. Ethological investigations of animals lower in the vertebrate scale are most closely related to our studies of human infants' behavior by direct observation. For the purposes of such a comparison, probably the point of greatest interest is to what extent human infants display stereotyped inherited reactions comparable to the instinctive acts of other animals demonstrated by the ethologists. In human beings, however, it is generally recognized that appetitive behavior modifiable by learning plays a proportionately much greater role than in other animals. The links between innate instinctive acts and the more flexible behavior of human adults are filled in by: (1) the appetitive behavior of the ethologists; and (2a) learning processes, or (2b) psychoanalytic reconstructions of the historical genesis of our patients' behavior.

Part Three

PSYCHOSOMATIC
MEDICINE

Chapter Twenty-Three

PSYCHOGENIC MATERIAL
RELATED TO THE FUNCTION
OF THE SEMICIRCULAR CANALS

The following is a dream reported by a patient who was in analysis following recovery from an acute psychosis. The dream has two parts. In the first, the patient is in a yellow cottage by the lake. His mother comes to visit him. There are two beds, one higher than the other, on adjoining sides of the room, the heads of the beds facing each other. The patient wonders how privacy can be maintained when his mother undresses.

In association he recalls that in his early childhood his own bed and that of his parents were arranged exactly as in the dream, except that the feet of the beds faced each other. When he was twelve, his mother took him to a crowded summer resort where they both slept in the same room. He was awakened in the night by two rats fighting on his face. As he awoke, one rat ran down each arm. He insists on the reality as well as the vividness of this experience.

This experience, we suspect, was based on a real one from a much earlier date. It probably was a nightmare, reproducing, with only a little disguise, a primal scene memory from early childhood. The two rats were his parents, and the probability is that when he was sleeping in the same room with them he once observed them during coitus and interpreted this as a fight. When he was twelve and again in the same room with his mother, this memory was revived as a vivid dream. His more recent material denies the reality of the scene by reversing the position of the beds.

Reprinted from *International Journal of Psycho-Analysis*, 10 (1929), Part 4.

In the second part of the dream, the patient's mother now becomes his wife and he takes her out in a boat in front of the cottage. There is an island in the lake. Suddenly the landscape begins to move like a panorama in a counterclockwise direction, but the scenes appear in the order in which they would appear if the landscape were moving in the opposite direction; the island then moves out of the way and the patient points out to his wife a place where he and his father, mother, and brother once went picnicking.

The lake, the cottage, and the picnicking place correspond to an actual site where he really went picnicking once with his father, mother, and brother; but there is no island in the real lake. The island in the dream had the shape of the female breast. From the picnicking place a picture was once taken of the patient and his brother seated in a boat as though they were rowing, but the picture was somewhat ridiculous, as it was so obvious that they were actually sitting very still. The revolving panorama recalls a fantasy he reported earlier of a snake in his rectum swaying his body. He is reminded also of a panorama of the Battle of Waterloo, and of a sketch showing Wellington smoking one pipe after another as one after another is shot out of his mouth. He has been told that Victor Hugo made the outcome of this whole battle turn on the nod of a peasant. He is also reminded of the view from the window of a moving train and of a top which was wound by pressing a spool over a projecting upright piece.

Our particular interest in this dream arises from the striking similarity of the scene of the revolving landscape in the dream (with the island moving in the opposite direction) to the apparent motion of surrounding objects after a revolving-chair test of the function of the semicircular canals. This suggests that the revolving landscape was a reaction to the patient's having turned over in bed.

In the remainder of this paper we make a more detailed comparison of the revolving landscape dream to reactions to the revolving-chair test; and then we discuss the relations of the revolving landscape to the patient's way of dealing with his primal scene fantasies.

The following material is from the analysis of a man of thirty who had been under analytic treatment since early in December 1927. The analysis had been begun during the course of a very mild depression without delusions which had developed during the convalescence from an acute excitement. The excitement during most of its course had been of the manic type but had taken on a distinctly schizoid coloring at its height.

In connection with the particular material which I am about to present, it is of interest to note that in 1919 there had been a nasal infection which had left a marked deafness of the left ear. I shall quote only those portions of his analytic material which have a bearing on my topic.

On April 13, immediately after defecation, he had a sensation as though he were swaying. This at first frightened him, then gave him a feeling as though he had seen something amusing. He was not dizzy. In association he thought of pictures of coils of intestine . . . seeing a monkey masturbate, snakes, a snake crawling into his rectum and shaking his whole body, sexual intercourse.

On May 7, three and a half weeks later, he reports a dream in two parts. The patient is in a yellow cottage by a lake. His mother comes to visit him. There are two beds, one higher than the other, on adjoining sides of the room, the heads of the beds facing each other. The patient wonders how privacy can be maintained when his mother undresses.

In association he recalls that in his early childhood his own bed and that of his parents were arranged exactly as in the dream, except that the feet of the beds faced each other. When he was twelve, his mother took him to a crowded summer resort where they both slept in the same room. He was awakened in the night by two rats fighting on his face. As he awoke, one rat ran down each arm. He insists upon the reality as well as the vividness of this experience.

I think we may well believe that the experience was a real one, but the reality belongs to an earlier date. The nightmare is a rather undisguised reproduction of the primal scene. The two rats were his parents, and the probability is that when he was sleeping in the same room with his parents he once observed them during coitus and interpreted this as a fight. When he was twelve and again in the same room with his mother, this memory was revived as a vivid dream. His more recent material denies the reality of the scene by reversing the position of the beds.

Let us now turn to the second part of the dream. The patient's mother now becomes his wife and he takes her out in a boat in front of the cottage. There is an island in the lake. Suddenly the landscape begins to move like a panorama in a counterclockwise direction, but the scenes appear in the order in which they would appear if the landscape were moving in the opposite direction; the island then moves out of the way and the patient points out to his wife a place where he and his father, mother, and brother once went picnicking.

The lake, the cottage, and the picnicking place correspond to an actual site where he really went picnicking once with his father, mother, and brother; but there is no island in the real lake. The island in the dream had the shape of the female breast. From the picnicking place a picture was once taken of the patient and his brother seated in a boat as though they were rowing, but the picture was somewhat ridiculous, as it was so obvious that they were actually sitting very still. The revolving panorama recalls the fantasy already reported of the snake in his rectum swaying his body. He is reminded also of a panorama of the Battle of Waterloo and of a sketch showing Wellington smoking one pipe after another as one after another is shot out of his mouth. He has been told that Victor Hugo made the outcome of this whole battle turn on the nod of a peasant. He is also reminded of the view from the window of a moving train and of a top which was wound by pressing a spool over a projecting upright piece.

In a position which would have been behind and to the right of the patient as he sat in the boat with his wife there used to be a small white shack with the inscription, "Hobo's Rest." The position of the shack corresponds to the position of the analyst, who sits behind the patient and a little to the right.

In this part of the dream we see the traumatic memory of the primal scene transformed in two ways, which are not, to be sure, altogether consistent with each other. (1) Instead of the motionless, frightened child in dread of castration, he is now the great Wellington replacing the penis everytime it is shot off, and the whole battle "turns on his nod." (2) It is the patient who has the mother, and the father analyst who is in the "Hobo's Rest." It will be noticed that, in both cases, it is his helpless passivity in the scene against which he is reacting and for which he is overcompensating.

But what is the meaning of the revolving landscape? Two thoughts suggest themselves. The rapid motion of the landscape is obviously an elaboration of the violent motion of the primal scene. Probably the confusion about the direction of the rotation reflects also the child's bewilderment at the unwonted sight. We have good reason to believe that he was both frightened and curious. In the dream he is pointing out to his wife a former picnicking place, a gesture obviously compensatory for the ungratified curiosity of the earlier scene. Besides, does not the island move out of his way on purpose to let him see? There is also a still more important conflict which might well contribute to his bewilderment. Several of the dream associations—the fantasy of the snake in his rectum, the top with the spool pressing down upon it, and the picture of Wellington with the pipe in his mouth—all these point to an identification with the mother in the passive role; but the whole trend of the dream is a most emphatic rejection of such desires on behalf of his narcissism. Such a conflict may well be expected to cause some bewilderment.

But why is this confusion represented precisely by a revolving landscape? The patient compares the impression with that of looking at a landscape from a moving train. This suggests the possibility that it is he himself who is being moved. We are reminded of the revolving-chair tests for the function of the semicircular canals.

The early reports in the literature upon the direction of the apparent motion of surrounding objects are somewhat contradictory. Purkinje, Hering, Breuer, and Hitzig reported that the apparent motion of the objects was in the direction opposite to that in which the subject had been rotated. Helmholz stated that, on the other hand, if the subject had had his eyes open during the rotation, the apparent post-rotatory movement of objects, though usually in the same direction as that of the previous rotation, was sometimes in the opposite direction; whereas, after rotation with eyes closed, the apparent motion was quite regularly in the opposite direction. According to Barany, individuals differ. He states that in association with a nystagmus with quick movement to the right (i.e., such as occurs after rotation to the left), objects appear with some persons to move to the right, with others back and forth, with others to the left, and with others not at all. Ewald noticed that a lantern post moved in one direction and the house behind it in another. An article by Leiri seems to reconcile some of these contradictions. Leiri, after turning about rapidly ten times to the right, seated himself quickly in a chair by the window and fixed his eyes on a vase there. He could then observe that the vase appeared to move to the left, that is, in the direction opposite to that in which he had himself been revolving; but the wall beyond appeared to move toward the right, in the same direction as that in which he had been turning.

Leiri attempts further to bring this observation into connection with the post-rotatory nystagmus. This consists, as is well known, of a quick movement in the direction opposite to that of the previous rotation and a slow movement in the same direction as that of the previous rotation, and corresponds rather closely to the nystagmus occasioned by trying to look at near objects from a train window. In the case of the train window, the eye executes a slow movement backward in the attempt to follow the objects backward, then recovers with a quick movement forward, that is, in the same direction as that in which the train is moving. The comparison suggests a connection, on the one hand, between the slow, nystalgic movement and the macular function of distinct vision, and, on the other hand, between the quick, nystalgic movement and the indistinct vision of the peripheral retina. This corresponds exactly to Leiri's observation that, after he had rotated himself rapidly to the right, the vase upon which his eyes were fixed appeared to move to the left. This corresponds to the slow movement of the post-rotatory nystagmus, which in this case would be to the right. The wall behind, however, which was observed only with the peripheral portion of the retina, appeared to move to the right, corresponding to the quick movement of the post-rotatory nystagmus which would be toward the left (after a rotation to the right).

After reading the description of this experiment and trying it upon myself, I suddenly realized that perhaps a new light was now thrown upon certain details of my patient's description of his dream which previously had seemed inadequately explained. Let me repeat the patient's description of the revolving landscape.

> Suddenly the landscape began to move like a panorama in a counterclockwise direction, but the scenes appeared in the order in which they would appear if the landscape had been moving in the opposite direction. Then the island moved out of the way.

It is unfortunate that this account is not more specific about the direction in which the island moved, as I failed to inquire about this, not realizing at the time that it would have any theoretical significance. However, the expression "moved out of the way" at least suggests a contrast with the direction of motion of the surrounding objects, and this was the definite impression which I received from his account. If this impression is correct, the description corresponds exactly to the impression one would expect the patient to get if he had just been rotated around to the left and had immediately fixed his eyes upon the island. The landscape as a whole moves to the left; the island moves "out of the way" to the right; but in spite of the apparent motion in opposite directions of landscape and island, there is actually no change in the relative position of the two, a phenomenon which might very naturally give the subjective impression that the scenes of the landscape were appearing in exactly the reverse order from what one would expect from the direction of the motion. It will be recalled that there has been much confusion in the scientific reports of the post-rotatory apparent motion of visually perceived objects, and that some of Barany's subjects even described this motion as oscillatory. It seems not at all unlikely that the patient's sense of contradiction with regard to the direction of the motion might be another individual's attempt to characterize the subjective impression of motion which results from a nystalgic oscillation of the eyes and to which there corresponds no actual change in the relative position of the objects with reference to each other.

But if we grant the similarity of the dream picture to that induced by a post-rotatory nystagmus, what help does this give us in the interpretation of the dream? Are we to suppose that the patient, by turning in bed, actually stimulated the semicirculatory canals sufficiently to cause the usual post-rotatory phenomena in his dream images? And even if he did, what meaning could this have as a reaction to the primal scene?

I suggest that we leave these questions unanswered for the present, until we have discussed certain other material which the patient later presented.

The following is a dream reported on May 16, nine days after the dream which we have been discussing. The patient had masturbated the night before, accompanying the masturbation with a fantasy about the prostitute with whom he had consorted for the first and only time in his life, just at the moment when a previous depression was giving way to the beginning of the excitement which led to his treatment in the hospital. The masturbation was followed by an impulse to commit suicide by swallowing some pins which were lying on the bureau. During the night he then dreamed as follows:

> He is on an ocean liner. Although the water is calm as glass, the boat rises and falls. The patient goes forward to see the bow cut the water, but he is unable to get far enough forward. Then he climbs to a crow's nest. He has a wheel in his hand and feels he is directing the boat. There is a sense of thrill at controlling so much power. Then the boat comes to a city, and he directs it through the streets of the city and can look over the roofs of the houses. Once the boat grazes a smoky, black building and bounds back to the other side. He turns to his brother (four years older)

who seems to be beside him. Then he is standing on the street where the boat had been. He sees the people streaming along as though they were a current set up by the boat which had just passed through.

He gives associations as follows. The people streaming through the streets remind him of spermatazoa, and the passage of the boat through the street, of coitus. He recalls an ocean trip when the water was clear as glass but he could see a current of water coming up from below. On another ocean trip, the deck steward, in return for a tip, gave another man the preference over the patient in the choice of chairs. This angered him during the whole trip. When in the navy he once tried to climb into a crow's nest but found it locked. Looking out upon the ocean gives him a feeling that he is so small and insignificant in comparison with the immensity of the expanse of waters. The dream further reminds the patient of his numerous fantasies of being in a boat—which is, in fact, a favorite feature in his masturbation fantasies. Often in these fantasies he pictures the boat as very small and cramped.

It will be noticed that this dream repeats many of the important features of the one last discussed. The patient is again in a boat. The coitus of the parents is now represented in transparent symbolism, and he has again a feeling that he is controlling all this display of power. On the other hand, his feelings of helplessness and insignificance are now plainly expressed; he feels so small in comparison with the immense expanse of water. The baffled curiosity for which he was compensating in the last dream is now first directly felt, then again over-compensated as he climbs into the crow's nest, which in real life he had found locked. In the discussion of the last dream we were led to surmise that the patient was representing himself as being passively moved. In this dream, the passive motion is directly represented but at the same time denied. The boat is rising and falling, although the water is calm as glass. Finally, the revolving landscape finds a sort of counterpart in the current of people of which the boat is a cause, and we have a hint of confirmation of our analogy with the post-rotatory effects, for here it is expressly stated that the current was set up by the passage of the boat upon which the patient had been carried.

Another feature which was barely hinted at in the last dream is now made entirely plain. The patient is in a boat, a city; his brother is with him, and he sees the spermatazoa streaming by him. It is quite plain that we are dealing here with a fantasy of intrauterine observation of parental coitus. This begins to throw a new light upon the passive motion to which the patient is being subjected.

Twelve days later, May 28, he complained of considerable nausea during the night, accompanied by a dream of trying to get rid of fibrous material stuck to his tongue.

Associations identified the tongue with a penis and with the head of a Latin professor, who liked to make obscene allusions in his classes and who later developed a paralysis of the tongue. The next day's material brought a boat fantasy, which expressed plainly the unconscious suspicion that the analyst was seeing too much of the patient's wife. The following night the patient was again nauseated and dreamed the following.

> He is on what seems like a Chinese riverboat, entering a coast harbor. Waves wash up over the starboard deck. A Chinaman is standing on a stool in the only dry spot. Then some Chinese women come back as though running away from a wave. The boat rocks and the patient asks his wife if she is seasick. She says, "No." He watches the boat cut the water. It passes very close to a red buoy.

Associations are as follows: He is reminded of seasickness on a French liner. He had already mentioned this in connection with the dream about the material adhering to his tongue. He recalls a trip on a Chinese riverboat, where the Chinese were packed very tightly together in steerage and pushed out without ceremony at the landing places. He recalls a number of storms at sea, in particular a monsoon, in which the water beat drearily on the starboard deck and the patient was seasick. The buoy reminds him of a nervous captain on a riverboat who almost ran over a buoy in trying to make a landing. The Chinese man, in the only dry spot, makes him think of himself, remaining in the hospital without regard for his wife.

This dream is obviously similar to the deeper latent sense of the dream last discussed; but the pressure of the passive impulses is now much stronger and the patient's narcissism is defending itself by physical rejection (nausea), and there is an attempt to project even this upon his wife. The imagination that the patient is the source of the motion is now no longer adequate. The best defense of this sort which he can now offer is to project himself into "the only dry spot." It will be noted that the nausea here has a double meaning: first, rejection of oral homosexual desires; second, seasickness, which may be considered perhaps as a rejection of the passive rotation which here appears again. It is also of interest to note that the waves come from the right side and hence must cause the boat to rotate from right to left. It will be recalled that the dream of the revolving landscape also seemed to point to a previous rotation from right to left.

For the next two months there was no material bearing upon our topic, but in the middle of July the patient's decision to discontinue masturbation brought out material which focused the discussion upon his homosexual impulses. With regard to the existence of these, however, he assumed a very skeptical attitude. On July 25 he reported a fantasy of instructing girls how to submit to coitus without repugnance. Then the homosexual material was interrupted by a period of three days (July 26 to 28) during which he complained of dizziness, faintness (from hunger, according to his own account), and slight nausea.

He recalled that sometimes before this, when the barber had turned his head quickly from left to right, he had had a sensation as though the room and the lights were spinning in the same direction. On another occasion, while sleeping on the couch, he had turned over in one direction and immediately felt as though he were revolving in the opposite direction. Once in childhood he dreamed that he was on the right side of the bed and in danger of falling out. He turned over to the left to save himself and actually did fall out. For the three nights in succession previous to this interview, he had gone to bed lying on top of the covers and waked up with the covers pulled over him. The next night he caught himself in the act of pulling them over him by rolling over in his sleep. As a child he used to spin around until he was dizzy and would fall. As he fell he would imagine himself dying a heroic death. Finally his· mother forbade this play. He used to swing in a swing and dream that when he was a man he would travel in a boat and write about it. He used also to sit motionless in the swing and imagine that the room was revolving about an iron bar. After discussing experiences of this sort for three days, the patient broke through his self-imposed restraint against masturbation for the first time in seventeen days.

It is quite evident from this material that he has unusually sensitive vestibular reflexes. When the barber turns his head sharply, or when he turns over in his sleep, he experiences the effects which most people would experience only after several revolutions. These in both cases reported, however, are of the normal type. The reader will recall that there was a considerable degree of deafness in his left ear, dating from a nasal infection in 1919. An examination in April 1927, a short time before his admission to the hospital, revealed air conduction moderately decreased on the right and markedly decreased on the left. A tuning fork held on the forehead was heard in the left ear. Reports from Barany tests stated that there was no pathological nystagmus and that responses to turning were normal. Both tympanic membranes appeared normal. The patient's deafness, therefore, is plainly a middle ear deafness and not caused by disease of the labyrinths.

An increased irritability of the semicircular canals is, moreover, reported to be the usual finding in neuroses in which vertigo is a symptom. Barany states, indeed, that "neurasthenia" increases in particular the duration of the *horizontal* nystagmus following rotation in the horizontal plane. The occurrence of a revolving visual field in dreams of patients subject to neurotic vertigo has also been described by Leidler and Loewy. It is of interest that a number of Leidler and Loewy's cases also gave a history of pleasurably toned fantasies and play, involving stimulation of the semicircular canals.

There is now also evidence that the patient is in the habit of turning over in his sleep, and interestingly enough, so far as we have evidence, always in the same direction, from right to left. It will be recalled that all of our dream material has pointed to rotation in this same direction.

Returning to the dream of the revolving landscape, we now have little reason to doubt that the dream is a reaction to the patient's having actually turned over in his sleep, and from right to left. But the question remains: How does this fit in with the sense of the dream? It will be remembered that the dream represents him as pointing out to his wife a former picnicking place where he had once been with his father, mother, and brother; but the analysis of the rotation phenomena pointed to the inference that he was really looking at the island. How can this discrepancy be reconciled? It will be recalled that the island was the shape of the female breast. The mother's breast is indeed a picnicking place for the infant. The island and the picnicking place are, except for the censorship, identical.

The sense of the dream is now clear. The dream is a reaction to the primal scene, not in the sense of identification with either mother or father, but by regression to the desire for the mother's breast.

But how are we to interpret his turning over to the left? We may perhaps use at this point some recent observations reported by Hoff. In an attempt to explain the fact that the vestibular symptoms developing under the influence of medinal or veronal often show a definite inequality in the irritability of the vestibular apparatus on the two sides, he finds that the individuals in question (in whom organic disease of the vestibular and cerebellar apparatus had been excluded) in every case slept invariably on the side corresponding to the more irritable vestibular apparatus. He then found that, out of 100 organically normal individuals, approximately 70 percent were able to sleep in only one position; interestingly enough, many of them were not aware of this, since the position was assumed only after they had already fallen asleep. When mechanical devices were used to compel the individual to sleep in some other position, it was found impossible in nearly every case to induce the individual to sleep. Only by procedures designed to cause excessive fatigue was the attempt to induce sleep successful, in a few cases; but even in these the sleep was much disturbed and the subjects awoke after a few hours, reporting dreams in which objects revolving about them, as well as a number of other phenomena referable to the vestibular apparatus, were the most conspicuous feature.

Let us return to our own material. The patient's tendency to turn to the left, combined with visual phenomena such as would be associated with a nystagmus with quick movement to the right, point rather definitely to the vestibular apparatus on the right side as the more irritable. In this case, according to Hoff's findings, we should expect him to sleep upon his right side. It then becomes quite understandable that his turning in his sleep should be so regularly to the left, for this would be, indeed, the only direction to which he could turn at all easily.

But the question still remains: What is the psychological significance of his turning in the context of the rest of the dream material? Two further thoughts suggest themselves. Perhaps his turning to the left is part of the primal scene itself. From the patient's description of the relative position of the beds, it would appear that the parents' bed lay toward the foot and to the left of his own. If the patient were lying on the right side, he would have to turn to the left in order to see his parents.

A second possibility is not inconsistent with this. Perhaps he is reviving memories of his mother's turning him to her to put him to the breast. The dream then becomes understandable as a condensation of the two experiences, the center of emphasis in the primal scene being displaced upon the one feature which it has in common with the suckling experience, i.e., the turning about and associated apparent revolution of surrounding objects.

We must also consider in this connection the well-nigh universal association, which is reflected also in language, between the right side of the body and what is morally right and acceptable. The right hand is the one which children are taught to use, and walking and standing "upright" are efforts requiring some self-mastery that are also encouraged by the parents. Perhaps, therefore, the left side is more readily associated with a regression to memories of being passively moved about.

I should like to emphasize another point in connection with this regression. The play and fantasies which I have quoted are evidence that not only the suckling, but also the being carried and turned about, have an erotic value for the patient. In fact, his dizziness and nausea for a period of three days appeared to absorb the greater part of his libido. It is, indeed, a matter of common knowledge that babies enjoy being rocked, that older children enjoy swings and merry-go-rounds, and that, when seasickness has been overcome, most of us enjoy the tossing and rolling of a boat at sea. Quite possibly also the visual impressions of the environment's apparent movement about them play a not unimportant part in the pleasure of such experiences, for we all know that infants are especially attracted to moving objects, and there is little reason to suppose that an infant at first distinguishes clearly between the apparent movements of its surroundings caused by its own movements and the actual movements of the objects themselves. I am inclined to suspect, therefore, that in the dreams which I have quoted, we have evidence of a visual and labyrinthine and kinesthetic delight in the phenomena of passive motion which, at least in this patient's case, seems to have played an important part, in association with oral eroticism, in the earliest postnatal stage of libidinal development, and to have later been brought into close association with his intrauterine fantasies.

It is interesting to note also the close connection between this delight in passive motion and the patient's homosexual material. I suspect that his condensation of the two tendencies in his intrauterine fantasies is more than a coincidence and depends upon a sort of structural unity between them. Possibly, the passive homosexual desires contain as one of their most important elements a later differentiation and modification of the infant's pleasure in passive motion.

The patient's lack of ability to distinguish between his own movement and that of surrounding objects, which is so striking a feature in this material, forms an interesting physical corollary with Tausk's conception of abolition of the ego-boundaries in deep regressive material. The absence of the ego-boundaries in Tausk's sense is also very strikingly illustrated in my patient's material and belongs, of course, just like the material with which we have been dealing, to the earliest period of postnatal development. It is this obliteration of ego-boundaries which makes so easy his transition, by identification, from feelings of utter helplessness and insignificance in comparison with his father, to an almost omnipotent identification with that father.

It is also of interest that the patient's nausea and dizziness appear only when his active defense against his passive tendencies begins. As long as he is content to reinterpret his passive experiencs and fuse them with fantasies of omnipotent identification with his father, so long do dizziness and nausea remain out of the picture; they appear for the first time only when he begins actively to reject his passive tendencies. This, after all, is consistent with the apparent organic meaning of dizziness as a symptom of threatened failure in the maintenance of equilibrium. Seasickness, for instance, is considerably relieved by one's lying down and thus giving up the attempt to maintain the upright position. The symptom of dizziness occurring so frequently at the end of an analytic hour, as Ferenczi describes, is, of course, quite consistent with this interpretation of dizziness as the expression of a conflict between passive desires (delight in passive motion, passive homosexual desires) and an ego which is struggling to assume a more active role. The more general conception of Bauer and Schilder, that psychogenic dizziness is "an expression of the irreconcilability of two spheres of psychic experience," is also not inconsistent with the suggestion here advanced.

BIBLIOGRAPHY

Barany, Robert. *Physiologie u. Pathologie des Bogengang-apparates beim Menschen.* 1907.

Bauer, J. and Schilder, P. Über einige psychophysiologische Mechanismen funktioneller Neurosen. *Deutsche Zeitschrift f. Nervenheilkunde,* 1919, Bd. 64.

Breuer, J. Über die Funktion der Bogengänge des Ohrlabyrinthes. *Med. Jahrbücher.* Wien, 1874. Quoted by Leiri.

Ewald, J. R. and Wollenberg, R. Der Schwindel. *Spezielle Pathologie u. Therapie, Nothnagel,* Bd. XII, 2 (1911, Auflage). Quoted by Leiri.

Ferenczi, S. Sensations of Giddiness at the End of the Psychoanalytic Session. *Further Contributions to the Theory and Technique of Psycho-Analysis.* London, 1926.

Helmholz, H. von. *Handbuch der Physiologischen Optik,* Bd. III. Hamburg, 1910.

Hering, E. *Beitrag zur Physiologie.* Heft I, 1861.

Hitzig, E. Der Schwindel. *Spezielle Pathologie u. Therapie, Nothnagel,* Bd. XII., 2. Wien, 1899.

Hoff, H. Zusammenhang v. Vestibularfunktion, Schlafstellung u. Traumleben. *Monatschrift f. Psychiatrie u. Neurologie,* 1929, Bd. 71.

Leidler, H. and Loewy, P. Der Schwindel bei Neurosen. *Monatschrift f. Ohrenheilkunde u. Laryngo. Rhinologie,* 1923, Bd. 57.

Leiri, F. Über den Schwindel. *Zeitschrift f. Hals. Nasen-und Ohren-Heilkunde,* 1927, Bd. 17. Several of the quotations in the text (as noted) have been requoted directly from Leiri, as the original articles were inaccessible to the writer.

Purkinje, J. Beitage zur Näheren Kenntnis des Schwindels nach heautognostischen Daten. *Med. Jahrbücher.* Wien, 1820. Quoted by Leiri.

Tausk, V. Über die Entstehung des Beeinflussungsapparates in der Schizophrenie. *Internationale Zeitschrift f. Arztliche Psychoanalyse,* 1919, V. Jahrgang.

Chapter Twenty-Four

PSYCHOGENIC FACTORS IN ASTHMA

The following paper was a preliminary report based upon investigations carried out by Drs. Alexander, Bacon, Eisler, French, Gerard, McLean, Mohr, Ross, Saul, Tower, and Wilson, supplemented by my detailed and comparative study especially of the dream material of twenty-four cases of bronchial asthma analyzed at the Chicago Institute for Psychoanalysis over periods of one to twenty-six months. Of these, six patients were men, ten were women, and eight were children, four boys and four girls. The patients chosen were those in whom allergic hypersensitivity had been previously demonstrated by means of allergic history, skin tests, etc., as judged by an experienced allergist.

When we pass our patients in review, our first impression is that they vary considerably both in their personality traits and in the type of emotional disturbances for which they sought treatment.

We found it much easier to demonstrate common features in emotional situations that seem to precipitate asthma attacks. In the cases that we have been able to analyze, we have found that the acute asthma attack occurs in place of a repressed cry in reaction to a temptation that threatens the patient with loss of the love of a mother figure. Apparently in a majority of cases, the temptation is a sexual one. The relation of the asthma attacks to the Oedipus complex differs somewhat according to the sex of the patient. In male patients, the typical conflict is between sexual urges toward the mother and the fear of losing the mother's love. A typical family constellation in the early childhood of these patients is one in which the mother is overprotective to the little boy and binds him to her in a dependent relationship, but immediately

Reprinted from *American Journal of Psychiatry*, 96 (1939).

rejects the first signs of his infantile genital interest in her. This creates a situation in which the first infantile stirrings of genital (phallic) sexuality become a temptation that threatens to deprive the little boy of that mother's love upon which he is so dependent. One is struck with the frequency with which the mothers of these patients play this double role, at once seductive and prohibitive. Four of our six adult male patients, for example, had continued to sleep with the mother until the age of puberty or later.

Fear of the father, on the other hand, seems not to play so great a role in connection with the asthma attacks. It is rather the loss of the father's love that is feared. The father seems, in fact, to play the role of a mother substitute.

In girls, the situations precipitating attacks seem typically to be ones in which the first stirrings of sexual interest in the father threaten the little girl with estrangement from the mother. A frequent early childhood constellation is one in which the father plays a somewhat seductive role but the mother binds the little girl to her in pregenital dependence upon condition that she betray no sign of awakening genital sexuality.

The birth of younger children and especially the discovery that the mother is pregnant also play an exceedingly important role in precipitating asthma attacks. It is not difficult to understand why this is the case. The possibility of another child already threatens the patient with the loss of the mother's love and stirs up aggressive impulses to take the unborn child from her, but these aggressive impulses in turn only increase the danger that the mother will withdraw her love.

The fact that the asthma attack seems to be an acute reaction to a conflict which is too intense for the ego to master enables us to understand better the defenses by means of which the ego is able to protect itself from asthmatic attacks during the symptom-free periods. These defenses vary a great deal, and the numerous possible defense mechanisms account for the great variation in the superficial clinical picture which we noted at the beginning of our discussion.

1) One type of defense is found in practically all cases. This is an urge to seek reconciliation with the mother by means of confession. This is but one example of the need of our asthma patients to seek reassurance that the mother will really not be offended in spite of the patient's unconscious wishes. Many of our patients were particularly good children seeking to assure themselves in this way of the mother's love. A disposition to win love by helping and giving to others is very common in our asthma patients and serves the double function (a) of

winning parental approval, and (b) of vicariously gratifying the pa-
tient's own need for love and reassurance by helping someone else as
the patient himself would like to be helped and loved. Other patients
develop a great facility for making use of rationalizations which were
presumably acceptable to their parents.

2) Another group of defense mechanisms offers a sharply contrasting
picture. These are defenses by the familiar method of attempting to
master a traumatic event which has been passively experienced by
active repetition of it. It is sexual temptation more than forbidden
sexual gratification that usually serves as the precipitating cause of the
asthma attack. It would seem that overt sexual activity already implies
a degree of mastery of the traumatic fear of losing the mother's love
that is sufficient to avert the asthmatic attack.

3) A third group of defense reactions may be described as attempts
on the part of the patient to withdraw from the whole temptation
situation and make himself independent of the mother by means of
autoerotic and particularly anal erotic substitutes. In many of our cases,
a marked periodicity is demonstrable in the course of the analysis. There
will be long periods during which the patient misses hours and comes
only infrequently to the analysis and during which the material is
characterized by anal erotic attitudes of independence and often by a
peculiarly impersonal attitude toward life. During these periods the
patient is free from asthma attacks. Then, perhaps after a long inter-
ruption of the analysis, the patient will begin to respond again to what
we have already referred to as the seductive phase of the transference.
Forbidden sexual impulses begin to be encouraged back into conscious-
ness. Finally, however, the temptation becomes intense enough to be-
come again a threat to the patient's bond to the mother, and another
asthma attack is precipitated.

Since earliest times, it has been suspected that psychological factors
play some role in connection with bronchial asthma. In the last few
decades, the discovery of the significance of allergic factors in this
disease has tended to divert interest away from earlier observations that
asthma is frequently associated with some sort of emotional instability
and that asthma attacks are often precipitated by acute emotional conflicts. In the present study, we wish to return to the problems presented
by these earlier observations. In so doing we have been interested, first

in determining the nature of the emotional disturbances associated with asthma and their relation to the attacks, but also secondarily in inquiring into the relation between these emotional disturbances and the allergic factors which have been more recently discovered.

The following report is based upon investigations carried out by Drs. Alexander, Bacon, Eisler, French, Gerard, McLean, Mohr, Ross, Saul, Tower, and Wilson supplemented by my detailed and comparative study especially of the dream material of our asthma patients. Twenty-four cases of bronchial asthma were analyzed at the Chicago Institute for Psychoanalysis over periods of one to twenty-six months. Of these, six were men, ten were women, and eight were children, four boys and four girls. The patients chosen were those in whom allergic hypersensitivity had been previously demonstrated by means of allergic history, skin tests, etc., as judged by an experienced allergist. In addition, Dr. Siegfried Bernfeld has supplemented our studies by analyzing and summarizing the case records of eight asthmatic children who have been under close observation since birth by the Institute of Child Welfare at the University of California at Berkeley.

Patients who undertake and continue through an analytic treatment must be patients who are suffering from some sort of emotional disturbance. It is impossible, therefore, to draw any significant conclusions from the fact that in all the patients that we analyzed the asthma was found associated with emotional difficulties of varying grades of severity. It will be interesting to inquire, however, whether the emotional conflicts and personality structure in these patients show any common features as contrasted with patients suffering from other forms of disorder.

An analysis tends, moreover, to mobilize emotional conflicts which may previously have been latent, and this might be expected to throw into relief the role played by emotional factors as contrasted with allergic factors in precipitating the attacks. It will be of interest, nevertheless, to inquire whether the emotional situations which seem to precipitate the attacks present any specific common characteristics. If they do, we may then inquire whether emotional conflicts of this specific character may perhaps also have been present as precipitating factors for other asthma attacks which preceded the analytic procedure.

When we pass our patients in review, our first impression is that they vary considerably both in their personality traits and in the type of emotional disturbance for which they sought treatment. A number of our patients were particularly good children and were characterized in adult life by an urge to help and give to others. Some of our children, on the other hand, were brought to treatment because of their particularly aggressive behavior. In one of our adult patients and in one of our children, the picture at the beginning of the treatment was of a compulsive character with mild compulsive neurotic symptoms. Still another, a man, sought treatment originally on account of conscious homosexual impulses. Upon superficial examination, therefore, there seems to be a considerable range of divergence in the personality picture presented by our asthma patients.

It is much easier at the outset to demonstrate common features in emotional situations that seem to precipitate the asthma attacks. Let me cite a few examples.

A male patient of Dr. Saul reports that he developed asthma for the first time shortly after marrying against his mother's opposition. Another attack is associated with his sleeping with his wife at a camp in a room separated by only a thin partition from the room of the director, an "old woman" who objected to the patient and his wife talking after 10 P.M.

A male patient of Dr. Catherine Bacon reported the following two dreams the day after he had had a basal metabolism test:

a. This morning. Was in a Catholic church. Three priests were in front of him and they had gleaming eyes. Their eyes were sparkling with delight. Patient was evidently becoming a Catholic. He thought of wife's remark Catholics are so glad to have a Protestant in their ranks. He thought the gleam was due to their getting him away from Protestants. Their eyes gleamed so brightly that it was like jewels. Remembers no color. He would have had more to this dream if he hadn't waked up wheezing.

b. This morning. He was also awakened from this by wheezing. This dream preceded the first one. A naked woman. She was lying down stretched in front of him with feet toward him and her legs stretched apart. She didn't represent a woman all the time, for part of the time her legs became writhing snakes.

Patient associates to the snakes in the dream reported second (actually the one which occurred first) fear of being poisoned by a rattlesnake; having an affair with a woman—he would be in danger of trouble and maybe disease; snakes that wrap themselves around a victim suggest the idea of a woman twining her legs around him and crushing him; "domination would come into that too," he adds. The dream is in reaction to the analysis as a temptation situation. Patient vainly attempts to ward off the sexual temptation by substituting phallic symbols for the female genitals, but the attempt fails and he awakens with asthma. The other side of his conflict is portrayed in the second dream (the one reported first). The three priests correspond to the three men present to observe patient's basal metabolism test of the day before. Their gleaming eyes portray the danger that they will see through patient and detect his incestuous wishes toward the analyst. The manifest dream is an attempt to defend himself from this danger. In the manifest dream the priests are not offended by patient's incestuous desires but their eyes are sparkling with delight at the prospect of converting him to a new faith. In the context it is easy to surmise that the new faith is the psychoanalytic "faith" which permits and encourages one to become conscious even of incestuous desires without fear of offense.

It will be noticed that in all three of these instances we find an identical conflict. In each case the patient is exposed to a temptation which would estrange him from a parental figure, usually the mother. In the dreams reported by Bacon's patient, we see this conflict portrayed particularly vividly. The patient is struggling desperately to ward off the temptation and the associated danger of losing the parents' love. He attempts to deny the temptation by substituting phallic symbols for the female genitals and then, in his second dream, he attempts to ward off the fear of loss of the parents' love by appealing to the tolerance of psychoanalysis for unconscious impulses and picturing the analysts as trying to take him into their fold—instead of expelling him from the church, as he really fears they will do. In both cases he awakens wheezing. It is only a short step to infer that the attack of asthma occurs when his defenses fail at the moment when he is suddenly exposed to the conflict between an acute temptation and his fear of losing the mother's love.

With this sort of fundamental conflict, we should expect that the tolerance offered by the analysis to the forbidden unconscious wishes would acquire an ambiguous meaning for the patient. At first the tolerant atmosphere of the analysis may be expected to quiet the patient's fears of losing the mother's love. Here at last is a mother who will not turn away from the patient. But very soon this same tolerance acquires a dangerous seductive character. Forbidden impulses thus encouraged into consciousness now awaken old fears that the analyst, the new mother, will behave like the original mother and will punish the patient's forbidden wishes by withdrawing love.

I regret that space does not permit me to give examples of the numerous dreams which could be selected to illustrate this double aspect of the transference. Over and over again, these patients become blocked just at the point where the unconscious material is leading up to a confession. They fear to make this confession and awaken with asthma.

Most of these patients have a very strong urge to regain the love of the mother by confession. In fact, this urge to confess sometimes goes to ridiculous extremes.

> For example, Saul's patient, to whom I have already referred, was at one time seduced by a girl almost to the point of having intercourse with her. Then the patient suddenly left her and rushed to his mother to confess the episode. The mother wept and made a great scene. A sequel to this incident is particularly instructive. After the interruption of his analysis the patient, who was a seasonal case, had lived through the spring and fall seasons, during which he was usually subject to asthma, without an attack. Then in January he responded to the telephone invitation of a girl from out of town and went to her hotel room, and they got into bed together. He had an orgasm but not intercourse, then fled in terror to his wife to whom he confessed only the nonsexual part of the story. During the succeeding two months he had a number of attacks of severe asthma. The attacks ceased when he finally gained spontaneous insight into the fact that they were a reaction to this incident.

Incidents of this sort occur frequently in the histories of our asthma patients. So long as this technique of winning back reconciliation with the mother by confession is successful, the patients appear to be protected from asthma attacks. But sometimes one is afraid to confess. Then, as in a dream, the confession is choked in one's throat and in its place occurs an asthma attack.

Confession is a defense that utilizes speech and speech is a respiratory mechanism. It is, therefore, perhaps not surprising that it should have so intimate a relationship with the asthma attacks. It is interesting to note, moreover, that there seems also to be a very intimate relationship between asthma and crying or laughing. There is much to suggest, in fact, that the asthma attack is really a sort of equivalent of a cry of anxiety or rage which has been inhibited and repressed. One of the first reactions of the child upon separation from the mother at birth is to cry, and during early infancy, and even later, crying remains the predominant reaction of the child in situations of helplessness when he can only wish for the mother to return to him. In later life this primitive cry is modified into speech and in confession retains the function of maintaining the bond between child and mother. For some reason, in the situations which provoke asthma attacks the child is unable to cry. Some of our patients state that they have not cried for years and others boast that they have never been afraid. In other cases it is apparently only in certain situations that crying is inhibited. Of particular interest, however, is the fact that we are sometimes able to observe the cessation of an asthma attack and the appearance of crying in its place. Such replacement of asthma attacks by crying is particularly apt to occur at times when the analysis is beginning to achieve some degree of resolution of the asthma attacks.

So far we have found that the acute asthma attack occurs in place of a repressed cry in reaction to a temptation that threatens the patient with loss of the mother's love. Is it possible to define more accurately the nature of this temptation?

It will be noted that, in all the instances cited, the temptation is a sexual one. The relation of the asthma attacks to the Oedipus complex differs somewhat according to the sex of the patient. In male patients, the typical conflict is between sexual urges toward the mother and the fear of losing the mother's love. A typical family constellation in the early childhood of these patients is one in which the mother is over-protective of the little boy and binds him to her in a dependent relationship but immediately rejects the first signs of infantile genital interest in her. This creates a situation in which the first infantile stirrings of genital (phallic) sexuality become a temptation that threatens to deprive the little boy of that mother's love upon which he is so dependent. One is struck with the frequency with which the mothers of these patients play this double role, at once seductive and prohibitive. Four of our six adult male patients, for example, had continued to sleep with the mother until the age of puberty or later.

Fear of the father, on the other hand, seems not to play so great a role in connection with the asthma attacks. It is rather the loss of the father's love that is feared. The father seems, in fact, to play the role of a mother substitute.

In girls, the situations precipitating attacks seem typically to be ones in which the first stirrings of sexual interest in the father threaten the little girl with estrangement from the mother. A frequent constellation in early childhood is one in which the father plays a somewhat seductive role, but the mother binds the little girl to her in pregenital dependence upon condition that she betray no sign of awakening genital sexuality.

It should be added that, because of the intense repression of sexuality in many of these cases, a superficial study of the attacks may overlook the importance of a sexual temptation in precipitating an attack. In such cases the patient will seem to have almost no interest in sex and the attack will be attributed to some other incident of a much more superficial character.

A patient of Dr. George Mohr's, for example, attributed her first asthma attack in the analysis to her worry about letting her child go with the father on a cold day without underwear. The preceding analytic material, however, pointed to the patient's first unconscious sexual transference wishes toward the analyst. The next attack of asthma some weeks later followed an exhibitionistic dream in which the patient was herself without underwear.

Sexual wishes arising out of the Oedipus complex are not, however, the only wishes that precipitate asthma attacks by threatening to disturb the patient's dependent relationship to the mother. The birth of younger children and especially the discovery that the mother is pregnant play an exceedingly important role in precipitating asthma attacks. It is not difficult to understand why this is the case. The possibility of another child already threatens the patient with the loss of the mother's love and stirs up aggressive impulses to take the unborn child from her, but these aggressive impulses in turn only increase the danger that the mother will withdraw her love.

In one of Dr. McLean's cases, a man, a period of asthma attacks dated from his discovery that a married woman with whom he was having a sexual relationship was pregnant. Another period of asthma attacks began during his wife's first pregnancy one year after his marriage, at which time the patient proposed an abortion but his wife refused. During the analysis, many attacks of asthma were stirred up by discussion of what the patient felt to be his wife's neglect of his children, a complaint which upon analysis proved to be a substitute for the unconscious complaint that his wife neglected him for the children.

It is interesting that it is sexual temptation rather than forbidden sexual gratification that usually serves as the precipitating cause of the asthma attack. Much of our material suggests that if the patient has gone so far as to commit himself to an overt sexual act this is apt to be already a sign that he has mastered the panic fear of loss of the mother's love to a degree sufficient to avert the asthmatic attack. The asthmatic attack seems rather to be a reaction of acute helplessness. At the moment of temptation the dependence upon the mother is so great that the threat of losing her completely overpowers the patient. The mechanism is similar to that postulated by Freud for acute anxiety. The asthma attack occurs only when the patient is overpowered by a mass of excitation which the ego is powerless to master.

The fantasy material of our asthma patients is full of symbolic representations of intrauterine fantasies in symptom-free periods as well as in the material accompanying asthma attacks, and the asthma attacks seem to be associated with material symbolic of interruption or disturbance of the protected intrauterine state. Alexander has attempted to check this impression statistically and finds that the proportion of symbolic intrauterine fantasies in the manifest dream content averages considerably higher in the asthma patients than in any other class of patients who were used as controls. The nearest approximation to the proportion found in asthma cases is in some cases of anxiety neurosis.

The fact that the asthma attack seems to be an acute reaction to a conflict which is too intense for the ego to master enables us to understand better the defenses by means of which the ego is able to protect itself from asthmatic attacks during the symptom-free periods. These defenses vary a great deal, and the numerous possible defense mechanisms account for the great variation in the superficial clinical picture which we noted at the beginning of our discussion.

1) One type of defense is found in practically all cases. I have already alluded to the urge to seek reconciliation with the mother by means of confession. This is but one example of the need that our asthma patients show to seek reassurance that the mother will really not be offended in spite of the patient's unconscious wishes. As already mentioned, many of our patients were particularly good children, seeking to assure themselves in this way of the mother's love. A disposition to win love by helping and giving to others is very common in our asthma patients and serves the double function (*a*) of winning parental approval, and (*b*) of vicariously gratifying the patient's own need for love and reassurance by helping someone else as the patient himself would like to be helped and loved. Other patients develop a great facility for making use of rationalizations which were presumably acceptable to their parents.

Still other patients utilize sickness and suffering in the well-known manner as means of regaining the sympathy and affection of the parents. One therefore finds very often that other symptoms, such as rheumatic pains or headache, will tend to protect the patient from attacks of asthma. In cases where the asthma has become more or less chronic, the mechanism seems to be one of a secondary adaptation to the symptom by means of which the child has learned to utilize the asthma attacks themselves as a means of regaining the mother's love for the patient. One of our male patients, in fact, was regularly taken into the mother's bed whenever he had an asthmatic attack.

2) Another group of defense mechanisms offers a sharply contrasting picture. These are defenses by the familiar method of attempting to master a traumatic event which has been passively experienced by active repetition of it. In this connection we have already noted that it is sexual temptation rather than forbidden sexual gratification that usually serves as the precipitating cause of the asthma attack. It would seem that overt sexual activity already implies a degree of mastery of the traumatic fear of the loss of the mother's love sufficient to avert the asthmatic attack.

Especially in a number of our children's cases, we can observe an attempt to master the fear by aggressive behavior. A little girl will ward off the dangerous temptation to father incest by castrative impulses toward the father, or a little boy will attempt to master his fear of seduction by the mother by aggressive attacks (anal, oral, or both) upon her. Similarly, our adult women patients defend themselves from the temptation to genital interest in the father by mechanisms of masculine protest and father identification such as are familiar to us in all types of neuroses in women; and in one of our male cases competitive attitudes toward the father served in a similar way to ward off the dangers arising from the patient's extreme dependence upon the mother's love.

Sometimes the aggressive impulses are direct reactions to the fear of suffocation and take the form of choking the mother. In a dream reported by McLean's patient, the patient urinated upon a hot stove in a boxcar as he saw two inspectors approaching and then ran away to watch with glee how they would be choked by the bad smell. Corresponding to this aggressive defense against the dangers arising from the patient's sexual impulses, this dream was not accompanied by asthma.

3) A third group of defense reactions may be described as attempts on the part of the patient to withdraw from the whole temptation situation and make himself independent of the mother by means of autoerotic and particularly anal erotic substitutes. In many of our cases a marked periodicity is demonstrable in the course of the analysis. There will be long periods during which the patient misses hours and comes only infrequently to the analysis and during which the material is characterized by anal erotic attitudes of independence and often

by a peculiarly impersonal attitude toward life. During these periods the patient is free from asthma attacks. Then, perhaps after a long interruption of the analysis, the patient will begin to respond again to what we have already referred to as the seductive phase of the transference. Forbidden sexual impulses begin to be encouraged back into consciousness. Finally, however, the temptation becomes intense enough to become again a threat to the patient's bond to the mother, and another asthma attack is precipitated.

In connection with these withdrawal mechanisms, it is interesting to note the reactions of our asthma patients to the danger of actual physical separation from the mother. It would seem that most asthma patients are particularly prone to attacks of asthma at times when they are undecided or in conflict as to whether or not to leave some mother figure. In the analysis we were early struck with the fact that asthma attacks tended to occur predominantly on weekends or during the period just preceding more prolonged interruptions of the analysis. Interestingly enough, during vacation periods, after the first few days, the patients were often singularly free from attacks. Then, just prior to the resumption of the analysis, the attacks would again begin to occur. In the history of these patients there would tend also to be a relative freedom from attacks during periods when the patients had actually achieved a physical separation from their mothers. It would seem that the precipitating situation is not the actual fact of separation from the mother but the indecision and conflict between the urge to cling to the mother and the need to separate from her.

> A case of Dr. Eisler's presented at the beginning of the analysis a related type of defense in the form of mild compulsive symptoms. It was not difficult to determine the relationship between these compulsive symptoms and the deeper fear of losing the love of the mother. The compulsive neurotic symptoms had arisen by the familiar mechanism of introjection of the mother and internalization of the conflict. The role played by the mother in the deeper conflict was now played by the patient's conscience and in place of the fear of loss of the mother's love there appeared guilt reactions with an anal erotic coloring, feelings of being impure. By means of this internalization of the conflict, the patient protected herself from the danger of an acute estrangement from the mother. The patient developed asthma attacks for the first time in the analysis only after this compulsive neurotic purity complex had been interpreted and worked through.

Summing up our findings: We have concluded that the asthma attack is precipitated as a rule by a temptation which threatens to estrange the patient from a mother figure, and our discussion of the numerous possible defenses against this conflict would suggest that the common feature in the otherwise divergent personalities of our asthma patients is the fact that the personality of these patients is built up in large part around the task of mastering by one means or another the patient's fear of being separated from the mother.

We may, perhaps, best conclude with a very few observations that have a bearing upon the relation between allergic and psychological factors in the etiology of bronchial asthma.

First, we have seen that asthma attacks tend to be precipitated by emotional conflict situations of a rather uniform and typical character. It would seem extremely improbable that these emotional conflict situations should in every case have coincided with an allergic stimulus which was absent during the often rather prolonged periods during which the same patient's emotional withdrawal from the analysis was marked and during which he also was free from asthma attacks. Moreover, a few patients experienced an initial relief from asthmatic attacks upon starting the analysis, apparently owing to the reassurance resulting from the analyst's interest in them; and most of our patients developed an aggravation of the frequency and severity of their attacks as the analysis, after working through the defensive mechanisms, approached the fundamental conflict that we have been describing. In a few cases whose attacks had been confined to a particular season, asthmatic attacks appeared during the analysis in other seasons of the year.

In some cases, the substances to which the patients were allergically hypersensitive proved also to play a significant role in their psychological material. A patient of Dr. McLean's whose skin test was strongly positive for ragweed recalled that at the age of six he had lost his brother in a hayfield where the brother remained all night before he was found. During the analysis the memory of this incident was frequently accompanied by severe wheezing. Other patients who showed marked hypersensitivity to cat fur also dreamed frequently of temptation situations in which the temptation was symbolized by a cat. Still another patient, who expressed a violent conscious resentment of children, displaced the greater part of her normal maternal interest upon cats and upon test developed an extreme allergic reaction to cat fur.

Finally, in a number of patients, as a result of analytic therapy the asthmatic attacks were greatly relieved and we could observe during the analytic sessions the gradual replacement of the asthmatic attacks by crying and then by a diminution of the fear of sexual temptation.

One patient of Dr. Wilson's who had previously shown a marked sensitivity to horse dander and in whom horses regularly elicited attacks of asthma later became able to ride horseback without any trace of asthma.

All these observations would suggest that psychological and allergic factors probably stand in a somewhat complementary relationship to each other in the etiology of bronchial asthma, that in some cases asthma attacks may be precipitated by allergic factors alone, in others by emotional factors alone, and that in still other cases cooperation of allergic and emotional factors may be necessary to produce the attacks.

Chapter Twenty-Five

BRIEF PSYCHOTHERAPY
IN BRONCHIAL ASTHMA

In the paper on brief psychotherapy in bronchial asthma, we began with the very significant relationship between asthma and confession. Throughout the lives of patients subject to psychogenic asthma attacks, there seems to run as a continuous undercurrent, more or less deeply repressed, a fear of estrangement from the mother. The cause of this fear is usually the patient's own forbidden impulses which he thinks will offend the mother. One device of which the asthmatic patient makes extensive use to protect himself against this danger of estrangement is confession of the disturbing impulse. If the mother or mother substitute accepts the confession without being shocked, then all is well for a time. If, however, the patient is too uncertain of the mother's tolerance to dare make his confession, then an asthma attack is likely to be precipitated.

This dynamic relationship between confession and asthma attacks has obvious implications for psychotherapy. The psychotherapeutic situation offers first of all an opportunity for the patient to confess what is disturbing him. If the asthmatic patient can gain confidence to confess fully and freely the impulses that are at the moment responsible for his fear of estrangement from some mother substitute, then we may expect his relief from asthma attacks until some new forbidden impulse arises to disturb him. This period of relief may be quite prolonged. When attacks occur again, the therapist's problem is to discover what

In collaboration with Adelaide M. Johnson, M.D. Reprinted from *Proceedings of the Second Brief Psychotherapy Council*, January 1944.

is the new disturbing impulse and to encourage the patient again to find relief by confessing it.

This theory suggests that we should be able to obtain satisfying therapeutic results with at least a considerable number of cases of bronchial asthma by means of briefer methods of psychotherapy. The objective in such therapy is to discover and help the patient to confess the particular matters that are disturbing him at the time of exacerbation of asthmatic attacks and then, as soon as relief is obtained, to diminish the frequency of treatments until other asthmatic attacks occur.

In the remainder of this paper we shall illustrate this kind of brief psychotherapy by two examples.

A study of the psychogenic factors in bronchial asthma was made several years ago by the Chicago Institute for Psychoanalysis. Of the dynamic relationships uncovered by this research, one of the most significant was that between asthma attacks and confessions. Throughout the lives of patients subject to psychogenic asthma attacks, there seems to run as a continuous undercurrent, more or less deeply repressed, a fear of estrangement from the mother. The cause of this fear is usually the patient's own forbidden impulses which he thinks will offend the mother. One device of which the asthmatic patient makes extensive use to protect himself against this danger of estrangement is confession of the disturbing impulse. If the mother or mother substitute accepts the confession without being shocked, then all is well for a time. If, however, the patient is too uncertain of the mother's tolerance to dare make his confession, then an asthma attack is likely to be precipitated.

This dynamic relationship between confession and asthma has obvious implications for psychotherapy. The psychotherapeutic situation offers first of all an opportunity for the patient to confess what is disturbing him. If the asthmatic patient can gain the confidence to confess fully and freely the impulses that are at the moment responsible for his fear of estrangement from some mother substitute, then we may expect his relief from asthma attacks until some new forbidden impulse arises to disturb him. This period of relief may be quite prolonged. When attacks occur again, the therapist's problem is to discover the new disturbing impulse and to encourage the patient again to find relief by confessing it.

This is an important principle in all psychotherapy. Many cases of psychogenic asthma, however, differ from other more complex psychotherapeutic problems in that the relatively uncomplicated cases of psychogenic asthma require little or no treatment other than that which aims to make the patient more and more secure in the confidence that nothing he may need to confess will be disturbing or offensive to the therapist.

The effect of such a therapy is at first merely symptomatic. By confessing what is disturbing him the patient gets relief for a time from his asthma attacks. Such symptomatic relief tends gradually to diminish deep underlying insecurity and dependence.

This theory suggests that we should be able to obtain satisfying therapeutic results with at least a considerable number of cases of bronchial asthma by means of briefer methods of psychotherapy. The objective in such therapy is to discover and help the patient to confess the particular matters that are disturbing him at the time of exacerbation of asthmatic attacks and then, as soon as relief is obtained, to diminish the frequency of treatments until other asthmatic attacks occur.

The following case, reported by Karl Hansen in 1930, is a very nice illustration of the efficacy of this kind of therapy. The patient was an English woman of forty-nine, married, and living in Germany. She had suffered periodically from asthma attacks since she was ten years old. Hansen reports the circumstances of original onset of the asthma attacks as follows: Just prior to the onset the patient's mother had become ill and died. During the mother's last illness the patient had had the sole responsibility for her care. The actual onset of the attacks seems, however, to have been precipitated by another incident. The patient was attending a school in England whose standards of honor were very high. She was the best student in the class. One day identical mistakes were found in the work of both the patient and the girl who sat next to her, and the patient was suspected of having copied. Even as an adult, she could not remember for sure whether she had been guilty. As she put it, "I didn't copy but my intelligence tells me that is the only way the identity of the two papers could be explained." In any case, much pressure was put upon her to confess but she stubbornly refused.

It was at this time that her asthma attacks began. They continued for about four years until she was fourteen years old. About this time, an American friend of her father, S, a man of considerable character, visited the family, won her friendship and confidence, and took her walking frequently with him in the country. In the course of her conversations with him the school incident and her feelings about it came to be talked over very freely. After that she ceased to have asthma attacks for a period of about five years.

Then at the age of eighteen she fell in love with F, whom she could not marry because he had other ties. Apparently in reaction to this situation she became engaged to G. She described G as a "splendid animal" whom she did not like but to whom she was strongly attracted sexually. A sexual relationship developed but she found this distasteful and was unable to decide either to marry him or to break with him.

Immediately after becoming acquainted with G, she began to have asthma attacks again, which continued for the three years she was engaged to him. They stopped when she broke off the engagement.

Then she married a German musician of great talent to whom she was attracted because of his many fine traits. The musician, however, was already ill at the time of the marriage and is described as a weak and dependent personality to whom the patient felt herself from the beginning in the role of sympathetic protectress and mother rather than wife. He was pictured as living in continuous high spirits, never tired or depressed, but under pressure to tell his wife everything that he felt. This made it necessary for her to maintain a continuous and often forced gaiety. She described the first months of the marriage as completely happy but never thoroughly free of the impressions made upon her by her memory of F. Even in the first months of her marriage she was thinking of F; she felt there was no one else like him.

A year later she gave birth to a son and was very happy. In her son she felt the first justification for her marriage. When the son was six months old, she took a trip to England and stayed not far from G. She avoided G but was pursued by him. She had no feeling for him, she said, but began to feel critical of her marriage. She began to suspect that her husband's illness was hereditary and decided therefore to have no more children by him.

After she had broken off her engagement with G, the patient had had no more asthma attacks for about four years, but immediately after she met G again the attacks returned. They continued to be severe for another four years and then gradually diminished.

During World War I, the patient was so busy with her household and so cut off from England that there was little to remind her of F. After the end of the war she entered into correspondence with S, the American friend of her childhood, and presumably continued in correspondence with him until he died a number of years later. Following his death and immediately after she had again seen F in England, her asthma attacks returned. They continued for three years until she first consulted Hansen.

In the first interviews Hansen was surprised by the amount that the patient was able to tell him and the freedom with which she could talk about herself. She said that since her youth she had longed for someone to whom she could tell all this.

On physical examination Hansen found evidence of chronic asthma, bronchitis, and "functional emphysema," but no temperature. There was a 4 percent eosinophilia. There was a strong positive allergic reaction to bed feathers and to horsehair.

After the patient had told her story to Hansen, there were no more asthma attacks for several months, but then there was a severe recurrence of attacks when she met F again. The attacks disappeared again after an interview with Hansen. After this the patient had been without attacks for two years at the time Hansen's article was written.

It will be noted that this individual had had prolonged periods throughout her life when she was free of asthma attacks, and that the periods of severe asthmatic attacks in every instance had their beginning in reaction to quite definite situations which brought to the surface her latent conflict. Such a case is obviously well suited for a method of psychotherapy that depends upon confession alone to achieve its results.

Our Institute case was not quite so favorable for this very simple method of therapy, because this patient, at the age of twenty-four, had already given in to his illness to the extent of renouncing the profession for which he had prepared himself, so that he was thoroughly dependent upon his father at the time he sought treatment. In accordance with this dependent attitude, he immediately developed a very strong dependence upon his therapist which made necessary a continuous therapeutic contact.

The following account of the therapy in this second case is based upon a summary prepared by Dr. Adelaide Johnson, who treated him.

When he first consulted Dr. Johnson, the patient was twenty-four years old and single. He had recently graduated from a medical school but felt himself quite unable to practice because of severe asthmatic attacks. Four years previously, skin tests had found him allergic to beef, pork, and chicken.

He had had a history of asthma since the age of fourteen. Before this age, he had weighed over 200 pounds but then went on a diet, reduced his weight to 155, and at that time began to develop asthmatic attacks. When he came for treatment, the patient was living with his father, a physician, his mother having died when he was three. Of this event he recalled only the mother's leaving home on a stretcher, his fighting with the attendants, and his crying as they took her to the hospital where she died of pneumonia.

After the mother's death, the patient and his brother moved next door to live with their father's sister and her husband. They lived there until the patient was nine. At this time the father married again, a young woman nineteen years his junior. The patient states that they were married six months before anyone was told. He resented the new wife and mother very much and first fought with her and was very mean to her, but as he came to know her he grew fond of her.

Four years before the patient came for treatment, the stepmother died of an ulcer. At the time he began treatment, he was extremely frank about his intense dislike for his father, which he attributed chiefly to the father's misuse of funds belonging to the patient's mother and stepmother. The patient also recalled that before his father's second marriage he had always sided with his aunt against his uncle, but rather early in the treatment he came to realize that the aunt was really a complaining, begrudging, and resentful person.

The aunt was very fat and the patient had always told her that he wished to be fat like her. At the time of the treatment, however, he resented her obesity and looked upon her refusal to diet as part of her greediness and infantilism. His own impulse to be fat like her throws some light upon his obesity in early adolescence before he began to diet. This attitude toward the aunt's obesity can probably be taken as an indication of a relationship which became plain later, that his obesity served the function of a defense against the conflict arising out of the attraction to his aunt and to his stepmother.

The patient was treated for a total of 45 interviews, for the most part at weekly intervals. Almost immediately the analyst had opportunity to point out the patient's tendency to develop a relationship of great dependence upon her. In the second hour the patient told how for eight years he had warded off attacks of asthma by rising late in the morning and leisurely sitting on the toilet, where he drank coffee slowly for an hour or so. If anything interrupted or rushed him he was certain to get an attack. Later in the same interview, however, a topic came up which was related to his anxieties about sexual impulses. He said that the only kind of girl he liked was an older girl who would take full responsibility for any sexual relations entered into and would not nag him afterward for attentions. Immediately after this statement he said, "I hope you will be critical of me and tell me just what to do so I don't do the wrong thing." The therapist said, "In other words you want me to be like the older girls who know what they are about, who see things clearly, who face the facts and relieve you of any responsibility for their acts." The patient laughed and said, "That's exactly what I want. You see I'm being dependent on you right away and I want you to be frank because I can't stand people to go round about things. I want to know where I stand with people."

The first asthma attack reported after the beginning of the treatment was attributed by the patient to the fact that he had to take his coffee rapidly and hurry around after he got up. He said he was watching himself to see whether he would have an attack and "sure enough I did." Later on in the same hour, however, he told of his extreme embarrassment with girls from the time he was six. Eventually he related this to the embarrassed uneasy feeling that he had had when his uncle teased him about being snuggled by his obese aunt.

When the therapist asked how his aunt accepted his efforts to be more independent, he said she would not stand for them. Any attempt on his part to "talk up" met with a whipping. She thwarted any adventurousness on his part. She "stuffed me with food."

At this point the therapist told him it seemed that his asthma came when his dependence was threatened, whether in relation to women or when he was left alone on a job (as will be reported later). She pointed out that his asthma began when he was fourteen, after he had reduced his weight and was therefore more attractive in appearance, and she wondered whether the asthma had something to do with impulses in him that might threaten a pleasant relationship with a mother person. After this interpretation, the patient recalled that when he was nine he realized that his stepmother was very pretty and nineteen years younger than his father. She encouraged him to fondle her breast and rest his head on her bosom. She would draw him closer and closer until the father in a rage would order him off to bed. From the ages of nine to fourteen, when he was so obese, this seductive situation continued, associated on the patient's part with intense conscious sexual desire for the stepmother. He did not think of her as a mother and longed to get into bed with her but feared that she would tell his father. In these years there was extreme fear of his father and of dogs. At fourteen, when he reduced drastically and felt more attractive physically, all the sexual play with his stepmother ceased and he had no further sexual feeling for her. It was at this time that his asthma began to be disturbing.

Two months after treatment started, the patient took a job in a department store under his brother's supervision. An asthma attack occurred the first night, when everyone went off and left him at midnight and he was alone at his work. To him this job signified an extension of the home, with dependence on his brother, although it did furnish an independent income. Attacks continued at night for some weeks when he was left alone.

The patient continued to feel elated about his treatment hours. He said nothing could make him leave them. The therapist at this point warned him about the possibility of later resistance. He protested, however, that he had told the therapist more than any other patient in so short a time. This the therapist interpreted as a wish to be the most cooperative of her patients and to confess all to her.

The patient failed to tell the therapist that he had had a mild asthmatic attack on the way to the office before the ninth hour, but he recalled this in the tenth hour. In discussing this attack, the analyst finally elicited from him the following confession. "Well, last Wednesday before I came here when I felt the attack coming on, I thought of sexual feelings in connection with the redhead and the Jewish girl and my aunt and my stepmother and practically every woman I know, and nothing clicked." The therapist pointed out that it was significant he should have thought of sexuality in relation to practically every woman except herself. This, however, he energetically denied. He emphasized instead his great dependence upon her.

At this point, three months after treatment began, the patient was very dependently attached to the therapist, was avoiding all girls, and was having almost no asthma. A month later he came in furious about having to meet his draft board. He was certain the men on the board would have no patience with the emotional basis for asthma. He felt all these men were as "dumb" as his father and he would die of asthma if he had to leave the therapist now. His asthma became worse. The analyst suggested that possibly he was angry at her for not intervening on his behalf with the draft board. In discussion of his intense anger, which soon appeared, he confessed that he had wished the therapist would "risk her reputation" in order to "save his life." The therapist's frustration of his dependence and her acceptance of his rage constituted one of the two major steps in his treatment. As a result the patient felt more independent.

It was after this hour that the patient for the first time was able to ask a "respectable girl" for intercourse, accept her refusal, and ask for another date. Never before had he approached a girl who he thought might refuse him. He now began steadily dating an attractive girl.

Soon he mentioned that his girl had a former beau whom she sometimes thought about. He did not want to be a "second fiddle" and he asked what the therapist thought about the girl. The therapist suspected that by means of this question the patient hoped to find out something about her own sexual experiences and her attitude toward them. This suggestion apparently took him by surprise but he immediately recognized its validity. "By George," he said, "that's right. I wouldn't have thought of it." For several hours after this, the patient was preoccupied with the faithlessness of women as illustrated by stories of married women with whom he had had intercourse. To this the therapist commented, "I doubt if you have as much conflict about women who are unfaithful as about women who are faithful to their husbands." He felt this to be true but added that he was not so easily downed by a rival as formerly. He went on for two or three hours to say that he could not be in conflict with the therapist because she was too old for him. When a friendly opportunity arose the therapist wondered if it were that he feared he was too young for her. He was evasive, blocked, and expressed amazement that he could not think of a thing to say for ten minutes. He said "only rarely" did he feel so uneasy talking to men or women as now. The therapist asked if it was necessary to bring the "men" in now, and with great heat he said, "Why not?" He was breathing heavily. The therapist mentioned some possible concern in relation to her husband. The patient appeared startled but immediately became more relaxed and said he had wondered about him.

About this time the therapist went on vacation. The second hour after she returned may be regarded as the turning point in the treatment. On this day the patient came to the office breathing heavily, perspiring somewhat, and obviously having a rather severe asthma attack. He had had several attacks during the week, always at night, and had taken ephedrine. Several mornings he felt his breathing a little impaired but no real attacks developed. He wanted to explain all this on the basis of his having had to rush around in the morning, especially that morning.

The therapist listened to him for a few minutes. He said he had not been out with a girl that week and he thought that could not be a factor. He mentioned nothing about the therapist. She commented that she thought his feelings toward her had been relatively flat since she returned from her vacation and he said that this was true. She wondered if there were some feelings about her having gone away that were not just clear. He said that he was sure this was not so, that he could not even remember one thing they talked about before she went away. Thinking that he was probably very angry at her, the therapist merely said that she was thinking of the fact he had mentioned, that when he found that the girl with whom he had been falling in love was still somewhat attached to a former beau, he had dropped her immediately. At this point the patient said, "Oh, yes, and probably that brings up your husband now. I was talking about your husband just before you went away and I felt he was too much of a rival in the picture. I felt that was one of the big factors inhibiting me in my feelings toward you."

At this point the asthma completely stopped. The patient breathed quietly, his face was no longer flushed, and he began to laugh. He said, "I can't believe it. I have never had an attack stop so suddenly even with ephedrine." He said, "You mentioned that thing and I thought of your husband and what we were talking about before you went away and in thirty seconds the attack had stopped." The patient was amazed. He said that at last he was convinced the therapist was involved in his attacks and when he had the asthma attacks in the morning or at night it must be that there were some thoughts of her he was not conscious of.

Hours followed full of resentment toward the therapist, with fears of humiliation, and speculations about her husband. He would like to marry her in order to have her take care of his attacks; there could be a sexual life also but he would not be in love with her. His bitterness and anger were mentioned briefly to him. At this time he wanted to call the therapist by her first name and to have her call him Dr. X. The feeling that the therapist would not be willing to concede him all his rightful prerogatives and respect as Dr. X was pointed out, and after this competition was worked through the patient and the therapist were both "Doctor."

After this he realized that he had begun to want to do things for women and to go out with them without any special interest in sexual intercourse. He finally came to tell the therapist that he could no longer be in love with her. There was much angry depreciation of her which she accepted without comment. After this he said he no longer felt the anxiety he used to feel when indicating to some girl he did not love her, whereas previously he had always feared this would throw the girl into a rage. From now on he felt a great sense of freedom, talked and acted with increased masculinity and independence, and was no longer hostile but friendly.

The patient has now been in the army for almost two years. He came to see the therapist two weeks ago. He looked fine. He had had one slight attack of asthma in a difficult situation a year and a half before. He is engaged and expects to marry soon.

It will be noted that this case differs from Hansen's in that this patient's dependence made necessary a more continuous contact between patient and therapist. As a result of this, the therapist had to do more interpretation than Hansen. The interpretations were directed primarily toward relieving the disturbance arising out of the frustrated dependence and out of the sexual wishes that the patient developed toward the therapist.

This case, however, illustrates, as Hansen's case did, the great relief that the patient received from confessing disturbing impulses; in fact, the therapist's interpretations in the main served the purpose of anticipating and thereby facilitating the patient's confession.

Chapter Twenty-Six

PHYSIOLOGY OF BEHAVIOR
AND CHOICE OF NEUROSIS

It is an old and often repeated observation, with which all analysts are familiar, that a dream will frequently anticipate the onset of a somatic symptom or even of an organic illness. In the following paper we illustrate this observation with a dream, reported by a forty-six-year-old male patient of Dr. Helen McLean, in which the patient's mother is beating an iron bar upon an anvil. This seemed to represent the patient's treatment, in which he seemed to be thinking of himself as the bar that is being beaten and bent. The patient agrees that he really is afraid of the analysis. He does not know what it is all about and feels helpless because he is in the dark.

It seems like a sort of continuation of the dream, therefore, when we learn in the next hour that two days later he developed lumbago, and in the fourteenth hour, a week later, he complained of a stiff neck so painful that he could talk of little else during the entire analytic hour.

There are three possible ways to explain the onset of these muscular and arthritic pains which occurred within a few days after this dream of violent muscular activity.

1) It may have been merely a coincidence. The difficulty with this view is that "coincidences" of this sort occur so frequently.

2) Freud (1925) has pointed out that an inflammatory or other pathological organic process may be unconsciously perceived some time before the symptoms to which it gives rise are sufficiently acute to attract conscious attention. This suggestion is supported by a number

Reprinted from *Psychoanalytic Quarterly*. 10, No. 4 (October 1941).

of observations in which dreams have seemed to predict organic lesions that developed later but that at the time even careful medical examination was unable to discover.

3) We may surmise that the violent activity in the dream may be reflecting some intense excitation in the muscles or in the associated nervous pathways corresponding to the wish to beat or be beaten of which the dream is an expression. The subsequent muscular and arthritic pains would in this case be at least in part the result of this intense functional excitation.

In confirmation of this third possibility, we may cite numerous dreams reported in the literature in which the dreamer awakened to find that he was acting out the impulse of which he had just been dreaming. Thus one might dream of a little boy masturbating and wake up to find that one was performing the act which his dream had attributed to the little boy; or he might dream that he was striking someone and wake up to find that he was beating the pillow.

We seem justified, therefore, in concluding that the manifest content of a dream may be a very valuable indicator of physiological excitations and tensions corresponding to the wishes and impulses of which the dream is an expression. Indeed, by careful study it is often possible also to gain some indications of the shift in the patterns of physiological tensions that have taken place during the dream work. For example, several dreams, reported in this patient's tenth hour, suggest that unconsciously the analyst has awakened the patient's sexual interest. In the dream reported in his twelfth hour, the iron bar that is being beaten and bent is probably a symbol of his erect penis, being beaten in punishment for this sexual interest. (Actually in his young manhood the patient's choleric father had twice beaten him for his sexual activities.)

Thus, this dream seems to imply that the dream work started with sexual excitation, very probably an erection, associated with sexual wishes stirred up in the analytic situation. He reacts to this sexual excitation with intense guilt and develops an impulse to beat himself or be beaten. This we suspect finds expression in some sort of tension or even activity in the muscles and in the associated nervous pathways. If we observe carefully, however, we note that this is not the final step in the dream work, for the manifest content of the dream does not represent the patient as beating or being beaten but rather as watching his mother beat an iron bar. If we follow literally the physiological implications of this fact we must suspect that this projection involves a further displacement of excitation away from genital excitement, and from the impulse to muscular activity, to the visual apparatus. We might compare the significance of such a displacement to that of a man who inhibited his impulse to beat up someone and attempted to relieve the tension by going to see a movie that was characterized by a good deal of violence.

In the remainder of this paper, we cite other examples in an attempt to sketch out the principles that determine the choice of physiological pattern in dreams and neurosis.

It is an old and often repeated observation with which all analysts are familiar that a dream will frequently anticipate the onset of a somatic symptom or even of an organic illness. As an example, I shall cite a dream of one of our asthma patients which Dr. Helen McLean has placed at my disposal.

The patient, a forty-six-year-old, rather inarticulate laborer, had just started an analysis for bronchial asthma. The following dream was reported in the twelfth hour of his analysis and was probably a reaction to the analyst's first interpretation of a dream in the tenth hour.

> I can't remember it. It was about father and mother. It seems mother was doing blacksmith work. She had hot iron and was hammering.

When the analyst reminds him that his father was a blacksmith, he adds a few details.

> Father was also in the dream but not so clear as mother. He was standing at the side of the shop—kind of dark. I plainly see my mother. She had hot iron and working at it, flattening it out and bending it, doing clean work, good job too.

In association he protests that his mother never did any blacksmith work, although she sometimes came to the door of the shop.

Owing to the patient's inarticulate character, he is quickly finished with his associations, so the analyst tries to help him out. She suggests that perhaps she seems like a woman doing a man's job.

It seems that the analyst is right. Probably the patient had been somewhat disappointed at being assigned to a woman analyst, but he has evidently been quite fascinated by the analyst's interpretation of his earlier dream and is beginning to feel that she can do as good a job as a man. He does not reply to the analyst's comment but continues to dwell admiringly upon the details of the mother's work in his memory of the dream:

Father was standing on one side. Mother took the iron out of the fire, performing the work on it—a long piece of heavy iron.

The iron resembled an iron bar used on locomotives to pull out clinkers. The mother was shaping it. There was a hook on the end of it.

If the mother's beating an iron bar on the anvil represents the patient's treatment, it would seem that the patient must be thinking of himself as the bar that is being beaten and bent. The analyst comes to this conclusion and remarks that if she is bending the patient like iron, he must be afraid. He partially confirms this interpretation. He agrees that he really is afraid of the analysis. He does not know what it is all about and feels helpless because he is in the dark.

My particular interest in presenting this material consists in its relation to the sequel. This dream, as we have seen, pictures vigorous muscular activity on the part of the mother and seems to represent the patient himself as being beaten upon an anvil. It seems like a sort of continuation of the dream, therefore, when we learn in the next hour that two days later he developed lumbago, and in the fourteenth hour, a week later, he complained of a stiff neck so painful that he could talk of little else during the entire analytic hour.

There are three possible ways to explain the onset of these muscular and arthritic pains which occurred within a few days after this dream of violent muscular activity.

1) It may have been merely a coincidence. The difficulty with this view is that "coincidences" of this sort occur so frequently.

2) Freud (1925) has pointed out that an inflammatory or other pathological organic process may be unconsciously perceived some time before the symptoms to which it gives rise are sufficiently acute to attract conscious attention. This suggestion is supported by a number of observations in which dreams have seemed to predict organic lesions that developed later but that at the time even careful medical examination was unable to discover.

3) We may surmise that the violent activity in the dream may be reflecting some intense excitation in the muscles or in the associated nervous pathways corresponding to the wish to beat or be beaten of which the dream is an expression. The subsequent muscular and

arthritic pains would in this case be at least in part the result of this intense functional excitation.

In confirmation of this third possibility, we may cite numerous dreams reported in the literature in which the dreamer awakened to find that he was acting out the impulse of which he had just been dreaming. Thus one might dream of a little boy masturbating and wake up to find that one was performing the act which his dream had attributed to the little boy; or he might dream that he was striking someone and wake up to find that he was beating the pillow. Some years ago Dr. Leon Saul (1935) collected a number of instances to show that symptoms that seem to be psychogenic in nature are often the result of activities during sleep of which the dreamer becomes conscious only later. Instances like these are sufficiently numerous, it seems, to warrant the assumption that activity represented in a dream is likely to indicate some sort of functional excitation or even activity of the organs that are involved in the dream activity and that subsequent symptoms involving these same organs will most probably be also the result of these functional excitations or tensions.

We seem justified, therefore, in concluding that the manifest content of a dream may be a very valuable indicator of physiological excitations and tensions corrresponding to the wishes and impulses of which the dream is an expression. Indeed, if we study the dream more carefully I believe that we can go further than this. By careful study I believe it is often possible also to gain some indications of the shifts in the patterns of physiological tensions that have taken place during the dream work. Let us take again as an example the dream of the mother beating the iron bar.

We have not yet asked why Dr. McLean's patient should have come to his treatment with the expectation that it was the analyst's job to hammer him into shape just as his father used to bend iron bars upon the anvil. This seems indeed to be an exceedingly masochistic concept of the analysis and would seem to imply that the patient was suffering from a very great sense of guilt and need for punishment. We cannot, in this short paper, give a very complete reconstruction of the latent content of this dream, but it will be of interest at least to make an attempt to trace the source of this sense of guilt.

We have not reported the content of the dream interpretation in the tenth hour for which this anvil dream of the twelfth hour expresses so much admiration. This patient's analysis had opened with a very considerable reluctance and embarrassment on the patient's part to bring into the discussion his discontent with his marital life and his great resentment of his wife, whom he criticized as fat and exceedingly sloppy in her dress and in her housekeeping, and very neglectful of their two children.

The dreams reported by the patient in the tenth hour dealt with this embarrassment at complaining about his wife to another woman. In one dream fragment which was particularly embarrassing to him he was trying to avoid his wife in a railroad station and another lady was sympathizing with him and asking why he had married her. The analyst interpreted this dream as the fulfillment of a wish that she sympathize with him in his desire to separate from his wife. In the discussion which followed, the analyst had occasion to point out that the patient had really married his wife in the expectation that she would take care of him like a mother. Now in the analysis the patient was unconsciously hoping that the analyst would play the mother role which the patient so missed in his wife's attitude toward him.

The patient must unconsciously have sensed in this interpretation an implication of sexual interest in the analyst, inasmuch as the next day he stated that he never put any value in dreams and spent most of the hour protesting that he could not stand the idea of "wives and mothers" talking about sex. However, his dream in the twelfth hour reveals that this was only one-half of his reaction to the analyst's interpretation. Deeper down, he was much impressed.

It is now easier to understand why the patient felt the need to be beaten by the analyst.[1] Unconsciously, he is intensely chagrined on account of the sexual interest which the analyst unconsciously awakens in him. The iron bar that is being beaten and bent is probably a symbol of his erect penis. Actually in his young manhood his choleric father had twice beaten him for his sexual activities, and in a dream much

1. Analysts will recognize in this dream a still deeper source of the patient's need for punishment. Later in the analysis he recalled that his resentment of his wife had begun during his wife's first pregnancy and had become more intense during a second pregnancy and that its deepest root lay in jealous resentment of the wife's relation to the two children. One of the central themes of the analysis was, in fact, the patient's intense resentment of his mother's pregnancies (he was the eldest of six children) and his unconscious impulse to take the unborn child from the mother's body. It will be noticed that this wish is symbolized in the iron bar with a hook at the end to remove clinkers from a furnace. Physiologically interpreted, this dream suggests that the mother is beating down his erect penis into a grasping hand—an interpretation which corresponds with his mother's actual attitude toward him, her sharp inhibition of his developing genital sexuality, and her urge to keep him a child, at least in the sexual sphere.

later in the analysis the patient himself is beating an iron bar which has the shape of a penis.

Let us now sum up the physiological implications of our reconstruction of the dream work. The dream seems to imply that the dream work started with sexual excitation, very probably an erection, associated with sexual wishes stirred up in the analytic situation. He reacts to this sexual excitation with intense guilt and develops an impulse to beat himself or be beaten. We suspect this finds expression in some sort of tension or even activity in the muscles and in the associated nervous pathways. If we observe carefully, however, we note that this is not the final step in the dream work, for the manifest content of the dream does not represent the patient as beating or being beaten but rather as watching his mother beat an iron bar. If we follow the physiological implications of this fact, we must suspect that this projection involves a further displacement of excitation, away from genital excitement and from the impulse to muscular activity, to the visual apparatus. We might compare the significance of such a displacement to that of a man who inhibited his impulse to beat up someone and attempted to relieve the tension by going to see a movie characterized by a good deal of violence.

The reader will perhaps ask me how literally I am inclined to accept this physiological reconstruction. Do I believe that the dream work was actually accompanied by physiological excitations and tensions such as I have described? On the basis of the analysis of the interrelations between a great many dreams, I would be inclined to believe that the physiological reconstruction we have made would correspond roughly to the actual course of distribution and displacement of functional excitation during the dream work; but I must admit that without examination of a great deal more material than I can present in a short paper, I would be unable to prove it. Nevertheless, I believe that there is a great deal of value in attempting to reconstruct the apparent physiological implications of our interpretations of dreams and other psychoanalytic material. The method, as I have indicated by this example, is to trace step by step the pathway from the wishes that motivate the dream to their expression in the manifest content of the dream and to pay careful attention to the organs or organ systems whose activity is implied in each of the steps of this process. We cannot, perhaps, be sure that what comes out will correspond in all details to the actual patterns of physiological excitation that accompanied the dream work, but I believe we have sufficient reason to suspect that it will have a fairly close relation to these physiological patterns and that it can form a good basis for further investigation (by comparison with other dream material of the same patient and by physiological experimentation, etc.) to test the rough hypotheses derived in this way.

Analysts will notice that what I am here proposing is merely an attempt to develop in very explicit form a procedure which analysts have long used in terms of Freud's original libido theory. We have long been accustomed to attempt to explain numerous psychological mechanisms by displacement of libido from one organ of the body to another. My only innovation in this procedure is to discard as unimportant the old and meaningless controversy as to whether the energy that is shoved about in these displacement processes is of a sexual nature or not. I think it is much more important to recognize that these displacements of energy are really of functional significance. As a matter of fact, every integrated activity involves the functional excitation now of one organ, now of another, according to the particular pattern of the activity. One moment we are looking, another we are thinking, and then there may be motor discharge. I believe it is introducing entirely unnecessary confusion to conceive of these "displacements of energy," when we encounter them in the dream work, as some sort of mysterious displacements of libido.

One of the most reliable ways of testing such hypotheses as these concerning the physiological excitations accompanying the dream work is by noting how far somatic symptoms that develop in the course of a psychoanalytic treatment correspond to what we might have expected from our physiological reconstructions. We have already discussed one example of such a correlation in noting that the forcible activity pictured in this anvil dream was followed within a few days by severe pains in all the muscles of the patient's body.

In fact, observations of this kind seem to suggest a very simple rule by which we may guess in many instances which organ will be chosen in a particular case for the somatic discharge of an emotional tension. We are all familiar with Stockard's experiments (1921), in which he demonstrated that developing organisms exposed to some more or less indiscriminate toxic agent would be most damaged at precisely those points that were developing most actively at the moment of exposure to the poison. A similar principle [2] would seem also to

2. I believe that this principle, which is already implicit in Freud's early papers, has been somewhere explicitly formulated, but I have been unable to find the reference.

obtain in our problem: symptoms resulting from the frustration of an activity are likely to involve especially the organs which are most active or most under tension at the moment of frustration. This principle is well illustrated in our reconstruction of the anvil dream. Our hypothesis in this case was that the dreamer was activated by a strong impulse to violent muscular activity but that the manifest content of the dream seems to represent an attempt of the dreamer to withdraw energy from these impulses to muscular activity and to content himself with a visual picture of the activities to which he is impelled. The attempted displacement to the visual apparatus already indicates an energetic effort to inhibit muscular discharge. In accordance with the principle just formulated, we should expect that symptoms developing at this time would involve the organs whose activity is being with difficulty inhibited—in this case the muscles and joints—and this proves in fact to be the case.

By contrast it will be of interest to describe a rather similar physiological pattern that seems to be followed regularly not by muscle and joint pains but by severe frontal headache. The physiological pattern in these cases also involves the displacement of excitation away from energetic muscular impulse to visual and intellectual activity; but in the cases to be cited, the inhibition of muscular discharge is much more complete. In the dream that we have just cited the patient seemed to be trying to satisfy his own need for violent activity by observing the violent activity of someone else. In the instances about to be reported, the inhibition of motility has gone much further. Instead of observing an active figure, the patient is fascinated by a motionless figure. The need for activity is not only projected; it is also denied. In accordance with our principle of expecting the somatic symptom in the organ that is most under tension, we find that in these cases the patients develop a headache.

I shall report the examples of this pattern only in anecdotal form.

A young man reports a dream which consists merely of a picture of female genitals with a penis. While discussing this dream in the analysis the next morning, the patient develops an intense frontal headache which continues for several hours. Associations to this dream indicate as usual that the dream is a defense against the feminine wish to be attacked sexually, a wish which is associated with a fear of castration. It will be noted that the feminine wish and castration fear in this dream are both projected and energetically negated. The patient is merely observing female genitals which have a penis. Both the projection and the denial are achieved by the substitution of a visual image. Correlating with this intense fixation upon a visual image, the patient develops a headache.

A young professional woman was much disturbed by a conflict of loyalty between a male and a female professional colleague, to both of whom she was much attached. The material at this time was obscure, but later material made it plain that she was disturbed both by sexual desires toward the man and by wishes to harm the woman. In the midst of this conflict she devoted herself intensely for a few hours to study in preparation for a lecture which she was giving that afternoon. During this time she developed a violent frontal headache which continued during the lecture and was not relieved until some time the next day. In this instance we see an energetic urge to distract interest from an intense emotional conflict. The method in this case is to become absorbed in intellectual activity. The result is a headache.

A young woman dreams of seeing a woman who is fascinated and petrified by the sight of a huge Negro man. The Negro, though motionless, seems about to attack her. While discussing this dream in the analysis the next day she develops an intense frontal headache. In this instance there is again a projection of the impulse to activity and an energetic denial of it.

The physiological mechanism implied in all these instances is one of attempting to distract energy from some conflict, involving the need for energetic motor discharge, by means of an intense intellectual preoccupation or visual fascination. In each of the two dreams cited, we note that the implied activity has been completely "frozen." An immobilized visual image replaces the 'urge for violent activity. The emphasis upon visual excitation as contrasted with muscular activity is thus much greater than in the case of the anvil dream, in which the patient is observing a scene of violent activity. In accordance with our principle, it seems consistent therefore that these patients should have developed severe headaches instead of muscular pains.

It is probable that, in all of the instances cited so far, we have pathological exaggerations of the normal alternation between thinking and activity that must play a very important role in the physiology of all kinds of behavior. By more careful and detailed study of such instances, we might work out the quantitative dynamic principles that regulate this normal oscillation between thinking and doing.

From our work at the Institute for Psychoanalysis we could cite a number of instances that seem to indicate the association of particular psychosomatic symptoms with rather specific patterns of distribution of physiological excitation insofar as these can be deduced from a recon-struction of the dream work.

One of the first examples was Alexander's (1935) demonstration of the frequency of dreams of unsatisfied desire for food in patients suffering from duodenal ulcer. It will be recalled that Alexander (1934) calls attention to the literature which cites physiological evidence of increased nocturnal gastric secretory activity in these cases, as well as the experimental production of ulcers by holding food just outside an animal's reach.

In our study of the psychogenesis of asthma attacks (1939), we were struck by the reciprocal relations between asthma and crying. It appeared that the asthma attack was very often a sort of substitute for a suppressed cry. Interestingly enough, the dreams of these patients very frequently represented the patient as talking. The talk usually had the meaning of an attempt to seek reconciliation by confession to a mother figure from whom some forbidden impulse threatened to estrange the dreamer. If the danger of estrangement of the mother figure were too great to be quieted in this way, the patient usually awoke with an attack of asthma. We note here again an example of the principle that the psychosomatic symptom involves the organ active at the time of frustration, in this case the respiratory apparatus involved in talking and crying.

In conclusion, I should like to bring these observations into relation with the wider field of psychosomatic research. At the present time an enormous amount of work is being done in the attempt to bridge the gap between the physiologist's detailed knowledge of the mechanisms of isolated reactions and the psychologist's attempts to work out the motivations that determine the larger patterns of behavior viewed as a whole. The two methods of research may be compared to two groups of workmen engaged in building a tunnel under a river together but start-ing from opposite ends. The physiologists are doing valiant work trying to piece together a detailed physiological mechanism in order to build up a synthetic picture of integrated behavior as a whole. Those of us at the psychological end, as in the present study, must seek to extract from our psychological material as many hints as possible as to the physiological mechanisms and dynamic principles involved in the trans-lation of motives into action. Sometime in the future we hope to meet somewhere under the river.

BIBLIOGRAPHY

1. Alexander, Franz: General Principles, Objectives and Preliminary Results. Chapter I of *The Influence of Psychologic Factors upon Gastro-Intestinal Disturbances: A Symposium.* Psychoanalytic Quarterly, 3 (1934): 501–40.

2. ———— and Wilson, George W.: *Quantitative Dream Studies.* Psycho-analytic Quarterly, 4 (1935): 371–407.

3. French, Thomas M.: *Psychogenic Factors in Asthma.* Am. J. of Psychiat., 94 (1939): 87–98.

4. Freud, Sigmund: *Metapsychological Supplement to the Theory of Dreams.* 1916. Coll. Papers, IV, p. 138. London: Hogarth Press, 1925.

5. Saul, Leon J.: *A Note on the Psychogenesis of Organic Symptoms.* Psychoanalytic Quarterly, 4 (1935): 476–83.

6. Stockard, C. R.: *Development Rate and Structural Expression: An Experimental Study of Twins, "Double Monsters" and Single Deformities, and the Interaction Among Embryonic Organs During Their Origin and Development.* Am. J. of Anat., 28 (1921): 115–275.

Chapter Twenty-Seven

CRITICAL SURVEY OF
THEORETICAL ASSUMPTIONS
ABOUT PSYCHOSOMATIC RELATIONSHIPS

One of Freud's earliest concepts of the psychogenesis of particular neuroses was a specificity hypothesis. In these early formulations, the specificity postulated was usually anatomical. When we later became interested in psychosomatic disorders, such assumptions seemed particularly inviting. It is easy to guess, for example, that a predisposition to peptic ulcer may be based on a hereditary predominance of oral eroticism in the sexual constitution. Colitis, with its symptoms of diarrhea and constipation, suggests a possible fixation on anal eroticism.

We ask next: Is the predominance of a particular erotic zone always inherited? The answer is probably no.

We know that oral deprivation or starvation often results in intense oral cravings that persist throughout life. Marked oral indulgence may have a similar effect.

Similarly, premature or unduly strict toilet training leads to fixations on anal eroticism. Or early somatically induced disorders of the bowel may predispose to later tendencies to respond to emotional conflicts with colitis or obstinate constipation, or both, alternately.

The initial assumption was that the predisposition for the somatic disease in question is based on a fixation on the activity of the particular organ or organ system involved. This concept leaves entirely out of account the role of the ego in the motivation of behavior. It also takes for granted that a growing child's need for love is somehow reducible to a craving for stimulation of some erotic zone, perhaps to a desire to be fed or cuddled. Even the child's growing capacity to give love (as well as to receive it) is felt to be somehow anatomically bound, perhaps to the genital zone.

At one period in the development of psychoanalytic theory, this kind of explanation was not only used to account for the genesis of particular neuroses but also expanded into a kind of characterology. The first and most convincing of these attempts to correlate character types with fixations on particular erotic zones was Freud's description (1908) of the "anal character." Later descriptions of other character types were significant but less clear-cut; for example, Abraham's (1924a) account of an "oral character," and Sadger's (1910) account of a "urethral character."

The concept of character types based on fixations on particular erotic zones did succeed in calling attention to a number of unexpected, very important relationships. It also ended by dramatizing—sometimes almost caricaturing—the one-sidedness of such an approach to the study of behavior. The anal erotic character, for example, should not be characterized as a "character." It is a "character neurosis." Normally, a person does not allow himself to be dominated for any prolonged period by any one erotic zone or physiological function.

On the contrary, a normal person uses all of his organs, combining and coordinating them in many different patterns in the service successively of many different goals.

We can best correct the one-sidedness of the literature on character types by analyzing the relations between play and work. For example, one does not always engage in muscular activity just for the fun of it. One must also work in order to earn a living or for other ulterior purposes.

The goal of earning a living is one that arises only relatively late in the course of ego development. After such a purpose has arisen, desires to play, to engage in functional activities for their own sake, may be either in conflict or in accord with efforts to achieve a serious purpose in real life. At times a person may feel his work to be onerous. Normally, there is more or less integration of work and play. Work becomes less onerous, it may even be enjoyed, when the functional activities that are required in order to achieve a serious purpose are pleasurable on their own account.

When we study behavior with this problem in mind, we can trace back its motives to interaction between two sets of factors: (1) to the needs of the organism as a whole (and serious purposes based on these needs); and (2) to delight in functional activity for its own sake.

Whenever behavior is dominated by serious purpose, then the "eroticism" of the various organs must play a subsidiary role, being used to facilitate the ego's efforts to achieve more serious goals.

What is important for our present discussion is the fact that the most important motives of behavior arise only in the course of ego development and cannot be traced back to cravings for stimulation of particular erotic zones. Alexander's vector theory was a first step toward recognition of this fact.

Of particular importance for our present discussion is the fact that many of the needs included under each of Alexander's vectors do not necessarily involve any one particular erotic zone. Examples of such needs or wishes that are not specifically "anatomically bound" are: (1) wishes to be loved, to be helped, to be taken care of; (2) impulses to give, to make an effort, or to attack; (3) urges to withhold, or to hide and protect things.

What is significant in each of these examples is the fact that no one of these wishes can be traced back to any single erotic zone. Fulfillment of any one of these wishes may be sought by way of any one of many different physiological patterns.

On reflection, we realize that wishes to be loved, for example, are not inherited "needs" but must emerge at some point in the course of ego development. When and how does this occur? For the answer to such a question we must turn to direct observation of children, to studies, like those of Spitz, on the development of the ego and of object relations in infants and young children. In the meantime, I propose as a working hypothesis the following general principles: A child cannot even wish for a mother's love until he has at some time experienced such love. This principle, I suspect, must be supplemented by another one: If a child has never experienced anything else, he can be secure in his mother's love, just as he takes for granted the air that he breathes. In other words, for a child to wish for a mother's love implies, first, that the child has already experienced such love, and then that he knows what it is to lose or to miss it.

From these two principles, another follows: The love that one child craves from the mother will not always be the same as the love that another child craves. Each will depend on the nature of the particular child's relation to his mother, on the kind of love that the mother has been able to give, and on what the child has later missed and longed for.

From facts like these it follows that the fixations on which the genesis of a neurosis is based are fixations on problems of adaptation

*involving two or more persons. A fixation on a particular erotic zone
or even on a vector tendency is usually only a part or one aspect of a
more comprehensive fixation on an interpersonal adaptive problem. As
a child grows, the pattern of his emotional relations to other people
must change step by step, first within the family, later increasingly outside. Each of these steps constitutes a problem. The solution for such
a problem does not depend on the child alone. It is a* problem of mutual
readaptation, *involving, sometimes, just the child and his mother, and
in other cases, the whole family group. For a particular child in a
particular family, one particular step in this mutual adaptation process
will offer unusual difficulties. In the most severe cases the problem will
remain permanently unsolved. If so, as the child grows older, he will
be disturbed whenever this problem arises, not only within the family
group, but also later when he becomes a member of other groups. In
other cases the fixation will be less intense. The child and his mother,
for example, may reach a fairly good adjustment, but only at the cost
of having to suppress disturbing internal tensions. If, then, at some
future time, the same problem arises in unusually severe form, the
solution achieved may break down and give rise to disturbing symptoms.*

*In the remainder of this paper we shall illustrate this thesis by com-
paring the genesis of several different kinds of psychosomatic disease.*

In the art of psychoanalytic interpretation we usually make certain
theoretical assumptions. The theories of the drives are some of the most
important of these. They are assumptions which deal with psychosomatic
relations.

Yet theories are not the foundation of science. Freud (1914, p. 77)
and many others before him have pointed out that the foundation of
science is "empirical observation alone." Every growing science is continually discovering new facts and new relationships between facts.
Therefore, theories, as well as all other scientific conclusions, need to be
checked repeatedly against new evidence.

Psychoanalysis is almost unique among sciences in that its predominant method of investigation is based on introspection and empathy.
Therefore, in psychoanalytic interpretation our first concern should be
to learn all that we can directly from empathic understanding of actual
behavior. Moreover, whenever we learn something new, our theories

should be carefully *re*checked against the new empathic understanding arising out of our new and pertinent observations.

In the last thirty-five or more years, there has been a great deal of empirical investigation, by Alexander, his co-workers, and many others, of relations between particular somatic diseases and psychodynamic patterns. What has not been sufficiently realized, I believe, is the light that this kind of empirical study can shed on psychoanalytic theory and, in particular, on the theories of the drives. Our purpose in the present paper, accordingly, will be to begin a review of the psychoanalytic theories of the drives insofar as they have been used in formulating propositions about associations between specific psychodynamic patterns and particular somatic diseases.

FIXATIONS ON EROTIC ZONES

One of Freud's earliest concepts of the psychogenesis of particular neuroses was a specificity hypothesis. For example, he postulated (1906) that hysteria developed in response to conflicts at the level of the Oedipus complex (genital or phallic phase). The obsessional neurosis or the predisposition to the development of this neurosis had its origin in fixation on the anal-sadistic phase of sexual development (Freud, 1913). Later, Abraham (1924b) traced melancholia back to an oral sadistic phase.

In these early formulations, the specificity postulated was usually anatomical. When we later became interested in psychosomatic disorders, such assumptions seemed particularly inviting. It is easy to guess, though perhaps more difficult to prove, that a predisposition to peptic ulcer may be based on a hereditary predominance of oral eroticism in the sexual constitution. Colitis, with its symptoms of diarrhea and constipation, suggests a possible fixation on anal eroticism. Exhibitionism, one of the partial sexual instincts postulated by Freud, was found to be closely related to eroticism of the exposed skin surfaces—as in blushing, for example. An association between neurodermatitis and exhibitionism was early recognized.

We ask next: Is the predominance of a particular erotic zone always inherited? The answer is probably no.

We know that oral deprivation or starvation often results in intense oral cravings that persist throughout life. Marked oral indulgence may have a similar effect.

492 PSYCHOSOMATIC MEDICINE

Neurodermatitis in infancy seems to be closely associated with lack of adequate caressing contact between the baby and his mother (see M. J. Rosenthal, 1952, J. Marmor, 1956). Other cases of neurodermatitis have received an unusual amount of seductive cuddling; or such seductive stimulation may have been followed by parental inhibition of cravings for physical affection. Whether from one or another of these causes, an unusual amount of what Mohr and Alexander call "contact hunger" seems to be characteristic of patients predisposed to neurodermatitis.

In our study we have also been impressed with the delight in muscular activity (sports and heavy muscular work) that has often been characteristic of patients who were later to develop rheumatoid arthritis. We have been impressed, too, with the frequency with which patients with rheumatoid arthritis have been subjected to an unusual amount of physical restraint (restriction of movement) by the parents in childhood. (This latter observation was first called to our attention by Margaret Gerard [1953], in her studies of the parents of arthritic children.)

Similarly, premature or unduly strict toilet training leads to fixations on anal eroticism. Or early somatically induced disorders of the bowel may predispose to later tendencies to respond to emotional conflicts with colitis or obstinate constipation, or both alternately.

In cases of bronchial asthma, Felix Deutsch (1939), in particular, has called attention to the frequency of early organic diseases of the respiratory tract as predisposing factors.

In all of these examples, the predisposition for the somatic disease in question is believed to be a fixation on the activity of the particular organ or organ system involved. This concept leaves entirely out of account the role of the ego in the motivation of behavior. It also takes for granted that a growing child's need for love is somehow reducible to a craving for stimulation of some erotic zone, perhaps to a desire to be fed or cuddled. Even the child's growing capacity to give love (as well as to receive it) is felt to be somehow anatomically bound, perhaps to the genital zone.

At one period in the development of psychoanalytic theory, this kind of explanation was not only used to account for the genesis of particular neuroses but also expanded into a kind of characterology. The first and most convincing of these attempts to correlate character types with fixations on particular erotic zones was Freud's description (1908) of the "anal character," which was later extensively documented and expanded by Jones (1919) and Abraham (1923). Later descriptions of other character types were significant but less clear-cut, for example,

Abraham's (1924a) account of an "oral character," and Sadger's account (1910) of a "urethral character."

Probably the least satisfactory of these character type descriptions was Abraham's portrayal of the "genital character" (1926)—which turned out to be based on a not very precisely defined correlation between psychosexual maturity and an ideal of maturity of character.

The concept of character types based on fixations on particular erotic zones did succeed in calling attention to a number of unexpected, very important relationships. It also ended by dramatizing—sometimes almost caricaturing—the one-sidedness of such an approach to the study of behavior. The anal erotic character, for example, should not be characterized as a "character." It is a "character neurosis." Normally, a person does not allow himself to be *dominated* for any prolonged period by any one erotic zone or physiological function. One does not eat all the time. One is also not preoccupied all the time with defecation or sphincter control. On the contrary, a normal person uses *all* of his organs, combining and coordinating them in many different patterns in the service successively of many different goals.

We can best correct the one-sidedness of the literature on character types by analyzing the relations between play and work (French, 1952, p. 136). Only the simplest play (autoerotic behavior) is motivated solely by delight in the functional activity of a single organ. For example, one does not always engage in muscular activity just for the fun of it. One must also work in order to earn a living or for other ulterior purposes.

The goal of earning a living is one that arises only relatively late in the course of ego development. After such a purpose has arisen, desires to play, to engage in functional activities for their own sake, may be either in conflict or in accord with efforts to achieve a serious purpose in real life. At times a person may feel his work to be onerous. Normally, there is more or less integration of work and play. Work becomes less onerous, it may even be enjoyed, when the functional activities that are required in order to achieve a serious purpose are pleasurable on their own account.

When we study behavior with this problem in mind, we can trace back its motives to interaction between two sets of factors (French, 1952, p. 135): (1) to the needs of the organism as a whole (and serious purposes based on these needs); and (2) to delight in functional activity for its own sake. Whenever behavior is dominated by serious purpose, then the "eroticism" of the various organs must play a subsidiary role, being *used* to facilitate the ego's effort to achieve more serious goals.

Motives That Are "Not Anatomically Bound"

What is important for our present discussion is the fact that the most important motives of behavior arise only in the course of ego development and cannot be traced back to cravings for stimulation of particular erotic zones. Alexander's vector theory (1935) was a first step toward recognition of this fact.

For example, he associated peptic ulcer with a receptive vector—including, besides desire for food, "the wish to receive help, love, money, a gift, a child, or the wish to castrate, to steal, to take away something." Somatically, Alexander postulated, the same group of wishes might disturb not only the stomach functions but also "other organic functions which involve incorporation, such as, for example, the inspiratory phase of the respiratory act or swallowing."

Colitis (mucous or spastic colitis was first studied) he associated with an eliminatory vector, including wishes "to give love, to make an effort, to help produce something, to give a gift, to give birth to a child—also the wish to attack someone (especially by throwing something at him). . . . Any of these impulses," Alexander postulated, "are apt to influence eliminatory organic functions such as urination, defecation, ejaculation, perspiration, the expiratory phase of respiration."

Constipation was considered as a manifestation of a retentive vector, as examples of which Alexander enumerated such tendencies as "collecting different objects, ordering and classifying them (as a sign of mastering them), also the fear of losing something, the rejection of the obligation to give something, the impulse to hide and protect things—and the mother's attitude toward the fetus. . . . All these may find expression in retentive physiological innervations," such as constipation (which is the most often recognized) and also "the retention of urine, retarded ejaculation and certain features of the respiratory act."

Our formulations for the somatic diseases have been very much influenced by this vector theory. However, Alexander's vector theory has one defect. It stresses the fact that many different impulses or motives may involve the same vector; but it does not concern itself with the question of what determines whether the receptive vector, for example, will take the form of receiving help or love or money, a gift, or a child, or of castrating, stealing, or taking away something. Erikson (1950), on the other hand, has paid more attention to this kind of question. Studying children, he distinguishes between the "mode" and the "zone" of an infant's response. The modes correspond rather closely to Alexander's vectors; but the same mode may involve any one of a number of zones (in the sense of Freud's erotic zones) or a constellation of different zones. Erikson tries to account for the ways that the infant's modes and zones succeed one another by studying how infant and mother interact with each other. For example, a mother may tend to withdraw from the nursing baby because she fears being nipped by the baby; and this may stimulate the baby's oral machinery, instead of relaxedly indulging in sucking, to develop a "biting" reflex prematurely and to try to hang on even before he has any teeth. On the other hand, the high premium of libidinal pleasure in both the baby's sucking and the mother's giving suck tends to give to the act of nursing a general aura of warmth and mutuality which is enjoyed and responded to with relaxation not only by mouth and nipple but by the total organisms of both baby and mother. These two examples illustrate how the zones and modes of the baby's responses are not just simple vector reactions of the baby but parts of total adaptive mutual interactions between baby and mother. Such is Erikson's contribution to our understanding of the significance of the zones and modes of the baby's responses.

Erikson based this understanding on the direct study of infant-mother relations. Alexander's essentially similar vector theory had been based on comparison of the vector tendencies in psychosomatic diseases and in the respective psychodynamic patterns underlying them. We shall now continue with further analysis of the implications of this comparison.

Of particular importance for our present discussion is the fact that many of the needs included under each vector do not necessarily involve any one particular erotic zone. Examples of such needs or wishes that are *not specifically "anatomically bound"* are: (1) wishes to be loved, to be helped, to be taken care of; (2) impulses to give, to make an effort, or to attack; and (3) urges to withhold, or to hide and protect things.

What is significant in each of these examples is the fact that no one of these wishes can be traced back to any single erotic zone. Fulfillment of any one of these wishes may be sought by way of any one of many different physiological patterns. Although Alexander did not particularly stress it, recognition of this fact is the basic contribution of his vector theory.

What are the sources of these deep and fundamental cravings which are not focused on any single organ?

Emergence of Such Cravings in the Course of Ego Development

We often—perhaps even habitually—think of these wishes as "needs" or "drives," born with the infant as he emerges from the mother's body. This assumption is probably based on the adult observer's subjective identification with the infant's behavior. We read back into the infant our own understanding, as adults, of the significance of his behavior. Yet wishes to be loved, for example, imply a conceptualization of which the infant is certainly not capable at birth. At birth the human infant is not even capable of realizing that the mother exists as a person. How then can he wish to be loved by her?

On reflection, we realize that wishes to be loved are not inherited "needs" but must emerge at some point in the course of ego development. When and how does this occur? For the answer to this question we must turn to direct observation of children, to studies, like those of Spitz (1965), on the development of the ego and of object relations in infants and young children. In the meantime, I propose as a working hypothesis the following general principles: A child cannot even wish for a mother's love until he has at some time experienced such love. This principle, I suspect, must be supplemented by another one: If a child has never experienced anything else, he can be secure in his mother's love just as he takes for granted the air that he breathes. Until he has experienced some (temporary) loss of the mother's loving care, he can be secure without being really aware of the love on which his security depends. In other words, for a child to wish for a mother's love implies, first, that the child has already experienced such love, and then that he knows what it is to lose or to miss it.

DIFFERENT KINDS OF DEPENDENCE

From these two principles, another follows: The love that one child craves from the mother will not always be the same as the love that another child craves. Each will depend on the nature of the particular child's relation to his mother, on the kind of love that the mother has been able to give, and on what the child has later missed and longed for.

Review and comparison of our patients with peptic ulcer and those with bronchial asthma or neurodermatitis have called our attention to two possible kinds of love that a child may crave from his mother and others.

One mother's love may be expressed predominantly in her feeding the child, and in her care for the child's other physical needs. In our patients with peptic ulcer, the patient's underlying dependence seems to have been focused on longings for this kind of love. This kind of longing for a mother's loving care should be distinguished, however, from a desire to receive one particular kind of care—to be fed, for example. The craving for a mother's loving care involves something more, longing for a sense of security. Whatever its physical needs may be, now or in the future, the child wishes to know that they will be fulfilled by an adequate mother. In our patients with peptic ulcer, we can usually find evidence that the patient, some time in his early life, has experienced this kind of security with his mother or with some other parental figure. In these patients, the underlying dependence seems to have been focused on the mother's physical care, on the security of knowing that mother is always on hand to provide for physical and material needs.

In the predisposition to bronchial asthma or neurodermatitis, longing for another kind of love seems to have played a more important part. What these patients seem to crave might be called "sympathic resonance." Such "sympathic resonance" is a kind of unity which is usually first experienced, if at all, between mother and child, later with other members of the child's immediate family, or with close personal friends. For these patients, close family ties and family solidarity are of particular importance. For example, they love to tell of activities in which the whole family has taken part as a unit. On the other hand, what they most fear or are most distressed by is estrangement or separation from the mother, finding themselves on the outside edge of a triangle, or excluded from close interpersonal groups. In a few extreme cases, the breakup of the family or of some other close personal group has been of central traumatic importance in the development of the patient's personality and in his later susceptibility to his somatic illness.

How do such longings for harmonious intimate relationships arise? According to our two basic working hypotheses, such longings imply first that a child must have experienced such a relationship, presumably with the mother. Later, his longings for such close harmony with the mother must have resulted from the experience or fear of losing it.

Consequently, in our asthma and dermatitis patients, longing for "sympathic resonance" with the mother is intimately associated with the experience or fear of losing it.

All this implies what we all know to be true—that a child, very early, has some way of sensing whether his mother really loves him. By what hints or signs is he able to do this? Of course, it is easy for a child to recognize his mother's displeasure if she has expressed it openly, for example, by punishing him. Yet a child is sometimes much more disturbed by subtle signs of estrangement from the mother when the mother's displeasure is not openly expressed. In such a case punishment may come as a very welcome relief, ending the estrangement that preceded it. In other cases, a mother may not be actually displeased with her child. In such a case, how has the child learned to sense the difference between a mother who really loves him and one who more or less mechanically gives him good physical care?

This leads us to the problem of empathic understanding between mother and child. How does such mutual "understanding" arise?

Benedek (1949) has described what she calls "symbiosis" (I like to call it "primary resonance") between mother and child. It begins even before the child's birth and is of central importance in the mother-child relationship in the months immediately following birth. Not only does the baby need the mother's love; the mother also needs the baby's response in order to achieve fulfillment in her mother role. The mother's nursing, Spitz (1964) emphasizes, is not just a mechanical act. It involves a most subtle intercommunication and interaction deeply satisfying to both baby and mother. At its best, this intercommunication develops quickly on the mother's side into a sensitive empathic understanding of the child.

The growth of the child's own capacity for empathy has not yet received anywhere near as much study as it deserves. Perhaps we should not speak of "empathy" on the child's side until the baby has begun to separate himself from his initial primary resonance with the mother, has learned to say no, and has begun to develop an independent personality of his own. Normally, while a child is learning to assert his own individuality, he also keeps trying to get back into resonance with the mother, then later with others. He delights in play that continues frankly the subtle interaction of the early symbiotic period. He is eager for his mother to share his fascination with new sights and may demand eagerly that his mother join him in even his simplest imaginative play, like "riding a horse." It is on this background that he begins to learn to talk—one of the most important objectives of which is to get back into the resonance with mother (and others) from which his growing capacity for individuality and independence might otherwise separate him.

We can bring our ulcerative colitis patients into this comparison by taking account of another factor, which involves the timing as well as the character and intensity of traumatic conflicts. In ulcerative colitis cases, the background, as a rule, is one of a very inadequate dependent relationship to the mother. Not infrequently there is a history of death or psychosis of the mother early in the patient's childhood. Engel (1952, 1955) has reported that patients in psychotherapy often develop exacerbations of their colitis when their therapists seem to abandon them by interrupting treatment. In a recent investigation of the parents of children with ulcerative colitis (by Mohr, Josselyn, Spurlock, and Barron [1958]), the children's mothers are described as "anxious and fearful persons who desperately and unsuccessfully attempt to control," except when they themselves are supported by dependable parental figures. The cases selected for interview in our most recent study were, as a rule, much less disturbed than many of those reported in the literature or in our own earlier, more intensive studies of ulcerative colitis. This may be the reason why early memories of the death, psychosis, or severe character disturbance of the mother were less frequently reported in the present research than in the literature. Late in our research, however (after all of our colitis cases had been interviewed and the discussions of all but two had been completed), review of our cases revealed a fact of which we had not been aware and which had not been mentioned in our diagnostic discussions. Our patients with ulcerative colitis had tended characteristically to play down, often very casually, the significance of emotionally disturbing events. This is part of the basic defense pattern that is most characteristic of these patients—they protect themselves from reactivation of their frustrated dependent cravings by turning away from emotionally significant relations to people. They turn anxiously, rather, to impersonal goals and to mechanical and impersonal patterns for dealing with interpersonal relations.

Review of our cases showed next that our peptic ulcer patients had usually started with a much more adequate dependent relationship to the mother. Somewhere in the emotional background of each of these peptic ulcer patients there had usually been a period in which the patient had felt secure in the loving care of a mother (or of someone else who could play a similar parental role). The conflict that predisposed the patient to develop a peptic ulcer seems to have begun later—when the patient, slowly or abruptly, was subjected to pressure, from the mother herself, from the father, or from the larger community, to renounce his secure and comfortable dependence and to assume responsibility for providing for himself and ultimately for others.

FIXATIONS ON UNSOLVED PROBLEMS OF INTERPERSONAL READAPTATION

This comparison of our peptic ulcer with our ulcerative colitis cases illustrates a principle which I would like to propose and to formulate as follows: A fixation on a particular erotic zone or even on a vector tendency is usually only a part or one aspect of a more comprehensive fixation on an interpersonal adaptive problem. As a child grows, the pattern of his emotional relations to other people must change step by step, first within the family, later increasingly outside. Each of these steps constitutes a problem. The solution for such a problem does not depend on the child alone. It is a *problem of mutual readaptation,* involving sometimes just the child and his mother, in other cases the whole family group. For a particular child in a particular family, one particular step in this mutual adaptation process will offer unusual difficulties. In the most severe cases the problem will remain permanently unsolved, and as the child grows older, he will be disturbed whenever this problem arises, not only within the family group, but also later when he becomes a member of other groups. In other cases the fixation will be less intense. The child and his mother, for example, may reach a fairly good adjustment, but only at the cost of having to suppress disturbing internal tensions. If then, at some future time, the same problem arises in unusually severe form, the solution achieved may break down and give rise to disturbing symptoms.

This, of course, is Freud's familiar concept of regression to earlier points of fixation. What I am adding is the hypothesis that the most significant fixations in each person's development are fixations on problems of mutual readaptation in interpersonal relationships.

To reconstruct the problem of mutual readaptation on which a particular patient is fixed, we should try to answer three sets of questions:

1) What was the nature of the relatively satisfactory interpersonal adaptation that preceded emergence of the problem?

2) (*a*) What disturbed this initial state of mutual adaptation? (*b*) What was the problem (traumatic conflict [1]) that resulted from this disturbance? (*c*) By what devices (defenses [2]) has the patient since tried to protect himself from full reactivation of this traumatic conflict?

3) What would be the ideal solution (taking account of both sides of the conflict) that would constitute a resolution of the traumatic conflict?

In the remainder of this paper, we shall illustrate the principles that we have just discussed by applying them to attempts to reformulate our concepts of the psychodynamic patterns associated with two of the somatic diseases studied at the Chicago Institute for Psychoanalysis.

REVIEW OF CASES AND BASIC FORMULATION FOR PEPTIC ULCER

Initial Formulation

In our initial formulation, Alexander (1934) stressed frustration of dependent cravings as the central feature in the psychodynamic background of patients with peptic ulcer. Coming into conflict with the patient's pride as he grew older, these dependent cravings have had to be repressed. Oral receptive wishes, when frustrated, have given rise to oral aggressive urges, and these in turn to guilt. The patient, in many cases, overcompensates for his dependent and acquisitive longings by hard work, ambition, and urges to take on responsibility and to take care of others. Excessive responsibilities increase in turn the secret longings to receive from others. When a certain threshold is exceeded, the receptive cravings take the regressive form of a wish to be fed, which then gives rise to onset or exacerbation of the somatic disease.

Further Questions

Dependent cravings are universal. Overcompensatory defenses against dependent wishes are also very common. We ask next: Is it possible to formulate this conflict more precisely? Are there perhaps different kinds of dependence? Perhaps comparison with other diseases could

---

1. As I use the terms, a conflict on which a patient is fixated is, by definition, a "traumatic conflict." It is a conflict for which the patient has never been able to find a solution. (See French, 1958, Chapter 7.)

2. I should like to call attention to the fact that I am using the word "defense" in a much more restricted sense than is usual. By "defense," I mean a device for protecting the patient against reactivation of a traumatic conflict. In the psychoanalytic literature, one speaks perhaps more frequently of defenses against one or another aspect of a conflict, against disturbing drives, impulses, or wishes. (See French, 1958, Chapter 8.)

help us define more precisely the dependency conflict in our patients with peptic ulcer.

A hint from physiology might also help us. Peptic ulcer is one of the most important reactions to generalized nonspecific stress as defined by Selye (1956). Do excessive responsibilities and the pressure of hard work constitute such a generalized stress? And does such stress perhaps activate peptic ulcers directly, rather than only by way of increased receptive cravings, taking the form of wishes to be fed?

COMPARISON WITH OUR ASTHMATIC PATIENTS

We turn now to a review of our cases. There is a difference between the dependent cravings in our peptic ulcer cases and in our patients with bronchial asthma. Our peptic ulcer patients desire food, physical care, material things, as expressions of a mother's love. [3] For our asthmatic patients, a sense of oneness with the mother, a sense of mutual understanding with the mother and others, is more important.

SECURE DEPENDENCE AND ANXIOUS DEPENDENCE

The dependent cravings in our peptic ulcer patients differ also from those in our patients with ulcerative colitis.

In our patients with ulcerative colitis, the underlying dependence is characteristically an anxious dependence. Both in the literature on ulcerative colitis and in the records of our own interviews, there is much evidence to suggest that the intense dependent cravings of our ulcerative colitis patients reflect a great deal of insecurity in their early dependent relationship to their mothers. These patients are reaching out for an affection that they never had or that they lost early as a result of traumatic events (such as the death or psychosis of the mother, for example).

In contrast to this insecurity, the dependent cravings of our peptic ulcer patients seem to be rooted in memories of a family background in which satisfaction of their need for loving care could be taken for granted. At least at some time in the emotional background of our peptic ulcer patients, there has usually been a period when the patient

---

3. The implied distinction is important. Our peptic ulcer patients do not have a coldly exploitative attitude toward the mother, merely using her as a means of getting material satisfactions. On the contrary, the peptic ulcer patients in our series are usually warmly appreciative of the parental care that they and their siblings have received, even though they may resent the same parent's domination or may be unconsciously rivalrous with siblings.

could feel secure in the loving care of a mother or of someone else who could play a similar protective role.

We should be careful not to confuse such security in the early family background with parental indulgence. Often the mothers and sometimes both parents of our peptic ulcer patients have been extremely indulgent. Yet a mother's indulgence may be undermined, as some of our ulcerative colitis patients show, by anxiety or neglect that makes her extremely inadequate as a source of real emotional security for her child. In the childhood history of many of our peptic ulcer patients, there has been poverty, sometimes even extreme physical deprivation (e.g., Case U23); but a mother's supporting warmth and one or both parents' steady struggles to make ends meet have stood as a buffer, protecting the child from the direct impact of such pressures from the external world.

The Basic Adaptive Problem in Peptic Ulcer Cases

Careful scrutiny of our cases suggests that the conflict that predisposes a patient to peptic ulcer is one that develops later. Sooner or later, slowly or abruptly, every one of these patients has been subjected to pressure to renounce his secure and comfortable dependence and to take on the task of providing for himself and in many cases also for others. These, of course, are demands that our culture makes on nearly every child that grows into an adult role in our social structure. What is characteristic of our peptic ulcer patients is that conflict over meeting these demands of our culture has become a central preoccupation in their lives. At least, it is a central preoccupation at times when their peptic ulcers have been activated, as was the case at the time when we interviewed these patients.

John Smith told the early Virginia settlers: "If a man will not work, neither shall he eat." In a particular case such pressure may have been exerted, either energetically or very gently and gradually, by the mother herself, or by the father or other members of the family, or by the patient's own ego-ideal (reflecting standards of the family or of the community at large). Sometimes sudden reverses of family fortune, or illness or death of parents, or the patient's leaving home, or marriage, or the birth of children, may have more or less abruptly increased the load of the patient's responsibilities. Such events may furnish the precipitating stimulus for onset or exacerbation of the patient's peptic ulcer.

In our initial formulation, we thought of these patients' excessive dependent cravings as the essential psychodynamic factor predisposing to this disease. We regarded their hard work, ambition, and urges to take on responsibility for others as merely overcompensatory reactions to these excessive dependent cravings. We did not ask why these patients' overcompensation had taken just this form. In our present formulation we are trying to take better account of these patients' ego functions and their development. We consider both the patients' frustrated dependent cravings and their pressure to work hard and take on responsibility as signs of fixation on a particular adaptive problem. Our concept is that a fixation on a particular erotic zone or on a particular vector tendency is usually only a part or one aspect of a more comprehensive fixation on an adaptive problem which has arisen at some point in the development of the integrative functions.

Our concept is, further, that the problems that are significant as emotional background for a predisposition to peptic ulcer are not concerned with individual development alone. They are problems of mutual readaptation, involving at first principally the child and his mother, and later, increasingly, the whole family group.

The interpersonal problems that are crucial in the development of patients who will later be predisposed to peptic ulcer are problems of distribution. Economists speak of distribution of goods and division of labor. Our peptic ulcer patients are concerned with distribution of parental love and distribution of responsibility for giving such loving care. How will the "available supplies" of loving parental care be distributed among the family group? How will the responsibility and the effort necessary to provide such care be divided among the family group? The steps in the development of family relationships that are likely to be significant in predisposing a particular person to peptic ulcer are changes in the family pattern that either decrease too rapidly his share of the "available parental care" or increase beyond his capacity the share of responsibility and effort that is required of him in order to provide such care for himself and others.

The concept just outlined of the psychodynamic background associated with peptic ulcer has the advantage of enabling us to recognize many different kinds of behavior occurring at very different periods of life as evidences, all of them, of a patient's preoccupation with this one single kind of problem. The mother of one patient, for example, seems to have applied pressure on him to "earn his feed" (reviewer's phrase), very, very gently but also very early. She told him that she had nursed him for two years. She also used to tell him that "I was big enough to pull out a chair for her to sit for my feeding" (Case U26). Many of these patients started to work very early. In some cases (U1, U3) this was necessary because the family was poor. In other cases (e.g., U12), the young or adolescent child wanted to earn extra money to buy indulgences that his family either could not afford or would not give him. Another young man (Case U19) received a much more energetic shove. Not long after he returned from serving in the army, he was asked by his stepfather, "When in the hell are you going to get off your ass and go to work?" The patient left home immediately and soon afterward came to Chicago to earn his way through college. Not long after this, he developed peptic ulcer while "carrying a full course load" and "working part-time in the Loop." "It was a real rat race," he said, and "touch and go as far as making ends meet, dollar-wise."

At the other extreme is a patient's (Case U1) nostalgic description of the wife of one of his close friends, who was willing to do anything for her husband and also to "welcome him with open arms even if he played cards with the fellows until 5 A.M." "She'll climb the walls and do all the work herself, bake his favorite cakes and make his favorite meals, everything catering to him. Well, she got a heart attack about five years ago. She's a young girl and we were all stunned by it." This story not only betrays this patient's own strong dependent cravings; it also gives emotionally charged recognition to the fact that, if he is to eat his favorite cakes, somebody must bake them. It gives evidence of his preoccupation with the problem of who is to do the necessary work. It helps us understand better a case reported by Rosenbaum (in Kapp, Rosenbaum, and Romano [1946], Case 5) who was able repeatedly to live out such a fantasy. This patient of Rosenbaum's seemed to have a knack for charming women into marrying and supporting him. When one woman finally got fed up and left him, he developed peptic ulcer.

Another variation on the same theme is our Case U13's account of going into business with his older brother. They broke up after a year because the patient felt that his brother was expecting him to do more than his share of the work.

We shall next discuss our attempts to reformulate our concepts of the psychodynamic patterns associated with essential hypertension. We shall begin with the formulations developed at the Chicago Institute for Psychoanalysis and then discuss a number of questions arising from these formulations. Following our earlier theoretical discussion, we shall try to reconstruct the traumatically interrupted basic adaptive problem which resulted in the patients' predisposition to their somatic disease.

AN ATTEMPT AT REVISION AND EXPANSION OF OUR FORMULATION FOR HYPERTENSION

Love, Loyalty, and the Fate of Fixations on Objects

Review of essential hypertension led us in an unexpected direction. According to our initial formulation, this disease develops on a background of chronic inhibited rage. Alexander (1934) initially brought this thesis into relation with Cannon's (1929) demonstration that fear and rage give rise to increase of blood pressure in the experimental animal. Normally, fear and rage are transient states in the life of an animal. In hypertensive patients the rage had been denied outlet and had become chronic. The result had been a persisting elevation of blood pressure.

Why, we asked, had they allowed their rage to become chronic? If these patients had been frustrated, why had they not long ago turned away from the situation that frustrated them and sought satisfaction elsewhere for their underlying needs? If they could find adequate satisfaction elsewhere, then they would not need to stay angry.

We sought the answer to this question in my early observation that hypertensive patients tend to become "fixated on obstacles." Even though an obstacle is insuperable, these patients are under compulsion to keep on struggling to overcome it, usually with great energy and persistence. They tend to hold grudges. Often they seem even to court frustration by espousing hopeless or lost causes. Such tendencies to "obstacle fixation" go a long way toward explaining why these patients are susceptible to states of chronic futile rage, rage that must be inhibited —and then gives rise to essential hypertension.

We then asked how such a tendency to become fixated on obstacles could have arisen. We arrived at the following hypothesis: In all of our cases, a tendency to become fixed on obstacles seems to have developed on a background of close personal relationships involving keenly felt obligations of mutual loyalty between two or more people. Typically, these relationships are those between parents and children, between husbands and wives, between older and younger brothers and sisters, sometimes between employers and faithful employees. A chronic elevation of blood pressure begins to develop when one party to such a relationship comes to feel that his own faithfulness to his obligations has not been appreciated or reciprocated, that his mother (or her father) has demanded too much of him (or her), or that he (or she) has been neglected by a parent or husband in sharp contrast to his (or her) own devoted acceptance of onerous responsibilities. Under such circumstances, the very stubbornness of his (or her) own loyalty keeps the patient chronically fixated on his (or her) frustration. Instead of turning away to a more satisfying relationship, he (or she) struggles to suppress his (or her) persisting rage, to overcompensate for it by gentle forbearance, friendliness, being exceedingly reasonable and fair. Then his (or her) blood pressure begins to rise and to remain elevated.

What is loyalty? Can we trace it back to its sources in childhood?

The dictionary definition of "loyal" is "faithful, true." Loyalty is defined as most nearly synonymous with "fidelity." It is related to, though of course not identical with, "allegiance" ("allegiance" has a legal rather than a psychological meaning).

For our present purpose, "loyalty" can best be defined as a strong and stubbornly persisting concern for the good of its object. Its object may be another person, a group (large or small), or a cause. One may be loyal to one's mother or one's father, to a wife, to a friend. One may be loyal to one's family (small or large). Loyalty to one's country is called patriotism.

It is astonishing that this concept of loyalty is hardly mentioned in the psychoanalytic literature. We have overreacted against the temptation of a century ago to overestimate sentimentally the tender and heroic possibilities of human nature. The love of Jonathan for David in the Old Testament and the love of Damon and Pythias in Greek legend are examples of the picture of love and loyalty that today we feel uncomfortable about accepting because it seems too beautiful to be true. Today we sometimes go to the other extreme, devaluating both tenderness and loyalty as only reaction formations against hostility.

Freud (1921, pp. 90–91) did not go so far. He speaks of "aim-inhibited love." He derives the solidarity of permanent groups (like an army or a church) from such aim-inhibited love of the leader. At other times, Freud contrasts the physical sexual and the "tender" components of love. My own concept of loyalty is close to these concepts of Freud.

As I conceive it, loyalty is one kind of love. Sometimes it is one aspect of more comprehensive forms of love. For example, it is one component of all mature sexual love (whether heterosexual or homosexual); it is part of what Freud called the "tender component" of love. Probably this "tender component" should be considered as having two parts. Tenderness for the love object is one. Loyalty is made of more earnest and sterner stuff.

I differ from Freud on only one point. As the phrase "aim-inhibited love" suggests, he often thinks of such love as a derivative of the sexual drive (presumably at the genital level of libidinal organization). He bases this inference on an undisputed fact: Both tenderness and loyalty to the love object are often enhanced when the lover postpones or denies himself final and complete gratification of his physical desire. In spite of this fact, my thesis is that both love and loyalty have a deeper source.

It is necessary to make one distinction before we try to trace this source. Both love and loyalty should be sharply distinguished from the desire to be loved. A desire for response from the love object is usually a concomitant of love, but both love and loyalty are spontaneous primary emotions. (In the more precise terminology of Shand [1914], both love and loyalty are "sentiments.") If one tries to please another person only *in order to be loved by him or for any other ulterior motive*, then his motivating urge is neither love nor loyalty.

Still, loyalty is usually—probably always—felt to be a mutual interpersonal relationship. X's continuing loyalty to Y is usually conditioned upon his belief that Y is loyal to X. If X's faith in Y's loyalty is shattered, this will be an intensely frustrating experience for X. As I have already indicated, this kind of frustration of a deep loyal attachment is the traumatic experience that serves as the predisposing "soil" for essential hypertension.

SOURCES AND DEVELOPMENT OF LOYALTY

From what sources does loyalty arise? To what extent can we trace the course of its development in the growing child?

For an answer to the first of these questions we shall attempt an analysis of universally known facts. The second question has not yet been adequately studied. We shall try again to piece together some tentative working hypotheses based on observations which we believe to be relevant.

We shall start with the group of drives that are usually called self-preservative. In the course of his development, a child learns progressively how to provide for his own needs and how to avoid or protect himself against dangers which might threaten him. At the very best, of course, his ability to take care of himself without help from others rarely even approximates that of a solitary beast of prey in the forest. What the human being is expected to achieve in the end is, rather, to fit adequately into one or more of the many roles in an extremely complex system of mutual interdependence that our society has provided or may have left open for him.

What happens next, after a person has achieved a certain limited capacity for taking care of himself? The answer to this depends on many circumstances. Whatever the circumstances, one quantitative factor in particular will play a decisive part. This factor is the adequacy of his integrative capacity for the social role or roles into which he is trying to fit. If his integrative capacity is not adequate, he will normally sink into one of the more dependent roles that society provides. If he cannot accept this solution, the resulting conflict will drive him into neurosis or psychosis. On the other hand, if a person's integrative capacity is more than adequate for the social role that he is in, he will normally rise into a role in which he is not only less dependent on others but must also accept more responsibility for taking care of others.

The notion of fluctuating degrees of dependence and of responsibility for others in a mutually interdependent society now forces us to expand considerably our concept of the self-preservative drives. What is the "self" that a particular person (at a particular time) is trying to "preserve"? For our present purpose, we shall skip over the very complex problems of social interaction that arise from the fact of division of labor in a society. In order to simplify our problem without distorting it, we shall use as our example the problem of earning a living. An adolescent boy may partially support himself. A young man may earn his own living. When he marries and has children, he must earn a living for his whole family, not for himself alone. If he goes into business he must provide a living, not for himself alone, but for a whole industrial establishment.

The same self-preservative drives, we assume, are involved in each of these examples. The examples differ chiefly in one quantitative factor—in the size of the "integrative unit" for which the individual concerned must make plans and must try to provide. In our series of examples, the "self" for whom the individual is struggling to earn a living is progressively expanding.

In an earlier discussion, we took for granted an urge to take care of children as a starting point for possible regressive modifications of behavior because of diminishing integrative capacity. We did not ask from what source an urge to take care of children might arise. Now we answer that question: Normally, urges to take care of others arise as a result of progressive expansion of the "self" as an integrative unit when integrative capacity increases.

LOYALTY AS THE SELF-PRESERVATIVE URGE "OFF CENTER"

We still have not accounted for loyalty and other tender components of object love. What our discussion suggests is that, in object love, the integrative unit for the self-preservative urges is projected out into the external world, just as Freud (1914) very early postulated that libido is projected out from a narcissistic center to objects in the external world, like an amoeba's protrusion of its pseudopods. In object love, we may say, the integrative unit for the self-preservative drives becomes "eccentric" (i.e., "off center," centered in the love object rather than in the person himself).

Examples of such projection, of such "decentering" of the integrative unit (at least for a short time), are numerous. At a movie (if it is artistically done), one often becomes so absorbed in the fortunes of the hero that he forgets his own identity. Indeed, empathy, in its simplest form, involves just such a projection ("decentering") of oneself. For the moment, one is interested only in what the other is feeling, wishing, or thinking. Of more importance for our present discussion is the example of a dog standing guard over his master's child. This is loyalty in its purest and simplest form. The dog's "self-protective" alertness is centered wholly on the child. Some suicidal depressions offer us examples that are equally pure, on the other side of their ambivalence. The underlying conflict is between murderous hostility and love for the object of that hostility (e.g., the mother). One way out of such a conflict might be to deflect the hostility onto some indifferent object ("take it out on the dog"). Why does the patient not avail himself of this possible outlet? The answer is: Because he has suddenly identified so completely and so primitively with what must be his mother's good that he can think of nothing else. His murderous self of a moment ago is his mother's enemy, and must be killed.

A corollary to this formulation accounts for another characteristic of loyalty responses. We have stated that X's loyalty to Y is usually conditioned on X's belief that Y is loyal to X. This is explained by the fact that X's love for Y has thrown X's self-love off center. After a time, X's self-love must be restored to equilibrium by evidence that Y is also loyal to him. Otherwise, frustration and rage result.

When we try to trace loyalty responses back to their sources in childhood, there are at least two features of such responses for which we must account. The first is the one that we have been discussing, its spontaneous "outgoing" character, the fact that it is oriented toward, and centered in, another person and is free of any self-seeking ulterior purpose. The other distinguishing feature of loyalty is its "steadfastness," its persistence. We contrast loyalty with all fleeting, temporary, "fickle" attachments. Probably a genuinely loyal attachment can be relinquished only after a prolonged mourning process (grief work). In our hypertensive cases, as in melancholia, this mourning process is blocked. This, I believe, is the reason why these patients become fixated on frustration and chronically persisting rage.

I suspect that the warm, outgoing character of love begins, fleetingly, very early, at least as early as the infant's first genuine smile. (To a discerning person, such a genuine smile is easy to distinguish from the hypocritical-seeming smile of the child who wants to get something. The seductive smile of the child who is eager to win love and response may be only slightly different from a smile that is a really spontaneous expression of genuine delight.)

The happy exuberance of outgoing behavior suggests Alexander's "surplus energy" concept (1940, 1948). My only addition would be that a surplus of integrative capacity is usually as much or more important than surplus energy. The essential point is that such responses can emerge only if the child is for the moment confident (Benedek, 1949), free from preoccupation with needs of whose fulfillment he is not sure.

The stubbornly persistent character of loyalty takes us back to another highly significant step in development, to the child's first choice of one object of attachment in preference to all others. Konrad Lorenz (1952) has described the process of "imprinting" in the young of many species; how the gosling, for example, becomes fixed on the first object that he sees after emerging from the egg, thenceforth following this object as it normally would follow the mother goose. The human infant does not at first distinguish his mother from others, not until somewhere between his fifth and his eighth month, according to Spitz. However, Spitz's (1946, 1965) reports of "anaclitic depressions" are clear evidence for the fact that, as early as the second half of the first year, attachments may be of such great intensity and persistence that the consequences of their interruption by death or abandonment by the love object may be catastrophic. Of particular interest for our present purpose is the fact that infants whose initial relationship to their mothers is less than satisfactory are much less likely to develop anaclitic depressions.

BIBLIOGRAPHY

Abraham, Karl. Contributions to the Theory of the Anal Character. *Int. j. psychoanal.* 4:400–18, 1923.
———. The Influence of Oral Eroticism on Character Formation. In *Selected Papers.* London: Hogarth, pp. 393–406, 1924a.
———. A Short Study of the Development of the Libido. In *Selected Papers.* London: Hogarth, pp. 418–501. 1924b.
———. Character Formation on the Genital Level of Libido Development. *Int. j. psychoanal.* 7:214–22, 1926.
Alexander, Franz. The Influence of Psychological Factors upon Gastrointestinal Disturbances: A Symposium. *Psychoanal. q.* 3:501–38, 1934.
———. The Logic of Emotions and Its Dynamic Background. *Int. j. psychoanal.* 16:399–413, 1935.
———. Psychoanalytic Study of a Case of Essential Hypertension. *Psychosom. med.* 1:139–54, 1939.
———. Psychoanalysis Revised. *Psychoanal. q.* 9:1–36, 1940.
———. *Fundamentals of Psychoanalysis.* New York: W. W. Norton & Co., 1948.
Benedek, Therese. Psychosomatic Implications of the Primary Unit: Mother-Child. *Am. j. orthopsychiat.* 19:642, 1949.
Cannon, Walter. *Bodily Changes in Pain, Hunger, Fear and Rage.* 2d ed. New York and London: D. Appleton & Co., 1929.
Deutsch, Felix. Production of Somatic Disease by Emotional Disturbance, *Research publications of research on nervous and mental disorders.* 19:271, 1939.
Engel, George L. Psychological Aspects of the Management of Patients with Ulcerative Colitis. *New York State j. med.* 52:2255–61, 1952.
———. Studies of Ulcerative Colitis: III. Nature of Psychological Processes. *Am. j. med.* 19:231–56, 1955.
Erikson, Erik H. *Childhood and Society.* New York: W. W. Norton & Co., 1950.
Freud, Sigmund. (1906) My Views on the Part Played by Sexuality in the

Etiology of Neuroses. Standard Edition, 7:269–79. London: Hogarth, 1958.

———. (1908) Character and Anal Eroticism. Standard Edition, 9:167–76. London: Hogarth, 1959.

———. (1913) Predisposition to Obsessional Neurosis. Standard Edition, 12:311–26. London: Hogarth, 1958.

———. (1914) On Narcissism: An Introduction. Standard Edition, 14:73–104. London: Hogarth, 1957.

———. (1921) Group Psychology and the Analysis of the Ego. Standard Edition, 17:90–91. London: Hogarth, 1955.

French, Thomas M. The Integration of Behavior, Vol. 1. Chicago: University of Chicago Press, 1952.

———. The Integration of Behavior, Vol. 3. Chicago: University of Chicago Press, 1958.

Gerard, Margaret (1953). Genesis of Psychosomatic Symptoms in Infancy. In *Emotionally Disturbed Child*. New York: Child Welfare League, 1956.

Jones, Ernest (1919). Anal-Erotic Character Traits. In *Papers on Psychoanalysis*. 5th ed. Baltimore: Williams & Wilkins, 1948.

Kapp, Frederic T., Rosenbaum, Milton, and Romano, John. Psychological Factors in Men with Peptic Ulcers (Case 5). *Am. j. psychiat.* 103:700–04, 1946.

Lorenz, Konrad. *King Solomon's Ring*. New York: Thomas Y. Crowell Co., 1952.

Marmor, J. (and others). Mother-Child Relationship in the Genesis of Neurodermatitis. *AMA arch. dermatology.* 74:599–605, 1956.

Mohr, George, Josselyn, Irene (and others). Studies of Ulcerative Colitis. *Am. j. psychiat.* 114:1067–76, 1958.

Rosenthal, M. J. Psychosomatic Study of Infantile Eczema: I. Mother-Child Relationships. *Pediatrics.* 10:581–92, 1952.

Sadger, J. Über Urethralerotik. *Jahrbuch für Psychoanalytische und Psychopathologische Forschungen.* 2:409–50, 1910.

Selye, Hans. *The Stress of Life*. New York: McGraw-Hill, 1956.

Shand, Alexander (1914). *The Foundations of Character*. London: Macmillan, 1920.

Spitz, René A. Anaclitic Depression. *Psychoanal. study child.* 2:313–42, 1946.

———. Derailment of Dialogue. *J. Am. psychoanal.* 12:765–66, 1964.

———. *The First Year of Life*. New York: International Universities Press, 1965.

Part Four

RELATIONS BETWEEN INDIVIDUAL PSYCHOLOGICAL PROBLEMS AND SOCIAL PROBLEMS

In a series of three papers, we discuss relations between individual psychological problems and social problems.

In the first we consider, in general, relations between psychic conflict in an individual and in society which may profitably be regarded as analogous phenomena. Moreover, most social conflicts usually involve large numbers of individuals in psychic conflicts, either overt or latent. Out of these emotional conflicts arise mass delusions and mass phobias analogous to those encountered by the psychiatrist in individual patients. The therapeutic effect of insight upon individual neuroses suggests an analogous possibility of favorably influencing "social neuroses" by free public discussion.

In the second paper, we attempt to analyze the psychodynamic problem of democracy. From a superficial reading of history, one inevitably gains the impression that rebellion against despotism plays a very important role in the motivation of the proponents of democracy. Enthusiastic democrats delight in such phrases as "Give me liberty or give me death" and love to picture themselves with their feet upon the necks of tyrants. Indeed, most democracies cherish the tradition of struggle against the arbitrary power of some individual or privileged class. On the other hand, only too many tragedies of history make it very plain that even the need to unite in the face of a common enemy is not always a sufficient motive to make cooperative action possible; and even if the common hatred for a despot is enough to unite men in rebellion against him, certainly this motive can no longer be trusted once the despot has been removed. Once the arbitrary power of a tyrant has been ended, there is only too much danger that some leader of the rebel forces will himself wish to seize despotic power. As example we may recall that our own American colonies in the Revolution were not always united in their struggle against the common enemy, and that for a number of years after the Revolution this country's very existence was threatened by jealousies and strife both within and between the states.

Self-government is self-restraint. If a people are to govern themselves, they must be able and willing, not only to rebel against the arbitrary authority of others, but also to submit to the legitimate authority of the laws that they themselves make and of those persons whom they choose to enforce them. The art of self-government is something that has to be learned. One of the most interesting conclusions from Kurt Lewin's recent experiments in group activity is the fact that, if a group has been accustomed to an autocratic regime, it takes time for it to adjust to a democratic organization of its activity. Adjustment to an autocratic "atmosphere" takes place much more quickly; but democratic attitudes are a product of learning and growth.

There is much to suggest that the democratic ideal must arise as a reaction formation against widespread motives that set every man against his fellow. As evidence for this conclusion, we may cite the enthusiasm of nascent democracies like the early American and French republics for the philosophical doctrine that all men are equal. Such doctrines imply, not only protest against the aristocratic pretensions of others, but also a renunciation of one's own desires to get the better of one's fellows. In the enthusiasm of early Jacksonian Democracy, it was the boast of one western town that there were no "principal citizens."

The success of a democracy depends upon a somewhat delicate psychodynamic equilibrium. On the one hand, it is of the very essence of democracy that it implies a renunciation of the more extreme forms of competitive struggle between its members. On the other hand, danger threatens if the self-assertive impulses of the members of the community are too much inhibited. A community whose members are ready too easily to surrender their individual interests to the supposed welfare of the state may become only too ripe for the usurpations of the next would-be tyrant. "The price of liberty is eternal vigilance."

History and common experience make it sufficiently plain that fear and rational expediency are not adequate motives to weld together a people in cooperative effort, even in the face of common danger. If a people have not already some sense of solidarity, then fear is apt to result in panic rather than in common action. The outlook is much better, however, if a people already have a memory and a tradition of successful communal effort.

In the third paper, we attempt a psychodynamic analysis of new ethical and political orientations, of orientations that cannot be accounted for by successful transmission of attitudes from one generation to the next but seem rather to arise spontaneously, often in strong opposition to existing attitudes and conventions.

The thesis that I propose in this paper is that the development of an ethical system cannot be understood in terms of individual psychology, but that it is always a group phenomenon, based on interaction, on a kind of resonance between the two or more persons who constitute the group. The underlying principle is the following: Whenever people become welded together into a group, they develop ethical sentiments of two kinds. (a) They condemn behavior and motives that threaten to bring members of the group into conflict with one another; and (b) they approve behavior and motives that foster common purposes and harmony between members of the group. In other words, according to this developing ethical system, anything that may stir up discord within the group is bad, and whatever makes for harmony within the group is good.

It is, of course, generally recognized that the ethical principles that are accepted by a group do in fact serve the function of binding the group together. I mean to assert something more than this. I am interested not so much in the functional significance of already established systems as in the psychodynamic sources from which developing ethical systems arise and from which they derive their power over men's lives. What I do assert is that each person's ethical sentiments arise and derive their power from his need for solidarity with one or more particular groups, and that the stronger the motives that bind a group together, the more powerful will be the ethical sentiments that arise from them. If we could know the circumstances under which a group is forming and the motives favoring and opposing group formation, we should be able to predict accurately, on the basis of these principles, what ethical principles will develop and also how strong a hold they will have on the members of the group.

Chapter Twenty-Eight

SOCIAL CONFLICT
AND PSYCHIC CONFLICT

Psychoanalysis has shown that the neuroses and many other mental disorders have their origin in psychic conflict, in conflicting motives within one and the same individual. In the study of social phenomena, similarly, considerable use has been made of the concept of social conflict, of conflicting interests, of conflicting motives within the social body. We often think of such social conflicts as conflicts between different individuals. The Marxian school tends to speak in rather simple terms of a class struggle, of a struggle between capitalist and proletariat classes, between those who own the tools of production and others without property whose interests demand the curbing of the unrestricted power of property-owners. Such a concept of a sharp division of society into conflicting classes may indeed be a useful one for the understanding of certain phenomena and in some cases may be a rough but essentially correct description of the facts.

But there are also those who insist that there is no fundamental conflict of interest within the social body. Such insistence upon the identity of interest of all groups within the community is perhaps more often used as a political slogan than advanced as a reasoned scientific conclusion, but the so-called "national governments" and totalitarian states have made us very familiar with the notion that there must be complete unanimity within the state.

In a more subtle form, the same idea enters as an implicit assumption in most political discussions. We proceed in our political dis-

Reprinted from *American Journal of Sociology*, 44, No. 6 (May 1939).

cussions as though there were no question of reconciling divergent needs and interests, as though we were in fact all agreed upon the goal of our deliberations and merely debating upon the best means to further this common goal.

There are also views intermediate between these two extremes. Very often, indeed, there are divergences of interest between different classes in the community, but the borderlines between these classes may be anything but sharply defined. In the conflict between property-owning and propertyless classes, there are very large numbers of individuals whose interests do not lie exclusively with either of these two groups. There are many people who have enough possessions to make them feel threatened by any attack upon the rights of property but who are yet not secure enough in their property rights to be indifferent to encroachment upon the rights of propertyless individuals. There are also many whose economic status would place them in the proletarian class but who, for other psychological motives, tend rather to identify with the capitalists. Communist writers complain that the so-called white-collar workers utterly ignore their own real interests by identifying themselves with the capitalist interests of their employers.

In psychoanalysis we distinguish between conscious and unconscious attitudes. Logically we should expect such individuals to be in conflict. Alongside of their conscious identification with property-owners and employers one might expect to find more or less envy of the more privileged classes and a less conscious identification with the under-privileged groups in their resentment and fear of encroachments upon the security and rights of the classes who have no property to protect them. Is there any evidence to confirm this deduction? Is there any evidence to suggest that social conflicts between classes involve many individuals, at least unconsciously, in conflicting class loyalties?

Certain communities are today striving most desperately to deny the possibility of any fundamental divergence of class interest and to devote themselves with utmost loyalty to the ideal of absolute national harmony. It is precisely in these communities that we find in its most extreme form the problem of antagonism to minority groups and a widespread belief that a large group of people is plotting to overthrow this supposedly harmonious and unanimous regime. We need not deny that there is an element of truth in this belief. There are indeed individuals in all these communities who are actually plotting revolution. The point of interest, however, is the fact that whole classes of individuals who have little or nothing to do with these revolutionary activities are nevertheless suspected of them. How is this fact to be explained?

At this point we are tempted to draw upon psychiatric and psychoanalytic experience. Every psychiatrist has encountered numerous individuals who, quite without objective grounds for their beliefs, are nevertheless firmly convinced that they are the object of systematic persecution by some widespread and malicious organization. Psychoanalysis has shown that such delusions of persecution are based quite regularly upon the mechanism of projection. One attributes to others motives against which one is struggling in oneself. A husband who is struggling against temptations to be unfaithful to his wife refuses to recognize the existence of such motives in himself but becomes convinced that his wife is unfaithful to him.

It would seem almost certain that in the mass delusions of today we are seeing the manifestations of a similar mechanism of projection. If this interpretation is correct, then we have a most impressive confirmation of our hypothesis that class conflicts within the social body actually involve large numbers of individuals in personal emotional conflicts. In a state where absolute unanimity and devotion to the commonweal are demanded of every individual, one cannot acknowledge even to oneself that one resents intensely this complete submergence of one's own individual needs to the needs of the state; but the resentment is there, nevertheless, and this fact receives projected recognition in the mass delusion that some other vaguely defined group of people is plotting incessantly to destroy the harmony and social solidarity for which all the rest of the community are striving so loyally.

In communities like our own we are not yet attempting to enforce such complete unanimity. In this country these mass delusions of persecution have not reached the same degree of intensity, but we all are aware of milder manifestations of the same phenomenon. Here, too, there are vague fears abroad of mysterious subversive elements in the community. We call them Communists, "reds," Bolsheviks. Here, too, of course, there has been a very small amount of objective justification for such fears. There are small groups who preach or who have preached revolution; but the brand of "Communist" and the vague fears attached to it have been extended to apply to very considerable numbers of individuals who have not even the remotest connection with any sort of a plot to overthrow the government.

At first thought these fears do not seem at all difficult to explain.

The liberal and radical victims of these suspicions will tell us that there is an active and deliberate effort upon the part of certain groups in the community to discredit any protagonist of the rights of the less privileged classes. Here, as elsewhere in the world, we are becoming more and more aware of the possibilities of widely influencing public opinion by means of propaganda; and the manufacture of propaganda —much of it deliberately misleading—has already become a major industry nearly everywhere in the world.

However, the widespread efforts to spread propaganda do not yet adequately explain why it is so effective. As Zilboorg [1] has pointed out in a recent article, propaganda can be effective only if it appeals to some strong and widely distributed motive in the people who read or hear it. After all, there are liberal and even radical magazines and newspapers which are trying very energetically and actively to combat the propaganda against the so-called "reds"; and every reader is at liberty to choose the kind of propaganda that suits him best. As a rule, however, those who are most susceptible to the vague fears of Communist activities will not even read the protests of liberals and radicals against this sort of propaganda; and, if they do, their minds are likely to be so closed that it is almost the same as if they had not read them. It would seem that the propaganda against so-called "Communists" is only augmenting fears that are already present in a latent form.

Why do people have this vague fear of Communists, and why is this fear so indiscriminate as to include even the most mild-spoken advocates of the need for changes in our social order?

A first answer to this question seems rather self-evident. Recent events have made us vividly aware of the fact that revolutions are nearly always accompanied by violent excesses on a large scale. We have a horror, therefore, of all attempts at violent overthrow of existing regimes. There is a deep-seated tradition in this country that it is better to proceed slowly by legal means with the reform even of very serious abuses rather than to incur the dangers of social upheaval and indiscriminate violence.

But the victims of this propaganda are for the most part not advocates of lawless violence but rather individuals who are urging, or actively engaged in the attempt to bring about, changes by legal means. It is precisely such advocates of lawful change who are our best pro-

1. Gregory Zilboorg, "Propaganda from Within," *Annals of the Academy of Political and Social Sciences,* 198 (July 1938): 116–23.

tection against revolution. If social discontent can find no legal outlet, then indeed we shall be in ever increasing danger of attempts to achieve by violence what cannot be achieved by legal means. How, then, can we account for the fact that just such advocates of peaceful and legal changes in our institutions can be so easily grouped together with advocates of violent revolution and can become the indiscriminate object of a fear of revolutionary agitators?

It is evident that it is not only revolutionary violence that we fear. We seem also to be afraid even of the ideas propounded by those advocating peaceful social change. We react as though we felt that even the thought of changes in our institutions were somehow subversive—as if we felt that even the most sober and unemotional advocacy of a need for such changes involved a threat of violent revolution.

But how can an idea be dangerous? Obviously, only if it somehow appeals to us or—what is often the same thing—if we fear that it will appeal to someone else. An idea that arouses no reverberations in the minds of others cannot possibly be dangerous. Any idea that we fear must therefore be one that awakens in us some powerful emotional response.

Let us turn again to analogies in psychoanalytic experience. We not infrequently encounter individuals who have a totally irrational fear of certain situations that other people find entirely harmless. A woman will be afraid to go out on the street unless she is accompanied by her mother or sister. A man will be thrown into a panic if a knife comes within his reach. Psychoanalysis has shown that the explanation of such fears is regularly based upon a fear of temptation. The woman is afraid to go on the street without a chaperone because she is afraid of her indiscriminate sexual impulses. The man is afraid of a knife because the sight of the knife reminds him of his desire to kill somebody with it.

It is legitimate to assume that our fear of subversive social ideas is based upon a similar mechanism. The advocate of social change is reminding us of problems that are not yet solved and that we are very reluctant even to think about. We do not like to be reminded that millions of people are out of work, that millions more are inadequately housed and fed and in other respects in dire need. We like still less to be reminded that very few of us are so secure that an unfortunate turn of fate might not reduce us to a similar situation of unemployment and want. It is distressing to realize that as society is now organized this sort of economic crisis recurs over and over at periodic intervals, that our methods of dealing with such crises are slipshod and ineffective, and that some of the reasons why they are ineffective are based upon the fact that we are afraid of interfering in any way with the rights of private property. We are unwilling to face the fact that any rational and fundamental solution of these problems will inevitably demand of us sacrifices that we are very reluctant to make. Still less do we like to face the fact that, if these problems do not find adequate solution, there is always danger that general popular discontent is likely to rise to a point where a violent revolution will occur. This whole complex of thoughts is distasteful to us, and one temporary solution is to try to push the whole problem from our minds—just as the patients we described a moment ago try to avoid going on the street unchaperoned or try to keep knives out of the reach of their hands. So long as we are successful in this we can have some peace, but the individuals who stubbornly insist upon reminding us of these problems threaten our peace of mind. The problems that we are trying to avoid thinking about contain within them the danger of revolution. Therefore, anyone who compels us to think about them is reacted to as though he were a revolutionary agitator.

With the help of psychoanalysis, we have arrived at a dynamic explanation of our fear of social innovators. The motives just considered concern exclusively the dynamics of the social situation, the state of organization of the community, and the like. Motives arising out of childhood situations that are of such predominant importance in the analysis of the individual—such motives seem here to be playing a much less significant role. This fact points to a methodological distinction of considerable significance for the application of psychoanalysis to sociological problems. In the analysis of the individual also we must always start by attempting to understand his reactions in terms of the patient's real dynamic situation in the present, but these reactions to a present real situation regularly turn out to be founded upon reactions to earlier childhood situations. These childhood situations, however, differ greatly in each individual case. In mass reactions, on the other hand, these more variable features of the individual childhood situation tend to cancel one another out. Only the more universal and invariable aspects of the childhood situations of the group remain of significance. The momentary dynamic situation of the group as a whole becomes, therefore, of greater proportional significance.

Can psychoanalysis give us any insight as to a rational therapy?

The patient with a paranoid delusion, as we know, is usually very difficult to help. The prospects of therapy for the patient suffering from irrational fears is usually much better. What is the principle of our therapy? What we usually try to do is to encourage the patient to talk about his difficulties, to help him to gain some understanding of what it is that he really fears, and finally to bring him to the point where he dares to face frankly and think freely about the impulses from which he has been fleeing in such a panic.

Can we draw any hints from this analogy that could help us find a rational therapy for our phobia against the advocates of social change? Our therapy for the individual is to encourage him to talk freely. The analogous therapy for our social problem would seem to be free public discussion. By encouraging the individual sufferer to talk freely we help him bring his conflicting impulses face to face. His forbidden sexual or hostile impulses must be brought clearly into consciousness and contemplated face to face with the protests of his conscience against them. Only so is it possible for him to find a new way of trying to reconcile the two opposing forces within him. Similarly, it would seem that any fundamental solution of our social conflicts must be based upon a frank recognition of the fundamental issues involved and of the conflicting motives between which we are torn in attempting to find a solution.

In the treatment of an individual patient, the solution found must take account of both of the opposing forces. No solution can be really stable that attempts to ignore either the instinctual demands or the claims of conscience. Cure of the neurosis depends upon the achievement of some sort of reconciliation between these opposing tendencies. In every case both instinctual demands and conscience must submit to some sort of modification.

Similarly in the social sphere any social order that hopes to maintain any real stability must find a way of reconciling the claims of those whose dire need makes imperative some change in the social order with the justifiable fears of more fortunate members of the community; for the fears of the latter are also well grounded, as too abrupt social change not only would destroy their own privileges but would also wipe away valuable institutions for which it might take decades or even centuries to find satisfactory substitutes.

But how is it possible to find a way of reconciling interests that are so bitterly opposed to each other? Only, I believe, by the same method that must be employed in the case of the individual patient—by frank recognition not only of divergent aims but also of the fundamental needs upon which they are based; by the freest possible public discussion in which the opposing groups attempt, not to outwit each other by clever propaganda, but honestly to understand the needs and points of view each of the other.

Is such a solution possible? The individual neurotic patient must usually seek help in order to gain insight into the problem that is so painful to him. Moreover, the psychoanalyst who attempts to give him this insight cannot do so with impunity. In the treatment of individual patients, pointing out unwelcome facts stirs up all sorts of resistances and resentments against the analyst who gives the interpretation. Even outside of the analytic situation, we all know with what bitter resentment Freud's discoveries have been greeted. The analyst who hopes for therapeutic success must therefore not only gain an adequate insight into the nature of the patient's conflict; he must also be ready to bear the brunt of the patient's resentment against unwelcome insights. Moreover, he must have the tact to know how much unpleasant truth his patient is able to tolerate at one time; for it is necessary that he retain the patient's confidence so that the patient may be induced to stick to the task of trying to understand himself in spite of his resentments. It is this latent trust of the patient in the integrity and understanding of the analyst that makes it possible for the patient to learn, step by step, to look frankly at problems which, without help, he would have been unable to face.

If social conflicts are to be solved, it is plain that our political leaders must play a similar role. They must have a comprehensive grasp of the conflict situation and of the fundamental and divergent needs upon which it is based; but they must also have the courage to bear the brunt of the public resentment against unwelcome insights and the tact to sense how much unpleasant truth a people can assimilate at one time. The art of real democratic [2] statesmanship is analogous to the art of therapy by insight—only it is many times more difficult.

But even with adequate leadership, is it going to be possible to find a solution for our social conflicts in the forum of public discussion?

2. Really successful autocracies also demand statesmanship of a high order. An autocracy, in order to be stable, must also find ways of reconciling and satisfying the fundamental needs of the people, but the solution can be imposed from above. The analogy in individual therapy would be treatment by environmental manipulation without any attempt to give the patient insight into his conflict. In a democracy, on the other hand, we strive toward the ideal of self-government by an enlightened public opinion.

Are not the passions that have already been aroused too violent to permit any sort of effective friendly discussion in a spirit of mutual willingness to make sacrifices for the sake of a harmonious solution? When we ask this question we are really asking another: Is democracy really possible? For the essence of democracy is not so much its ballot boxes and its machinery of representation, important though these are. The essence of democracy is rather this spirit of attempting to settle differences by mutual deliberation and of readiness to make mutual sacrifices for the common good. If passions run too high, this democratic method becomes, indeed, impossible. Democracy today is indeed threatened from without, but, if it is to maintain its own inner vitality, it can do so by only one method—by the frank recognition of our diverging needs and the freest possible public discussion.

Chapter Twenty-Nine

THE PSYCHODYNAMIC PROBLEM
OF DEMOCRACY

In the great struggle for existence in which we are now engaged,* one of the most potent psychological weapons employed by our enemies has been a direct attack upon the fundamental philosophy of democracy. The danger of such an attack lies, of course, in the fact that it appeals to doubts and feelings of disillusionment that have already been undermining our own faith in democratic institutions. Such doubts may conceivably become a serious threat to our morale in the war that we are now waging. It is important, therefore, that we face them frankly and courageously. Not only must we examine carefully the reasons for our skepticism; it will be well also to inquire into the deeper sources of our faith in the principles of self-government.

Doubts about whether it is possible for a people to govern themselves well are as old as the democratic dream itself. Indeed, during a great part of the world's history, it has been quite taken for granted that the task of government could safely be entrusted only to a divinely ordained ruler, or at best to some sort of superior ruling class. In the nineteenth century, however, following upon the American and French revolutions, there developed a rapidly spreading enthusiasm for democratic ideals and parliamentary institutions. By the end of the century, many were already developing a complacent and shallow faith that the world was progressing steadily toward universal acceptance of democratic principles. Even the Communists dreamed that a transitional period of dictatorship would be followed more or less automatically

* This paper was written in 1942.

by the extension of the principle of self-government beyond the political field and into the economic field.

In the last two decades, this shallow complacency has been rudely shaken. With a new content appropriate to our modern problems, the old doubts rise again. Democracy may indeed have worked fairly well so long as we were a nation of small and independent farmers; but in the world of today our social and economic life has become so much more complex. The whole world has become interdependent to a degree that could hardly have been dreamed of in previous times. Industry and our whole social life are therefore inevitably becoming much more highly and complexly organized. We have all become little cogs in a vast machine, and economic independence in the sense that our ancestors knew it has become a thing of the past. How, then, can it be possible for a whole people to be sufficiently well informed to be able to make intelligent decisions about such highly technical problems as those that face the governing bodies of the nations of the present day?

If democracy were a religious faith and nothing more, we should repudiate such doubts promptly and turn with renewed energy to battle for our democratic ideals; but the task of self-government requires intelligence as well as enthusiasm. It would seem better, therefore, to meet the challenge of these questions by attempting to analyze the interplay of forces upon which the successful operation of a democracy depends. If we can gain some notion of this interplay of forces, then we ought to be able to estimate more carefully the conditions under which the experiment of self-government by a whole people is most likely to be successful.

Such problems in social dynamics obviously belong in the field of the sociologist and political scientist who have experience in the study of dynamic interactions between social trends and institutions, and between mass movements and their leaders, in the light of the broad perspective of history. The psychologist's interest in such problems arises, of course, from the fact that the behavior both of leaders and of masses must ultimately be accounted for in terms of human motives. As psychologists, therefore, we shall do well to circumscribe our problem. In attempting to throw light upon the interplay of forces in a democracy, it will be well for us to restrict ourselves to a few rather elementary problems concerning motivations. What motives impel men to desire or to dream of democracy? What psychological problems must men face if they attempt to realize their democratic dreams? What

enthusiasm of nascent democracies like the early American and French republics for the philosophical doctrine that all men are equal. Such doctrines imply not only protest against the aristocratic pretensions of others but also a renunciation of one's own desires to get the better of his fellows. In some communities this intolerance of inequality may even tend to inhibit achievement and to put obstacles in the way of the acceptance of leadership. Both the conscience of an individual and a strong community pressure demand that he who achieves something noteworthy or who aspires to be a leader must take great care to make it clear that he is really no better than his fellows. In the enthusiasm of the early Jacksonian Democracy, it was the boast of one western town that there were no "principal citizens."

The motive for this reaction formation against inequality would seem to be some need for the security of solidarity with the group. In a considerably different emotional setup, we encounter a similar reaction formation in early childhood. The children of a family do not govern themselves. Nevertheless we find here, as in the democratic community, that great importance is apt to be attached to the idea of equality. Father and mother must not love any one child more than the others. The mechanism is simple. Each child renounces his own desires to get the better of brothers and sisters on condition that the other children must also content themselves with an equal place in the parents' affections.

There seems good reason to believe that similar mechanisms underlie the insistence of democrats upon the idea that all men are equal. Sometimes democratic leaders appeal to such motives quite consciously and frankly. As an example,[2] I may cite one of Lincoln's principal arguments against slavery: "If A can prove, however conclusively, that he may, of right, enslave B, why may not B snatch the same argument, and prove equally that he may enslave A? . . . You say A is white, and B is black. It is color, then: the lighter having the right to enslave the darker? . . . Take care. By this rule, you are to be slave to the first man you meet with a fairer skin than your own. . . . You do not mean color exactly? You mean the whites are intellectually the superiors of the blacks, and therefore have the right to enslave them? . . . Take care again. By this rule, you are to be slave to the first man you meet with an intellect superior to your own."

In this argument, we see Lincoln appealing quite frankly to the motive to renounce the claim to superiority over others, lest one be compelled, on the same principle, to accept domination by others. On the other hand, the attitudes against which Lincoln is protesting show plainly the underlying emotional conflict out of which these conflicting philosophies arise. Each person would like to be assured that he is at least the equal of others, while at the same time finding excuses to restrict as far as possible the number of those whom he will be constrained to recognize as equals. Logically, obviously, Lincoln has a very good case, but the problem is not one of logic but of emotional and sociodynamic equilibrium, and in the logic of many peoples' emotions the case for inequality is very strong.

Freud [3] many years ago suggested that what binds together such integrated groups as the church and the army is the common devotion of the members of the group to the leader and the confidence of each member that the leader is caring for all alike. Under these circumstances, strong bonds of identification develop between each group member and the leader and between the several members of the group with each other. So long as this devotion to the leader continues, the group maintains its solidarity; but if anything occurs to shake the confidence of the group in the leader or in his equal regard for each of the members, then the group suddenly disintegrates. This principle is illustrated by a number of recorded instances of acute panic spreading rapidly through an army when the commander in chief was killed or discredited.

Freud's analysis obviously fits an autocracy much better than a democracy. In a democracy there is a tendency to become resentful or suspicious of any leader who seems likely to gain too dominant an influence over the group. The leader must always remember that he has been chosen by the group and that he derives his authority solely from this fact. Obviously this is a point of danger in the sociodynamic equilibrium of a democracy.[4] As we have seen, if this reaction against inequality is excessive, it may put obstacles in the way of achievement and necessary leadership; but even if it is not excessive, the members of a democracy must renounce the security of knowing that they will be provided for by a good father. In renouncing the security of this common dependence upon a fatherlike leader, they tend also to undermine the basis of their solidarity with each other. Since the solidarity of the group can no longer rest upon common devotion to a supreme leader, some other principle must be found to bind its members together in cooperative effort. Freud and others have tentatively suggested that this unifying principle might be a common devotion to an idea. Is it possible, perhaps, that the love of democracy itself might be the bond best fitted to unite a people in the task of governing themselves?

The transition from autocratic to democratic institutions would seem to involve, for a people, much the same emotional readjustment as does the departure of the young man from the parental home to establish an independent economic existence and found a home of his own. As in the case of the individual, the community that throws off autocratic rule must renounce the security [5] of being children in the parental home, and must substitute in its place the pride of independence and achievement and the satisfaction of mutual devotion to each other and to the group as a whole. As in the case of the individual, too, this readjustment cannot take place suddenly in one step, but can only be the product of long training in the art of self-government.

We come thus to the realization that the success of a democracy depends upon a somewhat delicate psychodynamic equilibrium. On the one hand, it is of the very essence of democracy that it implies a renunciation of the more extreme forms of competitive struggle between its members. In order that all may be secure against being ruled by a tyrant, it is necessary that everyone must also renounce the desire to be a tyrant. The potential leaders, especially, must be trained from youth on to aspire to be the servants and not the masters of the people whom they lead, and to be loyal always to the principle that their authority is derived from their being the chosen and temporary representatives of those whom they govern.

On the other hand, danger threatens if the self-assertive impulses of the members of the community are too much inhibited. A community whose members are ready too easily to surrender their individual interests to the supposed welfare of the state may become only too ripe for the usurpations of the next would-be tyrant. "The price of liberty is eternal vigilance." In a really vital democracy, every citizen must be alert to detect and resist any attempt at arbitrary and unwarranted use of authority.

In recent years there has been much to remind us of the danger of a democracy's becoming soft, of its losing its will to self-assertion and self-defense against enemies both outside and inside its borders. Now that we are at war, we are becoming aroused to the necessity of aggressive action to defend our institutions against open attack. Times of war, however, put democratic institutions to their most severe test. The necessity of secrecy and the imperative need for effective leadership in acute emergencies make it necessary to put restraints upon public discussion and tend to encourage attitudes that are more appropriate in an autocracy. At no time is it more important to maintain the tradition that a people's leaders are their servants and not their masters and that a people must be alert against attempts to abuse authority. On the other hand, we must not forget that a rebellious spirit can foment revolutions and divide a people into warring factions; but if a people are to become capable of governing themselves, the spirit of rebellion must be supplemented by a strong loyalty to the common task of building a unified nation.

The central problem of democracy is the problem of how to build and how to foster and maintain such loyalties. Upon first thought it seems utterly impossible that the idea of self-government by a people of over a hundred million could have any meaning. In the town meetings of early American democracy, people met each other face to face, confronted each other with their conflicting purposes, and thus actively engaged in the process of forming public opinion and in the actual business of self-government. As the country has grown larger, however, and as its problems have become more complex, the idea of self-government has imperceptibly but progressively been losing much of its reality and its meaning. This is, of course, particularly true of our big cities, those enormous and chaotic masses of people who are strangers to each other and know nothing of each other's lives and interests. How can one speak of a public opinion when people of differing backgrounds and interests rarely meet together and perhaps never become acquainted with each other's views? What meaning has the vote if one feels that its influence is infinitesimal in comparison with a great statistical mass of votes cast by people who have little real contact with each other and little influence upon each other's opinions?

Under these circumstances, we develop attitudes that are not so dissimilar to those of the subjects of an autocratic government. Most of us realize that the task of government is really a very intricate and complex one, requiring many kinds of expert knowledge which most of us cannot possess. We depend to a great extent for our information and our opinions upon streams of propaganda that are no doubt in part motivated by considerations of public interest, but may to a great and unknown extent have been influenced by our enemies or by people who are dominated by motives of private gain, merely masquerading as lovers of the public good. Instead of participating in the task of governing ourselves, we seem to be faced with the alternative either of passively yielding or futilely rebelling against overwhelming social forces that are quite beyond our control.

The crux of the problem of democracy would seem to be this

question: Is it possible for a great people, with widely diverging interests, and spread over a vast territory, to form and make effective a really intelligent public opinion? The difficulties seem twofold. (1) How can the great mass of the people become sufficiently well informed to be capable of intelligent opinions upon the extremely complex problems that face modern governments? (2) How can people with diverging opinions and interests be brought into vital enough contact with one another to participate in agreeing upon some sort of common policy, instead of merely trying to overwhelm each other statistically at the ballot box?

Let us consider first whether it is possible today for a people to be well enough informed to govern themselves intelligently. On this point, I believe a great deal of our pessimism is based upon a rather widespread misunderstanding. We speak of "public opinion" and habitually think of our political deliberations as though the task of arriving at a political decision were primarily an intellectual one. Making use of such phrases as "the public interest," "the commonweal," we often proceed in our political discussions as though we were all agreed upon the goal of our deliberations and merely debating about the best means to further this common goal. Quite the contrary is the fact. It is an age-old maxim that politics, like religion, is a topic that it is futile to discuss. The reason is obvious. Political "opinions" are not merely opinions arrived at by intellectual reasoning based upon ascertainable facts. On the contrary, most political discussions start from conflicting emotional attitudes and divergent assumptions as to what are desirable aims of public policy. The task of agreeing upon a public policy is not primarily an intellectual one. It is comparable to the task of an individual who is attempting to find a solution for an emotional conflict. It is not a question of concurring in a method of reaching a goal upon which all are agreed, but rather a question of agreeing upon a goal to reconcile as far as possible conflicting demands.[6] The prerequisite of a fruitful political discussion, therefore, must be a frank recognition of diverging goals and interests. The phrases "public interest" and "commonweal" can have sense only if they are used to denote some sort of synthesis of conflicting needs and interests. If one starts with the assumption that all are agreed in advance upon what is the "public interest," then obviously and inevitably political argument must be futile.

From this it follows that the problems that the people in a democracy must solve are not the same highly technical problems that confront the political expert. It is futile to expect that even the most enlightened public discussion can result in wise and consistent decisions concerning the details of public policy. The people must choose or decide upon the elementary goals of public policy. It then becomes the task of the expert to find out how these goals can best be achieved. Of course, the expert can also be of great service to the people in helping them make their choices. A large section of public opinion may be enamored of a goal that may be quite unattainable or whose consequences are not fully realized. It is the duty of the expert to keep the public informed about the feasibility and the consequences of proposed projects. In fact, one of the most important functions of democratic leadership is to clarify issues for public discussion, to make clear to everyone just what is involved in the decisions that a people must make. In our own American history, the discussions in *The Federalist* and Lincoln's debates against Douglas offer us classic models of this sort of leadership at its best. Once the issues and consequences have been made clear, however, the choice that a people must make is not a technical nor an intellectual one at all, but rather a choice of what is desired. Even in an autocracy, the art of good government might be described as that of making shrewd guesses about how the conflicting needs of a population can best be harmonized; but in a democracy it is necessary that people themselves should get together and agree upon how their conflicting wishes can best be reconciled. Obviously such an ideal is much nearer possible attainment than would be the fantasy of a vast people attempting to solve in detail the complex problems that every modern government must face.

Since the central task in a democracy is to reconcile conflicting needs, we must now return again to the question we have asked so often. What psychological forces can perform this integrative task? If differences are to be reconciled, someone must be willing to make sacrifices. The motive for such sacrifices must be the wish to preserve the unity of the group, must spring from loyalty to the group. Whence arise such loyalties? How can they be built up and fostered?

I believe that history and common experience make it sufficiently plain that fear and rational expediency are not adequate to weld a people together in cooperative effort even in the face of common danger. If a people have not already some sense of solidarity, then fear is apt to result in panic rather than in common action. The outlook is much better, however, if a people already have a memory and tradition of successful communal effort. It seems to be a principle of rather general validity that people learn to love activities that they habitually and successfully practice, and nothing seems to bind together a group so effectively as the consciousness or memory of having successfully braved dangers or performed difficult tasks together. We can thus understand why it takes time for a people to learn the art of self-government. The very rivets that bind together the structure must be forged one by one. Each difficulty successfully overcome, each conflict satisfactorily adjusted, becomes a sort of reservoir of confidence, of community pride—a bond uniting a people in common loyalties that may serve to prepare them for even greater difficulties in the future. Starting with practice in local self-government in the early town meetings, the American colonists elected colonial legislatures that carried on parliamentary struggles with royal governors. Then finally united, though often somewhat halfheartedly, to wage what was ultimately a successful revolution, and, after a period of threatened disintegration, succeeded in agreeing upon a governmental framework that made possible a really effective federal structure. Thus, step by step, we can trace the process by which we grew in the sense of national unity and of our capacity to reconcile our differences and govern ourselves.

It follows that a people's capacity for self-government tends to grow with practice. Correspondingly, the greatest danger to a democracy arises when different sections of the people get out of touch with each other, when they seek to outwit each other by clever propaganda and become fascinated with the dishonest art of selling people something which it is against their interest to buy. If democracy is to survive, we must cultivate the art of confronting divergent views in lively public discussion and in a spirit of readiness for mutual sacrifices for the common good. We must develop a keen and widespread interest in the problem of how the great mass of us can be stimulated to question the source and motives of propaganda and to think for ourselves about public questions, instead of being merely passive recipients of opinions that someone wants to plant in our minds. We are now engaged in the task of defending democracy against external enemies. But even now and increasingly in the postwar period, we must realize that this is not enough; the art of self-government must be practiced and developed and loved, if it is to survive. But if we can learn to adapt the art of vital public discussion to the complexities of modern life, then we too shall have made our contribution to the faith of our people that even in these difficult times we can govern ourselves.

NOTES

1. Kurt Lewin, Ronald Lippitt, and Sibylle Korsch Escalona, *Studies in Topological and Vector Psychology I,* University of Iowa Studies, 16, No. 3 (February 1940). (Iowa City: University of Iowa Press, 1940). Lewin and Lippitt, "An Experimental Approach to the Study of Autocracy and Democracy: A Preliminary Note," *Sociometry,* 1 (1938). Lewin, "Experiments on Autocratic and Democratic Atmospheres," *The Social Frontier,* 4, No. 37 (1938).

2. See Carl Sandburg, *Abraham Lincoln: The Prairie Years* (New York: Harcourt, Brace & Co., 1926).

3. Sigmund Freud, *Group Psychology and the Analysis of the Ego* (London: International Psycho-analytical Press, 1922).

4. This point is particularly stressed by Robert Waelder, "Democracy and the Scientific Spirit." *American Journal of Orthopsychiatry,* 1940, X, 451–57.

5. See Franz Alexander, "The Social Problem and the Individual," *Parent Education,* 3, No. 4 (February 1937); "Psychiatric Aspects of War and Peace," *American Journal of Sociology,* 46, No. 4 (January 1941); "John Dollard's Hostility and Fear in Social Life," *Social Forces,* 17, No. 1 (October 1938); and "Defeatism Concerning Democracy," *American Journal of Orthopsychiatry,* 11 (1941), 643–51.

6. The point of view of this and the following paragraph has been extensively discussed by Mary P. Follett in *The New State—Group Organization, the Solution of Popular Government* (New York: Longmans, Green & Co., 1934) and succeeding works. See also Thomas M. French, "Social Conflict and Psychic Conflict," *American Journal of Sociology,* 44, No. 6 (1939), reprinted as Chapter 28 of this volume, for further elaboration of this point.

Chapter Thirty

PSYCHODYNAMIC ANALYSIS
OF ETHICAL AND
POLITICAL ORIENTATIONS

I

We usually think of ethical principles as traditions handed down from one generation to another: Parents teach their children what is right and what is wrong and enforce their precepts by punishing bad behavior and rewarding good behavior. The parents' teaching is also reinforced by the child's tendency to identify himself directly with a parent's ethical attitudes, either because of admiration for the parent and ambition to emulate him or as an expression of love and loyalty.

These motives account fairly well for the cases in which ethical attitudes are successfully transmitted from one generation to the next, but they do not account for the very frequent cases in which children refuse to take over the ethical standards of their parents. Very often children espouse ethical or political attitudes in direct opposition to their parents; and, at least in our culture, the generally prevailing standards tend to change considerably from one generation to the next. The most fundamental and perplexing question of all is: How do ethical systems get started? How do we account for new religious and new political and ethical movements that seem to arise spontaneously, often in strong opposition to existing attitudes and conventions?

Reprinted from *American Journal of Economics and Sociology,* 12 (1952).

II

Of course, a psychiatrist has little opportunity to study such mass phenomena directly. Yet he does have many opportunities to observe how a particular individual's ethical, political, and religious attitudes fit into the pattern of his emotional life as a whole, and sometimes he is able to trace back a rather unusual ethical orientation to the situation out of which it arose.

One transitory phenomenon of this kind has been reported by Hanns Sachs.[1] Most people prefer to keep their daydreams to themselves, but Sachs studied two sisters who shared between them a daydream which they continued to elaborate together during the whole of a long summer vacation. During this vacation they were spending almost all their time with a single young man, Max, who evidently was fond of both of them but showed little preference for either one. This man had as friends three brothers, but took great care not to introduce them to the girls. Under these circumstances, the two girls spun out together a long series of daydreams in which the recurring theme was one of the three brothers' pursuing them and their outwitting Max, compelling him to introduce the brothers to them. "But this seems very strange," they commented, "as we really cared much more for Max than for the others."

What was the motive for this fantasy? And why did the two girls take pleasure in sharing it? Sachs points out that the motive was revenge against Max for stirring up their jealousy of each other. In the daydream they contrived to stimulate Max's jealousy. In this way they protected themselves from their own jealousy of each other by turning their resentment against the disturber who was stimulating their jealousy.

III

Sachs uses this episode to illustrate the dynamic principle that makes it possible for a daydream, which is usually private, to become a work of art, which is communicated to others. I believe that the same episode

1. Hanns Sachs, *Gemeinseme Tagträume* (1920), English translation in *The Creative Unconscious* (Cambridge, Mass.: Sci-Art Publishers, 1942), Chap. 1, "The Community of Daydreams."

illustrates equally well the principle that underlies the genesis or espousal of an ethical system.

To avoid misunderstanding, let me state at the outset that I am talking, not about ethical sentiments that a person merely professes, but about those he lives by and that cause him to feel guilty or even punish himself if he acts contrary to them. Such genuine ethical reactions, I believe, are always motivated by a loyalty to a group that derives its power from the need of the members of this particular group for solidarity with one another and with the group as a whole.

In other words, I believe that the development of an ethical system cannot be understood in terms of individual psychology, but that it is always a group phenomenon, based on interaction, on a kind of resonance between the two or more persons who constitute the group. The underlying principle is the following: Whenever people become welded together into a group, they develop ethical sentiments of two kinds. (*a*) They condemn behavior and motives that threaten to bring members of the group into conflict with one another; and (*b*) they approve behavior and motives that foster common purposes and harmony between members of the group. In other words, according to this developing ethical system, anything that may stir up discord within the group is bad, and whatever makes for harmony within the group is good.

It is, of course, generally recognized that the ethical principles that are accepted by a group do in fact serve the function of binding the group together. I mean to assert something more than this. I am interested not so much in the functional significance of already established systems as in the psychodynamic sources from which developing ethical systems arise and from which they derive their power over men's lives. I assert that each person's ethical sentiments arise out of and derive their power from his need for solidarity with one or more particular groups,[2] and that the stronger the motives that bind a group together, the more powerful will be the ethical sentiments that arise out of them. If we could know the circumstances under which a group is forming and the motives favoring and opposing group formation, we should be able to predict accurately, on the basis of these principles, what ethical principles will develop and how strong a hold they will have on the members of the group.

---

2. If he is loyal to more than one group at the same time he may, of course, find himself torn between conflicting ethical sentiments.

IV

This paper is only a preliminary report of a thesis for which I hope to present much more extended evidence later. I shall here restrict myself to illustrating these principles first by one more family constellation, then by a few examples of mass phenomena, and finally by several instances in which attitudes arising in childhood in the family group may be continued in political dreams in later life.

I have studied a number of times a family situation in which a young woman has a charming but undependable alcoholic father and a loyal and dependable but usually less attractive mother. Under such circumstances, a strong bond of dependence and loyalty established between mother and daughter is threatened by jealousies arising out of the fascination of both with the charming father. In this situation a kind of feminist code develops: Women and loyalty are good. Father and alcohol and all men, especially charming and seductive ones, are bad.

Schiller, in his play *The Robbers,* has portrayed an almost identical situation except that the sexes are reversed: The solidarity of a robber gang is threatened when their leader falls in love with a beautiful girl. The play ends with the gang compelling the leader to shoot the girl.

A rather trivial example is the resentment student groups feel against the "grind." Many groups also resent people who are "too good." Carl Sandburg tells of a western town which boasted that it had no "principal citizens."

In times of national danger, patriotism and the demand that everyone love his country become intense; and hatred of traitors and slackers may rise to white heat.

When patriotism or some other ethical sentiment requires a greater surrender of self-interest to the common good than the members of the group are capable of, then the situation is ripe for scapegoat phenomena like the intense hostility against the Jews under the Nazis in Germany: National Socialism made tremendous demands upon its adherents and upon all Germans for subordination of the individual to the state. Probably large numbers of individuals could not help resenting what was demanded of them; yet such resentments could not be tolerated and had to be repressed. However, a person may be all the more ready to see in others what he cannot tolerate or recognize in himself. So the Nazi who could not acknowledge his own repudiation of the excessive demands of the state made the Jew a symbol of all the disloyal sentiments that he could not tolerate in himself.[3]

V

The ethical sentiments that dominate human behavior do not always originate as mass phenomena in the present but often have their roots in the group orientations of early childhood. The first group to which the child belongs is the family, and we now know that early orientations to the significant persons in the family may set the pattern for a person's social relationships throughout life. Even what looks like simple transmission of parental attitudes by precept and instruction may be only a special case of the principle of group orientation that we have just been discussing. Most children have a strong need for harmony and solidarity with one or both parents. When such a need is dominant, the child will tend to incorporate and make his own the ethical sentiments of the parent.

As the growing child steps out from his parents' home into the larger community, he finds other social situations that are similar in many ways to the family circle which he is leaving; and it is natural that he should at first try to adapt to the larger group in accordance with the pattern of the family group with which he is already familiar. In the schoolroom, for example, he has the problem of sharing the teacher's interest with other children, just as he had to share the mother's love and care at home. However, he must now reconcile himself to the facts that the classroom is not so intimate a circle as the home, that he must share the teacher with a larger number of rivals, and that he must now earn the teacher's approval by achievement instead of receiving affection as a matter of course in the home.

VI

Thus the ethical orientations that we acquire in early childhood in the family group tend to undergo gradual modification and elaboration as we emerge from the family into the larger and more complex groups of the world outside. Yet many of us remain fixated on ethical systems that arose in adaptation to the early family situation. For example,

---

3. I have developed this thesis at greater length in "Social Conflict and Psychic Conflict," *American Journal of Sociology,* 44 (May 1939), which appears as Chapter 28 in this volume.

the basic Christian precepts to love God and one's neighbor are quite frankly extensions of the injunctions that most of us learned to respect early in childhood—a child ought to love his father and his mother and his brothers and sisters.

My clinical experience would suggest that many political ideologies are built around a nucleus the deepest roots of which are in early childhood orientations to the family group. A political fantasy that has particularly interested me is what I like to call the naïve socialist dream: that the state is a bounteous mother able to care for and feed all her children.

One of the commonest problems in childhood is the problem of rivalry of brothers and sisters for the mother's love. Yet each child knows that the mother's love can be retained only on condition that he renounce or at least suppress his hostility to the other children. The dream of a bounteous mother who has love enough for all is the logical and ideal solution for this conflict and one which in some cases is realized in the early family situation.

Yet even when such ethical orientations persist after a child has left the parental home, they are sooner or later confronted with the realities of the larger community. Society and the state prove to be anything but the bounteous mother of the socialist dream. The most naïve reaction to this disillusioning fact is a simple one: It is all the fault of the wicked capitalists.

However, most socialists are not so naïve as this. At the other extreme are creative socialist thinkers who recognize frankly the difficulties in the way of realizing their socialist dreams and devote their energies and often a great deal of ability to working out plans to achieve them.

Still, like everything else that is human, these carefully thought out schemes always have their flaws; and many people in the community do not accept them. For adequate understanding of the socialist thinker's task, one must realize that his problem is not only an administrative one but also one of psychological adaptation: Who will play the roles of bountiful mother and what will be their incentive to undertake such tasks? Undoubtedly the greatest obstacle to the realization of socialist dreams is the fact that most people are as yet unwilling to subordinate their own individual interests to those of the whole community to the extent that would be necessary for the success of a socialist state.

For this kind of problem, socialist thinkers and leaders have not yet found adequate answers. When they are frustrated in their aims, these socialist thinkers, too, often revert to the naïve socialist's explanation: It is all the fault of the wicked capitalist.

Even more important is the emotional adjustment of the great majority of devoted socialists, who are neither naïve dreamers nor creative thinkers and organizers. One is often impressed with the stubborn dogmatism of many socialists. Why are they so dogmatic? The answer follows readily from our analysis of the psychology of the socialist dream. This dream arose as a solution for a problem of central importance in childhood. For many socialists the faith that the socialist dream is realizable is essential for emotional equilibrium. Unable to think out a plan for themselves, they cling to the program and thinking of the leader. Yet doubts cannot be entirely quieted. Dogma is a compulsive reaction against doubt.

VII

This kind of dogmatism, reinforced by a tendency to blame the capitalists for all difficulties, is a very natural reaction as long as socialists continue to be a minority group. The same dogmatism and the same paranoid fear of capitalists persist when a Communist minority seizes power and sets aside the democratic processes which might force them to relinquish their control to an electoral majority. But when a labor government must keep a parliamentary majority in order to continue its socialist experiment, neither dogmatism nor blaming the capitalists is of much use.

Such a democratic socialist experiment can succeed only if a majority of the people are willing to make the necessary sacrifices of private interest in order to achieve the hoped-for advantages of cooperative effort on a national scale. For example, as long as government owner- ship of the mines is only a program proposed by an opposition party, even those who favor the project may not realize how it will really affect them—but when a labor government has actually taken over the mines, it may find itself forced to appeal to the miners not to desert their jobs for other employment. As the implications of a cooperative project in terms of personal sacrifice are more vividly realized, public opposition to it must be expected to increase. Just as a psychoanalyst must expect a period of protest against a disturbing interpretation before his patient can assimilate and make use of it, so a socialist leader must recognize that it takes time for a people to awaken fully to the consequences of a great cooperative project, so that they can choose with open eyes whether or not to commit themselves to it.

However, this sketchy outline of the psychodynamic background of some socialist attitudes is intended only as a foretaste of what more thorough studies might teach us about a number of the prevalent political dreams and programs.

INDEX

Abraham, Karl, 468, 491–492
Abreaction, 385
Adaptation, mutual, 500–501
"Adaptation to Reality in Early Infancy" (Benedek), 272
Adaptive principle (biology), 162, 170, 178
Adaptive problem: of integrative functions, 504, 506; interpersonal, 490; mutual readaptation, 500; response, 219, 223
Aggression, 262–263, 428; attacks, 460; character, 499; motives, 280; oral urges, 501; "simple reversal of," 265
Agitator, revolutionary, 525
Alexander, Franz, 32, 34–35, 121, 192, 318, 357–359, 361–366, 377, 450, 453, 459; "contact hunger," 492; contributions of superego, 38–39, 43; "emotional shame," 417; empirical investigation, 491; feelings of inferiority, 233–234, 260; frequency of dreams, 485; frustration, 501; inhibited rage, 506; new concepts of personality structure, 50; problems of psychoanalytic technique, 71; "surplus energy" concept, 511; vector theory, 489, 494–496
Alimentary salivary reflex. See Salivary reflexes.
American Journal of Psychiatry, 450
American Journal of Sociology, 545, 570
American Psychoanalytic Association, 426
American Psychoanalytic Society, 149
American Revolution, 518, 531
Amiel, Henri Frédéric, 272
"Anaclitic depressions," 511–512
Anal erotic character: fixations on, 492; neurosis, 487–488, 493
Analysis: fear of, 402; marked periodicity, 452, 460; problem of termination, 401

"Analysis of an Infantile Neurosis" (Freud), 413
"Analysis of the Dream Censorship," 288, 295
Analyst, therapeutic functions, 31
Analytic process, 400, 402
Anger, 7
Annals of the Academy of Political and Social Science, 523
Anxiety, 363–364, 399; acute, 401; gradual relation, 400; objective, 136–137; release of, 158
Arthritis, rheumatoid, 492
Asthma, bronchial, 450–451, 463, 492, 497–498; acute attacks, 457–459; brief psychotherapy, 464–474; emotional disturbances, 453; psychogenesis, 485; psychological factors, 452
Autocracies, 538; demand high-order statesmanship, 527; Freud's analysis, 534. *See also* Freud, Sigmund.
Autocratic behavior, simplest play, 493
Autocratic government, 535, 536, 538; regime, 518, 532

Bacon, Catherine, 450, 453
Barany, Robert, 539, 441, 445
Basal metabolism test, 454
Bauer, J., 448
Behavior, 240, 408, 415; adaptive goal-seeking, 149, 165; aggressive, 233–234, 454, 460; of animals, 296–297; appetitive, 427, 430–431; attitudes, 394, 396; autoerotic, 493; chain of causation, 383; clinical approach, 377; cognitive, 157, 217–220, 272, 487–489, 492, 494; compensatory, 261; complexity, 6; conscious behavior, 120; criminal, 260, 263; destructive, 426; disintegration of, 156; dynamic analyses, 150, 376; dynamics of purposive,

Frustration (*cont.*)
ternal and internal, 151–152, 158; fixation upon traumatic, 172; goal concept, 153–154; mobilization, 364–365; reactions to, 149–150, 155, 171, 173, 190–191; theory of drives, 186–87. *See also* Cognitive field.

Functional pathological states, production of, 15

Gemeinseme Tagtraume (Sachs), 542
Generalizations phenomena, 10, 12; scientific, 384
Genetic analysis: inherited drives, 183; source, 213
"Genital character," 493; excitations repressed, 10; sexuality, infantile, 451
Gerard, Margaret, 450, 453, 492
Gestalt school of psychology, 107, 168; psychologists, 216, 218, 220, 307
Goal-directed behavior, 217, 223, 427; activity, 161; character, 151, 163; cognitive field, 168, 186; disintegration, 224; drives, 170; integrative capacity, 174–177; motivated, 294, 300, 306, 327; strivings, 149–150, 160, 162–163, 165–167, 210, 215, 262; subsidiary goal, 171–173, 221. *See also* Behavior.
Goal-seeking mechanism. *See* Disintegration.
Goals: behavior, 300–301; compensatory, 159; competing, 177; concept, 153–154; "motivating pressure," 223–226; negative, 261; presentation, 22–23, 30; primary and secondary, 158; psychological, 150; wishes, 217, 220. *See also* Behavior.
Goethe, Johann Wolfgang von, 52
Gratification, 35, 153, 214, 232, 259, 452; displaced, 389; emotional, 409; erotic, 397; from external world, 144–146; of sublimation phenomena, 27–28; substitute, 10, 54, 69, 91, 93–94, 140, 145, 154; symbolic, 37; symptoms, 10, unrecognized, 425; vicarious, 139
Guidance of behavior. *See* Behavior.
Guilt, 283, 363, 366, 394, 409, 417, 479; dream censorship, 241; inferiority in direct conflict, 234; oral aggressive urges, 501; punishment, 264–265; reactions, 231, 233, 258, 261; reactive motive, 267, 327, 405–406

Hallucinations, 427, 430. *See also* Dreams.
Hallucinatory fulfillment, 54–56, 58–59; sensation, 385
Hamilton, Samuel, 412
Hannibal, 158, 261

Hansen, Karl, 466, 468, 474
Healy, William, 121
Helmholz, H. von, 439
Heredity, 165; activate hereditary pattern, 428–429; fundamental biological tendencies, 183; goal-directed urges, 170; heredity pattern, 428, 429, human, 426; predominance of oral eroticism in sexual constitution, 487, 491
Hering, E., 439
Heterosexual interest, 366, 507
Historical reconstruction, 325, 413–415
History of an Infantile Neurosis (Freud), 122
Hitzig, E., 439
Hoff, H., 446
Homosexual, 507–508; desires, 448; impulses, 385; material, 447
"Hope and Repudiation of Hope in Psychoanalytic Therapy," 295
Hopes, 295, 304–305; become conscious, 285; case history, 324, 336; earliest of "virtues" guiding ego, 272–273; evaluation and influence on behavior, 271; integrative capacity, 292; mobilization by, 364–365; motivation and integration of all behavior, 271, 273; overt expression, 286; preconscious, 270, 283; in psychoanalytic therapy, 287; reality based, 324–325; reawakened, 288; repudiation, 274, 289; therapeutic, 279, 291, 365, 368. *See also* Behavior; Ego.
Horney, Karen, 420
Hostility, 507; repressed feelings, 376, 387
Hunger, 7
Hunt, J. McV., 373, 389
Hypersensitivity, allergic, 450, 453
Hypertension: essential, 508; inhibited rage, 505
Hypnosis, 135, 384–385; cathartic, 367; mood, 335
Hysteria, 297, 384, 412–413; conflicts, 491; treatment, 367
Hysterical symptoms: precipitate of a traumatic memory, 237, 239; reminiscences, 236

Id, 11, 230; function in dreams, 121; instinctual impulses invade ego, 39, 134–135, 232–233. *See also* Ego; Impulses; Superego.
Identification, 252, 254; aggressive and competitive masculine, 399; conscious, 521; hysterical, 253; omnipotent, 448; with capitalists, 520; with father, 460
"Imprinting" process, 511